Chaim Herzog and Shlomo Gazit

THE ARAB-ISRAELI WARS

Chaim Herzog was the President of Israel and a major
general in the Israeli army, and he served as his country's ambassador to the United Nations. His other books
include *Battles of the Bible* and *The War of Atonement*.
He passed away in 1997.

Shlomo Gazit served as the Israeli Head of Military Intelligence and was personally involved in negotiations with
Egypt and the Palestinians. He lives in Israel.

Also by Chaim Herzog

BATTLES OF THE BIBLE
(with Mordecai Gichon)

DAYS OF AWE

ISRAEL'S FINEST HOUR

JUDAISM: LAW AND ETHICS

LIVING HISTORY

THE WAR OF ATONEMENT

WHO STANDS ACCUSED?

The
Arab-Israeli Wars

The
Arab-Israeli Wars

War and Peace in the Middle East
from the 1948 War of Independence to the Present

CHAIM HERZOG

UPDATED BY SHLOMO GAZIT

Introduction by Isaac Herzog and Michael Herzog

Vintage Books
A Division of Random House, Inc.
New York

Cartography by Dalia and Menahem Egozzi
Original picture research by Andrea Stern

Library of Congress Cataloging-in-Publication Data
Herzog, Chaim, 1918–
The Arab-Israeli wars.
Bibliography: p.
Includes index.
1. Israel—History, Military.
2. Jewish-Arab relations—1949–
I. Title.
DS119.2.H47   1983   956'.04   83-47817

ISBN 1-4000-7963-2

www.vintagebooks.com

Printed in the United States of America
10 9 8 7 6 5 4 3 2 1

CONTENTS

LIST OF MAPS

PREFACE

In the course of the preparation of this book I have drawn on my own personal experiences, because in one way or another I have been involved in all the wars described therein. For some forty years, ever since my boyhood, I have been involved in the conflict, first in Palestine and later in Israel. From the day on which I took a solemn oath, as I was inducted as a fifteen or sixteen year old boy into the Haganah, in an atmosphere of unforgettably solemn and awesome conspiracy in the dark cellars of the Alliance School in Jerusalem in the mid-1930s, I have been associated in one way or another with Israel's defence effort. It was my privilege to be one of those who served in the historic days of the War of Independence, in a struggle that must surely live on forever in the history of the Jewish people. I was also privileged to be part of the team that created the Israel Defence Forces as a regularly constituted army after that war, concentrating as I did on the organization of the Intelligence Corps.

Like all Israelis of my generation, I trace my life as a series of periods, some long, some short, between wars. In each of the wars, I found myself in differing roles, all of which contributed to a background that has enabled me to appreciate to some degree the overall historic context of the period through which we have been living. The path I followed led me to the United Nations, where I was privileged to serve as my country's ambassador during some of the very bitter struggles that Israel has had in the international political field. Here too, I participated in the defence of Israel in its continuing struggle for existence.

The Middle East conflict has been a tragedy for all involved in it. Neighbours, instead of devoting themselves to the task of advancing the lot of the common man in a backward area, are pitted against each other in armed confrontation. For over thirty years this senseless waste of lives and wealth has been the fate of this area. The struggle in the Middle East transcends its local nature because of its global implications for world peace: from a military and political point of view it has a direct bearing on East-West confrontation. Thus, world attention has been focused on this struggle in its every aspect. From a professional point of view, it has been one of the principal areas in the world of development and advance in military science. From a political point of view, it has reflected the various trends and pressures bearing upon the vital oil production centre of the world. It is a confrontation that no student of political or military science can afford to ignore.

Apart from my extensive personal experience and involvement, I have gathered material for this book over the years, and have interviewed many of the principal figures featuring in this account on both sides of no man's land, in Israel, in Egypt, in the United Nations and in Britain. I have also had recourse to the considerable body of published literature on the subject, a select list of which appears in the Bibliography. This new work, of course, rests on the foundation of previous publications of mine over the years.

If this book, apart from giving a professional insight into the major battles that Israel has fought, enables the reader to understand more clearly and more thoroughly the struggle in the Middle East, its purpose will have been achieved.

Finally, I should like to add a word of appreciation to my publishers and to all those involved in the editorial process, and of course to Mrs. Joan Gahtan, my secretary, who laboriously and faithfully typed all the drafts of this book.

C. Herzog, Herzliyah, 1982.

INTRODUCTION
To Revised Edition

Two decades have passed since the first edition of this book was printed. During this period, the Middle East has witnessed a series of dramatic events that have shaken the region and affected the entire globe. The Iran-Iraq War, the Gulf War and the war in Iraq, the war in Afghanistan against al-Qaeda, the Oslo Aaccords between Israel and the PLO, the first and second *Intifada* (the violent Palestinian conflict with Israel), the peace agreement between Israel and Jordan, the withdrawal of Israeli troops from Lebanon and the futile, repetitious efforts for peace between Israel and Syria.

Over the past few decades, two major events have reshaped the international arena: the fall of the USSR, marking the evaporation of the Cold War, and the horrendous attack on the heart of the free world on 11 September 2001. These events have had a profound impact on the Middle East and signify the transition of the general global orientation from one based on Cold War alliances to one based on the struggle between the free world and the forces of evil, whose weapons are hatred, terror and weapons of mass destruction.

As this new edition goes to press, the shifting sands of the Middle East are blowing again. The US has a massive presence in Iraq where America is trying to stabilize a tormented and oppressed nation and rebuild its institutions. The main American objective is to institute a new regime based on the values of democracy, thus establishing a new model of democratic governance in the region. The Iranian regime is racing towards the development of nuclear capability and fostering the proliferation of global terror, espousing a philosophy of hatred and creating instability throughout the Middle East. Iran's most noted allies, who are actively involved in the conflict with Israel, are the Hizballah from Lebanon and the Hamas and Islamic Jihad terrorist groups operating from within the Palestinian areas.

The Middle East is also the world's breeding ground for suicide bombers. The suicide bombers act as human precision-guided munitions. This relatively new weapon has been employed *en masse* against Israel by Palestinian terror groups, but its use is spreading throughout the Middle East and around the world. Indeed, the Middle East has become the global hotbed for Islamic fundamentalist terror, which is posing a threat to all pragmatic regimes in the region – such as that in Saudi Arabia – and to the entire free world.

The above, in a nutshell, clearly indicates to what extent the Middle East remains one of the most volatile and unstable areas of the world, where the clash of liberalism and democracy versus fundamentalism and dictatorship is most poignantly played out.

While the first edition of this book chronicled a gripping, classic story of conventional warfare, recent additions to the book include accounts of new types of violent conflict with unconventional battle norms. Since September 2000 the world has watched the bloody clash between Palestinians and Israelis, immediately following the collapse of what seemed to be a very promising peace process. This is not a standard type of military conflict, but rather a conflict in which there is no defined frontline and which influences the daily life of every citizen. Such a conflict embroils suicide bombers, men and women of all ages, civilian casualties on both sides, modern security measures, riots and clashes, new technologies and a lot of media attention. While there are many – often greater – conflicts taking place in all corners of the globe, it seems that the world has given added weight to this conflict. This generations-long fixation on the Arab-Israeli conflict calls for this new edition, so as to remind readers of its roots and provide an objective description of its background.

Although the region has experienced a lot of bloodshed, one cannot ignore the rays of hope and the endless efforts towards peace in the Middle East. Peace accords and truces have been signed. When the first edition of this book was published, the peace between Israel and Egypt was just at its inception. More than two decades later, one can firmly state that this peace has withstood great upheavals and storms. The same can be said for the courageous peace between Israel and Jordan. While endless initiatives have been introduced to reach a peaceful agreement between Israel and Syria and between Israel and the Palestinians, we must continue in this mission until a solution is reached. The Oslo accords led to a substantial Israeli withdrawal from Palestinian territories and the establishment of the Palestinian Authority, with the ultimate vision of creating a Palestinian state living peacefully side by side with Israel. The peoples of both sides are fatigued and ready for a major breakthrough that will lead to an amicable solution. An agreement cannot be brought about by terror and violence, but only through negotiations with both parties making painful concessions for peace.

Like many citizens of the region, we sincerely hope and pray that such a moment will come about – sooner rather than later. We hope that the legacy of great leaders such as Yitzhak Rabin, Anwar el Sadat and King Hussein will be fulfilled and that the brave risks they took for peace will not be in vain. And it is also the painful legacy of all those who lost loved ones on the battlefield or in terror attacks, leaving a trail of broken hearts and shattered bodies and souls.

Our late father, Chaim Herzog, was regarded as one of the leading commentators on strategic and military issues around the globe. Throughout the decades, he published many books and articles on these subjects. He had a fascinating military career as a soldier and officer in the ranks of the British Army in the war against the Nazis, including the landing at Normandy, the liberation of concentration camps, the intense battles at the crossing of the River Rhine and the invasion of northern Germany. He then moved on to become one of the founding officers of the Israeli Army, fighting in the battles for Jerusalem in 1948 and later establishing the Israel Defence Force's military intelligence. He retired with the rank of major general. During the Six Day War (1967) he became a world-renowned military commentator, bringing the true story of the war to every house in Israel and to the world at large. In the mid-1970s, he served as Israel's ambassador to the United Nations, partaking in some of the most heated debates concerning the Middle East. He reached the pinnacle of being the sixth president of the State of Israel, where he witnessed peaks of hope and moments of grave pain in the history of the Middle East conflict.

In his autobiography, *Living History*, which he managed to publish prior to his death in 1997, he said of himself:

'I have been many things – statesman, diplomat, businessman, commentator, lawyer, family man – but perhaps more than anything, I consider myself a soldier. If one has a great cause, I believe nothing is so noble as the willingness to fight and sacrifice for it.'

This book also tells the story of such sacrifice for the sake of the establishment and the preservation of the State of Israel.

This edition includes some new chapters added by Major-General (Res.) Shlomo Gazit. A longtime friend and fellow officer of Chaim Herzog, General Gazit reconstructed Israeli military intelligence following the trauma of the surprise Arab attack at the start of the Yom Kippur War (1973). He is a distinguished military analyst and commentator who has written and published extensively on the Arab-Israeli Wars and strategic issues pertaining to the Middle East and is involved with many academic and public ventures dealing with related matters. He has kindly agreed to review and update the original chapters of the book and add developments in the conflict since the publication of the first edition in the early 1980s. We are grateful to him for his contribution without which this updated version could not have come about.

We also acknowledge with thanks the outstanding work of a friend of Chaim Herzog, Lionel Leventhal, and his son Michael, both of Greenhill Books. They have devoted much time and effort to publish this new edition of *The Arab Israeli Wars*.

A popular song in Israel tells of the promise of a soldier writing to his young daughter from the front line: 'I promise you, my little girl, that this shall be the last war.' This telling book is a token of our personal prayer that peace will prevail against all the setbacks we have witnessed. We know that many people in Israel and throughout the Middle East share in this hope.

Our beloved father dedicated the original edition of this book to us, his children, with the heartfelt wish 'May you know war no more' It is also our deepest wish for our children that they will one day see a new peaceful era in the region and that the saga depicted in this book will not call for additional chapters in the future.

These pages are devoted with love and esteem to our late father – a soldier, freedom fighter and statesman who dedicated his life to his country and people, who fought for them and dreamed of peace.

Brigadier-General Michael Herzog
Isaac Herzog, MK
Tel Aviv, 2004

PROLOGUE

On 29 November 1947, the United Nations General Assembly voted 33:13 (with 10 abstaining and one absent) to partition the territory of Palestine west of the River Jordan, there to establish a Jewish state and an Arab state, leaving Jerusalem to be an internationally administered area. The Jewish community, mindful of the nightmare of the recent holocaust in Europe, which had left in its wake hundreds of thousands of displaced Jews across that continent, received the decision rapturously and gave public expression to their joy on what was for them a historic day. But the Arab countries did not rejoice; instead, they rejected the resolution and announced their decision to fight to prevent its implementation. The next day, as the Jewish community continued its celebrations with the prospect of national independence in sight, a bus carrying Jewish passengers was attacked by rifle fire on the road from Petach Tikva to Lod and five of the passengers were killed. Thus began Israel's War of Independence — a Jewish population of some 650,000 ranged against a Palestinian Arab population of approximately 1.1 million, supported by seven Arab armies from across the borders.

The rioting, which erupted on 30 November 1947 and developed into an Arab invasion of Palestine, brought to a head an intermittent struggle between the Jewish and Arab populations in Palestine that dated back to 1922, when the League of Nations granted the Mandate to Britain.

The age-old yearning of the Jewish people to return to the land of the Bible and the land of their forefathers found its modern, political expression at the end of the nineteenth century in the form of the Zionist movement. It was this organization, led initially by Dr. Theodore Herzl and subsequently by Dr. Chaim Weizmann and other outstanding Jewish leaders, that spearheaded the fight for international recognition of Jewish expression in Palestine. It was, in fact, the national liberation movement of the Jewish people.

In November 1917, the British Government issued the Balfour Declaration enunciating Britain's support for the establishment of a national home for the Jewish people in Palestine — which was to be established without prejudice to the rights of the Arab inhabitants of the country. This policy, which was enthusiastically supported by many leaders of British opinion (such as Lloyd George, Churchill, Balfour and others), received added emphasis because of Jewish support, particularly in the United States, for the Allied cause in the World War. Hussein Sharif, the leader of the Arab world during the First World War, did not oppose the return of Jews to Palestine. His son, Feisal, who represented the Arab world at the Paris Peace Conference, wrote to Justice Felix Frankfurter of the United States: 'There is room in Syria for us both. Indeed I think that neither can be a success without the other.'

During the First World War, promises of independence were made to Arab leaders by the Allies, and these were later implemented in Syria, Lebanon and Iraq. But many Arabs believed that the arrangements promised were also to relate to the area of Palestine within the framework of a 'Greater Syria'. In 1922, the Council of the League of Nations granted a Mandate to the British Government, entrusting it inter alia with the task of ruling Palestine and implementing the Balfour Declaration. At the time of the Declaration, approximately 85,000 Jews lived in Palestine. A proportion of this population had lived for centuries in the country and, indeed, for over a hundred years the Jewish population had constituted the majority of the citizens in the city of Jerusalem. Under the British Mandate, Jewish immigration (although limited by the authorities) swelled the Jewish population sevenfold until, by 1947, it numbered something over 600,000 souls. From some several hundred thousand, the Arab population had grown during this period to over a million, the higher standard of living in Palestine created by the Jewish immigrants having attracted Arabs from surrounding countries. The Palestine Mandate granted to Britain included the entire area of Transjordan, on the east bank of the River Jordan, as well as the area on the west bank. In 1922, the British Secretary of State for the Colonies, Winston Churchill, created an emirate under Emir (later King) Abdullah in the area of Transjordan that was later to become the independent state of Jordan. Thus, 80 per cent of the mandated area of Palestine was allocated as an autonomous area to the Arabs of Palestine.

But over the years — in 1922, 1929 and 1936 — Arab disturbances broke out in Palestine, incited by the extremist Mufti of Jerusalem, Haj Amin el-Husseini. In 1937, a British Royal Commission headed by Lord Peel concluded that there was no prospect of the Jews and Arabs living side by side and of reconciling their national aspirations: it therefore recommended the partition of Palestine into a Jewish state, a continued Mandate for Jerusalem and the annexation of the remainder of Palestine to Transjordan. While the Jewish community was prepared to contemplate such a solution, the Arab community was not.

The Second World War brought about a hiatus in the struggle, however. The Jewish population volunteered for service in the British forces, and over 30,000 saw service. The war saw a holocaust wrought by Nazi Germany in which six million Jews were put to death in the gas chambers of eastern Europe. The remnants who survived clamoured to leave Europe and to come to a national home in Palestine. But the British Government was committed to a policy that severely limited Jewish immigration to Palestine and limited the sale of land for settlement by the Jewish population: thus, the new British Labour Government after the war found itself on a collision course with the Jews in Palestine.

In 1945, after the British Government had rejected President Truman's call for the admission of 100,000 Jewish displaced persons from Europe to

Palestine, the Jewish population in Palestine began armed opposition to the Mandate authorities. This struggle was led by the nascent Israeli army, the Haganah,* and concentrated primarily on breaking the barrier against the so-called 'illegal' immigration. There were also two dissident underground organizations: the 'Irgun Zvai Leumi' ('National Military Organization', generally known as the 'Irgun' or 'IZL'), led by Menachem Begin (who some thirty years later would head the Government of Israel and would sign a peace treaty with the President of Egypt); and the 'Lohamei Herut Israel' ('Fighters for the Freedom of Israel', better known as 'Lehi' or the 'Stern Group'**). These pursued a more active policy, which included direct attacks against British personnel.

In April 1946, a commission appointed jointly by the United States and British Governments recommended authorizing the entry of 100,000 Jewish refugees into Palestine and the abolition of the restrictions imposed by the Government of Palestine since 1939 on Jewish purchase of land. But the commission's recommendations, which were unanimous and were endorsed by President Truman, were not accepted by the British Government. The conflict in Palestine escalated: the Haganah mounted an operation to destroy all bridges and road links with neighbouring Arab countries, while the British stepped up countermeasures, arresting all the known Haganah commanders. And, as Jewish resistance became more formidable, Britain was forced to increase its military presence in Palestine. Exhausted both physically and economically from the Second World War, faced with the vast task of reconstruction after a long and cruel struggle, its resources depleted, its empire disappearing, the British Government now found itself involved in a major armed conflict in Palestine requiring the maintenance there of approximately 100,000 troops. It decided therefore to hand back the Mandate to the world community. On 18 February 1947, the British Foreign Secretary, Ernest Bevin, announced to the House of Commons that Britain had decided to refer the entire problem to the United Nations.

In the meantime, hostilities mounted in intensity: the Irgun blew up the King David Hotel, the British headquarters in Jerusalem, with heavy loss of life; the death sentence was imposed for the illegal possession of arms; members of the Jewish underground were hanged; and the Irgun retaliated by hanging two British sergeants. In August 1947, the British Government apprehended an illegal immigrant ship, *Exodus*, and, before the eyes of a shocked world and an infuriated Jewish population, returned the refugees (homeless victims of the Nazi regime) to German soil.

Following the British Government's referral of the matter to the United Nations, the General Assembly appointed a special commission on Palestine, which proceeded to the area, met the local populations and received testimony from the various parties involved. As a result, the commission proposed the partition of the country into Arab and Jewish

---

* Haganah means 'defence'; in full, it was called Irgun Hahaganah, meaning 'Defence Organization'.
** Named after its leader, Avraham Stern, who was killed by British police in Tel Aviv during a search in 1942.

states with an international trusteeship for Jerusalem. The United Nations General Assembly accepted this, and it was finally voted as the Partition Resolution of 29 November 1947. While the Jewish population welcomed it, the Arab states rejected it out of hand and vowed to destroy any emerging Jewish state in its infancy. Thus originated the War of Independence in which the conflicting political aims of the two peoples were to come to a head: the stage was set for the tragedy of the Middle East.

BOOK I

THE WAR
OF INDEPENDENCE
1948–1949

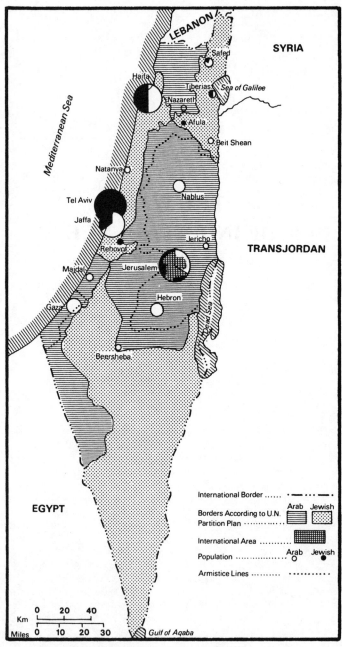

The U.N. Partition Plan (U.N. Resolution, 29 November 1947)

1

CONFRONTATION IN PALESTINE

As Britain prepared to withdraw her forces in May 1948, and as the Jewish community in Palestine braced itself for the inevitable Arab onslaught, there emerged a factor that was to influence Israel's military considerations throughout the initial part of the War of Independence. The leadership of the British armed forces had expressed itself in unequivocably hostile terms about the struggle of the Jewish population. They controlled the country's major arteries and strongpoints; their ships patrolled the eastern Mediterranean and the coast; and the Royal Air Force controlled the skies above Palestine. Furthermore, their forces included two Arab elements, namely the Arab Legion and the Transjordan Frontier Force. Both these units were to play no small part in favour of the Arab forces during the ensuing hostilities.

Israeli forces and dispositions

The most vulnerable aspect of the Jewish position lay in tenuous lines of communications between settlements, and it was inevitable that these would become the first targets for Arab attacks. The Jewish population was concentrated mainly in long strips of agricultural communities in eastern Galilee, across the valley of Jezreel and down the coastal plain to the south of Tel Aviv. In many towns and areas there was no clear dividing line between Jewish and Arab populations; the institutions and offices of government and major utilities such as electricity and oil refineries were common to both. Particularly vulnerable were communications with the isolated settlements of western Galilee and the Negev and the links between Jerusalem's 100,000 Jews and the coastal plain (not to mention those linking the outlying Jewish Jerusalem settlements with the bulk of the Jewish population in the city proper). Nor were the official frontiers secure. Controlled primarily by units of the Arab Legion and the Transjordan Frontier Force, the long land borders could not be closed effectively to the passage of Arab forces and military supplies into Palestine. The Legion numbered some 8,000 troops, while the Frontier Force was 3,000 strong; in addition, the British Palestine Police numbered some 4,000. Nominally, the British forces were responsible for law and order in the country, but both Jewish and Arab irregulars were by now operating freely within the areas under their respective control.

Over the years, the Jewish armed forces or militia had grown, sometimes with the connivance and assistance of the British and sometimes 'underground', despite the British. At the outset, locally organized defence units had been established throughout the country in order to defend Jewish settlements, but these had gradually been amalgamated into a national organization, the 'Haganah'. The Arab revolt of 1936–39 brought into existence the field companies of the Haganah, which were the first units activated on a national country-wide basis, to counter the effects of the uprising and to protect the oil pipeline crossing the valley of Jezreel on its way from Iraq to a terminal at Haifa. They were inspired by a British Army Captain, Orde Wingate (later to become famous as leader of the 'Chindits' in Burma during the Second World War), who set up 'Special Night Squads' to fight against the Arab guerrillas bent on sabotaging the pipeline. There also existed auxiliary forces known as the 'Jewish Settlement Police', who assisted in the defence of Jewish settlements and the maintenance of the lines of communications between them. Numbering some 2,000 men, officered by the British and financed by the Jewish Agency, they were organized in sections and armed only with small-arms.

In May 1941, the Haganah created a full-time military force known as the 'Palmach' (from 'Plugot Mahatz' or 'shock troops'). This force was under the exclusive control of the Haganah, and was led initially by Yitzhak Sadeh, a large and flamboyant Haganah leader who, by personality and example, was a major driving force in its creation. (Later, with the establishment of the Israel Defence Forces, his record as a military leader in conventional operations did not live up to the promise of these early years.) He gathered around him a group of youngsters destined to be the leaders of Israel's armed forces — indeed, many of the men who were later to lead Israel's army into battle received their first training in the ranks of the Palmach — men such as Yitzhak Rabin (later Chief of Staff and Prime Minister), Chaim Bar-Lev (later Chief of Staff and a minister in the Israeli Government), David Elazar (Chief of Staff in the 1973 Yom Kippur War) and many others. It was in one of the first operations of the force, acting with the British to oust the Vichy French from Syria, that Moshe Dayan (later to become Chief of Staff, Minister of Defence and Minister of Foreign Affairs in various Israeli Governments, and to command Israel's army in the 1956 Sinai Campaign) lost an eye. In command of one of two select reconnaissance units of the Palmach sent to secure a bridge across the River Litani, his binoculars were hit by a French sniper's bullet as he was surveying the bridge. In command of the second unit that day was Yigal Allon, later to become commander of the Palmach and subsequently Deputy Prime Minister and a minister in several Israeli Governments.

During the Second World War, many Jews had volunteered for service in the British armed forces, either as individuals or in Palestinian units. In 1944, a Jewish Brigade Group was established and saw action in Italy against the Germans. The wartime experience acquired by some 30,000 volunteers, in all arms of the British forces, later proved to be invaluable in the creation of the Israel Defence Forces, providing as it did much of the organizational, training and technical background that hitherto had been absent in the Haganah. By the time that Rommel's army — which had threatened to overrun Egypt and enter Palestine — had been defeated by the British in 1942, the Palmach under Yitzhak Sadeh comprised a force of over 3,000, including some 2,000 reserves. In 1947, at the time of the United Nations Partition Resolution, the Palmach numbered over 3,000 men and women with approximately 1,000 on active reserve who could be called up at a moment's notice. (In 1944, a naval company, 'Pal Yam', and an air platoon had been established within the Palmach organization.)

In mid-1947, David Ben-Gurion, Chairman of the Jewish Agency for Palestine (which was, in effect, the government of the Jewish population in Palestine), began preparing the Haganah for the expected war. By six months before the outbreak of hostilities, he had created military districts or commands astride the possible invasion routes of the Arab armies, established brigades on a territorial basis and set out the guidelines for the acquisition of arms and the training of forces. Thus, by February 1948, the 'Golani' Brigade was operating in the Jordan valley and eastern Galilee; the 'Carmeli' Brigade covered Haifa and western Galilee; the 'Givati' Brigade the southern lowlands; the 'Alexandroni' Brigade the Sharon central area; the 'Etzioni' Brigade the Jerusalem area; and the 'Kiryati' Brigade covered the city of Tel Aviv and its environs. In the course of the following months, three other Palmach brigades were created out of the independent Palmach battalions: the 'Negev' Brigade in the southern lowlands and the northern Negev; the 'Yiftach' Brigade in Galilee; and the 'Harel' Brigade in the Jerusalem area.

It is well to recall that, when one talks about brigades and military units, one is not depicting a normal military line-up. The entire Haganah operation was an underground one, and its military organization and deployment had to be carried out under the vigilant eyes of British troops and police in the full knowledge that the possession of weapons was a crime punishable by death. Moreover, British soldiers carried out raids on Jewish villages and towns from time to time, revealing secret storage dumps of weapons. Ingenious, devious means of transporting and storing weapons were an essential facet of Haganah skills. The Arabs did not suffer from this disability, because they were less in confrontation with the British forces and often moved around freely in the areas under their control openly armed. In this respect, they benefited considerably from the active support of the units of the Arab Legion, which were part of the British forces. A modest domestic war industry was created in which small-arms such as Sten guns and hand grenades were manufactured, but the disadvantage with which the Jewish forces set out to do battle is emphasized by the fact that the total armament at the Haganah's disposal in 1947 consisted of 900 rifles, 700 light machine-guns and 200 medium machine-guns with sufficient ammunition for only three days' fighting — even the standing force, the Palmach, could only arm two out of every three of its active members. At this stage, heavy machine-guns, anti-tank guns and artillery were but a dream: not one existed in the Jewish forces.

The total Jewish force that could be mobilized from an overall Jewish population of 650,000 was some 45,000, but these included some 30,000 men and women whose functions were limited to local defence, particularly in the villages throughout the country — they could at no time be included in the field forces. The effective force that the Jewish population could field on a national basis on the outbreak of hostilities therefore numbered approximately 15,000. The air platoon of the Palmach consisted of eleven single-engined light aircraft manned by twenty Piper Cub pilots plus some twenty fighter pilots with Royal Air

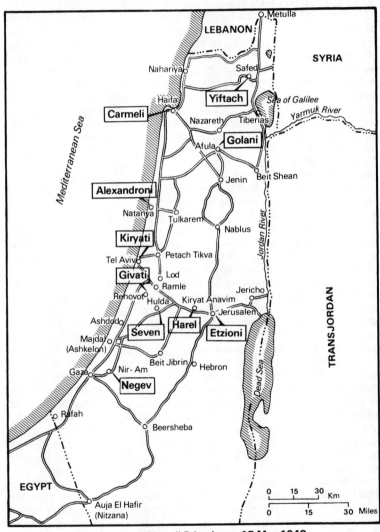

Deployment of Israeli Brigades on 15 May 1948

Force experience. These civilian aircraft were the nucleus of the Israeli Air Force. No airport or landing strip was at their exclusive disposal, and only two airfields in the country, Haifa and Lod (Lydda), could be used by civilian aircraft. The naval company numbered some 350 sailors with Royal Navy and 'illegal' immigrant-running experience, with a few motor boats and a number of frogmen.

In addition to the Haganah, there existed in Palestine the two Jewish dissident organizations, who did not accept the authority of the Jewish Command. The 2,000-4,000 members of the Irgun, under the command of Menachem Begin, continued with militant anti-British activity even when the official Jewish policy was not to engage in such activity. Pursuing a policy of constant attack on British police posts, government and army installations, it was trained primarily to carry out small-unit, commando-type raids, but had very little experience in large-scale, open fighting. The 500-800 member Lehi, or Stern Group, was even more extreme in its dissident policy, and remained consistently anti-British throughout the war. The ultimate integration of these two units into a unified Israeli Army was not to be accomplished without severe problems and some internecine bloodshed.

Arab forces and dispositions

The bulk of the Arab population in Palestine was led by Haj Amin el-Husseini, exiled Mufti of Jerusalem. His openly-declared purpose was to destroy the entire Jewish community of Palestine or to drive it into the sea. Born in Jerusalem in 1893, his active participation in the Arab nationalist movement dates from about 1919, and he led the anti-Jewish riots in Jerusalem in April of the following year, for which he was jailed by the British authorities. But the British High Commissioner at the time, Sir Herbert Samuel, attempted to appease the nationalists and to improve the balance of power between the rival Arab families by appointing him Mufti of Jerusalem in 1921. Husseini, however, made use of his new power to encourage an extreme policy: he took an active part in organizing the anti-Jewish riots in 1929, and headed the Arab Higher Committee that directed the 1936 rebellion. In 1937, the British dismissed him and outlawed his Committee, but he escaped to Damascus, from where he led the rebellion. In 1940, he moved to Iraq, where he took part in the pro-German coup of 1941, after the failure of which he escaped to Germany. At the end of the war, he made his way to Cairo, from where he began to organize the Arabs in Palestine once more. (After the Arab defeat in 1948, he was to remain in exile, primarily in Egypt and Lebanon, his influence waning rapidly until his death in exile in his late seventies.)

Most Arab villagers carried weapons and could be mobilized by the Faza'a, an Arab alarm system whereby each sheikh could call up the males in his district for an operation, whether for defence or attack, on a purely guerrilla basis. The Palestinian Arabs had two paramilitary organizations, the Najada and the Futuwa, which operated openly as scout movements.

Within their framework, a certain amount of urban guerrilla training was given to their members, but they were to be no match for the Haganah. They could, of course, rely on the backing of the local Arab population and benefited also from a loose co-operation with the Arab Legion and the Transjordan Frontier Force. From time to time, the Arab forces were able to make use of a number of deserters from British units: posing as British regular troops on duty and travelling around in stolen British Army vehicles, these were used to cross into heavily-populated Jewish areas in the cities, particularly Jerusalem, and introduce bombs, which created considerable damage and heavy casualties. Thus, of the three major attacks that succeeded in Jerusalem, two – the blowing-up of the *Palestine Post* building and the attack in Ben Yehuda Street in which some fifty people were killed and most of the area destroyed — were carried out by such deserters. The third attack was perpetrated at the Jewish Agency Headquarters by the use of a United States consular car, which was driven into the courtyard. (On the other side, when the war developed, a small number of deserters from the British forces joined the Haganah, in one case bringing the first tank, a Cromwell, to join Israel's armed forces.)

The Mufti's two guerrilla forces, known as 'The Army of Salvation', each about 1,000 men strong, were led by his cousin, Abd el Kader el-Husseini, and Hassan Salameh, who had undergone a certain degree of military training with the Germans during the war. Arriving in Palestine to begin the 'jihad' ('holy war'), Abd el Kader began operations in the area of Jerusalem while Salameh became active in the Lod-Ramle district. To complicate the Arab military picture further, there existed in southern Palestine a radical and somewhat disorderly group of guerrillas organized by the extreme fanatical Moslem Brotherhood of Egypt, who maintained but a tenuous liaison with the other Arab parties. Backing these Arab forces was the military potential of the Arab world, which numbered several hundred aircraft in the air forces of Egypt, Syria and Iraq, plus British and French artillery and armour. In addition, they had ready access to arms, ammunition and spares, in contrast to the embargo that affected the Jewish forces.

As the date of the British withdrawal from Palestine drew near, the decision was taken by the Arab League that its member states would intervene militarily in Palestine. But the preparation for war against the infant Israeli state took place against a background of the inevitable inter-Arab differences, intrigues and manoeuvrings of the various rulers against each other. In April 1948, they appointed King Abdullah of Transjordan to be Commander-in-Chief of the invading armies: not only did he control the most effective of the Arab armies, the Arab Legion, but he also enjoyed the initial advantage of having part of his forces already in Palestine, within the framework of the British Army. This served to increase the other leaders' suspicions of his motives, for there was little doubt of his desire to reunite the west and east banks of the River Jordan and create a Palestinian-Jordanian kingdom. There was always the possibility that he would enter into active co-operation with the Mufti of Jerusalem. In sum, the various Arab countries were more divided than united, their common cause being limited to opposing Jewish settlement in Palestine, and the creation of a Jewish state. It was a pattern that was to continue over the years.

By far the most effective and best-trained Arab force was the Arab Legion, commanded by Lieutenant-General Sir John Bagot Glubb (better known as 'Glubb Pasha'), a veteran of the First World War. Fluent in Arabic, he and a group of British officers had transformed the Legion from a desert frontier force into a modern army. His total identification with the highly-individualistic Bedouin tribesmen and his personal authority had helped to create a formidable force by applying British discipline and organization to the inherent qualities of the Bedouin. The Legion at that time comprised over 10,000 troops organized in three brigade groups, a number of armoured battalions and artillery elements. The Egyptian Army was nominally the strongest of the Arab armies and was prepared to commit an expeditionary force of some 5,000 troops, consisting of a brigade group with an armoured element. In the north, the Syrian force numbered 8,000 troops, in two infantry brigades with a mechanized battalion of French-built tanks, and a small air force. The 2,000-man Lebanese contingent allocated to the Palestine operation included four infantry battalions with limited artillery and armoured forces, while the Iraqi Army assigned 10,000 men − four infantry brigades, an armoured battalion and supporting troops, in addition to an air unit.

In order to offset the danger, as they saw it, created by King Abdullah's ambition and his military potential, the kings and presidents of the Arab countries also decided to create an Arab Liberation Army, which would operate in Palestine even before the evacuation of the British. To lead this force, they appointed General Taha Al Hashimi of Iraq, but he proved little more than a figurehead; the real leader of the force, which ultimately came to be identified with his name, was a former Syrian officer of the Ottoman Turkish Army, Fauzi el-Kaukji. He had been a leader of the Arab irregulars during the 1936 revolt in Palestine, and had led the Arab guerrilla forces based on the area of Nablus. Although a most disorganized commander administratively, he had shown qualities of leadership and courage − in addition to certain flamboyant characteristics bordering on the theatrical, which gave him the reputation of being something of a clown. (From a purely professional military point of view, his performance in the 1948 war was to be mediocre, to say the least.)

Thus, the Arab armies that were to invade Palestine, in addition to the crack Transjordan Arab Legion, Kaukji's Arab Liberation Army and the Mufti's Army of Salvation, were: the armies of Lebanon, Syria, Egypt and Iraq; contingents from the Saudi Arabian Army were subsequently attached to the Egyptian expeditionary force. All these various elements co-ordinated their activities to a degree, while at the same time pursuing their individual partisan aims − a situation that did not always allow for effective military control over, and co-operation between, the 30,000-plus troops committed to the invasion. Well-equipped by 1948 standards with small-arms, artillery, armoured and air elements, and well-organized in conventional modern military terms, they nevertheless made a striking contrast to the Israeli forces — a proportion of which had only small-arms, and in which no artillery, armour or air units of any consequence existed whatsoever. Such were the very unevenly matched forces that were ranged one against the other at the outset.

Attempts have been made by Arab historians to portray the situation as one in which the military advantage lay with the Jews because of interior supply lines and a flexible mobilization system. But the first of these assumptions ignores the fact that all the Jewish lines of communication were highly vulnerable because of a large, armed, hostile population sitting astride them. The second assumption misses the fact that the bulk of the Arab forces were regular military organizations equipped with conventional modern military weapons of the time. The Jewish loss of one per cent of its population is perhaps the best indication of the intensity of the struggle and its one-sided nature. Ranged against professional Arab armies was a civilian population fighting as a militia. The avowed and openly proclaimed purpose of the Arab forces was to drive the Jewish population into the sea: the new Jewish state found itself fighting a war for its very existence — a war that was to become its War of Independence.

Military confrontation

The war erupted as a series of city riots, bloody urban encounters, hit-and-run operations that left scores of dead, maimed and wounded civilians on both sides, attacks on the Jewish urban transport systems and major attempts to cut communications between the various Jewish centres. Many outlying Jewish settlements were cut off. Despite the fact that military logic would have called for the shortening of lines of communication by abandoning such settlements, a decision in principle was taken by the Haganah that none would be voluntarily abandoned. It was appreciated by the Jewish leadership that abandoning villages, even for sound strategic reasons, could have very serious consequences of a far-reaching nature, for it was obvious that the final borders of the new Jewish state would be decided above all by the actual physical presence and location of a Jewish population. Thus, despite the heavy risk involved, until the entry of regular Arab armies into the war not a single Jewish settlement was abandoned.

The first major Arab attempt to capture a Jewish settlement was made in January 1948, when the Arab Liberation Army attacked Kfar Szold, a village in the eastern part of upper Galilee, a few hundred yards from the Syrian border. The Arabs controlled the entire area from the high ground, and threw their 1st 'Yarmuk' Battalion against the village. The British, who could not condone this blatant invasion of British-controlled territory from a neighbouring country, sent an armoured unit to the aid of the hard-pressed settlers and the invading Arab force withdrew.

In the same month, a force of 1,000 men under Abd el Kader el-Husseini mounted an attack against Kfar Etzion, the principal village of a group of four Jewish villages, fourteen miles south of Jerusalem. The main supply routes to this area from the city had been closed by Arab units, and the only form of communication was by means of Piper Cub light aircraft landing on a makeshift airstrip. The main attack was mounted against Kfar Etzion by some 300 Arab fighters, while diversionary attacks were mounted against Massuot Yitzhak and Ein Zurim. The preparations for the attack had been observed in advance by the Jewish forces and, accordingly, the reserve company of Palmach fighters stationed there was deployed in ambush along the probable Arab line of approach towards the village of Ein Zurim. The Arab attack on Kfar Etzion was blunted by the settlers, who held their fire until the main Arab force was within close range. At that point, the Palmach force ambushed one of the Arab contingents following up, and this suffered very heavy casualties. The entire Arab force broke and withdrew. Meanwhile, the Haganah in Jerusalem had organized a Palmach platoon of 35 men to rush to the aid of the beleaguered villages. While making their way across the Hebron Hills they were engaged and surrounded by Arab forces and, in a desperate struggle, fought until they were wiped out to the last man.

Similar attacks were mounted by Kaukji's force against the isolated village of Yehiam in western Galilee and against Kibbutz Tirat Tzvi in the Beisan valley. In an effort to impress the Palestinian Arab population, Kaukji proclaimed his forthcoming victory against Tirat Tzvi with a considerable fanfare, and threw the 1st 'Yarmuk' Battalion into the attack. But the defenders had been alerted and were ready. Once again, a mobile Jewish force moved out in a wide circle and hit the attacking Arab force in the flank, causing it to withdraw in disarray, leaving behind 60 dead and a large amount of equipment.

Parallel to these attacks on the villages, the Arabs intensified their terrorist attacks using Europeans (British deserters, Poles, Germans and Yugoslavs) to drive vehicles loaded with bombs into Jewish populated areas. Thus they spread destruction and death in the main cities, particularly in Jerusalem. Jewish forces were not slow to react and in one action destroyed the Arab Headquarters in Jaffa.

The main Arab effort was meanwhile directed towards disrupting the Jewish lines of communication, and a number of main axes throughout the country were by now completely closed to Jewish traffic. The main thrust of the Arab effort was directed towards cutting the road link between Jerusalem and the coast, while by mid-March the Jewish settlements in the Negev had been completely cut off on land, and the only communication with them was maintained by two Piper Cub aircraft. Gradually, Jewish forces developed a system of convoys with home-made armoured vehicles, but the nature of the tortuous winding main road to Jerusalem, rising up to a height of almost 3,000 feet in the Judean Hills, rendered the task of defending the slow-moving convoys increasingly difficult. (The logical solution to such a situation, namely that of capturing and holding high ground covering both sides of the route, was not possible in the early stages because the British forces would have intervened in force against such Jewish moves.) The burned-out wrecks of the primitive armoured vehicles and trucks have been preserved. They lie to this day on both sides of the route leading to Jerusalem through the hills, in mute testimony to the bitter and bloody struggle that raged there and the inordinately high sacrifices incurred in the battle to keep open the lifeline of the Jewish population in Jerusalem.

Similar battles were taking place simultaneously on all the main supply routes to the outlying Jewish settlements. By late March, the Etzion group of villages in the Hebron Hills had finally been cut off, while in Galilee 42 members of a convoy trying to supply the isolated village of Yehiam were wiped out. It too was cut off. And, at the end of the month, seventeen people were killed in a major convoy en route to Jerusalem. The Negev, Jerusalem, and parts of western Galilee were now isolated from the main Jewish centres of Palestine. The Jewish population was desperately fighting — against heavy and seemingly hopeless odds — for its existence. The triumphant Arab forces had won the first round; they were on the offensive. Jewish losses in this first phase included 1,200 dead.

But the struggle against odds in this first phase had not been in vain. For, at considerable sacrifice and by fighting-off repeated Arab attempts to capture Jewish settlements, the Jewish community had gained one of the most precious assets, namely time: time in which to organize order out of the chaos; time in which to mobilize; time in which to train; and time in which to mount a major effort to smuggle into the country the arms so vital to continue the struggle. Gradually, the plans for moving over to the offensive were being laid.

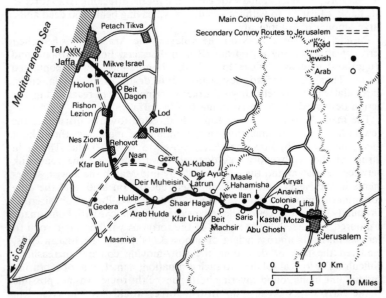

The Road to Jerusalem (to 15 May 1948)

The struggle intensifies

The most pressing military problem facing the Haganah Command was the siege of the Jewish community of Jerusalem and the fact that the lines of communication with that community had been severed. It became evident that the convoy system was no longer effective and that a new approach would have to be adopted. As plans were being laid for the breaking of the siege of Jerusalem, Kaukji, who had now consolidated his forces in the Nablus area, began to take the offensive in an endeavour to cut the Jewish lines of communication between Tel Aviv and Haifa and the north. His first move was against the Jewish agricultural settlement of Mishmar Haemek, which lay before the Hills of Ephraim, south of the Carmel ridge, overlooking the valley of Jezreel. The north-south coastal route running between the sea and the Carmel range was by now closed to Jewish traffic; consequently, were Kaukji's offensive to succeed, he would be in a position to close off the valley of Wadi Milek, through which all Jewish traffic from Tel Aviv to Haifa now had to pass. Haifa would be isolated.

On 4 April 1948, a force numbering over 1,000 men, including the 'Kadisia' Battalion and units from the 1st 'Yarmuk' Battalion under Mohammed Safa, and the 'Hittin' Battalion commanded by Madlul Abas, supported by seven pieces of artillery supplied by the Syrians (the first artillery to be used in the War of Independence), occupied the hills dominating the village of Mishmar Haemek. After an artillery bombardment supported by small-arms fire, the infantry advanced, but was stopped in its tracks along the fence of the village by the defenders' fire. That night, a company from the 'Golani' Brigade infiltrated across the fields into the village to reinforce the defenders. All the next day, the village was shelled; at night, additional Jewish reinforcements arrived. Following a cease-fire negotiated by the British to enable the evacuation of the women and children from the village, the 1st Battalion of the Palmach readied itself in the neighbouring village of Ein Hashofet for the counter-attack. Using the Haganah field force that had reinforced the village as a firm base, both in the village itself and in the nearby Mishmar Haemek forest, Yitzhak Sadeh, who was in command of the operation, decided on a line of indirect approach to hit the enemy's lines of communications — a conventional counterattack was out of the question because of the superiority of the Arabs in weapons and the complete absence of artillery on the Jewish side. For five days and nights the battle raged, as Palmach units occupied Arab villages and high ground behind Kaukji's front-line. Some of these villages and positions were fought-over repeatedly, changing hands several times. Indeed, the Arabs mounted eleven consecutive attacks on one stronghold in the mountains: by night, the Jewish forces would capture the position; by day, Kaukji's forces would exploit their considerable advantage in numbers and weapons to recapture it. But, as the bloody struggle waged to and fro in the mountains around the battlefield, the 1st Palmach Battalion was gradually gaining the upper hand.

On 12 April, Kaukji mounted yet another determined attack against Mishmar Haemek, but the attacking force was ambushed in the woods covering the approach to the village. At the same time, the Haganah forces captured two Arab villages behind and to the east of Kaukji's forces. In the midst of the battle, Kaukji suddenly realized that he was cut off. Desperate attacks were launched against the Haganah forces holding the village of Mensi in his rear, while his efforts against Mishmar Haemek were redoubled in order to draw off the Jewish troops in his rear. With difficulty, he succeeded in breaking the ring that was closing behind him. It was a narrow escape. Unwilling to risk being trapped again, Kaukji decided to cut his losses and withdraw to Jenin.

Parallel to this attack on Mishmar Haemek, and at Kaukji's request, the Druze battalion in his army commanded by Shahib Wahab attacked the village of Ramat Yohanan to the north in order to relieve the pressure on

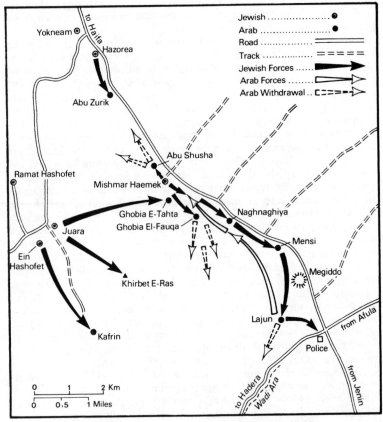

The Battles of Mishmar Haemek, 4–12 April 1948

Kaukji's forces around Mishmar Haemek. A fierce battle was fought for two days, during which units of the 'Carmeli' Brigade were on the verge of breaking. Time and again, wave after wave of Druze* troops stormed the village incurring severe casualties. But the breaking point of the Druze force came sooner than that of the Haganah.

The Arab attempt to isolate Haifa had failed, and Kaukji's forces had suffered yet another humiliating defeat despite the heavy odds in their favour. The tide was turning.

Operation 'Nachshon'

Parallel to the events in Mishmar Haemek, the first major Haganah operation was being mounted. The situation in Jerusalem had become desperate. The Arab siege had been intensified and food supplies in Jerusalem were running out. The city was dependent on water supplies from the coastal plain, and the pumping stations were especially vulnerable. It became evident that only a major operation could open the road to Jerusalem, but it was an operation that had to be undertaken. Failure in the Jerusalem sector would be fatal to the Jewish struggle. Despite the scepticism and opposition of many members of his staff, Ben-Gurion insisted on what was for the Haganah an operation of a scope and size hitherto unknown. Until that date, Haganah activities had never been much above those of company level; no battalion-size operation had been undertaken. Ben-Gurion now insisted on a brigade-size operation – which would mean draining manpower from many parts of the country, concentrating arms and leaving several fronts open to Arab attack.

The plan, Operation 'Nachshon',** called for the opening of a corridor some six miles wide in the coastal plain and some two miles wide in the mountains. It would be secured by the occupation of high ground and Arab villages bordering the road, so that convoys would be free to move back and forth on the main route. For this purpose, a brigade force was organized, numbering about 1,500 men in three battalions. One battalion was to be responsible for the area between Hulda and Latrun on the coastal plain; a second would take care of the area from Latrun to Kiryat Anavim (the mountainous ascent to an area some ten miles from Jerusalem); the third battalion would remain in reserve. Command of the

---

* An Arabic-speaking national religious community. The Druze religion originated in the 11th century in the Isma'iliyya (an extreme branch of Shi'i Islam), but is considered by most as having seceded from Islam. It is a secret cult, its tenets being known fully to the religious heads of the community alone. The Druze stress moral and social principles rather than ritual or ceremony. Altogether, there are currently some 350,000 Druze in Syria, Lebanon and Israel: about 180,000 in Syria, or about 3 per cent of the population; some 150,000 in Lebanon, or 3.6 per cent of the total population; and 33,000 in Israel, or 1 per cent of the population. This bitter battle brought to an end the Druze participation in the war on the Arab side; Druze forces were later to be a very loyal element in the Israel Defence Forces.
** Called after Nachshon Ben-Aminadav, the head of the tribe of Judah during the exodus from Egypt, who was reputed to have been the first to have dived into the Red Sea as Moses parted it for the passage of the children of Israel. He thus served as an example and an inspiration to those who followed.

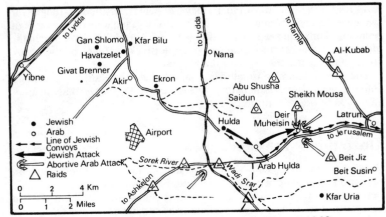

Operation 'Nachshon' (Western Sector), 3-15 April 1948

operation would go to Shimon Avidan, the commander of the 'Givati' Brigade.

By a fortuitous set of circumstances, the first shipment of arms from Czechoslovakia was smuggled into the country on the night of 1 April at Beit Daras, a secret airstrip in the south. The arms predicament of the Haganah at the time is emphasized by the fact that the 200 rifles and 40 light machine-guns that were unloaded from the aircraft constituted a major improvement in the Haganah's arms situation. Two days later, the first ship arrived with Czech rifles and light machine-guns. These were surreptitiously unloaded and distributed, frequently before the grease had been removed, to the units in the field.

Two very important actions preceded Operation 'Nachshon'. First, in the area of Ramle, a Haganah commando unit blew up the headquarters of Hassan Salameh, area commander of the Mufti's Army of Salvation. Many of Salameh's key personnel died in the attack, and the ability of his force to disrupt the Haganah preparations on the coastal plain was severely impeded. Second, an Arab village near Jerusalem, Kastel, built on the site of a Roman fortress dominating the road between Jerusalem and Kiryat Anavim, was captured. Operation 'Nachshon' itself began on the evening of 5 April. Blocking units moved out to cover seven Arab villages, while larger forces captured the villages of Arab Hulda and Deir Muheisin in the general area of Latrun. At the same time, the Palmach attacked the village of Beit Machsir on the high ground in the area of Bab el Wad, the opening in the mountains where the road winds up to Jerusalem. At midnight, 60 trucks loaded with civilian and military supplies left Hulda and, moving slowly to Jerusalem past the forces fighting for control of the hills, reached the capital city after a ten-hour drive. The Arabs counterattacked on the night of 7/8 April, their main thrust being in the area of Motza below Kastel. Abd el Kader el-Husseini had rushed back from Damascus, where he had been mobilizing financial support and acquiring additional weapons, and he now led the attack on Kastel, which changed hands in fierce struggles a number of times. After six days of continuous fighting without relief or rest, the remnants of the Jewish forces were finally forced back with only one commander, a section leader, alive. But, at the last moment, the situation was dramatically reversed. Abd el Kader el-Husseini was himself killed as he approached a position he thought had already been taken by Arab forces. Demoralized, the Arabs fell back. Next day, a counterattacking unit of the Palmach found Kastel unoccupied, and supplies could be moved into Jerusalem.

The success of Operation 'Nachshon' was important for a number of reasons. The supplies that arrived in the city enabled the beleaguered garrison and population to hold out for another two months. From a military point of view, Operation 'Nachshon' was the first in which a Jewish force of formation level had been activated. It was the first time in which the Haganah had attacked for the purpose of taking control of territory. The operation itself had a major psychological effect on the Arab forces, the results of which would be seen in the coming weeks of fighting. But, above all, the operation prepared the way for the implementation of what the Haganah called 'Plan D' — the seizure of strategic points that might influence battles along the axes of the impending Arab invasion.

The relief of Jerusalem was short-lived, however. Two large convoys of supplies and reinforcements reached Jerusalem within the framework of Operation 'Nachshon' and, by 20 April, three further such convoys had helped to improve the situation in the city and had brought up the Palmach 'Harel' Brigade. But 20 April saw a halt to this flow of men and supplies: only part of a convoy managed to reach the city, while the rear end was obliged to turn back. The road to Jerusalem was once again sealed off in the area of Bab el Wad. The siege of Jerusalem had commenced.

While Operation 'Nachshon' was being carried out, one of the more controversial episodes in the war took place. An attack was mounted by an Irgun unit with members of Lehi on the Arab village of Deir Yassin, on the western edge of Jerusalem. In the course of the fighting, over 200 of the villagers were reported to have been killed. There have been numerous conflicting reports about the attack on Deir Yassin. Certainly, it became a weapon in the hands of the Arabs over the years in their attacks on Israel, and the words 'Deir Yassin' were used over and over again by the Arabs to justify their own atrocities. The Irgun version maintains that they called on the village to surrender, but that when fire was opened on them, inflicting casualties, they found themselves involved in a military attack. The Jewish Agency and the Haganah High Command immediately expressed their deep disgust and regret.

During the month of April 1948, the pendulum had swung in favour of the Haganah. In two major actions, the Haganah had activated forces larger than any before — a brigade group in Operation 'Nachshon' and forces equivalent to two battalions at Mishmar Haemek. In both these operations, the Jewish forces had been successful. The adverse effect on the morale of the Arab forces was considerable.

Plan D

The Arab strategy during April and May was to harass the Jews — to hold on to positions such as on the Jerusalem road, but not to enter into major military confrontations. They preferred to await the withdrawal of the British forces and the conclusion of the Mandate, when the Arab armies would invade the country. Meanwhile, the Haganah was obliged by the accelerated withdrawal of the British forces to advance the moves envisaged in Plan D. Part of this called for the reorganization of the Haganah, establishing regional commands and mobile brigades. By the time of the British withdrawal, the Haganah and Palmach field forces would number some 40,000 fighters under arms.

The Palmach forces were now under the command of Yigal Allon, a son of Galilee, born in the final month of the First World War in the shadow of historic Mount Tabor. One of the early commanders in the Palmach, he

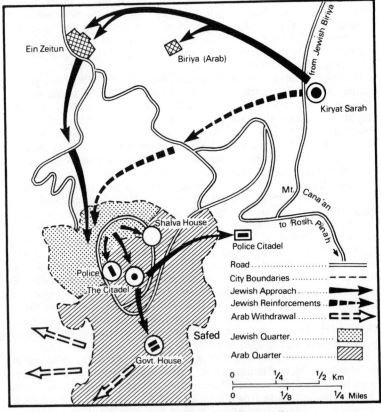

The Conquest of Safed and its Surroundings
(Operation 'Yiftach', May 1948)

had been trained in Wingate's Special Night Squads and had commanded a reconnaissance unit leading the Allied advance to the River Litani against the Vichy French in 1942. He was a young, handsome, dashing figure, a natural leader, and he became at the time a symbol for the Jewish youth. As commander of the Palmach, he proved to be the most effective Jewish military leader in the War of Independence. His generalship was outstanding. (When the state was established, he achieved general officer rank; but, because of political differences with David Ben-Gurion, he did not continue in the service and for this reason alone did not reach the top military position. He entered politics, serving in ministerial positions in various governments, including that of Deputy Prime Minister under Golda Meir and Yitzhak Rabin, and also as Foreign Minister. He died in March 1980 of a heart attack while running a campaign to become leader of the Israel Labour Party.)

The operational aspects of Plan D called for the securing of all areas allocated to the Jewish state under the United Nations Partition Resolution — plus areas of Jewish settlement outside those planned borders, in order to be in a suitable position to meet the invading Arab armies by deploying defenders across the axes of advance. The areas vacated by the British automatically became autonomous Jewish or Arab regions; thus, for instance, the area between Tel Aviv and Petach Tikva to all intents and purposes became the first district of the State of Israel, in the same way as did areas such as the triangle based on Nablus or the area of Hebron on the Arab side. In the implementation of Plan D, the Haganah went over to the attack in various parts of the country. In mid-April, units of the 'Golani' Brigade captured the city of Tiberias. When they cut the city in two, isolating a major part of the Arab population, the Arabs chose to evacuate the city and, with the assistance of units of the British Army, were transported east to Transjordan. Thus began the great tragedy of the Arab refugee population, which was to plague the Middle East for decades after the war.

On 30 April, Allon launched Operation 'Yiftach' to capture the strategically-important town of Safed in Galilee. The Jewish quarter there (with a population of some 1,500), had been under siege since February, for sited above it was the Arab town of some 10,000 inhabitants. On the eve of the British withdrawal from Safed on 15 April, the Palmach had infiltrated a platoon of troops to strengthen the depleted Haganah garrison. As the British forces had withdrawn, the major tactical positions in the city had been taken over by the Arabs — a police fortress on Mount Cana'an, an ancient fortress in the town and an additional strategically-sited building, Shalva House. Allon realized that failure to capture Safed could affect the entire military situation in northern Galilee. The strategic Nebi Yusha fortress overlooking the Huleh valley was also in Arab hands, and attacks on it on 15 April by both Palmach and Haganah forces were driven off with heavy loss of life.

On 28 April, Haganah forces captured the police fortress in Rosh Pinah and a neighbouring army camp. Bypassing Mount Cana'an, Palmach forces occupied the villages of Birya and Ein Zeitun to the north of Safed, and from here opened a corridor leading into the Jewish quarter of Safed through which the first supplies were manhandled by the soldiers and carried into the starving quarter. The Jewish forces in the area were now strengthened by an additional Palmach battalion.

The first attack mounted on 5 May against the police fortress on Mount Cana'an failed, so Allon withdrew his forces and reorganized them. Then, on 10 May, a simultaneous offensive was mounted against the three strategic positions in Safed — the citadel on Mount Cana'an, the municipal police station in the old quarter and Shalva House. Aided by an unseasonably heavy rainfall, the Palmach forces fought all night, attacking in waves up the hilly streets of the town, fighting from house to house and from room to room. By the morning of the next day, the strongpoints were in Jewish hands and the by-now-familiar mass Arab evacuation from the town began. With the imminence of invasion by the Arab armies, the capture of Safed had been vital to maintain the Jewish position in north-east Galilee.

Operations in pursuance of Plan D spilled over into the northern Jordan valley with the seizure by the 'Golani' Brigade of the fortified police posts

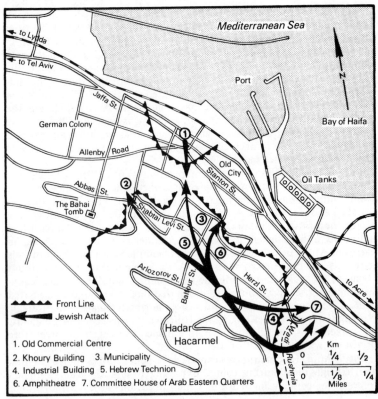

The Battle for Haifa, 22 April 1948

at Zemach, south of the Sea of Galilee, and Gesher, to the south of it on the River Jordan. Farther south, Haganah troops seized Beit Shean, while a number of villages were captured to the west in the mountains of lower Galilee, thus giving depth to the area under Jewish control running north and south along the Jordan. At the same time, the Haganah secured the Mount Tabor and southern Carmel regions.

On 21 April, the British forces in Haifa evacuated their positions and concentrated in a number of military camps and in the port of Haifa. Operation 'Scissors' for the capture of the whole of Haifa was initiated by the 'Carmeli' Brigade. Mounting an attack from the high ground of the Carmel, the Jewish forces surprised the Arabs and succeeded in cutting Arab Haifa into three parts, whereupon the Arab commander of the city fled to Beirut. Major-General Hugh Stockwell, commander of the British 6th Airborne Division, convened a meeting of the Arab and Jewish notables of the city. The Jewish demand was for the Arabs to surrender and hand over their arms; at the same time, they urged their Arab neighbours to remain and to continue to live peacefully in the city. The Arabs went into caucus and were subjected to the urging of the representatives of the Mufti and of Kaukji, who advised them that an Arab military invasion was imminent, that the Jews would be wiped out and that their property would be 'fair game' for the Arab population. They could return to their homes after the Jews had been driven out. The Mufti's consideration in giving this tragic advice was that the resultant stream of refugees would move the neighbouring Arab countries to go to war, a development that was not at that point wholly certain. Following the Arab decision, the Jewish mayor addressed them movingly, and promised them that they could continue to live peacefully side by side with their Jewish neighbours; but the Arab leaders persisted. General Stockwell and some of the leading Arab citizens also attempted to dissuade them, but again these efforts were unsuccessful. A five-day truce was arranged and a mass evacuation began. Out of an Arab population of 100,000, only a few thousand Arabs opted to remain in Haifa.

In Operation 'Ben-Ami', units of the 'Carmeli' Brigade, after securing Haifa, now seized Arab strongholds north of there and northeast of Acre, partly isolating that town. At the same time, they struck towards the north-east to establish direct communication with the Jewish settlements in western Galilee, such as Yehiam and Hanita. Napoleon Hill, east of Acre, had been constructed as an artillery emplacement overlooking the city fortifications by Napoleon Bonaparte during his siege of the city in 1799. A Jewish force now reached Shavei Zion by sea, took the hill and moved southwards towards Acre. On 17 May, after a few hours of mortar shelling, the city that Napoleon had failed to take when it was defended by Sir Philip Sydney, fell to the forces of Israel three days after the establishment of the state.

With a population of 70,000 Arabs, the city of Jaffa was adjacent to, and a continuation of, the Jewish city of Tel Aviv, and had been allotted by the United Nations Partition Resolution to the Arab state. Plan D did not call for the capture of the city, but it did call for the reduction of a number of Arab villages east of it (manned by Iraqi volunteers), which created a wedge between the Jewish areas to the north-east and south-east of Tel Aviv and endangered the road to Jerusalem. Jaffa was thus a thorn in the Jewish side. Arab attacks were being mounted constantly on the outlying areas of Tel Aviv, and snipers from Jaffa's high buildings covered the main thoroughfares inside Tel Aviv, so that innocent passers-by could be picked off. However, as long as there was some prospect that the Arab armies would not invade the country and that the Arabs might ultimately reconcile themselves to the Partition plan, the Haganah refrained from attacking Jaffa. Instead, they chose to create a situation whereby the Haganah forces would control all approaches to that city. Accordingly, with the purpose of isolating it, of linking-up the brigade areas to the north and south of Tel Aviv and of opening the road to the international airport of the country, Lod (which had been allocated to the Jewish state), orders were issued to secure the area around Jaffa. In the last week of April, while the 'Kiryati' Brigade pinned down the forces defending Jaffa with feint attacks, the 'Givati' Brigade from the south and the 'Alexandroni' Brigade from the north began to mop-up along the approaches to the city.

Then, in the early morning of 25 April, without notifying the Haganah and without any prior co-ordination, the Irgun (IZL) concentrated a force of 600 men and launched an attack against Jaffa along the coastal strip connecting the two cities in the Manshiya area. However, stubborn Arab opposition forced the Irgun Command to approach the Haganah and reach an accord whereby all Irgun positions would come under the command of the Haganah area commanders. They also undertook not to initiate any actions unless agreed upon beforehand with the Haganah. Then, with limited Haganah support, the Irgun renewed the attack, cutting the Manshiya area in half. At this point, British forces intervened, bringing in a tank battalion and an artillery battalion and threatening to take action against Tel Aviv. An agreement was finally reached for the Haganah to replace the Irgun and the British forces to take up positions between the two cities. Thus, British and Haganah forces faced each other on the border of Tel Aviv for two weeks until the conclusion of the British Mandate. After this, the city of Jaffa surrendered, the bulk of the Arab population having already fled. A few thousand Arabs remained. The surrounding areas had already been cleared by the Haganah, and the central coastal area of Palestine was now in Jewish hands.

The fighting between the Jews and the Arabs had been very fierce, with little quarter being given on either side. The Arab leaders had openly declared that their purpose was to drive the Jewish population into the sea, to annihilate them. The Arab masses had been particularly affected by the uncontrollable hysteria that characterized the leadership as they suddenly and unexpectedly faced defeat. As a result, they had experienced a complete psychological collapse, moving from an extreme of euphoria to one of doom, depression and despair. They fully expected that the fate they had promised the Jewish population would be meted out to them. In

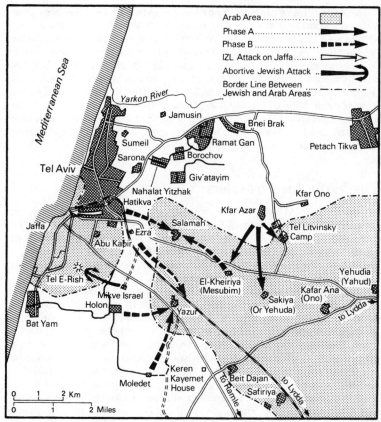

Mopping up around Jaffa, April — May 1948

every case, their leaders abandoned them and were the first to flee, advising the population to follow them and promising them that they would return after the invasion of Palestine with the victorious Arab armies; then, they would not only regain their homes but participate in the looting of the Jewish property that would ensue.

The Jews endeavoured, particularly in Haifa and in other places, to dissuade the Arab population from following their leaders in this. But the Arabs were torn by doubts and beset by an atmosphere of panic. Rather than risk what they believed might occur after the collapse of Arab resistance, they decided in most cases to take advantage of the presence of the British forces and to be evacuated under their aegis. Part of the Arab population (in all, about 150,000) resisted the urge to flee during the war; they remained and became citizens of Israel. The Israeli Arab population has grown today to some 550,000, constituting almost 15 per cent of the total population of Israel.

The Arab refugee problem created by the events of 1948 has been dealt with very frankly and openly by many Arab writers. In his memoirs,* Khaled al-Azm, Prime Minister of Syria in 1948 and 1949, writes: 'Since 1948 we have been demanding the return of the refugees to their homes. But we ourselves are the ones who encouraged them to leave. Only a few months separated our call to them to leave and our appeal to the United Nations to resolve on their return.' And, writing in *Falastin al-Thawra* (official publication of the PLO) in March 1976, Abu Mazer, a member of the PLO Executive Committee, noted: 'The Arab armies entered Palestine to protect the Palestinians . . . but instead they abandoned them, forced them to emigrate and leave their homeland. . . .'**

The battle for Jerusalem

As the British Mandate drew to a close, bitter fighting erupted in Jerusalem. The newly-formed 'Harel' Brigade of the Palmach under the command of Yitzhak Rabin had moved up to Jerusalem with three large supply convoys. A fair-haired, shy, agricultural student, Rabin was a disciple of Yigal Allon and served under his command in numerous capacities. He had risen through the ranks in the Palmach, and the command of a brigade awarded him in his twenties was but an indication of the very heavy turnover in the ranks of the fighting units and of the rapid rise of the young leaders. Dour and taciturn, with little ability to establish a rapport with his fellows, he was nevertheless endowed with a sharp mind and very incisive powers of analysis. He was later to occupy many positions of command in the Israel Defence Forces, rising to the position of Chief of Staff, in which capacity he was Israel's Commander-in-Chief in the 1967 Six Day War. He was later Israeli Ambassador to Washington and, after the resignation of Mrs. Golda Meir's Government in 1974 following the aftermath of the 1973 war, he became Prime Minister, serving until 1977.

Various outlying Jewish areas were being supplied by convoys from the city of Jerusalem, but communications between them were becoming more and more tenuous. One of these areas was the Mount Scopus complex, which included the Hadassah Hospital and the Hebrew University, the route to which passed through the suburb of Sheikh Jarrach, which was controlled by British-manned posts. On 13 April, a convoy en route to the Hadassah Hospital with some eighty civilians, mostly doctors and nurses, was ambushed. British forces were stationed but a few yards away from the ambushed convoy, but they refused to intervene despite the repeated appeals addressed to them. The author of this book, who was responsible at the time for liaison between the Jewish Agency and the Haganah, and the British Mandatory Administration and military headquarters, attempted repeatedly to move the British authorities to call off the

* Khaled al-Azm, *Memoirs*. vol. I, pp. 386-87, Beirut.
** Abu Mazer, Article in *Falastin al-Thawra*. March 1976.

attackers and to rescue those besieged in the home-made armoured cars, which were becoming death-traps. The Jewish Governor of Jerusalem at the time, Dr. Dov Joseph, describes these efforts:

'The attack took place less than two hundred yards from the British military post responsible for the safety of the road. The soldiers watched the attack, but did nothing. Twice, at 1pm and at 2pm, British military cars passed and were hailed by Dr. Chaim Yassky, Director of the hospital. Neither of them stopped. When the Jewish Agency liaison officer appealed to the British military headquarters to let us send Haganah men to the scene, he was told the Army had the situation in hand and would extricate the convoy. A Haganah intervention would only make the fighting worse. Finally, two Haganah cars which tried to reach the convoy

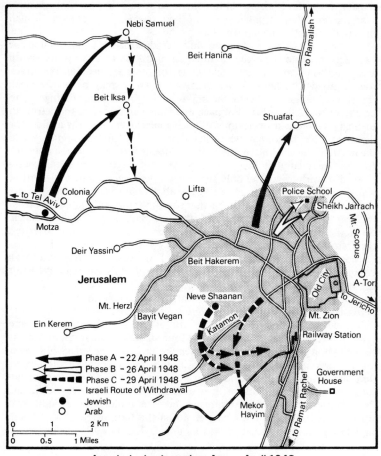

Attacks in the Jerusalem Area , April 1948

were ambushed and two cars which tried to come down to help from Mount Scopus were mined, but all their occupants engaged the attacking Arabs. At noon the Arabs were reinforced. By 1.45pm Dr. Judah Magnes, President of the University, telephoned General Macmillan with a desperate plea for help. The reply was that military vehicles were trying to reach the scene but that a large battle had developed. By three o'clock the two buses were set on fire and most of the passengers who had not already been killed were burned alive.'*

The battle could be seen from the rooftops throughout Jerusalem by an anguished population as it continued for some seven hours and as, one by one, every individual in the convoy was massacred. Encouraged by this success, the Arabs seized further areas to the north of Jerusalem. The area of the Hadassah Hospital and Hebrew University on Mount Scopus was to remain an enclave within Arab-controlled areas for the next nineteen years, a small Jewish police garrison there receiving its supplies through the good offices of the United Nations.

To the north of the city, meanwhile, Yitzhak Sadeh, commanding the Palmach forces in the area, mounted an operation to link up the Jewish areas and to occupy the strategic village of Nebi Samuel. But the attack was repulsed with heavy losses because of poor timing by the Palmach forces. (Failure to appreciate the importance of meticulous timing was to be a frequent failing of the Palmach and Haganah forces, to the detriment of many subsequent operations.) Sadeh's next operation was against the district of Sheikh Jarrach, which lay along the British evacuation route to the north of the city and on the route to Mount Scopus. Here the Palmach forces succeeded, but they were ordered out by the British and were obliged to withdraw. The only successful operation mounted at the time was the capture of Katamon, a large Arab district to the south of the city that cut off the Jewish districts farther south: the 4th and 5th Battalions of the Palmach 'Harel' Brigade and the 4th Battalion of the Jerusalem 'Etzioni' Brigade moved against the Iraqi forces occupying the district and the Iraqi Arab Liberation Army irregulars were driven out of the Greek Orthodox St. Simon's Monastery after a fierce struggle. Desperate Arab counterattacks were beaten off when 'Etzioni' Brigade reinforcements arrived — the fierceness of the battle can be gauged by the fact that, of 120 men who attacked the monastery, only 20 were able to march back to Jerusalem, 40 were dead and 60 were stretcher cases.

The Jewish settlements to the north of the city, Neve Yaakov and Atarot, were now cut off, as were the four villages to the south of the city in the Etzion group, south of Bethlehem; to the west, the village of Hartuv was likewise isolated. Since 20 April, the supply route to the city of Jerusalem from the coastal plain (which was by now a major battlefield) had been severed; the toll of lives in the city was rising every day, and Jewish supplies of food, water, arms and ammunition were dwindling. It was essential to break the stranglehold on the Jerusalem-Tel Aviv road, and so Operation 'Maccabee' was mounted. The 'Givati' Brigade, which

* Dr. Dov Joseph, *The Faithful City*, p. 77, 1962.

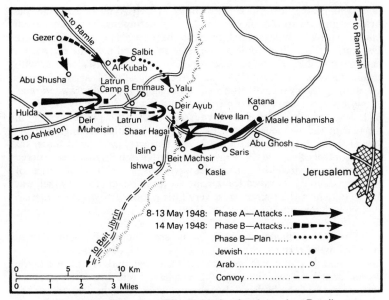

Operation 'Maccabee' (The Battle for the Jerusalem Road)
May 1948

had been fighting around Jaffa and was designated to meet the Egyptian invasion along the coastal road, was to allocate one battalion to the operation; this would take control of the road between Hulda and Latrun, organize the convoy to Jerusalem and bring it to Bab el Wad at the entrance to the mountains. At the same time, the 5th and 6th Battalions of the 'Harel' Brigade were ordered to capture the high ground astride the mountain road leading up to Jerusalem between Bab el Wad and Abu Ghosh and the village of Beit Machsir. When this phase had been completed and the convoy readied, the Jewish forces would then capture Deir Ayub between Bab el Wad and Latrun.

The operation began as planned on 8 May, with the 'Givati' Brigade element completing its part of the mission on the Hulda-Latrun road. The 'Harel' forces captured the high ground north of the road, but, because of poor timing, were not in a position to attack Beit Machsir — a vital point because of its control of the area at Bab el Wad — as planned. The entire operation was therefore postponed for 24 hours. In an endeavour not to draw Arab attention to it, the 'Harel' forces withdrew from the high ground they had occupied; but the Arabs had noted everything that had occurred. As the 'Harel' troops withdrew, Arab troops quietly moved into the vacated positions. Subsequent attacks by 'Harel' units on the 9th and 10th failed to take Beit Machsir. The element of surprise had disappeared.

A third desperate attack by the 'Harel' force finally captured Beit Machsir, but losses were so considerable that they were in no position to continue with the next phase, the capture of Deir Ayub. Meanwhile, the Arabs went over to the offensive and, with the support of artillery from Kaukji's forces, endeavoured to push back the Haganah forces. In desperation, the 'Givati' unit was ordered to try and pass the convoy up through the hills, giving it close protection. But Kaukji's forces, with armoured cars and artillery, seized the high ground above Latrun, inflicting losses on the 'Givati' force and obliging it to withdraw. Parallel to this move, his men also stormed the positions already held by the 'Harel' Brigade in the hills above Bab el Wad. Some of the most bitter fighting in the War of Independence now took place, with positions changing hands several times. When the battle was over, however, the 'Harel' force was still in control of its position. Once again, the 'Givati' Brigade was ordered to capture the area of Latrun. However, as a result of a series of misunderstandings between Kaukji and the Arab Legion force, which was due to take over the Latrun area, very little opposition was encountered: by 16 May, the entire route from Hulda to Jerusalem was open to the Jews.

But now the golden opportunity was missed. The Israeli Command had failed to make ready a convoy to take advantage of the new situation. Indeed, had developments been correctly assessed, and had success in the Latrun area been exploited as it should have been, the entire strategic position both of the besieged Jewish population in Jerusalem and of the Arab position in the hills of Samaria might have been completely different. The failure to exploit the 'Givati' success in the Latrun area at this point was a major error for which the Israeli forces were to pay dearly, for in the meantime new Arab forces had entered the arena. On 14 May, the Egyptian Army had crossed the border into the south of Palestine, so the units of the 'Givati' Brigade that had taken the Latrun area were immediately rushed southwards to block this new invasion. At the same time, Glubb, mindful of the vital strategic importance of Latrun, was moving his advance forces cautiously towards that place via Ramallah, and into other parts of Samaria. Because of the Israeli error in leaving the area of Latrun unmanned, troops of the 4th Battalion of the Arab Legion, which had crossed into Palestine on 15 May, were able to occupy the Latrun area on 17 May without encountering any opposition, and the road to Jerusalem was once more blocked. As the news spread that the Arab Legion forces were advancing from the east and from the north, Jewish Jerusalem braced itself for an invasion.

To the south of the city, the Jewish Etzion settlements between Bethlehem and Hebron had been under siege for several weeks, receiving supplies only by parachute or Piper Cub light aircraft. The beleaguered garrison consisted of 280 male and female settlers, reinforced by a Palmach platoon and a Haganah field force company, giving a total of approximately 500 fighters. On 4 May, an independent Arab Legion company attached to the British Army in the Hebron area, assisted by an irregular infantry force from neighbouring Arab villages, attacked the position near the 'Russian Monastery' and other strongholds held by the Jewish settlers near the Jerusalem-Hebron road, killing twelve of the

Haganah forces and wounding many more. On 12 May, the Arab Legion mounted its final attack and, of the 32 soldiers defending the monastery, only eight men, all wounded, were able to withdraw. By 13 May, the Arab Legion had seized high ground to split the main defence areas of the Etzion villages one from the other, while an Arab Legion force penetrated Kfar Etzion. They were followed by the Arab villagers, who massacred prisoners, both men and women being lined up and shot in cold blood: three men and a girl, who managed to escape under cover of darkness, were all who survived from the entire population to tell the tale.

When it became clear that the situation of the defenders of the Etzion village area was hopeless, negotiations were conducted in Jerusalem

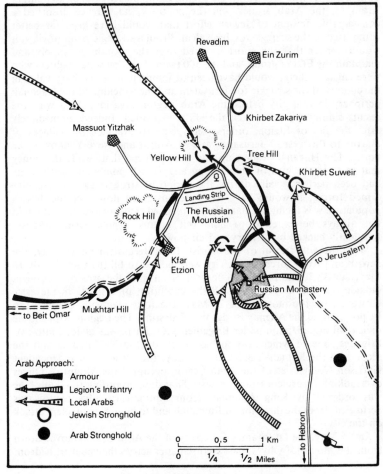

Last Battle of Etzion Bloc , 12 May

through the mediation of the International Red Cross for the surrender of the other settlements there. On 14 May, the Etzion survivors were taken prisoner by the Arab Legion, while the wounded were handed over to the Red Cross for transfer back to Jerusalem. The villages were plundered, looted and destroyed by the Arabs, and the area did not revert to its settlers until June 1967, when the Jewish settlements in the area were re-established.

The destruction of the Etzion villages raised many questions in the Jewish community about the wisdom of a policy that insisted the areas be held to the last man or woman. The argument in favour of such a policy was that such an outpost threatened Arab lines of communication and pinned down Arab forces, but the Etzion group placed little or no military strain on the Arab armies. On the contrary, its defence absorbed a considerable amount of Jewish effort that would have been far better committed to the struggle for Jerusalem. From a strategic point of view, it would appear that the effort invested over the months to supply and maintain the Etzion group, and the 500 trained and seasoned fighters who were engaged there, would have been of infinitely more military value in the context of the struggle for Jerusalem and the widening of the Haganah periphery in that city before the Arab Legion invasion. As it was, the results simply did not match the effort expended. Indeed, immediately after the fall of Etzion, orders were given to evacuate the villages of Hartuv to the west of Jerusalem and of Atarot and Neve Yaakov to the north. The Haganah leadership had now realized that, while the policy that rejected the idea of abandoning any Jewish points and settlements had been perfectly valid during the period of struggle against irregular armed forces, it would have to be reconsidered now that the Jewish population was facing regulars. It was realized that isolated villages could not always be expected to hold out against regular army attacks, frequently backed by artillery and air power.

With the withdrawal of the British from Jerusalem on 14 May, the Jewish and Arab forces in the city were poised to fill the vacuum. By 16 May, Jewish forces had taken control of most of the area of Jerusalem outside the Old City walls, with the exception of districts in the east. However, on the morning of 15 May, the four regiments of the Arab Legion crossed the Allenby Bridge into Palestine. The Legion, with a loose divisional organization under Brigadier N.O. Lash, was divided into two brigades, one of which was to base itself on the Nablus area and the second on the Ramallah area. On 17 May, the 1st and 8th Independent Garrison Companies of the Arab Legion occupied the Mount of Olives overlooking Jerusalem from the east. That day, according to Glubb,* he was ordered by King Abdullah from Amman to advance towards Jerusalem from the direction of Ramallah and to launch an artillery attack on the city.

On 18 May, the 1st Infantry Company of the Arab Legion moved down from the Mount of Olives, past Gethsemane, across the valley of Kidron,

---

* Sir John Bagot Glubb, *A Soldier with the Arabs*, p. 110, 1957.

past the reputed tomb of the Virgin Mary, and then up the slope where St. Stephen is said to have been stoned outside the city walls. Passing through St. Stephen's Gate, they entered the old walled city of Jerusalem and joined the battle for the Jewish Quarter in the Old City. On the same day, Glubb issued orders to his divisional headquarters to attack Sheikh Jarrach at dawn on the 19th, in order to break through and establish contact with the Old City from that direction. At the same time, the 8th Infantry Company on the Mount of Olives was ordered forward into the Old City. On the morning of the 19th, armoured cars led the advance on Sheikh Jarrach, captured French Hill overlooking the northern approaches to the city, and then advanced on the Police School, which was held at the time by Irgun forces. The school fell to the Legion, which exploited success by occupying Sheikh Jarrach, thus linking-up with the Arabs in the Old City and cutting the only Jewish supply route to Mount Scopus. (It was to remain cut off for the next nineteen years, until the Six Day War of 1967.) The armoured car squadron at the head of the Arab Legion column advanced into the city, reaching the Damascus Gate, and there poised itself for the final assault into the Jewish part of the city. The Arab Legion embarked on a systematic shelling of Jerusalem, and the final battle for Jerusalem was joined.

The Arab Legion shelling was directed against what its commanders believed were important Jewish centres, such as military barracks, the Jewish Agency Headquarters, electricity transformers, etc. However, all these targets were sited in the midst of civilian neighbourhoods, and there was also a considerable amount of indiscriminate shelling. The purpose was, of course, to break the morale of the defending population — indeed, life became almost untenable in besieged Jewish Jerusalem. The area was hit by more than 10,000 artillery and mortar shells, and was peppered day and night by bullets that whistled through the air and ricochetted after they had hit the solid stone buildings. There was not a house or an apartment in Jewish Jerusalem that did not have its collection of spent bullets and shrapnel. People hurried through the streets during the lulls in the firing, but the sight of a person walking along the street and suddenly being felled by a stray bullet became commonplace. The streets for the most part of the day were comparatively empty. The water pipeline from the coast to Jerusalem had been blown up, so water from wells and cisterns had to be delivered to homes by lorry — one pail of water per family per day. Families collected weeds from their gardens and the open spaces and cooked them over open fires, for there was little fuel and no electricity. Cemeteries were inaccessible because of the intensity of fire, and people were buried where they fell, in back gardens. The city was administered by the Civilian Governor, Dr. Dov Joseph, a prominent lawyer who had been an active member of the Jewish Agency. His administration played no small part in preparing the city for the siege and in guiding it during these times of hardship. The quiet and determined spirit that characterized other besieged cities in similar circumstances (such as London in the Second World War) was reflected in Jerusalem under siege.

The Mandate ends

Meanwhile, the British evacuation of Palestine was proceeding according to plan. The British withdrew from successive areas in the country without being able to transfer administrative authority to anybody, leaving a vacuum and, in many areas, utterly chaotic conditions. The police force had ceased to exist; postal services had broken down (and Palestine was no longer a member of the International Postal Union). By Friday 14 May, only a small British garrison was left in Jerusalem protecting the High Commissioner, in addition to an enclave retained in Haifa. On that day, the British garrison evacuated Jerusalem, and the High Commissioner, General Sir Alan Cunningham, flew from Kalandia Airport (now Atarot) outside Jerusalem to Haifa, whence he sailed on a Royal Navy vessel. Palestine was now free of British troops and British authority, with the exception of a small enclave at Haifa port, which remained for some weeks in order to complete the final British withdrawal.

The United Nations Palestine Commission, which had been appointed to implement the Partition Resolution, had sent an advance party under Dr. Pablo Azcarate (formerly Republican Spanish Ambassador to Great Britain). The Commission reported that the refusal of the Mandate Government to co-operate with it in the orderly transfer of power under the Partition Resolution had brought Palestine into a state of complete chaos. Desperate political moves were initiated in the United Nations to avert what was seen as an impending disaster and bloodbath, including a trusteeship proposal put forward by the United States of America. A Consular Truce Commission was appointed in which the United States, France and Belgium were members. Its efforts, however, were to be of little avail. Unsuccessful appeals were made to the British to postpone their departure, and events in Palestine moved forward inexorably to their inevitable conclusion.

Meanwhile, the Jewish leadership was debating whether or not to declare independence on 14 May, the date of the British withdrawal. Pressures were exerted on the Jewish representatives in Washington and elsewhere to postpone what might be a precipitate action and thus avoid forcing the Arab armies to go to war. But David Ben-Gurion, head of what was known then as the 'People's Directorate' (later to become the provisional government of Israel), decided that the historic opportunity that had been created must be seized, and his view prevailed against opposition in the Directorate. On Friday 14 May, David Ben-Gurion convened the Provisional Council (later to become the Knesset or Parliament) in the Municipal Museum of Tel Aviv on Rothschild Boulevard (Jerusalem, of course, being under siege and completely cut off). He declared the establishment of a Jewish state in Palestine to be known as the State of Israel. Early the next morning, he broadcast to the United States of America; as he spoke, the sound of Egyptian aircraft bombing Tel Aviv could clearly be heard.

No parallel development occurred on the Arab side. Having rejected the idea of an Arab state in part of Palestine, they joined together to destroy the embryonic State of Israel. A few days before the final British evacuation, Golda Myerson (later Mrs. Golda Meir), a member of the Executive of the Jewish Agency for Palestine (and a prominent leader of the Labour Party) had been sent by Ben-Gurion to meet King Abdullah. She was accompanied by Mr. Ezra Danin, whose task at that time was to maintain contact between the Jewish Agency and various Arab leaders, including the King. Disguised as an Arab woman, Mrs. Myerson had crossed into Jordan in the area of the power station at Naharayim at the confluence of the Jordan and Yarmuk rivers. At her secret meeting with King Abdullah, she had endeavoured to dissuade him from joining the invasion and to set the basis for future Jordanian-Israeli co-operation, but the King was by now committed. She returned to Tel Aviv to report the failure of her mission and the inevitability of an invasion. On the night of 14/15 May, the armies of five Arab states (Egypt, Jordan, Syria, Lebanon and Iraq) crossed the borders and began the invasion of Palestine.

The Jewish forces had now linked-up in most parts of the country to create a measure of territorial depth, but there were two particularly vulnerable elements in Israel's defence posture. One was Jerusalem, which was now being pounded by Arab Legion artillery and fighting as a desperate, beleaguered garrison, with food and supplies already at a minimum. The other problem area was the Negev, in the south, where the Jewish settlements were under siege.

In the first week of May, following the urging of the Political Committee of the Arab League (which decided to invade Palestine immediately on termination of the Mandate on 15 May), the Chiefs of Staff of the Arab armies met in Damascus and approved an invasion plan. King Abdullah of Jordan was Commander-in-Chief of the Arab armies, but this appointment was no more than a title on paper: in practice, each army intended to act in its own national interest and to take orders from its own General Staff rather than from the overall commander. Indeed, the plan evolved not so much as a co-ordinated attack as a division of Palestine into areas to be occupied by the respective Arab armies. The Lebanese were to strike along the northern coast towards Nahariya. The Syrians would cross to the north and south of the Sea of Galilee and head for Zemach, with the occupation of Galilee as their objective. The Iraqis would cross the Jordan south of the Sea of Galilee and, moving through the Arab 'triangle', advance to Netanya on the Mediterranean coast and cut the Jewish state in half. The objective of the Jordanian Arab Legion was the seizure of Nablus and the district of Samaria by one brigade, while the second brigade would seize Ramle on the approaches to Tel Aviv in the central coastal plain; the third brigade was to remain in reserve. The Egyptians would advance in two columns: the main body, from El-Arish, would march along the coastal plain and seize Gaza and then advance northwards to Tel Aviv; the other, reinforced by the Moslem Brotherhood volunteers, would strike towards the north-east through Auja, Beersheba and Hebron, to engage the Jewish forces defending the southern approaches to Jerusalem. In addition, Kaukji's Arab Liberation Army, numbering some 10,000 troops backed by 50,000 Palestinian Arab irregulars, would be available for local defence. All these Arab forces were equipped with modern weapons; three of them, Egypt, Iraq and Syria, had air force support; two, Egypt and Syria, were equipped with tanks; Jordan, Lebanon and Iraq had armoured car contingents. All five armies had a modern artillery component and all had been trained by European instructors (primarily British and French) as modern forces. Kaukji's had an artillery and armoured car element, while the Egyptian Army included units of the Saudi Arabian Army.

Facing this multi-pronged Arab attack advancing on all the major routes into Israel were the infant Israel Defence Forces — more like a partisan force, with a hodge-podge of various types of non-standard equipment, with a wide range of small-arms, with a primitive communication system, with practically no artillery, armour or heavy equipment, and with but an embryonic air unit of light liaison aeroplanes. However, the Arab armies did not have an effective central command: co-ordination between them was loose and, at times, ineffective. The Israeli forces had the advantage of operating along internal lines and were, as the fighting continued, gradually being fashioned into a co-ordinated fighting force that could move reserves from front to front. Above all, the Israelis were consciously and literally fighting for their lives and those of their women and children, and enjoyed outstanding and committed leadership.

The Israeli forces now consisted of nine operational brigades, deployed as follows: three Palmach brigades, the 'Yiftach' in eastern Galilee, the 'Harel' in the Jerusalem Corridor and the 'Negev' in the south. The 'Golani' Brigade was in southern Galilee, the 'Carmeli' in western Galilee, the 'Alexandroni' along the coast between Haifa and Tel Aviv, the 'Kiryati' north and north-east of Tel Aviv, and the 'Givati' to the south. Jerusalem was held by the 'Etzioni' Brigade. In the course of formation was the 7th Brigade under Colonel Shlomo Shamir, at the western end of the Jerusalem Corridor. Yitzhak Sadeh was creating an 8th Armoured Brigade and, in the north, the 'Oded' or 9th Brigade was being formed. Approximately 40,000 Jewish troops thus organized faced the Arab invaders. Apart from the large variety of small-arms, the heaviest equipment of any consequence in the Israeli forces was the 3-inch mortar, of which there were 195, while the 'artillery' units had acquired some Hispano-Suiza 20mm guns and some French 65mm howitzers without sights dating from the beginning of the century. A few Messerschmitt aircraft had been acquired, but were still abroad. Armoured units included some scout cars and a number of crudely home-made armoured vehicles. The battle for the existence of Israel was about to begin.

2
TO THE FIRST TRUCE
15 May to 11 June 1948

The Israeli War of Independence was fought simultaneously on a number of fronts; in the north, against the Syrians, Lebanese and the Arab Liberation Army; in the centre, against the Iraqi Army, the Arab Legion and elements of the Arab Liberation Army; and in the south, against the Egyptians and other irregular Arab elements. Jerusalem was still under siege, and the battle to supply the beleaguered city continued. Fortunately for the Israelis, co-ordination between the Arab forces on the various fronts was lacking. The war itself was broken up intermittently by a series of cease-fires and truces in June and July 1948, so it is convenient to divide the narrative of these events according to the truces and, within these periods, to describe developments in each sector.

The northern front

The first major Arab attack against an area of concentrated Jewish settlement was carried out by the Syrians in the upper Jordan-Beisan area. The tactical advantages in choosing this line of approach were threefold: first, the dominating high ground that controlled the planned battlefield was on their side of the border; second, many of the Jewish agricultural settlements lay east of the River Jordan, thus obviating any Arab necessity for a special river-crossing operation. Third, a breakthrough in this area would enable the Syrian forces to link-up with the Arab population concentrated in Galilee around the Arab city of Nazareth. This would enable them to establish a firm and potentially friendly jumping-off ground from which to move in the direction of Haifa, a major port and one of the terminals of the oil pipeline from Iraq to the Mediterranean. The fighting in the area had begun with abortive attempts by the Arab Legion, moving from Transjordan, to take the strategic police post of Gesher. On 14 May, the Arab Legion attacked and captured the power station at Naharayim.

The Iraqi expeditionary force, moving into the 'West Bank' area towards the sector allotted to it in the Arab plan, endeavoured to bridge and ford the Jordan in the area of Gesher. But, following a series of bitter battles that were fought for a whole week by the settlers of Gesher and by units of the 'Golani' Brigade, the Iraqis withdrew, choosing to cross the river in an area controlled by the Arabs to the south.

The Syrian attacks began on 14 May with heavy artillery bombardments on the settlements in the area south of the Sea of Galilee and on the settlement of Ein Gev, isolated on the eastern shore below Mount Susita. Apart from the villagers, the only Israeli unit available to defend the area was the 2nd Battalion of the 'Golani' Brigade — a single battalion to defend the upper Jordan valley against an invasion by two Arab armies. Even worse, one company of that battalion was still mopping-up in the area of Mount Tabor, some twenty miles to the west. The first objective of

Battles from the Invasion to the First Truce

the Syrian attack force, which consisted initially of an infantry brigade supported by a company of tanks, a battalion of armoured cars and an artillery regiment, was the village of Zemach. Two infantry companies occupied an abandoned military camp south of the village, while a mixed force of armour and infantry advanced on the settlements of Shaar Hagolan and Massada. In a desperate battle, the initial Syrian advance was halted — but only at the cost of all but one member of the force covering the villages. Then, to keep the Syrians guessing and to make time to evacuate the women and children from the area, the settlers resorted to a ruse. Concentrating all their lorries and tractors, they ran convoys by night, ascending in darkness the mountains to the west of the Sea of Galilee and then returning towards the Jordan with their lights full on. This deception was repeated several nights running.

On 18 May, the Syrian 1st Brigade, commanded by Brigadier-General Husni el Zaim (who was a year later to lead the first of many military revolts in Syria), mounted a determined attack against Zemach. The defenders, with two 20mm anti-tank guns, faced an attack led by some thirty armoured vehicles and Renault tanks, which picked-off the defending Haganah positions one by one with point-blank fire. At the same time, a mixed infantry and armoured force outflanked Zemach. When one of the two defending anti-tank guns was put out of action by Syrian fire, part of the force abandoned its positions and retreated from Zemach, leaving behind many casualties — ultimately, most of the defending force was wiped out. The Syrian force had now opened the door to the Jordan valley, and the situation looked very desperate indeed for the outgunned and outmanned Israeli settlers and troops defending the area. The villages of Degania A and Degania B had now become the front-line of defence. Reinforcements from nearby villages were rushed to the area, plus part of the 3rd Battalion of the 'Golani' Brigade and a company of the 'Yiftach' Palmach Brigade. At night, the villages of Shaar Hagolan and Massada were evacuated. When they were taken over by the Syrians, they were looted and destroyed by the Arab camp followers. Meanwhile, an attempt by the Palmach to recapture the police post in Zemach was beaten off.

In Tel Aviv, a delegation of the settlers in the area attempted to impress on David Ben-Gurion the seriousness of the situation. Ben-Gurion reportedly replied: 'We do not have enough guns, and not enough airplanes. There is a shortage of men on all fronts. The situation in the Negev is very serious and it is serious in Jerusalem and upper Galilee. The whole country is a front-line. We have no possibility to send reinforcements.' The Haganah's Chief of Operations, General Yigael Yadin, agreed: 'There is no alternative but to let them reach twenty to thirty yards from the gates of Degania and to engage them at point-blank range in close combat.' After the war, Yadin was to succeed General Yaakov Dori as the second Chief of Staff of the Israel Defence Forces. He was later to be credited with the special type of organization that characterized the IDF and the very effective reserve system that was to be created in Israel. (He resigned as Chief of Staff in the early 1950s, following disagreements with

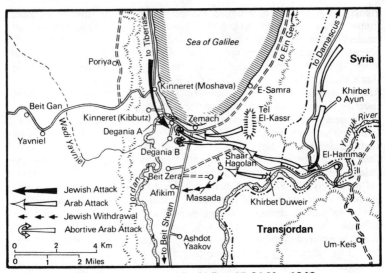

The Battle for the Jordan Valley, 15-21 May 1948

David Ben-Gurion on issues affecting the budget and size of the Israeli armed forces. After some years of archaeological research and teaching, he entered the political arena in 1977 as head of a newly-formed centre party, and achieved the position of Deputy Prime Minister.) In the War of Independence he was a pivotal figure as Ben-Gurion's adviser, and effectively dominated the General Staff.

The Arab attack on the Deganias began at dawn on 20 May with a heavy artillery bombardment. The main thrust was directed against Degania A, in which the total defending force numbered 70 men. The attack was led by an infantry company spearheaded by five tanks and an armoured car unit. The armoured cars opened fire, pinning down the defenders and giving covering fire to the infantry, while the tanks fired point-blank at each of the defending pillboxes and positions, forcing the defenders out of them and into the communication trenches. Now the tanks pushed forward, breaking through the outer, unmined fence: one of the Syrian armoured cars was knocked out by the remaining 20mm anti-tank gun from the flank; a Renault tank was damaged and withdrew; but the attack continued, and soon had reached the Israeli trenches. The defenders, fighting desperately to defend their homes, engaged the tanks with 'Molotov cocktails' and PIAT anti-tank shells. The leading tank was hit by a 'Molotov cocktail' and stopped in its tracks, but its gun continued to fire until yet more 'Molotov cocktails' destroyed it. (That tank has never been moved from there: it stands in silent testimony to the bravery and self-sacrifice of a handful of desperate defenders.) Fortunately for the Israelis, the bulk of the Syrian infantry had not kept up with the armoured advance. Exposed to the Israeli fire, they sought in vain for a break in the defences. But the Israelis held on, and gave not an inch. At midday, the Syrians pulled back from Degania A, having lost two more armoured cars, and concentrated their attack on Degania B.

Here, eight tanks and armoured cars moved forward in attack, this time led by two infantry companies. The infantry were driven off and, again, a large Syrian armoured force attacked with infantry support but was driven back. At noon on that day, the first artillery of the Israel Defence Forces made its debut on the battlefield. The crews had never even trained on them — the guns had been unloaded but a few days earlier in Tel Aviv and rushed to the north. From the hills overlooking the Sea of Galilee, the first practice shots were fired into the water to 'zero in'. They were then aimed at the area occupied by the Syrian support weapons and armour concentrations. The effect of their first shells on the Syrians (who, until now, had held a monopoly of artillery on the field of battle) was immediate: they withdrew, abandoning Zemach, Shaar Hagolan and Massada, which were re-occupied immediately by Israeli forces.

The Israelis had won the battle for the Jordan valley by 23 May. The Syrians never again attempted to invade the country in the area south of

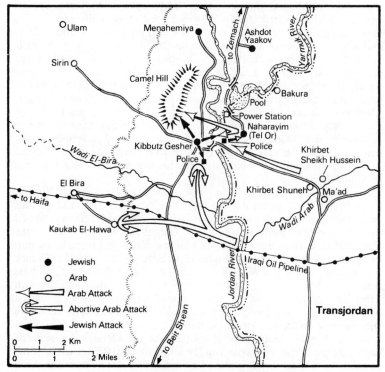

The Jordan Valley — Gesher, 15-22 May 1948

the Sea of Galilee; instead, they switched their major efforts to the north, in the area of Mishmar Hayarden. The significance of the victory at Degania lay less in the fact that the main thrust of the Arab invasion in the Jordan valley area had been blocked than in the electrifying effect it had on the whole of the Jewish population in the newborn State of Israel. Degania, situated on the River Jordan where the waters emerge from the southern shore of the Sea of Galilee, is known as the 'Mother of the Kibbutzim', for it was the first co-operative settlement of the type known as the 'kibbutz' to be established in Palestine in 1910. The fact that this first major battle against an invading army was taking place at Degania was seen in many ways as an omen. The disparity in numbers and equipment had not prevented a handful of settlers from beating back an attack by a regular Arab army. The morale-boosting effect of this success was to be decisive in the desperate days that followed.

Parallel to these events, on the western side of the 'finger' of Galilee, the Lebanese attacked on 6 June and occupied the villages of Malkiya and Kadesh. The Israeli forces meanwhile took the police post at Nebi Yusha, in order to cover the approaches from Lebanon into eastern Galilee. The 'Yiftach' Palmach Brigade under Colonel 'Mula' Cohen then took the initiative, surprising the Lebanese from behind by cross-country infiltration of armoured vehicles. The enemy withdrew in disorder, leaving behind a considerable amount of weapons and ammunition, and Malkiya and Kadesh were once more in Israeli hands. Meanwhile, on the night of 18/19 May, forces of the 'Yiftach' Brigade launched a successful pre-emptive attack against a supply base in Syria in the area of the Bnot Ya'akov Bridge, where the Syrians were concentrating supplies in preparation for an attack against the eastern flank of the Galilee 'finger'. Meanwhile, as the situation of Jerusalem and the Corridor was worsening, the 'Yiftach' Brigade was rushed southwards in the first week of June to face the Arab Legion in the area of Latrun on the road to Jerusalem, and was replaced by the 'Oded' or 9th Brigade, which had been created hastily, following the mobilization of settlers and new recruits. It was commanded by Colonel Uri Yoffe.

Following a reorganization in Syria, with Brigadier-General Husni el Zaim becoming Commander-in-Chief, the Syrians — mindful of their failure against Degania in the Jordan valley — changed their strategy. On 6 June, a co-ordinated, three-pronged Arab attack was mounted against Galilee. The Syrians moved against Mishmar Hayarden with the purpose of cutting the main north-south road in the centre of the 'finger' of Galilee. The Lebanese attacked Malkiya, which would give them control of the heights overlooking the main north-south artery from the west. The Arab Liberation Army directed its attacks against Sejera to the south, which would have had the effect of cutting the only road in Israeli hands linking the centre of Israel with eastern Galilee.

The Lebanese Army took the defenders of Malkiya by surprise, capturing the lightly-held village in the initial assault. The attacking force consisted of almost two brigades of Lebanese and Arab Liberation Army units. Subsequently, Kadesh fell, and the reinforcement route for the ALA into central Galilee was thus opened. However, when the Lebanese attempted to capture Ramat Naftali, they were beaten back after a bitter battle waged literally along the perimeter fence of the village for an entire day.

On 6 June, Mishmar Hayarden, one of the early Jewish settlements founded in 1884 on the River Jordan opposite the bridge of Bnot Ya'akov, was attacked by a Syrian force of two infantry battalions supported by artillery and tank units. Jewish settlements in the area came under heavy artillery barrages and air bombardment. The initial Syrian attack was beaten back by the defenders of Mishmar Hayarden, but the Syrians rapidly recuperated and renewed the attack on 10 June (at the same time as Israeli forces were desperately defending Ramat Naftali to the west). The Syrian attack force was increased to two brigades, and the defending 'Oded' Brigade units were very hard pressed. The Syrians now crossed the Jordan in a two-pronged attack, one moving towards Mahanayim to cut off Mishmar Hayarden from the rear, while the second attacked north and south of the settlement. Led by eight tanks, this prong rapidly reduced the defence positions with point-blank fire, and a battalion of the Israeli 'Carmeli' Brigade, which was rushed to the area, was unable to deploy in time to save the day. In a well co-ordinated attack, with the advantage of overwhelming numbers, the Syrians overran the outer defences of Mishmar Hayarden and, late in the day, with most of the defending force dead and only twenty Israeli prisoners taken, Mishmar Hayarden fell to the Syrian Army. The Syrians advanced towards the main road, but were then blocked by units of the 'Oded' Brigade and the newly-arrived 'Carmeli' reinforcements.

On the same day (10 June) Ein Gev, isolated on the eastern shores of the Sea of Galilee and defended by approximately 100 men and women bearing arms, was attacked by a Syrian battalion with artillery support. The attack was launched from three directions. It was beaten off, heavy casualties being incurred by the Syrians in an exploit that − even in the context of a conflict characterized by extraordinary exploits − is remarkable for the courage and ingenuity of the defenders.

By now, a United Nations negotiated truce had been agreed upon by both sides. As the fighting had been heavy and bitter, and the losses had been considerable, the imposition of such a truce came as a rather welcome respite − a 'priceless month's respite', as Glubb* puts it − to the armies in the field. In particular the Israelis required a period for recuperation and reorganization, and time in which to receive and absorb the growing stream of equipment that was being acquired abroad. However, the cease-fire that came into force on the evening of 11 June was not honoured by the third prong of the Arab attack in Galilee − Kaukji's ALA. He had been alarmed at the attempt by units of the 'Golani' Brigade to take the village of Lubya, a move that endangered his line of communication from Nazareth northward. The Israeli attack had failed but, to prevent a recurrence, Kaukji launched a pre-emptive strike against the Jewish village of Sejera near Lubya. In the course of the fighting, Kaukji's

* Ibid.

forces succeeded in cutting the road to Kfar Tabor, and a bitter hand-to-hand struggle took place in Sejera. Casualties on both sides were heavy, and the Israeli troops were nearing exhaustion when Kaukji's forces at last broke and withdrew. The Arab attacks continued for almost two days into the truce, but the Israeli forces held.

Thus ended the first phase of the fighting in Galilee. The Israelis had achieved their strategic purpose of blocking the Arab invasion. Arab successes at Mishmar Hayarden and Malkiya were not in proportion to the effort and cost, while the Arab Liberation Army had been soundly defeated at Sejera. This had been a phase in which the initiative had been almost entirely in the hands of the Arabs: yet, at its conclusion, they had very little to show for it. Meanwhile, the Jewish irregulars were gradually being honed into an army in the very heat of battle.

The central front

Meanwhile to the south, the Iraqi force of an infantry brigade and an armoured battalion, which had forded the Jordan near Gesher on 15 May and been repulsed, had withdrawn into Transjordan and moved south to the Damya and Allenby Bridges (which were held by the Arab Legion). Crossing the river to Nablus, they concentrated and awaited reinforcements, which arrived by the end of May, bringing their strength up to two infantry brigades and an armoured brigade. On 25 May, the Iraqis struck from the hills of Samaria past Tulkarem in the direction of the Mediterranean – their purpose to cut the State of Israel in two. The Jewish settlement of Geulim was taken; on 28 May, their armoured spearheads reached Kfar Yona and Ein Vered as they pushed along the Tulkarem-Natanya road; Kfar Javits also came under attack. The Iraqi forces were only six miles from Natanya and the Mediterranean when they were at last brought to a halt by the units of the 'Alexandroni' Brigade, which recaptured Geulim.

To counter this threat to Israel's narrow 'waistline', the Israeli Command decided to mount an operation threatening the Nablus triangle and the northern flank of the Iraqi expeditionary force. The plan called for a co-ordinated attack by two battalions of the 'Golani' Brigade and two battalions of the 'Carmeli' Brigade on the town of Jenin (at the northern point of the triangle), while a diversionary attack would be launched by the 'Alexandroni' Brigade to the west through Wadi Ara, thus threatening Tulkarem. The attack from the north was to be led by General Moshe Carmel, commanding the northern front forces of Israel. A leader in the Haganah, he had commanded its forces that had captured Haifa in Operation 'Scissors'. He had acquired his military experience and training in the ranks of the Haganah, initially commanding the 'Carmeli' Brigade and subsequently Northern Command. After the War of Independence he was to enter politics, serving for many years as Minister of Transport in various Labour-led coalitions. Upon his appointment to lead Northern Command, Carmel's 'Carmeli' Brigade was taken over by Colonel

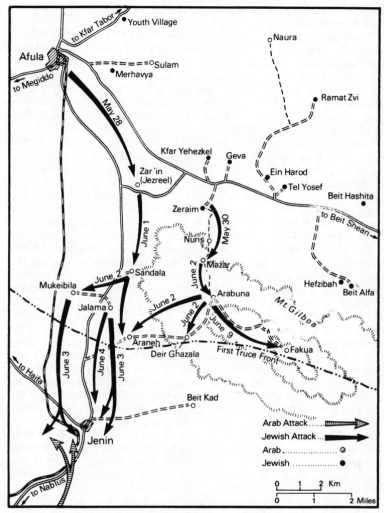

The Battles for the Approaches to Jenin , 28 May—9 June 1948

Mordechai Makleff. As a child of nine, Makleff had witnessed the Arab massacre of his whole family at Motza in the Jerusalem Hills in 1929, and he had saved himself by jumping from a window. He had served as an officer in the Jewish Brigade Group in the British Army during the Second World War; after the War of Independence, he was to be the Deputy Chief of Staff under General Yadin and to succeed him as Chief of Staff for a year. He was later to direct his undoubted administrative ability to the construction of the Dead Sea potash works, which grew to be one of Israel's principal export industries.

The Israeli attack was mounted during the night of 31 May/1 June along the traditional highway that has been the route of invaders from Galilee into Samaria throughout history. The 'Golani' force captured the villages in the Mount Gilboa range north-east of Jenin, occupying Zar'in. At the same time, they seized Megiddo and Lajun, clearing the high ground and the area to the north of Jenin. The 'Carmeli' Brigade was to pass through the 'Golani' lines from the north and take control of the hills dominating the town of Jenin from the south-west and the south-east — control of these hills meant control of Jenin. Iraqi resistance to the 'Carmeli' Brigade attack was very strong and supported by aircraft, while Israel's primitive 65mm artillery did not have the range to reach the Iraqi concentrations preparing for a counterattack. The excessive heat and the troops' inability to dig slit trenches for personal protection on the exposed, sun-scorched rocky terraces impaired the effectiveness of the Israelis holding the high ground to the west of the city. Nevertheless, the 'Carmeli' force persevered and captured the town in the early hours of 3 June.

The Iraqis now brought up reinforcements, whose weight began to tell in the battle. This was the critical phase, which could have brought success had the 'Alexandroni' diversionary attack taken place as planned. Inexplicably, it did not. It was designed to split the Iraqi force and would, in all probability, have done so. But no effective attack was mounted from the west by the 'Alexandroni' Brigade, and the situation of the western 'Carmeli' unit became very precarious, with losses mounting as the Iraqi pressure grew and their forces overran the 'Carmeli' advance positions. The excessive heat, the inability to bring water forward to the positions over the exposed open terraces covered by Iraqi artillery, the ineffective range of the Israeli artillery, the involvement of Iraqi aircraft and now the ominous move of a new Iraqi column to the area of battle — all increased the precariousness of the situation. Carmel advised Headquarters that holding on in this desperate situation would be worthwhile only on condition that a major effort were made by the 'Alexandroni' Brigade to capture Tulkarem. He was therefore given permission to withdraw from the town of Jenin. This was effected with heavy losses, but the Israeli forces continued to hold all the positions north of Jenin after the Iraqis had regained the town.

A major opportunity to achieve a foothold in the foothills of Samaria, possibly to roll back the Iraqi Army, and thus to widen Israel's 'waist' along the coast, was lost by the complete failure of the 'Alexandroni' Brigade — whose leadership seems to have been unimaginative and to have lacked aggressiveness. This was the prime cause of the failure of the Israeli forces to take Jenin and thus threaten Nablus, and for any major dent to be made in the Arab positions overlooking the coastal plain. On 4 June, the 'Alexandroni' Brigade did capture the large village of Kakun, however, just north of the Natanya-Tulkarem road. Repeated Iraqi counterattacks were beaten back and the village remained in the hands of the Israelis.

The battle for Jerusalem

On 15 May, with the announcement of the Arab invasion of Palestine, Kaukji assumed that his task at Latrun, blocking the road to Jerusalem, had been completed. He withdrew from his positions in order to reorganize without so much as co-ordinating with the Arab Legion — whose commander, Glubb, only realized that this had happened a few days later, on 18 May, when the 4th Battalion of the Legion entered Latrun. An invaluable opportunity had thus been lost by the Israeli Command: for two to three days, this absolutely vital and pivotal point in the defence of Jerusalem had been abandoned by the Arab forces and could have been seized by the Haganah, but no advantage was taken of this situation. The inexperience of the senior commanders, inadequate organization at the regional level, and an almost total absence of effective field intelligence (not to mention of intelligence at the command level), all combined to cause a costly error of a type that was to claim the lives of many in the course of the war.

As the Arab Legion moved into Palestine, the isolated Jewish settlements to the north of Jerusalem, Atarot and Neve Yaakov, were abandoned. Similarly Kibbutz Beit Haarava and the potash works at the northern end of the Dead Sea were evacuated by sea to Sdom, at its southern end. To the south of Jerusalem, the Etzion group of villages had fallen.

The Arab Legion now concentrated on reducing the city of Jerusalem. From the heights north of the city including French Hill, Arab Legion artillery pounded the Holy City incessantly. The Irgun forces had been driven out of Sheikh Jarrach and, in the Old City, Jordanian forces isolated the Jewish Quarter. At the same time, they launched a major attack to break into the Jewish city in the area subsequently known as the Mandelbaum Gate. A parallel attack was directed from the Damascus Gate at the Old City wall towards the monastery of Notre Dame. The 3rd Regiment of the Arab Legion advanced with armoured cars against the Musrara Quarter along the road leading from the Damascus Gate to the Notre Dame Monastery, passing between the Old City wall and the Monastery, which they pounded with anti-tank guns over open sights. In the desperate battle that ensued, of the 200 Arab Legion infantry who had set out to take Notre Dame at noon on 23 May, nearly half were killed or were stretcher cases. The leading company lost all its officers and NCOs except one. The Jewish defenders, armed with 'Molotov cocktails' and PIAT anti-tank projectors, fought back desperately. As the first Arab armoured cars came abreast of the Monastery opposite the New Gate in the Old City wall, the wall of the Monastery was blown up and collapsed on them, after which they were destroyed by 'Molotov cocktails'. The debris, covering the road entirely between the Monastery and the Old City wall, rendered the road impassable and blocked the Arab Legion advance. Indeed, the burnt-out hulks of the armoured cars and the debris proved to be effective anti-tank obstacles in the narrow street. At 17.00 hours on 24 May, Glubb called off the Legion attack. The 3rd Regiment had incurred

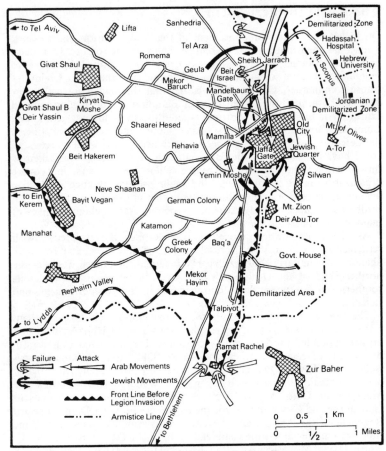

Battles In Jerusalem up to the First Truce

severe losses. Glubb had little or no reserves and considered that, having regard to the Israeli pressure on Latrun and the additional threats to Samaria, it would be unwise to become bogged down in one of the more complicated forms of warfare, street fighting. He decided to cut his losses and not to press any farther in western Jerusalem. Thus, a few hundred yards from the centre of the Jewish city in Jerusalem, the Arab Legion was halted. The Jewish city had been saved by the stubborn struggle of the defenders of Notre Dame.

To the south, the Arab Legion joined the forces of the Moslem Brotherhood who had advanced through Hebron and Bethlehem to the southern outskirts of Jerusalem as part of the eastern arm of the invading Egyptian forces. On 21 May, the first attack had been mounted against

Kibbutz Ramat Rachel on the southern outskirts of Jerusalem; in the subsequent days, the village had fallen three times to Arab forces only to be retaken each time in fierce and bloody battles by units of the 'Etzioni' Brigade, the Irgun and the Palmach.

The main thrust of the Arab Legion was now directed against the Jewish Quarter of the Old City in Jerusalem. Situated in the south-east part of the Old City, this was bordered on the east by the Temple Mount, including the El Aqsa and Omar (Dome of the Rock) Mosques, on the west by the Armenian Quarter, and on the north by the Moslem Quarter. To the south it was bordered by the Old City wall between the Zion Gate and the Dung Gate. Since March, it had been supplied by means of convoys escorted by British troops. The Security Council of the United Nations had declared the Old City an open, demilitarized zone: but, with the withdrawal of the British, the Arabs rejected this decision, and drove out the Jewish units defending the area of Mount Zion.

After the first Arab Legion forces entered the Old City, the Jerusalem Haganah Command diverted the force due to counterattack at Sheikh Jarrach, and ordered it to attack Jaffa Gate in order to break into the Old City. As a diversionary attack, a company of the 4th Battalion of the Palmach 'Harel' Brigade commanded by Colonel Uzi Narkiss was ordered to attack Mount Zion. (Nineteen years later, General Narkiss would be GOC Central Command, whose forces in the Six Day War broke into, and captured, the Old City of Jerusalem against fierce Arab Legion resistance.) As occurred far too frequently, the operation against the Jaffa Gate was late in starting, and the preparations gave adequate warning to the Arab forces. There was also little or no co-ordination between the main attack on the Jaffa Gate on the evening of 18 May, and the diversionary attack of the 'Harel' force from a base in Yemin Moshe. Consequently, the frontal attack on the Jaffa Gate incurred heavy losses and was beaten back. However, the attack on the Jaffa Gate had at least diverted the attention of the Arabs from the Palmach force stealthily climbing the steep slopes of Mount Zion on the night of 18/19 May. The attacking company, led by Major David Elazar, took the Arabs by surprise, captured Mount Zion, reached the Zion Gate early in the morning, blew a breach in the gate and linked-up with the defenders of the Jewish Quarter. After this, the exhausted Palmach force, which had been fighting without respite in the hills to the west of the city, insisted on being relieved: it withdrew out of the city back to its base, and was relieved by a reinforcement of 80 men of the 'Etzioni' Brigade. But this force was poorly trained and unequal to the bitter struggle in the narrow alleys of the Old City. The next day, the battalion of the Arab Legion that had entered the Old City reinforced the Arab counterattack, and the area the Palmach had taken at the Zion Gate was recaptured. The Jewish Quarter was once again besieged.

The man who commanded the successful Palmach break-in at the Zion Gate, Major David Elazar, known as 'Dado', had come to Israel as a child from Yugoslavia during the Second World War, where his father was a major in Tito's partisan forces. He was to rise through the ranks of the Israel Defence Forces, commanding the operations of the Israeli Northern

Command in the Six Day War against the Syrian forces on the Golan Heights, and ultimately being appointed Chief of Staff of the IDF. In 1973, he commanded the Israel Defence Forces in the Yom Kippur War, proving his mettle as a cool, calm and determined commander in the face of great adversity, demonstrating exceptional ability as a general. However, the so-called Agranat Commission (page 236) after the Yom Kippur War found him at fault, and he submitted his resignation. Not long thereafter, in his 48th year, he died from a heart seizure.

With a population of 1,500 civilians and a total Haganah and Irgun force of some 300, the defenders fought desperately in the narrow alleys of the Old City. Hand-to-hand fighting took place from house to house and from room to room. Renewed attacks were mounted by the forces on Mount Zion in order to break into the Old City, but they failed, as did attacks some days later on the Zion Gate and on the New Gate in the north. Ammunition ran out and, as one position after another was fought over and abandoned, the area defended by the Jewish forces narrowed down to some 200 square yards around the Nissan Bek Synagogue and Misgav Ladach Hospital, whose cellars were packed to overflowing with wounded. By 28 May, with only 300 rounds of ammunition left, and 36 men capable of manning positions, the commander of the Quarter gave in to the pressure and pleading of the Rabbis, and allowed them to negotiate with the Arab Legion for surrender. When the surrender was effected, the officers of the Arab Legion were unwilling to believe the sight they saw, and to credit such a handful of fighters with holding off their forces at such high cost. A few fighters were taken as prisoners of war. Thereafter, 1,190 civilians led by old Rabbis carrying Scrolls of the Law made their weary way down the slopes of Mount Zion, a long and sad procession — old people, women and children, followed by the walking wounded and the severely wounded, stretcher-borne by Arab Legion soldiers. The Arab mobs proceeded to loot and burn the Jewish Quarter, destroying in the process some 58 Jewish synagogues. The Jewish holy places in the Old City were to remain closed to the Jewish population for nineteen years until the city was retaken in the 1967 Six Day War and the holy places for three religions were opened to all.

The capture of the Jewish Quarter of the Old City was the only success of any significance achieved by the Arab Legion. The Jewish lines in the meantime had been stabilized. Glubb, mindful of the mounting casualties in the street fighting, had realized that tying down his force in house-to-house fighting could be a very costly endeavour. He therefore had decided to concentrate on starving the Jewish City into surrender by tightening his hold on the Jerusalem road, particularly at Latrun. Electricity supplies in the city were down to a minimum of a few hours a day, and the water-pumping stations had been shut off by the Arabs since 12 May. There was no news because the radio was cut off. There was widespread hunger and thirst and, at night, total darkness. Twenty-four hours a day the city was under artillery bombardment. There was no food in the shops. The entire population lived and slept in the cellars and the shelters, and there were no sanitary arrangements because of the lack of water. As supplies ran out, it became clear to all that the limit of human endurance was not far off unless the siege could be lifted.

The feeling of desperation that animated those defending Jerusalem was reflected in the decisions of the Israeli General Staff. During the week preceding the establishment of the State, a new brigade was formed: the 7th Brigade, under General Shlomo Shamir. A product of the Haganah, he had served as an infantry officer in the Jewish Brigade Group with the British Army in the Second World War. (The author of this book served as his operations officer and deputy during May and June 1948.) The 7th Brigade was centred around an armoured battalion equipped with half-tracks, which had just arrived in the country, and various armoured cars acquired from the enemy in the fighting. This armoured battalion was commanded by General Haim Laskov. He too was a product of the Haganah, had served as an infantry officer in the Jewish Brigade Group in the British Army, and had created the framework within which the Haganah forces and the new army were trained. A tall, heavily-built, soldierly-looking man who was seldom seen without a pipe in his mouth, he was a great devotee of the British Army tradition, which he endeavoured on all occasions to represent and to further. He had organized the first Officers' School of the Israel Defence Forces, and was later to serve as a regular soldier, devoting his life exclusively to soldiering. He was to follow Moshe Dayan as Chief of Staff of the armed forces in 1958.

A second infantry battalion was scraped together from personnel from different brigades, while a third battalion was officered by the staff of part of the training establishment and manned by new immigrants as they arrived on boats from the camps in Cyprus to which they had been sent after trying to enter Palestine illegally before the end of the Mandate. These troops had received little or no training — in fact, in many cases they were given their initial weapons training only a day or two before being thrown into battle. The brigade was not given a chance to organize or train properly, and was sent into battle within a week of being formed. Equipment was minimal, and one vital item was almost totally absent: a supply of water bottles. The absence of these in the excessive 'khamsin' heatwave that was to envelop the battlefield was to prove tragic.

Unorganized and ill-equipped though it was, the 7th Brigade was entrusted with the main effort to open the road to Jerusalem and move a convoy of supplies to the beleaguered city. On taking the area of Latrun, it was to advance into the mountains along the road towards Ramallah; this, it was estimated, would relieve the pressure on the north of Jerusalem. The attack was to be co-ordinated with operations by the 'Harel' Brigade in the Jerusalem Corridor, striking north from Kiryat Anavim and Bab el Wad towards Ramallah, and by the 'Etzioni' Brigade in Jerusalem itself. Mindful of the inherent weakness of the new brigade, the General Staff attached a battalion of the 'Alexandroni' Brigade to it. By 23 May, the Brigade was concentrated in the area of Hulda and Naan, while a large convoy loaded with supplies stood by at Ekron, ready to move up to Jerusalem. However, at the request of the Brigade's commander the

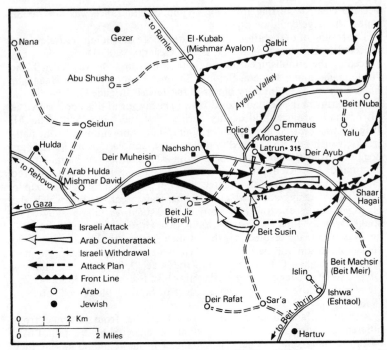

The First Attack on Latrun, 23 May 1948

planned attack was postponed for 24 hours, during which the Arab Legion reinforced its 4th Battalion under the command of Lieutenant-Colonel Habis el Majali (who was in later years to become Commander-in-Chief of the Arab Legion). The Legion now became responsible for the defence of Latrun and moved the 2nd Battalion to the area of Deir Ayub and Yalu.

The Israeli plan called for the 'Alexandroni' Battalion to capture the police station and village of Latrun, which was behind a spur crowned with the ruins of a castle dating from the period of the Crusades. A battalion from the 7th Brigade was to cover its right flank in order to secure the Jerusalem road. But, as occurred on numerous occasions with tragic results during the War of Independence, timing was faulty: the 'Alexandroni' Battalion, which was entrusted with the main effort, instead of attacking towards midnight and using the cover of darkness, was delayed. The Battalion reached its jumping-off position and was ready to move only by 04.00 hours on the 23rd when the first rays of dawn appeared. By the time the advance units reached the Latrun-Jerusalem road, they were in full view of the defending Arab Legion in the Latrun area above the road. Completely exposed, the Israelis came under withering fire that obviated any possibility of attack. Thus began a tragic withdrawal, during which most of the hundreds of casualties suffered were

On 14 May 1948 in Tel Aviv Museum, David Ben-Gurion, the country's first Prime Minister, declared the independence of Israel. The following day, the new state was invaded by five neighbouring Arab nations. (Braun)

Far left: Fauzi el-Kaukji, the Syrian-born commander of the Arab irregular forces in Galilee. (Jerusalem Post) **Left, top:** Emir (later King) Abdullah of Transjordan believed that peace could be achieved between the Arab and Jewish populations of Palestine. His beliefs resulted in his assassination by Arab extremists outside the El Aqsa Mosque in the Old City of Jerusalem in 1951. (Jerusalem Post) **Left, below:** The Mufti of Jerusalem, Haj Amin el-Husseini, was extreme in his support for Arab nationalism and in his attempts to whip up revolutionary fervour among his supporters to oust the Jews from Palestine. He died in exile in Beirut in 1974. (GPO) **Above:** Major Gamal Abd al Nasser (on his left, his battalion commander) served in the ill-fated Faluja pocket which surrendered to Israeli forces on the southern front. (Cohen) **Below left:** Lieutenant-Colonel Izaak Bey Dessouky, commander of the Egyptian forces in Gaza, after his capture by Israeli forces. (GPO) **Below right:** Anwar el Sadat, a young infantry major in the 1948 War, was one of Nasser's closest collaborators in the Free Officers Revolution of 1952 which overthrew King Farouk. Later, as President of Egypt, Sadat was to become the main architect of the peace process. (Camera Press)

Above: Brigadier-General Yaakov Dori was Israel's first Chief of Staff and commanded the Israeli Army during the 1948 War of Independence. He subsequently became President of the Technion in Haifa. (GPO)

Above left: Lieutenant-Colonel Yigael Yadin at a briefing. He was Chief of Operations of the Haganah and of the Israeli Army and, in 1949, he succeeded Dori as Commander-in-Chief. (Zahal Archives)

Below left: Colonel Yigal Allon visiting troops near Abu Ageila in 1948. Allon became commander of the Palmach and of the southern front.

Right, top: A mobilization centre in Jerusalem. All males aged 17 to 55 were called upon to report for army duty. (GPO)

Right, below: Besieged Jerusalem was governed by a civilian committee under the chairmanship of a Canadian-born lawyer, Dov (Bernard) Joseph (centre, with moustache). (Zahal Archives)

Far left, top: Tracer fire illuminates the walls of the Old City of Jerusalem immediately before the unsuccessful Israeli attempt to breach the Zion Gate. The cone-topped building is the Church of the Dormition, which stands exactly opposite the gate. (Braun)

Far left, below: Arab Legion soldiers parading in East Jerusalem, 1948.

Left: The first supply convoy reaches the outskirts of Jerusalem after the siege has been finally broken, just before the festival of Passover, April 1948. (Jerusalem Post)

Below: Provision of water was one of the most pressing problems of besieged Jerusalem. Trucks bearing tanks doled out a small daily ration. (GPO)

Above: Kastel Hill, some six miles west of Jerusalem, whose capture by the Israelis was a crucial turning-point in the battle for the city. (GPO)

Right: Abd el Kader el-Husseini, a cousin of the Mufti, was the most charismatic and respected commander of the Arab forces. His death during the fierce fighting for Kastel Hill dealt a severe blow to the Arabs' morale. (Jerusalem Post)

Far right, top: Nebi Yusha police fortress in upper Galilee.

Far right: A group of defenders of the town of Safed in northern Galilee, made up of members of the Palmach and a cross-section of civilian residents of the town. (Zahal Archives)

Left, top: The village of Mishmar Hayarden on the Jordan, after its destruction by the Syrians.

Left, below: The defenders of Kfar Etzion at prayer in their positions.

Above: Israeli troops accept the surrender of an Arab village during the Auja campaign in October 1948. (GPO)

Right: Members of the Palmach in an American-built M3 half-track during Operation 'Yoav' in the Negev. (Zahal Archives)

Left, top: Israeli troops in an assortment of American and locally built armoured fighting vehicles approach the Israel-Egypt border, Sinai, 1948. **Left, below:** Israeli troops occupying abandoned Egyptian trenches at Huleiqat on the southern perimeter of the surrounded Faluja pocket in the Negev, October 1948. (GPO) **Above:** Israeli forces advancing in the Negev Desert. **Below:** Brigadier-General Mohammed Said Taha Bey, known as 'The Tiger', negotiating the evacuation of Egyptian troops from the Faluja pocket at the stronghold of Iraq Suedan. On his left is Lieutenant-Colonel Yitzhak Rabin, who later became the victorious commander of the IDF in the Six Day War of 1967.

Left: Captain Avraham ('Bren') Adan raises an ink-drawn flag at the hamlet of Um-Rashrash, later the town of Eilat, on the northernmost tip of the Gulf of Aqaba. As a major-general, 'Bren' Adan was a divisional commander on the southern front during the 1973 War. (GPO)

Right, top: The cease-fire lines in Jerusalem are negotiated in the presence of UN mediators on 5 December 1948 by members of the Arab Legion, commanded by Lieutenant-Colonel Abdullah el-Tel (second from the left), and the Jerusalem Brigade of the IDF, commanded by Colonel Moshe Dayan. (GPO)

Right, below: Demarcation of the cease-fire lines in the Latrun salient. UN mediators oversee negotiations between officers of the Arab Legion and the IDF. Israel was represented by the author (then Operations Officer of 7th Brigade), far right, and, on his right, Colonel Assaf Simhoni, who became commander of the southern front in the Sinai Campaign of 1956 and was subsequently killed in an aircrash.

Israel's military delegation to the Armistice Commission's deliberations in Rhodes. From left to right, Major Yehoshafat Harkabi (later to become Chief of Intelligence), Major Arieh Simon, Colonel Yigael Yadin (then Chief of Operations of the IDF) and Lieutenant-Colonel Yitzhak Rabin. (GPO)

incurred. At the same time, the battalion of the 7th Brigade to the right of the 'Alexandroni' Battalion came under flanking fire from Arab Legion forces and Arab irregulars who had occupied the villages of Beit Jiz and Beit Susin — to the rear of the attacking forces — which had previously been assumed to be empty. The heat was oppressive. There were no water supplies and the troops carried no water bottles, an especial hardship for the immigrants, who were completely unaccustomed to the weather and conditions. The Arab Legion artillery pounded the area mercilessly as the units tried to extricate themselves. Numerous acts of heroism and self-sacrifice were recorded. Sniping from the flanks and rear intensified. It was only with the greatest difficulty that the remainder of the force was extricated. The units, broken, in disarray and followed by stragglers, gradually struggled back to the area of high ground held as a firm base by one of the companies of the 'Alexandroni' Battalion. The first battle for Latrun, entered into as it was with inadequate preparation, ill-trained forces and poor co-ordination, was a serious defeat for the Israel Defence Forces at the hands of the Arab Legion. Had the 7th Brigade been given even one more week in which to train and organize itself into a fighting force, the results may well have been different.

Encouraged by its success, the Arab Legion on 26 May attacked one of the principal Haganah strongholds to the north of the Jerusalem road, drove out the 'Etzioni' garrison and captured Radar Hill (known as such because the British forces had erected a radar station on it during the Second World War) in the area of Biddu. This gave the Legion an ideal observation post overlooking the main Jerusalem road, which it could henceforth interdict with artillery fire.

Despite the critical situation on all fronts, Ben-Gurion decided to give priority to the Latrun front and, a week later, the 7th Brigade was ordered to the attack again. In the meantime, detachments had occupied Beit Jiz and Beit Susin in order to secure their flanks. The 'Alexandroni' Battalion was withdrawn and replaced by a battalion from the 'Givati' Brigade. The new plan called for the 'Givati' Battalion, using Beit Susin as its firm base, to move across the Jerusalem road, capture Deir Ayub and thereafter take Yalu: from there it would be possible to cut the Latrun-Ramallah road, the main supply route of the Arab Legion positions in Latrun. Simultaneously, Laskov's armoured battalion followed by an infantry battalion would capture the police station and village of Latrun and neutralize the Trappist Monastery below the village of Latrun at the base of the hill on the Jerusalem road. The Israeli attack was to be supported by four 65mm guns and a number of 120mm mortars that had just arrived in the country.

Deir Ayub fell to the 'Givati' attack without opposition. However, as the force moved on to Yalu, it came under flanking fire that wounded a number of soldiers in the leading platoon. Panic ensued and, without permission, the 'Givati' Battalion withdrew in disarray, abandoning also Deir Ayub. Unaware of the failure of the operation's eastern flank, Laskov's armoured forces fought bravely, reached the outskirts of Latrun village, and penetrated the courtyard of the police post. However, the untrained and inexperienced infantry failed to follow through the murderous fire of the Legion artillery. The armour persisted in its attack under point-blank fire from the defence positions on the roof of the police fortress. Flame-throwers were used in the attack, but the engineers whose task it was to demolish the wall of the police station were hit and immobilized by fire from nearby Emmaus (the scene of one of the great battles of the Maccabees two thousand years earlier). Laskov's attacking force, without its supporting infantry and without the benefit of what would have been a major diversion at Yalu, saw victory snatched from its grasp at the last minute, and was obliged to withdraw. Indeed, it later transpired that the move against Yalu and the assumption that the armoured forces would be followed by a major infantry assault had alerted the Arab Legion, which had even thrown its clerks and cooks into the battle. Hastily, orders had even been issued to prepare for an Arab withdrawal from the area to avoid being cut off at Yalu.

But Latrun remained in Arab hands, and the Israeli Command remained concerned about its strategic importance. A second attack was therefore ordered, to be commanded by Colonel David Marcus (known also by the pseudonym of 'Mickey Stone', to avoid complications in the United States), a retired officer from the United States Army and a graduate of West Point who had come to help the new Israeli Army. Courageous, athletic and extrovert, he had little field experience, since most of his senior appointments had been staff jobs: his effectiveness lay in his leadership, for he was capable of adapting himself to the informal and ill-organized type of partisan army that was being created out of an underground force under fire. Furthermore, he actively participated in many operations, and thus gained the respect of Israeli commanders who regarded outsiders with very considerable suspicion. He arrived at the 7th Brigade with orders issued by Ben-Gurion to the effect that, after suitable co-ordination had been effected (it being assumed that this would take place in the first lull or truce in the fighting), Marcus would take charge of the entire Jerusalem front with the 7th, 'Harel' and 'Etzioni' Brigades under his command. His report on the second Latrun attack to the Chief of Operations, General Yadin, read: 'Plan good, artillery good, armour [Laskov's Battalion] excellent, infantry disgraceful.' Some two weeks later, however, with the beginning of the first truce, Marcus moved up to Jerusalem in order to visit the troop formations that were to come under his command and to establish his headquarters. He spent the night with a Palmach force in Abu Ghosh and, in the darkness, went outside the perimeter wrapped in a blanket. On his return, he was challenged in Hebrew by a sentry; when he replied in English and vaulted over the stone wall, the sentry fired one shot from his Sten gun, which entered Marcus's heart. Thus, his inherent ability, enthusiasm and leadership qualities, which could well have made him a very important commander in the Israeli forces, were lost. Accompanied by two Israeli officers (one of them Moshe Dayan), his body was taken back to the United States to be buried at West Point.

Following the capture of Beit Susin, patrols of the 7th Brigade reconnoitred towards the hills of Jerusalem and met patrols of the 'Harel'

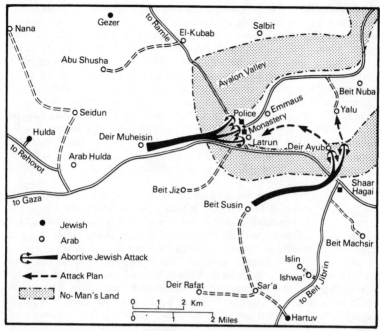

The Second Attack on Latrun, 30 May 1948

Brigade probing down towards the coast. Only a narrow strip of mountainous territory separated the areas controlled by the two brigades, so the 7th recommended the construction of a 'Burma Road' linking them. (Indeed, the author of this book brought the plan back to Tel Aviv for consideration by David Ben-Gurion, specifying the route it was believed the new road should take, after a commanders' reconnaissance by David Marcus, Shlomo Shamir, the Brigade Engineer and the author.) A similar proposal was brought forward by Amos Horev, Operations Officer of the Palmach. A slightly-built, determined man, whose youthful appearance belied his years and experience, he was later to become a general, the Chief of Ordnance and subsequently the Quartermaster-General of the Israel Defence Forces and President of the Technion, the Haifa Institute of Technology.

David Ben-Gurion gave immediate instructions to assemble the maximum available number of earth-moving vehicles in order to exploit the possibility of building a road as proposed. Isolated units and individuals made their way across the stretch separating the two brigade areas. The area, impassable to transport, was immediately east of Beit Susin, where there was a steep rocky drop of 400 feet. Immediately, large convoys of flour, meat on the hoof and other supplies were driven to Beit Susin under cover of darkness; there they were manhandled by hundreds of porters mobilized in Jerusalem, and taken by mule to the Hartuv road. At the same time, hundreds of engineers and road-construction workers and all available bulldozers were concentrated in the area. Speed was essential: on 11 June, a United Nations negotiated truce, the so-called 'First Truce', was due to come into effect. This would enforce a complete status quo, which meant that no supplies would be allowed to move up to Jerusalem through any route that had been blocked off (such as the Latrun route) without United Nations and Arab supervision. Hence, it became absolutely vital for the Israelis to have a road open and in operation before the truce came into effect. The result, the 'Burma Road', was first traversed — with great difficulty, jeeps and lorries frequently having to be manhandled over rocks — on 10 June by a convoy that drove straight through from Tel Aviv to Jerusalem with American correspondents on board.

A further attempt was made to take Latrun just before the truce, when the 'Yiftach' Palmach Brigade was moved from Galilee to the Jerusalem Corridor. After a number of delays, the operation was finally mounted on 9 June in co-ordination with an attack by a battalion of the 'Harel' Brigade from the mountains overlooking Latrun from the east. A series of errors ensued: the 'Harel' Brigade occupied the wrong position so that the 'Yiftach' Brigade, moving towards what it believed was a position held by a friendly force, instead came under heavy Arab Legion fire. The attack broke up in disarray. The fourth attack on Latrun had failed. The Arab Legion counterattacked and, on 10 June, captured the settlement of Gezer, thereby endangering Hulda, the main Israeli base for operations in the area. The village was looted and destroyed by the time forces of the 'Yiftach' Brigade recaptured it that same evening. Then, at 10.00 hours on 11 June, the United Nations cease-fire came into force.

The Arab Legion had failed to take Jewish Jerusalem; the Israelis had failed to break the Arab stranglehold at Latrun. However, at the last minute, by a combination of improvization and ingenuity, the Israeli forces facing Latrun had succeeded in creating a road that had raised the siege of Jerusalem and opened up the route for supplies and reinforcements to Jewish Jerusalem from the coastal plain.

The southern front

The Egyptian invasion was mounted along the two classic routes that have been traversed over forty times in history by invading armies moving from Egypt to Palestine — the northern Sinai route along the coast towards Gaza and the eastern route towards Beersheba. The irregular Egyptian forces of the Moslem Brotherhood commanded by Lieutenant-Colonel Ahmed Abd-el-Aziz, a regular cavalry officer, had already been operating in the south of Palestine before the conclusion of the Mandate. King Farouk of Egypt had long come to the conclusion that a military adventure with what appeared to be tremendous odds on his side would divert public opinion from the internal problems of his country (which were becoming more and more complex) and would help to consolidate his own position. Participating with a comparatively large force would enable him to thwart King Abdullah's probable ambitions to take advantage of the situation and seize control of Palestine. In this approach, he was supported by his Prime Minister, Nokrashi Pasha, who chose to ignore the military problems posed by the invasion and the glaring inadequacies of the Egyptian Army, commanded by Lieutenant-General Mohammed Haidar.

The Egyptian invasion force itself was led by Major-General Ahmed Ali el Mawawi, and consisted of five infantry battalions, a force of British-manufactured Crusader tanks and artillery, with an air force including three squadrons of fighters, one squadron of bombers and some reconnaissance aircraft in support. The ground force, which consisted of the 3rd Division, was divided into two brigade groups: a large one, numbering some 5,000 men, was routed along the coastal road while a smaller one, some 2,000 men plus the Moslem Brotherhood unit, advanced on the interior road towards Beersheba.

Of the 27 scattered Jewish settlements in the south of Palestine and Negev Desert at the time, only five had more than 30 defenders. The defence of the area rested on two Israeli brigades. The southern brigade, the 'Negev' Brigade of the Palmach, consisted of two battalions totalling approximately 800 men. (After the invasion began, the 'Negev' Brigade was strengthened by a jeep-borne commando force, which was to be the nucleus of the future 3rd Battalion of the Brigade.) It was equipped with small-arms, light mortars and two 20mm guns that had just arrived in the country. One battalion was responsible for the area south of the Beersheba-Gaza road and the other for the area north of that road. All were equipped only with small-arms. The 'Negev' Brigade was commanded by Colonel Nahum Sarig. A tough, dour farmer, a member of a kibbutz and a product of the Palmach, he had led his Brigade in the desert in the days preceding statehood, under conditions of blockade and siege, with considerable ability. (Years later, in the 1973 Yom Kippur War, he was to lose one son in the fighting, while another son, although wounded, was to lead a brigade in the counterattack on the Golan Heights that brought the Israel Defence Forces within range of Damascus.)

The second Israeli brigade was the 'Givati' Brigade, which was unusually large by Israeli standards and consisted of five battalions, totalling over 3,000 men. This had no heavy equipment at its disposal and was responsible for the defence of the southern part of the country immediately north of the Negev Desert (in other words, the area immediately north of the road from Majdal or Ashkelon to Beit Jibrin). It was commanded by one of the more impressive Jewish commanders in the War of Independence, Colonel Shimon Avidan. A native of Germany who had moved to Kibbutz Ein Hashofet in Palestine, he had volunteered for, and served in, the International Brigade during the Spanish Civil War. A slight, fair-haired, determined man, with a toothbrush-like moustache, he was a natural leader. After the war, in which he distinguished himself as an outstanding commander, he was to resign from the Army because his extreme left-wing philosophy proved to be irreconcilable with Ben-Gurion's policies.

On 14 May, the Egyptian Army crossed the border in a great fanfare of publicity. King Farouk published a special postage stamp to commemorate the march of the Egyptian Army up the coast towards Gaza, and the Egyptian press and radio heralded daily the great military victories of the advancing Egyptian forces as they entered Gaza, Majdal and Beersheba without encountering any Jewish force — indeed, the fall of Tel Aviv seemed to be but a matter of days away. While a token force was landed by sea at Majdal, the bulk of the main column passed Rafah along the coastal road towards Gaza, and the secondary column crossed the border at El Auja and moved towards Beersheba. The assumption of the Egyptian command was that the capture of the main Jewish centres of population in the north would bring about the automatic collapse of all the villages in the Negev. Their planning envisaged the first major battles at the approaches to Tel Aviv and Jerusalem.

However, because it posed a potential threat to their lines of communication, the Egyptians first attacked the isolated Jewish village of Kfar Darom to the south between Khan Yunis and Gaza. Defended by 30 youths, and cut off for months, the village had already withstood a major attack by the Moslem Brotherhood, supported by artillery, on 10 May. The defenders had held their fire until the attackers reached the barbed-wire fence surrounding the village and then, with hand grenades and small-arms, had fought back. When the defenders, orthodox Jews, had run out of hand grenades, they had even filled the small velvet bags in which they normally kept their phylacteries, worn during morning prayers, with TNT and thrown them as grenades at the attackers. Meanwhile, the Egyptian artillery supporting the attack had erred, so that instead of hitting the village its shells had landed among the attackers, causing chaos. The Brotherhood had broken, leaving some 70 dead and wounded on the battlefield. The morale-raising effect of this gallant defence on the isolated settlers throughout the Negev had been electrifying. However, an attempt to reinforce the settlement was intercepted by the Egyptians with the result that, while a small number of reinforcements did arrive, they brought with them comparatively large numbers of wounded to the already-overcrowded underground infirmary of the village. Then, on 15 May, the Egyptian Army attacked, led by a troop of tanks and two troops of armoured cars, but the infantry failed to keep up with the armour. As a result, the attack was broken: a number of armoured vehicles were disabled, and the infantry fell back with heavy losses. Thereafter, the Egyptians refrained from attempting to attack the village, but occupied all the high ground around it, to bring it under blockade. (Towards the end of the First Truce, when it was clear that fighting was about to be renewed, it became evident to the Israelis that there was no point in maintaining an isolated position so far behind the Egyptian lines, and the village was evacuated. The day after the stealthy evacuation of the village by the Israelis, the Egyptians opened up with a long artillery barrage, and then launched an attack . . . only to find Kfar Darom empty.)

Meanwhile, the Egyptians also mounted an attack on Nirim, east of Rafah. This village, with 45 defenders, was attacked by an Egyptian infantry battalion, a troop of armoured cars and 20 Bren Gun Carriers supported by artillery, mortars and an air bombardment. A short battle ensued, and the Egyptians withdrew leaving 30 dead behind. The next day, the attack was renewed with similar results. The Egyptians concentrated thereafter on shelling the village from a distance.

Such indifferent military performance on the part of the Egyptians was a pattern to be repeated on many occasions during the war. There is no doubt that the Israeli successes were a function, not only of Israeli ingenuity, flexibility and courage, but also of the ineffectual handling of the Arab forces (with the outstanding exception of the Arab Legion) on many occasions. The Egyptian forces advanced and attacked according to the textbook — literally. When, as is customary in the course of battle, unforeseen developments faced their leaders in the field, they did not have the flexibility to adapt themselves to the new circumstances. Accordingly, the Egyptian performance in attack was characterized by a slavish adherence to the book, and poor leadership that was unable to adapt itself rapidly to changing circumstances and in turn engendered a hesitant approach during critical phases in the field of battle. At a higher level, there was a marked failure to co-ordinate the various elements, such as armour, infantry and artillery, with the result that the forces could not benefit from mutual support. By contrast (as will be seen in the accounts of the developments in the war at a later stage), when the Egyptians were on the defensive, their performance was good. In such actions, where they were firing along fixed lines, where the artillery fire-plan was clearly set out in advance and the field of battle was planned, the Egyptian commanders and soldiers acted courageously and conducted defensive battles very effectively.

Their experience at Kfar Darom and Nirim convinced the Egyptians that it would be poor strategy on their part to engage every Jewish settlement, and so they pushed forward along the main road to the more populous centre of the country, bypassing the Jewish villages en route. However, they could not ignore Yad Mordechai because of the position of the kibbutz on the Gaza-Ashkelon highway, which blocked the Egyptian advance northwards. This village (named after Mordechai Anielevitz, leader of the Warsaw Ghetto uprising in 1943) was attacked on 19 May by the main Egyptian column after an additional brigade group had arrived to reinforce it. The Egyptian 1st Battalion attacked and, after a fierce battle, captured the forward outpost, the defenders of which were forced to withdraw; when the Egyptians attempted to penetrate the perimeter of the settlement, they were driven back in bitter hand-to-hand fighting. On 20 May, the attack was resumed, and four separate assaults were beaten back by the settlers: casualties rose, reaching 38 killed and wounded on the second day. The shelling continued intermittently.

On 23 May, the defenders succeeded in beating back an attack by two infantry battalions backed by armour, but the fighting was now taking place within the built-up area of the village. Machine-guns in the hands of the settlers were by now unserviceable, and reserves of ammunition were depleted — indeed, many positions were now without ammunition. Accordingly, in the early hours of the morning of 24 May, the 180 surviving settlers and the Palmach reinforcements that had reached them withdrew under cover of darkness. Yad Mordechai fell to the Egyptians. For five days, a force amounting to little more than an infantry company had fought off a regular army force consisting of two infantry battalions, one armoured battalion and an artillery regiment, and had inflicted approximately 300 casualties. The most valuable achievement, however, was that five days had been gained — five vital days in which feverish fortification work took place to the north and in which the desperate efforts to bring in equipment, aircraft and guns from abroad were beginning to bear fruit. Had the Egyptians not been held up at Yad Mordechai, the stabilization of the lines in the area of Ashdod would have been a somewhat doubtful proposition. The battlefield around Yad Mordechai is today a national shrine. The water tower, peppered with holes created by bullets, shrapnel and shells, has been preserved as it was immediately following hostilities, as a reminder of the very heavy cost paid by the brave defenders who fought the Egyptian invasion.

The Egyptian force now encountered the 'Givati' Brigade, which had in the meantime cleared its area of operations and taken a number of Arab villages between Beer Tuvia and Negba and also captured the old British Army camp of Sarafand (near Tel Aviv). The Iraq Suedan police fortress (near Faluja) had been handed over by the British to the Arabs and was to be a thorn in the side of the Israelis for months, for it was an important position on the vital Majdal-Faluja-Beit Jibrin lateral road, which linked the two arms of the Egyptian attack. This road commanded the routes linking the southern area with the Negev, and was therefore vital from the point of view of supply to the Israelis operating there. Iraq Suedan fortress, with its dominating position on this axis, was vital to both sides — hence the bitter fighting for it which was to take place over the coming months.

On 29 May, the Egyptian 2nd Brigade under command of Brigadier-General Mohammed Neguib (later to be the first President of the Republic of Egypt) moved northward. Non-combatants were evacuated from the Jewish villages in the general area that is now Ashdod.* In the meantime, the first four Messerschmitt fighter aircraft, which had arrived in Israel from Czechoslovakia and had been assembled but a day earlier, were directed against the advancing Egyptian columns. One of the pilots manning them was Ezer Weizman, a native of Haifa, and nephew of the first President of Israel, Dr. Chaim Weizmann. He had received his training in the Royal Air Force in the Second World War, and his ebullient, outgoing and outspoken nature combined with many mannerisms acquired in the Royal Air Force to mark him out as a special type. He was later to prove a very forceful commander of the Israeli Air

---

* The area that is today the city and port of Ashdod was a series of barren, windswept sand dunes on the coast. An Arab village called Isdud existed in the area, but the Jewish city and port of Ashdod was established and built in the 1960s and 1970s.

Force. After his military service he was to enter politics, rising to be Menachem Begin's Minister of Defence in the Likud Government formed in 1977, and establishing very close personal relations with President Anwar el Sadat of Egypt. At the time that Weizman was strafing an Egyptian military column in Ashkelon, Sadat was serving as a junior officer in the Egyptian Army who had but recently emerged from imprisonment by the British as a supporter of the Nazis.

Although the Israeli air attack was ineffective because of faulty guns and bomb fuzes, the psychological effect on the Egyptians was enormous: they had no idea that the Israelis had aircraft. The Egyptian advance stopped at the blown bridge about two miles north of the village of Isdud, and orders were given to dig in. Israeli 65mm artillery shelled the Egyptian concentrations from the flanks; 'Givati' units mounted commando raids; and the Egyptian expeditionary force moved over from attack to defence. A major attack was mounted on 2 June by the 'Givati' Brigade against the Egyptian concentrations, and the attackers experienced for the first time on this front the effect of the concentrated defensive fire of a regular army. The plan was over-ambitious and co-ordination between the three attacking columns was faulty: the attack failed with heavy losses to the Israeli force including over 100 killed and wounded, and a number being taken prisoner. Nevertheless, this was the turning-point on the southern front. The Egyptian Command, whose forces were due to advance northwards to Yibne, decided to consolidate, reinforce the existing lines and concentrate subsequent efforts on isolating the Jewish forces in the Negev from the rest of the country.

This decision sealed the fate of the village of Nitzanim. Once the Egyptian commander had decided against any further advance northwards (the Israeli forces having in the meantime occupied the Arab village of Yibne), the Egyptians directed their attention to tidying-up along their lines of communication. On 7 June, Nitzanim's 150 defenders, half settlers and half soldiers, was attacked by an Egyptian force consisting of a reinforced battalion, a company of armoured vehicles and a regiment of field guns, supported by aircraft. When the Israeli's sole anti-tank weapon, a PIAT, was put out of action, there was nothing left to stop the Egyptian armour breaking into the village courtyard, followed by the infantry. Nitzanim fell to the Egyptians, and subsequent attempts by units of the 'Givati' Brigade to retake it failed with heavy losses. An Egyptian counter-attack drove an Israeli company from Hill 69, a key position controlling the road to the Ashdod area, and the Egyptians endeavoured to sweep on towards Beer Tuvia. But here the defenders stood firm.

The main Egyptian objective now was to cut off the Negev completely from the north and to lend added emphasis to the eastern Egyptian push via Hebron and Bethlehem towards Jerusalem. In addition to military considerations, those of inter-Arab rivalry were coming to the fore: the Egyptians now determined to place the emphasis on acquiring as much territory as possible in order to prevent it being taken by King Abdullah of Jordan. Accordingly, the Majdal-Faluja-Beit Jibrin road became vitally important as a lateral axis — it would both seal off the Negev from the north and enable the Egyptian forces to reinforce their eastern effort on the Beersheba-Hebron-Jerusalem road. The Egyptians thereupon proceeded to fortify the villages and high ground controlling the Majdal-Beit Jibrin road. This action brought them up against Kibbutz Negba. The village had been attacked on 21 May and another major assault was launched on 2 June (the day the 'Givati' force attacked the Egyptians in the area of Ashdod). Leading the attack was a battalion of the Egyptian 1st Brigade, commanded by Brigadier Said Taha Bey, also known as 'The Tiger', a Sudanese officer who was later to command the Egyptian defence of the Faluja pocket. The attack led by armour succeeded in reaching the inner fence of the village, but the appearance of an Israeli jeep-borne commando unit on the flank of the attack caused an Egyptian withdrawal. In the attack, in which over 1,000 Egyptians fought against some 140 defenders, the Egyptian losses were over 100 dead and wounded. These heroic stands against heavy odds, proving what could be done by a determined defence, were by now a vital element in bolstering the national morale of the emerging Israeli state.

A day before the United Nations truce was due to begin, the 'Givati' Brigade improved its position by capturing a number of villages threatening the narrow corridor to the south; the 'Negev' Brigade once again launched its 7th Battalion against the police fortress at Iraq Suedan (but in vain); and to the south, Beer Asluj on the Auja-Beersheba road was taken in a surprise attack by units of the 'Negev' Brigade. However, the Egyptians ultimately succeeded in improvising an alternative route bypassing Beer Asluj and renewing the link between the international border, Sinai and Beersheba. The Egyptians also made desperate efforts to improve their position before the truce came into effect. They took control of the high ground commanding the 'junction' (the intersection of the Majdal-Faluja and Kaukaba-Julis roads), thus blocking the road south to the Negev. The Palmach forces captured Kaukaba and Huleiqat south of the junction, while the 'Givati' force captured Hill 113 near the junction. But this situation did not change the fact that the Negev remained cut off. This was serious for the Israelis. All through the fighting, the road to the Negev had been kept open, but now, as the truce began, the Negev was isolated and the Egyptians had established control of the east-west lateral road between Majdal and Faluja.

The first truce

The first truce came as a welcome respite for the hard-pressed Israeli forces, but above all it was most welcome in Jerusalem. When the truce began, no more than three days' supply of food remained in the city. The United Nations organized convoys under Arab Legion inspection, which allowed a certain amount of supplies to move up into the city, but the 'Burma Road' bypassing Latrun was meanwhile improved and civilian supplies, military equipment and reinforcements moved along it freely and without inspection to the city.

Both sides succeeded in bypassing the limitations imposed on them by the truce and augmented their stocks of military equipment in addition to recouping their losses. King Abdullah undertook a tour of Arab capitals in an endeavour to consolidate his command and to achieve greater unity in the conduct of the war. In effect, what he was trying to obtain was Arab approval for him to annex the Arab parts of Palestine; not surprisingly, he was totally unsuccessful in his mission — even encountering a refusal on the part of King Farouk to his request that, as Supreme Commander, he should visit the headquarters of the Egyptian expeditionary force in Palestine. Farouk maintained that such a visit was out of the question as long as he, King Farouk, had not visited his own troops — a venture he considered too risky at the time. Thus, while the individual Arab armies regrouped, rested and re-equipped themselves, very little was achieved at the level of overall command.

Similar efforts were afoot in the Israel Defence Forces to reorganize and regroup. The Army was reorganized, and underwent intensive training as war matériel arriving from Europe (particularly from Czechoslovakia) was absorbed. Artillery units were being added, and a hodge-podge of tanks and armoured vehicles acquired from various countries throughout the world was gathered together in order to create the 8th Armoured Brigade. The Air Force, which was receiving aircraft, had already shot down some Egyptian Dakotas sent to bomb Tel Aviv, and had driven off an Egyptian naval force that had bombarded the city.

During the truce, an incident occurred that brought to a head the problems of indiscipline in the Israeli forces. David Ben-Gurion had viewed the possible appearance of private armies as the greatest danger that could threaten the stability of the emerging nation and, on 28 May, 'Order No. 4' promulgated by the Israeli Provisional Government had created a national army. This was to be known as the 'Israel Defence Forces' (IDF), and the law specifically prohibited the establishment or maintenance of any other force. But it was not put into effect without a struggle. During the first truce, the Irgun brought in a landing ship named *Altalena*, which had sailed from Europe with some 900 recruits aboard and loaded with arms and ammunition. Ben-Gurion ordered them to hand over the arms and ammunition to the Israel Defence Forces, which would assume responsibility for the new recruits. The result was an incident off Kfar Vitkin and a confrontation with units of the IDF: the ship sailed and ran aground on the beach in the centre of Tel Aviv; the Irgun refused to obey the instructions of the IDF units, and fighting broke out. Fifteen men were killed and *Altalena* was eventually sunk by gunfire. On 28 June, an oath of allegiance was taken by all of the armed forces, and the Irgun ceased to exist as a separate force.

3
TO THE SECOND TRUCE
18 July to 15 October 1948

The United Nations mediator, Count Bernadotte of Sweden, meanwhile proposed a formula for peace, hoping to convert the truce into an armistice that would eventually lead to a peace treaty. The plan that he presented awarded all of Galilee to the Israelis and the Negev to the Arabs, with Jerusalem remaining under the authority of the United Nations and the Arab portion of Palestine to be administered by Transjordan. This was rejected by both the Arabs and the Jews, and the two sides prepared themselves for the inevitable clash that would come on the conclusion of the 28-day truce, which ended on Friday 9 July. As this date drew closer, the IDF planned to go over to the offensive. Until now they had been reacting to Arab attacks and Arab initiatives. Now they would take the initiative into their own hands.

The northern front

Occupying the bridgehead of Mishmar Hayarden was a Syrian force consisting of an infantry brigade, supported by armour and artillery. An additional brigade held the heights overlooking the east bank of the River Jordan. The Lebanese Army was deployed from Rosh Hanikra on the coast to Bint Jbeil near Malkiya in the east, thus ensuring the supply and reinforcement lines of Kaukji's Arab Liberation Army, which was concentrated primarily in the centre of Galilee.

Five IDF brigades were deployed along the truce lines in the north and centre of the country: the 'Alexandroni', 'Golani', 'Carmeli' and 'Oded' Brigades plus the 7th Brigade, which had been transferred from the Latrun sector to western Galilee. The Israeli plan envisaged two operations: Operation 'Dekel' ('Palm Tree') directed against the weakest link in the Arab chain, Kaukji's ALA; and Operation 'Brosh' ('Cypress Tree') directed against the Syrian Army, which posed the most serious threat, for the Syrian bridgehead was but a mile from the vital north-south road in eastern Galilee. This bridgehead had been heavily reinforced during the truce, so the plan chosen envisaged an encircling operation in an endeavour to cut off the bridgehead from its sources of supply. The main effort of the operation, commanded by Moshe Carmel (now a Brigadier-General), was to be carried out by the 'Carmeli' Brigade under Colonel Mordechai Makleff, reinforced by detachments from the 'Oded' Brigade, which would make a diversionary attack on the Syrian bridgehead from the west. The main force of the 'Carmeli' Brigade would cross the River

Jordan to the north of the bridgehead and take the customs house position overlooking the Bnot Ya'akov Bridge. Following the isolation of the bridgehead, it would be reduced by an all-out attack.

The attack was launched after nightfall on 9 July. One of the battalions managed to cross the Jordan with difficulty, but the engineers failed to build the planned pontoon bridge because of heavy Syrian artillery fire. The second battalion was delayed and, at this point, word was received that the Syrians were about to launch an attack in the direction of Rosh Pinah. The Israeli forces were behind schedule, and it was obvious that they could not capture the customs house before daylight. Accordingly, an order was given to withdraw to the west bank of the Jordan and the encirclement of the Syrian positions was called off. There has been criticism of this decision, because it is reasonable to assume that, had the Israeli attack on the east bank of the Jordan developed, the Syrians would have hesitated to mount an attack against Rosh Pinah when their lines of communication across the river would have been endangered by the Israeli penetration. The argument in favour of the Israeli withdrawal was that there was no chance, because of the approach of daylight, for the Israeli forces to reach the Syrian customs house, a move which would have effectively cut the Syrian lines of communication.

At dawn, the Syrian force counterattacked, strongly supported from the air. The Syrian brigade on the heights to the east of the Jordan in the meantime attacked the Israeli forces that were still on the eastern bank. For two days these units desperately fought-off the Syrian attacks until they too were obliged to withdraw to the west bank. Various positions in the area were fought over bitterly, with heavy casualties being incurred as the Syrians advanced to threaten Mahanayim and Rosh Pinah. For two days, a see-saw battle was fought, with some positions changing hands four times. On 14 July, Makleff's force made another attempt on the bridgehead, this time by a flanking attack from the south, but this attempt also failed. When the second truce came into effect after nine days of fighting, the two exhausted armies faced each other in stalemate, occupying roughly the same positions from which they had launched their respective attacks ten days earlier.

Farther to the west, the Israel Defence Forces launched Operation 'Dekel' to dislodge Kaukji's Arab Liberation Army from the strategic positions it held in the centre of Galilee, in the area of the village of Sejera, a vital link along the main Israeli route leading to the north, via Kfar Tabor to Tiberias. While the 2nd Battalion of the 'Golani' Brigade was conducting a holding operation, Kaukji planned to take Sejera at all costs. Concentrating the greater part of his force, he mounted repeated attacks against the stubborn defence of the 'Golani' Battalion, which had no supporting arms for most of the battle (apart from the last three days it had heavy mortar support). The attack reached its crescendo on 14 July, when Kaukji's forces mounted no less than eight successive attacks backed by armoured vehicles and Iraqi aircraft. All were repelled.

The 'Golani' Brigade was commanded by Nahum Golan, a member of a kibbutz in Galilee, who had grown up militarily in the Haganah and had

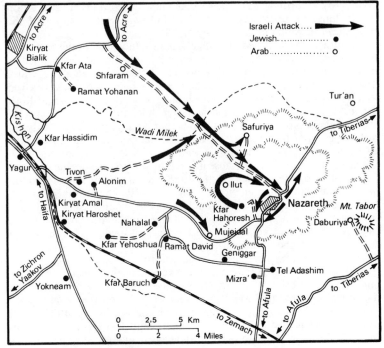

Operation 'Dekel' — The Capture of Nazareth, 16 July 1948

acquired some military experience in the British Army. A quiet-spoken, self-effacing commander, he led his brigade with distinction in many of the decisive actions in the War of Independence. The standards of the Brigade carry the battle honours of many of the major battles in Israel's wars: it was to reach the Gulf of Aqaba in the War of Independence, to break through the Egyptian lines at Rafah in the Sinai Campaign, to storm the seemingly impregnable Syrian fortifications on the Golan Heights in the Six Day War, and to mount the costly attacks on Mount Hermon and retake this vital position after it had been lost at the beginning of the Yom Kippur War in 1973.

The outcome of the battle at Sejera was finally decided by the threat posed by the advance of the Israeli forces moving towards Nazareth from western Galilee. Basing itself on the coastal road and plain in western Galilee north of Haifa, a force under the command of Haim Laskov (now a Brigadier-General), consisting of the 7th Brigade and a battalion from the 'Carmeli' Brigade, advanced along the inland road from Acre to establish itself in co-operation with local Druze villagers in the hills to the east. The 7th Brigade was by now under command of Colonel Ben Dunkelman, who had come from Canada as a volunteer. He had won the

British Distinguished Service Order leading Canadian troops in the Hochwald on the Rhine in the Second World War, having landed with the Queen's Own Rifles of Canada on the beaches of Normandy on D-Day, 6 June 1944. A heavily-built, soft-spoken but determined officer, he had found acceptance by both Israeli command and troops after participating in various operations, particularly in organizing the mortar support of the Palmach units in the hills of Jerusalem. Dunkelman returned after the war to his family business in Canada. He was undoubtedly one of the few outstanding brigade commanders in the Israel Defence Forces and with the 7th Brigade achieved the most prominent command position awarded to a volunteer from abroad in the course of the war.

As soon as it became evident from the disposition of the Lebanese Army that the Lebanese would not intervene from the north, Laskov directed his forces eastward towards Nazareth, taking Shfaram on the Acre-Nazareth road on 14 July. The next day, a detachment from the 'Golani' Brigade made its way up into the hills from its base in Nahalal, clearing the Arab forces from the area, and linked up with Kfar Hahoresh, west of Nazareth, which had been isolated by Arab forces for a number of months. The main defences of Nazareth were concentrated on the approaches from the Jezreel valley, whence the Arabs always assumed Israeli attacks would come. But the threat from Kfar Hahoresh and the advance of Laskov's column (which in the meantime had captured the village of Zippori, four miles north-west of Nazareth), coming as it did through what Kaukji had considered to be the safe Arab hinterland of Nazareth, disrupted the Arab dispositions. On 15 July, Kaukji hastily reorganized his forces and despatched his mobile reserve, a company of armoured cars, to meet the new Israeli threat at his rear. The single self-propelled 20mm gun mounted on a half-track with the 7th Brigade engaged the armoured cars at a distance of 500 yards and destroyed six of the eight attacking vehicles. The Arab forces withdrew, as did the Nazareth garrison: on the morning of the 16th, the town of Nazareth surrendered.

Laskov's advance across Galilee had forced Kaukji to divert his attention from Sejera and, from 18 July, the ALA forces began their withdrawal, abandoning lower Galilee and withdrawing to the north-east. On 18 July, the second truce declared by the United Nations came into effect, leaving a central enclave in northern Galilee, based on the Lebanese border and stretching southwards to the valley of Beit Netofa, in the hands of the Arab Liberation Army.

The central front and Jerusalem

The main military problem facing the Israelis on the conclusion of the first truce was posed by the strongest and most effective Arab army, the Arab Legion. This was besieging the city of Jerusalem; from the towns of Lod (Lydda) and Ramle, Arab forces also posed a direct threat to Tel Aviv, the main Jewish population centre. Furthermore, the main railway junction of the country was at Lod, in addition to the only international airport. Two Arab Legion infantry battalions supported by armour and artillery were concentrated in the Latrun sector; Ramle and Lod were well fortified and held mainly by local Arab forces, irregular units, several hundred tribesmen from Transjordan, and small detachments of the Arab Legion.

A blow at the Arab Legion was the essence of Operation 'Danny' , planned as the main Israeli offensive to be mounted on the resumption of hostilities. Its aim was to relieve Jerusalem again and remove the threat to Tel Aviv. The first phase was to occupy the areas of Lod and Ramle; the second phase called for the capture of Latrun and Ramallah with the object of raising the siege on Jerusalem. The operation was to be carried out by Yigal Allon, commander of the Palmach, and the forces allotted were the 'Harel' and 'Yiftach' Brigades with the 'Kiryati' Brigade and the 8th Armoured Brigade in support. Elements of the 'Alexandroni' and 'Etzioni' Brigades were also attached to the operation. From the north, the 8th Armoured Brigade supported by battalions from the 'Alexandroni' and 'Kiryati' Brigades was ordered to capture Lod Airport and exploit success into the foothills to the east, in the area of the military camp at Beit Nabala; the 'Yiftach' Brigade was to provide the southern flank of the pincer movement.

Under Colonel 'Mula' Cohen, who had successfully commanded the Brigade in the battle for Safed and the fighting in Galilee, the 'Yiftach' attack commenced from the south at nightfall on 9 July, and cleared several Arab villages in the area. To the north, the 8th Armoured Brigade under Colonel Yitzhak Sadeh, fielded a battalion of tanks — the first used in the IDF, including ten French H-35 light tanks and two British Cromwells brought over by deserters. These and a number of armoured cars advanced with units of the 'Kiryati' Brigade and the 'Alexandroni' Brigade operating on the flanks, and took the airport.

The two pincer movements were to meet at Ben Shemen, a Jewish children's village that had been isolated for months. The 'Yiftach' Brigade from the south reached there, but the 8th Armoured Brigade from the north encountered severe difficulties because of numerous technical problems, which the inexperienced troops operating the tanks had difficulty in overcoming. In the meantime, while the pincer movement in the north was held up, the 89th Mechanized Commando Battalion, under Lieutenant-Colonel Moshe Dayan, pressed forward towards Lod, where units of the 'Yiftach' Brigade were now encountering difficulties. Dayan's battalion, mounted on half-tracks and jeeps and including an armoured car captured from the Arab Legion, stormed through the town firing in all directions and then retraced its noisy path back through the town. This daring operation unnerved the defenders, enabling 'Yiftach' Brigade units to take advantage of the ensuing panic during which the bulk of the population of Lod fled en masse. The town surrendered to the 'Yiftach' Brigade, but rose in arms again when an Arab Legion unit counter-attacked, but the Israelis beat off the attack and secured the town. The next day, Ramle surrendered and was occupied by units of the 'Kiryati' Brigade.

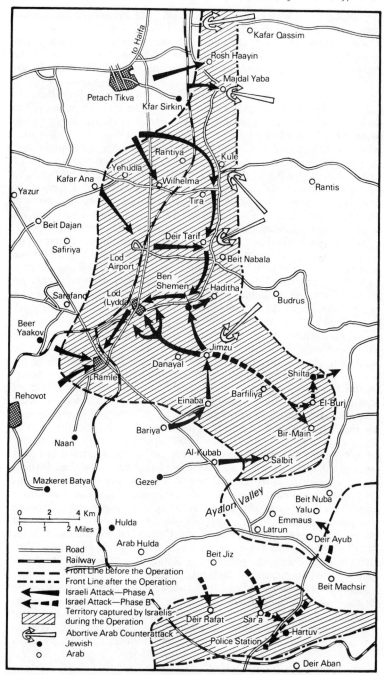

Operation 'Danny' — Western Sector, 9-12 July 1948

Glubb, commander of the Arab Legion, had meanwhile been under considerable pressure to reinforce Lod and Ramle, but the only forces on which he could draw were the two battalions at Latrun, the 4th and 2nd Regiments — to have any effect it would have been essential for him to deploy a full battalion. He was of the opinion that, should the Israeli attack succeed, then it would not be possible for him to prevent the Israeli forces from breaking through at Latrun and advancing to Ramallah. He did not believe that a single battalion could resist such an advance. His decision not to reinforce placed him under considerable pressure, and was to be the subject of bitter reproaches from the rest of the Arab world. After the fall of Lod and Ramle, Arab Legion troops were stoned and insulted in the streets of Ramallah, and Glubb himself was accused of treachery at a meeting of the Jordanian Cabinet in the presence of King Abdullah. However, having regard to the forces available to Glubb at the time and his appreciation of the vital and pivotal importance of Latrun in the Arab position to the west of Jerusalem, there is no doubt that his decision from a military point of view was in fact a correct one.

An Arab Legion company, the 5th Independent Infantry Company, had in fact been in the police station at Lod, but during the fighting Glubb had ordered its withdrawal. It had been the counterattack of this unit coupled with the appearance of a troop of Arab Legion armoured cars on reconnaissance on the outskirts of Lod that had brought about the revolt of the Arab population in the town — believing as it did that the Arab Legion had returned in force.

In the meantime, the 'Harel' Brigade under the command of Lieutenant-Colonel Joseph Tabenkin had captured a number of villages in the Jerusalem Corridor preparatory for its principal mission of raising the siege of Jerusalem and capturing Ramallah. It became clear, however, from the debates in the Security Council of the United Nations, that yet another cease-fire would soon be imposed. (This pattern was to repeat itself on many occasions in the future military history of Israel, because the automatic majority mobilized in the United Nations over the years by the Arabs and the Communist bloc would inevitably carry the day against Israel's interests. For, as was to occur on many occasions, when it appeared that the Jewish forces were hard-pressed, the United Nations organization dragged its feet and saw no urgency whatsoever in bringing the hostilities to a conclusion; but, when it appeared that the Israelis were gaining the upper hand, the entire machinery of the community of nations was galvanized into action to prevent the Israelis from exploiting their success.) The new developments in the United Nations indicated to the Israeli Command that but a few days were left in which to complete their mission. Accordingly, the plan to take Ramallah was shelved. The forces were now to concentrate on capturing Latrun.

Glubb, as previously indicated, had very wisely decided to conserve his forces at the outset of Operation 'Danny' and not to dissipate them by attempting to reinforce the garrisons in Lod and Ramle. Aware of the strategic importance of Latrun, he concentrated and indeed reinforced his forces in that area and to the north of the Jerusalem Corridor, ordering back to the Latrun area elements of the 1st Regiment, which had captured Kule only to lose it later in an Israeli counterattack.

The fourth attack on Latrun took place on the night of 15/16 July. The 'Yiftach' Brigade, supported by an armoured battalion from the 8th Armoured Brigade and by elements of the 'Kiryati' Brigade, captured the area north of the Latrun enclave, including the villages of Barfiliya, Salbit, El-Burj and Bir-Main, thus opening the way to bypassing Latrun on the road to Ramallah. Appreciating the danger of such a possibility, the Legion forces reacted by counterattacking. The Legion, determined to hold on at all costs to Latrun and only too aware that the Israeli plan was to isolate or encircle it, mounted some of the fiercest counterattacks launched by the Legion during the War. Many stories of bravery in these battles were later recounted. One was about the troop of armoured cars commanded by a young Bedouin who fought in the village of El-Burj: despite receiving numerous wounds, he fought on until his armoured car was a hopeless wreck; in hospital, more than 100 pieces of metal were removed from his body. On the Israeli side, a withdrawing company on the Latrun ridge left three seriously wounded men on the battlefield. A medical orderly, disobeying orders, remained with them. The bodies of all four were later found on the hill.

Meanwhile, the main 'Harel' effort was directed against the Latrun ridge which was held by one of the three Legion battalions (the 1st, 2nd and 4th) now concentrated in the general area of Latrun. The 'Harel' forces were hard-pressed as a result of an Arab Legion counterattack mounted by units of the 2nd Regiment on El-Burj and Beit Sira, and the Israeli attempt to take Latrun failed.

As the new truce approached, the 'Yiftach' and 'Harel' Brigades widened their respective areas of control. A distance of but two miles now separated the 'Yiftach' outposts west of the Latrun road from the 'Harel' outposts poised in the Jerusalem Hills to the east of the Latrun road. Yigal Allon resolved therefore to mount yet a further frontal attack on Latrun. While the 'Harel' units occupied the heights above Beit Nuba, from the west, the 'Yiftach' Brigade attacked with the support of the 8th Armoured Brigade. As a result of an error in communications, however, this support — which suffered losses from an anti-tank gun on the roof of the Latrun police station — withdrew, and the infantry did not persist in the attack. This was the last Israeli effort to capture Latrun. It continued to block the main highway to Jerusalem for the next nineteen years, until it fell to Israeli forces in the Six Day War.

Despite this setback, however, the ten days of fighting in Operation 'Danny' had improved the situation of the Israeli forces immeasurably: Ramle and Lod, with its international airport, were now in Israeli hands; the direct threat to Tel Aviv had been averted; and the Jerusalem Corridor had been broadened towards the south. On the night before the truce became effective, Hartuv had fallen, opening up an additional road to the city. In addition, most of the railway to Jerusalem had been cleared. Nevertheless, the threat against the main road to Jerusalem remained so long as the Arab Legion continued to control Latrun.

In Jerusalem itself, operations were mounted with a view to widening the southern part of the Corridor in the areas of Malha and Ein Kerem, with the purpose of taking complete control of the railway line from Tel Aviv to Jerusalem. On the night of 9/10 July, a company of the Gadna (a youth battalion consisting of boys aged sixteen and seventeen), which had fought throughout the siege of Jerusalem, took the area later to be known as Mount Herzl, which dominated Ein Kerem. Malha, to the south, was taken too. For its part, the 1st Brigade of the Arab Legion, led by units of the 3rd Regiment, attacked in the Mandelbaum area, occupying a number of buildings. On the last night before the truce, an additional Israeli attack was mounted on the Old City. An Irgun unit managed to break through the New Gate, but was able to advance only a short distance within before being obliged to withdraw. A simultaneous attempt by an 'Etzioni' unit to break into the Zion Gate also failed.

The southern front

During the truce, the Egyptian expeditionary force was strengthened to a force of four brigades. The 1st Brigade was responsible for the area of the coastal road from the international border north through Gaza to Majdal; the 2nd Brigade was responsible for the most northerly sector, in the area of Ashdod; the 4th Brigade, based on Faluja, controlled the lateral axis from Majdal via Beit Jibrin to Hebron; while a fourth brigade, consisting

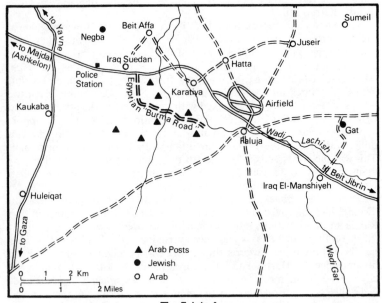

The Faluja Area

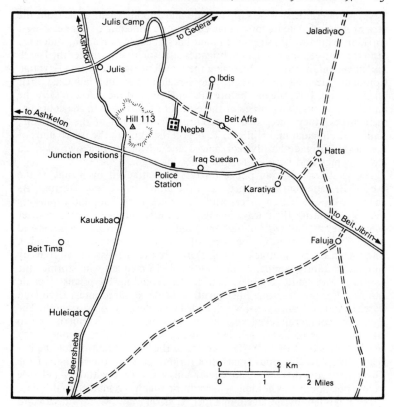

Negba and its Surroundings

of Moslem Brotherhood volunteers, was deployed along the Beersheba-Hebron-Bethlehem axis to Jerusalem's southernmost approaches.

Facing these forces were two Israeli brigades. The 'Givati' Brigade, responsible for the area north of the road from Majdal to Beit Jibrin, was deployed with two battalions north and east of the Ashdod area stretching in a wide arc from Gal-On in the south-east near the lower slopes of the Judean Hills, to Yavne in the north-west, and the remaining two battalions in reserve. The 'Negev' Brigade, under Colonel Nahum Sarig, was responsible for the area south of the Gaza-Beersheba road with a commando battalion maintaining the supply routes to the various isolated settlements.

In anticipation of the conclusion of the first truce, both sides laid plans to mount offensives immediately on resumption of hostilities during the night of 9/10 July. The plan of the Israeli forces, under the overall command of Colonel Shimon Avidan (commander of the 'Givati' Brigade), called for the opening of the road to the Negev, cutting the

Egyptian lateral east-west supply route and forcing them back from the area of Ashdod. The Egyptian plan called for a widening of their east-west corridor, which would strengthen their lines of communication, widen the distance between the two Israeli brigades and isolate still further the Israeli settlements in the Negev. Observing the Israeli preparations, the Egyptian Command decided to pre-empt the Israeli attack and launched their offensive on 8 July, the day before the conclusion of the truce, to seize the initiative and take advantage of the element of surprise. In the course of their attack, they succeeded in capturing in the area of the 'junction', Kaukaba, Huleiqat and Hill 113. Taken off their guard, the Israeli units of the 'Givati' Brigade hastily reorganized and advanced their own planned attack, which had been set for the following night.

The vital Iraq Suedan police fortress was attacked by a unit of the 'Negev' Brigade, but here once again the attack was late in starting. As dawn broke, combat engineers with Bangalore Torpedoes and explosives were still fighting their way through the numerous layers of perimeter fence. They withdrew, but fighting continued as 'Givati' units cleared several Arab villages in the area of the 'junction' and fought-off a determined Egyptian attack on Beit Daras. In the final assault on Ibdis by an Israeli infantry company, there were only 18 men left who stormed the positions with hand grenades, causing the defending Egyptians to panic and flee. For the first time, the 'Givati' Brigade captured intact Bren Gun Carriers and anti-tank guns, which added considerably to its strength. The Egyptians counterattacked heavily, recapturing Beit Affa, but failing to take the village of Ibdis, despite putting in what proved to be one of the heaviest attacks of the war. The success of the 'Givati' unit in holding out against considerable odds, marked a turning point in the history of the 'Givati' Brigade: thereafter, no 'Givati' unit was ever to withdraw in battle from a position it was holding − a tradition that has remained to this day.

The Egyptian divisional commander, General Mawawi, now decided to launch an all-out frontal attack on Negba, which he saw as a pivotal point and the key to the Israeli defence system in the general area of the 'junction'. Following an intense artillery barrage designed to soften up the settlement, which was defended by approximately 150 fighters, he launched the largest concentration of Egyptian forces deployed in attack to date, consisting of three infantry battalions, one armoured battalion and an artillery regiment. With the Egyptian 9th Infantry Battalion in the lead, Negba was attacked simultaneously from four different directions. The first attack was halted when the Egyptians were almost at the perimeter fence; the second attack was halted when the Egyptians were already at the inner fence; but, as evening drew on, the Egyptians were compelled to withdraw, leaving 200 casualties on the battlefield.

At the same time, the Egyptians launched attacks against Gal-On on the Israelis' eastern flank and against Beerot Yitzhak near Gaza. This settlement was manned by approximately 70 armed settlers, reinforced by a 'Negev' Brigade platoon. The Egyptian Command decided that it had threatened their lines of communication for too long and must therefore be eliminated. But the appearance of an Israeli commando battalion with artillery reinforcements broke the Egyptian attack on Beerot Yitzhak; once more the invaders withdrew, leaving a further 200 casualties in the field.

For five days, some of the fiercest fighting in the War took place, with the Egyptian forces launching attack after attack on the crossroads. Sudanese units serving within the Egyptian Army took Hill 105 near Negba, but were driven off by a counterattack mounted by the commando unit of 'Givati' Brigade's 'Samson Foxes'. However, the failure of the Egyptians at Negba and Beerot Yitzhak — with very heavy losses in each case — left its mark on Egyptian morale. Thereafter in the war, the Egyptian forces were to assume a defensive role, with the Israelis exploiting the psychological advantages they had achieved. In the meantime, both sides were by now completely exhausted, following days of intense fighting and heavy losses. As the second truce approached, unsuccessful attacks were mounted again by Avidan's forces against Huleiqat, Kaukaba and Beit Affa, but attacks did succeed against Hatta and Kharatiya. Heavy fighting took place around Kharatiya as the Egyptians launched an abortive counterattack.

The truce came into effect on the evening of 18 July. The Israelis had succeeded in opening a somewhat tenuous, narrow corridor to the Negev and had blocked the east-west road between Majdal and Beit Jibrin; but the Egyptians had succeeded in overcoming this problem by occupying high ground near Kharatiya and building their own 'Burma Road' bypass.

The second truce

In reviewing the operations during the ten days of fighting in July, one notes a marked advance in the Israel Defence Forces, as the Air Force grew with the acquisition of some Messerschmitt fighters from Czechoslovakia and three B-17 Flying Fortresses (which, during this period of fighting, bombed Cairo and Damascus). Gradually, the Israeli infantry were beginning to learn how to fight with armoured and artillery support. An army was gradually being forged out of a partisan force, in the very heat of battle.

Meanwhile, Count Bernadotte, the United Nations mediator, was actively pushing his proposals, which would have removed the Negev from Israel, giving it western Galilee in return; would have passed Ramle and Lod back to Arab rule; and would have placed Jerusalem and the international airport at Lod under United Nations control. The Israeli Government realized that, as long as the Negev was cut off from the centre of Israel, it would be impossible to fight these political proposals. It was clear that the ring closing the Negev (which was, however, not tight enough to prevent Israeli units infiltrating each night past the Egyptian positions) must be broken and the region firmly linked back to Israel. Then, on 17 September, after signing the report to the Security Council in which he put forward new proposals that included granting 'enforcement ability' to the United Nations representatives, Count Bernadotte was driving through Jerusalem to Government House, which was in an area recognized by both sides as a demilitarized zone, as declared by the United Nations, when his convoy was halted in the Katamon quarter. A jeep blocked the road, three men jumped out and opened fire, killing Bernadotte and a French assistant. The assailants, who were generally assumed to be Jewish, escaped and were never apprehended, but David Ben-Gurion decided to take advantage of the shock brought about by the murder, and to act forcefully. The Irgun, which had continued to exist independently in Jerusalem (unlike in other parts of Israel), was ordered to disband within 24 hours and to hand over its arms to the Israel Defence Forces. Some 200 members of Lehi, including its leaders and commanders, were detained.

The international reaction to the murder of Count Bernadotte placed Israel in a very difficult position politically. What were recommendations in his report now became a political testament, with added emphasis. Israel faced a delicate situation. Indeed, Israel's hands might have been tied by fear of the international reaction to the murder had the Egyptians not intervened in a manner that solved Israel's Negev problem. They persisted in an obstinate refusal to allow Israeli convoys free passage into the Negev, contrary to the conditions of the truce — hence, Israeli military operations became justified. So the lack of appreciation on the part of the Egyptians of the very difficult situation in which the murder of Bernadotte had placed the Israelis opened the way for the Israeli operations that were finally to dislodge and defeat the Egyptian Army.

The Israel Defence Forces had, in the meantime, been reorganized into four regional commands: the northern front under Brigadier-General Moshe Carmel; the central front under Brigadier-General Dan Even; Jerusalem and the Corridor under Brigadier-General Zvi Ayalon; and the southern region under Brigadier-General Yigal Allon.

4

THE DECISION

Decision in Galilee

In the northern sector of the War, the area under the control of Kaukji's Arab Liberation Army was a major enclave, resting in the north on the Lebanese border; in the east, southwards from near Metulla to a point but a few miles to the west of the Sea of Galilee; thence westwards, via Eilabun turning northwards, back to the Lebanese border, past Majdal Krum and Tarshiha. His forces were now reduced to 3,000-4,000 men divided into three brigades: the 1st 'Yarmuk' Brigade, supported by Lebanese volunteers, was operating in the hills south of the Acre-Safed road; the 2nd 'Yarmuk' Brigade was deployed facing Safed between Meron and Sasa; and the 3rd 'Yarmuk' Brigade held the western side of the pocket, based on Tarshiha. Between them, these forces disposed of a limited number of 75mm field guns and some armoured cars. On 22 October, Kaukji launched a surprise attack with his reorganized forces in the area of Manara, in the hills to the west overlooking the 'finger' of Galilee. The strongpoint of Sheikh Abed was taken, the village of Manara isolated, and an Israeli counterattack repulsed. The Lebanese Army, meanwhile, still had four battalions along the border, and the three Syrian brigades manned the eastern border south to El-Hamma.

The Israelis now determined to clear Galilee of Arab forces, destroy Kaukji's ALA and establish an Israeli defensive line along the international Palestinian-Lebanese border. The forces available to General Carmel, commanding the northern front, were now four brigades: the 7th Brigade, the 'Oded' Brigade (which had been brought back north from the Negev), and the 'Golani' and 'Carmeli' Brigades. There were now four artillery batteries, two with 75mm guns and two with 65mm guns. The Israeli offensive was codenamed Operation 'Hiram' after the King of Tyre (an ally and friend of King David and King Solomon, who had sent cedars to build the Temple in Jerusalem). It was mounted on the night of 28/29 October, and took the form of a pincer movement, the arms of which would meet at Sasa near the Lebanese border and close off the Arab pocket in Galilee. The 7th Brigade would move from Safed to Sasa, while the 'Oded' Brigade from the west would take Tarshiha and then close in on Sasa. At the same time, diversionary attacks were to be mounted by the 'Golani' units from the south in the direction of Eilabun. To the northeast, the 'Carmeli' Brigade would occupy the attention of the Syrians.

The 7th Brigade, under the command of Colonel Ben Dunkelman, consisted of an armoured battalion and two infantry battalions, including

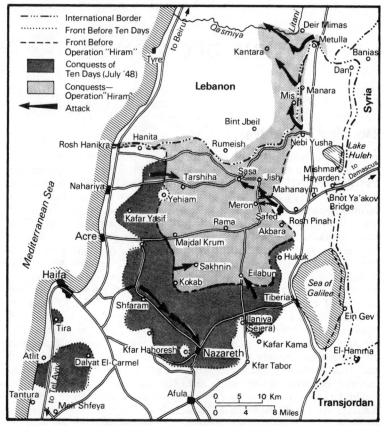

Operation 'Hiram,' 29-31 October 1948

a company of Circassians.* Moving from Safed on the evening of 28 October, it was engaged in a bitter infantry action at Meron as a result of which the Arabs withdrew, leaving 80 dead on the battlefield. The Brigade advanced and captured Jish (the site of Gush Halav, one of the fortresses that had held out against the Romans during the Jewish rebellion in the second century AD). A Syrian battalion, which had been hurriedly moved down from Lebanon to reinforce the Arab defences, was ambushed by Israeli units before it could deploy for attack, and withdrew in disorder leaving over 200 dead on the battlefield. The 7th Brigade pushed on to Sasa, and completed its mission as the eastern arm of the pincer movement. The western operation of the pincer movement, mounted by

---

* One of the peoples of the Caucasus. Their region was formerly part of the Turkish Empire. The Moslem Circassians dispersed over Syria, Jordan and Palestine, and were partially assimilated by the Arabs.

the 'Oded' Brigade, was less successful: it failed to capture Tarshiha, and a Druze company attached to it found itself in serious trouble. However, the news that the 7th Brigade had taken Sasa in their rear unsettled the Arab defenders of Tarshiha, and they withdrew towards Lebanon, abandoning all their heavy equipment. The next day, 30 October, the 'Oded' Brigade mounted a new attack and Tarshiha surrendered, enabling the western arm of the pincer movement to close on Sasa.

The second phase of Operation 'Hiram' was now implemented. 'Golani' forces advanced northwards from Eilabun and, by the evening of the 21st, reached the Tarshiha-Sasa road. The Arab Liberation Army had, in fact, ceased to exist. Carmel ordered his forces to follow-up at once: the 'Oded' Brigade was ordered to mop-up and clear the area between Nahariya and Sasa, south of the Lebanese border, while the 7th Brigade moved rapidly from Sasa north-eastwards towards Malkiya, which had been the scene of very heavy fighting early in the war. The defending Arab forces broke and fled. The IDF now controlled the entire Lebanese border from Nebi Yusha in the east, to Rosh Hanikra on the Mediterranean coast. The siege of Manara was lifted, and units of 'Carmeli' Brigade crossed the border into Lebanon, capturing fourteen Lebanese villages and reaching the River Litani. (This area was later to be used as a bargaining factor in the armistice negotiations before it was eventually returned to the control of the Lebanese.)

At dawn on 31 October, Operation 'Hiram', the last operation to be undertaken in the north during the war, came to a close. Kaukji's ALA had been totally defeated and eliminated, its remnants having been taken prisoner or driven out of Galilee. Arab casualties in the operation had included some 400 killed and 550 prisoners. The Lebanese Army had, in fact, withdrawn from the war, and Israel held a strip of territory in the Lebanon from the Litani south to Malkiya. The Syrians retained their bridgehead at Mishmar Hayarden, but apart from this the entire area of the Galilee was in Israel's hands. For all practical purposes, the war along Israel's northern borders had come to an end.

The southern front: the Faluja pocket

As Allon prepared his plans for a major offensive in the Negev, a very intricate operation was carried out under the very noses of the Egyptians. The 'Yiftach' Brigade moved to the Negev through the Egyptian lines to relieve the 'Negev' Brigade, which had borne the brunt of the fighting in the south for the previous nine months. Both sides endeavoured to improve their positions during the truce, and fighting broke out as the respective opposing sides resisted such attempts. A typical battle was the one that took place in the area of Khirbet Mahaz, a hill overlooking the main road running from north to south through the Negev, and which was within artillery range of the airfield at Ruhama, a vital supply link for the Israeli forces in the Negev. After a fresh force from the 'Yiftach' Brigade had occupied the area of Khirbet Mahaz, the Israeli positions were

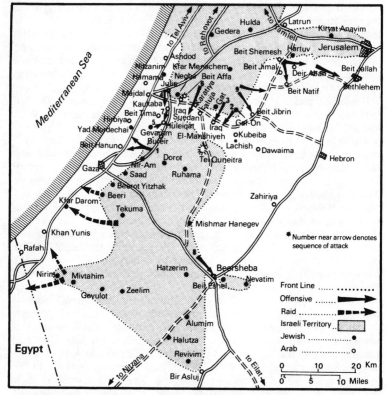

Operation 'Yoav', 15-22 October 1948

unsuccessfully attacked seven times by Egyptian forces, particularly by the 6th Infantry Battalion, whose operations officer at the time was a Major Gamal Abd al Nasser. (When he assumed the Presidency of Egypt after participating in the Revolution of the Free Officers that deposed King Farouk in 1952, Nasser was to describe how the idea of a revolution germinated within him and his colleagues of the Free Officers movement during the long nights in the field in Palestine, and particularly when he was later besieged in the 'Faluja pocket'.)

The Israeli offensive against Egypt in the south was codenamed Operation 'Yoav'. Under Allon's command were the 'Givati', 'Negev' and 'Yiftach' Brigades, in addition to two battalions from the 8th Armoured Brigade. (At a later date, the 'Oded' Brigade was moved from the northern front to take part in the operations.) Allon's plan was to force open a corridor to the Negev, cut the Egyptian lines of communications along the coast and on the Beersheba-Hebron-Jerusalem road, isolate and defeat the Egyptian forces in detail, and drive them out of the country.

On 15 October, an Israeli supply convoy under United Nations supervision (in accordance with the agreed terms) set out on its way to the Negev, through the Egyptian lines at the 'junction'. As anticipated, the Egyptians opened fire on the convoy, but the incident was merely a convenient signal for operation 'Yoav' to commence. That evening, Gaza, Majdal and Beit Hanun were bombed, and part of the Egyptian Air Force at El-Arish was put out of action. The commando battalion of the 'Yiftach' Brigade mined the railway between El-Arish and Rafah and various roads in the Rafah-Gaza area, and harassed Egyptian installations and camps. At the same time, two battalions of the 'Givati' Brigade forced a wedge southwards to the east of Iraq El-Manshiyeh, thus cutting the road between Faluja and Beit Jibrin. On the morning of 16 October, a tank battalion of the 8th Armoured Brigade, supported by an infantry battalion of the 'Negev' Brigade, launched a major attack against Iraq El-Manshiyeh in an attempt to open the corridor to the south-east. This attempt failed because of the lack of experience of the Israeli forces in co-ordinating armour and infantry: much of the armoured force was damaged when it was caught exposed in an artillery 'killing ground' previously prepared by the Egyptians, and the Israeli force was obliged to withdraw. In the course of the action, one of the two Cromwell tanks that had been acquired from the British Army was damaged, and the second Cromwell was involved in the task of extricating it from the battlefield. Very heavy losses were incurred in this attack, which had all the indications of slovenliness, lack of co-ordination and poor overall command. Of the total attacking force, only about 50 men managed to make their way back to the Israeli trenches. In addition to the heavy casualties, four Hotchkiss tanks of the small Israeli tank force were lost, and all the remaining tanks were damaged.

Allon drew his conclusions from this defeat and decided to return to the area near the 'junction' in an endeavour to break through in the area of Huleiqat. The Egyptian defences around the 'junction' were based on the Iraq Suedan fortress and consisted of Hill 113 and Hill 100 overlooking the 'junction' in the north, two mutually-supporting positions to the west held by a company and, to the south, the fortified hilltop villages of Huleiqat and Kaukaba, which were held by a reinforced company of Saudi Arabians. Allon decided to concentrate his attack on Hill 113 and the 'junction' strongholds, a battalion of the 'Givati' Brigade being assigned the task of capturing these vital points. Each position was attacked by a company advancing under the cover of artillery fire, following diversionary attacks designed to give the impression that the main attack would come from the direction of the Negev, to the south. The Egyptians were taken by surprise when the main Israeli attack came from the opposite direction. On the night of 16/17 October, the Israeli forces stormed the positions in bayonet attacks and, by midnight, following a fierce hand-to-hand battle, Hills 113 and 100 were captured. The attack on the 'junction' positions ran into trouble, the Egyptian resistance being more determined and protracted, but by dawn on 18 October both positions were in Israeli hands. The Egyptians counterattacked four times, but in vain. That night, the 'Givati' units exploited their success further by capturing Kaukaba, but an attack by the 1st Battalion of the 'Yiftach' Brigade on Huleiqat failed. The planned corridor to the south remained blocked.

Meanwhile, the 'Yiftach' Brigade forces, which had succeeded in cutting the coastal road at Beit Hanun, threatened the Egyptian forces to the north with complete encirclement. The Egyptians began to evacuate the Ashdod and Majdal areas, using an alternative route along the beaches, and they succeeded in concentrating the evacuated brigade in the area that later became known as the 'Gaza Strip'. The reaction on the part of the other Arab countries to the plight of the withdrawing and encircled Egyptian forces led to the inevitable inter-Arab recriminations, and this convinced the Israeli Command that other Arab armies would not intervene to help the Egyptians. Accordingly, the 'Oded' Brigade was moved south from Galilee, and was thrown into an unsuccessful attack on the Egyptians in the hilly area of the Kharatiya bypass. With pressure developing at the United Nations for a new cease-fire, Allon decided' to concentrate all his efforts on opening the corridor to the south by cracking the 'hard nut' at Huleiqat. Despite the heavy losses and exhaustion of the troops, Allon decided that the task would be carried out on the night of 19/20 October by the battle-seasoned 'Givati' Brigade. The result was to be one of the most fiercely-fought battles in the Negev.

The Huleiqat defence system was manned by a reinforced Egyptian battalion and included a Saudi Arabian infantry company backed by a heavy weapons support company (armed with machine-guns, mortars and Bren Gun Carriers). To wrest this complex from the enemy, the 2nd Battalion of the 'Givati' Brigade was reinforced by an additional company from the 4th Battalion. Commanding the 2nd Battalion of the 'Givati' Brigade and in charge of the operation was Zvi Tzur, later to rise to the position of Chief of Staff of the Israel Defence Forces in 1961. (A very able administrator, General Tzur was to be General Dayan's right-hand man during his period as Minister of Defence from 1967 to 1974.) The six hills held by the Egyptians were mutually supporting, and the problem of the Israeli attackers was to isolate each one and then to reduce them individually. The initial bayonet assault on the hill held in part by the Saudi Arabians, took the position by storm. A considerable quantity of equipment was discovered there, including some thirty Vickers machine-guns, which were immediately put to use by the Israeli forces, who turned the hill into a fire-support base. On all six hills, the fighting was characterized by bitter hand-to-hand combat, with the trench systems being cleared by repeated bayonet and grenade attacks. In the fighting for the last hill, ammunition ran out and men were locked in desperate 'cold-steel' encounters – Saudi Arabian soldiers even resorting to biting their attackers!

Thus did the Huleiqat complex fall to the 'Givati' attack and, on 20 October, the road to the Negev was finally opened. Near Huleiqat today stands a monument bearing the insignia of the 'Givati' Brigade and the inscription: 'As you travel southwards don't forget us.'

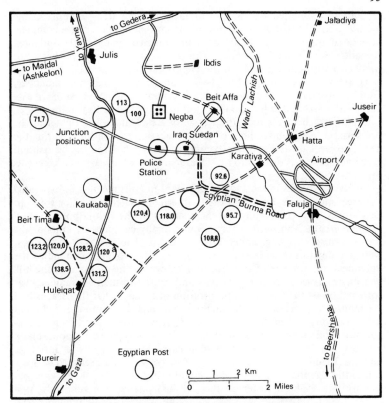

Positions in the Area of the Egyptian Junction

An attack mounted simultaneously to take the Iraq Suedan police fortress on 20/21 October failed for the fifth time, again with serious losses. However, following up the Huleiqat success, Allon immediately prepared a task force to move on Beersheba, with the purpose of isolating the eastern Egyptian force in the Hills of Hebron and cutting its lines of communication: once fragmented, the Egyptian forces in the Negev could be dealt with in detail.

The force that moved on Beersheba consisted of major elements of the 8th Brigade, the commando battalion and two other battalions of the 'Negev' Brigade. At dawn on 21 October, the Israeli forces approached Beersheba from the west, while a diversionary operation was mounted from the direction of Hebron to the north. After fierce fighting, the 500-strong Egyptian garrison broke and, by 09.00 hours that morning, Beersheba — capital of the Negev — had surrendered to Israeli forces. The eastern part of the Egyptian Army was by now dismembered, with its main supply lines cut. In fact, the Egyptian expeditionary force was now broken up into four isolated forces: one brigade in the Rafah-Gaza area; one brigade about to withdraw southwards from the Majdal area; a complete brigade of approximately 4,000 men, under the command of the Sudanese Brigadier Said Taha Bey, confined in the so-called 'Faluja pocket'; and some two battalions isolated in the Hebron-Jerusalem area.

To relieve the Faluja pocket, the Jordanian Arab Legion commander, Glubb, proposed a battalion-sized operation: but inter-Arab rivalry prevailed — Abdullah had no intention of relieving the Egyptians. On 22 October, Israeli forces took the village of Beit Hanun and tightened the pressure on the Egyptian lines of communication to Ashdod. During the next two weeks, the Egyptians completed the evacuation of the Ashdod area and Majdal, retiring into the general area of what was to be known as the 'Gaza Strip'.

The Israeli forces in the Judean and Hebron Hills meanwhile expanded the area under their control in the southern Jerusalem Corridor south to Beit Jibrin, thus completing the encirclement of the Faluja pocket. On 9 November, the Iraq Suedan fortress was finally captured by units of the 8th Armoured Brigade, under Yitzhak Sadeh. The mistakes of the past were avoided this time. In the afternoon, with the setting sun blinding the defenders, the fortress of Iraq Suedan, known as 'the monster on the hill' and having resisted so many attacks and caused so many casualties, was softened up by the heaviest concentration of artillery that the Israelis had yet managed in the War, including newly-acquired 75mm guns, light and heavy mortars and machine-guns. The roof was swept clean by machine-gun fire, and every aperture in the building was engaged by point-blank artillery fire. After two hours of concentrated, non-stop fire, infantry, half-tracks and two tanks reached the fortress wall and breached it. They found the Egyptian garrison stunned and in shock as its soldiers emerged to surrender. 'The monster on the hill' had finally been subdued. As a result, the Faluja pocket was reduced to the area between Faluja and Iraq El-Manshiyeh, which continued to be held by the besieged brigade until the armistice agreement between Israel and Egypt, which was signed on 24 February 1949.

Hitherto, the commander of the Faluja pocket, Brigadier Said Taha Bey, had refused offers to meet the Israeli commanders, but now he met the southern front commander, Yigal Allon, at the village of Gat. Allon's offer to allow the Egyptians full military honours and a free return to Egypt if they surrendered, was refused. Said Taha Bey maintained that, while he knew the position was hopeless, his task now was to save the honour of the Egyptian Army. The Egyptian Government, replied Allon, was not worthy of as brave an officer as Taha Bey.

To reinforce the Israeli units on the southern front, the 'Golani' Brigade was now brought down from the lush green hills of Galilee to the barren desert of the Negev. The 'Givati' Brigade — which had borne the brunt of the fighting in the northern Negev and had performed magnificently — was relieved and replaced by the 'Alexandroni' Brigade which, from mid-November, was entrusted with enforcing an effective siege of the pocket and frustrating the numerous attempts made by the Egyptians to bring in supplies by parachute or camel convoy. A plan to help the besieged forces break out to the Hebron Hills was clandestinely brought through the lines by a British officer of the Arab Legion, Major Lockheed. However, the supreme command of the Egyptian forces rejected it, maintaining that it was impracticable. They were also innately suspicious of any plan in which a British officer, albeit as an ally, was involved. Besides, the pocket was pinning down considerable Israeli forces. An attack by the 'Alexandroni' Brigade was beaten off on the night of 27/28 December. Characterized by numerous errors and ineffective co-ordination and communication, the attack was rapidly fragmented and unified command lost. Some of the isolated Israeli units were wiped out. The attack was a disaster, and a morale booster for the besieged Egyptians. Henceforth, the Faluja brigade remained under siege without any further Israeli attacks until the end of the war.

The southern front: the 'Horev' offensive

The Egyptian Command prepared to break the stalemate. Having withdrawn and redeployed its forces in the area along the coast south of Beit Hanun, concentrating primarily in the area of Gaza-Rafah, it planned to launch an attack from the Gaza area to relieve the Faluja pocket. As a prelude to the operation, Egyptian columns occupied a number of dominating points, particularly in the south-west. Very heavy fighting took place and, in a series of counterattacks on 5 December, the Israeli forces succeeded in occupying a number of strategic positions along the Gaza front-line in what was known as Operation 'Assaf', units of the 8th Armoured Brigade and 'Golani' Brigade fighting-off heavy infantry and armoured Egyptian attacks. As a result, the Israeli line was strengthened and much improved.

Late in November, the Israeli forces had also extended their control to the east of Beersheba, across the desert towards the Dead Sea and down Wadi Arava, running south along the Jordanian border, thus relieving the southern Dead Sea potash plant at Sdom which had been cut off for well-nigh six months. (This area, on the shores of the Dead Sea, included Masada, scene of the heroic last stand of the Jews in their uprising against the Romans, in AD72.)

Meanwhile, political pressure was mounting in the United Nations Security Council to force Israel to withdraw to the lines of 14 October — which would mean allowing the Negev to be cut off again. This political pressure, in which Britain played a major rôle, coupled with the Egyptian moves towards Faluja (which led to the eruption of a series of battles along the Gaza front), convinced the Israeli Command that it was essential to drive the Egyptians out of the country and to remove the threat that an Egyptian concentration in the Gaza area would constitute against the security of the Negev and against Israeli security in general. Above all, the Israelis were conscious of the fact that the British Government refused to reconcile itself to the incorporation of the Negev in Israel; indeed,

Bernadotte's plan to allocate the Negev to the Arabs in exchange for Galilee was still an option favoured by some of the Western powers. Accordingly, the Government of Israel decided to mount an additional military operation in the Negev designed to destroy the invading Egyptian forces and to create a military situation that would force the Egyptians to come to the negotiating table.

The five Egyptian brigades that now comprised the Egyptian expeditionary force, were dispersed as follows: one brigade of approximately 4,000 men besieged in the Faluja pocket; two reinforced brigades in the Gaza area; and one brigade in the area around Abu Ageila and El-Arish. There were also approximately 2,000 men, remnants of the Moslem Brotherhood battalions, still isolated in the Hebron-Bethlehem area. Thus, the Egyptian forces in Palestine were deployed in a wide arc, with the western arm sweeping from the Gaza area southwards to the area of El-Arish and Abu Ageila, and the eastern arm northwards from Abu Ageila to Bir Asluj. The main concentration of Egyptian forces was in the Gaza area, to the defence of which the Egyptian Command revealed considerable sensitivity. It was clear to Allon that a head-on attack against Gaza would be a very costly venture. As he saw it, the key to bringing about the collapse of the Egyptian dispositions would be to cut the lateral communications between the eastern and western forces. The concept — Operation 'Horev' — was to strike with this aim in view, to roll back the forces on the eastern road from Bir Asluj southwards and then, in a broad sweep into the Sinai Desert, to close in on El-Arish from the south and thus cut off the entire Egyptian force from its sources of supplies and reinforcements.

The forces at the disposal of the southern front commander for Operation 'Horev' consisted of five brigades: the 8th Armoured Brigade, commanded by Yitzhak Sadeh; the 'Negev' and 'Golani' Brigades and the 'Harel' Brigade; which had been moved south from the Jerusalem Corridor. The 'Alexandroni' Brigade continued to besiege the Faluja pocket. The Israeli Command sought a way to avoid committing forces to potentially costly operations against one strongly-held Egyptian position after another, for the Egyptians held a series of strongpoints in the area of Bir Asluj, particularly at Bir E-Tamile and Mishrefe to the south of Bir Asluj, on the road to El Auja. The Egyptian positions were deployed along the main road connecting El Auja and Beersheba — but the Israeli Command was aware of the existence of the remains of an ancient Roman road which would bypass them, running as it did almost in a straight line from Beersheba to El Auja. It had been covered by the sands over the centuries and would require considerable repairs to render it usable, but an advance along this road would bypass all the Egyptian positions in the area of Bir Asluj and cut their lines of communication to El Auja. In order to divert Egyptian attention from the activity engendered by the forces engaged in repairing the Roman road, and to mislead the Egyptians as to the direction of the principal Israeli effort, a major assault by 'Golani' forces was directed against the Gaza area at Hirbet Main. The 'Golani' troops were ordered to hammer a wedge into that area to prevent the

Egyptians from using the main coastal road. In the east, the 8th Armoured Brigade, supported by a battalion from the 'Harel' Brigade, would capture El Auja, and follow-up in the direction of Abu Ageila in the Sinai Peninsula. Furthermore, units of the 8th Armoured Brigade were to cut the lateral road from Rafah to El Auja and, simultaneously, two battalions of the 'Negev' Brigade were to capture the Bir E-Tamile and Mishrefe strongpoints astride the main road north of El Auja. An air and naval bombardment of Egyptian bases and concentrations would add to the pressure.

On 22 December, in the midst of a heavy downpour of rain in the coastal area and a violent sandstorm in the desert to the east, Operation 'Horev' was launched. A battalion of the 'Golani' Brigade surprised and

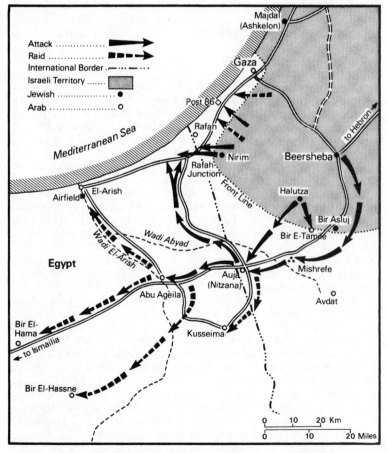

Operation 'Horev', 22 December 1948 to 8 January 1949

captured Hill 86 controlling the Gaza-Rafah road. The Egyptians mounted a concentrated counterattack with armour, artillery and half-tracks mounting flame-throwers, forcing the 'Golani' unit to withdraw under heavy pressure. However, the operation had the effect of concentrating Egyptian attention on this sector. Air attacks were mounted against the Egyptians in the western sector only, and naval units shelled Gaza. The Egyptians were by now convinced that the main Israeli effort was to be directed against their forces nearest the coast. Meanwhile, Israeli engineers were working around the clock, moving the sand that had accumulated over the old Roman road (known as the 'Ruheiba trail') and laying wire netting on it. By 25 December, an armoured force was able to move gingerly along the ancient road. Simultaneously, a commando unit executed a broad sweep into the eastern desert, emerging from the east to capture the Mishrefe stronghold, thus severing the lines of communication of the Egyptian forces based on Bir Asluj. A unit of the 'Negev' Brigade captured Bir E-Tamile, the defenders of which withdrew northwards to Bir Asluj.

The armoured brigade operation against El Auja did not succeed until 27 December. Parallel to this, the 'Negev' Brigade moved against the remaining Egyptian positions between Bir Asluj and El Auja, which cut off Beersheba from El Auja. By the afternoon of 27 December, the capture of these positions had been completed and the 'Negev' Brigade moved along the Beersheba-Auja road, linking-up with the armoured brigade before the day was over. The entire Beersheba-Auja road was now in Israeli hands, and the first phase of Operation 'Horev' had been completed. The Egyptian eastern front had collapsed completely, all the forces in the area either being taken prisoner or fleeing.

The extent of the Egyptian defeat was not yet appreciated abroad, because the Egyptian Government persisted in misleading its own people with false claims of victory. Political pressure on Israel had therefore not yet mounted. At the same time, it was clear that this new situation must be exploited to take advantage of the confusion into which the Egyptian camp had been thrown and to prevent the restabilization of the Egyptian forces in the Sinai Peninsula. On the night of 28 December, the 'Negev' Brigade, supported by the tank battalion of the armoured brigade, crossed the border into Sinai with the mission of taking Abu Ageila. After overcoming resistance at Um-Katef, the commando battalion of the 'Negev' Brigade entered Abu Ageila without encountering opposition. The next day, a unit of the 'Negev' Brigade advanced northwards to El-Arish with the tank battalion leading, overcoming opposition at Bir Lahfan and reaching the airfield at El-Arish, while to the south 'Harel' units reached the village of Kusseima. The Israeli forces poised to hit El-Arish from the south now regrouped to prepare for the next phase. Their purpose was to create a threat at El-Arish and Rafah that, coupled with pressure from the 'Golani' Brigade along the Gaza front, would encourage the Egyptians to withdraw their remaining forces from south-west Palestine.

In the meantime, on 29 December, the Security Council of the United Nations ordered another cease-fire. Egyptian appeals to the other Arab

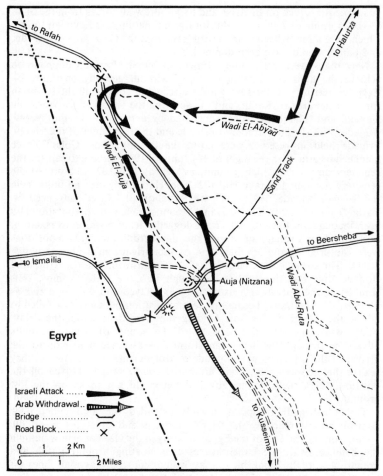

**The Conquest of Auja (Nitzana) — Operation 'Horev',
27 December 1948**

contingents to mount diversionary attacks against Israel were in vain, but
the Egyptian salvation was to come from a totally unexpected quarter. On
1 January 1949, the United States Ambassador to Israel delivered an
ultimatum from the British Government: unless Israeli forces withdrew
from the Sinai, the British would be obliged to invoke the provisions of the
Anglo-Egyptian treaty of 1936, and to come to the aid of the Egyptians.
(Ironically, the Egyptians had been mounting a campaign to abrogate the
treaty, a goal that was in fact achieved seven years later by President
Nasser.) Unwilling to take unnecessary political risks, and mindful of the
inherent weakness of the new State, Ben-Gurion ordered General Allon to

postpone the attack on El-Arish and to withdraw all forces from the Sinai by the morning of 2 January. But for this ultimatum, the Egyptian forces, which were already beginning to withdraw from the Gaza area in disorder and panic, would have been doomed.

New plans were accordingly drawn up by the Israeli Command to achieve the aims of Operation 'Horev' without actually operating on Egyptian territory. Efforts were to be directed at cutting off the Egyptian forces in the area of Rafah, and to capturing the Rafah crossroads. The 'Golani' and 'Harel' Brigades, supported by a battalion of the 'Negev' Brigade, with the 8th Armoured Brigade and the remainder of the 'Negev' Brigade held in reserve, were given the mission. The 'Golani' force launched its attack on the night of 3/4 January 1949, aiming to capture the cemetery and nearby high ground, as well as Hill 102; it captured the cemetery but failed to take Hill 102. The 'Harel' Brigade and units from the 'Negev' Brigade, led by the 4th Battalion of 'Harel', advanced on Rafah from the south. Their advance reconnaissance and preparation had been inadequate, but they advanced doggedly from position to position, capturing four strongpoints during the night. Additionally, two positions were captured by the 5th Battalion of the Brigade in a fierce bayonet attack. The struggle took place in a violent sandstorm, but the Armoured Brigade that was due to break through into the Rafah camps, thus completing the operation, was once again delayed and did not arrive as planned. Furthermore, because of communication difficulties, it failed to advise the 'Harel' forces now holding the crossroads about the delay. Thus, when the 'Harel' troops heard the sound of armoured units advancing through the heavy sandstorm they assumed it to indicate the arrival of the 8th Armoured Brigade reinforcements — too late did they realize that it was an Egyptian armoured counterattack. Driven off the position, the Israelis counterattacked but could not make up the lost ground.

'Golani' Brigade troops meanwhile extended the area under their control, almost reaching the 'Harel' outposts and thus closing off the Rafah camps. The fate of the Egyptian army in the Gaza area now hung in the balance, with the Israeli forces consolidating around Rafah and preparing for the final blow that would cut the Egyptian lines of communication. As the Israelis deployed for the final push, the blinding sandstorm that was raging finally became so bad that operations were impossible. However, the Egyptian Command had already drawn its own conclusions: the bulk of the army was now doomed, and it was but a matter of hours before it would be cut off from its supplies and destroyed by the Israeli forces. Acknowledging the inevitable, the Egyptian Government declared its willingness to enter into negotiations for an armistice agreement.

International pressure in the United Nations and elsewhere was now mounting against Israel, and the British sent a patrol of fighter aircraft to reconnoitre the Sinai and ensure that the Israelis had withdrawn from Egyptian territory. Israeli pilots patrolling the border with Egypt encountered British Spitfires, which (according to the Israeli pilots' reports) were strafing Israeli transport inside Israel. A series of dogfights ensued as the Israeli fighter aircraft engaged the British patrol over Israeli air space in the Negev. In all, five British Spitfires were shot down, four in aerial combat and one by ground fire. Two British pilots lost their lives, two were taken prisoner by the Israelis and one succeeded in making his way to the Egyptian lines. (One of the Spitfires was shot down by a young pilot in the first Israeli Fighter Squadron, 101, Ezer Weizman, in later

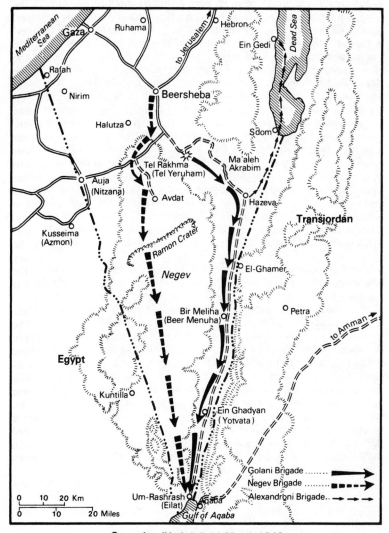

Operation 'Uvda', 6-10 March 1949

years to command the Air Force and become Minister of Defence.) Later that day, an RAF patrol consisting of one Mosquito with an escort of Hawker Tempests came looking for the missing Spitfires. They too were engaged by aircraft of 101 Squadron, and one of the Tempests was shot down. The British reaction was violent and threatening: the Israelis found themselves with no choice but to agree to a cease-fire, which came into force on 7 January.

The area of the Negev, with its apex at the northern tip of the Gulf of Aqaba, where the distance between the Egyptian and Jordanian frontiers is some six miles, had been allocated to the State of Israel by the Partition Resolution, but it had not all been brought under actual Israeli control. The Jordanians, with whom preliminary discussions were being conducted at the time, maintained some military control in the southern part of the Negev, and demanded that that area be allocated to Jordan. The Israelis now saw that the most propitious time in which to establish control over the area would be between the signing of the armistice agreement with Egypt and the opening of the armistice negotiations with Jordan. Accordingly, in March 1949, the 'Negev' Brigade and the 'Golani' Brigade mounted Operation 'Uvda'. Because of the cease-fire, the strictest instructions were issued to ensure that Jordanian forces in the Negev were in no way to be engaged and no hostile activities were to be mounted against them. The operation was thus envisaged as a series of manoeuvres that would outflank the small Jordanian patrols in the area and make their positions untenable. The main force, the 'Negev' Brigade, moved south through the wadis and mountains of the central Negev, while the 'Golani' Brigade moved southwards along the Wadi Arava route parallel to the Jordanian border.

Some Jordanian patrols opened fire, but the Israeli forces, which outnumbered them considerably and had set up a makeshift airfield for supplies in the centre of the Negev Desert, easily bypassed them. By 10 March, the small Jordanian outposts had withdrawn across the border, and Um-Rashrash, a desert outpost situated on the Red Sea coast, was evacuated. Two hours later, the Israeli forces arrived there and Captain Avraham ('Bren') Adan, a battalion commander in the 'Negev' Brigade, shinned up a makeshift pole and affixed to it an improvised flag — a white sheet with the Shield of David drawn on it in ink — marking the assumption of Israeli authority in what was later to be the port of Eilat. Adan, a small, wiry, fair-haired man, hailing from the kibbutz of Nirim, where he had first fought against the invading Egyptian forces, and a veteran of the wars of the Negev, was later to command the Israeli Armoured Corps and subsequently one of the divisions that crossed the Suez Canal in the 1973 War leading to the encirclement of the Egyptian Third Army.

SUMMARY
The Israeli Victory

The armistice agreement with Egypt was signed on the Island of Rhodes on 24 February 1949. The front-lines as they were at the end of the fighting became the armistice borders, and the strip of coastline at Gaza remained in the hands of the Egyptians. Israeli control of the Negev was now unquestioned. The besieged Egyptian brigade at Faluja marched out with its arms, receiving full military honours from the Israelis, and returned to Egypt. Then followed the armistice agreement with Lebanon on 23 March 1949, Israeli forces withdrawing from the area held in Lebanon; the armistice agreement with Jordan on 3 April 1949; and finally the armistice agreement with Syria, on 20 July 1949, whereby Syria withdrew from the Mishmar Hayarden bridgehead, which was to remain demilitarized.

The War of Independence was over. The State of Israel was established within borders constituted by the lines agreed upon in the armistice agreements. These agreements, which were envisaged as a prelude to a peace treaty to be signed within six months, were to continue for years and indeed were to lapse because they were not honoured by the Arab signatories. Every compromise proposal towards peace proposed by the Israelis over the years was rejected out of hand by the Arabs. The crux of the problem became, and remained, the refusal of the Arab States to recognize the right of the Jewish State in the Middle East to exist.

Several attempts were made over the years by the Palestinian Arabs to assert themselves, but in vain. In 1949, the representatives of the Palestinian refugees attempted to bring their case before the Palestinian Conciliation Commission meeting in Lausanne, and sought a compromise with Israel; but their action was disowned by the Arab governments. On numerous occasions, Ben-Gurion offered to meet the Arab leadership (as indeed did all future Israeli prime ministers) in order to work out a compromise, but until President Sadat's historic trip to Jerusalem in November 1977 no Arab leader was prepared to take such a step.

Two large refugee problems were created as a result of the conflict, each encompassing approximately 800,000 persons: a Palestinian Arab refugee problem and a Jewish refugee problem, the latter created upon the establishment of the State of Israel when the Jewish populations in Arab countries were exiled from their countries. The Jewish people and the State of Israel solved the Jewish refugee problem rapidly and re-established the Jewish refugees, primarily in Israel. But the Arab governments chose to perpetuate the Arab refugee problem, to use the Arab refugees as political pawns over the years, and to allow generations to be born and to grow up in miserable refugee camps in the Middle East supported by international charity. (It is sobering to reflect that just one day's Arab oil revenues, even in 1949, would have sufficed to solve the entire Arab refugee problem. But this was not to be.)

The Israeli nation had been forged in the heat of a bloody war. A heavily outnumbered populace had defended itself against seemingly overwhelming odds, losing in the process one per cent of its population. In Israel's War of Independence, 6,000 were killed, of whom over 4,000 were members of the armed forces. (This was as if 2,500,000 people had been lost in battle by the United States, or 500,000 people by Great Britain, or 35,000 people — almost the total of American dead in the Vietnamese War — by Israel today.)

Israel's victory was the result of the self-sacrifice and determination of a people to fight for its existence. The spirit that animated the people and the courage it reflected were the function of a rare form of determined and inspiring leadership. David Ben-Gurion belongs in history to the class of Churchill, Roosevelt and De Gaulle — a powerful, charismatic leader with sufficient vision to see several steps ahead and to grasp the basic issues facing the nation, with sufficient courage to lead against the most impossible odds and to demand the most extreme sacrifices from his people. He was, moreover, endowed with sufficient personality and power of leadership to weld together elements of different outlooks and philosophies to one common purpose. He had the necessary historic vision and understanding to appreciate already in late 1945 that there was no chance of an agreed settlement with the British, and that therefore the Jews in Palestine must prepare for the creation of a national army and for a full-scale war. Had he not grasped the significance of the new developments, events would have overtaken the Jews of Palestine and found them completely unprepared, both politically and militarily. While Ben-Gurion's colleagues, and indeed his political opponents, were thinking in terms of commando raids and small-unit warfare, Ben-Gurion realized that there would be no compromise and that he would have to go the whole way. Above all, he knew what he wanted, and was unwilling to compromise — hence his insistence at all stages on preparation for an all-out war, and his clear understanding of the meaning of statehood, which at times clashed with the confusion and contradictions of some outdated Zionist ideologies. He made mistakes, but his faults were those of a very great man. Without his foresight, imagination and determination, it is doubtful whether disaster could have been averted.

In retrospect, with a number of outstanding exceptions such as Yigal Allon and Shimon Avidan, the Israeli generals were inexperienced and unimaginative, but this failing was compensated to a degree by the overpowering personality, ability, vision and understanding of the issues by Ben-Gurion, and by the extraordinary bravery of the Israeli military leadership in the field. The main brunt of the fighting in the War of Independence was borne at battalion and company level. The norms of leadership, the personal example and the self-sacrifice that were later to characterize Israeli officers and NCOs in battle were established in the War of Independence. Many outstanding generals who were to lead the Israel

Defence Forces in four more wars, emerged from the ranks of the battalion, company and platoon commanders in the War of Independence. What was to all intents and purposes a partisan army based in the main on the Haganah, to which were added elements of the Irgun and Lehi, grew into a conventional army in the heat of battle. The basically civilian nature of the force that fought for the villages, homesteads and towns of Palestine set the future pattern. The IDF continued to be a civilian army comprising a comparatively small regular component and a large reserve force. This very effective organization of a reserve army was created, after the establishment of the State, by General Yigael Yadin, the second Chief of Staff of the armed forces. Based on reservists, it gave rise to the comparatively 'easygoing' atmosphere for which the Israeli Army was later to be noted. The formative period of the IDF, fighting for the life of a nation in a war of bitter struggles and much suffering, left its mark: the fact that war was to continue sporadically for the next 30 years before the first peace treaty with an Arab country would be signed dictated the character of the armed forces, which saw little purpose in outward trappings and military pomp, and viewed the Army as a fighting machine, a necessary evil with which to defend independence, and no more.

The disadvantages under which the Israeli Army operated during the War of Independence — its weakness in manpower, its lack of modern weapons, and the necessity to fight on many fronts at the same time — evolved a military philosophy based on flexibility, the use of surprise and innovation. Fighting by night became almost second nature to the Israeli forces, because darkness neutralized to a degree the advantages enjoyed by the Arab forces. Indeed, the Israeli attacks during the War of Independence were nearly all mounted at night. Speed, commando-type operations, the use of outflanking manoeuvres — all of these combined to emphasize the character and mode of operation of the emerging Israeli armed forces. Coupled with this was a flexibility of thought that encouraged the leader in battle to adapt himself to the vicissitudes of war at a moment's notice and to take advantage of changing circumstances in the field. A rigid approach and over-dependence on higher command had no place in the Israeli forces. Thus emerged the Israel Defence Forces, which was to become a major military factor in the Middle East, a factor that would not only be of local significance but would also become an important strategic element in the region.

On the opposing side, the Arab Legion stood out as the outstanding army, British-officered and led as it was; but even after the British left some years later, it continued to be the most effective Arab army, well led, brave and satisfactorily organized. All the Arab armies apart from Kaukji's Arab Liberation Army proved to be highly effective in defence, and this was to characterize them over the coming years. But their failing in attack arose out of the fact that, when their set-piece attack encountered unexpected obstacles, the junior leadership in the field was incapable of adapting itself rapidly enough to the changing circumstances of the battle. Above all, the inter-Arab bickering — which over the years was to erupt sporadically in internecine strife — plagued the Arab forces. While they all fought against the Israelis, they were inevitably looking over their shoulders at their allies in an atmosphere of mistrust. They could thus never really take full advantage of their overwhelming superiority, while the Israeli forces, operating on internal lines of communication, were able to take advantage of this situation, switching forces from front to front and developing attacks against one Arab force conscious of the fact that there would be no concerted military pressure brought to bear on them on other fronts.

In the War of Independence the fate of Israel hung precariously in the balance. It was saved by the great and historic leadership of Ben-Gurion, leading a nation endowed with a desire to live, and prepared to make every sacrifice to achieve this end. That sacrifice was made in the War of Independence, but it would continue to be exacted in the years to come.

BOOK II

THE SINAI CAMPAIGN OF 1956

THE SINAI CAMPAIGN
OF 1956

During the seven years following the signing of the armistice agreements, instead of peace treaties being achieved as envisaged in the preambles to the agreements, the rift between Israel and the Arab states widened, and the relations along Israel's borders (apart from that with Lebanon) deteriorated. The Arabs persisted in their policy of refusing to accept the fact that Israel existed as a sovereign state, a member of the international community and an independent entity. Whilst the War of Independence, as a war, had been fought and was physically-speaking over, its causes and the motives behind the enmity of the Arab states against Israel continued to exist and to brew. Within months of the signing of the 1949 armistice agreements, border incursions, raids, economic warfare and other violations became the order of the day. By 1954, it was clear that the incursions of 'fedayeen'* murder groups were not isolated incidents, but, like the economic sanctions against Israeli commercial and maritime interests, were organized and implemented with the knowledge and co-operation of the Arab governments.

New régimes: the rise of Nasser's Egypt

The major Arab defeat in 1948 exacerbated many of their internal problems, bringing to the fore the extreme elements and creating an atmosphere of unrest and near-revolution in many of the Arab countries. In July 1951, King Abdullah of Jordan, who had secretly initialled an agreement intended to lead to a peace accord with Israel, was assassinated, struck down by the agents of the Mufti of Jerusalem, Haj Amin el-Husseini, on the steps of the El Aqsa Mosque on the Temple Mount in Jerusalem. (His grandson Hussein, who was to be proclaimed King of Jordan a year later, was at his side.) In Egypt, the Egyptian Prime Minister, Nokrashi Pasha, was assassinated in the aftermath of the War. The Syrian Government was overthrown by General Husni el Zaim in 1949, and he in turn was overthrown in 1951; thereafter, Syria was to be torn by frequent military revolutions. In Egypt, a group of so-called 'Free Officers' led by Lieutenant-Colonel Gamal Abd al Nasser seized control of the government on 23 July 1952 and sent King Farouk into exile. For a period, the officers appointed as their leader General Mohammed Neguib,

---

* Arabic for suicide squads or commandos, and a term based on medieval Islamic concepts. In the modern period, it designates commando and sabotage groups, guerrillas and terrorists engaged in political murder.

who had emerged from the 1948 War as a popular figure, but he was soon deposed and full authority over the new republic was assumed by Nasser. (One of the leading members of the Free Officers group who participated in the revolution was Lieutenant-Colonel Anwar el Sadat, later to be the President of Egypt and the first Arab leader to sign a peace treaty with Israel.) In Jordan, moves made by the British Government to induce the Kingdom to join the Western Middle East alliance known as the 'Baghdad Pact' provoked riots in December 1954. This extreme reaction was brought about by an anti-Western, pro-Nasser change of direction in the Jordanian Government: Glubb Pasha and the British officers serving in the Arab Legion were dismissed summarily, and thereafter armed incursions from Jordan by fedayeen groups frequently attacked objectives in Israel.

The rise of Nasser to power in Egypt was welcomed at first by Israel. Indeed, the aims of the revolution and initial contacts with Nasser's regime inspired hope for the future. But Nasser's mixture of radicalism and extreme Arab nationalism, coupled with an ambition to achieve leadership in the Arab world, pre-eminence in the world of Islam and primacy in the so-called 'non-aligned' group of nations (which, with Presidents Tito and Nehru, he founded), gradually came to expression in a bitter, blind antagonism to Israel. It was to lead Egypt to tragedy.

In late 1955, a massive arms transaction between Egypt and Czechoslovakia was concluded, whereby Egypt received modern weapons. This, as Nasser declared, constituted a major step toward the decisive battle for the destruction of Israel. Egypt received 530 armoured vehicles (230 tanks, 200 armoured troop carriers and 100 self-propelled guns), some 500 artillery pieces, and up to 200 fighter, bomber and transport aircraft, plus destroyers, motor torpedo-boats and submarines. Thus was established the first major Soviet foothold in the Middle East. This arms agreement with the Eastern bloc was a major boost to Nasser's ambitions. He was now establishing himself as the leading element hostile to 'Western imperialism' in the Middle East, and becoming a serious embarrassment to the British and French in the area. Besides supporting radical governments in Africa and backing the fedayeen raids on Israel, he was active in helping the FLN* revolutionaries in Algeria against French rule. This, however, created a bond of common interest between Israel and France, as a result of which Shimon Peres (then the dynamic Director-General of Israel's Ministry of Defence) was able to promote various areas of co-operation between the two countries. Israel now began to receive shipments of arms from France (although sufficient only to avoid Egypt's superiority in weaponry from exceeding four to one on the eve of the Sinai campaign).

Egypt meanwhile blocked the navigation of Israeli vessels in the international waterways of the area in violation both of the 1949 armistice agreement and of international law. In order to reach the Red Sea and maintain commercial and maritime contacts with the Far East and Africa, Israeli vessels had to navigate through the Straits of Tiran, which Egypt had blocked by installing a coastal artillery battery at Ras Nasrani. Egypt

* Front de Liberation Nationale, the Algerian revolutionary movement against the French, which was proclaimed on 1 November 1954.

President Gamal Abd al Nasser of Egypt, the leader of the Free Officers who overthrew King Farouk in 1952. He opened Egypt's doors to the Soviet Union and led Egypt into two wars with Israel in 1956 and 1967.

Above: King Hussein of the Hashemite Kingdom of Jordan shakes the hand of his implacable enemy, Ahmed Shukeiri, the Palestine delegate of the Arab League, later a founder of the Palestine Liberation Organization. (UPI)

Right: President Aref of Iraq with Nasser. (UPI)

Far right, top: A refugee camp in Gaza. The Arab governments have for political reasons perpetuated this crucial problem in the Middle East, opposing any attempt to dissolve the camps and resettle the refugees.

Far right, below: The '101 Unit' of the IDF was specially created to combat fedayeen raids. Its commander was Ariel Sharon (left), later to become a major-general and commander of the southern front in 1973. On his left is Lieutenant-General Moshe Dayan, then Chief of G Branch (Operations) of the IDF.

Above: An Israeli pilot climbing into a French-manufactured Mystère IV A single-seat fighter—an aircraft that played a key rôle in the Sinai Campaign. (Zahal-Bamahane) **Below:** A British-manufactured Archer self-propelled anti-tank gun of Second World War vintage, captured from the Egyptians. In the background is a Soviet-built T34/85 tank. (GPO)

had also barred all passage by Israeli vessels through the Suez Canal — despite a Resolution of the United Nations Security Council in 1951 censuring Egypt's policy on this issue. But, even after this Resolution, Egypt, aided politically by the Soviet Union, extended the maritime limitations, impounded Israeli vessels, cargo and crews.

In the course of negotiations with Great Britain, Nasser negotiated the withdrawal of British troops from the Suez Canal Zone, where they had been stationed for over eighty years by treaty. He was also negotiating with the United States Government and with the British Government for a loan from the International Bank for Reconstruction and Development to finance the construction of a dam on the River Nile above Aswan. This would supply electricity, control the Nile floods and by irrigation increase considerably the area of arable land in Egypt. At the same time, he conducted parallel negotiations on this project with the Soviet Union. But his attempt to play off West against East on this issue aroused the wrath of the United States Secretary of State, John Foster Dulles, who in July 1956 withdrew the American offer to finance the dam. Infuriated, Nasser nationalized the Suez Canal on 27 July 1956 by seizing control from the Suez Canal Company, in which the British Government held a majority share, and abrogating the Anglo-Egyptian Treaty. Seeing the seizure of the Canal as a threat to their strategic interests — including their oil-supply routes — the British and French began to prepare contingency plans. Forces were moved to Malta and Cyprus in the Mediterranean in preparation for the seizure of the Canal Zone and, indirectly, to bring about Nasser's downfall. Such a campaign, whilst objectively-speaking independent of the local Arab-Israeli problems, naturally had its implications — a factor that undoubtedly contributed to the decision-making process prior to the start of the campaign.

By this time, the Israeli leadership had reached the conclusion that Nasser was heading for an all-out war against Israel. This could be the only explanation for the joint military command established in October 1955 between Egypt and Syria (to be expanded in 1956 to include Jordan). The blockade of the Suez Canal and the Gulf of Aqaba was part of an all-out economic war against Israel, while the fedayeen incursions into Israel were becoming more frequent and exacting greater numbers of casualties — some 260 Israeli citizens being killed or wounded by the fedayeen in 1955. The Egyptians would very rapidly absorb the weapons supplied by the Soviet bloc. It was clear that Israel could not allow Nasser to develop his plans with impunity. Accordingly, in July 1956, David Ben-Gurion decided that he had no option but to take a pre-emptive move, and gave instructions to the Israeli General Staff to plan for war in the course of 1956, concentrating initially on the opening of the Straits of Tiran.

Israel meanwhile mounted diplomatic efforts to expedite the supply of arms from France. According to Moshe Dayan, the Chief of Staff at that time, the Israeli military attaché in Paris cabled on 1 September 1956, advising him of the Anglo-French plans against the Suez Canal and informing him that Admiral Pierre Barjot, who was to be Deputy Commander of the combined Allied forces, was of the opinion that Israel should be invited to take part in the operation. Ben-Gurion's instructions were to reply that in principle Israel was ready to co-operate. An exploratory meeting took place six days later between the Israeli Chief of Operations and French military representatives, while Shimon Peres continued talks in Paris with the French Minister of Defence, Maurice Bourges-Maunoury. At the end of the month, an Israeli mission headed by Foreign Minister Golda Meir, and including Peres and Dayan, met a French mission that included the French Defence Minister and the French Foreign Minister, Christian Pineau. As the preparations were set afoot to strike at Egypt, Franco-Israeli meetings became more frequent. Then, on 21 October, at the invitation of the French, Ben-Gurion flew to Sèvres in France, accompanied by Shimon Peres and Moshe Dayan. At these negotiations, in which the French Prime Minister, Guy Mollet, participated, they were joined by a British mission consisting of the British Foreign Minister Selwyn Lloyd and one senior official. After much discussion, during which Ben-Gurion was very hesitant because of his innate lack of trust in the British, the plan was arranged in such a way that Israel's first moves would not be interpreted as an invasion, and its forces could be withdrawn should the British and French allies not fulfil their part of the agreement.

A further factor affecting considerations was the way in which both the United States and the Soviet Union were preoccupied in such a manner (or so it was estimated) as to limit their freedom of action at the time. The United States was in the throes of a presidential election, during which it was assumed that President Eisenhower would not take any vital international decision that might prejudice his chances of re-election. Similarly, the Soviet Union was busy during the three months prior to the campaign, quelling the national urge for liberalization that had begun to come to expression in Poland and Hungary.

By October 1956, the Egyptian threat to Israel had taken on an increasing active form. Fedayeen raids reached an all-time high, in both intensity and violence, and the Israeli reprisal policy did not supply any final, secure or convincing answer. This and the prevailing global situation placed Israel in a position in which it had to take advantage of the circumstances in order to break the Egyptian stranglehold on its commercial sea routes and along its border areas. The aims were to be threefold: to remove the threat, wholly or partially, of the Egyptian Army in the Sinai; to destroy the framework of the fedayeen; and to secure the freedom of navigation through the Straits of Tiran. Only thus would Israel place itself in a comfortable bargaining position for the political struggle that would undoubtedly ensue.

The arena of war and the opposing forces

The Sinai Peninsula is a parched desert area in the form of an inverted triangle, serving as both a connecting corridor and a dividing barrier between Egypt and Israel. It provides either side with an ideal jumping-off ground in an attack against the other. The northern side, on the Mediterranean coast, is 134 miles long; its western side, along the banks of the Suez Canal and the Gulf of Suez, is 311 miles long; and its eastern side, along the Gulf of Aqaba, is 155 miles long. Topography in the northern half ranges from undulating sand dunes and ridges, palm groves and salt flats along the coastal plain, to a central hilly area with a vertical range of ridges reaching heights of up to 3,500 feet. Here there are but limited axes for passage, through which Egypt had constructed main roads, utilizing the negotiable passes between the high ridges and the deep, powdery-sandy wadis. These routes ran eastwards from the Suez Canal area: from Kantara to El-Arish in the north, and from Ismailia to Abu Ageila in the centre. Farther south, they had built a road connecting the southern Canal town of Suez with the village and training base of Nakhle, east of the steep Mitla Pass. North-south connecting roads had been constructed in the west, between Kusseima, Kuntilla and Ras El-Naqb, parallel to the Israel-Egypt frontier, and in the central plain connecting El-Arish to Bir El-Hassne and Nakhle.

The lower half of the peninsula represents the most extreme forms of desert topography — steep, saw-tooth mountain ranges, deep powdery wadis devoid of water, greenery and negotiable roads. The only passable road built in this area by the Egyptians had been, in fact, the coastal road connecting Suez, Ras Sudar, A-Tor and Sharm El-Sheikh along the coast of the Gulf of Suez.

The nature of the territory dictated over the centuries the course of warfare in the Sinai, a form of warfare concentrated on the negotiable routes and on the critically-strategic ridges overlooking such routes. In the Sinai, there are no rivers, forests or jungles: the conflict is predetermined by the demands of the desert, and this in fact is clear from the battles waged there in 1956.

The Egyptian military presence in the Sinai up to 1953 had been purely defensive, with no more than one reinforced battalion, the principal task of which was to combat the widespread drug-smuggling operations. This ended abruptly when Nasser constructed roads — not for civilian use but to ensure efficient passage for military transport. Air bases were located in the Sinai to place the Egyptian Air Force in close proximity to potential targets; and army camps were built at strategic centres on the main axes, with large storage warehouses, in order to ensure a rapid and effective supply system.

On the eve of the campaign, in October 1956, the Egyptian force in the Sinai was based on two infantry divisions, — the Palestinian 8th Division based in the Gaza-Rafah area, and the 3rd Infantry Division, deployed in the El-Arish–Abu Ageila area. An armoured brigade based in Bir Gafgafa alternated between its base and Bir El-Hama, west of Abu Ageila, on the central Sinai axis, while an infantry brigade held the high ground west of the Mitla Pass, around the port of Suez. Other commanding sectors of the central and southern parts of the Sinai Peninsula were patrolled by a light Mobile Frontier Force which was mounted on armoured jeeps and troop carriers.

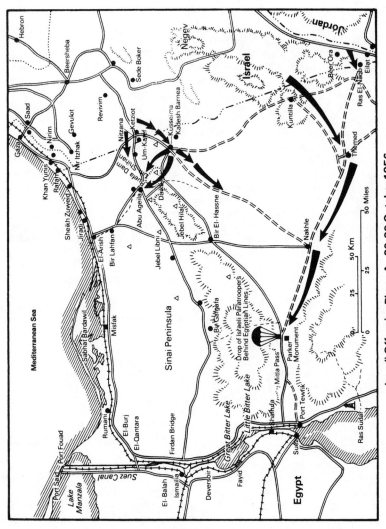

Israeli Offensive Phase A, 29-30 October 1956

Against this force, Israel put into the field some ten brigades — six infantry (1st, 4th, 9th, 10th, 11th and 12th), 202 Parachute Brigade, the 7th Armoured Brigade and two mechanized brigades, the 27th and 37th.

The war — the Mitla battle

Usually, wars begin with a major offensive — an armoured invasion, air attacks, artillery shelling, naval bombardment and rapid movement on a number of fronts. But the Sinai war does not fall into the category of a war that exploded into being — and perhaps this is the reason why it is known as the 'Sinai Campaign'. On the contrary, it started quietly and hesitantly. For the first twenty-four hours, Egypt was not even certain whether it was in fact a war, or merely a reprisal for a fedayeen raid. This opening, it will be recalled, was adopted so as to give the Israelis an opportunity to call off the operation and withdraw their forces should it become evident that her Anglo-French allies were not implementing their part of the plan.

In order to introduce the element of surprise, and to explain away an Israeli mobilization that must have become evident for all to see, the impression was created that Israel intended to mount a major attack against Jordan in retaliation for terrorist actions that had been launched from Jordanian territory. On 10 October, following the murder of two Israeli farm workers in an orange grove near the border, the Israel Defence Forces launched a heavy attack on the frontier town of Kalkilya, in which a Jordanian Arab Legion police fort was attacked. Israeli losses in this attack were heavy: 18 killed and over 50 wounded. Tension rose as King Hussein asked the commander of the British forces in the Middle East to send the RAF to the Arab Legion under the terms of the Anglo-Jordanian Defence Treaty. An Iraqi division moved to enter Jordan, and the British chargé d'affaires informed Ben-Gurion that if Israel took further military action against Jordan, Britain would go to Jordan's aid. Ben-Gurion's reply was that if the Iraqis entered Jordan, Israel would reserve its freedom of action. Israeli preparations for the Sinai Campaign were thus understood as preparations to mount military operations against Jordan — particularly since Jordan had, but a few days earlier, acceded to Egyptian pressure and joined the Egyptian-Syrian military pact against Israel.

The campaign started on 29 October 1956, at 17.00 hours, with a daringly-planned paratroop drop deep into the central Sinai at the eastern entrance to the Mitla Pass, 156 miles from Israel and 45 miles from the Suez Canal. The drop was made by a battalion of 395 paratroopers of the crack 202 Parachute Brigade under the command of Lieutenant-Colonel Rafael ('Raful') Eitan. Sixteen Dakotas transported the four paratroop companies, escorted by ten Meteor fighters; at the same time, twelve Mystère jets patrolled the length of the Suez Canal. Contrary to many reports, no French aircraft participated at any stage in the Sinai operations. Two hours before the parachuting of the forces at the Mitla

Pass, four Israeli piston-engined P-51 Mustang fighters of Second World War vintage carried out a hair-raising operation to cut Egyptian communications: descending to twelve feet above the ground, they cut with their propellers and wings all the overhead telephone lines in the Sinai connecting the various Egyptian headquarters and units.

Such a bold opening to the war was based on a sound evaluation of the enemy. From a local strategic point of view, it separated the southern Sinai from the northern sector, which held the main concentration of Egyptian military forces in the Sinai. It thereby blocked major transit and reinforcement routes from the Suez Canal through the Mitla Pass and along the backbone of the Sinai north-eastwards towards Bir El-Hassne, El-Arish and the Abu Ageila region, and eastwards towards Nakhle. From an overall strategic and psychological point of view, the actual drop did not necessarily constitute an immediate threat to the main deployment of Egyptian forces in the Sinai. The assumption was that the Egyptians would not consider this to be the opening of a war, but merely a major reprisal raid as the Israelis claimed — albeit deep into Egyptian territory. Consequently, the Egyptian war machine would not be moved into operation immediately. This element of surprise was vital to Israel in view of the limited amount of time available before the United Nations and the superpowers would react. By the same token, no opening air-strike was undertaken to neutralize the Egyptian Air Force — in order to underline the impression that this was a major reprisal raid and no more than that. From a diplomatic point of view, the depth of the raid was intended openly to threaten the Suez Canal, thereby furnishing the Anglo-French forces with their pretext for intervention to protect it.

This move was a classic application of some of the basic principles of war. The element of surprise was complete — indeed so great was the surprise that for 24 hours the Egyptians were kept guessing: what was the real purpose of the operation? Was this merely a reprisal raid or all-out war? If so, where would the main Israeli attack fall? The Israelis were in a position to retain the initiative and maintain momentum, while the enemy forces were still not in a position to realize what was in fact happening.

Eitan's paratroop battalion deployed into a defensive locality, east of the entrance to the Mitla Pass, receiving additional supplies by parachute drop during the evening of 29 October, including four 106mm recoilless anti-tank guns, two 120mm heavy mortars, eight jeeps for reconnaissance, ammunition and personal equipment. They had good reason to be confident, for their leader was by now a highly-regarded figure in the Israeli Army. A tough, hard-bitten warrior looking every inch a soldier, he had achieved the reputation of being a 'soldier's soldier'. A farmer from the village of Tel Adashim in the valley of Jezreel, he is simplistic in approach and very unsophisticated. A squat, trim man, brave, uncompromising, showing the scars of war, short-spoken and dour, he was invariably to be found at the head of his men in battle. He led many of the reprisal raids before the Sinai Campaign, some of which, because of their unique character, became almost legendary. In the 1967 War, a sniper's bullet in the heavy fighting in the Gaza Strip was to cut a deep furrow in his skull; in the Yom Kippur War, he would command the division fighting the Syrian invasion in the Golan Heights to a standstill; in 1978, he would be appointed Chief of Staff of the Israel Defence Forces.

The next phase, directly linked to the first, while still maintaining the fiction of a major reprisal operation, was the establishment of a direct supply route from Israel to the paratroop battalion. This was achieved by the remainder of 202 Parachute Brigade, commanded by Colonel Ariel ('Arik') Sharon. The remaining battalions of the Brigade were assembled along the Jordanian border in order to strengthen the impression of an impending attack against the Jordanians. The plan was for the leading unit to cross the Egyptian border in the Sinai at the same time that the parachutes of Eitan's battalion were opening over the Mitla Pass. Thus, ten hours before Eitan's H-Hour over the Mitla Pass, Sharon's 202 Parachute Brigade moved out of its concentration area near the Jordanian border and began to traverse the distance of more than 65 miles across the deserts and wadis of the Negev Desert. The Brigade crossed the Egyptian border some eighteen minutes behind schedule, and proceeded to develop its drive across the Sinai along the route passing Kuntilla, Themed and Nakhle. The force consisted of two parachute battalions, two half-track battalions, one AMX light tank company, a field artillery battalion with 25-pounder guns, and a battalion of heavy mortars.

The route to Mitla involved passing three Egyptian-defended localities. The first, Kuntilla, close to the Israeli border, was attacked by the brigade reconnaissance unit, the advance guard attacking from the *west* with the late-afternoon sunset behind them. After a few shots, the defenders, an Egyptian infantry platoon, vacated the post. Despite numerous organizational problems owing to the nature of the sandy desert route, bogged-down vehicles, delayed petrol supplies and mechanical break-downs, the advance guard continued to the Themed post, a strongly-fortified position surrounded by minefields and barbed wire, and manned by two infantry companies. By the time Sharon's force reached Themed, only two out of thirteen tanks were operative. The post comprised high ridges on each side of the road, each ridge with entrenched positions for machine-guns and artillery. The assault came at dawn on the 30th, this time utilizing the rising sun to dazzle the defenders, whose field of view was in any event limited by the smoke and dust covering the column advancing from the east. The frontal attack was led by the remaining AMX tanks, accompanied by half-tracks and jeeps, and resistance collapsed after a 40-minute battle. The final strongpoint was Nakhle — which was both the headquarters of an Egyptian Frontier Force battalion, and a training base for fedayeen terrorist squads. After driving-off an aerial attack by Egyptian Vampires and MiGs, Sharon ordered an artillery barrage on Nakhle and, by 17.00 hours on 30 October, the post had fallen without further fighting. That night, at 22.30 hours, the two elements of the Parachute Brigade were reunited and an overland supply axis to the Mitla Pass was in operation.

Colonel Sharon was a colourful figure who had in a way become a legend in the Israel Defence Forces. A heavily-built, swashbuckling type, who invariably spoke with great authority and would suffer no criticism or opposition within his command, he had created and led in the early 1950s a special commando-type paratroop unit known as 'Unit 101', which carried out many spectacular operations across Israel's borders in reply to the attacks by the fedayeen and regular Arab forces. Following the mass release of personnel after the War of Independence and the beginning of the creation of a regular armed force, many weaknesses had been revealed in the combat effectiveness of the Israeli Army. Unit 101 had been established not only to undertake reprisal actions but to set combat standards that would be a model for the Israel Defence Forces and, indeed, to convert the combat standards that had characterized the Palmach operations into the normal standards of the Israeli Army. Sharon had gathered around him a unit of tough, brave, dedicated young soldiers based entirely on volunteers, in which daring and sacrifice were bywords. Gradually, a very high standard of combat effectiveness had been introduced into the Israel Defence Forces. Later he had been given command of 202 Parachute Brigade, the first of its kind in the Israel Defence Forces, and thus he embarked on a very eventful military and political career. A very independently-minded and assertive character, Sharon was later in his political career to be accused of dictatorial tendencies by his opponents. He was to be accused, both in this and later campaigns, of insubordination and dishonesty. He can best be described as a Patton-like, swashbuckling general, who rose in the ranks of the Israel Defence Forces, proved himself to have an uncanny feel for battle, but at the same time to be a most difficult person to command. Few, if any, of his superior officers over the years had a good word to say for him as far as human relations and integrity were concerned, although none would deny his innate ability as a field soldier. Probably because of this, he never achieved his great ambition, to be Chief of Staff of the armed forces. After leaving the armed forces, he was to enter the arena of politics, becoming a central and very controversial figure in Menachem Begin's Cabinet in 1977. After Mr. Begin's victory in the elections held in June 1981, he appointed Sharon Minister of Defence. We shall encounter him in many of the battles of Israel from this point onwards.

By the morning of 30 October, despite a certain feeling of uncertainty in the Egyptian camp as to the intentions of the Israelis, and even before the Egyptian Minister of Defence and Commander-in-Chief, General Abd el Hakim Amer, had decided to return to Egypt from a visit to Jordan, the Egyptian 2nd Brigade was despatched from Suez to attack the intruders at the Mitla Pass. Of this Brigade, the 5th Battalion reinforced by a company from the 6th Battalion, with additional support weapons in the form of heavy machine-guns, recoilless weapons and heavy mortars, advanced from the Canal to the Mitla Pass, despite heavy interdiction from Israeli planes. After losing much of its vehicles and equipment, the Battalion succeeded in entering the Pass and deploying in the natural caves honeycombing its northern and southern sides. Such caves, and natural stone emplacements covering the narrowest parts of the nineteen-mile long, steep, winding pass, were invisible to the Israeli pilots who consequently were unable to provide Sharon's brigade with an accurate picture of the Egyptian deployment.

With a strongly-defended Israeli emplacement at the eastern entrance to the Mitla Pass, blocking Egyptian reinforcement routes into the Sinai thereby, it would appear to have been strategically or tactically unnecessary at this stage to advance into the Pass, or further westward, until similar progress had been made along the parallel northern El-Arish–Kantara and central Abu Ageila–Ismailia routes. Indeed, 31 October was the day on which the major operations on the central axis at Abu Ageila had been planned. Such action would require concentration of all available air power, and there was no room at this stage for any other major action. This is perhaps why the next stage in this part of the campaign has remained so controversial, highlighting as it does questions of tactical logic seen against a background of impressive human bravery.

The eastern exit of the Mitla Pass was not the most favourable position, tactically speaking, to have chosen to hold. The terrain was unsuitable for defence, especially in view of its vulnerability to the increasing number of Egyptian air attacks, and the danger of attack from the north (from the direction of Bir Gafgafa) where an Egyptian armoured force was based, some 30 miles distant. Sharon consequently sought to improve his position and requested permission to despatch a reconnaissance force into the Pass. After discussing the matter with Lieutenant-General Moshe Dayan, Chief of Staff, he received permission to send a patrol on condition that the force avoid any involvement in serious combat.

Towards noon on 31 October, a combat team commanded by Major Mordechai ('Motta') Gur was sent in. It consisted of two half-track mounted rifle companies, three AMX-13 tanks, the brigade reconnaissance unit travelling in trucks, one 120mm heavy mortar battery and one battery of 25-pounder field guns. On entering the Pass, the unit encountered heavy concentrated fire from the emplacements on both sides, but nevertheless continued to advance, assuming that the opposition would be minimal. Within minutes, however, it was drawn into a bitter battle. Gur and the two half-tracks before him were hit. The crews found cover by the side of the road in the wadi, trapped, unable to advance or retreat. The remainder of the advance guard, including two tanks, raced through the Pass under murderous fire, while the rear section of the force, which Gur had placed at the entrance (and included the heavy mortars and petrol and ammunition stocks), came under Egyptian aerial attack. The fuel trucks went up in flames. For seven hours, from 13.00 until 20.00, the paratroopers fought a desperate battle. Gur ordered mortar fire on the ridges, and Sharon despatched an infantry battalion to assist him. It scrambled up the sides of the Pass, taking each emplacement and cave by hand-to-hand fighting, under ferocious cross-fire from emplacements on the opposite and adjacent ridges and positions. In the early evening, to draw Egyptian fire away from his comrades and to enable them to extricate themselves, a soldier volunteered to drive a jeep through the Pass: he was fatally wounded by numerous hits. Such acts of heroism characterized this battle, in which 38 Israeli paratroopers died and 120

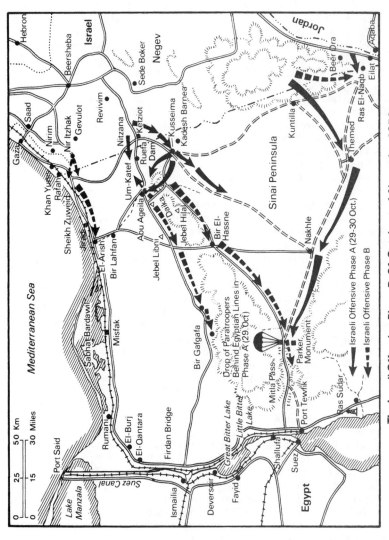

The Israeli Offensive Phase B, 31 October to 1 November 1956

were wounded, and some 200 Egyptian soldiers fell. The remainder of the Egyptian 5th Battalion of the 2nd Brigade succeeded in withdrawing and escaping across the Suez Canal.

This tragic operation, which had been completely unnecessary from a tactical or strategic point of view, brought in its wake some serious recriminations between Dayan and Sharon. Dayan maintained that he had been misled by Sharon, who had requested and received permission to send a patrol into the Pass. Taking advantage of this approval, the paratroop commander had engaged in what Dayan termed 'a subterfuge' by calling the operation a patrol in order to get the approval of the General Staff. Dayan was heavily criticized at the time for not disciplining Sharon.

Gur, who led the reconnaissance force in the Mitla Pass, was ten years later to command 55 Parachute Brigade in the Six Day War in the capture of Jerusalem, and to lead his men in taking the Old City and reaching the holiest Jewish shrine — the Wailing Wall. The Yom Kippur War found him serving as Military Attaché in Washington. After the war and the resignation of General David Elazar as Chief of Staff, Lieutenant-General Gur was appointed Chief of Staff of the Israel Defence Forces, and was to command them in the so-called 'Litani Operation' against southern Lebanon in 1978. Following the completion of his military service, he too entered the political field. Tall, well-built, eminently self-confident and very articulate, he also achieved renown as a writer of children's books.

After licking its wounds and resting for 48 hours, Sharon's brigade was called upon to take part in the finale of the campaign — the assault on Sharm El-Sheikh and the reopening of the Straits of Tiran. On the night of 2/3 November, while the Israeli 9th Infantry Brigade was undertaking its marathon trek along the mountainous coastal route from Ras El-Naqb to Sharm El-Sheikh, Sharon received orders to hand over the responsibility for the Mitla-Nakhle axis to the 4th Infantry Brigade, and to despatch a battalion through the Mitla Pass westward to Ras Sudar on the coast of the Gulf of Suez. At the same time, he was ordered to send two paratroop companies to be dropped at A-Tor, 120 miles farther south on the Gulf of Suez, and 40 miles north of Sharm El-Sheikh, to meet the 9th Brigade and assist in the assault on Sharm El-Sheikh, thereby completing the destruction of the Egyptian military presence east of the Suez Canal. The two paratroop companies seized A-Tor during the night, secured control of the airfield and prepared it for the landing of an infantry battalion, complete with equipment, prior to the advance on Sharm El-Sheikh.

The battle of Abu Ageila

The second major battle of the campaign — and possibly the most vital and decisive — was the battle to neutralize the main concentration of Egyptian forces in the Sinai, the defended localities of Kusseima/Abu Ageila and Um-Katef, and to overrun the central axis from Kusseima to Ismailia. This defensive front has been described by the American military commentator General S. L. A. Marshall, in his commentary on the Sinai

Campaign,* as the 'Abu Ageila hedgehog'. It comprised three successive, strongly-fortified sand ridges overlooking the main crossroads facing east, protected by deep trenches, bunkers, double-apron concertina barbed wire fences, minefields and fortified by field artillery and tank-destroying weapons. This front blocked the main central axis — the axis that, if opened, would ensure the success of the campaign. Gaining control of these positions would also open up an alternative transport and supply route from Israel to Sharon's 202 Parachute Brigade at the Mitla Pass. The task was entrusted to the 38th Divisional Group, comprising the 4th and 10th Infantry Brigades and the 7th Armoured Brigade, together with an artillery group and a battalion of engineers. It was commanded by Colonel Yehuda Wallach, who had previously commanded the famous 'Givati' Brigade of War of Independence fame (and was later to become Professor of Military History at Tel Aviv University.)

On the evening of 29 October, after an exhausting trek through twelve miles of the Israeli Negev, two battalions of the 4th Infantry Brigade (a reserve brigade based primarily on troops from the Tel Aviv area under the command of Colonel Joseph Harpaz) commenced their advance towards the two Egyptian posts close to the Israeli border that served as the main southern forward defence positions for the Egyptian 3rd Infantry Division based on El-Arish, commanded by Brigadier Anwar abd Wahab al Qadi, and the key to the vital central axis. The front, consisting of two fortified hills and the Kusseima outpost, was defended by two battalions of Egyptian border guards, an infantry company and a jeep company, all under the command of the Egyptian 6th Brigade (Brigadier Gaafer el Abd) which controlled the Abu Ageila/Um-Katef 'hedgehog'. After discovering that the first two hill emplacements (the Sabha emplacements) were empty, the 1st Battalion of the 4th Brigade moved towards the Kusseima outpost, some eleven miles distant. The difficult territory had taken its toll, however, and only by early morning did the Battalion actually begin its assault, encountering heavy return fire from the outpost. The assault was completed by both lead battalions of the Brigade and immediately thereafter an armoured task force of the 7th Armoured Brigade arrived, despatched by the GOC Southern Command, Major-General Assaf Simhoni, to ensure the speedy completion of the assault. The original plans had not envisaged the entry of the crack 7th Armoured Brigade until the campaign had entered its second day when the assault on the 'hedgehog' was at a further advanced stage, but the addition of armour at this earlier stage was considered necessary in order to press forward with the preliminary phase of the campaign, and ensure the establishment of a firm base as a jumping-off line in Egyptian territory.

A tall, gruff, unkempt farmer, son of a kibbutz, whose mother was a prominent labour leader, General Simhoni, who had come up through the ranks of the Palmach, was a rising star in the Israel Defence Forces. In his moment of success, after reviewing a victory parade of the 9th Brigade at Sharm El-Sheikh on the conclusion of the Sinai Campaign, Simhoni was

---

* General S. L. A. Marshall, *Sinai Victory*, 1958.

to fly north, accompanied by his liaison officer, in a light aircraft to the village of Kfar Giladi in upper Galilee. The aircraft ran into heavy winds which whipped up a sandstorm across the desert and blinded Simhoni, who was in the pilot's seat: the aircraft was blown eastwards off its course, and in the blinding storm crashed in the mountains of Jordan, killing its occupants. The bodies were later returned by the Jordanians to Israel.

As originally planned, the 4th Brigade sent out its advance units from Kusseima to Nakhle, to establish contact with Sharon's brigade, and thereby open up a second land axis to the paratroopers. Meanwhile, encouraged by the progress of operations, General Simhoni decided to alter the original plans and to maintain the momentum created by the 7th Armoured Brigade. Its commander, Colonel Ben Ari had been an outstanding combat officer in the Palmach during the War of Independence. (In the Six Day War, he would command the 10th ('Harel') Brigade capturing the area north of Jerusalem; and in the 1973 War he would serve as Chief of Staff to General Gonen, Commander of

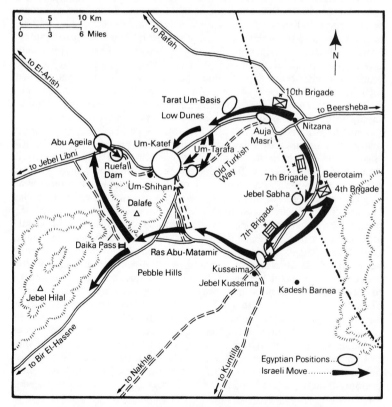

The Battle for the Abu Ageila Stronghold, 31 October 1956

the Southern Front. A tall, commanding, soldierly figure, he was later to serve as Consul-General of Israel in New York.)

A task force was now despatched along the road from Kusseima to Abu Ageila to test the southern defences of the 'hedgehog'. This task force, part of a battalion commanded by Lieutenant-Colonel Avraham ('Bren') Adan, came under heavy fire from well emplaced anti-tank weaponry – especially Archer tank destroyers – in the Abu Ageila/Um-Katef emplacements. It soon became evident that any attempt to assault this front directly from the south, with the limited forces and equipment available to this advance task force of the 7th Armoured Brigade, would be doomed to failure and would incur heavy casualties. Leaving a force of armoured infantry to dig in, and after conferring with the Chief of Staff (Moshe Dayan) and the GOC Southern Command, Adan ordered a second armoured task force to continue to advance in a westerly direction, and to find a weak point – a soft spot in the south-western underbelly of the 'hedgehog' – well away from the prickly defences of the southern and eastern fronts. By the early afternoon of 30 October, the reconnaissance company of the second armoured task force had discovered a narrow defile, or pass, which would bring the forces behind the Egyptians' western flank. This passage, the Daika Pass, was very narrow and negotiable by tracked vehicles only. Egyptian sappers had destroyed a bridge over a wadi crossing it, so engineers of the Armoured Brigade had to prepare the ground for passage. By late evening, the reconnaissance unit had crossed the defile and found itself on the main road, leading from the Suez Canal to Abu Ageila, west of the 'hedgehog', having in fact cut off the Egyptian supply route to the locality from the Suez Canal area.

While a third task force was sent in a south-westerly direction to cut off a suspected advance by Egyptian armour from the direction of Bir El-Hassne, the remaining forces of the second armoured task force passed through the Daika defile, with orders to overcome the Abu Ageila defences and advance to the Ruefa Dam emplacement,* covering Abu Ageila and Um-Katef. Such a task was risky – very risky – in view of the fact that only tracked vehicles could negotiate the narrow sandy defile, leaving behind the wheeled vehicles with supplies, engineering equipment, ammunition and petrol. Such a tenuous, delicate supply line for such a vital stage of the assault on this front was a gamble: air-dropped supplies were out of the question, since Sharon's paratroop requirements in the Mitla monopolized the airborne lift capacity of the air force. The only way to solve Adan's supply problem was to open a direct axis from the east. That evening, the 10th Infantry Brigade was ordered to cross the border and attack the eastern outer ring of the 'hedgehog' defences, which consisted of two outposts, Auja Masri and Tarat Um-Basis. These collapsed without any fighting, leaving the 10th Brigade to make its way towards the main defences of the Um-Katef side of the 'hedgehog'.

By 05.00 hours on 31 October, at the break of dawn, the second armoured task force completed its western approach to Abu Ageila.

---

* The Ruefa Dam had been built by the British to collect the winter flood-waters in Wadi El-Arish for use by the Bedouin.

Because it served as the Egyptian Area Command HQ, Abu Ageila was a vast and intricate system of camps and bunkers surrounded by barbed wire, minefields and pre-ranged artillery 'killing grounds' extending to a distance of seven miles on each side. The reinforced brigade defending the locality comprised two infantry battalions of the Egyptian 6th Brigade, two reserve battalions, a National Guard brigade, a field artillery battalion with twenty-four 25-pounders, anti-aircraft guns, a jeep company and twenty-three Archer tank destroyers. The element of surprise had by now disappeared, for the Egyptians were aware of what was afoot and had the time and opportunity to prepare for the assault. When the half-tracks of the second armoured task force reached within two miles of Abu Ageila, the Egyptian defences opened up with a concentrated artillery barrage, supported by additional fire from the Ruefa Dam, which covered the Israeli attack on its right flank. Armoured infantry continued to advance in half-tracks while the tanks covered both the Ruefa Dam barrage and an Egyptian armoured advance, coming up from the north, on the El-Arish–Abu Ageila road. Within an hour, Abu Ageila fell. The advancing Israeli forces were now harassed by a constant barrage of heavy artillery from Um-Shihan, another fortified post within the 'hedgehog'. This was co-ordinated with repeated attempts by Egyptian armour to break through from the north — attempts that were foiled by Israeli joint armour-air force action.

The first task force, which had been ordered to dig-in south of the 'hedgehog', should now have come in to reinforce Adan in the neutralization of the dangerous Ruefa Dam emplacement. However, reports arrived of an armoured column of the Egyptian 1st Armoured Brigade led by Colonel Talat Hassan Ali advancing along the central axis from Bir Gafgafa towards the 'hedgehog'. This force, according to the reports, consisted of two battalions of Soviet-built T-34 tanks, a company of Soviet-built, heavy SU-100 tank destroyers and a battalion of motorized infantry on troop carriers. The first task force was immediately despatched to block the approach of this force. It discovered the column with difficulty, however, for Israeli aircraft had already attacked it and caused havoc, forcing it to turn around and return to Bir Gafgafa and, from there, to cross the Canal, leaving rearguard ambushes at Bir El-Hama, and Bir Gafgafa. Ben Ari, leading the task force, chased the column until its retreat over the Canal and, after clearing the central axis, halted the chase ten miles from the waterway opposite Ismailia.

With the threat of Egyptian armour attacks having been taken care of, and the central axis blocked to any Egyptian armoured advance, the second task force of the 7th Armoured Brigade was left to continue the assault on the 'hedgehog'. On the evening of 31 October, the order came to take the Ruefa Dam. This position consisted of more than twenty well-entrenched tank guns, ten of which were Archers, six 25-pounders, seven 57mm guns and two 33mm cannon. The second task force opened a frontal attack from the direction of Abu Ageila to the Ruefa Dam at sunset. The tanks moved forward in a cloud of dust in the failing light, and came up against concentrated anti-tank firepower that proved to be very effective and, in fact, succeeded in hitting every Israeli tank in the task force. Urged on by its commander, the force nevertheless persevered in the attack and, as darkness fell, the battle continued, illuminated by burning ammunition stores and vehicles. As the Israeli tanks and half-tracks broke into the Egyptian positions, many of the tanks were without tank cannon or heavy machine-gun ammunition, but the Israelis continued their advance, crushing the Egyptian positions with the tank tracks, lobbing grenades at the defending Egyptians and firing at them with personal weapons from open turrets. Before this determined attack, the Egyptian defences collapsed.

The exhausted and decimated Israeli crews set about repairing and resupplying their tanks, only just in time to meet a counterattack from Um-Katef supported by fire from Um-Shihan. This Egyptian attack failed, leaving in its wake four Archers burning and 37 men dead on the battlefield. By the morning of 1 November, with most of the tanks repaired, the second task force was ordered to block any attempt by the Egyptians to move out of the remainder of the 'hedgehog' under Egyptian control — Um-Katef and Um-Shihan, along the northern road, to El-Arish.

The task of capturing the remaining Um-Katef/Um-Shihan pocket was entrusted to the 10th Infantry Brigade, which two days earlier had taken the eastern outer defensive front of the 'hedgehog' (Auja/Masri and Tarat/Um-Basis) without resistance. The aim was to complete the destruction of the 'hedgehog' and to open up a direct axis to facilitate the transport of supplies to the 7th Armoured Brigade — which Dayan was becoming very impatient about. Unfortunately, the 10th Brigade, a reserve unit, was neither trained nor equipped to deal with a stronghold position in the desert, even though it was now reinforced by part of the 37th Armoured Brigade from GHQ Reserve. When the reconnaissance unit of the 10th Brigade reinforced by an infantry company and ten half-tracks launched its assault on Um-Katef on the morning of 1 November, the Egyptian defenders replied with a heavy artillery barrage that drove it back. A second attempt by night failed after two battalions lost their way searching for the northern and southern flanks of the Um-Katef position. By morning, one of the battalions, which had finally reached Um-Katef, was once again pushed back by heavy artillery fire, while the other only succeeded in capturing a remote emplacement, some one-and-a-half miles from the main defensive area. A combination of faulty intelligence at Southern Command, lack of an effective battle plan and the insufficient concentration of resources contributed to the failure of the 10th Brigade (and later of the 37th Brigade) to break through. Dayan had put pressure on GOC Southern Command, and this pressure had been passed on, but the attacks had failed. The commander of the 10th Brigade was replaced, as Dayan felt that the unit had not made the necessary effort to enter into combat. The 37th Armoured Brigade arrived late on the scene with its full complement of tanks, but it too failed to push its way through. A gallant but ill-conceived frontal attack by half-tracks led by the Brigade commander, Colonel Shmuel Galinka, only caused extensive casualties, including his own death. The Egyptians, however, were by now fearful of being cut off. During the night they slipped away and, by the morning of 2 November, after routes had been cleared through the minefields, a task force of the 10th Brigade found the place empty.

By completing the assault on the Abu Ageila/Um-Katef system of defences, the Israelis had captured the core of the Egyptian defensive front in the Sinai, opened up a good-quality supply route to the forces at the Mitla Pass and along the central axis, and had cut off the Egyptian garrison in the Gaza Strip. There remained the task of clearing up the Egyptian forces in the north-west, in the Rafah area and the Gaza Strip, and then of opening the Straits of Tiran, at the southern tip of Sinai — all this within a strictly-limited political timetable imposed by the United Nations, United States and Soviet pressure, and by the planned Anglo-French military action against the Canal Zone.

The battle for Rafah

When the Israeli General Staff made its final preparations for the assault on the Rafah area, it did so knowing that battles were raging at Mitla and Abu Ageila. No element of surprise existed. The Egyptians awaited the oncoming attack behind a labyrinth of multiple minefields and inter-defensive, mutually-supporting emplacements on hard earth ridges and hillocks. The locality was manned by the Egyptian 6th Infantry Brigade, under the general command of the 3rd Division based at El-Arish, plus a tank company, two Frontier Force companies, one battalion of 25-pounder field artillery, seventeen Archers, Czech 105mm recoilless anti-tank guns, anti-aircraft weapons and units of the Palestinian Volunteer 87th Brigade.

To deal with this front, a divisional task force under Brigadier-General Haim Laskov was created, comprising the 1st 'Golani' Infantry Brigade under command of Colonel Benjamin Gibli, and the 27th Armoured Brigade under Colonel Chaim Bar-Lev, with additional artillery and engineer units. The 'Golani' Brigade included three infantry rifle battalions, one battalion of 120mm mortars and twelve anti-tank guns, with an additional tank company from the 27th Armoured Brigade. The 27th Armoured Brigade itself comprised one motorized infantry battalion, two companies of Super-Sherman tanks, one company of Sherman tanks and one AMX-13 light tank company.

Colonel Gibli had previously been a Director of Military Intelligence, whose name had been linked to the so-called 'affair', in which an Israeli spy ring operating in Egypt in 1954 was arrested, most of its members receiving long terms of imprisonment and two being executed. An argument had developed as to who gave the order for the group in Egypt to carry out acts of sabotage, and there followed serious political repercussions, leading to the resignation of the then Minister of Defence, Pinchas Lavon, and to the removal of Colonel Gibli from all intelligence functions. A ministerial enquiry into the whole affair at the request of

David Ben-Gurion in the early 1960s ultimately led to one of Israel's most serious political crises, the resignation of Ben-Gurion, and his splitting from the Labour Party which he had led. (Colonel Gibli was later to head a large industrial manufacturing group controlled by the General Federation of Trade Unions.)

Colonel Bar-Lev, a quiet, dour, very slowly-spoken and determined individual, had been an outstanding battalion commander in the Palmach 'Negev' Brigade in the War of Independence. A native of Yugoslavia, he later commanded the 'Givati' Brigade and moved on to command the

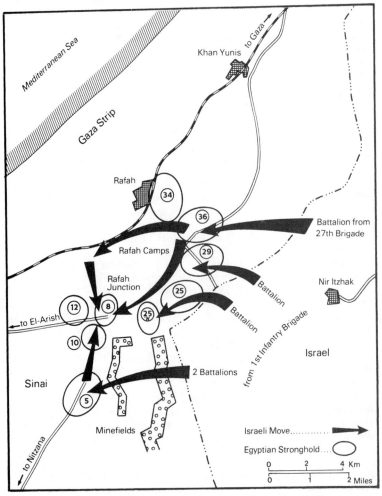

The Battle of Rafah, 31 October to 1 November 1956

Armoured Corps. A graduate of Columbia University, New York, in Business Administration, he was to be Deputy Chief of Staff to General Rabin in the Six Day War, and Chief of Staff of the Israel Defence Forces in 1968. During his period of office, he constructed the defensive line at the Suez Canal that was to be associated with his name, the so-called 'Bar-Lev Line'. He later entered politics, being appointed Minister of Trade and Industry, but in the Yom Kippur War of 1973 he was called back to uniform and played an important part in stabilizing the southern front.

The assault on Rafah was meticulously planned, and required strict timing in order to co-ordinate the movements of the two brigades. It was to be carried out in three stages. A southern force of the 3rd and 4th 'Golani' Battalions was to open a gap in the extensive minefields adjacent to the international border to allow armour to pass through and reach the Rafah-Nitzana road south of the Rafah junction. A central force of the 1st and 2nd 'Golani' Battalions was to clear the fortified hills adjacent to the Rafah-Gaza road, and a force of the 27th Armoured Brigade was to strike through the flank of the Rafah camps* to the north, meet the 'Golani' forces at the junction and advance south-westwards towards El-Arish and Kantara.

The 4th Battalion was the first to cross the border, just before midnight on 30 November, passing precariously through the minefields: after encountering difficulties in identifying two Egyptian positions guarding and covering them, the Battalion took control of the entry route, enabling the 3rd Battalion, on half-tracks and 6 × 6 trucks, reinforced by a company of Super-Sherman tanks of the 27th Armoured Brigade, to cross. However, the half-tracks struck mines and blocked any farther advance through the minefield, providing the Egyptian multiple emplacements in the vicinity with a static, flaming target for artillery and tank fire. Under an intense barrage, Israeli sappers crawled along the route and cleared a path while the soldiers of the 3rd Battalion, led by Lieutenant-Colonel Meir Pa'il (in later years a lecturer in military history at Tel Aviv University and a very vociferous and effective member of the Knesset for the left-wing Sheli Party) found temporary cover behind bushes and sand dunes. The advance was hampered by yet more mines, which destroyed two Super-Shermans. Only after five hours of arduous delicate manoeuvring through the minefields, illuminated by huge Egyptian searchlights and under a heavy, accurate artillery barrage, did Pa'il's Battalion finally find its way to the main road connecting Rafah and Nitzana. By 05.30 hours, the Battalion had successfully assaulted a large emplacement overlooking the road, and commenced movement towards the Rafah junction. This was protected by three fortified positions, which were taken in an assault by the 3rd and 4th Battalions, who thereupon established a bridgehead and dug-in to await the arrival of the tanks of the 27th Armoured Brigade.

In the central area, the 1st and 2nd Battalions assaulted stronger emplacements adjacent to the Gaza–El-Arish road. Because of

* In the Second World War, Rafah had been a major British Army centre, with numerous camps.

malfunctioning explosive equipment, the soldiers had to cut their way through rolls of concertina wire under heavy and medium machine-gun fire. Only then, with supporting fire from a tank platoon borrowed from the 27th Armoured Brigade, could they advance through various key, fortified, hill emplacements, and take the vast military camps and storage depôts, left behind by the British from the Second World War, behind the junction.

The motorized infantry battalion of the 27th Armoured Brigade, comprising four rifle companies and a troop of AMX tanks, went into action along the northern road at 04.00 hours against two strongly-fortified anti-tank positions on ridges covering the road. These positions, held by a reinforced platoon and two rifle companies with seventeen anti-tank guns, fell after two hours of bitter hand-to-hand fighting in the communication channels and bunkers. The battle was fought chiefly with bazookas, which succeeded in destroying the seventeen Egyptian anti-tank positions. By 10.00 hours on 1 November, the 'Golani' and 27th Armoured Brigade forces met at the junction, in the presence of the Chief of Staff, General Dayan, who had accompanied the 27th Armoured Brigade during its advance. Dayan describes in his *Diary** the enthusiasm of the troops as the dust-covered infantry men of the 'Golani' Brigade met the advancing units of the 27th Armoured Brigade: 'We fell into each other's arms in the classic tradition of a Russian movie.' But within thirty minutes, units of the 27th Armoured Brigade were on their way westwards towards El-Arish. A seven-jeep reconnaissance unit led the Brigade, followed by engineers, infantry on half-tracks and two troops of AMX light tanks, and an artillery troop of four 105mm self-propelled guns. At El Jiradi, a few miles east of El-Arish, the Brigade encountered a strongly-defended set of emplacements, based on an infantry company equipped with Archer tank destroyers, anti-tank artillery and a battery of 120mm mortars. This force held up the Brigade for an hour, during which time the position was taken by a flanking operation from the south and rear, in a combined armour and aerial attack.

General Dayan decided not to enter the town of El-Arish that evening, but to wait for the dawn at a distance of some three miles north-east of the town. His hesitation was influenced by the fact that the Israeli Southern Command was not certain of the strength of the Egyptian military force in the town. It was known that, in addition to the Egyptian 4th Brigade led by Colonel Saad ed-Din Mutawally of the 3rd Division based in El-Arish, reinforcements had been despatched from west of the Canal and, despite constant Israeli air attacks on the advancing column, the 1st Motorized Division had reached the town. Another reason for Dayan's delay was the necessity to concentrate, reorganize and deploy the Brigade, which had scattered along the Rafah–El-Arish road. No doubt, the knowledge that an Israeli armoured brigade was hovering on the outskirts of the town had its own psychological effect on any Egyptian defenders therein. At noon on 1 November, in fact, orders had been received by the Egyptian garrison

---

* Moshe Dayan, *Diary of the Sinai Campaign*, 1966.

in the Sinai to withdraw to the western bank of the Suez Canal, following the first Anglo-French air attacks on bases and airfields in Egypt.

Dayan describes in his *Diary** the gruesome scene in the military hospital in El-Arish, with the bodies of soldiers who had been abandoned in the midst of operations and treatment littering the building. Sporadic sniping continued and, as Dayan was standing at the open window of a building looking out on to the street, an Egyptian soldier fired a burst from his machine-gun, killing Dayan's signalman who was at his side.

Thus, on the morning of 2 November, when the 27th Armoured Brigade entered El-Arish and continued westward, the only factors to hamper its progress were the hulks and wreckage of armour and lorries destroyed by the heavy air bombardment of the previous days. By that evening, a task force had completed its advance 100 miles westward, reaching Romani and halting just ten miles east of the Suez Canal. En route, the task force had collected valuable war booty left new and intact by the retreating Egyptian forces − 385 vehicles, including 40 Soviet-built T-34 tanks and 60 armoured cars. Direct contact was now established with the 7th Armoured Brigade on the central axis, and with 202 Parachute Brigade, which had advanced through the Mitla Pass to the banks of the Gulf of Suez. With the backbone of the Egyptian military forces in the Sinai broken, Dayan could now give the order setting into motion the final stages of the campaign − to clean up the 25-mile-long, 6-mile-wide Gaza Strip, and to free the Straits of Tiran − all this against the background of mounting political pressure directed from the United Nations Headquarters in New York.

The battle for the Gaza Strip

Despite Egyptian strength in the Strip − 10,000 troops comprising the Palestinian 8th Division under Major-General Youssef el Agroudi − it was not expected that the Gaza Strip would pose a severe military problem following the fall of Rafah. The defence of the Strip was allotted to the Palestinian 86th Brigade, based on Khan Yunis in the southern portion of the Strip, and the Egyptian 26th National Guard Brigade (with eight 120mm heavy mortars and two motorized border platoons) based on the city of Gaza in the north: these maintained fourteen fortified locations along the borders of the Strip and three battalion defence locations around Khan Yunis.

The Israeli 11th Infantry Brigade commanded by Colonel Aharon Doron − (later to be the Adjutant-General of the armed forces and subsequently Vice-President of Tel Aviv University) was given the task of taking the Gaza Strip. It disposed of two infantry battalions and an armoured combat team from the 37th Armoured Brigade, a company of Sherman medium tanks and a company of infantry on half-tracks. Previous to this, the Brigade had been occupied fighting and foiling

* Ibid.

fedayeen raids, which, surprisingly, were being carried out in even greater numbers than before.

The order to launch the attack came at 06.00 hours on 2 November – at the same time as the 27th Armoured Brigade entered El-Arish. The assault began from the south, with the 120mm mortar and tank barrage on the fortified ridges overlooking the city of Gaza. (The main Ali Montar ridge had gained renown in the First World War when Allenby's British forces had lost some 10,000 men in three ill-fated attacks on the Turkish positions there.) Although the Egyptian forces on the ridges replied with heavy fire, an Israeli tank squadron, together with half-tracks, broke through the outer defences, crossed the south-western corner of the Ali Montar ridge and moved rapidly towards the northern border of the Gaza Strip at Beit Hanun. At the same time, an infantry battalion entered the city to mop-up pockets of resistance, followed by tanks which soon occupied the centre of the city. By noon, through the mediation of a member of the United Nations Mixed Armistice Commission, the Egyptian Governor of the city of Gaza surrendered and proceeded to persuade the remainder of the Egyptian garrison in the city to lay down its arms. He thereby avoided unnecessary fighting within the city, which, in addition to its residents, housed some 200,000 refugees in primitive camps that the Egyptians had maintained in the environs of the city. Soon, the Egyptian Governor of the Gaza Strip, General Fuad Al Dijani, handed in his surrender and, by late afternoon, an Israeli Military Government had been established.

By early evening, the Brigade was moving towards Khan Yunis. Here the Palestinian 86th Brigade found itself surrounded by Israeli forces in Rafah to the south and in Gaza to the north. Despite their plight, the defenders chose to fight from their emplacements on the outer ridges of the locality. Consequently, the armoured combat team of the Israeli 11th Brigade found itself under a heavy barrage that lasted until the dawn of 3 November. The team despatched a combat group along the eastern flank of the locality, while an infantry battalion entered a neighbouring refugee camp and thereby penetrated the locality. By 13.30 hours, the mopping-up was complete, and the advance guard of the Brigade reached the outer perimeter of the 'Golani' Brigade defences north of Rafah.

The battle for the Straits of Tiran

The final act was a story of ingenuity, physical endurance and tenacity by a dedicated group of 'old soldiers' – veterans of the War of Independence. It also demonstrates the prime importance of the politico-strategic planning that enabled the achievement of one of the major aims of the campaign within the tight schedule dictated by considerations of international political pressure.

The finale started, in fact, on the opening night of the campaign when Sharon's paratroopers were pushing their way from Kuntilla towards Themed, and when the 4th Brigade was en route to Kusseima. Parallel to these northerly moves, close to the border at Kusseima and Kuntilla, a southern move had been planned from Ras El-Naqb, south-east of Eilat, as the starting point for the final assault on the Gulf of Aqaba and the Straits of Tiran. On that same evening of 29 October, a reconnaissance company of the 9th Infantry Brigade — a reserve brigade raised from the farmers of the valley of Jezreel under the command of Colonel Avraham Yoffe — set out from Eilat, seized the vital road junction just east of Ras El-Naqb, connecting roads from Kuntilla, Themed and Ras El-Naqb and, after clearing minefields, stormed and took the police fort in Ras El-Naqb itself. The route to the southern Sinai was now open.

The remainder of the Brigade thereafter reached Ras El-Naqb, but not directly from Eilat — a move that would have betrayed, at this early stage, the intention of the Israeli forces in the area. Instead, the Brigade moved by a roundabout route, across the Israeli Negev Desert from the north, via Kuntilla (which had earlier fallen to Sharon's 202 Parachute Brigade on its way to Mitla).

Colonel Yoffe, a tall, heavily-built, bluff, Falstaff-like character, had served as an officer in the British Army in the Second World War, and had held command positions in the Haganah and in the Israel Defence Forces. A farmer, son of farmers, a native of Yavniel in Galilee, he was recognized as an authority on wildlife. He was later to serve as GOC Southern Command and, in the Six Day War, would command one of the divisions that penetrated the central front in the Sinai. He was for a short while to be a Member of Parliament, but his main occupation would be that of head of the Israel Nature Preservation Authority, in the course of which he established wildlife and game reserves throughout the country.

The task allotted the 9th Infantry Brigade was in many ways the most difficult of the campaign — to advance along the rough west coast of the Gulf of Aqaba, an area of steep, saw-tooth ridges dropping straight into the sea; an area strewn with huge boulders, deep sand, and ravines; excruciatingly hot, devoid of water and, above all, a camel route that had not been designed for passage by a fully-motorized infantry brigade. The length of the route was approximately 150 miles over difficult and frequently well-nigh impassable terrain. Such a trek required self-sufficiency in supplies, water and petrol, at least until such points as would permit the landing of supplies by sea were reached. The Brigade consisted of 200 vehicles and 1,800 men, formed into two infantry battalions on half-tracks and 6 × 6 trucks, a reconnaissance unit, an artillery battery, one heavy mortar battalion, an anti-aircraft troop, engineers, workshop and service detachments. A tank unit would be transported by naval landing craft that had been specially transported by rail and road from Haifa to Eilat. This force was to face a defending garrison of 1,500 Egyptians comprising two infantry battalions emplaced in stone and concrete fortifications with an extensive collection of artillery, based on Sharm El-Sheikh and its outer position at Ras Nasrani.

The Brigade covered the first 60 miles along Wadi Watin as planned, widely spread out with units seven miles apart in order to reduce dust and ensure constant mobility. After passing the oasis of Ein El-Furtaga the brigade met the major physical obstruction — a steep uphill climb through Wadi Zaala, with deep, boulder-strewn, powdery sand in which most of the vehicles sank and had to be pushed, pulled or shifted by hand. Upon reaching the large coastal oasis of Dahab, on 3 November, the advance guard found itself faced with a camel-riding section of the Egyptian 'motorized' Frontier Force — the desert police force — which set up an ambush there. Because of a lack of caution, the 9th Brigade suffered a number of casualties here.

After resting and refuelling from landing craft sent by sea from Eilat to Dahab, the Brigade set out at 18.00 hours on 3 November, passing through the narrow Wadi Kid, a goat track flanked by steep walls, only two yards wide in some places. Here, as expected, the Egyptians had placed a platoon with bazookas and machine-guns to block any possible advance by small Israeli units, and had mined the route. But, after a few shots, the isolated Egyptian unit withdrew, the obstacle was overcome and the sappers proceeded to widen the defile in order to enable the Brigade to pass through. By noon on 4 November, they were at Ras Nasrani, there to discover that this heavily fortified citadel, with its reinforced concrete bunkers, communication trenches, minefields and concertina wire, had been vacated by the Egyptian garrison, which had withdrawn westwards in order to regroup for the defence of Sharm El-Sheikh. This may have been due to the fact that elements of 202 Parachute Brigade were meanwhile advancing from A-Tor in the north, so that concentrating the Egyptian forces on Sharm El-Sheikh became strategically necessary for its defence. Sharm El-Sheikh was a rear supply-base, complete with large storehouses and airport, but hardly equipped to withstand an armoured attack.

The assault on the outer defences of Sharm El-Sheikh, which were built on a chain of hills, Tsafrat-el-At, about three miles to the north, commenced in the early afternoon of 4 November, in co-ordination with the Parachute Battalion, which had closed in from the north-west and halted fifteen miles north of Sharm El-Sheikh in order to prevent any attempted push to the west by the Egyptian force stationed there. The outer defences of Tsafrat-el-At fell to the 9th Brigade reconnaissance unit after an aerial rocket and machine-gun attack. (Air co-operation in this final move encountered no opposition owing to the fact that the activity of the Egyptian Air Force in the Sinai had been neutralized both by Israeli action and by the Anglo-French bombing of Egyptian air bases west of the Suez Canal.) At 03.30 hours the next day, the 91st Battalion assaulted the outer defences of Sharm El-Sheikh on the western flank of the locality — without any clear picture of the extent of the enemy defence works. Consequently, heavy Egyptian fire, from three fortified positions, and an extensive minefield caused heavy casualties. The 91st Battalion withdrew, moving in darkness, with the wounded loaded in half-tracks. Part of the withdrawing force stumbled on one of the anti-tank positions that had so successfully engaged them in their assault, only to discover that this position had in the meantime been vacated by the Egyptian forces, leaving behind anti-tank weapons and an open telephone line to the Egyptian Headquarters!

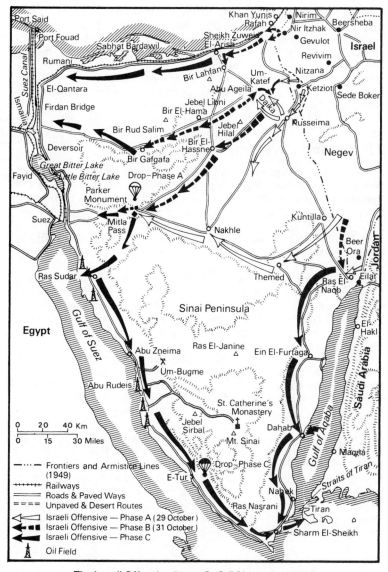

The Israeli Offensive Phase C, 2-5 November 1956

One hour later, at 05.30 hours, and following a 120mm mortar and aerial barrage, the half-track company and reconnaissance unit, followed by infantry units, set out along the western flank to mop-up the emplacements, whilst the 92nd Battalion broke through on the eastern flank, reaching the airport. Thereafter, the Brigade took control of the locality and, by 09.00 hours on 5 November, the Egyptian command post had been taken and units of Sharon's 202 Parachute Brigade, which had moved down along the Gulf of Suez from Ras Sudar via A-Tor, met up with Yoffe's 9th Brigade in Sharm El-Sheikh.

By 09.30 on 5 November, the war in the Sinai was over and the Straits had been opened. The following day, in compliance with the demands of the United Nations, a cease-fire came into force.

The air and naval war

On 29 October, Egyptian air power was 60 per cent greater than that of Israel, with a correspondingly larger number of jet fighters (MiG-15s and Vampires) than Israel (Mystère IVs, Ouragans and Vautours). However, despite their quantitative and qualitative advantages, Egyptian aerial activity was minimal — possibly owing to the fact that, from the evening of 31 October, British and French aircraft were bombing targets in Egypt, especially air bases, leaving the Israeli Air Force free to roam at will over the Sinai.

During the first 48 hours, some 164 air encounters took place, generally involving Egyptian MiGs and Israeli Mystères, but also Vampires and Ouragans: in these battles, five Egyptian MiGs and four Vampires were shot down. Israeli losses were caused primarily by heavy, concentrated ground fire, which succeeded in bringing down two Mystères and nine piston-engined planes.

The Israeli Navy was quantitatively and qualitatively as inferior proportionately to the Egyptian Navy, as was the Air Force — especially after the Egyptian Navy had received two Russian Skoryy-class destroyers and a number of submarines. Israel had received two British ex-Second World War destroyers in 1956. The one and only spectacular naval event of the campaign occurred at the end of its second day, on the evening of 30 October, when the Egyptians despatched the 1,490-ton, 27-knot frigate *Ibrahim el Awal* to shell the port and oil refineries of Haifa with its four 102mm guns. The frigate reached Haifa at 03.40 hours on 31 October and, from a range of six miles, fired 160 shells. At 05.30 hours, Israeli frigates arrived on the scene, commenced pursuit and, together with the Air Force, engaged the Egyptian vessel. They succeeded in damaging its turbo-generator and rudder and, at 07.20 hours, the frigate struck its flag and surrendered to the Israeli Navy.

Britain, France and the United Nations

Meanwhile, the Allied forces had planned an operation that obviously envisaged heavy opposition on the part of the Egyptians, and indicated their adherence to the set-piece type of battle they apparently anticipated. Consequently, the Allied task force set sail only on 1 November from

Valetta harbour in Malta. There is no doubt that the results would have been completely different had the British Prime Minister, Anthony Eden, taken the advice of General Sir Charles Keightley and Lieutenant-General Sir Hugh Stockwell (who had been in command of British forces in Haifa in 1948 and was now commander of the Allied land forces) to effect the landing on 1 November as was originally planned. This would have changed the entire pattern of developments and would have avoided many of the political issues.

The British forces at sea included an infantry division, a parachute brigade group and a Royal Marine Commando brigade, while the French forces included a parachute division, a parachute battalion and a light mechanized regiment. There were also the naval forces of both countries and air forces operating from the British and French aircraft carriers and from Cyprus. As this force was making its way slowly across the Mediterranean, to be joined en route by French units from Algeria and British units from Cyprus, political pressure from the Russians and in the United Nations increased, and the political limitations imposed on the British and French forces grew. They were hampered by a growing degree of hesitation on the part of the political leadership, particularly in Britain, where the Government came under very heavy attack both from the Opposition and from its own benches.

From 31 October, after the British and French Governments delivered an ultimatum calling for a withdrawal of forces from both sides of the area of the Suez Canal, their air forces attacked air bases in Egypt, destroying many Egyptian aircraft. The attacks directed by the Allies were exclusively against Egyptian air bases; at no point did the French or British aircraft become involved in support of the Israeli forces advancing in the Sinai.

Mounting efforts in the United Nations Security Council were being made to bring about a cease-fire, and twice the British and French vetoed such moves. Meanwhile, the Anglo-French force was sailing slowly across the Mediterranean, but it was losing in the race against political pressure. Under the pressure of events, Stockwell advanced the dropping of the parachute forces in the area of Port Said and Port Fouad by a day — to 5 November. Because of growing hostile public opinion in Britain and elsewhere, limitations were imposed on the types of guns that could be used by the naval vessels to shell the landing areas in support of the troops that were now sent in to land. On 6 November, the first British troops landed on the beaches of Port Said, while the French troops landed at Port Fouad. The Egyptian commander of Port Said, Brigadier Mogui, who had been taken prisoner, refused to issue a general order to surrender. General Stockwell thereupon decided to advance his forces southwards by helicopter and by parachuting troops into Ismailia and Abu Suweir. But, just as these operations were about to be mounted, the British Government caved-in under international political pressure, and agreed to a cease-fire at midnight on 6/7 November. The French were left with no alternative but reluctantly to follow the British. Thus ended the Sinai-Suez War of 1956.

There now began protracted negotiations, in which Israel attempted to obtain guarantees in respect of the two major developments that had brought about the war — the blockade of the Straits of Tiran and the fedayeen operations into Israel from Egyptian-controlled territory. The creation of a United Nations Emergency Force was proposed by the Canadian Government and accepted by the United Nations. Although Israel attempted to hold on to the essential areas of Sharm El-Sheikh and the Gaza Strip, United States pressure forced her to withdraw from these positions in return for 'real guarantees' of passage through the Straits and United Nations participation in the administration of the Gaza Strip. Both the Gaza Strip and Sharm El-Sheikh were to be placed in the control of United Nations Emergency Forces. Israeli withdrawal was carried out in stages.

In Gaza, the withdrawal of the Israeli forces led to a period of violence in which those who had allegedly 'co-operated' with the Israeli occupying forces, from November 1956 until the Israeli withdrawal in March 1957, were summarily executed. The United Nations soldiers in the Strip lost all control of the roaming fedayeen gangs and, indeed, of the entire situation. Within two days of Gaza being transferred to the United Nations, Nasser had nominated a military governor for the Strip who, without asking the UN, moved in with his headquarters — the United Nations did not even demur, and this weakness sowed the seeds for future problems in the area. Within a short time, the Mayor of Gaza was dismissed and replaced by a pro-Egyptian. At the same time, the UN, under pressure of the Egyptians, ordered its forces to vacate the Strip and only to patrol its borders. The UN Emergency Force took up positions along the borders between Israel and Egypt, and at Sharm El-Sheikh.

Israeli shipping did, at last, move freely through the Straits of Tiran to and from Africa and Asia. A comparative lull set in along the Israel-Egyptian border, until ten years later when the 'real guarantees' of passage through the Straits were to be forgotten as Nasser ordered the United Nations forces out of Sinai. As they departed, the threat of war was to loom again.

SUMMARY
'A Work of Art'

The Sinai Campaign was in many ways classic. The opening phase was a brilliant application of the strategy of the indirect approach. Captain Sir Basil Liddell Hart, who coined this strategy, characterized the opening moves in the Sinai as one of the most brilliant applications of such an approach in the history of warfare — he considered the Sinai plan to have been 'a work of art'. It was also the first opportunity accorded to the Israel Defence Forces to prove that what it had built since the War of Independence was an effective fighting force retaining the originality of movement and thought that had prevailed in the Israeli forces as they fought for the establishment of Israel in 1948–49. A marked degree of flexibility also characterized the main decisions in battle, with commanders proving themselves capable of adapting rapidly to changing conditions. This was particularly evident in the manner in which the task forces of the 7th Armoured Brigade were handled during the breakthrough at Abu Ageila. The Israeli reserve system, which had mobilized the Army for operations against Egypt in Sinai and had yet managed to keep the objectives of the operation secret, had proved itself. Israel succeeded at the same time in maintaining command of the air, before it became evident to the Egyptians that the British and French air forces were likely to become involved. But perhaps the most important point to note was that the tradition established in the War of Independence — whereby the officers invariably led and set a personal example in battle — was implemented in this campaign. A very high percentage of the casualties were incurred by the officers and NCOs and, in all phases of the battle, senior officers were to be seen leading their men under fire.

The Egyptians, who by and large had suffered many reverses during the operations against the Israelis, could maintain that they had not been defeated by the Israelis because they had been obliged to withdraw under the Anglo-French threat. Indeed, Nasser's stand against the onslaught gained for him considerable political prestige, which he portrayed as a highly successful outcome in the final analysis of the war.

The Sinai Campaign also marked the inauguration of the United Nations Emergency Force for peace-keeping purposes. For ten years, the Force performed a valuable task. The failure in 1967 was not that of the Force on the ground, but rather that of the Secretary-General of the United Nations and of that organization itself. A new and important element, which was to become part of the Middle East scene, had been introduced.

BOOK III

THE SIX DAY WAR
1967

PROLOGUE

The period following the Sinai Campaign in 1956 was one of comparative quiet along the Israel-Egypt border, both along the Gaza Strip and the international border in the Sinai, largely because of the United Nations presence. However, this situation did not necessarily mean that the Middle East was quiet and had achieved a period of calm. The contrary was true.

Within a year of the conclusion of hostilities and the withdrawal of Israel from the areas occupied in 1956, a series of almost continuous upheavals in the Arab world began. In 1958, King Feisal of Iraq was deposed and brutally assassinated together with his uncle Abdul Illah and members of his family. The bodies were dragged through the streets of Baghdad by the jubilant mob. General Nuri Said, the Prime Minister of Iraq and one of the most astute and central political figures in the Arab world, who had led the country since its establishment as an independent state after the First World War, went into hiding dressed as a woman, but was discovered and torn to pieces by the rampaging mob. A weak revolutionary régime led by General Abdul Karim Kassem enabled the Soviet Union to achieve its first foothold in that oil-rich state and make its first moves in attempting to establish a position on the Persian Gulf. President Nasser continued to foment unrest in many parts of the Arab world, primarily at that time in Lebanon and Jordan. As a result of these activities, a civil war broke out in Lebanon and, at the urgent invitation of President Chamoun of Lebanon, the United States Sixth Fleet landed a force of marines in Lebanon to stabilize the situation and protect the régime, while the British Army flew forces across Israel (with Israel's approval) to Amman in order to bolster King Hussein's régime. In February of the same year, following the rise to power of the Ba'ath Party in Syria, Egypt and Syria had united to establish the 'United Arab Republic' with two regions, a northern one in Syria and a southern one in Egypt. Syria thereby became the northern centre for the development of Nasser's activities against Israel, for he was hampered in this respect along the Israel-Egyptian frontier by the presence of UN troops.

From Syria, Nasser also developed his efforts to bring about the downfall of the Hashemite monarchy in Jordan and, in September 1960, his agents succeeded in killing the Jordanian Prime Minister, Hazza al-Majali, who had taken a strong stand against Nasser: they introduced a bomb into the Prime Minister's office which blew up at approximately the time that King Hussein had planned to visit the Prime Minister's offices. This was one of many Syrian attempts made at the time against King Hussein personally and his régime, masterminded by Colonel Fuad Serag el Din, the Syrian Chief of Intelligence. On one occasion, King Hussein was piloting his aeroplane across Syrian territory and saved himself, according to his own description of the incident in his memoirs, by a series of aerobatic manoeuvres that enabled him to break away from Syrian fighter aircraft bent on shooting him down. King Hussein was incensed by the death of his Prime Minister, to whom he had been deeply attached, and who was a member of a distinguished Bedouin family that had produced many of Hussein's military leaders. Driven by a consuming hatred, the King concentrated three brigades, the bulk of his army at the time, along the Syrian border, with the intention of invading and avenging his Prime Minister's death. Secret overtures were made at the time by the Jordanians to the Israelis through the mediation of the author of this book — who was at the time Israeli Chief of Military Intelligence — advising of the possibility that such an invasion of Syria might take place, and requesting that no advantage be taken of the fact that the front-lines between Israel and Jordan would be denuded of Jordanian forces. King Hussein was finally dissuaded from undertaking this venture (which, having regard to the comparative strengths of the two armies, might have been a very costly one) by the efforts of the United States and British ambassadors, who spent many hours talking him out of it.

After a few years of smarting under what was in effect Egyptian occupation, with Field-Marshal Abd el Hakim Amer acting as Nasser's Pro-Consul in Syria, the Syrians revolted against the Egyptians in October 1961, and Syria became once more an independent nation.

While Israel's border with Egypt remained comparatively quiet, the centre of Arab activity against Israel developed along the Syrian, and later along the Jordanian, border. The Syrians shelled Israeli settlements from their advantageous positions on the Golan Heights, laid mines and developed a minor war of attrition along the frontier. On 1 February 1960, after a long period of calm since 1956, the Israel Defence Forces carried out a reprisal raid against Syrian posts in Khirbet Tawfiq, on the Sea of Galilee. But the Syrians continued to attack fishing boats on the lake, shell villages in the Huleh valley, and fire on agricultural workers in the demilitarized zone along the frontier.

In 1964, an Arab Summit Conference in Cairo attended by the heads of state decided as a matter of policy to proceed actively with the diversion of the waters of the River Jordan; at the same Conference it was decided to set up a Palestinian movement, which would be known as the 'Palestine Liberation Organization'. At this Conference, and at the Casablanca Conference that followed it, some £400 million ($1,100 million) was allocated for the purpose of implementing these decisions. In recognizing the Palestinian movement, the Arab states gave official standing to Ahmed Shukeiri, head of the PLO and, following the decisions of the Conference, he proceeded with the establishment of a Palestinian Army.

In 1965, the PLO was formally established at a Conference in Jerusalem, and the Palestine Covenant, which became the political basis for the movement, was enunciated. It was to be amended in 1968 so as to include in its objectives not only the State of Israel, but also implicitly

King Hussein's Jordan. At the time, Jordan was in control of the West Bank and Egypt was in control of Gaza: had they so desired, they could have established a Palestinian state in these areas. However, this was not to their purpose, nor was it to the purpose of the PLO, which was unwilling to accept any compromise then or later in regard to those sections of the Palestine Covenant calling for the destruction of the State of Israel. Indeed, the policy of the PLO was to endeavour to create a situation along the Israeli border that would draw the Arab states into a war against Israel. This policy did not always accord with that of the Arab states and, consequently, the PLO was restrained from time to time by them. However, the Syrian Government soon 'adopted' the PLO, a development that enabled this organization to grow and become a major factor.

The work on the diversion of the Jordan waters proceeded apace both in Lebanon and in Syria, where a canal was dug to divert the waters of the Hazbani in Lebanon and the Banias in Syria into the River Yarmuk in Jordan, thus depriving Israel of two-thirds of the water in the Jordan. Israel had on many occasions declared that the closing of the Straits of Tiran or the diversion of the Jordan waters would themselves be considered acts of war. Israel reacted to the diversion operations with a series of engagements in which long-range artillery and tank fire was directed against the diversion works, obstructing the progress on the canal construction. In November 1964, Israeli aircraft were sent into action against those sectors of the diversion works that were out of artillery range. However, the Arab states were unwilling to be drawn into an all-out war as a result of this Syrian initiative; indeed, Israel's activities ultimately brought the work to a halt, for it became clear to the Syrian leadership that pursuit of the diversion ultimately must mean war with Israel, for which the Arab leadership was showing little enthusiasm.

The internal upheavals in Syria meanwhile brought to the fore extreme elements in the Ba'ath Party, and the Syrians continued to send saboteurs to Israel through Jordan and Lebanon. King Hussein was at times unable or unwilling to control his own borders and prevent the incursions against Israel. In November 1966, after a number of such raids, the Israel Defence Forces struck at the village of al-Samu in the Hebron Hills, a centre from which terrorist attacks had been mounted; this was the first Israeli reprisal raid ever to be carried out in daylight utilizing both armoured and air elements. Following this attack, there was an outburst of unrest in Jordan; heavy criticism was directed against the leadership of King Hussein, and various hostile elements began to plot against him. His régime appeared to be tottering and, in response to his appeal, was bolstered by additional military aid from the United States.

The confrontation

Syrian attacks along the northern frontier continued, as did infiltration into Israel from Syrian-based camps, via Jordan and Lebanon. In April 1967, their shelling of farming operations in the demilitarized zones along the Sea of Galilee were stepped up, with increasing fire being directed against Israeli border villages. On 7 April 1967, unusually heavy fire was directed by long-range guns against Israeli villages, and Israeli aircraft were sent into action against them. As the Israeli aircraft attacked the artillery positions of the Syrian Army, the Syrian Air Force was scrambled into action and attempted to intercept the Israeli attacking planes. An air battle developed between the French-manufactured Mystères of the Israeli Air Force and the Russian-manufactured MiGs of the Syrian Air Force. In a series of dogfights, six Syrian aircraft were shot down. Commenting in a public interview on this air battle and on the Syrian provocations, the Israeli Chief of Staff, Lieutenant-General Yitzhak Rabin, issued a stern warning to the Syrian Government, indicating that Israel would not remain passive in the face of the Syrian attacks and provocations, and that, should activity on the part of the Syrians continue, Israeli reaction would be such as to endanger the very existence of the régime in Damascus. This warning, against a background of the shooting down of the six Syrian aircraft, gave rise to considerable apprehensions in the Syrian capital. They felt that Israel might attempt to take advantage of what appeared to be the comparative weakness of the Syrians and the lack of unity evident at the time in the Arab world, in order to launch an attack.

Fearful of Israeli reaction to their provocations, the Syrians now tried to impress on the Egyptians their apprehension of an impending Israeli attack. They also turned to the Russians, and urged them to make similar representations in Cairo. But, early in May 1967, Nasser was at one of the low-points of his career. For five years, his forces had been involved in the civil war in the Yemen without success against ill-armed tribesmen; his forces there were led by Field Marshal Abd el Hakim Amer, as they supported the left-wing revolutionaries. Other elements in the area (notably from Saudi Arabia and reportedly some Western powers) provided aid to the Royalist forces in the Yemen. Nasser was in conflict with King Hussein, whom he described in a speech on 1 May as an 'agent and slave of the imperialists'. His relations with Saudi Arabia were near breaking point, and he could make no headway in the struggle against Israel. Against this background came the urgent request for assistance from Syria — strengthened by the appearance in Cairo on 13 May of a Soviet delegation, which informed the Egyptians that Israel had indeed massed some eleven brigades along the Syrian frontier. The Soviet Ambassador to Israel was invited by the Prime Minister of Israel, Levi Eshkol, to accompany him to the area bordering the Syrian frontier so that he would convince himself that the information about the concentration of Israeli forces was totally untrue. Indeed, instead of eleven brigades being concentrated there, there were hardly eleven companies in the area. The Soviet Ambassador, however, declined the invitation. The Russians were interested in pressing Syria's case for political reasons of their own, and had no intention of helping Israel to deny their allegations. The Soviet Union was particularly interested in strengthening the régime in Syria, which had afforded the Soviet Union its first major foothold in the

Middle East. By influencing Egypt to threaten Israel from the south, the Russians gambled on strengthening Syria's security and hence the government in Damascus.

In Israel, there was no sense of urgency. Indeed, in a press interview the Chief of Staff of the Israel Defence Forces at the time, Lieutenant-General Yitzhak Rabin, forecast a long period of quiet for Israel. Israel's 19th Independence Day on 15 May was celebrated with the comfortable feeling that the Chief of Staff's prognostications were correct.

However, two days later, in a well-publicized mass demonstration, Nasser proceeded to move large forces through Cairo en route to the Sinai. Within a few days, by 20 May, some 100,000 troops organized in seven divisions (with over 1,000 tanks) had been concentrated along Israel's south-western border. Hysteria seized the Arab world. Nasser was again at a peak of popularity, as one Arab government after the other volunteered support and was caught up in the enthusiasm of the impending war. On 17 May, Nasser had demanded the withdrawal of the United Nations Emergency Force, and the Secretary-General of the United Nations, U Thant, had acceded to the request within two days without demur. Nasser had demanded that the UN forces withdraw from a number of points along the border. U Thant's reply had been that he could not accept any limitation, and that all or none of the forces would remain. Without consulting the General Assembly or Security Council, in a move that was to haunt him to his dying day, U Thant acted: UN forces withdrew.

Once again, after ten years, Israel faced Egyptian forces directly along the frontier. On 22 May, Nasser declared the Straits of Tiran closed to Israeli shipping and to shipping bound to and from Israel. That such an act would be a declaration of war had been made clear by Israel. The major powers attempted to establish a naval force in order to implement the assurances made to Israel in 1957, but no force or action emerged. On 26 May, Nasser told the Arab Trade Union Congress that this time it was their intention to destroy Israel. Contingents arrived from other Arab countries, such as Kuwait and Algeria. Israel was soon ringed by an Arab force of some 250,000 troops, over 2,000 tanks and some 700 front-line fighter and bomber aircraft. The world looked on at what was believed by many to be the impending destruction of Israel. But no international action was taken. Every effort was made by the Soviet and Arab delegates to the United Nations to pre-empt any effort that might be made by the West to intervene and obstruct the Arab plans; they went out of the way to minimize the seriousness of the situation and to permit developments to take their course. The Israeli Government, headed by Levi Eshkol, made urgent efforts to solve the crisis by diplomatic means, despatching Foreign Minister Abba Eban to the heads of government of the Western great powers. But the mission was in vain. A sudden change in French policy emerged, and the traditional sympathy of the French Government for Israel disappeared, against the background of a new French bid for Arab support. For years, as long as the French had been involved in the war in Algeria, in which the Algerian rebels enjoyed massive support from the Arab world (particularly from Egypt), a community of interest had developed and existed between France and Israel. However, with the conclusion of hostilities in Algeria and the French withdrawal from that country, President de Gaulle did not perceive any further common interests with Israel, and indeed declared that France's interest now was to gain favour in the Arab countries and develop relations with them, particularly commercial and military. Thus, in Israel's hour of crisis, her ally, France, without any word of warning, turned her back on her. Israel, it seemed, was on her own.

Israel was thrown into a crisis, as its reserves remained mobilized, denuding the country of its manpower, and grave doubts existed as to the ability of the Eshkol Government to decide upon a war and to wage a war. The Chief of Staff, General Rabin, at one point collapsed, allegedly because of nicotine poisoning, and for some forty-eight hours was inactive, his place being taken by Major-General Ezer Weizman, formerly commander of the Air Force and at that time Chief of the General Staff Operations Branch.* Political pressures grew, in the face of what was interpreted by the public as hesitation on the part of the Government. Finally, Eshkol acceded to public pressure and formed a National Unity Government, co-opting General Moshe Dayan to his cabinet as Minister of Defence and Menachem Begin, the leader of the Opposition, as Minister without Portfolio.

Meanwhile, the Arab armies mobilized, as additional contingents joined Nasser's forces. Two battalions of Egyptian commandos were flown from Egypt to Jordan, and moved to the Latrun area in order to operate against Israel's main artery — the Jerusalem-Tel Aviv road. While hysteria developed in the Arab world, King Hussein of Jordan, who but a few weeks earlier had been characterized by President Nasser in a May Day speech as a lackey of the imperialists, flew to Cairo in order to achieve a reconciliation. He later explained to Western diplomats that what he had done was to take out an insurance policy, having regard to the hysteria that now gripped the Arab world. Signing a defence agreement with President Nasser, he agreed to the appointment by the Egyptians of an Egyptian general, General Abdal Muneim Riadh, as joint commander of the Arab forces operating on the Jordanian front. King Hussein flew back to Jordan on 30 May, accompanied this time by a sworn enemy, namely Ahmed Shukeiri, the vociferous leader of the Palestine Liberation Organization, the PLO. And, three days later, General Riadh arrived with his staff to take over his new command.

The Arab forces were poised to attack, and the new Israeli Minister of Defence, General Dayan, made it clear that every day of delay in launching a pre-emptive strike against Egypt would mean heavier casualties for the Israeli forces. But doubts have been expressed as to whether or not the Egyptians really intended to attack Israel and as to what might have happened had Israel not taken pre-emptive steps. For

---

* In 1974, when Yitzhak Rabin was proposed as Prime Minister of Israel by the Labour Alignment following Golda Meir's resignation, General Ezer Weizman published a statement maintaining that General Rabin's behaviour at the time of crisis in 1967 rendered him unfit to occupy the post of Prime Minister.

Israel, from a strategic point of view, faced by a mobilized military offensive alliance surrounding the country on at least two borders (the Jordanian and the Egyptian) against the background of mass hysteria, war was inevitable. It will be recalled that one of the deciding factors in 1956 that brought Ben-Gurion to a decision to go to war was not only President Nasser's behaviour but also the development of a military alliance against Israel, which first included Egypt and Syria, and which, in the week before the final decision to attack was taken, included the Jordanians. Here, in 1967, a similar development was again taking place, with Jordan joining the offensive alliance that had already been forged between Egypt and Syria. This situation was one that left Israel, in the view of its military commanders, with very few options. Furthermore, the Government of Israel had frequently made it quite clear that the blocking of the Straits of Tiran would be interpreted by Israel as an active declaration of war by the Arab countries.

In retrospect, it is now possible to evaluate correctly Nasser's estimate of the situation and his plan as he moved towards a confrontation. Indeed, it was possible to obtain a very clear insight into his thinking by analysing carefully the articles of Mohammed Hassanein Heikal, Editor of *Al Ahram*, who was Nasser's closest confidante at that time. Nasser's thinking was set out by Heikal in an article which he published in *Al Ahram* on 26 May. It is clear from this and from a subsequent analysis of statements made in Egypt that, when Nasser ordered the United Nations Emergency Force to withdraw on 17 May, he did so on the basis of three assumptions:

1. That, after the United Nations forces would be withdrawn at his request, he would close the Straits of Tiran to Israeli shipping.
2. That, following this action, the Israelis would be likely to try to open the Straits by force and break the blockade. This would lead to war.
3. That, in the event of an outbreak of war, the ratio of forces and the state of preparedness of his forces guaranteed Egypt military success. Nasser was convinced that, in a combination of both the military and political struggle that would ensue, he would gain the upper hand.

The pre-emptive strike

The morning of 5 June 1967 found Israel's armed forces facing the massed Arab armies around her frontiers. Israel's citizen army had been quietly and efficiently mobilized over several weeks to defend the country against the impending Arab attack which every Arab medium of mass communication announced was imminent. At 07.45 hours on Monday 5 June, and for the ensuing three hours, the Israeli Air Force commanded by Major-General Mordechai Hod, undertook a pre-emptive attack designed to destroy the Egyptian Air Force and its airfields. Flying in low, under the Arab radar screens, Israeli aircraft destroyed the Egyptian Air Force. Later it was to deal with the air forces of Jordan and Syria and to destroy aircraft of the Iraqi Air Force, mostly on the ground. The actual hour of the attack was chosen on the assumption (a correct one as it later turned out) that it would find most Egyptian Air Force Command personnel in their cars en route after breakfast from their homes to their bases. In the main attack, nineteen Egyptian air bases in the Sinai, in the Nile delta, the Nile valley and Cairo area were attacked in some 500 sorties, destroying 309 out of 340 serviceable combat aircraft including all 30 long-range Tu-16 bombers, 27 medium-range Illyushin Il-28 bombers, 12 Sukhoi Su-7

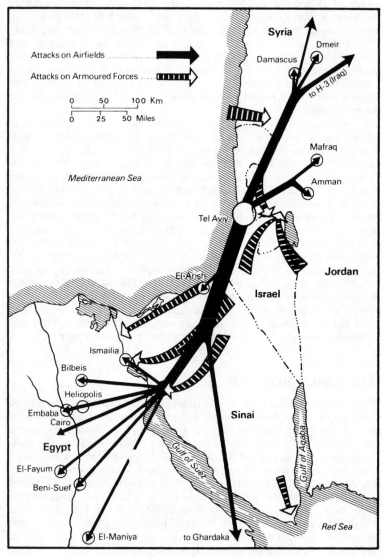

Israeli Air Strikes, 5-10 June 1967

fighter bombers, some 90 MiG-21 fighters, 20 MiG-19 fighters, 25 MiG-17 fighters, and a further 32 transport aircraft and helicopters.

That morning, unaware of the scope of the catastrophe that had befallen the Egyptian Air Force, and believing the optimistic reports of victories emanating from Cairo, the Jordanian, Syrian and Iraqi Air Forces commenced hostile operations. Syrian bombers attacked the oil refineries in Haifa Bay and an airfield at Megiddo; the Jordanians attempted to strafe a small airfield near Kfar Sirkin; and the town of Natanya on the Mediterranean coast was attacked by Iraqi aircraft. The Israeli Air Force thereupon directed its attention to these Air Forces. By the evening of that day, the Jordanian Air Force had been wiped out, with 22 Hunter fighters, 6 transports and 2 helicopters destroyed; the Syrian Air Force had lost 32 MiG-21, 23 MiG-15 and MiG-17 fighters, and 2 Illyushin Il-28 bombers, constituting two-thirds of its total strength; while numbers of aircraft were destroyed in an attack on an Iraqi Air Force base at H3. By nightfall on the second day of the war, 416 Arab aircraft had been destroyed, 393 of which were destroyed on the ground; 26 Israeli aircraft had been lost in action. Of the total number of Arab aircraft lost in the war, 58 were downed in aerial dog-fights.

This brilliant operation accorded Israel complete superiority in the air. Thereafter, the Israeli Air Force was free to devote itself to providing close combat support for the advancing ground formations during the remaining days of fighting on the various fronts. Unlike his two predecessors in command of the Air Force (Major-General Dan Tolkowsky and Major-General Ezer Weizman), General Hod was not a product of the Royal Air Force. He had served in the Palmach, and joined the Palmach air unit, which was a nucleus for the future Israeli Air Force. He was sent, as were many others of his class, to train in a special course at an airfield in Czechoslovakia on the eve of the War of Independence and in the early stages of that war, when the Czechs were supplying arms and actively aiding Israel by making available facilities in order to train the embryonic air force. General Hod, a native of Kibbutz Degania, was a graduate of the first class that had trained to fly in Czechoslovakia, the supplier of the first Messerschmitt aircraft to Israel, which played such an important part in the War of Independence. He subsequently trained in the 1950s at a Royal Air Force flying school in Britain, where he emerged as the outstanding pilot of his class. He rose through the ranks of the Air Force, attending courses abroad and, some months before the outbreak of the Six Day War, replaced Major-General Weizman, who moved over to the General Staff as No. 2 in the capacity of Chief of the Operations Branch. General Hod proved to be a dynamic and forceful commander of the Air Force. In his very outspoken manner, which came to expression in a staccato type of speech, he imposed his views (as did indeed his predecessor) frequently on the General Staff, ensuring a marked preference from a budgetary and other points of view, for the Air Force. He was innovative and daring, and these traits of character came to very clear expression in the daring and very brilliant plan evolved for the opening of the Six Day War.

1

THE SECOND SINAI CAMPAIGN

The theatre of war in the Sinai was essentially unchanged since the last war — the northern sandy area with the main coastal route and the railway; the central hilly and valley area criss-crossed by roads and tracks; and the southern mountainous area. But, since the 1956 Campaign, the Egyptians had invested considerable funds and energy in restoring the roads and fortifications destroyed in that campaign, and in transforming all of the north-west Sinai into one large fortified area, designed to provide a firm base for an attack on Israel. Additional roads had been constructed following the lessons learned from the 1956 Campaign. A mountain pass, the Gidi (which runs parallel to the Mitla Pass), had been cut through the range of mountains that run parallel to the Suez Canal in order to ensure additional flexibility in movement of forces. Additional roads running from north to south had been added to connect the main trans-Sinai arteries. Giant strongpoints had been established, including air bases, training camps, storage depots — all combining to form one solid fortified framework, stretching back from the border with Israel deep into the heart of the central Sinai. The Gaza Strip had been converted into a fortress, with dug-in tanks and artillery covering all approaches. The Egyptian forces pouring into the Sinai at the end of May and beginning of June 1967 entered bases well prepared in advance, fully equipped and supplied. In a matter of days, the entire force was ready to move into battle from these previously-prepared positions.

The Egyptian forces in the Sinai were five infantry and two armoured divisions, totalling some 100,000 soldiers equipped with over 1,000 tanks and hundreds of artillery pieces. The infantry was deployed forward along the main axes, close to the border with Israel, while the armoured formations were to the rear, primarily in the central Sinai and covering also the southern flank of the front. The northern axis was defended by the Palestine 20th Division commanded by Major-General Mohammed Hasni, which was deployed in the Gaza Strip, and the 7th Infantry Division under Major-General Abd el Aziz Soliman, which was responsible for the area south-west of the Strip, from Rafah to El-Arish. To the south, along the central axis, the 2nd Infantry Division, led by Major-General Sadi Naguib, was deployed in a vast fortified locality covering the area stretching from Kusseima to Abu Ageila, and including the Um-Katef stronghold (an area that had figured prominently in the Sinai Campaign of 1956). The 3rd Infantry Division, under Major-General Osman Nasser, was west of the northern and central divisions in the Jebel Libni/Bir El-Hassne area, providing the necessary depth in deployment. To the south, the 6th Mechanized Division, commanded by Major-General Abd el Kader Hassan, was in position along the Kuntilla-Themed-Nakhle axis — the same axis along which the opening breakthrough of the 1956 Campaign had been undertaken by the paratroop brigade under Colonel 'Arik' Sharon.

The two armoured fists of the Egyptian Army in the Sinai were deployed in strategic depth. The crack 4th Armoured Division, led by Major-General Sidki el Ghoul, was concentrated in Wadi Mleiz between Bir Gafgafa and Bir El-Tamade, a central air and logistics base deep in the Sinai. The second division-sized armoured task force, Force Shazli, named after its commander, Major-General Saad el Din Shazli, was moved forward close to the Israeli border, between Kusseima and Kuntilla, and held in readiness to break into Israel and cut off the southern Negev area and the southern port of Eilat from the remainder of Israel.

The Israeli Southern Command, under Major-General Yeshayahu Gavish, consisted of three divisions commanded respectively by Major-Generals Israel Tal, Avraham Yoffe and Ariel 'Arik' Sharon. General Gavish, a graduate of L'Ecole de Guerre in Paris, and whose limp came from a wound received in the War of Independence, was a highly articulate and brilliant officer. Indeed, he was considered to have been one of the more outstanding officers in the Israeli Command. In the 1956 Sinai Campaign, he was Chief of the Operations Division in the General Staff and, as such, had been the liaison between the then Chief of Staff, General Dayan, who insisted on being forward with his troops during the fighting, and the General Staff. After the Six Day War, Gavish was to be very much in the running to become Chief of Staff after General Bar-Lev's tour of duty, and was favoured by General Moshe Dayan over General Elazar. However, Dayan, although Minister of Defence, was unable to assert himself in the face of the combined preference of Golda Meir, the Prime Minister, and General Bar-Lev, the retiring Chief of Staff, for General Elazar. As a result, General Gavish retired from the armed forces to become Deputy Director-General of the Koor Industrial Group, the largest industrial group in the country.

General Tal, a small, squat soldier, had served in the British Army in the ranks of the Jewish Brigade Group. A strict disciplinarian, he rose in the ranks of the Israel Defence Forces ultimately to command the Armoured Corps. A graduate in philosophy from the Hebrew University, he soon came to be regarded in the Israel Defence Forces as something of a technical genius: he was twice awarded the coveted Israel Prize for important inventions in the field of security, and later was to design the Israeli main battle tank, the Merkeva (Chariot), one of the most advanced tanks in the world. (Its concept was to be based on the lessons learned by the Israeli armoured forces in their various wars, and particularly in the Yom Kippur War.) A certain degree of controversy grew around him following the Yom Kippur War, in which he served as the Deputy Chief of Staff to General Elazar. Later, he became adviser to the Minister of Defence on development and organization, also becoming regarded as an international authority on armoured warfare.

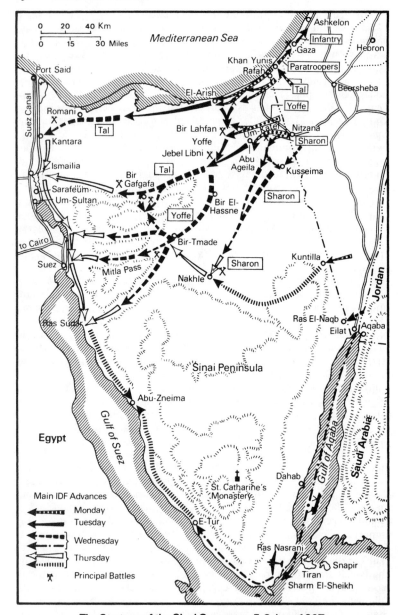

0 20 40 Km
0 15 30 Miles

Mediterranean Sea

Ashkelon
Infantry
Gaza
Hebron
Khan Yunis
Rafah
Paratroopers
Port Said
El-Arish
Tal
Beersheba
Yoffe
Romani
Tal
Bir Lahfan
Um-Katef
Nitzana
Kantara
Yoffe
Sharon
Jebel Libni
Ismailia
Tal
Abu
Ageila
Bir
Gafgafa
Kusseima
Sarafeum
Um-Sultan
Bir El-
Hassne
Sharon
to Cairo
Yoffe
Bir-Tmade
Kuntilla
Suez
Sharon
Mitla Pass
Nakhle
Ras Sudar
Ras El-Naqb
Eilat
Aqaba

Sinai Peninsula

Jordan

Abu-Zneima

Egypt

Gulf of Suez

Saudi Arabia

Gulf of Aqaba

Dahab

St. Catharine's
Monastery

Main IDF Advances
Monday
Tuesday
Wednesday
Thursday
Principal Battles

E-Tur

Ras Nasrani
Snapir
Tiran
Sharm El-Sheikh

The Strategy of the Sinai Campaign, 5-8 June 1967

The overall strategy of Southern Command was based on a three-pronged break-in by means of three principal phases. The first phase was to open the northern and central axes by destroying the fortified Egyptian infrastructure along them and thereby breaking the back of the Egyptian forces in the Sinai; the second phase was to penetrate into the depths of the Sinai; while the third stage was to take the two mountain passes leading to the Suez Canal and thereby cut off the Egyptian Army from recrossing the Canal. (The Egyptians were not expecting a direct frontal assault. Indeed, they anticipated an opening move similar to that of the 1956 Campaign. The Egyptian Commander-in-Chief in the Sinai, General Abd el Mohsen Mortagui, had decided to deploy the special armoured divisional task force, Force Shazli, close to the border between Kusseima and Kuntilla, so that he could counter immediately by striking into Israel.) In the northern sector, General Tal's Division was to assault the fortified area of Rafah/El-Arish. In the centre, General Sharon would take the Um-Katef/Abu Ageila complex on which the Egyptian defensive deployment hinged. Elements of General Yoffe's Division would negotiate the sandy, apparently impassable area between the northern and central axes, thus isolating the two main Egyptian defensive locations and preventing lateral passage of reinforcements or any attempt at co-ordination between the two Egyptian divisions, the 7th and the 2nd, under assault.

The northern area of Rafah/El-Arish was a defensive locality surrounded, as in 1956, by deep multiple minefields and heavily-fortified lines, with infantry brigades dug-in behind a complex of anti-tank weapons sited in concrete emplacements along the outer perimeter. To the rear of the positions, in addition to artillery, over 100 tanks were defensively deployed. The general impression created by the Israeli deployment of forces, which in the southern sector were moved to and fro along the border openly and demonstratively, succeeded in misleading the Egyptians as to the probable planned main thrust of the Israeli forces — the impression was given that the attack would be launched to the south. As a result, there was an element of surprise when the opening attack took place along the northern axis in the area of Rafah.

Tal's breakthrough in the northern sector, which was launched at 08.00 hours on 5 June, was achieved by avoiding the minefields around the fortified locations and by breaking into the Rafah area from the north-east near the town of Khan Yunis. This was carried out by the 7th Armoured Brigade commanded by Colonel Shmuel Gonen at the junction of the Egyptian 20th and 7th Divisions, and Rafah was taken after a fierce tank battle. Parallel with this, a parachute brigade reinforced by a battalion of tanks, led by Colonel 'Raful' Eitan (indeed the same Brigade in which he led a battalion in the 1956 Sinai Campaign) made a wide, southerly, flanking sweep around Rafah, which was defended by two brigades heavily reinforced by artillery, turning northwards and advancing on the position from the rear over sand dunes the Egyptians had considered impassable. Taking the Egyptian artillery park by surprise, Eitan's brigade broke into artillery concentrations and mopped-up position after position. Meanwhile, Gonen's 7th Armoured Brigade advanced westwards to the next Egyptian defensive locality at Sheikh Zuweid, which was manned by an infantry brigade of General Soliman's 7th Division and a battalion of Russian-built T-34 tanks. While a battalion of Centurion tanks drew the Egyptian fire, a battalion of Patton tanks outflanked the position from the north and the south, and it fell to Gonen's forces. Before El-Arish, Gonen's forces came upon the heavily-fortified, solid-concrete defences of El Jiradi — the strongest Egyptian position in the vicinity of El-Arish. The Brigade attacked and overcame these defences, then continued to push towards El-Arish. However, the Egyptian forces, which had dispersed among the sand dunes in the desert, regrouped and counterattacked the position, reoccupying it. While Tal's advance forces were advancing on El-Arish, his rear units were engaged in a struggle for the El Jiradi positions, which changed hands several times. General Tal thereupon concentrated other available forces, which finally occupied the position after bitter hand-to-hand fighting. By the early morning of 6 June, the road was open as a supply route to the Israeli forces already in El-Arish. These were the advance forces of General Tal's division, which continued along the northern axis of advance and reached El-Arish during the night of 5/6 June.

The following day, part of Tal's forces continued their sweep westward along the northern axis, in the direction of Kantara on the Suez Canal, whilst the other part of the division under Colonel Gonen moved south to the El-Arish airfield, which fell after a tank battle, opening the road to Bir Lahfan, thus opening an eastern road south to Abu Ageila and a western road south to Jebel Libni. Colonel Gonen, a tough, rough-spoken officer, invariably wearing tinted or sun glasses, was to emerge from this war with an outstanding reputation. A native of Jerusalem, the son of Orthodox parents, he was a student as a young boy at a strictly Orthodox Theological Seminary in Jerusalem. He received his baptism of fire in the War of Independence at the age of 16 in the siege of Jerusalem. In the Sinai Campaign, he served as a company commander in Ben Ari's 7th Brigade, which he now commanded. He trained in the United States at the School of Armor at Fort Knox (as, incidentally, did most of the senior Israeli officers in the Armoured Corps) and, in summer 1973, he was to replace General 'Arik' Sharon as GOC Southern Command. A few months later, the Yom Kippur War broke out. In his appearances before the Agranat Commission (page 236) and also in his subsequent public appearances, Gonen maintained that he had inherited a Southern Command that had suffered from neglect on the part of his predecessor, General Sharon. Be that as it may, he was to become an unfortunate 'casualty' of the Yom Kippur War, bringing the career of a courageous, tough, able and professional soldier to an abrupt end.

To General 'Arik' Sharon's division was entrusted the breakthrough along the central Nitzana-Ismailia axis. This axis was vital: from it radiated the roads leading to El-Arish in the north and to Nakhle in the south. A major fortified complex barred the way, based upon interconnecting fortified positions extending from Um-Katef to Abu Ageila in the west, and Um-Shihan in the south, with an outer perimeter close to the Israel border at Tarat Um-Basis and Um Torpa. In this locality, the Egyptian 2nd Infantry Division was firmly entrenched.

Sharon's initial assault on 5 June, with an armoured and mechanized infantry force against Tarat Um-Basis, destroyed the Egyptians' eastern perimeter positions. Sharon's forces were now before the main defensive positions of the locality, and he brought forward the divisional artillery units to soften them up by persistent bombardment. An armoured reconnaissance group meanwhile moved along the northern flank, over sandy dunes that (as in other places) the Egyptians had misjudged and considered impassable. After a heavy battle, in which a battalion position armed with anti-tank weaponry was overcome at the third attempt, the group bypassed the fortified locality to its south and reached the road junctions leading from Abu Ageila towards El-Arish in the north and to Jebel Libni to the south-west. There, it dug-in. In a parallel move to the south, Sharon sent an additional reconnaissance unit with tanks, jeeps and mortars to block the road connecting Abu Ageila and Kusseima. The result of these two moves was to sever all Egyptian axes of reinforcement from El-Arish, Kusseima and Jebel Libni — and, of course, all possible lines of retreat from Abu Ageila in any direction.

At dusk on 5 June, the order was given to begin concentrated artillery fire. A paratroop battalion was flown by helicopter into the rear area of the locality in order to neutralize the Egyptian artillery, and then tank units advanced directly from the east, accompanied by infantry who proceeded to clear the enemy trenches and positions. When the infantry reached the road from the north, the tank unit that had blocked that line of Egyptian resupply and retreat now attacked from the rear. Israeli armour and infantry met in the centre of the locality: by 06.00 hours the following morning, after what was probably the most complicated battle in the history of the Arab-Israeli Wars, the central axis from Um-Katef to Abu Ageila was in Israeli hands. Mopping-up operations took a further 24 hours, but the road was now open for units of Major-General Yoffe's division to cut deeper along the central axis, towards Jebel Libni.

While the two Egyptian divisions were fighting desperately against the forces of Tal on the northern axis and Sharon on the central axis, the third Israeli division, under Yoffe, was achieving what the Egyptians had considered to be an impossible task. Part of the Division advanced with vehicles and equipment across the soft sand dunes between the northern and central axes, covering a distance of 35 miles in nine hours. By the next evening, 6 June, the force had reached the area of the Bir Lahfan junction, connecting the Jebel Libni and Abu Ageila-Kusseima roads to El-Arish. The mission of the force was to prevent any lateral movement by Egyptian forces between the two axes, and to block any reinforcements from the Egyptian concentrations in the Jebel Libni area. Such reinforcements in the form of an Egyptian armoured force, comprising an armoured brigade and a mechanized brigade, did in fact move along the central axis leading from Ismailia towards Jebel Libni in the early evening. It came upon Yoffe's leading brigade, under Colonel Yiska Shadmi, lying in wait in hull-down positions at the Bir Lahfan crossroads. Battle was joined, and a fierce armoured confrontation raged around the junction, terminating in the complete rout of the Egyptian force, and opening the road for the remainder of Yoffe's division to proceed south-west towards Jebel Libni.

With the outbreak of war, Egyptian propaganda had begun to put out euphoric stories about the impressive victories that had been achieved by the Arab forces. Tel Aviv was reported to be under heavy air attack, the oil refineries in Haifa were declared to be on fire, and numerous alleged victories were reported from the field of battle. The Egyptian public received the news of the first day of the war with enthusiastic joy. On the second day of war, with news already filtering through, past the Egyptian news media that continued to publish stories of continued successes, a more sober tale began to be heard in the streets of Egypt. (The third day of the war was to mark a radical change, with dismay, chagrin and outrage reflected in the reaction of the population.) Field Marshal Amer, the Commander-in-Chief of the Egyptian forces, about whom there had been many stories concerning his addiction to drugs, lost his nerve, and he began issuing conflicting orders direct to the field commanders in the Sinai. President Nasser continued during the day to receive the fabricated optimistic reports from the front-line and, indeed, in a telephone conversation in the morning hours, encouraged King Hussein to launch his forces along the Jordanian front, advising him that the Egyptians were now well on their way across the Negev and planned to meet the Jordanian forces pushing down from the Hebron Hills.

According to subsequent speeches by Nasser and by revelations in the trials of the various Egyptian commanders that took place after the war, President Nasser was unaware of the calamity that had befallen the Egyptian Air Force in the early hours of the morning until 16.00 hours that afternoon. Later, in order to explain away the stunning defeat the Arab Air Forces had experienced at the hands of the Israeli Air Force, President Nasser and King Hussein fabricated a story in which they alleged that United States air units had participated in the attack on the Egyptian Air Force. This gauche attempt to explain away a defeat that was now staring the Arab leaders in the face was confounded by the Israelis, who monitored the radio-telephone conversation between the two Arab leaders and two days later released it. King Hussein subsequently admitted that the Israeli tape of the conversation was authentic, and withdrew the allegations, which had by now given rise to a wave of anti-American and also anti-British demonstrations throughout the Middle East.

The conflicting orders that Field Marshal Amer issued to units in the Sinai created an atmosphere of panic among many of the senior commanders, who decided in many cases to save their own skins, abandon their formations and flee for safety across the Suez Canal. Many of them were later to be court-martialled and severely punished. Field Marshal Amer himself was to commit suicide when it became clear to him that he too would have to face trial.

As evidence mounted of signs of demoralization at higher command levels of the Egyptian Army, General Gavish met his three divisional commanders, Tal, Yoffe and Sharon, and urged them to develop new and

Above: A unit of the Palestine Liberation Army marching through the city of Gaza on their way to take up positions along the Egyptian-Israeli frontier. (AP)

Below: The days preceding the Six Day War. Tel Aviv children help fill sandbags for use in their school's shelter.

Left: The President of Israel, Zalman Shazar, with Israel's generals, June 1967. Standing, left to right: Lieutenant-Colonel Arieh Raz (the President's aide); the author; Major-General Elad Peled; Major-General Yeshayahu Gavish; Major-General Israel Tal; Major-General David Elazar; Major-General Ezer Weizman; Major-General Shmuel Ayal; President Shazar; Major-General Rehavam Zeevi; Lieutenant-General Yitzhak Rabin; Major-General Mattityahu Peled; Major-General Shlomo Erel; Major-General Ariel Sharon; Brigadier-General Yaakov Hefetz; Major-General Shlomo Goren, Chief Chaplain. Kneeling and seated, left to right: Major-General Amos Horev; Major-General Yaakov Peri; Major-General Chaim Bar-Lev; Major-General Avraham Yoffe; Major-General Aharon Yariv; Major-General Moshe Goren; Major-General Mordechai Hod; Major-General Uzi Narkiss. **Left, below: 1,** Major-General Yeshayahu ('Shaike') Gavish, commander of the southern front. (GPO) **2,** Major-General Israel Tal ('Talik'). (Newsphot) **3,** Major-General Ariel ('Arik') Sharon. (Zahal-Bamahane) **4,** Major-General Uzi Narkiss, commander of the central front, with Teddy Kollek, the Mayor of Jerusalem. (Y. Aharonot) **5,** Major-General Avraham Yoffe (left) meeting Bar-Lev in the Sinai. (GPO) **Above:** Lieutenant-General Yitzhak Rabin, Commander-in-Chief of the IDF, and (left) Major-General David Elazar. (GPO) **Below:** Israel's Prime Minister, Levi Eshkol (in black beret), visits the northern front; on his right is the Minister of Defence, Moshe Dayan, and the front commander, Major-General David Elazar, who became Commander-in-Chief of the IDF during the 1973 War. (GPO)

The Six Day War was won virtually in the first few hours. The IDF knocked out the Egyptian Air Force at the onset of the war, allowing the Israeli Air Force air superiority. The photograph below shows a typical scene of devastation along a road near the Mitla Pass, after an attack by the Israeli Air Force. (Rubinger)
Inset: A French-built Mirage III. (GPO)

Above left: An Israeli Navy Dabur-class patrol boat passing through the Straits of Tiran near Sharm El-Sheikh. (GPO) **Below left:** Centurion tank crews preparing for action in the Negev. **Above:** Israeli paratroopers waiting to emplane in Nord transport aircraft en route for action in the Sinai. At the last moment, they were diverted to the Jerusalem front, where they carried out the attack on the Old City. (GPO) **Below:** Israeli troops advancing towards the Suez Canal are strafed by some of the surviving Egyptian MiG-17 fighters. (GPO)

Among the prime objectives of the IDF were the recapture of two important positions lost in the War of Independence in 1948.

Left: Soldiers guard the approaches to the Etzion bloc, a group of kibbutzim that had been wiped out in 1948. (GPO)

Below: An IDF Super-Sherman tank at the monastery of Latrun, the scene of some of the bitterest fighting in 1948. (Zahal-Bamahane)

Right, top: Colonel Mordechai ('Motta') Gur (bareheaded), the paratroop commander, surrounded by his staff on the Mount of Olives overlooking the Old City of Jerusalem before the break-in and capture. (Jerusalem Post)

Right, below: The paratroopers begin their attack along the Old City walls. (Shimon Fuchs)

Left, top: The paratroopers prior to breaking into the Old City.

Left: Israeli forces enter the Old City through St. Stephen's (Lion's) Gate. (GPO)

Above: Paratroopers dash across the esplanade of the Temple Mount on which is built the Dome of the Rock and the El Aqsa Mosque. One wall of the mount is the Western ('Wailing') Wall. (Y. Aharonot)

Right: The first paratroopers arrive at the Western Wall. One of Israel's main aims was to restore this site—the most sacred to Jews the world over—to Israeli sovereignty for the first time since the destruction of the Temple in AD70. (Jerusalem Post)

Above: Parachuting supplies to advance units of the IDF who have already reached the Golan Heights. (Zahal-Bamahane) **Below:** The Syrian fortifications along the eastern ridge of the Golan Heights occupied a commanding position above the Israeli settlements in the Jordan valley and Galilee. This knocked-out Syrian tank—a German Mark IV of World War Two vintage—is at Tawfiq, overlooking Kibbutz Tel Katzir on the eastern shore of the Sea of Galilee. (GPO)

more rapid pursuit plans so as to cut off the Egyptian forces before they could make good their escape across the Sinai. The second day of fighting, however, was spent in consolidating the previous day's gains. General Tal's forces, which had veered southwards through the El-Arish airfield, reached Bir Lahfan en route to Jebel Libni. Bir Lahfan fell after once again apparently impassable sand dunes had been crossed in order to outflank the Egyptian forces. Jebel Libni constituted one of the major Egyptian bases deep in the Sinai, encompassing several fortified army camps and an air base, and straddling a central road junction with connecting north-south and east-west roads. Here and in Bir El-Hassne, some twelve miles to the south, General Mortagui had deployed the Egyptian 3rd Infantry Division supported by tank units. The forces of both General Tal from the north and General Yoffe from the east now attacked this elongated, heavily-fortified concentration. By dusk on 6 June, most of the camps in the Jebel Libni complex had fallen, and Yoffe's force continued southwards to Bir El-Hassne. Sharon's forces in the meantime continued to mop-up the Um-Katef area. Thereafter, they turned south towards Nakhle, in order to deal with the Shazli armoured divisional task force between Kusseima and Kuntilla.

Major-General Saad el Din Shazli was a commando officer highly regarded by President Nasser. In 1960, he had commanded a battalion of the Egyptian commandos within the framework of the UN forces in the Congo. The Egyptian battalion did not acquit itself particularly well in this operation, but Colonel Shazli had continued to enjoy considerable popularity and standing, and was later to command Egyptian forces in Yemen. His force in 1967 was given the major offensive task of cutting the Israeli Negev in the south, to the north of Eilat. In the weeks before the outbreak of the war, during the so-called 'waiting period', he engaged in flamboyant demonstrations of Egyptian armoured power before the world press, belittling the Israeli forces facing him. He was to participate in the planning of the 1973 Yom Kippur War, as Chief of Staff of the Egyptian Armed Forces. His nerve apparently broke in that war, after the Israeli bridgehead was established across the Suez Canal in Egypt proper, and he quarrelled with President Sadat during a meeting when, according to President Sadat, Shazli in a state of hysteria urged the withdrawal of the Egyptian forces from the east bank of the Suez Canal. President Sadat refused to accept his recommendations, and ultimately relieved him of his command. He was sent into 'exile' as Ambassador to Great Britain, and later to Portugal, but subsequently resigned and called for a revolt against President Sadat. After that he was engaged by Colonel Gaddafi of Libya, presumably to rally around him the Egyptian anti-Sadat forces.

By the end of the second day's fighting, the main Egyptian defences manned by elements of three divisions had been overrun, and Israeli forces were advancing into the depths of the Sinai towards the major armoured concentrations in the centre, which constituted the last major obstacle before the Suez Canal.

Along the northern axis, Tal's forces moved rapidly on 7 June towards Kantara on the Suez Canal, meeting resistance only at a distance of some ten miles west of the Canal, where Egyptian tanks, anti-tank guns and a few aircraft laid an ambush for the advancing columns and put up a spirited fight. The Egyptian armoured force, which had concentrated at Kantara East, launched an attack on the advancing Israeli task force, which had raced along the northern coast from El-Arish under Colonel Israel Granit. His force had been joined by a detachment of the paratroop brigade under the command of Colonel 'Raful' Eitan. Rapidly sizing up the situation, the commander of the Israeli task force executed a fire and movement tactic. Part of Granit's armoured force blocked the main road by fire and engaged the Egyptian armoured forces in a tank battle at extreme ranges, while the paratroopers on half-tracks and jeeps mounting recoilless rifles outflanked the Egyptian forces that were engaging the Israeli fire-base. The Egyptian armoured force was destroyed, and Granit's task force broke through to Kantara. By the morning of the following day — the fourth day of the war (8 June) — the banks of the Suez Canal had been reached.

Apart from this independent northern advance, the main effort of the combined Israeli forces in the Sinai now shifted towards the destruction of the huge Egyptian armour concentrations that remained in the central Sinai. General Gavish ordered a co-ordinated two-divisional force to deal with these: Tal's division moved directly westwards towards the major base of Bir Gafgafa, while Yoffe's division moved south to Bir El-Hassne and Bir El-Tamade. From there, Yoffe advanced westward on a parallel course to that of Tal, towards the Mitla Pass. Sharon's division, which had meanwhile mopped-up Um-Katef, pushed south towards Nakhle, compelling Force Shazli and the tanks of the 6th Division to move towards the trap that was being laid by Tal and Yoffe at the Mitla Pass — the only route out of the Sinai. The Israeli forces were in fact funnelling the withdrawing Egyptian forces to the Mitla Pass, where Tal and Yoffe's forces were waiting to destroy them. The move of Sharon's forces against the Shazli armoured force and the armoured units of the 6th Division forced them to move rapidly in order to avoid an armoured engagement that would have held up their withdrawal.

Tal's forces overran the Bir El-Hama infantry base and, farther west, the Bir Rud Salim position. Near the main concentration of armour at Bir Gafgafa, the roads connecting Bir Gafgafa to the west and south (possible supply and reinforcement routes) were soon blocked by Tal's tank battalions. Tal's forces came upon an Egyptian armoured concentration that was attempting to fight its way out of the Sinai towards Egypt, a small Israeli armoured force attempted to draw the Egyptian armour and cause it to counterattack so that it would fall into a trap laid by outflanking armoured forces. But the Egyptian force refused to react, so the Israelis launched a frontal attack that was successful after a battle lasting some two hours.

Yoffe's forces had by now completed mopping-up Jebel Libni and were moving south to Bir El-Hassne, thereby blocking the retreat of the Shazali armoured force. Threatened by the dual advance of Yoffe's and Sharon's forces, the remaining Egyptian armour retreated towards what it considered to be a safe and direct exit towards the Canal, the Mitla Pass. During this retreat, Israeli aircraft strafed the retreating columns without cease, wreaking havoc amongst the Egyptian forces in the narrow confines of the Pass.

Yoffe's forces moved rapidly to the Mitla Pass seeking to block its entrance and destroy the mass of armour that was expected to attempt to retreat through it. The routes back from the Sinai converging on the Mitla Pass were gradually becoming crowded with the withdrawing Egyptian units of the 3rd Infantry Division, the 6th Infantry Division, Shazli's divisional task force, and some elements of the 4th Armoured Division. General Ghoul, commander of the Egyptian 4th Division, meanwhile did his best to create some order in the chaos that was developing along the route.

Meanwhile, Colonel Shadmi's advance units were desperately racing towards the eastern opening of the Mitla Pass in order to lay an ambush there for the converging Egyptian troops and block their passage westwards across the Suez Canal. The Israeli Air Force, which had complete control of the skies, had a field day here, as aircraft strafed and bombed the vast concentration of Egyptian vehicles converging on the Pass. First hundreds and then thousands of burning vehicles were piling up in the area, leaving little or no room for any of the units to manoeuvre. On its way to the Pass, the forward task force of nine tanks under Colonel Shadmi had run out of fuel, and reached its destination with four of the tanks being towed by the others. They dug-in and blocked the approaches, holding out against desperate Egyptian forces trying to force their way through the Pass and, in the process, almost overwhelming Shadmi's isolated unit. (Shadmi was eventually to be joined by the remainder of Yoffe's forces, and only one Egyptian tank succeeded in breaking through this trap — all the others were destroyed.)

In the confusion that ensued in the general area of the approaches to the Mitla Pass, as Israeli forces struggled to reach Shadmi's small unit holding out and blocking the Pass, and Egyptian units equally desperately tried to reach the Pass and break through in order to reach the Suez Canal, an Israeli tank company became entangled with a column of Egyptian tanks. It was by now dark, and it was impossible to distinguish which tanks were Egyptian and which were Israeli. The Israelis realized that they had blundered into the midst of an Egyptian column, but the Egyptians, who were now rushing westwards in a panic-stricken drive, were unaware of the identity of the tanks that had joined them in the dark. The Israeli commander ordered his unit to continue in the column as if nothing untoward were happening along the road for a short distance and then, on a given order, to veer off the road sharply to the right. They were then to switch on their searchlights and shoot at any tank that remained on the road. This they did: in the process, they destroyed a complete Egyptian tank battalion. Meanwhile, Shadmi's forces fought a battle against heavy odds all through the night, being saved by the ammunition and fuel that they were able to pick up on the battlefield from the abandoned Egyptian tanks.

Sharon's forces, in the meantime, continued their push southwards towards Nakhle. At one stage, they encountered an entire Egyptian armoured brigade, the 125th Armoured Brigade of the 6th Mechanized Division, abandoned with all its equipment in perfect condition and in place. The troops had fled. Unknown to Sharon, the commander of this brigade, Brigadier Ahmed Abd el Naby, was taken prisoner with a number of his men by units in General Yoffe's division. When queried about abandoning the tanks intact, he replied that his orders had been to withdraw, but no instructions had been received about destroying the tanks! Outside Nakhle, Sharon's forces caught up with an infantry brigade and an armoured brigade detached from the Egyptian 6th Division. In the ensuing battle, some 60 tanks, over 100 guns and more than 300 vehicles were destroyed. Sharon's force regrouped and moved to link up with Yoffe's division near Bir El-Tamade.

Tal's forces, en route from Bir Gafgafa westwards towards the Canal, came upon Egyptian armoured reinforcements making their way eastwards from Ismailia bent on launching a counterattack to delay the Israeli advance to the Canal. Tal's leading tanks were thin-skinned AMX tanks, and they fought a holding battle against what proved to be an Egyptian armoured division with Russian-built T-55 medium tanks. When the Israeli reinforcements arrived, they engaged the Egyptian brigade from long range, approximately 3,000 yards, because of the poor manoevrability in an area of sand dunes. The Egyptian brigade was spread out to a depth of some 4 miles and, after a battle lasting some six hours, it was wiped out. With his leading brigade deployed on a wide front, Tal advanced towards the Suez Canal.

The final day's fighting saw the completion of the destruction of the Egyptian armoured forces in the Sinai and the final advance to the Canal. Tal's two forces linked up on the road running along the eastern bank of the Suez Canal, but, as they did so and as the Israeli forces approached the Canal, the Egyptian forces in the area of Ismailia attacked the Israeli forces from across the Canal with heavy artillery concentrations and anti-tank missile fire. An active exchange of fire over the Canal developed.

Yoffe's forces on the central axis broke through the Gidi Pass after encountering opposition from some 30 Egyptian tanks that were supported by the remnants of the Egyptian Air Force. Parallel to this move and simultaneously, his forces pushed their way past the impressive concentrations of destroyed tanks and vehicles, through the Mitla Pass towards the Canal. Another unit of Yoffe's division moved south-west to the Gulf of Suez, at Ras Sudar. Assisted by a parachute drop, the combined forces took the area and immediately advanced southwards along the coast towards Sharm El-Sheikh. This time there had been no dramatic dash from Eilat to Sharm El-Sheikh as by Yoffe's 9th Infantry Brigade in the 1956 Campaign (which was not dissimilar to his move across the sand dunes on the night of 5/6 June to the Bir Lahfan junction in this war). The naval task force of three Israeli torpedo-boats, which set out by sea from Eilat as part of a concentrated three-prong assault (paratroop, air and naval), discovered on 7 June that Sharm El-Sheikh had been deserted and that the Egyptian naval blockade at the Straits of Tiran, which had deterred the naval forces of the western powers from taking action to open the Straits of Tiran, was non-existent. The paratroopers landed at Sharm El-Sheikh airfield and advanced northwards along the Gulf of Suez to meet up with Yoffe's forces coming south from Ras Sudar.

Meanwhile, a fierce battle was being fought for the Gaza Strip. The battle for this small area, 25 miles long by 8 miles wide and densely inhabited, had been fought and won during the first two days of the fighting, when Tal and Yoffe were planning the assault on Jebel Libni. When the armoured forces broke-in initially opposite Khan Yunis on 5 June and turned south-west toward Rafah, a parachute brigade reinforced by armour moved northwards along the Strip towards the town of Gaza, fighting through the villages and refugee camps, many of whose inhabitants, reinforcing the Palestinian division, were equipped with weapons. Parallel to this action, Gaza was attacked from Israeli territory west of the town, close to the line of Egyptian border posts on the eastern ridges of the Ali Montar. On the evening of the attack, the forces advancing northwards from Khan Yunis had taken Ali Montar ridge from the south, ascending it under heavy fire. In heavy hand-to-hand fighting, the towns of Khan Yunis and Gaza were taken the following day, and control of the Strip was finally achieved by the early hours of the morning of the third day of the War.

The Israelis estimated that Egyptian casualties in the Six Day War totalled some 15,000. The Egyptians put the figure at somewhat less — approximately 10,000. The Israelis captured over 5,000 soldiers and over 500 officers. Approximately 800 Egyptian tanks were taken in the Sinai, of which at least two-thirds were destroyed. In addition, several hundred Russian-made field guns and self-propelled guns were taken, together with more than 10,000 vehicles of various types. Some months later, President Nasser admitted that some 80 per cent of the military equipment in the possession of the Egyptian Army had been lost in the battles in the Sinai. The Israeli losses on this front numbered some 300 killed and over 1,000 wounded.

A United States electronic intelligence ship, *Liberty*, was stationed at the outset of the war off the coast of Sinai, and was steaming slowly some fourteen miles north-west of El-Arish. The Americans had not notified either of the sides as to the purpose or the mission of the ship, or indeed of the fact that the ship was operating in the area. It will be recalled that when General Tal's forces broke through along the northern axis in the direction of El-Arish, the Egyptian forces regrouped and retook some of the positions that had been captured by the Israeli forces. A certain atmosphere of confusion was created by this situation. On 8 June, fire was directed at Israeli forces in the general area of El-Arish. Israeli forces reported that they were being shelled, presumably from the sea. The Air Force was alerted, and identified a naval vessel sailing off the coast of Sinai in the general area that had received artillery bombardment. The silhouette of the ship was similar — particularly to a pilot flying at high speed in a jet fighter aircraft — to the silhouette of ships in the service of the Egyptian Navy. Without further ado, the Israeli aircraft attacked this strange naval vessel, which had not been identified as friendly, killing 34 members of her crew and wounding 164. The ship managed to limp back to Malta. After a military enquiry, the Israelis expressed regret and offered to pay compensation to the United States Government and to the families of those who had been killed or injured. But attempts to imply that this was a premeditated attack on the part of the Israeli forces do not stand up to examination, especially having regard to the particularly close relationship that existed at that time between the Governments of Israel and the United States, and to the almost tacit agreement expressed in a circuitous way by President Lyndon Johnson to the Israeli Government, that he would 'understand' if Israel saw no way out of the impasse but to embark on war. The blame would appear to have been primarily that of the United States authorities, who saw fit to position an intelligence-gathering ship off the coast of a friendly nation in time of war without giving any warning whatsoever and without advising of the position of their ship.

2

THE WAR WITH JORDAN

Unlike in 1956, the Sinai Campaign of 1967 constituted but one theatre of conflict in a war that was waged on three fronts. The war with Jordan was fought on territory of a very different character from the Sinai, and over cities and towns of a religious and historic connotation for Jews, Moslems and Christians. The structure of the territory in the West Bank area is based on a central mountainous ridge running from north to south; to the east of this, there is a steep drop to the River Jordan and, farther south, to the Dead Sea. Here, few roads permit passage from the west bank of the river towards the Mediterranean coast: the mountainous nature of the terrain makes it a difficult proposition for an army facing determined opposition. To the west of this ridge lies a fertile, populated plain, parts of which were controlled by Jordan no more than eight or ten miles from the coast, at the point where the coastal plain commenced its gentle climb towards the central ridge. Passage through and across this western area is comparatively easy, while artillery positions on the hills and ridges facing the coastal resort areas and towns covered centres of population such as Natanya, Herzliya and Tel Aviv. Farther south, a spur of Israeli territory thrust into the area held by Jordan — the Jerusalem Corridor. This Corridor was flanked by high ridges fortified by the Jordanians.

The dispositions of the Jordanian Army were based on two major defensive sectors. The northern sector comprised the region of Samaria, and was based on the main cities of Nablus, Tulkarem and Jenin. The southern sector based on the Judean region extended along the spine of the Judean Hills south from Ramallah through Jerusalem and Hebron. The forward elements of the forces in both regions were deployed along the coastal strip leading to the narrow 'waistline' of Israel. The Jordanian Army comprised eight infantry brigades and two armoured brigades under the Commander-in-Chief, Field Marshal Habis el Majali. Major-General Mohammed Ahmed Salim, the Arab general in command of the West Front, had deployed his forces in the field as follows. Six infantry brigades defended the West Bank, with three holding the district of Samaria, two stationed in and around Jerusalem and a sixth in the Hebron Hills south of Bethlehem. A further infantry brigade was deployed near Jericho, just west of the River Jordan, while the mobile striking force of the Jordanian Army, the 40th and 60th Armoured Brigades, were held back in the area of the Jordan valley, with the 40th Brigade, commanded by Brigadier Rakan Inad el Jazi, responsible for the northern part of the West Bank and the 60th Brigade, commanded by Brigadier Sherif Zeid Ben Shaker, directed towards Jerusalem and the area south of it. (Brigadier Ben Shaker

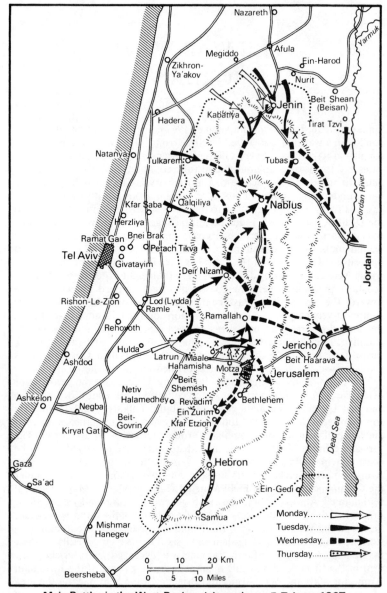

Main Battles in the West Bank and Jerusalem , 5-7 June 1967

was one of the outstanding officers in the Jordanian Army, highly regarded by his cousin, King Hussein. He was in later years to become the Commander-in-Chief of the Jordanian armed forces.) Batteries of 155mm 'Long Tom' guns were sited to cover Tel Aviv in the south and Ramat David airfield in the north. As Nasser moved his divisions into the Sinai and signed a pact with King Hussein, the Jordanians advanced their field artillery to the ridges covering the coastal towns and Jerusalem, and readied their armoured forces in the Jordan valley, with one brigade near Jericho and the other by the Damya Bridge, further north, with a battalion in the area of Nablus. In addition to Jordan's 270 tanks and 150 artillery pieces, an Iraqi infantry brigade was stationed in Jordan: this was to grow within a week to three infantry brigades and an armoured brigade.

Facing these forces were elements of two Commands in the Israel Defence Forces: Central Command, under Major-General Uzi Narkiss, disposed of the 16th Jerusalem Brigade in that city, commanded by Colonel Eliezer Amitai, a reserve infantry brigade near Lod under Colonel Moshe Yotvat, and a reserve infantry brigade commanded by Colonel Zeev Shaham in the area of Natanya. Under Colonel David Elazar's Northern Command were seven brigades, and these were responsible for the borders with three countries, Syria, Jordan and Lebanon. This deployment included a brigade covering the Lebanese border, two brigades deployed in eastern Galilee facing Syria and one brigade facing Samaria in the area of Nazareth. An armoured brigade was held in reserve for the Syrian front, while an armoured division under Major-General Peled, comprising two armoured brigades, was held in reserve in central Galilee. Held in General Staff Reserve was the 'Harel' Mechanized Brigade, under Colonel Uri Ben Ari, who had commanded the 7th Armoured Brigade so successfully in the 1956 Sinai Campaign, and part of 55 Parachute Brigade, under Colonel Mordechai 'Motta' Gur, which was being held ready for an air drop against El-Arish or Sharm El-Sheikh.

The war with Jordan came on Israel unexpectedly. A message from Prime Minister Eshkol of Israel had been sent to King Hussein on the morning of 5 June through the offices of General Odd Bull, chief of the United Nations observers, assuring him that if Jordan kept out of the fighting, Israel for its part would not initiate hostilities. However, King Hussein's commitments under the new alliance with Egypt, and the atmosphere of hysteria in the Arab world that already made the destruction of Israel a reality in the Arab mind, joined together to force the King's hand. He had joined the alliance with President Nasser with some misgivings. Less did he desire to join the alliance, than to be 'odd man out' — a situation that would label him as a traitor to the Arab cause. King Hussein had agreed, further, to appoint General Riadh of Egypt as the Commander-in-Chief of his forces. He behaved with a certain degree of hesitation because he was not completely sure of the wisdom of the step he was taking; indeed, this hesitation was to come to expression on a number of occasions during the conduct of the war. However, such doubts as King Hussein may have had were overcome by an assurance he received from President Nasser in a telephone conversation that morning (5 June) that scores of Israeli aircraft had been downed (at which moment the Egyptian Air Force lay, unbeknown to Nasser, in smoking ruins), and that Egyptian armoured forces were pushing across the Negev in a move to join up with the Jordanian forces in the Hebron Hills. King Hussein ordered his armed forces to attack.

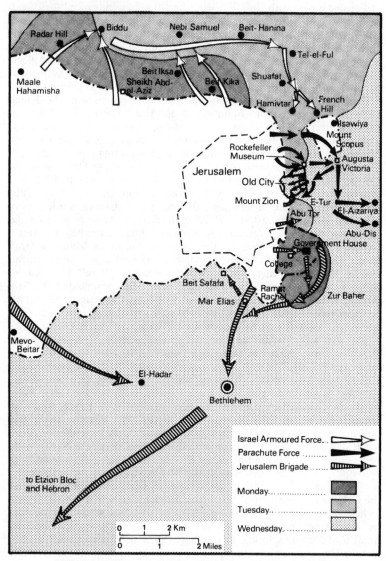

Main Israeli Moves in the Jerusalem Area , 5-7 June 1967

The encirclement of Jerusalem

At 11.00 hours on 5 June 1967, the Jordanian Army launched a barrage of artillery and small arms fire from positions along the winding armistice line against targets inside Israel, including the cities of Tel Aviv and Jerusalem, and its forces crossed the border south of Jerusalem, occupying the United Nations observers' headquarters in Government House, supposedly a demilitarized zone.*

In charge of the Israeli Central Command was Major-General Uzi Narkiss. He had served with distinction with the Palmach, and had in fact commanded the battalion that had broken into the Old City at the Zion Gate in the War of Independence in 1948. Major David Elazar ('Dado') commanded the company in his battalion that actually broke in. A graduate of the French Ecole de Guerre, General Narkiss, a short, slightly-built man, combined a sharp analytical mind with a keen military understanding. He had served as Deputy Director of Military Intelligence and also as Defence Attaché to France.

Narkiss ordered the Israeli artillery to reply to the Jordanian bombardment, and a force of the 16th Jerusalem Brigade was sent to oust the Jordanians of the 'Hittin' Brigade from Government House. Units of the 16th Brigade stormed the area, relieved the United Nations personnel who had been cut off inside, and the impetus of the attack continued towards the village of Zur Baher, lying astride the main Hebron-Jerusalem road — which, in fact, linked the Hebron Hills and the area of Hebron with the rest of the Jordanian kingdom. The Jordanians in the Hebron Hills would now have only secondary roads and mountain tracks as a means of communication with the Jerusalem area and with other parts of the West Bank. The action of the Jerusalem Brigade had thus cut off the area of the Hebron Hills, which was to have been a jumping-off ground for the Jordanian forces in the direction of Beersheba and the Negev, with a view to linking up with the Egyptian forces that were supposed to be advancing across the Negev.

With Jerusalem again under bombardment from the guns of the Arab Legion, and Ramat David airfield and the centre of the city of Tel Aviv being shelled by the long-range Jordanian guns, orders were given by the Israeli General Staff to General Narkiss to move over to the offensive. As part of the plan to isolate Jerusalem from the bulk of the Jordanian Army to the north, Colonel Ben Ari's 10th ('Harel') Mechanized Brigade was ordered to move up into the Jerusalem Corridor to break through the Jordanian lines in the area of Maale Hahamisha and to seize the mountain ridge and road connecting Jerusalem with Ramallah. This area is the key to the control of the Judean Hills and Jerusalem, for it overlooks the

---

* Government House was the official residence of the British High Commissioner of Palestine. It is situated on the so-called Hill of Evil Counsel to the south of the Old City of Jerusalem. In the War of Independence, it was declared a demilitarized zone, and has been recognized ever since as such by the Arabs and the Israelis. The United Nations took it over during the War of Independence and established in it the headquarters of the UN Truce Supervision Organization. To this day it serves as the UN Headquarters.

descent to Jericho and controls all approaches to the city. (This was the area that Joshua, in his campaign to occupy the hills of Judea, saw as his first priority when he crossed the River Jordan; and it was also the area that the British 90th Division in the First World War occupied before Allenby took Jerusalem.) The 'Harel' Brigade under Ben Ari, who had achieved renown at the head of the 7th Armoured Brigade in the 1956 Sinai Campaign, advanced towards the central region up between three mountainous spurs abutting the Jerusalem Corridor at Maale Hahamisha − Radar Hill, Sheikh Abd-el-Aziz and Beit Iksa. Indeed, Colonel Ben Ari was back again fighting over familiar territory. In 1948, he had been a company commander in the Palmach 'Harel' Brigade that had fought over the area north of the Jerusalem Corridor. The strategic Radar Hill had been taken by the Arab Legion in fierce fighting at the time. In vain, Ben Ari had led his company in five counterattacks on the position − and for the ensuing nineteen years this dominant feature, which in effect controlled the Jerusalem road to the coast, had been in the hands of the Arab Legion.

The area chosen by Ben Ari was difficult mountainous terrain, with well-fortified positions of the Arab Legion covering all approach routes. Ben Ari's forces advanced up the main Jerusalem road from the coast and, without any pause, turned northwards along the three parallel axes and stormed the Legion positions, the tanks neutralizing the Arab bunkers at point-blank range and the armoured engineers and infantry overcoming them. This operation began in the afternoon hours of 5 June; by midnight, after hours of heavy fighting, the breakthrough had been achieved and, in the morning of 6 June, Ben Ari's brigade was well established on the strategic ridge (facing the hill at Tel El-Ful overlooking Jerusalem, on which a palace for King Hussein had been in the course of construction). The Brigade now controlled an area with roads leading to Jericho in the east, to Latrun in the west, to Ramallah in the north and to Jerusalem in the south. Parallel and simultaneous to this operation, units of Yotvat's infantry brigade from the Lod area had occupied the Latrun complex, putting to flight the Egyptian commandos who had begun to operate from the area against Israeli targets. Thus, for the first time after so many bloody battles that had failed in the War of Independence, Latrun was in Israeli hands, and the Latrun-Ramallah road was under Israeli control.

King Hussein's air force had attacked targets in Israel that morning at 11.00 hours, its main target being a minor Israeli airfield at Kfar Sirkin near Petach Tikva. In attacking, King Hussein was a victim not only of his own folly but of the duplicity and false reporting of his Arab allies. He had received false information, cabled by Field Marshal Amer from Egypt to the Egyptian General Riadh early in the morning, advising that 70 per cent of the Israeli Air Force had been wiped out; he had also been advised by Nasser of the failure of the Israeli attack and of the armoured advance of the Egyptians across the Negev towards the Hebron Hills. The Syrians, who let him down, as he described quite vividly in his memoirs on the war, and who despite all their promises did not send any forces to support him over a period of a week, announced that their air force was not yet ready to operate. The Iraqis advised him that they had already taken off and bombed Tel Aviv, causing much destruction there – a claim that was completely false. King Hussein, for his part, launched his aircraft against Israel in an unsuccessful attack. Thereupon, the Israeli Air Force, having eliminated most of the Egyptian Air Force, directed its attention to the Jordanian Air Force, attacking the Jordanian bases at Mafraq and Amman. Jordan's Air Force, numbering some 22 Hawker Hunters, was wiped out and Jordan was left without air support in the ensuing fighting.

This allowed the Israeli Air Force to focus its attention on close ground support. Since orders were that on no account should air attacks be mounted in the vicinity of Jerusalem, Israeli Air Force strikes were directed towards the Jordanian reserves in the Jordan valley and the interdiction of forces moving along the Jericho-Jerusalem road to reinforce the Jordanian units battling in Jerusalem. The Israeli air attacks forced the Jordanian West Bank HQ to withdraw to the east of the River Jordan. The road from Jericho to Jerusalem lay strewn with the tanks of the Jordanian 60th Brigade, which had tried in vain to move up to the Jerusalem area.

Colonel 'Motta' Gur's 55 Parachute Brigade had now been assigned fully to General Narkiss's Command. Its mission would be to break through in the built-up area north of the Old City of Jerusalem at Sheikh Jarrach, the Police School and Ammunition Hill. This was the area that controlled the road leading up to the Mount Scopus enclave, where a small force of 120 Jewish policemen had been isolated for years (and only supplied under the auspices of the United Nations). Such a move would also complement Ben Ari's operation and would doubly sever the link between Ramallah and northern Jerusalem leading into the Old City. The Arab Legion was only too aware of the bitter battles that had been fought over this area in 1948 and of the strategic importance of these districts in northern Jerusalem. Accordingly, over nineteen years they had constructed a vast complex of most formidable defence works with the purpose of ensuring that no Israeli attack could break the link between the area of Ramallah and the Old City of Jerusalem. The buildings and positions in this area were honeycombed with a complex of reinforced concrete defences, in many cases several stories high, all interconnected by deep trenches and protected by minefields and barbed wire.

Since the conclusion of hostilities in 1948, Jerusalem had been divided between two warring elements: barbed-wire in profusion, fortifications, trenches and battlements cut through the city, and across them each side watched the other warily. The western part of the city was predominantly Jewish, with over 100,000 inhabitants, and was the tip of the Israeli salient connected to the coast by the Jerusalem Corridor. The city itself was surrounded on three sides by Jordanian military positions, which controlled the approaches from the high ground on each side. In particular, the Jordanian Arab Legion threatened the Corridor, primarily at Latrun, which it had held since the battles of 1948, and from the high ground north of the Corridor covered the road linking Jerusalem to the coastal plain. The Arab part of Jerusalem was held by the Arab Legion centring in particular on the historic Old City, with its shrines and holy places revered by all three major religions, and also the eastern, predominantly Arab part of Jerusalem. There were two enclaves in Jerusalem that added to the military problems of the commanders there. The first was Mount Scopus, an Israeli enclave on the site of the Hebrew University and the Hadassah Hospital; it had been completely surrounded in 1948, but had held out successfully against all Arab attacks. The second enclave was the area of Government House, which had been the residence of the British High Commissioner of Palestine and had continued after the British withdrawal as the headquarters of the United Nations Truce Supervision Organization following the war and the signing of the armistice agreement. It was situated to the south of the Old City on a spur known as the Hill of Evil Counsel, jutting eastwards and controlling the road linking Jerusalem and Bethlehem, which had been built by the Jordanians.

Jerusalem was defended by a very heavy concentration of Jordanian forces. The responsibility for the defence of the Old City lay with the 27th Infantry Brigade of the Arab Legion under the command of Brigadier Ata Ali. The area of Ramallah north of Jerusalem was held by the 'El Hashim' Brigade, which detached some forces to the northern suburbs of the city. One battalion of tanks of the 60th Armoured Brigade was stationed just outside Jerusalem across the Kidron valley. The 'Hittin' Brigade, which was responsible for the Hebron area south of Jerusalem, had also detached a battalion to be responsible for the area between Jerusalem and Bethlehem. Surprisingly enough, there was no Jordanian central command for the whole area of the City of Jerusalem.

When General Narkiss was finally given permission to commence hostilities after the Jordanian forces had opened fire and taken Government House, he set into motion the contingency plans of the Israel Defence Forces. These envisaged a move by the Jerusalem Brigade under command of Colonel Amitai to seize an area to the south of the city, which would cut the communications between Bethlehem and Jerusalem and threaten the Jordanian communications from Jerusalem to Jericho. Colonel Ben Ari's Mechanized 'Harel' Brigade was to seize the high ground and the ridge between Jerusalem and Ramallah, thus effectively cutting off Jerusalem from both Jericho and Ramallah. The main effort against the eastern part of the city and the Old City would be made by Colonel Gur's parachute brigade. One of the outstanding qualities of the Israel Defence Forces was emphasized by the flexible manner in which Gur's brigade, poised to parachute into El-Arish or Sharm El-Sheikh, had its mission changed at a moment's notice and was, literally in a matter of hours, moving up to Jerusalem. Its commanders had moved ahead and were reconnoitring the built-up area far from the desert sands where they had anticipated operating, and planning to overcome heavily-fortified positions in one of the most difficult types of military operation — fighting in built-up areas.

During the afternoon of 5 June, after the Jordanian Air Force had been wiped out, Israeli aircraft repeatedly attacked Jordanian positions around

Jerusalem, and particularly all reinforcements on the road from the River Jordan at Jericho towards the city. All Jordanian line communications had been destroyed and, by evening, their main radio transmitter at Ramallah had been put out of action. In the meantime, the headquarters of the West Bank forces had been forced by the Israeli air activity out of

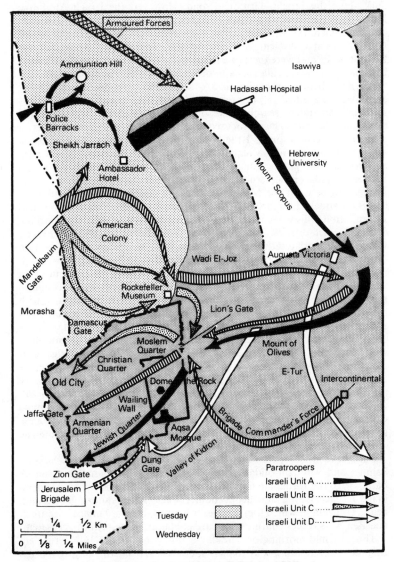

The Battle for Jerusalem, 5-7 June 1967

the West Bank, and had moved over to the East Bank of the River Jordan. Brigadier Ata Ali, commanding the Jordanian 27th Brigade in the general area of Jerusalem, desperately pleaded for forces to reinforce his troops, which were now fighting against heavy odds, and soon elements of the 60th Armoured Brigade and an infantry battalion began to move up after dark along the Jericho-Jerusalem road. However, the Israeli Air Force illuminated the road with flares and then proceeded to destroy the relief column, which was wiped out. The Jordanians were aware of the arrival of Gur's forces in Jerusalem, and realized that a major offensive would now take place. Efforts were therefore made to send up infantry reinforcements by desert tracks and side roads in order to avoid aerial interdiction.

An hour before midnight on 5/6 June 1967, the historic battle for Jerusalem was joined. A pre-prepared plan of artillery and mortar fire was set in motion and, as searchlights from the western part of Jerusalem and the Mount Scopus enclave focused their beams on target after target, a numbing concentration of Israeli point-blank fire reduced Arab position after position. Shortly after 02.00 hours, Gur's paratroopers, led by artillery fire and the reconnaissance unit of the Jerusalem Brigade and backed by tanks of the Jerusalem Brigade, advanced across no-man's land in the area between the Mandelbaum Gate and the Police School. One battalion attacked the heavily-fortified complex of the Police School and Ammunition Hill, while in the north a second battalion advanced into the Sheikh Jarrach district. The Jordanian forces fought fiercely. After Gur's forces had negotiated the fields of mines that the Jordanians had laid on the approaches to the positions, a series of close-combat battles developed as Israeli forces worked their way along the trench positions, moving from room to room, clearing bunker after bunker, fighting on the roofs and in the cellars. For four hours, this desperate see-saw battle was fought, with the troops of both sides fighting incredibly bravely. The battle on Ammunition Hill has become part of the military saga of Israel.

As dawn approached, Gur threw in his third battalion to the southern sector at Sheikh Jarrach, together with tanks of the Jerusalem Brigade. It fought its way towards the area of the Rockefeller Museum facing the northern sector of the Old City Wall, in the area of the Damascus Gate and Herod's Gate. By mid-morning, the area had been cleared, and Israeli forces controlled the area between the city wall and Mount Scopus. Communications were now reopened with the besieged enclave, and the paratroopers were established in the valley below Mount Scopus and the Augusta Victoria Hill facing the Old City wall.

Parallel to these operations, Ben Ari's 'Harel' Brigade had taken Nebi Samuel and was consolidating along the Jerusalem-Ramallah road. A battalion of the Jordanian 60th Armoured Brigade that had been stationed in the Jerusalem area launched a counterattack. After a short, fierce battle near Tel El-Ful in which they lost several tanks, the Jordanians withdrew, and Ben Ari's forces continued towards Shuafat Hill, north of Jerusalem.

Thus, by mid-morning on Tuesday 6 June, units of the 16th Jerusalem Brigade were holding Zur Baher south of Jerusalem, cutting-off the Hebron Hills from Jerusalem; Gur's paratroopers were poised between

Mount Scopus and the Old City; and Ben Ari's armoured force was in control of the northern approaches from Ramallah to the city. Brigadier Ata Ali's brigade was now divided up into three isolated units — in the Old City, on Shuafat Hill and in the general area of Augusta Victoria, which was on the ridge between Mount Scopus and the Mount of Olives. There was a small unit also in the Abu Tor area, just south of the Old City's walls overlooking the Jerusalem railway station. He was advised by King Hussein personally that efforts would be made to relieve Jerusalem, and he accordingly decided to hold on and fight. Meanwhile, the Qadisiyeh Infantry Brigade that was concentrated in the area of Jericho began to move towards Jerusalem along the mountain roads and tracks. En route, however, the Brigade was spotted by the Israeli Air Force using flares, and heavy casualties were inflicted on it in repeated attacks. The timetable of the relief column was so disrupted by these attacks that by the time it approached Jerusalem it was already too late to be of any assistance to the Jordanian forces in the Old City.

The West Bank: Samaria

Facing the northern sector of the West Bank, Major-General Elad Peled, at the head of his armoured division, which included two armoured brigades, waited to discern the main Jordanian thrust. None was forthcoming, however, from either the Syrians or the Jordanians.

The Jordanian forces in the Samaria sector comprised three infantry brigades, one reinforced armoured brigade, two independent battalions of infantry and two independent armoured battalions. The key town of Jenin in the north, over which such heavy fighting had taken place in the War of Independence, was held by the Jordanian 25th Infantry Brigade reinforced by a tank battalion. This brigade was responsible for the approaches southwards to the Jordan valley from Tubas in the north. The Princess Alia Brigade based on Nablus was responsible for deployment in the coastal plain in the area of Tulkarem. A further brigade, with headquarters in Ramallah, defended Latrun and the northern part of the Jerusalem Corridor. The main armoured reserve was the 40th Armoured Brigade based at the Damya Bridge on the Jordan.

Judea and Samaria can be likened to a giant staircase leading up from the sea to the central watershed plateau and down again, though in much steeper steps, to the Jordan valley. From the shore of the Mediterranean, the first step, one ascends through the foothills (the 'shephela' in the Bible) to the third step (the lower slopes) and the fourth step (the upper slopes) to the plateau. On the descent, the lowest step (from the slopes to the Jordan valley) is a steep, near-perpendicular cliff of varying height. From the air, the relief of the central massif looks like a huge fishbone: the spine is the watershed, and the wadis (river beds) running down from the watershed to the Mediterranean and the Jordan valley or Dead Sea, are like the ribs emanating from the spine. The two principal towns influencing the strategy of the Israeli forces in the campaign were Nablus and Jenin, which were also main crossroads. Jenin is located at the foot of the hills of Samaria, controlling the approaches to the valley of Jezreel to the north. Southward of the town is the Dotan valley, which opens west to the coastal plain. In history, this valley was the main route for the armies invading Samaria from the north. Nablus, some 18 miles south of Jenin, lies in a valley between the two mountains mentioned in the Bible, Mount Gerizim and Mount Ebal. Two roads run between Nablus and Jenin: the eastern road passes through Tubas, while the western road runs through Silat ed Dhahar and Dir Sharaf.

In the afternoon of 5 June, General Elazar, GOC Northern Command, ordered Major-General Peled to attack the Jordanians with the immediate purpose of neutralizing the artillery units in the Dotan valley, which were endangering the Ramat David air base. As a young officer in the Palmach, Peled had distinguished himself in the fighting for Safed during the War of Independence in which he was severely wounded. A graduate of the French Ecole de Guerre, he later commanded the renowned 'Golani' Infantry Brigade and, after his retirement from the Army, was to serve as Director-General of the Ministry of Education under his former Palmach commander Yigal Allon, who was Minister of Education. At a later stage, he entered municipal political life and was elected Deputy Mayor of Jerusalem under Mayor Teddy Kollek.

Peled's forces crossed the Armistice Lines at 17.00 hours. The attack was accompanied by a concentrated Israeli Air Force bombardment of the upper Dotan valley artillery concentrations west of Jenin. An armoured brigade under Colonel Moshe Bar-Kochva, followed by an infantry brigade under Colonel Aharon Avnon, advanced on two axes, one towards Ya'abad to the west and southwards of Jenin, and the second towards Jenin from the west. At the same time, a diversionary operation was mounted by an infantry attack from the Beit Shean valley southwards, posing a threat to the Damya Bridge — this might have endangered the entire Jordanian deployment by preventing the Jordanians initially from concentrating their forces to meet the main Israeli thrust against Jenin. The Israeli plan to attack Jenin was based on a wide outflanking movement from the south, with a view to taking the high ground overlooking the city.

The Israeli armoured infantry under Colonel Bar-Kochva reached the Jordanian artillery concentrations, and after a fierce battle, took the area; his tank column then moved on to take the Kabatiya junction, thus cutting Jenin off from Nablus and most of the West Bank. The Jordanian armoured forces counterattacked, attempting a double envelopment of Bar-Kochva's forces, and an armoured battle took place at night. But the Israeli armoured forces, with their 105mm-guns mounted in old Sherman tanks, proved more than a match for the Jordanian US-made Pattons: Bar-Kochva counterattacked the enveloping Jordanian forces and put them to flight. In conjunction with units of Avnon's infantry brigade, Bar-Kochva's forces now advanced into Jenin against a well-camouflaged Jordanian anti-tank concentration backed by 30 Jordanian Patton tanks. After beating off a Jordanian counterattack, in which the Jordanian forces fought with considerable bravery, Bar-Kochva's forces moved to occupy the hills controlling Jenin from the south-east, while other units of the brigade occupied the hills to the south-west.

Meanwhile, as the Israeli forces reached the Police Station north of Jenin, the brigade reconnaissance unit reported a force of some 60 Jordanian Patton tanks advancing northwards from the direction of Tubas. Bar-Kochva moved his forces southwards to the Kabatiya junction and prepared to meet them, while Avnon's infantry brigade continued to mop-up in the city and completed its capture by 13.00 hours. The advancing Jordanian armoured forces entered into battle with Bar-Kochva's reconnaissance battalion, outflanked it and surrounded it completely. Bar-Kochva's forces, which had been on the march for 24 hours and had engaged in very heavy and intense fighting, were in urgent need of regrouping and resupply. But now they were faced with a battle against a fresh Jordanian armoured force that established itself in a firm defensive position in and around Kabatiya while besieging Bar-Kochva's reconnaissance battalion. Peled sent in air reinforcements to relieve the pressure on Bar-Kochva and allow him time to regroup and reorganize. The battle of Kabatiya was joined against the Jordanian force comprising units of the Jordanian 25th Infantry Brigade, under the command of Lieutenant-Colonel Awad Mohammed El Khalidi, and armoured reinforcements. The Jordanians threw back repeated Israeli attacks as fierce fighting continued in the area of the junction for some twelve hours. After nightfall, however, an Israeli tank company moving round the flank of the Jordanian forces succeeded in punching a hole through the Jordanian circle that had closed off the reconnaissance battalion. The surrounded troops moved out of their besieged position and rejoined the main body of Israeli forces, while the armoured battle continued at close range. Gradually, Bar-Kochva's forces overcame the Jordanians at Kabatiya and broke through, advancing from the north towards Nablus.

As Bar-Kochva's brigade was battling for Jenin and Kabatiya, Peled moved a second armoured brigade under the command of Colonel Uri Ram, passing it to the east of Mount Gilboa and Jenin with the purpose of opening up the Jenin-Tubas road in order to advance on Nablus from the east. After overcoming the forward Jordanian anti-tank concentrations, Ram's forces broke through Tilfit and were then engaged in a long-range static armoured battle that continued throughout the day. The Jordanians engaged Ram's advance units from high ground near Zababida, from which positions the Jordanian field of fire covered the road and the entire valley. Colonel Ram deployed along the heights on the eastern side of the valley. He sent small armoured units down into the valley to draw the Jordanian fire, so that the muzzle flashes of the guns would give away their locations. The battle raged till dusk. Towards evening, a Jordanian tank company that was observed moving was attacked by an air strike. As darkness fell, using the burning Jordanian tanks as reference points, Ram developed a night attack and reached the village of Akaba. The Brigade advanced and took Tubas by surprise. Ram left the bulk of his force at the junction covering the road from the Damya Bridge, on the assumption that the Jordanian 40th Armoured Brigade could approach from that direction, and also because he was aware of further armoured units which had been unaccounted for behind him in the area of Tubas. Accordingly, he advanced to Nablus with only his reconnaissance battalion and a tank company.

The reports of the reconnaissance force were that the city of Nablus was quiet, and so Ram ordered them to enter the city. To the utter amazement of the Israeli troops, they were greeted by the citizens of Nablus crowding both sides of the road, cheering and applauding — mistaking the Israeli troops for an expected Iraqi armoured force that was due to move up as reinforcements from Damya. When an Israeli soldier tried to disarm an Arab and shooting erupted, the citizens of Nablus soon realized their error, and sporadic firing broke out. For some six hours, a confused battle took place in and around the western approaches to the city. Jordanian planning had always taken into account that the main danger to Nablus would be from Israeli forces attacking from the coast and not from the east. So Jordanian armoured forces were deployed to the west of the city along the road leading from the coast, while Jordanian infantry were deployed east of the city. So, at the eastern approaches, Ram's forces fought Jordanian infantry, while on the western approaches an Israeli armoured force met and engaged Jordanian tank units. A close-range tank battle developed while units of the 'Golani' Infantry Brigade, which had been advancing with the armoured forces, entered the centre of the city and, in intense house-to-house combat, subdued the city by the evening of 6 June.

The fall of Jerusalem

Meanwhile in Jerusalem, Gur's forces, having cleared the approaches to the Old City and having been deployed in the valley between Mount Scopus and the Old City, prepared for the final assault in what was to be an action of major historic and religious significance in the history of the Jewish people. First, however, it was necessary to ensure control of the ridge overlooking Jerusalem from the east, Mount Scopus, the Augusta Victoria Hill and the Mount of Olives. (It was from this hill that the Roman legions under Titus surveyed the city walls of Jerusalem some two thousand years earlier, in the year AD70, before launching their attack on the city and on the Jewish Temple.) Time was running out as the pressures mounted in the United Nations Security Council to impose a cease-fire.

The Jordanian Governor of the Jerusalem district, Anwar el Khatib, was becoming desperate. He had been in touch with King Hussein, who had promised him (as he had promised the commander of the 27th Infantry Brigade responsible for the defence of the Jerusalem area, Brigadier Ata Ali) reinforcements. These were despatched but never arrived, because of the Israeli Air Force interdiction along the Jericho road. He had protested the use of the area of the Dome of the Rock, housing the Mosque of Omar and the El Aqsa Mosque, as ammunition dumps, but to no avail, and now he was seriously concerned lest the fighting should set off these supplies, which could destroy the entire area holy to the three great religions. When the reinforcements failed to arrive from Jericho, Ata Ali realized that the situation was hopeless. He decided to withdraw his forces and thus save them. Gradually, the bulk of the Jordanian forces withdrew in a skilful evacuation. But Governor Khatib refused to accompany them: two days later, he was to present himself in Jerusalem to the author of this book, who was appointed the first Israeli Governor of the West Bank, and to recount the tense and dramatic tale of the battle for Jerusalem as seen on the Jordanian side. (Incidentally, the removal of the military supplies, high-explosives and ammunition from the area of the mosques was to take several days.)

At 08.30 hours on 7 June, Gur's three battalions attacked. Two of the battalions, supported by concentrated artillery fire and air support, launched a two-pronged attack against the Augusta Victoria Hill: one battalion supported by tanks broke into the Jordanian positions from the direction of Mount Scopus, while a second battalion scaled the slopes of the Augusta Victoria positions from the valley between the Hill and the Old City. At the same time, the third battalion pushed along the city wall from the Rockefeller Museum towards St. Stephen's Gate, where it was planned to break into the Old City and the Temple Mount. Advancing in this two-pronged attack, the paratroopers supported by tanks swept across the Augusta Victoria Hill and the Mount of Olives and then down its slopes to the northern end of the Kidron valley below the city walls. Part of the force then took up defensive positions blocking the road from Jericho. A Jordanian infantry brigade had moved up that road during the night in order to strengthen the Jordanian forces in Jerusalem, but at first light had been engaged by the Israeli Air Force and by Israeli artillery from the Jerusalem area. The force was scattered and forced to withdraw before it could even deploy.

Gur in his half-track now took the lead of the third battalion which, supported by a platoon of tanks, was approaching St. Stephen's Gate, and led the entry into the Old City. He was rapidly followed by the three battalions of his Brigade. From the wide, open area of the Temple Mount, Gur's units spread out in order to mop-up such areas of resistance as might remain, but, apart from occasional snipers, little resistance was encountered. The bulk of the Jordanian forces had withdrawn. Thus, by 10.00 hours, the Israeli forces had reached the holiest of Jewish shrines — the Wailing Wall. A brief and very moving ceremony to mark what was considered by Israelis to be one of the great moments in a very long national history took place on this historic occasion. At this point, the Arab lay leaders presented themselves to Colonel Gur and informed him that there would be no further organized resistance. Meantime, as Gur's forces entered the Old City, units of the 16th Jerusalem Brigade under Colonel Amitai were mopping-up to the south of the city from Mount Zion to Silwan and the Dung Gate. The Brigade then advanced southwards, overcoming the Mar Elias positions and, encountering but light resistance, took in quick succession Bethlehem, Etzion and Hebron.

Pushing south from Hebron, the Jerusalem forces linked up on 8 June with units of the Israeli Southern Command.

To the Jordan valley

While the Israeli forces were occupying the Old City and taking the Hebron Hills, Ben Ari led his brigade into Ramallah. His forces were soon to be relieved by units of Colonel Yotvat's brigade which advanced from Latrun. Two of Ben Ari's battalions now moved along separate routes down the Jordan valley towards Jericho, where they charged through the town with guns blazing and broke the scattered resistance. From there, they fanned out to the Jordan bridges, and then moved north along the Jordan valley to meet forces moving southward from Northern Command. Ben Ari's third battalion pushed northwards towards Nablus where it met the forces from Northern Command, which had captured that city. Jordanian armoured units withdrawing from the Hebron Hills tried to reach the bridges north of the Dead Sea along tracks through the Judean Desert, but their tanks were finally abandoned as the troops endeavoured to escape on foot.

Farther north, on the morning of 7 June, Colonel Bar-Kochva renewed his assault on the Kabatiya junction, supported by a concentrated Israeli Air Force attack. The battle lasted some four hours. After losing an additional 25 tanks in the battle (which meant that the Jordanian 40th Armoured Brigade had already lost more than half its tanks in and around Nablus), and threatened by the advance from the west of Colonel Shaham's brigade approaching Nablus from Kalkilya, the Jordanians began to withdraw towards the Damya Bridge. Peled now advanced some of his forces southwards from Nablus towards Ramallah, where they met up with Ben Ari's brigade advancing northwards, while units from Bar-Kochva's brigade moved into the Jordan valley and took control of the Damya Bridge. Thus, the Israeli forces now held all three bridges across the Jordan, ensuring their control of the West Bank.

Dishevelled, weary, and with several days' growth of stubble, King Hussein appeared on television and made a desperate plea to his nation 'to fight to the last breath and to the last drop of blood'. But he had, in fact, already made the decision to accept the cease-fire call issued by the United Nations: that evening, at 20.00 hours on 7 June, both Israel and Jordan formally accepted.

The conquest of the West Bank had been completed. King Hussein had lost half his kingdom because he had allowed Jordan to be dragged into war by the wave of hysteria in the Arab world and had signed a military accord with Egypt which ten days later he was deeply to regret. He had been given a clear opportunity to stay out of the war and a fair warning of the consequences of not doing so, in the message the Israeli Prime Minister Levi Eshkol had transmitted to him through the good offices of the United Nations on 5 June. He had chosen to ignore this warning and instead to base himself on false intelligence made available by the Egyptians. He had furthermore weakened his standing internationally by conniving with President Nasser in putting out the false story about United States and British military support for Israel. His Egyptian allies had misled him and his Syrian allies had betrayed him — for, despite his desperate pleas, the brigade the Syrians had promised him had never materialized. The Iraqis, although stationed in Jordan, did not enter the conflict. He was to give bitter expression to his feelings in his book, *My 'War' with Israel* (1969). Jordanian casualties in the fighting were estimated by the Jordanians at over 6,000 in killed and missing; Israeli casualties were approximately 550 killed and 2,500 wounded.

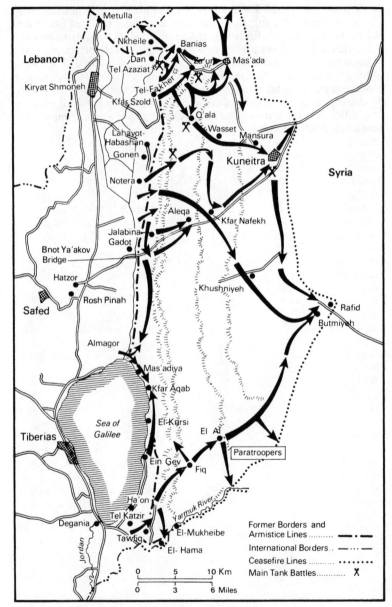

Main Battles in the Golan Heights, 9-10 June 1967

3

THE GOLAN HEIGHTS

The Golan Heights constitute a plateau some 45 miles long from Mount Hermon in the north, which rises to a height of some 9,000 feet, to 600 feet above the Yarmuk valley in the south. To the east, the rough, boulder-strewn lava surface of the plateau rises gently towards the Damascus Plain. To the west, the escarpment — averaging 1,500-2,500 feet in height and dominating the Huleh valley, the Sea of Galilee and the entire northern 'finger' of Israel stretching up to the Lebanese border — drops suddenly down to the Jordan valley. The area is interspersed with volcanic hills called 'tels', the highest of them being Tel Abu Nida, which rises to a height of 3,600 feet above Kuneitra. Over a period of nineteen years the Syrians had converted the area of the Golan Heights into a deep defence zone, with bunkers and tank and gun emplacements sited along the heights overlooking the cease-fire line with Israel. These very formidable defences stretched back along the main axes leading to Damascus, and the Syrian Army manned the entire zone permanently. The fortifications in the rear were no less formidable than those in the front-line. Over the years, the front had erupted from time to time as the Syrians, taking advantage of their position on the Heights, would harass Israeli settlements below in the valley with tank and artillery fire.

With the outbreak of the Six Day War, the Syrians, who had in fact been the major element in causing the Egyptian mobilization and deployment in Sinai, behaved in a very controlled manner. They wanted to appear to be involved by issuing bombastic war communiqués, but at the same time they did everything to avoid becoming too heavily involved. The Syrian Air Force attempted to bomb the Haifa oil refineries, whereupon the Israeli Air Force reacted and destroyed the bulk of Syria's aircraft. During the period in which the Israeli forces were fighting in the Sinai and the West Bank, Syrian artillery kept up a heavy, constant bombardment of the Israeli forces in eastern Galilee. Artillery exchanges developed all along the front. On three different occasions, the Syrians mounted probing, company-size reconnaissances in force against two Israeli kibbutzim and were beaten back. Syrian artillery and armoured units engaged the Israeli villages in the valley below the Golan Heights as they had done over the years. But no major move of Syrian forces took place. King Hussein characterized in his memoirs the behaviour of the Syrians as downright treachery, describing how, despite his pleas for reinforcements and Syrian promises, not one Syrian brigade had been moved to Jordan by the end of the war. And, as the true picture of the Israeli successes against the Egyptians and the Jordanians emerged, the

Syrians restricted themselves to shelling Israeli units and villages along the border, and to a few 'reconnaissances in strength' in the area of Kibbutz Dan and the village of Sha'ar Yashuv.

The Syrian forces were organized in three divisional groups. Eight brigades were concentrated on the Golan Heights west of Kuneitra, with three infantry brigades forward and three infantry brigades behind them. In addition, the strike force of the Syrian Army, namely two armoured brigades and two mechanized brigades, were moved forward, part along the road between Kuneitra and the Bnot Ya'akov Bridge, and part in the area of Kuneitra itself. Each of the infantry brigades included an armoured battalion of tanks in addition to self-propelled assault guns. Facing this force was Major-General David Elazar's Northern Command, consisting of three armoured brigades and five infantry brigades (including GHQ Reserve); in addition to the Syrian frontier, however, these troops guarded the northern border with Jordan and the Lebanese border.

The Israeli Minister of Defence, General Dayan, was hesitant about launching an attack against Syria, which might draw the Russians into armed conflict; but, as the war proceeded, pressure grew from the villages in northern Israel to reply in strength to the Syrian harassment and to occupy the Heights from which this was taking place. Only after the Egyptians had collapsed in the Sinai and the Jordanians had been ejected from the West Bank were orders given by General Dayan to General Elazar to attack. On Friday morning, 9 June, forces of the Israeli Northern Command attacked, the Israeli Air Force leading, while Syrian forward positions were reduced one after the other according to plan by open-sight tank fire. The Israeli main effort in the northern part of the sector was in the Tel Azaziat/Q'ala/Za'ura area, the aim being to open a road through Banias at the foot of Mount Hermon, which would in turn provide access to the Mas'ada-Kuneitra road from the north. This area was chosen because it was steep enough for the Syrians to have fortified it comparatively lightly against armour, and yet it was not steep enough to be impassable, as would be the case farther south: the Syrians in their deployment had obviously relied on the difficulties of the terrain in their defensive calculations. At the same time, secondary attacks were mounted by reserve infantry units against the Dardara/Tel Hillal/Darbashiya complex immediately north of the Bnot Ya'akov Bridge.

The northern sector of the Golan Heights front was entrusted by General Elazar to a divisional task force commanded by Brigadier-General Dan Laner, who was his Chief of Staff in Northern Command. Laner had been an outstanding officer in the Palmach, and a comrade in arms with Elazar in many of the fierce battles fought in the War of Independence. (A tall, attractive officer with a commanding appearance, a member of a kibbutz, he had taken short spells in the regular army but was not a regular army officer. He was to prove his ability as a divisional commander in the battles fought in the Golan Heights in 1973, leading one of the major prongs that counterattacked and advanced towards Damascus.) His force consisted of an armoured brigade commanded by Colonel Albert Mandler and the 'Golani' Infantry Brigade commanded by Colonel Yona Efrat.

(Colonel Mandler was to die in the 1973 War leading the division that held the line of the Suez Canal.)

Mandler's brigade moved to the attack from the area of Kfar Szold along a single axis leading towards Q'ala-Za'ura, under concentrated Syrian fire. Parallel to Mandler's advance, the infantry units of the 'Golani' Brigade were entrusted with the task of clearing all Syrian positions in the Kfar Szold/Za'ura/Banias triangle. The approaches to the Syrian lines were completely dominated by formidable concrete emplacements and positions at Tel Azaziat, which covered by fire the entire north-eastern area of the Huleh valley. The only way to overcome this position was to outflank it, to capture the Syrian positions behind it and then advance on it from the rear. To do this it was essential to overcome another formidable position in the rear, Tel Faher. As the infantry force worked its way round the foothills of the Hermon, a series of desperate battles — in which men of 'Golani' Brigade revealed extraordinary bravery — were waged over the various fortifications constituting the Tel Faher position. Surrounded by three double-apron, barbed-wire fences and several minefields, it was criss-crossed with trenches, machine-gun and anti-tank positions and dug-outs. It was cleared only after fierce hand-to-hand fighting. In the first attack on a fortification, the position was taken, but only three men out of the attacking forces survived unhurt; in the attack on a second position, the commander of the assault and most of his officers and NCOs were put out of action. Under withering fire, some of the Israeli troops, many of whom died in the process, threw themselves on the coils of concertina wire, creating a human bridge over which their comrades could cross and attack. As the battle waged to and fro, the brigade reconnaissance unit was thrown into action and, by 18.00 hours, Tel Faher had been taken by units of the 'Golani' Brigade in one of the fiercest battles ever waged by this crack infantry force. Backed by a few tanks, an additional force of the 'Golani' Brigade continued the attack from the rear against Tel Azaziat and, as darkness fell, that key position was in the hands of the Israelis, who now proceeded to move towards Banias.

Meanwhile, led by bulldozers and engineering units, Mandler's brigade fought its way up the steep ascent under concentrated artillery fire. The entire column moved up along a single axis, led by an engineer detachment with a company of bulldozers. All the bulldozers were hit in the action, and each one of them lost several crews during what proved to be a most costly advance: despite this, somehow or other the advance continued. The Israeli losses were heavy, and the leading armoured battalion suffered considerable losses. Nevertheless, Mandler's units pressed forward, taking Na'mush and over-running the Syrians in their positions. The unit then moved south-east towards Q'ala. A young lieutenant, bleeding from his wounds, commanded the last two tanks in the battalion still operational in the final assault. The Syrians held on desperately. The Israeli survivors of knocked-out tanks in the leading battalion followed the remaining tanks fighting as infantry. The remainder of Mandler's brigade bypassed the attack of the lead battalion on Q'ala and advanced on Za'ura. As this force moved from Za'ura on Q'ala, the Syrians withdrew rapidly. Thus, by the end of the first day of fighting, the 'Golani' Brigade and Mandler's brigade were holding a line along the first crest of the northern Golan Heights.

Farther south, two infantry brigades attacked across the Jordan at Mishmar Hayarden and took Darbashiya, Jalabina and Dardara. They captured the Upper Customs House, thus enabling units to open up the route for armoured forces. As soon as this was accomplished, units of Colonel Uri Ram's armoured brigade, which had moved up from the fighting in the West Bank against the Jordanians, pushed up the hill, taking the village of Rawiya. At the same time, paratroop units captured the Syrian positions east of Darbashiya, enabling an additional armoured penetration that could now reach the main road between Kuneitra and the Bnot Ya'akov Bridge.

The next morning, on 10 June, Colonel Bar-Kochva's armoured brigade, which too had arrived from the West Bank, joined the 'Golani' Brigade to attack Banias and move on Ein Fit and Mas'ada on the southern slopes of Mount Hermon. Parallel to this, Mandler's brigade moved eastward from Q'ala towards Kuneitra, while Ram's brigade, advancing to Kfar Nafekh, attacked also towards Kuneitra. Thus, the Israeli forces in the northern half of the Golan Heights were advancing in an arc towards Kuneitra: the 'Golani' Brigade and Bar-Kochva's brigade through Mansoura; and Mandler's brigade via the road junction at Wassett.

At mid-morning on 10 June, the Syrian forces broke and began to blow up their positions. Panic developed as the Israel Air Force intensified its attacks, and the Syrians began to flee. Many abandoned tanks were encountered by the Israelis as they advanced. Kuneitra was occupied by Mandler's forces without any fight by 14.00 hours. Part of the 'Golani' force was meanwhile helicopter-lifted to the lower peak of Mount Hermon, some 7,000 feet high, and occupied that strategic position.

Parallel to these operations, General Elad Peled had launched his division — which now included Colonel Avnon's infantry brigade and Colonel Gur's paratroop brigade moved up from Jerusalem, in addition to some armoured units — on the morning of Saturday 10 June. The attack took place in the southern area of the Golan Heights in the area of Tawfik and the Yarmuk valley. Following heavy air bombardment, armoured and paratroop forces attacked and overcame Tawfik; then, leap-frogging by helicopter, paratroopers took Fiq and El Al and moved eastwards towards Butmiyeh and Rafid junction. Infantry and paratroop units mopped-up after them and also in the area along the eastern shore of the Sea of Galilee. Gradually, the line was stabilized and a perimeter acceptable to the Israeli General Staff on the Golan Heights overlooking the Damascus Plain was achieved in time to accept the United Nations imposed cease-fire, which became effective at 18.30 hours. The perimeter now extended from the western peak of the Golan Heights along a line east of Mas'ada, Kuneitra and Rafid junction, turning westwards into the Yarmuk valley to the Jordan valley.

SUMMARY
A Vindication

Following the Six Day War, the strategic situation of Israel had changed radically — for the first time in its history, Israel had the benefit of defence in depth. In the south, the Sinai Desert acted as a buffer. The Israeli control of the West Bank down to the River Jordan moved potentially hostile forces from the coastal strip and narrow 'waistline' of Israel and the areas surrounding the city of Jerusalem, and created an additional buffer for Israel's defences. In the north, the threat now posed was that of Israeli artillery and armour towards Damascus, as opposed to the situation hitherto of a Syrian threat against northern Galilee in Israel. Cards were now placed in Israel's hands, in the form of the territories that had been used as a jumping-off ground for attack on Israel, which it was believed, if played correctly, could open the way to negotiations for peace.

The results of the war were a vindication of years of hard work on the part of commanders of Israel's armed forces and also of very effective military planning, which had taken place in the Israeli GHQ. The comparatively long period of waiting for several weeks under conditions of tension had enabled the Israel Defence Forces to mobilize effectively and to be prepared for the initial strike. (Thus many of the mistakes that were to characterize the opening days of the 1973 War were avoided in 1967.) At the same time, because of the astounding victory that was achieved, there was a tendency to sweep many of the shortcomings of the Israel Defence Forces under the carpet and not to deal with them. (This too was to have its effect in 1973.) In general the victory in the Six Day War was such an astounding and unexpected one that the Israeli Command tended to credit itself with many achievements that were in some cases more a result of Arab negligence, lack of co-ordination and poor command at the higher level, than of Israeli effectiveness.

The outstanding event of the Six Day War was the initial air strike when the Israeli Air Force, commanded by Major-General Mordechai Hod, in a carefully-planned attack, took the Egyptian and other Arab air forces by surprise and, after three hours of concentrated activity, had gained complete superiority in the air on all fronts. This move paved the way to victory for the ground forces. Another major element was the bravery of the Israeli soldiers in such classic battles as the struggle of the paratroopers in east Jerusalem, particularly at Ammunition Hill, against a brave and determined enemy, and of the incredible armoured and infantry assault on the Golan Heights, particularly in the northern part of the sector. A measure of the example and leadership ability within the Israel Defence Forces can be gauged from the fact that 23 per cent of the casualties in the

Israel Defence Forces were suffered by officers and NCOs: one of the main secrets of Israel's success lay, and lies still, in the fact that the officers and NCOs are invariably at the head of their men in battle. Again, in this war, as far as the higher command level was concerned, the Arab forces were completely outgeneralled by the Israelis.

This war had been brought on by President Nasser of Egypt. In his evaluation of Egypt's prospects and in the manner in which he conducted the war, particularly at the outset, he made a number of cardinal errors. In the first place, he became convinced by his own oft-repeated argument that the Israelis had been successful in the 1956 Sinai Campaign thanks to the involvement of the French and British; as a result of this, in planning for the war, he tended to underestimate the Israel Defence Forces. His second error lay in the fact that he exaggerated the strength of his own forces and of the Arab armies. As General Dayan later put it, Nasser was blinded by the apparent strength of the vast amount of equipment he had received from the Soviet Union. The fact that Egypt and other Arab armies had succeeded in mastering sophisticated modern aircraft, electronic equipment and masses of armour, caused him to exaggerate and to lay excessive emphasis on the equipment, as opposed to the men who had to use it. A further mistake was that he tended to see wars in the mirror of the Second World War, or as reflected in his experience in the Faluja pocket in the 1948 War. He did not envisage a rapid, hard-hitting war of manoeuvre in the desert, but saw it more (as the deployment and fortifications of his forces would indicate) as a long-drawn-out slogging match. Finally, he did not appreciate the decisive importance of the first strike, and this is borne out by the gradual, cautious opening of hostilities on the part of the Arab forces, in which no use was made of the powerful potential of a first strike. All of these mistakes combined to bring about the false and misleading evaluations that guided Nasser, both in the moves leading up to the war and in its conduct.

The Egyptian Command was later to analyse these errors, and the planning stages and opening phases of the 1973 War were to prove that President Sadat and his generals had understood Nasser's mistakes and had learned the lessons of the Six Day War.

Above all, from a political point of view, a major factor in bringing on the war lay in the direct involvement of the Soviet Union, whose leaders immediately after the war blocked any move by the Arab states, even after President Nasser had announced his resignation (later to be withdrawn by popular appeal of the Egyptian masses), to enter into negotiations with Israel for a peaceful resolution of the conflict. On 19 June 1967, the Israeli Cabinet unanimously voted to return the whole of Sinai to Egypt in return for peace and demilitarization and special arrangements at Sharm El-Sheikh, and the whole of the Golan Heights to Syria in return for peace and demilitarization. Moves were afoot, too, to enter into negotiations with King Hussein of Jordan in respect of the West Bank. But all of these were blocked by the Soviet Union: President Nikolai Podgorny, together with a large military staff, came to the Middle East and immediately set about the task of reconstructing the Egyptian and Syrian armies. This

Soviet move influenced the Arab reaction to the Israeli peace moves. The Arab Summit Conference at Khartoum on 1 September 1967 passed 'the "three noes" resolution' — no negotiations with Israel, no recognition of Israel, no peace with Israel. Thus, Russian intrigue and Arab intransigence prepared the ground for a further renewal of hostilities in the area.

BOOK IV

THE WAR OF
ATTRITION

THE WAR OF
ATTRITION

The conclusion of the Six Day War, with its resultant trauma for the Arab world, created an atmosphere, particularly in Israel, indicating that an end had been reached in the wars of Israel with the various Arab countries. Indeed, as was pointed out at the end of the previous chapter, the imminent opening of peace negotiations was envisaged. From a military point of view, Israel was now in a much stronger position than it had ever been and, in the eyes of most Israelis, this fact enhanced the prospects for peace negotiations. This time Israel would be negotiating from strength.

As a result of the Six Day War, the area controlled by Israel had increased some four-fold. In the north in the Golan Heights, the Israeli forces controlled an area some twenty miles in depth, which removed the Syrian artillery threat to Israeli villages, and furthermore increased Israeli control of one of the three main sources of the River Jordan. In the West Bank of the Jordan, the front-line had hitherto cut the capital city of Jerusalem in half and had brought Tel Aviv, the centre of Israeli commerce and the area of Israel's densest population, to within artillery range of the armistice lines. It created a ten-mile-wide waistline opposite Natanya. Now, Israeli forces were deployed along the natural frontier of the River Jordan. A Jordanian attack against Israel would now have to take into consideration not only the river crossing, but an ascent of some 3,000 feet over a distance of some 40 miles into the Judean Hills through most inhospitable barren territory before reaching any centres of population. In the south, Israel controlled the Sinai Desert, which included at its southernmost tip the strategically placed Straits of Tiran at the entrance to the Gulf of Aqaba. The area included the oilfields of the Gulf of Suez capable of supplying a high percentage of Israel's oil requirements. Most important of all, this vast wasteland provided an ideal buffer to guarantee Israel's security against any recurring threat from Egypt. The electronic warning period given to Israel in respect of an air attack from Egypt had increased four-fold, to sixteen minutes. (Indeed, the vital importance of the Sinai as a buffer area was demonstrated when the Egyptians attacked across the Suez Canal in 1973.)

Israel's belief that the war had come to an end and that peace would now reign along the borders was soon dispelled. Three weeks after the conclusion of hostilities, the first major incident occurred on the Suez Canal. Thus began a war, known as 'The War of Attrition'. While not as spectacular as a conventional war (and it did not therefore attract world-wide attention), this was waged from 1967 until the cease-fire between Israel and Egypt in August 1970. Many actions in this 'war' were to prove to be complete innovations in the history of warfare. The anti-aircraft defence system that protects the Soviet empire was tested out by the Israel Defence Forces flying Western-type aeroplanes, and was found wanting. The battlefield around the Suez Canal became a major proving ground for the military equipment of the two superpowers. In many ways — from the point of view of the development of military equipment and science — the War of Attrition was perhaps more significant than other struggles in which Israel was hitherto involved.

At the beginning of July 1967, the United Nations Security Council was in session on the Middle East conflict. The Soviets emphasized to the Egyptians, with an eye to the discussions in the United Nations, that it was important to create the impression that the war was not over: hence Israel would be pressurized to withdraw in order to enable the Egyptians to open the Suez Canal to international shipping. The first shots were fired on Saturday 1 July 1967. On a number of occasions, Egyptian forces ambushed Israeli patrols moving along the exposed narrow dyke on the Suez Canal; at places but a few yards wide, this links Kantara in the south with Port Fouad in the north. Egypt chose this area, a narrow neck of land some eighteen miles in length, bordered on one side by the Suez Canal and on the other side by swamps, in which to engage Israeli forces that would be exposed and hence be without any possibility of retaliation.

On 1 July, an armoured infantry company commanded by Major Uriel Menuhin advanced northwards along the dyke in order to drive off an Egyptian ambush, which had sited itself on the eastern bank of the Suez Canal in the general area of Ras El-Aish, some ten miles south of Port Said. Despite the fact that it was attacked by artillery and armoured fire from the west bank of the Canal, the Israeli force continued to carry out its mission and drove off the Egyptian forces. However, in the ensuing artillery engagement, Major Menuhin was wounded. Despite his wounds, he continued to command the force and engaged the units on the other side of the Canal, directing the fire of his tanks. In this operation, he was wounded a second time. As the Israeli force was in the process of withdrawing on the evening of the second day, having accomplished its task, the half-track carrying the wounded company commander was hit again and he was killed. In total, the action cost the Israelis one killed, the unit commander, and thirteen wounded.

Thus it continued, battle being joined with the Egyptians intermittently engaging Israeli patrols along the eastern bank of the Canal with flat-trajectory fire from tanks, coastal artillery fire from Port Said, and field artillery fire. At times, these actions escalated, and Israeli air units were thrown into the combat to deal with the sources of Egyptian fire. During one of these engagements, 120 Egyptian troops attempted to cross in rubber dinghies at the northern end of the Canal, but they were repulsed by Israeli forces. The fighting that broke out in this area included naval operations off the coast of Sinai opposite Rumani, in which the Israeli naval flagship *Eilat* and two torpedo-boats were engaged by Egyptian torpedo-boats. Two of the Egyptian torpedo-boats were sunk in one such engagement.

On 11 July, Israel and Egypt agreed to establish United Nations observation posts on both sides of the Canal. Israel maintained that the cease-fire line ran down the middle of the waterway. Accordingly, on 14 July, Israeli naval dinghies were lowered into the Canal to the south of Kantara as a test probe to see if the Egyptians would accept the Israeli definition of the cease-fire line. The Egyptians opened fire on them and there followed a major tank and artillery exchange with the Israeli Air Force also joining in the battle. Israeli dinghies and Israeli ships were hit. In the air battles that ensued, four Egyptian MiG-17s and three MiG-21s were shot down by the Israeli Air Force. Israel suffered some nine men dead and 55 wounded. This phase came to an end in mid-July, and thereafter no naval forces were introduced by either side into the Canal.

Gradually, life settled into a routine along the Canal, and relationships even began to develop between the forces on the opposing sides. Visitors at the time were amazed to see soldiers of the two armies sitting peacefully engaged in fishing, each on their side of the Canal. In many cases, the troops talked to each other and exchanged at first epithets and later pleasantries across the Canal.

'Defensive rehabilitation'

At this stage the Arab political policy towards Israel was established at the Khartoum Summit Conference. On 1 September 1967, this Conference laid down the basis for Arab policy in 'the "three noes" resolution': no recognition of Israel, no negotiations with Israel and no peace with Israel. Addressing a mass demonstration in the square before the People's Assembly in Cairo, President Nasser declared that all that had been taken by force could only be returned by force, and added an additional 'no' to the three of Khartoum: 'no concessions on the legitimate rights of the Palestinian people'. He formulated Egyptian military policy as one based on three phases: the 'defensive rehabilitation' phase, the 'offensive defence' phase and, finally, the 'liberation' phase. He made it perfectly clear for all who would listen, that the lull along the Canal was a temporary one and that the hostilities would be resumed when it suited the Egyptians.

The second major outbreak of hostilities began in September 1967, when the Egyptians opened fire from the fortified Green Island in the north of the Gulf of Suez on Israeli shipping traversing the waters within the Israeli sector. The Egyptians wanted to emphasize their adherence to the decisions of the Khartoum Conference and to symbolize Nasser's determination to maintain this policy. The fire spread, and heavy artillery battles developed along the Suez Canal as far north as Kantara, which, together with Ismailia and Suez, came directly under fire. Thousands of citizens abandoned their homes and, as the fighting developed over the months, a major refugee problem was created for Egypt, reaching proportions of some 750,000 people.

Again, a lull set in. After this brief outbreak, the guns fell silent until, in the autumn of 1967, an event once more focused world attention on the

Egyptian front. On 21 October 1967, the Israeli flagship, the destroyer *Eilat*, was patrolling at a distance of 14½ nautical miles off Port Said. At 17.32 hours, a Styx surface-to-surface missile was fired from a Komar-class Egyptian missile-boat anchored inside Port Said harbour. *Eilat*'s radar had not revealed any suspicious activity or movement because the attacking missile-boat was in fact anchored inside the harbour and, despite evasive action ordered by the captain of the vessel when the missile was sighted, the missile hit the ship in the area of the boiler, killing and wounding officers and crewmen and cutting-off the electric current. The ship began to list. Two minutes later, a second missile hit *Eilat*, causing additional damage and casualties. With the ship listing heavily, the survivors amongst the crew tended to their wounded comrades and engaged in rescue and repair activities while they awaited ships of the Israeli Navy, which were speeding to the rescue. Some two hours after the first missile had hit the ship, a third missile was fired in the midst of the rescue operations, and this struck amidships. Fire broke out and a series of explosions shook the ship, causing heavy casualties. Shortly thereafter she sank.

Eilat, previously HMS *Zealous* of the Royal Navy, a destroyer displacing 1,710 tons, had seen active service in the Second World War before being sold to Israel in 1956. Of 199 crew members aboard *Eilat*, 47 were listed as killed or missing and 90 were wounded. The incident aroused world-wide interest, because it was the first occasion in history in which a warship had been sunk by missile fire. The age of naval missiles had dawned. This encounter foreshadowed the first naval missile battles in history between the Israeli Navy and the Egyptian and Syrian Navies in the 1973 War. More significance than this should not be read into the incident, however, because the Egyptian missile-boats, by virtue of remaining static inside Port Said harbour, had not been detected on *Eilat*'s radar; nevertheless, much interest was aroused at the time, for this was the shape of naval things to come.

This had been a planned, premeditated attack. Its significance was not lost on Israel both because of losses incurred and also because of the departure in military policy that it obviously reflected. The Egyptian move must have taken into account a massive Israeli reaction and presumably assumed a renewed outbreak of intense fighting along the cease-fire line. Israeli reaction to this event was indeed fierce, but unexpected. The Egyptians had prepared themselves for a reaction in the area of Port Said at the northern end of the Canal. Acting on this assumption, the Israeli Command reacted at the other extremity. Four days later, on 25 October 1967, a heavy concentration of Israeli artillery opened up along the southern end of the Suez Canal: the Egyptian refineries in Suez, petrol depots and petrochemical installations came under fire and went up in flames. For a period of days, all attempts to extinguish the fire failed, as benzine and asphalt burned, destroying plant, buildings and factories. The Egyptians themselves estimated the loss in the region of over £36 million ($100 million) and announced that 11 people had been killed and 92 wounded. The Israeli retaliation had been a heavy one, greater apparently than the Egyptians had bargained for. The cost was considered by the Egyptians to be excessive, so a period of comparative calm descended along the Suez Canal—a period that lasted with sporadic outbreaks of artillery and patrol activity and occasional air battles, for almost a year into the summer of 1968.

September 1968 saw the conclusion of the first phase proclaimed by Nasser, namely that of 'defensive rehabilitation'. During this period, the Soviets succeeded in reorganizing the Egyptian Army and in completing its re-equipment. Within a comparatively short period, the Egyptian Army regained the total strength it had enjoyed before the outbreak of war in June 1967. Now, however, because of the more modern equipment which had been supplied, it was much stronger, for it had improved considerably its military posture by absorbing MiG-21 fighters in place of the MiG-17s and MiG-19s, and T-54 and T-55 tanks in place of the T-34 and T-54 tanks that had been lost to Israel in the Six Day War. This resupply of the Egyptian Army was paralleled by a larger Soviet involvement in Egypt. Initially, hundreds of military advisers were assigned to the Egyptian Army, but their numbers gradually ascended to thousands. At the outset, they limited their attention mainly to advice on organization and training, but they soon became involved in all aspects of the Egyptian armed forces – including that of operations. Mindful of the shortcomings of the Egyptian Air Force, and anxious to involve the Soviet military command as deeply as possible in the defence of Egypt, Nasser even proposed to the Russians that a Soviet Air Force general assume command of the air defences of Egypt. However, aware of the complications from an inter- national point of view to which such a move could give rise, the Russians turned down the proposal. Meanwhile, considerable quantities of Soviet aid continued to flow to Egypt as the Egyptian Army recovered physically, and from an equipment point of view, from the setbacks of the 1967 War. The stage was set now for the opening of the next phase in Nasser's plan.

'Offensive defence' and the Bar-Lev Line

The economic damage that had been caused to Egypt as a result of the War was enormous. The blocking of the Suez Canal, the extensive damage caused to the cities along the Canal and the complete cessation of tourism, not to mention continued total mobilization of one of the largest armies in the world, combined to have a crippling effect on Egypt's economy. The losses caused to its economy during that initial period were estimated at approximately £250 million ($750 million). However, the massive Soviet aid made available to Egypt, and also the combined aid of the oil-rich Arab countries, which came to a total of approximately £90 million ($250 million) a year, enabled Egypt to overcome some of its economic difficulties.

The new phase opened at the beginning of September 1968. Some 150,000 Egyptian troops were by now concentrated along the Suez Canal. The Egyptian commanders and the Soviet advisers considered that the time had now arrived for action to raise the morale of the Army and eliminate the psychological effects of the 1967 defeat. The move coincided with Nasser's drive to raise the morale in the country as a whole, and to enhance the prestige of the Army. The time had now come, it was felt, to imbue the defensively-minded Egyptian forces with a new spirit, for morale was at a low ebb. (Testimony to this state of affairs was the number of Egyptian deserters crossing the Canal and giving themselves up to the Israeli forces.) On 8 September 1968, an Israeli patrol discovered a mine just north of Port Tewfik, at the southern extremity of the Canal, and exploded it. This was the signal for a co-ordinated Egyptian fire-plan along 65 miles of the Suez Canal to be activated. Over a thousand Egyptian artillery pieces together with mortars and tanks opened a highly-concentrated barrage on Israeli targets along the Canal. Israel's losses in the sudden onslaught were 28 men killed and wounded. On the Egyptian side, the civilians had been warned to take shelter in advance, but the Egyptians admitted the loss of 26 dead and 104 wounded. This offensive was co-ordinated with a major propaganda offensive on the part of the Egyptians who hailed it as 'a great victory'. The offensive was resumed some weeks later when again the Egyptians opened up with a heavy artillery barrage along the Canal, but this time their attack was coupled with the landing of Egyptian commando units on the Israeli-held bank. Israeli casualties rose to 49 killed and wounded, and the Egyptian media heralded once again a major victory.

The Egyptians disposed of a wide range of conventional Soviet artillery. Facing them, the Israel Defence Forces had 105mm howitzers mounted on the chassis of French AMX tanks, 155mm howitzers mounted on the chassis of the United States Sherman M4 tanks, and Israeli 160mm mortars also mounted on Shermans. However, the Israelis were outgunned by an overwhelming concentration of Russian-supplied artillery on the Egyptian side. (This tendency of the Israeli Command not to place adequate emphasis on the importance of artillery was to prove a very costly mistake, which would come to full expression in the 1973 War.) Because the Israeli units were so heavily outgunned by the Egyptians along the Canal, the strategy of indirect approach was chosen by the Israelis.

On the night of 31 October, Israeli commandos flown in by French Sud 321 helicopters penetrated to the heart of the Nile valley some 220 miles from the nearest Israeli-held area, and attacked three targets — the bridges of Kina and Najh Hamadi across the Nile and an electric transformer station near Najh Hamadi. These were some 300 miles south of Cairo and 150 miles north of Aswan. The operation against the bridges and the transformer station was a complete success, and it served to emphasize the existence of the 'soft under-belly' of Egypt. The warning was a clear one: wide areas of Egyptian territory were wide open to Israeli attack. In Egypt itself, there was a wave of criticism about inadequate security arrangements. Indeed, on 1 November, the day after the Israeli operation, an order was issued in Cairo creating a militia to protect vital points throughout the country. The Egyptians drew their conclusions from this operation and ceased operations along the Canal. Comparative quiet returned.

This lull gave Israel the much-sought-after opportunity to improve its defensive posture along the Suez Canal and to create the fortifications necessary to withstand the massive artillery barrages to which the Israeli forces had been subjected. Intensive discussions took place in the Israeli General Staff on the type of fortification system that should be built along the Canal. Lieutenant-General Chaim Bar-Lev, the Chief of Staff, entrusted Major-General Avraham ('Bren') Adan with the task of heading an inter-service team to bring to the General Staff a proposal for the creation of a defensive system in Sinai. Before this team went down to Sinai, Major-General Yeshayahu Gavish, GOC Southern Command and the commander of the victorious Israeli forces in the Sinai in the Six Day War, weighed the problems posed by the defence of the peninsula. Having regard to the losses incurred as a result of the Egyptian shelling, it was obvious to him that the troops holding the line must be given adequate cover in strongpoints; the main problem facing him, however, was whether to keep his forces on the water line or to maintain them in depth away from it. While holding the water line in strength created a series of fixed objectives under constant observation of the Egyptians, at the same time it gave the Israeli forces the advantage of observation and an ability to deal immediately with any crossing attempt by the Egyptians. Gavish came to the conclusion that it would be advisable to hold positions on the water front, particularly at all points that were probable crossing areas, since he felt there would be no problem for the Egyptians to cross along the entire length of the Canal, and the Israelis must be prepared to answer this possibility.

Adan set about planning the defence of the line along the Suez Canal. He drew up the original plans for the fortifications, which were to be built in such a way as to give a maximum degree of observation (good visual observation by day and electronic observation by night) while exposing a minimum number of troops to enemy artillery fire. He planned individual fortifications for fifteen troops, at a distance of seven miles from each other, with mobile armour patrolling between them and with artillery and armour deployed to the rear ready to move forward and destroy any attempt to cross. These fortifications were conceived as a warning outpost system. They were not seen as a line of defence, hence the limitation to fifteen troops, the distance between them and their limited defensive facilities.

Gavish accepted Adan's plan, with the proviso that at the northern end of the Canal all possible crossing points be covered by groups of fortifications. The Israeli defence plan based on this warning system along the Canal was brought to the General Staff for approval, and Major-General Ariel Sharon, Director of Training in the General Staff, and Major-General Israel Tal, attached to the Ministry of Defence, opposed it. They proposed to deploy only with armour at a certain distance from the Canal, and to control it by mobile armoured activity. Gavish later explained publicly his attitude to this problem. He saw the line acting in time of war as a series of observation posts and fortifications along all possible axes of advance, which would delay the enemy before he came on a series of defensive infantry brigade localities with their concentrated force of armour along the line of the passes, from the Mitla Pass in the south to Baluza in the north. During a war of attrition and in periods of cease-fire, the fortifications would serve as observation posts (affording protection from artillery fire during the former), as well as centres for electronic warning and control, and as bases for armoured patrols. As part of the defences along the Canal, Gavish initiated a system of oil installations, which could be activated from inside the fortifications to set the Canal alight.* It was always Gavish's opinion that, if the Canal was to be considered a physical barrier, there was no option but to establish a physical presence along it. In his view, one of the main dangers that Israel would have to face would be a sudden Egyptian move to gain a foothold, however narrow, along the east bank, followed by an attempt to achieve an immediate cease-fire by international agreement. Furthermore, since the Israeli concept invariably called for mounting a counter-offensive into the enemy's territory, it was important for them to be sited in force along the Canal itself, rather than to be in a position that would require fighting before they reached it.

In the ensuing debate there was no suggestion of leaving the Canal, but there was an argument as to the mode of deployment, with General Sharon supporting the system of mobile defence along the Canal. General Bar-Lev decided in favour of the fortifications, and the team headed by Adan proceeded to supervise the construction of the line, which was finished on 15 March 1969.

Thus the so-called 'Bar-Lev Line' came into being. The creation of this line was the largest engineering operation ever undertaken in Israel. Every effort was made to take advantage of the lull that the Israeli raids in depth in Egypt had forced on the Egyptians. Already, before the completion of this line (which included fortifications built to accommodate battle teams of all arms, enabling them to withstand the heaviest possible artillery barrages and at the same time to control the eastern bank of the Canal), the Egyptians began to appreciate its significance. Accordingly, they began to interfere with the work on the Israeli side by sniping, patrolling, mining and other hostile activities. In March 1969, it became obvious that the Egyptians were preparing to renew the battle along the Canal and, in mid-March, the artillery barrages increased in frequency. Nasser announced with a fanfare the opening of the 'liberation' phase of the 'War of Attrition'. It was to continue almost without let-up for a year and a half until the cease-fire in August 1970.

Jordan and the PLO

It is impossible to evaluate the developments along the Suez Canal and the Bar-Lev Line accurately without relating to this situation the developments on Israel's other borders, and in particular the border with Jordan. Indeed, the number of hostile actions against Israel instigated by the

* See page 232.

Jordanian Army, the Iraqi Army (which was stationed in Jordan), and units of the PLO, reached hundreds. Of all the hostile actions directed against Israel during 1968–69, approximately half initiated in the Jordan valley and in the valley of Beit Shean, in Jordan. Thus, a very considerable proportion of Israel's defensive effort at the time was being invested in activities along this border. However, the comparative intensity of the military activity along the border with Jordan compared with the comparative lull along the Suez Canal, created a considerable amount of strain within the inter-Arab relationship.

Thus, for several months, the Israelis were fortifying their positions along the Suez Canal, dismantling the railway lines leading across the Sinai to Kantara and using the rails to fortify the bunkers along the Suez Canal, moving millions of tons of earth in order to create a line that would defend Israeli soldiers and reduce losses to a minimum. Simultaneously, the Jordanian front was flaring up from time to time, and Israeli forces were being engaged all along it. There was a definite pressure on the part of the other Arab countries on Egypt, which, despite the warlike statements being uttered by its leaders about the 'War of Attrition', was allowing the Israelis to fortify themselves along the Suez Canal with impunity and in comparative quiet.

Along the Jordanian border, military activities had been stepped up by the PLO. Immediately after the conclusion of the Six Day War, they estimated that an ideal situation had been created for them. They could now operate from within a population of some three-quarters of a million Arabs in the West Bank who would serve as their base; furthermore, as a result of their activities, they estimated that they would be in a position to incite the civilian population in the West Bank to rise against the Israeli occupation and to engage in hostile activities, and possibly break out ultimately in revolt. However, the effectiveness of the Israeli military government (which was a very benign one) was emphasized by the fact that the Arabs were allowed to rule themselves and live in peace and security provided that they did not in any way affect Israeli security adversely by their actions. This policy, coupled with a very efficient security control and an effective system of patrolling by the Israel Defence Forces in the uninhabited deserts and open spaces of the Jordan valley, created a situation whereby the position of the PLO in the area became untenable. One by one, their possible bases of operation in the West Bank were eliminated. So the PLO had no alternative but to abandon the area of the West Bank, where they could not hope to set up a base, and to move to the East Bank of the Jordan. There they set up their bases, mounted operations from them across the river and returned after the conclusion of the operations.

These operations, coupled with recurring and increased artillery attacks against Israeli patrols in the Jordan valley and against Israeli villages and villagers working in the fields in the upper Jordan valley and the valley of Beit Shean, created a serious military problem for Israel. After a school bus had been blown up in March 1968, with children dead and wounded, the Israel Defence Forces decided to mount an operation against the main base that the PLO had created in the area of Karameh, to the east of the River Jordan, and also in the area south of the Dead Sea. The village of Karameh had been almost completely evacuated of its civilian population, and was populated now by the various units of the constituent terrorist organizations of the PLO. In addition, many of the headquarters were

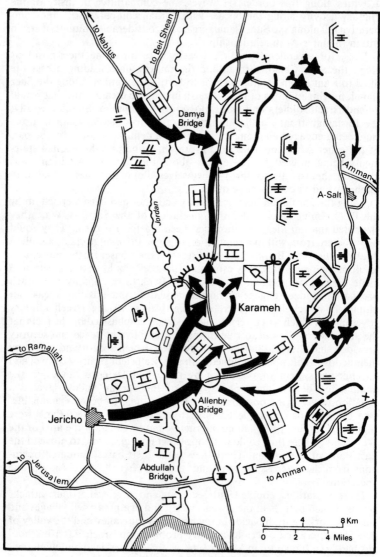

The Karameh Operation, 21 March 1968

concentrated in this area. On 21 March, the Israel Defence Forces struck at Karameh. The first Israeli forces to cross the river advanced rapidly to the east: their task was to block any advance or reaction on the part of the Jordanian Army. All day long, very heavy armoured battles were conducted between the Israeli forces and the Jordanian armour. The task of capturing Karameh was entrusted to a paratroop force moving on half-tracks supported by tanks. An additional paratroop force was landed by helicopter to block the retreat routes of the PLO units from Karameh. By 08.00 hours, the Israeli forces had taken control of the township, and it was discovered to be an even larger PLO base than had previously been imagined. Meanwhile, the Jordanian forces had withdrawn into the hills and were conducting a battle against the Israeli armoured units, utilizing the benefit of the high ground on which they were sited. From midday, the Israeli forces withdrew, and completed their withdrawal from the East Bank by 21.00 hours that evening. The battle had been a bitterly fought one, in which a number of tactical errors had been made by the Israeli Command; despite this, however, the purpose of the mission had been achieved.

Parallel to this operation, an Israeli action took place to the south of the Dead Sea against the Jordanian village of Safi and nearby positions. During this day of operations on 21 March, the Jordanian Army lost 40 killed and the PLO some 200 killed, while some 150 suspected members of the PLO were brought to Israel for interrogation. The Israeli losses came to 28 killed and 69 wounded, in addition to the loss of four tanks and two armoured cars and an aircraft that was shot down, although its pilot succeeded in parachuting to safety.

The operation in Karameh exposed the vulnerability of the PLO units deployed along the River Jordan, and so they moved their concentrations up into the mountains. This imposed additional strains on them and made their operations into the West Bank even more involved and difficult than they had been hitherto. At this point, the Israeli Air Force was sent into action to bomb their concentrations in the area of Es Salt, and this obliged them to move their units farther to the east and higher up into the mountains, to spread out in a larger number of bases and to take refuge

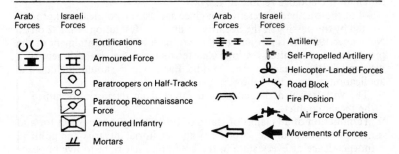

Arab Forces	Israeli Forces		Arab Forces	Israeli Forces	
ʊ ʊ		Fortifications	⚏ ⚏	⚌	Artillery
▤	⊥⊥	Armoured Force	╞	╞	Self-Propelled Artillery
	◇	Paratroopers on Half-Tracks		⚓	Helicopter-Landed Forces
	▱	Paratroop Reconnaissance Force	⋏⋏⋏⋏	⋏⋏⋏⋏	Road Block
	⊠	Armoured Infantry	⌒⌒	⌒	Fire Position
	⫫	Mortars			Air Force Operations
			⇦	⬅	Movements of Forces

from the Israeli attacks by attempting to concentrate within areas of Jordanian civilian population. This ultimately gave rise to very considerable amount of friction between the terrorists and the Jordanians, and was to have its effect on the course of events that was to lead to an explosion between the PLO units in Jordan and the Jordanian armed forces.

The successful activities of the Israel Defence Forces in preventing the penetration of terrorist units bent on sabotage across the Jordan, and also the offensive operations of the Israeli forces against such concentrations of the PLO as could be identified had their effect, and the scope of operations by the PLO units across the river was considerably reduced. But the shelling and harassment by means of artillery and Katyusha rocket fire continued. Many of these events flared up into major exchanges, with the Israeli artillery engaging centres of population as far away as the town of Irbid in northern Jordan. Towards the end of 1968, in the month of December, long-range artillery of the Iraqi Expeditionary Force also took a hand in shelling centres of civilian population in Israel. Artillery duels ensued, and the Israeli Air Force finally attacked the Iraqi force, inflicting on it eight dead, and fourteen wounded and considerable damage to equipment and vehicles.

The scope of these hostile actions against Israel along the various borders can be gauged from the fact that, between September 1968 and March 1969, there were some 534 such incidents; of them, 189 emanated from Jordan and 123 from the Gaza Strip. Only 29 originated in the West Bank, and 47 along the Suez Canal.

At the same time, however, the PLO mounted terrorist activities against Israeli objectives abroad, beginning with the hijacking of an El Al airliner to Algeria in July 1968. Thus began a comparatively new form of international terror limited, as time went on, not only to Israeli targets, and one that was soon adopted by terrorist organizations throughout the world. It is a development that continues to pose a very serious threat to society throughout the free world. The PLO was to act as a central training, supply and operational force for many of the terrorist organizations that were to plague the free world in the years to come. These terrorist activities were furthermore to be financed above all by Colonel Moamar al Gaddafi's régime in Libya.

All of these activities were taking place against the political background created by the passing in the Security Council of Resolution No. 242 on 22 November 1967. This resolution affirmed, inter alia, that fulfilment of the principles of the United Nations Charter required the establishment of a just and lasting peace in the Middle East, which should include the application of both the following principles:

'1. The withdrawal of Israel's armed forces from territories occupied in the recent conflict.

'2. Termination of all claims or states of belligerency, and respect for and acknowledgment of the sovereignty and territorial integrity and political independence of every state in the area and their right to live in peace within secure and recognized boundaries free from threats or acts of force.'

The resolution instructed the Secretary-General of the United Nations to appoint a special representative to implement the provisions of the resolution; the appointee was a Swedish diplomat, Gunnar Jarring, who for the next couple of years began to shuttle between the various capitals in the Middle East attempting to implement the resolution. His efforts were in vain, but the resolution itself, which was accepted both by Egypt and Jordan on the Arab side, and by Israel, was to provide ultimately the basis for the achievement of the first peace treaty in the Middle East in 1979.

The 'liberation' phase

The relative quiet that had reigned along the Suez Canal since October 1968 was broken in March 1969. Several Egyptian aircraft penetrated Israeli air space on reconnaissance, and one of them was shot down. A concentrated artillery exchange developed and spread along the Canal, on the second day of which the Egyptian Chief of Staff, General Abd al Muneim Riadh, and several of his staff officers were killed while in a forward position in Ismailia supervising the new offensive. Once again, casualties were suffered by both sides, and Egyptian towns, ships in the Gulf of Suez and installations sustained further considerable damage. After a short lull for a few weeks, the Egyptians renewed the War of Attrition on 10 April 1969; thereafter, it continued without respite for a period of sixteen months.

At this point, President Nasser declared that Egypt no longer recognized or adhered to the cease-fire that had been in existence since 1967. Indeed, on 1 May in his annual May Day speech, Nasser declared that 60 per cent of the Bar-Lev Line had been destroyed by Egyptian fire and that the Egyptian Army had now moved from the phase of 'active defence' to the 'liberation' phase. The War of Attrition was now on with a vengeance.

The Egyptian policy was based on evaluations of what they considered to be certain basic vulnerabilities in the Israeli national character and military approach. Basing themselves on the assumption that the Israeli armed forces have always shown their true strength in a war of movement in which speed and manoeuvrability are of the essence, the Egyptians came to the conclusion that the Israel Defence Forces would be at a disadvantage in a static war of attrition, in which manoeuvrability was of little value and in which Egypt possessed a marked superiority over Israel in the main weapon for such a type of war, artillery. The Egyptians were also aware of the extreme sensitivity of the Israeli population to loss of manpower. They realized that, by creating a constant drain on Israeli manpower by means of attrition, they would be striking at what they considered to be the Israeli Achilles' heel. Accordingly, their purpose was to wear out the Israel Defence Forces by constant attack and thus to bring about a reduction of morale both in the Israeli armed forces and in the civilian hinterland; to destroy as much of Israel's war equipment as possible; and to impose as heavy an economic burden as possible on Israel. This situation, they believed, would ultimately soften up the Israel force to such a degree that sooner or later situations would be created in which it would be possible for chosen Egyptian forces to cross the Canal and seize a bridgehead on the eastern bank. Furthermore, there was a consideration that the continuous conflagration along the Canal would keep the issue alive before the United Nations and thus intensify political pressure on Israel.

To meet this military policy, Israel enunciated its own policy, which was best expressed by the vast expenditure invested in the Bar-Lev Line along the Suez Canal, with its complex system of fortresses, patrol roads, and earth walls, approach roads, underground control centres and tank and artillery positions all sited for mutual support. The first principle of Israel's defence was to ensure complete control of the water line along the Canal and to be in a position to beat back any Egyptian attempt to cross the Canal or to establish a bridgehead. The second purpose of such a system of defence along the Canal was to keep to an absolute minimum the number of casualties Israel would have to suffer. For this purpose, the Israeli fortresses were constructed to withstand the heaviest possible Egyptian barrage. Furthermore, the new deployment would be such as to enable Israel to wage its 'counter-War of Attrition' against the Egyptians and force them to return to an acceptance of the cease-fire. But, as the Egyptians had foreseen, this new policy required the Israeli forces to adapt themselves to the unaccustomed strategy of static defence, in place of the tactics based on speed and manoeuvrability on which they had as a matter of principle based themselves hitherto. So the construction of the Canal line continued. It included the construction of an earth wall designed to prevent Egyptian observation of Israeli activities and preparations along the Canal. The Egyptians harassed the Israeli engineering forces attempting to complete the wall, obliging the Israelis at a certain point to roll a succession of railway wagons into position and fill them with earth as a basis for the wall. Both sides at this stage adopted a more active policy, each sending patrols across to the enemy side. One attempt by Egyptian commandos to capture an Israeli fortress was foiled.

The artillery exchange continued along the Canal, with both sides suffering losses. Because of the very considerable strength of the Israeli fortresses along the Canal, the Egyptian artillery failed to penetrate or destroy any of them, however. Accordingly, the Egyptians adopted a policy of steady harassment of all signs of life and movement along the Canal with the purpose of making things as difficult as possible for the Israeli forces and inflicting as many casualties as possible. So Israel returned to the strategy of indirect approach, carrying out daring commando raids deep inside Egyptian territory. They cut the high-tension lines between Aswan and Cairo, and attacked the dam at Najh Hamadi, a bridge near Idfu and Egyptian coastal bases at Ras Adabiah on the western shore of the Gulf of Suez. In one such raid, 29 Egyptian soldiers were killed.

The Egyptians, for their part, conducted a very active strategy of offensive operations, which were carried out with increasing frequency, on the Israeli-held east bank of the Canal. Mines were laid and units crossed to ambush Israeli patrols and traffic moving along the north-south road

Above left: Lieutenant-General Chaim Bar-Lev, Chief of Staff of the IDF during the War of Attrition, after whom the Israeli fortifications along the Suez Canal—the Bar-Lev Line—were named. (Israel Sun)

Above right: Major-General Ezer Weizman, commander of the Israeli Air Force and Deputy Chief of Staff of the IDF during the War of Attrition.

Right: Major-General Abd al Muneim Riadh, Chief of Staff of the Egyptian Army, was killed during an artillery duel across the Suez Canal in March 1969. (AP)

Top left: An Israeli patrol drives northwards along the Suez Canal; the Canal is on the left of the dirt-track. (GPO) **Below left:** Some of the many merchant ships marooned since the Canal's closure during the previous year, in 1967. (Zahal-Bamahane) **Above:** Dense smoke rising from the oil refineries in the town of Suez after an assault by Israeli artillery in 1968. (Jerusalem Post) **Below:** Israeli forces carried out a major reprisal raid in March 1968 against a terrorist base in the town of Karameh, east of the Jordan. Casualties on both sides were heavy. (Zahal-Bamahane)

Above: An Israeli Sa'ar-II class guided-missile patrol boat. Each boxlike canister contains one Gabriel antiship missile. These boats were known as 'Cherbourg vessels', because the Israelis managed to spirit them out of Cherbourg harbour while they were under embargo. (Israeli Navy)

Right: Deep inside one of the bunkers along the Bar-Lev Line, the fortifications on the Israeli side of the Canal. (Zahal-Bamahane)

parallel to the Canal. In July, one of the many Egyptian attempts succeeded in penetrating an Israeli tank laager south of Port Tewfik, inflicting eleven casualties. It was during this phase, on 24 May 1969, that an Egyptian MiG-21 was shot down while flying at a height of 22,000 feet by an Israeli-operated Hawk ground-to-air missile. This was the first time

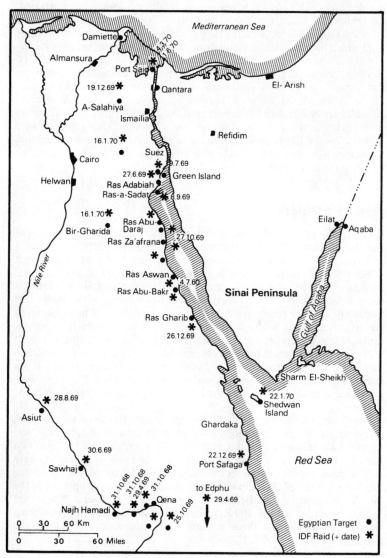

IDF Raids in Egyptian Territory

in the Middle East conflict that a Hawk missile had been used to bring down an enemy aircraft; first deployed in the United States air defence system in 1959, the Hawk missile had been in Israeli service since 1964.

By July 1969 it became evident to the Israeli commanders that their counter-plan was not having the desired effect, and so a new approach was decided upon. This envisaged massive air retaliation coupled with stepped-up raids of a scope not mounted hitherto. On 19 July, Israeli forces attacked Green Island, an artificial island fortress in the northern Gulf of Suez which had been built originally to protect the approaches to the Suez. It was built as a fortress, heavily fortified, manned by approximately 200 Egyptian troops and, on the face of it, appeared impregnable. Nevertheless, Israeli commandos succeeded in landing on the island and, in an action characterized by great bravery — one of the most daring and difficult ever undertaken in the history of the Israel Defence Forces, replete with daring actions — the fortress was captured. Heavy losses were inflicted on the Egyptian defenders, at a cost of 16 casualties killed and wounded to the Israelis; then the attacking force blew up the fort and its installations and withdrew.

'Flying artillery'

From a military point of view, the most significant change in Israeli policy was the decision to throw the Israeli Air Force into the battle and utilize it as 'flying artillery' rather than to increase the strength of ground artillery.* This policy was to prove later to have been a grave error. Preconceived concepts that placed excessive emphasis on armour and air as against a more balanced force came to expression at this point, with results that were to prove very costly in the 1973 Yom Kippur War. While this policy was to prove to have been a major error in Israeli calculations from a long-range, strategic point of view, from a short-range tactical point of view it proved to be an unmitigated success. But, in the longer term, it created an imbalance in the Israel Defence Forces, with insufficient emphasis on supporting arms such as artillery and armoured infantry. The Egyptians' preponderance in artillery continued to be a major factor in the balance of power.

Israeli air operations inevitably brought on an Egyptian air reaction, and dogfights developed along the Canal. In the course of July 1969, five Egyptian aircraft were shot down: two MiG-21s, one Sukhoi Su-7 and two MiG-17s (the latter pair by anti-aircraft fire). The main Israeli targets were the Egyptian artillery emplacements and the SAM-2 surface-to-air missile bases that protected them. In less than two months after the opening of the Israeli air offensive, the Israeli Air Force completed over 1,000 sorties against Egypt, as against 100 Egyptian sorties in the same period, during which the Israelis lost three aircraft as against a loss of 21 by the Egyptians.

* The main aircraft used by the Israelis in this rôle was the McDonnell Douglas A4 Skyhawk.

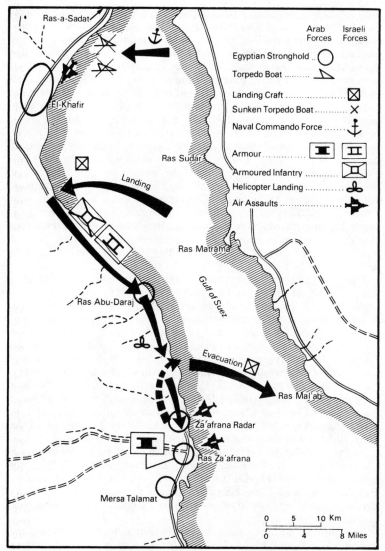

**Armoured Raid on the Western Shore of the
Gulf of Suez, 9 September 1969**

Meanwhile, the war raged along the Canal. Sniping, patrols, ambushes and intermittent shelling were all taking their toll and casualties on both sides rose. Between 8 and 11 September 1969, the Israelis mounted an operation that once again was unusual in its scope and nature. It opened with Israeli frogmen sinking two Egyptian torpedo-boats at anchor at Ras-a-Sadat on the Gulf of Suez. Next day, an Israeli armoured battalion task force sailed across the Gulf of Suez in tank landing craft bound for the Egyptian coast on what was to prove to be one of the most imaginative operations undertaken to date by the Israel Defence Forces — an armoured raid in depth into Egypt. Landing at dawn on 9 September 1969 at A-Dir on the western shore of the Gulf of Suez, the armoured task force took the Egyptians by complete surprise. Many of the Egyptian units encountering this armoured force did not react because the last troop movements they ever expected to meet were Israeli forces on their side of the Gulf. Control and co-ordination of Egyptian forces along the Gulf proved to be inadequate, a fact that was exploited to the full by the Israeli raiders. By early morning, the force had reached its main objective, a military camp known as Ras Abu-Daraj. In the course of the assault, which was backed up by Israeli air attacks, the camp installations were destroyed, including the main objective of the raid, the radar tower in the camp. Having cleared Ras Abu-Daraj, the Israeli force continued south to Ras Za'afrana, where more radar installations were destroyed. At that point, the Israeli force embarked on landing craft and returned safely to its base in the Sinai.

This raid came as a great shock to the Egyptians, emphasizing once again the vulnerability of the Egyptian defence system and the fact that Israel did not feel bound to fight along fixed lines. For over ten hours, the Israeli armoured force had operated at will in Egyptian territory, traversing some 30 miles in the process, destroying twelve Egyptian outposts and warning stations and inflicting over 100 casualties on the Egyptian forces. It proved to have been one of the more daringly conceived Israeli operations, well planned, with a high degree of inter-arm co-operation. By the time the Egyptians fully appreciated what was happening, the triumphant Israeli force was on its way back to the Sinai. Nasser himself suffered a heart attack after this operation, and there were major changes in the Egyptian Command, including the dismissal of the Chief of Staff and the commander of the Navy.

As the War of Attrition continued, the number of air battles increased. On 11 September, the Egyptians lost eleven aircraft (seven MiG-21s, three Sukhoi Su-7s and one MiG-17) for the loss of one Israeli aircraft. Still the Egyptians mounted their commando attacks across the Canal, artillery duels continued, and the Israelis conducted a number of long-range raids into upper Egypt.

The most spectacular operation in this period was undoubtedly the assault on the radar station at Ras-Arab for the purpose, not of destroying the position, but of capturing and removing the equipment, the total weight of which was seven tons. The acquisition of this latest P12 type of Russian radar would prove to be invaluable for the Israelis and for the Western powers in electronic countermeasure warfare. The Israeli force crossed the Gulf of Suez to Egypt, and reached the area of the radar station in CH-53 helicopters. The Air Force bombed targets in the vicinity to divert attention, while the raiding party made its way to the radar station. The attacking force overcame the Egyptian garrison, killing some and capturing others. Then, in a race against time, the raiding party managed to extricate the caravans containing the radar equipment, which had been partially buried in the ground; the principal trailer was harnessed by special steel hawsers to a helicopter, and the second trailer was lifted by a second helicopter. Both helicopters succeeded with great difficulty in transporting the very heavy equipment to the eastern shores of the Gulf of Suez. For the first time, the military establishment of Israel (and of many Western countries) were afforded an intimate view of a Russian P12 radar installation.

The opening days of 1970 afforded evidence of the fact that the Israeli strategy of counter-attrition was beginning to have its effect upon the Egyptians. The daring Israeli raids had to a degree knocked the Egyptian Command off balance, and the immediate effect of the massive use of Israeli air power proved to be very telling indeed. The Egyptians activated their surface-to-air missile system based on the Soviet SAM-2 type missile, but, three times in the course of the period between the opening of the offensive in July 1969 and January 1970, the Israeli Air Force succeeded in destroying a considerable part of the Egyptian air defence system. Israeli aircraft were beginning to range far and wide inside Egypt and to engage Egyptian targets in depth. The effect on the Egyptian public was marked, and the internal effect on Nasser's régime became a matter of concern for him. In the Kremlin and elsewhere in the Soviet empire, they watched with growing concern as Western-type equipment flown by Israeli pilots operated with comparative impunity against a system of air defence similar to that protecting the Communist bloc against the West. The effects of the blows that Israeli forces inflicted on the Soviet-supplied Egyptian defence system was being noted by the military establishments throughout the Soviet bloc. The Israelis pounded the Canal positions. In the period under review, 48 Egyptian aircraft were lost as against five Israeli aircraft. The Israelis had seized the initiative. And, as the Israeli offensive persisted, a note of growing desperation could be detected in Egyptian public reaction − even more in Egyptian reports to the Soviet Union.

The Israeli counterattack against the War of Attrition waged by the Egyptians and the other Arab countries in violation of the cease-fire agreement was proving to be a considerable success in its first phase, namely from July to September 1969. During this period, Israel achieved complete superiority in the air as a result of a number of decisive air battles. This was followed by the second phase, which entailed the destruction of Egyptian anti-aircraft missile and radar defences in order to give Israel a comparatively free hand over Egyptian air space. The third phase was basically a psychological phase, that of bringing home the facts of the situation to the average Egyptian citizen by means of attacks on military installations in the neighbourhood of Cairo and other cities and, what was perhaps of greater importance, to the second line of Egyptian forces including reserve formations and units not directly affected by the fighting along the Suez Canal. This phase began on 7 January 1970.

The developments in the fighting along the Suez Canal, where the Israeli Air Force now had a comparatively free hand over Egyptian air space, the Egyptian anti-aircraft system lay to a considerable degree in ruins and Israel was gradually gaining the upper hand in the War of Attrition, were hidden from the Egyptian public by a controlled press and media. The purpose of the new Israeli offensive was to bring home to the Egyptian public the true facts and thus give rise to pressures from below in favour of reinstating the cease-fire agreement. The Israeli attacks were mounted against military targets deep in Egypt, including supply and ammunition depots, headquarters, military training centres, all within a radius of 25 miles of Cairo. Again and again these targets were attacked, and the citizens in Egypt's capital city were alerted frequently by air-raid warnings. The Egyptian public gradually realized that the Israeli Air Force was operating freely in the skies of Egypt.

Meanwhile, as Israeli attacks were being mounted in depth against Egypt, the battle along the Canal and the Gulf of Suez was being waged sporadically. On 22 January, units of the Israel Defence Forces attacked and occupied the island of Shadwan, situated some 20 miles from Sharm El-Sheikh in the straits linking the Gulf of Suez with the Red Sea. In the course of the battle, 30 Egyptian soldiers were killed and many others taken prisoner, while two Egyptian torpedo-boats of the P183 type were sunk. After occupying the island for 30 hours, the Israeli force withdrew, bearing with it all the military equipment including the radar installation on the island, which they had dismantled, and 62 prisoners. Israeli casualties were three dead and six wounded. The cumulative effect of such attacks against Egypt on all sectors was having its effect and, indeed, the Israeli forces along the Canal suffered the lowest number of casualties in January 1970 in any given month since the opening of the War of Attrition: six killed. A growing tone of concern could now be detected in Egyptian public statements. Nasser appealed to the Soviet Union.

Soviets and SAMs

In December 1969, the Soviet Chief of Anti-Aircraft Forces had come to inspect the somewhat embarrassing situation that had been created by the failure of Soviet-supplied weapons to withstand the Israeli air attacks. Nasser made a secret visit to Moscow in January 1970, emphasizing the seriousness of the situation that had developed and appealing for additional Soviet aid. During this visit, he posed the military dilemma facing the Egyptians as well as the problems that might face his régime if the Israeli attacks were to persevere. Soviet response was immediate and unhesitant. Indeed, the Soviets seized on Nasser's desperate situation to develop their own plans for additional penetration in the area. By mid-February, some 1,500 Soviet personnel had arrived with consignments of the latest anti-aircraft system, including the new SAM-3 missiles. These missiles, with their increased mobility and effectiveness, were manned by Soviet and not Egyptian troops and were sited both in the Canal zone and in depth in Egypt. The Soviet forces in Egypt rose to some 15,000 troops, which were engaged in air defence, manned missile and air installations, and assumed responsibility for the protection of Egyptian strategic depth, initially by missiles and later with Russian-piloted aircraft. Thus was created a situation whereby Israeli penetration of Egyptian air space could spell a clash with Soviet forces. The SAM-3 missile was designed especially for use against low-flying aircraft; it could be mounted on a mobile platform or sited in heavily-protected underground bunkers. Because it was complementary to the longer range SAM-2 missile it effectively closed many of the 'holes' in the Egyptian defence system and made the task of the Israeli Air Force that much more difficult.

During this period in early 1970, the battles, patrolling activities by both sides, mining and artillery attrition were intensified along all the sectors. During February, in Israel's southern port of Eilat, Egyptian frogmen operating from Aqaba in Jordan succeeded in sinking an Israeli Navy auxiliary vessel and damaging a landing craft; an Egyptian patrol in depth succeeded in taking prisoner two Israeli canteen employees; and an Israeli force crossed the Canal at Al-Kaf, south of Port Said, attacking artillery batteries and bunkers. Early in the month, an Israeli mixed patrol of armour and infantry, moving along the eastern bank of the Canal, was ambushed by an Egyptian patrol that had taken up positions on the Israeli side of the Canal. In the ensuing action, the commander of the Israeli force and four of his troops were killed, and a short battle ensued. Some days later, an Israeli patrol engaged an Egyptian reconnaissance unit that had penetrated as far as the Mitla Pass: all the Egyptians were either captured or killed. At the same time, the Egyptian Air Force mounted its 'hit and run' attacks across the Canal and, in one of these attacks, caused eleven Israeli casualties. The increased air activity over the area of the Canal led to many dogfights during the month of February, in the course of which eight Egyptian and two Israeli aircraft were shot down. The month of March saw the fighting grow in intensity, as in air battles the Egyptians lost twelve aircraft.

Meanwhile, the process of 'Sovietization' was growing, as additional Soviet forces poured into Egypt and the new anti-aircraft system became more operative and effective. These developments were a natural corollary to the traditional Soviet policy that had led to the Six Day War and had militated against any form of compromise on the part of the Arabs in negotiating with Israel. The Soviet Union was achieving one of its strategic aims — to establish Soviet forces in the Mediterranean and along the vital strategic waterway of the Suez Canal, thus enabling them to control the main link between the Mediterranean and the Indian Ocean. The developments in Egypt created a convenient pattern within which the Soviet strategic aim could be realized, particularly within the context of the confrontation with China, which gave the Indian Ocean additional importance within the overall strategic pattern.

In an attempt to exert pressure on the Egyptians and induce them to agree to a cease-fire, Moshe Dayan, Israel's Minister of Defence, proposed to the Ministerial Defence Committee that Israel carry out air attacks on army bases deep inside Egypt. According to Dayan, the attacks during the months of January, February and March 1970 had caused Egyptian morale to collapse and confronted Nasser with a dilemma: on the one hand he realized that his army was in no position to prevent the Israeli operations and, at the same time, he was not prepared to declare a cease-fire and enter into peace negotiations with Israel. In his memoirs,* Dayan points out that Nasser then flew to Moscow and asked the Russians to send him Soviet troops. Thus he confirms that it was the Israeli bombing in depth of Egypt that brought about the massive entry of Soviet troops into Egypt.

From a short term point of view, the Israeli deep penetration bombing had contained a certain logic; but, from a long term point of view, it would appear to have been a major error. Politically, it failed to achieve its objectives, for Nasser's authority was in no way damaged. Although Egyptian installations were at times in ruins, the Egyptians persevered with attacks along the Canal. Whether or not the natural course of events would have led to increased Sovietization in Egypt, it is difficult to say, but there is no doubt that the Israeli decision to bomb Egypt in depth constituted a major turning-point in the Middle East, and created a situation that encouraged President Nasser to open up Egypt, not only to Soviet advisers, but also to Soviet combat units. In April 1970, Soviet-piloted MiG-21s began to fly operationally in defence of central Egypt to protect these areas from Israeli air attacks. The voices of Russian pilots became commonplace on the ether in the Middle East. And, indeed, to avoid the danger of a clash with aircraft of the Soviet Air Force, Israeli air attacks in depth over Egypt ceased in April 1970. The renewed sense of security that the increased Soviet presence instilled in their hard-pressed ally led to an intensification of their air activity over the Sinai. As the Egyptians began to launch a series of hit-and-run raids against Israeli targets, air battles developed over the Sinai. In one of the first encounters, three Egyptian Sukhoi Su-7s raiding Israeli targets were shot down.

The renewed Egyptian offensive, mounted with the knowledge of an immediate Soviet air back-up over Egyptian air space, created a swing of the pendulum in the battle: in the three months of March, April and May 1970, 64 Israeli troops were killed and 149 wounded, while Egyptian ambushes on the Israeli bank of the Canal cost Israel eighteen dead, six wounded and six prisoners. As the fighting rose in intensity, the Israeli Air Force, adapting itself to the new situation created by this new Soviet deployment in Egypt by adopting new tactics to deal with the ground-to-air missile system, launched its most intensive bombing attacks to date over a period of eleven days, beginning on 30 May, against the Egyptian positions along the Canal. Within a period of one week, more than 4,000 bombs were dropped on Egyptian positions and, on the seventh day of successive bombing on the northern sector, the Israeli Air Force attacked for a continuous period of some 14½ hours. On 12 June, Israeli ground forces crossed the Canal and seized an area along a mile-and-a-half front

* Moshe Dayan, *The Story of My Life*, p. 449, 1976.

south of Port Said, destroying the Egyptian positions in the area before withdrawing.

The struggle along the Suez Canal became one of major importance for the Soviet Union, and the leadership closely followed every phase of the battle, for the entire system of air defence upon which the Soviet Union, and indeed the Soviet empire, relied for its defence was now being put to the test in Egypt by a small Israeli Air Force equipped with Western equipment. Indeed, the experience being gained in these battles was proving to be invaluable both for the Russians and for the Western powers — in particular, for the Americans, who were closely monitoring the lessons being learned from the battles in the skies of Egypt and over the Canal. Nasser's confidant, Mohammed Hassanein Heikal, Editor of *Al Ahram*, described vividly a meeting in the Kremlin in which there was an argument between Leonid Brezhnev and Nasser as to how many Israeli aircraft had been shot down as a result of the new Soviet tactics the day before. There was a disagreement, whereupon Brezhnev brusquely ordered Marshal Grechko, the Soviet Defence Minister, to produce the evidence. He for his part immediately produced reports setting out in great detail the story of the shooting down of Israeli aircraft the day before. The issue had become important enough for it to be a central one at the centre of power of the Soviet empire.

As the Israeli attacks intensified, the Soviets decided upon a new strategy of air defence. They planned a completely new defensive system to deal with the Israeli attacks. At the end of June, a major redeployment of Soviet-Egyptian air defences of the air space over the Suez Canal and in its vicinity was completed. The effect was immediate: on 30 June, two Israeli aircraft were shot down during an attack on the Canal area; one of the pilots was rescued by helicopter from Egyptian territory, and three aircrew members were taken prisoner. On 5 July an additional plane was shot down with the crew being taken prisoner. Hitherto, the Egyptian air defence had been spread out and deployed all along the 100-mile length of the Suez Canal. Now, the Russians had created a box some 20 miles deep and 45 miles long covering the central and southern sectors. Missiles were sited in 'packs' that gave mutual covering fire, and the entire system was reinforced by heavy concentrations of conventional anti-aircraft weapons. A solution was found to the vulnerability of the SAM-2 missile, sited as they had been in fixed positions in easily-discernible concrete emplacements: hastily created earth positions were scraped out by earth moving machinery, and the missiles themselves were moved into the chosen launching site under cover of darkness as close as possible to the estimated launching time. Now, many missiles could be fired at single targets, unlike the situation that had obtained hitherto in Egypt and in Vietnam, where only one or two missiles were launched against single aircraft. Moreover, the SAM-2 Guideline missile was of an improved range and was far more accurate than its predecessor. Each SAM-2 battery consisted of six launchers and was linked to a radar system for advance warning and interception. Several dozen four-barrelled anti-aircraft guns of the 23mm ZSU type were deployed with the batteries, and these proved to be very effective. (Indeed, of the Israeli aircraft shot down that week by anti-aircraft fire, three were shot down by these guns, rather than by SAM-2 missiles.) While the SAM-2 was deployed against medium-altitude attacks (with an improved capability of up to 60,000 feet) the SAM-3 GOA missile was a low- to medium-altitude weapon, sited in batteries consisting of eight missiles on four twin launchers, which could be mobile or fixed, with a slant range of 18 miles and with two types of radar being used.

Once the skies of Cairo became the responsibility of Soviet-piloted MiG-21s, the Egyptians could concentrate a greater number of anti-aircraft batteries along the Canal. But, despite the losses now being incurred, the Israeli Air Force continued to attack this new system, destroying five SAM batteries early in July.

The new anti-aircraft deployment in Egypt was not only a reply to the immediate problems facing the Egyptians in their attacks of the Canal, but was the expression of a strategic development that would only be fully appreciated three years later on 6 October 1973, with the opening of the Egyptian offensive in the Yom Kippur War. The new heavy concentration of anti-aircraft weapons in the central sector was sited in the form of an ellipse some 18 miles in depth with the farthest missile of this concentration some 30 miles east of Cairo and the nearest some 12 miles west of the Canal. It was clear that the next phase would be to leapfrog towards the Canal, a move that would place the missiles in a position to be effective over the front-line yet be out of range of Israeli artillery. Thus, they would be a factor in Israel's attacks against the Egyptian artillery concentrations. It became clear that, in addition to a policy of achieving air parity with Israel, the anti-aircraft capability of the Egyptian forces along the Suez Canal had become a vital element in developing future Egyptian offensive strategy. The increased reach of the missile system would bring the air space over the Israeli front-line within range of Egyptian missiles. The stage would be set, as far as the anti-aircraft phase was concerned, for the ultimate crossing of the Suez Canal by the Egyptians.

As the Soviet penetration grew, Soviet involvement in the fighting in the air defence of Egypt increased considerably. A marked improvement in the air-defence system of Egypt was evident. The number of air battles increased, and Russian-piloted aircraft tangled on 25 and 27 July with Israeli aircraft. On 30 July, an air battle developed between Israeli forces and Soviet-piloted MiG-21s. An Israeli patrol was flying over the northern sector of the Gulf of Suez when it came under attack from eight MiG-21s flying in two formations; in the course of the dogfight that ensued, five Soviet aircraft were shot down for no loss on the part of Israel. According to Moshe Dayan,* the Israeli pilots thought the Soviet pilots lacked experience and flexibility: they behaved in battle as they had been taught in training exercises, and stuck to the book, flying in pairs, close together, and not breaking off fast enough. The five pilots bailed out and landed on the Egyptian side of the Gulf. When they were finally found, one was unhurt, two were wounded and two were dead. In order to avoid an

* Ibid.

escalation, no communiqué on this aerial encounter was issued, and nor indeed did the Egyptians or Russians mention a word of it in public. There was considerable consternation in the Soviet Union, but the Egyptians openly rejoiced at the Soviet discomfiture: they heartily disliked their Soviet allies, whose crude, gauche behaviour had created bitter antagonism, and whose officers looked down on the Egyptian officers, treating them with faintly-concealed disdain. The commander of the Soviet Air Defences and the commander of the Soviet Air Force rushed to Egypt on that very day.

The cease-fire

Meanwhile, political negotiations had been afoot on the basis of the United States' so-called 'Rogers Plan'. Originally proposed by the American Secretary of State, William Rogers, in December 1969, this plan envisaged a peace treaty between Israel, Egypt and Jordan, in which there would be almost complete Israeli withdrawal from occupied territories, leaving open the questions of the Gaza Strip and Sharm El-Sheikh. An acceptance of this plan required an agreement for a cease-fire for a period of three months. Nasser returned from a visit to the Soviet Union in July a frustrated and very sick man. He was beginning to realize the scope of the political cost for Russian involvement in Egypt. The strain and cost of the War of Attrition were beginning to tell, and he believed he could use a cease-fire to advance his military plans. He announced that he was willing to accept the Rogers Plan, and Jordan joined him in accepting a cease-fire. On 31 July 1970, Israel also accepted the American initiative and agreed to the cease-fire, which came into operation at midnight on 8 August 1970.

Nasser's acceptance of the proposals came as a surprise to many. Dr. Henry Kissinger[*] feels that Nasser may have feared an Israeli pre-emptive strike. He and his Soviet advisers may have interpreted the White House press statements by President Nixon and Dr. Kissinger as indicating a danger of American involvement. However, he feels it more likely, in the light of later events, that Nasser and the Soviets may have decided from the outset to use the cease-fire offer as a cover for moving forward the missile complex with minimum risk. For Israel, the standstill was a crucial part of the cease-fire agreement, and neither party was entitled to reap military advantage by bringing missiles forward. While the exchange of fire had gone on across the Suez Canal, the Egyptians had not been able to build any new missile sites close to the Canal. If they were now to do this under the cover of the cease-fire, they would be in a better position to resume the war successfully after the lapse of the three-month period.

Israeli fears of Egyptian and Soviet duplicity were far from groundless. It became evident that, during the period between the date on which Nasser accepted the principle of the cease-fire and the actual cease-fire itself, a large-scale forward movement of missile sites had been carried out

* Henry Kissinger, *White House Years*, p. 582, 1979.

by the Russians and the Egyptians. During the period immediately before the cease-fire came into effect and immediately thereafter, the Israelis complained to the United States about the very considerable violations of the agreement, but the United States was sceptical about them. In the light of later evidence, Dr. Kissinger was to admit that 'It is probable that our hesitant first response encouraged Nasser to accelerate the forward deployment of missiles . . .' This evaluation was a most accurate one. From all the evidence that has been accumulated since, it would appear that Nasser's aim was indeed to attempt the next phase of his plans – the seizure of part of the east bank of the Suez Canal under cover of the missiles. He obviously fully intended to use the three months of the cease-fire to deploy his missile forces in such a way as to facilitate the crossing of the Suez Canal by his ground forces and to neutralize the Israeli Air Force over the Canal. However, on 28 September 1970 President Nasser died, and this immediately affected the military situation and developments in the area. Contrary to what Nasser had originally planned and intended, the cease-fire was to remain in force until his successor moved the Egyptian forces across the Suez Canal on 6 October 1973.

Thus came to an end a bitter and hard-fought conflict in which the Israeli and the Egyptian armies had been pitted against each other for some three years. This war was a decisive proving ground for new weapons, new methods and new military strategies in many fields. Indeed, the whole strategy and theory of modern air-defence was tested in a brutal confrontation, and a new policy was evolved by the Russians that was to withstand the test of war in 1973. For, on the basis of the new system that had proved itself in July 1970 along the Suez Canal, the Russians created a more developed and sophisticated system both in Egypt and in Syria, a system to which was added the highly-mobile SAM-6 missile. Unlike the SAM-2 and SAM-3, this was proof against many of the electronic counter-measures activated by the Israeli forces.

Israel, for its part, had withstood the battles despite the heavy casualties it had incurred between June 1967 and August 1970 – more than 500 killed and 2,000 wounded on all fronts – and had adapted itself to a hitherto alien type of warfare. When the cease-fire due to last for 90 days commenced, the Israeli Command decided to take advantage of this period of grace in order to reconstruct those parts of the Bar-Lev Line that had been damaged in the War of Attrition and to strengthen it. General 'Arik' Sharon had in the meantime taken command in the south, relieving General Gavish; and, following his suggestions, a second line of fortifications was constructed some five to seven miles behind the Line. Extensive works were undertaken, and a very considerable effort was invested in order to create the necessary infrastructure, for a total cost of approximately £200 million ($500 million).

There were those, like General Israel Tal, who were unhappy with these stepped-up construction activities. They felt that the fortifications were becoming a series of fixed targets under constant observation, with visible supply lines that invited attack. At best, they constituted only a shelter, and the Israeli artillery, it was maintained, was inadequate to support them. It was further pointed out that they could not prevent a water-crossing by day or by night because they were isolated and not mutually-supporting. Again, the proposal was put forward suggesting a system whereby mobile armoured forces with artillery and anti-aircraft support would be responsible for sectors, with tanks in observation points along the water line. But these reservations were not accepted, and construction continued of the complex system in the Bar-Lev Line. With the appointment of General David Elazar ('Dado') as Chief of Staff in January 1972, when he relieved General Bar-Lev, the matter was raised again. While General Elazar favoured the system of fortifications, a form of compromise emerged. There was a complete absence of hostile activity along the Canal, and this inactivity tended to quieten any reservations there may have been about the reduction in the number of fortifications and troops along the Canal. It accorded with a growing feeling of security and public expressions about the excessive burden being caused by the defence budget, and the necessity to look for savings. Wherever there was a group of fortifications, only one now remained active with a minimum number of soldiers manning it; of 26 fortifications, some ten were closed and blocked by sand in such a manner as to require a number of weeks to activate them again. Because of this compromise, the dividing line between the Bar-Lev Line acting as a warning system, or as a defensive system designed to block the enemy, gradually became hazy and clouded: such lack of clarity was to exact its cost in the first hours of the fighting along the Canal in 1973.

The period of quiet that continued along the Canal from 1970 to 1973, the dramatic decision of Nasser's successor, President Anwar el Sadat, to expel the Russians in July 1972, a failure to read correctly the intelligence picture, and an inability to show sufficient flexibility in evaluation – all these led to the lowering of the Israeli guard over the years. The original concept of the Bar-Lev Line was frittered away, and its implementation was weakened considerably. And all the time, Egyptian preparations were advanced discreetly and inexorably.

SUMMARY

The Israelis fought the War of Attrition along three borders. That with Jordan flared up considerably in the north Jordan valley area, with PLO units operating, on occasions supported by Jordanian units, with impunity from Jordanian territory against Israel. This sector saw some major operations, such as the Israeli operation against the central PLO training and operational camp in Karameh in the Jordan valley in Jordan. It only quietened down after King Hussein, after escaping an assassination attempt on him by the PLO, and realizing that the PLO had created a 'state within a state' and that his throne was thereby gravely endangered, launched an all-out attack on the Palestinians in August and September 1970. At that point Syrian armoured units under the guise of Palestinians invaded Jordan. As the Syrian invasion of Jordan developed and the Jordanian Army fought off the attackers in an attempt to stem the invasion, clear and unequivocal indications were given both to the Syrians and the Soviet Union that neither the United States nor Israel would view with equanimity a Syrian invasion of Jordan. At one stage, the United States, which was acting in close concert with Israel, indicated that it would approve Israeli intervention by military force to save King Hussein's forces. Both an air intervention and the use of ground forces were contemplated. Meanwhile, an Israeli mobilization, American troop dispositions in Europe and elsewhere, and the movement of the United States Sixth Fleet to the Levant coast, with numerous flights from the Fleet to Israeli airports, had been noted by the Russians. All of these moves, together with the indications that Israel might be obliged to move, impressed the Russians sufficiently to advise the Syrians to pull back. To this must be added the brave resistance put up by the Jordanian Army, and in particular by the 40th Armoured Brigade, which had acquitted itself so well in the northern part of the West Bank during the Six Day War.

The PLO in Jordan was eliminated as a military force. The organization moved from Jordan to Lebanon. With its departure, the War of Attrition along the Jordanian front came to an end, but began to develop from Lebanese territory. The stage was set for the decimation of the Lebanese state by the PLO and its occupation later by the Syrian armed forces.

Frequent military actions took place too in this period along the Syrian front. However, the main theatre of operation in which a major war was fought was the Egyptian front where the fighting went far beyond its local significance: hence, the description of the War of Attrition on the Egyptian front to the exclusion of the other fronts is intentional. It is well, however, to recall that, while waging war along the Canal, Israel was at the same time fighting from time to time battles on the Jordanian front and also on occasion on the Syrian and Lebanese fronts.

Nasser had planned to use the three months of the cease-fire for a breathing space, in which he could make the necessary dispositions of the anti-aircraft missile forces in the Canal area to enable him to take advantage of the new situation created and make some spectacular move across the Canal. He, of course, took into consideration the fact that the Israeli Air Force would be neutralized by a new deployment of the Soviet-supplied anti-aircraft forces. However, he died before he could implement his plan. He was replaced by President Anwar el Sadat, who was generally regarded as a stop-gap appointment until somebody strong could take over. But Sadat soon proved himself to be the wily and courageous man that the world grew later to know. He was the first Arab leader ever to talk of a possible peace with Israel. At the same time, however, he began to lay the plans for a major operation across the Suez Canal, which he believed would be essential if he were to hope to break the political log-jam that had developed in the area and had brought about a stalemate between Egypt and Israel.

Carefully, Sadat made his plans and prepared Egypt for war. He realized at a certain point that he required complete freedom of action to be able to go to war, and therefore decided to free himself from Russian supervision and restraints: in July 1972, he expelled the Russian military personnel from Egypt. (Thereafter, he did not neglect to mend his fences with the Russians, however, in order to guarantee his military sources of supply.) Sadat set in motion all the moves towards war — the political planning, the military planning and the outstandingly clever and sophisti-cated deception plan that he had evolved. This plan included a strict observance of the cease-fire along the Suez Canal, a situation which President Sadat rightly appreciated must lead to a lowering of the Israeli guard. At the same time, he began to exercise units of the Egyptian Army in the actual tasks and operations they would have to perform on the day of the Canal crossing. Many units, for a period of almost three years, rehearsed daily the function that they would perform on the day of the opening of the October or Yom Kippur War.

Israel was lulled into a false sense of security. The Egyptian leadership did everything it could to encourage the Israelis in their preconceived notions so as to strengthen this sense of security. And thus, as quiet descended along the Suez Canal and Egyptian and Israeli troops gradually returned to the peaceful occupations of fishing opposite each other in the Canal, and even at times developing a camaraderie between the troops of the opposing armies, President Sadat set in motion the preparations for the next Middle East war.

BOOK V

THE YOM KIPPUR WAR
1973

PROLOGUE

The origins of the Yom Kippur War can be traced back to the conclusion of the 1967 Six Day War. The lessons of that resounding defeat were not lost on the Arab leaders; but it was President Sadat who conceived a long-range strategy to recover the area of Sinai for Egypt and the territories lost to the Arabs in the 1967 War, which would be based on a combination of political and military moves. He came to the conclusion that, whatever military action would be taken by the Egyptians, however limited it would be, the Israeli reaction would be a massive one. Thus, there was no alternative left to the Egyptians but to mount the largest attack possible.

The Israeli military evaluation all along was that the possibility of a major Egyptian attack across the Canal existed, but it was assumed that, having learned the lessons of the 1967 War, the Egyptians would not embark upon a new war until they felt capable of striking at Israeli airfields and neutralizing the Israeli Air Force. For this they would require squadrons of medium bombers and medium fighter-bombers (such as the Jaguar, Phantom and MiG-23) capable of dealing simultaneously with the Israeli airfields. In other words, it was estimated that, until they had an adequate number of squadrons of this type of aircraft available, they would not embark on a new war. Because of this, and believing that the Egyptian Air Force would not receive the necessary reinforcements before 1975, Israeli Intelligence assumed that there was no real danger until approximately 1975. However, President Sadat came to the conclusion that because of his internal political problems he could not wait until then, and therefore he sought an alternative solution.

During a mission carried out by General Ahmed Ismail Ali, the Egyptian Minister of War, to Moscow in February 1972, the Russians proposed such an alternative. The Israeli Air Force was to be dealt with by the creation of one of the densest missile 'walls' in the world, composed of a mixture of various types of Soviet ground-to-air missiles SAM-2, SAM-3 and SAM-6, in addition to conventional anti-aircraft weapons, which would provide an effective umbrella over the planned area of operations along the Suez Canal. This would to a very considerable degree neutralize the effects of Israeli air superiority over the immediate field of battle.

The second problem facing Egypt in the event of hostilities was the ability of the Israeli Air Force to strike deep into Egypt. To counter this possibility, Egypt would be supplied with Soviet SCUD surface-to-surface missiles, having a range of 180 miles, which would threaten populated areas within Israel. It was assumed that the existence of such a capability in the hands of the Egyptians would deter Israel from deep raiding.

A Soviet mission came from Moscow to Cairo immediately thereafter, and the first SCUD missiles supplied to Egypt arrived in approximately April 1973. This was the final military deciding factor in President Sadat's decision to go to war; indeed, in a press interview in April 1973, he gave public expression to this fact and to his decision in principle to initiate a war. At an early stage, he had convinced President Assad of Syria to join with him in planning the attack, which would take the form of simultaneous assaults on both Israel's northern and southern borders. The joint planning began early in January 1973 and, after the supply of the SCUD missiles to Egypt, the Russians instituted a crash programme for the supply of SAM surface-to-air missiles to Syria. Approximately fifty such batteries were supplied in order to cover the approaches to Damascus.

Indications of Egyptian preparations for war in May 1973 did not go unobserved by Israel. But Israeli intelligence evaluated that this was again a case of moving to the brink, and that nothing would really happen. However, the Chief of Staff, General David Elazar, would not accept this evaluation and ordered partial mobilization. Nothing happened. President Sadat decided to postpone the war until the next propitious period of tides in the Suez Canal, which would be in September or October of 1973. The general reaction in Israel was that intelligence had proved to be correct. Accordingly, when the developments in May were being analysed and reviewed, there was a tendency to emphasize the fact that once again the intelligence evaluation had been vindicated. Against this atmosphere of self-satisfaction, the indications available — that the war had only been postponed until the autumn — were ignored. The Israeli military establishment — and particularly its Minister of Defence, General Dayan, and the intelligence department — became captives of a preconceived concept that the Egyptians would not and could not go to war until certain preconditions had been satisfied, and tended to adapt developments noted along the borders to this idea. Thus, in midsummer, General Dayan expressed an opinion that no war with Egypt was imminent. (This evaluation was in contrast to his directive, issued to the General Staff after the false alarm in May, that it should plan for the possibility of an Egyptian-initiated war in the autumn of 1973.) The Egyptian deception plan was conceived to encourage such Israeli misconceptions, and thus a series of foreign press interviews in Egypt and leaks to the press invariably confirmed such statements as had been made in Israel in support of the Israeli concept.

The Egyptians, in fact, mounted a classic 'misinformation' campaign, which proved to be effective. It was based on a careful analysis of the preconceived ideas obtaining in Israel and expressed from time to time by Israeli military leaders. Thus, statements by General Dayan about the lack of preparedness of the Egyptians and an analysis by General Rabin belittling the prospects of war were highlighted in the media coupled with evaluations emphasising the lack of preparedness of the Egyptian Army. Clare Hollingworth, the defence correspondent of the London *Daily Telegraph*, published an article with a Cairo dateline describing the poor maintenance of equipment in the Egyptian Army and the resultant lack of preparedness. A special staff, which had been assembled for this purpose, monitored the operation and guided it in such a way as to confirm those preconceived concepts, not only in Israel but also in Washington and elsewhere. There were many impressive aspects to the Egyptian preparations for the assault, but none as original in concept and in execution as the misinformation plan.

The Egyptians had meanwhile studied and absorbed the lessons of the Six Day War: with the Russians, they concluded that they could answer the problem of the Israeli Air Force over the battlefield by the creation of a very dense 'wall' of missiles along the Canal, denser even than that used in North Vietnam. The problem posed by Israeli armour was to be answered by the creation of a large concentration of anti-tank weapons at every level, from the RPG shoulder-operated missile at platoon level up to the Sagger missiles with a range of some 3,000 yards and the BRDM armoured missile-carrying vehicles at battalion and brigade level. A very thorough plan for anti-tank defence against the Israeli armoured forces was evolved. The question of the rapid mobilization of Israeli reserves would be answered by the use of the weapon of surprise. From a political point of view, the Soviet Union would ensure using the United Nations Security Council to bring about a cease-fire in the event of the attack going badly, and to prevent any interference in the event of everything going well. Supplies from the Soviet Union were guaranteed, with ships leaving Soviet ports loaded with follow-up supplies before the outbreak of war, and a Soviet military airlift beginning a few days after the outbreak of the war. President Sadat furthermore convinced King Feisal of Saudi Arabia that war was essential in order to activate the oil weapon. In other words, contrary to popular opinion, the oil weapon was not used because of the war. One of the reasons for the war was that it would guarantee the measure of unity in the Arab world necessary in order to activate the oil weapon.

In August 1973, the final phases of planning began. Yom Kippur Day — 6 October, the Jewish Day of Atonement — was chosen both because of an assumption that Israeli preparedness would be at its lowest on that day, and because it coincided with the appropriate tides and currents in the Suez Canal.

In mid-September, a dogfight developed between Israeli and Syrian aircraft over the Mediterranean, during which thirteen Syrian aircraft were shot down. Syrian mobilization and concentration of forces in the Golan Heights was thus explained away as being in preparation for a reaction to the air battle. In Egypt, major exercises were under way, but Israeli intelligence did not evaluate them as anything more serious than manoeuvres. The type of exercise and concentration of Egyptian forces along the Suez Canal had occurred in the past without anything serious developing. These repeated exercises were part of the Egyptian deception plan, which was so successful that it succeeded in deceiving not only Israeli intelligence but the intelligence organizations of many countries in the world, including that of the United States. Indeed, 95 per cent of the Egyptian officers taken prisoner by Israel knew for the first time that this exercise would turn into a war only on the morning of 6 October.

The defence concept of Israel had always been dictated by the inability of the country to maintain a large standing force at any given time. Her defence was based on three elements: intelligence, which should give sufficient warning to mobilize reserves; a standing army, which would fight the holding phase of an enemy attack; and an air force, which had a large regular component. These three elements were designed to win time and hold the line until the reserves moved in and took over. On this occasion, one element in the plan went wrong — intelligence.

At 14.00 hours on 6 October 1973, the Egyptian and Syrian Armies were to strike simultaneously. The equivalent of the total forces of NATO in Europe would be flung against Israel's borders. Such a concentration along the northern and southern frontiers of Israel had given rise to concern, particularly on the part of the Chief of Staff, General Elazar, despite calming evaluations by military intelligence which tended to explain it away in a logical manner. Nevertheless, on Friday 5 October, General Elazar asked, and obtained permission from a hastily convened meeting of several members of the Cabinet, for the armed forces to be put on 'Alert C', which maintained the standing army at the highest degree of preparedness and allowed for a limited mobilization of reserves in certain units such as the Air Force. Early in the morning of 6 October 1973, when intelligence information was received confirming that an attack would be launched that day against Israel, a meeting took place between the Minister of Defence, General Dayan, and the Chief of Staff, General Elazar. At this meeting, Elazar asked for permission to mount a pre-emptive air attack against Syria and to order general mobilization. General Dayan turned down the proposals, but, after much argument with Elazar, who pressed for total mobilization so that he could undertake an immediate counterattack, he did agree to a mobilization solely for defensive purposes. The subject was brought to the Prime Minister, Golda Meir, for a decision, with General Dayan proposing the mobilization of no more than 50,000 men. Elazar pressed his case once more. The Prime Minister supported Dayan's stand on a pre-emptive attack and turned down the proposal, but compromised between his position and that of Elazar by ordering the mobilization of 100,000 men. (In fact, Elazar took advantage of this authorization to issue mobilization orders for a much larger number of troops.)

At 14.00 hours, as the Israeli Cabinet was assembling to discuss developments, information was received that the war had begun. The fact that the surprise attack had taken place on Yom Kippur facilitated the mobilization of Israel's reserves, as most of them were either in the synagogues at prayer or at home. Thus, a nation at prayer rushed to the units and assembly areas, changing prayer shawls for battle kit on the way. Israel was again fighting for its existence.

1

THE SOUTHERN FRONT

On 1 July 1973, Major-General Shmuel Gonen was appointed GOC Southern Command, replacing Major-General Ariel Sharon who had retired from the regular army to go into farming and politics. A tough, abrasive Sabra,* born in Jerusalem, Gonen had spent the early years of his life in an orthodox seminary, a yeshiva. In the Six Day War, he had commanded the 7th Brigade in a series of battles across the Sinai Desert, which marked him out as one of the outstanding commanders in the Israeli forces. Wounded several times, an avid marksman with a large collection of small arms, he was known as a strict disciplinarian who could behave at times in an impossible manner towards his officers and yet who inspired in his men a confidence that led them to follow him in battle. 'Gorodish', as he continued to be known in the army by his original family name, was regarded with a mixture of respect and dislike. He was a stickler for the little matters that make up discipline and went out of his way to combat the negligence that had begun to affect the Israel Defence Forces. He had had many close brushes with death and was known to be fearless under fire.

Southern Command was responsible for the whole of the southern part of Israel — the Negev and the Sinai — behind the Suez Canal. 180–240 yards wide and 50–60 feet deep,** the Canal constitutes what General Dayan described as 'one of the best anti-tank ditches available'. The east bank is a wind-swept desert, while the west bank, along which a sweet-water canal runs, has a cultivated belt running parallel to it. The banks are steep and concrete-reinforced, the highest level of the water being six feet below the bank. Earth and soil (removed both by the digging of the Canal and by subsequent dredging operations) was concentrated along the east bank in the form of a dyke some 18–30 feet high. (Israeli engineers had raised this rampart at the critical areas to a height of 75 feet.) The tides change frequently, the difference in the water level varying between one foot and six feet in various parts of the Canal, a fact of great importance in carrying out crossing operations.

From the Canal, the desert rises in an undulating manner for some five miles to a line of sandy hills and thence stretches back to a mountainous and hilly ridge, through which a number of passes, such as the Mitla Pass

---

* A native-born Israeli is known as a Sabra: this is a cactus pear, prickly outside, sweet inside.

** Since the withdrawal of the Israeli forces from the area of the Suez Canal in 1975, under the Interim Agreement between Israel and Egypt, the Egyptians have widened and deepened the Canal so that supertankers can negotiate it.

and the Gidi Pass in the south, lead. The northern area from about Kantara to Port Said is a salty marsh area, criss-crossed by a number of routes that the Israeli Army had constructed. Parallel to the Suez Canal along the entire route runs a road bearing the codename 'Lexicon' on the Israeli military maps; parallel to it some five miles to the east runs a road known as 'Artillery Road'. (The various outstanding features in the desert had been given codenames, as had the various fortifications along the Canal, and they will be referred to by these in this account.) The area is criss-crossed by a considerable network of roads, both lateral and perpendicular.

With his appointment as GOC Southern Command, Gonen handed over command of his reserve division to his predecessor in Southern Command, General Sharon. Gonen was most unhappy with much of what he found in Southern Command, especially with the staff work and the level of discipline, and he began to institute a number of changes. On reviewing the defence system along the Suez Canal, he proposed the reopening of fourteen fortifications that had been blocked up, and received approval in respect of a number of them.

During the first months of his appointment, Gonen set priorities in the construction budget in his Command, allowing first of all for the construction of tank ramps along the second line of defence, thus enabling tanks to engage in depth from a second line an enemy crossing the Canal. Major-General Mandler, commander of the division holding the Canal line, had been pressing for this approval for over a year, but it had been delayed in the Ministry of Defence. A second priority was given to preparation of the infrastructure necessary for a possible Israeli crossing of the Suez.

During his visits along the Canal, Gonen noted that the Egyptians had elevated the ramp on their side to a height of some 130 feet, from which they could look straight over the Israeli rampart and down on to the Israeli fortifications and the tank ramps protecting them: these had been out of sight to the Egyptians when first built. The raised rampart also afforded them observation of the second line of defence along the so-called Artillery Road five to eight miles back. Gonen's answer to this was to order the building of earthworks that would hide activity in the second line of defence from the eyes of the Egyptians; he also ordered the construction of long-range observation towers 230 feet high to enable the Israeli forces to look over into the Egyptian front-line area. But it was to prove too late.

When General Gavish had been in command, underground oil storage tanks were ordered to be constructed under the strongpoints, with pipes leading from them so that the Canal could be sprayed with a film of oil that could then be ignited electrically from inside the fortification and turn parts of the Canal into a moat of fire. In 1971, however, when only two such installations had been built, it was decided that the speed of the current in the Canal would inhibit the effectiveness of this device, so the construction of additional facilities was discontinued. Nevertheless, when the General Staff decided to abandon the project early in 1971, Southern Command was authorized to test one installation in the Canal in order to create an appropriate psychological effect on the Egyptians. Impressed they certainly were, with the result that they devoted much thought and planning over the years to overcome this 'obstacle'.

For years, the Egyptians kept a close watch on the system, which gradually silted up and became clogged with sand. On 11 July 1973, the Egyptian 8th Infantry Brigade intelligence issued a circular on the subject: according to the document (which fell into Israeli hands during the subsequent war), the Israelis had neglected the equipment and all maintenance activities had ceased since the end of 1971. The Egyptians had noted the construction of twenty such facilities along the Canal, but patrols sent over to investigate had discovered them all to be dummies. The pipes in the equipment which had been identified had been cut or bent under the weight of the earth piled on top, so that no liquid could flow through them; they were covered in rust and clogged with sand, while construction work on the fortifications had closed up whole parts of the system. The summary concluded, correctly as it happened, that the Israelis had abandoned the idea of using the equipment and were leaving it in the area for psychological warfare purposes. Nevertheless, much was subsequently made by Ahmed Ismail, the Egyptian Minister of War, and by General Shazli, the Egyptian Chief of Staff, of the ingenuity with which they had neutralized this equipment all along the Canal. Indeed the story of how Egypt planned to deal with this problem and how 'in fact' it was overcome was the subject of long and detailed descriptions by Ismail and Shazli after the war and of admiring descriptions by many war reporters.

When he came to the Command in July, General Gonen decided to try to revive the system. He gave orders to his chief of engineers to check the two existing installations, to clean them out, repair the tanks and find cheaper alternatives to achieve the same purpose. A simpler and more effective method was devised and tested in September, but in the event there was no time in which to apply it. In the course of the preparations on the eve of war on 5 October, Gonen gave instructions for these two systems to be set into operation. An engineering team headed by Second Lieutenant Shimon Tal reached the Hizayon strongpoint at Firdan on the morning of Saturday 6 October, and explained to the men in the position how to operate the system. Since the controls were in the fortification that had been blocked up and de-activated, the troops were told that they would have to run along the Canal several hundred yards, open the pipe manually and throw a phosphorescent grenade into the oil on the water. Having explained the system at Hizayon, Tal continued southwards to Matzmed at Deversoir. But, while he was demonstrating how to operate the installation, the Egyptian artillery barrage fell on them.

The deception

Israeli Intelligence was in a good position to evaluate developments in the Arab world, and had developed an efficient collection system over the years. Following Sadat's elevation to the presidency of Egypt, there had been four periods of escalation in which it had noted major Egyptian mobilization and preparations to go to war. There had been numerous emergencies along the line and, on every occasion, the Israeli forces had invariably been strengthened and moved forward to the line in accordance with the operational plans existing at the time. A major mobilization involving the Egyptian home front was less frequent, however.

The first major mobilization to take place during Sadat's period was at the end of the 'Year of Decision' — 1971 — when the Egyptians planned a surprise attack by fifty bombers on Sharm El-Sheikh (cancelled by Sadat because of the outbreak of the Indo-Pakistan War). During this alert there was a general mobilization of reserves, civilian vehicles and civil defence in the cities; GHQ and all Egyptian field forces were engaged in manoeuvres. Formations of tanks were advanced to the Suez Canal, as well as bridging and water-crossing equipment. Earth-moving activity took place along the water, positions were prepared for tanks and artillery, and the approaches to the Canal were opened up in the southern sector. The Egyptian media announced that war was inevitable, to the accompaniment of warlike statements by the leadership. A year later a second major mobilization took place, during December 1972, when Sadat planned an operation in which a paratroop brigade was to seize and hold territory in the Sinai until the United Nations intervened. During this mobilization too, the field forces went on manoeuvres, soldiers were called back from leave, work was stepped-up on the ramps and fortifications along the Suez Canal, with the preparation of areas for the launching of crossing vehicles and bridging equipment. A war atmosphere was created in the media, but neither the reserves nor the civil defence in the cities were mobilized; nor were ground units advanced to the Canal with their bridging and crossing equipment. The third and fourth periods of escalation and mobilization both took place in 1973 — in April-May and September-October.

Egyptian capability to attack Israel without advance warning existed — and indeed in the discussions that took place with members of the Israeli Cabinet in the days before the actual outbreak of war, General Zeira and his Director of Research, Brigadier-General Aryeh Shalev, acknowledged its existence, while indicating the low probability of its happening. The presence of the Egyptian Army in strength along the Canal was not in itself an indication of impending war, for this deployment had been in effect since 1969; nor, it was argued, were the signs of escalation a definitive signal, as three previous mobilizations had taken place since 1971 without the subsequent aggressive strike. The sole key to providing an advance warning now lay in the evaluation of Egyptian intentions, which in effect meant estimating what Egypt's head of state, President Sadat, might decide. Such a task could hardly be made the exclusive responsibility of the Director of Military Intelligence. The mistake of all involved in intelligence and at the policy-decision level was in not relating the simultaneous increase in capability both in the north and in the south to Syrian and Egyptian intentions.

The Israeli intelligence community followed with interest the development of the major exercise in Egypt, while at the same time being somewhat concerned by the large concentration of forces in Syria, although all the indications were that Syria was simply nervous about a possible Israeli reaction to Syrian operations in retaliation for their shooting down of thirteen Syrian aircraft on 13 September. The assumption, however, was that there was no real danger from Syria, who would never attack on her own. All they saw as they looked towards Egypt were preparations for an exercise, special precautions being taken for fear that an Israeli attack might be in the offing. There were numerous indicators that should have given rise to concern, but these were offset by perhaps twice the number of signs showing that there was no cause for alarm. Towards the end of September, however, information was received from various sources indicating that the Egyptians were preparing for an all-out war. In many cases, the intelligence material went into details of various developments about to occur. But, when these did in fact occur, they were ignored.

With the commencement of the Egyptian manoeuvres, the Israeli forces along the Suez Canal noted an increased degree of activity. A growing stream of information about the Egyptian preparations along the Canal began to flow back daily from their positions. Lieutenant David Abu Dirham, commanding one of the most northerly fortifications, Orkal, some five miles south of Port Fouad, reported that a ship was unloading artillery, equipment and ammunition at the port. Reports came in of artillery being moved into forward positions, unoccupied surface-to-air and surface-to-surface missile positions being manned, minefields being cleared along the Canal and Egyptian soldiers diving into the water to blow up underwater mines. The reports described improvement works on the various descents to the water, earth-moving activity, preparation of areas for crossing and for bridges and pontoons. However, as the Egyptians cleared mines at seventy points along the Canal, they laid them at others; some descents to the water were opened, others were closed. On the other hand, the normal daily routine − both of soldiers and of civilians − continued without any change; Egyptian soldiers continued to fish and to wander along the banks of the Canal without helmets; civilians continued their work as if nothing untoward were happening.

As the Egyptian exercise began, Israeli forces were placed on alert along the Canal, and Southern Command Headquarters issued instructions to ensure that all standing orders for such an alert were carried out. All mobilization systems were checked. Leaves were cancelled. General Gonen visited the Canal on 2 October and issued a number of orders to ensure a higher state of alert. He asked for permission to take a number of precautionary steps, some of which were turned down, but orders were issued to increase guards and security around all camps in the Sinai and to ensure that Operation 'Shovach Yonim',* which would be put into effect should

---

* Shovach Yonim ('pigeon loft' in Hebrew) was the codename for the battle deployment plan of the regular forces in the Sinai in preparation for hostile activity. This included full alert and manning of all positions in the fortifications along the Canal, the assumption of battle positions by the artillery, and the forward movement of the entire armoured division towards the Canal, thus allowing an armoured element to join each fortification and armoured units to take up their positions along the ramps in order to cover the areas between the fortifications.

the enemy move — and which had not been tested for some time — was familiar to all forces. Orders were also issued to accelerate the assembly of a preconstructed bridge, to be used in the event of an Israeli crossing of the Canal, and to place ambushes along the rampart.

According to the Agranat Commission's* report, on 1 October, Lieutenant Benjamin Siman Tov, the order-of-battle officer in Southern Command intelligence, had submitted a document to Lieutenant-Colonel David Gedaliah, intelligence officer of Southern Command, analysing the deployment on the Egyptian side as an indication of preparations to go to war, the exercise notwithstanding. Again, on 3 October, he submitted a document pointing out a number of factors that indicated the exercise might be a cover-up for preparations for war. But Gedaliah did not distribute this junior officer's evaluation, and it was omitted from the Southern Command Intelligence report. In fact, the Director of Military Intelligence, General Zeira, did not learn about Siman Tov's evaluation until March 1974, during the Agranat Commission hearings (whereupon he invited Tov, who had been removed from Southern Command Intelligence, to his office, heard his story, and promoted him to the rank of captain).

On 5 October, the division requested reinforcements, which were to include additional troops to man the strongpoints along the Canal and forces for deployment in the passes some twenty miles east of it. In reply, they received a signal from Southern Command Headquarters repeating a signal from GHQ, to the effect that the Egyptian exercise was nearing its conclusion.

Meanwhile, Soviet broadcasts emphasized that the Israeli concentrations along the Syrian border were there with the intention of attacking Syria. Israeli intelligence estimated that Syrian apprehension as to the possibility of an Israeli attack had grown in the past twenty-four hours, and that the Syrian deployment was a result of their belief that, for political reasons (caused by Israel's growing isolation in the world and the increased co-operation between the front-line Arab countries), Israel might launch a pre-emptive attack. Similarly, Egyptian fears of an Israeli attack were also emphasized, as was the fact that, for the first time since the War of Attrition, a major naval exercise in both the Mediterranean and the Red Sea was taking place.

At dawn on 5 October, it was noted that the Egyptian Army along the Suez Canal had reached a degree of emergency deployment and dispositions such as had never been observed previously by the IDF. An addition of 56 batteries of artillery, bringing the total in the forward areas up to 194, was noted. Furthermore, it was reported that all five infantry divisions were fully deployed, that all five concentration areas for bridging and crossing equipment were partially filled up, and that the ramps prepared on the sand ramparts enabling tanks to fire into the Sinai were

* A public commission of enquiry headed by the President of the Supreme Court of Israel, Shmuel Agranat, which was appointed by the Government of Israel to enquire into the various aspects of the outbreak of the Yom Kippur War and the conduct of the war in its early stages.

occupied by platoons of tanks along the entire Canal. Mobile pontoon units were identified and the forward movement of additional concentrations of forces recorded. Reading all the various indications, the senior intelligence officer of the Israeli Navy expressed the opinion to his commanding officer early in the week that war was imminent. His appreciation was not accepted by GHQ.

On 30 September, the situation had been discussed at GHQ. General Tal expressed grave reservations about the soothing intelligence estimate, while General Zeira maintained that the probability of war was low, explaining that the Syrian concentrations were related to the incident of 13 September, when Syrian aircraft were shot down by Israeli aircraft, and that the Egyptians were simply preparing for a major exercise. But Tal was disturbed. He invited Zeira and Shalev to a meeting in which he again maintained that he did not accept their evaluation. They, however, did not accept his approach.

There was one other Middle Eastern element that could provide indications of imminent war, involved as it was in the military developments in the area: the Soviet Union. Three days before the war, a Soviet reconnaissance satellite was launched and proceeded to orbit above the Sinai, the Suez Canal and the Syrian-Israeli border area in addition to the area of Galilee. Each day its orbit was altered to take in the different sectors of Israel's two front-lines. On Wednesday morning, 3 October, President Sadat summoned the Soviet ambassador, Vinogradoff. At approximately the same time, President Assad summoned the Soviet ambassador in Damascus to meet him. The two presidents indicated to the ambassadors that war was imminent, without entering into details. On 4 October, units of the Soviet fleet stationed in Alexandria and Port Said began to move out. This mass exodus strengthened the suspicions of Israeli Naval Intelligence. In the meantime, information was received of the arrival of giant Soviet Antonov An-22 aircraft in Cairo and Damascus and the evacuation by air of the Soviet families stationed there. The explanation of all these Soviet moves by Israeli Intelligence was: either they indicated a knowledge on the part of the Soviets that war was about to break out (and the evacuation and naval withdrawal might be a Soviet move designed to deter the Egyptians from such an action, since at the end of the 'Year of Decision' in 1971, during a previous general mobilization in Egypt, Soviet vessels had evacuated Port Said); or it might be that the Egyptians, together with the Syrians, had finally decided to liquidate Soviet presence in Egypt, although this did not seem very feasible.

On Saturday 29 September, at the Czech-Austrian border, two Palestinian gunmen held up a train carrying Russian Jews from Moscow to Vienna. They took as hostages five Jews and an Austrian customs official, and demanded facilities to fly themselves and the hostages to an Arab country. In the course of the negotiations, Bruno Kreisky, Austria's chancellor (himself a Jew), initiated a proposal to close the transit centre for Jewish immigrants at Schonau, near Vienna. The hostages were released and the gunmen were set free. Israel was horrified and outraged, and the event dominated all the media. The Israeli Government became completely absorbed in this problem: Golda Meir flew to Strasbourg to address the Council of Europe and then, despite the misgivings of some of her Cabinet members, flew to Vienna in an abortive attempt to persuade Kreisky to reconsider his decision. She returned to Israel on Wednesday 3 October, and immediately convened a Cabinet meeting to discuss the Austrian developments. It is not clear to this day whether or not this operation was part of the general deception plan to divert Israel's attention from developments along the front. The operation was carried out by a little-known Palestinian terrorist organization, but the fact that it was linked to Saika, the Palestinian guerrilla organization controlled by the Syrian Army, lends credence to the assumption that the operation was part of the overall deception plan. However, whether or not it was planned, the operation certainly did help to divert government and public attention from the ominous developments along the borders of Israel.

On Thursday evening, General Zeira brought the news of the evacuation of Soviet families from Egypt and Syria to the Chief of Staff; Zeira had been away ill for two days, and this new information gave him an uncomfortable feeling.

Early on Friday morning, military correspondents of the Israeli press were briefed not to exaggerate the reports coming from abroad about large Arab concentrations along the borders, but to indicate that the Israel Defence Forces were taking all necessary steps in the light of developments. That same morning however, General Elazar decided on a 'C' state of alert, the highest state of alert in the standing army; it was the first time that he had declared such a state of alert since he had become Chief of Staff. At the same time, a conference was held with the Minister of Defence. Zeira described the Soviet airlift, reflecting that this could indicate a final break between the Arabs and the Soviet Union, but that he did not consider this as very probable. He went on to say that the Soviets were obviously aware of the fact that the possibility of a conflagration existed; it may be that they had accepted the Arab claim that Israel was about to launch an attack, which they had incidentally echoed in their broadcasts. This, however, seemed unlikely, because in such a case the Soviets would doubtless have approached the Americans, who in turn would have made approaches to Israel counselling moderation. There had been no American approaches; so, Zeira concluded, it was conceivable that the Soviets were aware of the possibility of an Arab attack and feared for their families in the consequences of an Israeli counterattack. Nevertheless, the feeling of Intelligence was that the probability of an Arab attack was very low.

General Elazar had been convinced all along that he could expect adequate warning for mobilization from Military Intelligence, and an evaluation of the information that poured in during the fateful days of the first week in October vindicates his assumption. Yet, after the war, he was to maintain that a considerable amount of material indicating the probability of war had *not* reached him. There were, according to Elazar's testimony before the Agranat Commission, items of information on Friday morning indicating the imminence of war, but these had not reached him until Saturday morning. Had he received this information, he maintained, he would have mobilized on Friday morning. In fact on Friday, he still considered that he would receive adequate warning in the event of war. Two days previously, on 3 October, he had addressed the Israeli press, who had asked him if the regular forces would be adequate to deal with the attack should war break out. He answered that they would not; at best, together with the Air Force, they could prevent a collapse in the event of a complete surprise. However, it was generally assumed that Israel would have adequate warning time in which to mobilize her reserves.

From Thursday evening, Zeira was torn by doubts, but he invariably comforted himself with the knowledge that the standing army was on the alert and that its strength was considered sufficient by GHQ to be able to withstand an initial assault. In this, he saw an additional insurance policy as far as the intelligence warning was concerned. On Friday 5 October, a meeting of the General Staff took place. The intelligence picture was again presented, but the probability of war breaking out was regarded as 'the lowest of the low'. A staff conference at Southern Command, which took place at 15.30 hours reviewed all the preparations that had been made and discussed all the relevant operational plans. It was decided that next day half of the staff would visit the Suez front, while the other half visited other parts of the Command.

That night, the political and military leaders of Israel went to sleep with an uneasy feeling, but few dreamt that the country was facing an imminent attack. Had they been able to overcome their preconceived notions in time, the entire history of the next few days would have been very different. At 04.00 hours on the morning of 6 October, the strident buzz of the telephone ringing by his bedside awoke General Zeira. He listened to the voice at the other end and immediately dialled three numbers, one after the other, waking the Minister of Defence, the Chief of Staff and the Vice Chief of Staff (General Tal). He recounted the information he had just received — that war would break out that evening on both fronts towards sundown.

The onslaught

The total strength of the Egyptian Army (one of the largest standing armies in the world) included some 800,000 troops, 2,200 tanks, 2,300 artillery pieces, 150 anti-aircraft missile batteries and 550 first-line aircraft. Deployed along the Canal were five infantry divisions and a number of independent brigades (infantry and armour) backed by three mechanized divisions and two armoured divisions. Each infantry division included a battalion of tanks for every one of the three brigades, making a total of 120 tanks in every infantry division. The three mechanized divisions included two mechanized brigades and one armoured brigade, a total of 160 tanks per division. The two armoured divisions were composed of two armoured brigades and one mechanized brigade, with a total of about 250 tanks per division. There were also independent tank brigades, two paratroop brigades, some 28 battalions of commandos and a marine brigade.

The Egyptian Second Army was responsible for the northern half of the Canal and Third Army for the southern half. The Second Army front was

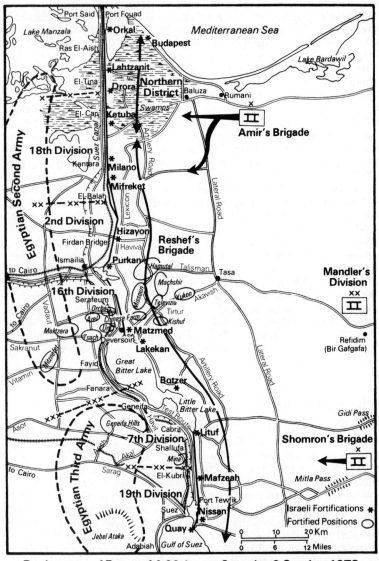

Deployment of Forces, 14.00 hours, Saturday 6 October 1973

held by the 18th Infantry Division from Port Said to Kantara and the Firdan Bridge; by the 2nd Infantry Division from the Firdan bridge to the north of Lake Timsah; and by the 16th Infantry Division from Lake Timsah to Deversoir at the northern end of the Great Bitter Lake. The dividing line between the two armies ran through the centre of the Great Bitter Lake. Third Army had under command the 7th Infantry Division, responsible for the sector of the Bitter Lakes to half-way down the southernmost section of the Suez Canal, and the 19th Infantry Division south to, and including, the city of Suez. Each of the assaulting infantry divisions was reinforced for the crossing by an armoured brigade, drawn in part from the armoured and mechanized divisions.

Every move in the first phase, which was to take place between 6 and 9 October, had previously been planned and prepared to the minutest detail. Ten bridges were to be thrown across the Canal, three in the area of Kantara, three in the area of Ismailia-Deversoir and four in the area of Geneifa-Suez. A division would cross in a sector some four to five miles wide. The first wave would be entrusted with seizing and holding the earth ramparts; when the second wave reached these, forces of the first phase were to advance 200 yards and remain in their positions; within an hour of the attack, third and fourth waves would move to join the first and second waves. As soon as the support units of the attacking battalion had crossed, the entire force would advance. The first waves of the attacking infantry divisions were to establish themselves one to two miles in depth, following which special infantry units trained for the purpose were to attack and capture the strongpoints. Each bridgehead was ultimately to be five miles wide and three and a half miles deep. They were to remain so until the arrival of the tanks and the artillery, when they would be enlarged to a base of ten miles wide and five miles deep.

At H-Hour on 6 October, 240 Egyptian aircraft crossed the Canal. Their mission was to strike three airfields in the Sinai, to hit the Israeli Hawk surface-to-air missile batteries, to bomb three Israeli command posts, plus radar stations, medium artillery positions, the administration centres and the Israeli strongpoint known as 'Budapest' on the sandbank east of Port Fouad. Simultaneously, 2,000 guns opened up along the entire front: field artillery, medium and heavy artillery and medium and heavy mortars. In the first minute of the attack, 10,500 shells fell on Israeli positions at the rate of 175 shells per second. A brigade of FROG surface-to-surface missiles launched its weapons, and tanks moved up to the ramps prepared on the sand ramparts, depressed their guns and fired point-blank at the Israeli strongpoints. Over 3,000 tons of concentrated destruction were launched against a handful of Israeli fortifications in a barrage that turned the entire east bank of the Suez Canal into an inferno for 53 minutes.

At 14.15 hours, when the aircraft had returned from their bombing missions, the first wave of 8,000 assault infantrymen, moving exactly as they had been trained dozens and (in many cases) hundreds of times, stormed across the Canal. Along most of the front, they crossed in areas not covered by fire from the Israeli strongpoints or organized for action; in most places they avoided such fortifications, bypassing them and pushing eastwards. At the same time, commando and infantry tank-destroyer units crossed the Canal, mined the approaches to the ramps, prepared anti-tank ambushes and lay in wait for the advancing Israeli armour.

In some areas Israeli resistance was heavy; in other areas it was comparatively light. Initial Egyptian estimates had been that the crossing would cost some 25,000–30,000 casualties, including some 10,000 dead, but their casualties in the initial crossing, which totalled only 208 killed, were lower than any Egyptian planner had imagined. (In the Second Army area, the crossing went according to plan with few hitches, but in the area of Third Army there were some problems caused by the Israeli rampart proving to be wider than the Egyptians had estimated and also by the nature of the soil at the southern end of the Suez Canal, which, instead of disintegrating under the high-pressure water hoses, tended instead to become a morass of mud.) The commander of one of the two infantry divisions in Third Army who encountered strong Israeli reaction later recounted that he lost 10 per cent of his men in the initial assault, although he had estimated that he would lose 30 per cent. He related the story of a lone Israeli tank that fought off the attacking forces for over half an hour, causing very heavy casualties to his men when they tried to storm it. When the finally overcame it, the Egyptian general recounted how, to his utter amazement, he found that all the crew had been killed with the exception of one wounded soldier, who had continued to fight. He described how impressed he and his men were by this man, who, as he was being carried away on a stretcher to a waiting ambulance, saluted the Egyptian general.

Less successful were the Egyptian commandos, who were landed in depth along the entire length of the front from the area of Port Fouad in the north down to Sharm El-Sheikh at the southern tip of the Sinai Peninsula. Their purpose was to harass the inevitable Israeli counterattacks, and tank-hunting units were ordered into position to prevent the Israeli tanks from deploying according to plan on the ramps between the strongpoints. A special operation in this phase was the crossing of the Great Bitter Lake by 130 Marine Brigade: its amphibious vehicles attempted to bypass Israeli forces and link up with commando forces in the area of the Mitla and Gidi Passes. However, fourteen helicopters loaded with Egyptian commando forces were shot down by the Israeli Air Force, and Israeli forces throughout the Sinai were rapidly organized to deal with the threat.

Defending the Bar-Lev Line

Facing the initial onslaught of the Egyptian Army was the division of Major-General Avraham ('Albert') Mandler. A very fine and sensitive personality, he was known as one of the most disciplined and considerate officers in the IDF. A tall, taciturn, ruddy-faced officer, aged 45, with piercing blue eyes, he had commanded the armoured brigade that had performed the almost impossible in breaking the Syrian line holding the

Golan Heights in 1967. Now, as war broke out again, the forces at his disposal totalled some 280 tanks in three brigades, with a special command including an infantry brigade holding the northern area of marshland. However, the bulk of these forces were held as 'immediate reserves' in the eastern Sinai, ready to be activated by the 'trip-wire' of the Bar-Lev Line.

The full impact of the Egyptian crossing along the 110 miles of the Suez Canal fell upon a total of 436 Israeli soldiers in a series of fortifications seven to eight miles apart, and three tanks actually on the waterfront. They were men of the Jerusalem Brigade, serving their annual reserve duty, and constituted a typical cross-section of average Jerusalemites. Because Jerusalem had absorbed a large proportion of new immigrants of late, many of the men serving in the fortifications were inexperienced soldiers with little or no battle experience.

At midday on Saturday 6 October, warning was flashed to Mandler's divisional headquarters in Sinai advising of an imminent artillery bombardment and instructing all forces to be on the alert. Brigadier-General Pinko, Mandler's deputy, again pressed his commander to instruct all forces to activate the 'Shovach Yonim' plan and move forward to the Canal. At midday Mandler agreed and the instructions were issued. Arriving back at his headquarters at 13.45 hours from the General Staff meeting in Tel Aviv, General Gonen called Mandler and reviewed the various orders that had been issued. In closing, he told him that he felt that the time had come for him to begin moving his armoured brigades down to the front. Mandler replied laconically, 'Yes, I suppose we had. We are being bombed at this moment.'

Reports describing massive artillery bombardment, air attacks, crossings of the Canal and fighting were meanwhile pouring in from the strongpoints along the Canal. Some fortifications (particularly where the officers were in charge) reported in a matter-of-fact manner; others, whose officers had been killed at the outset, were in some cases hysterical. In some, NCOs, and in one case a private soldier, took command and led the men in battle. All pleaded for air and artillery support and for armoured reinforcements. All were promised that these were on the way.

By 15.00 hours it was clear to Mandler that the Egyptians were staging a major attack all along the front. And, an hour later, it was evident that the crossing of the Canal was a major amphibious operation taking place along its full length. Gonen tried to read the battle in his headquarters as the reports flowed in and the highly developed communication system in the Command provided a clear picture of what was going on in every strongpoint along the Canal. For two hours, he tried to identify the enemy's main effort; in fact, the Egyptians had estimated that the absence of such a main effort would itself delay the Israeli counterattack. By 16.00 hours, it was clear to Gonen that there was no main effort, but that the crossing was more successful in the northern sector of the Canal than in the southern sector.

Meanwhile, the sixteen manned fortifications of the Bar-Lev Line continued to bear the brunt of the attack. In those fortifications in which the troops had manned the firing points, the Egyptians were beaten back, but the Egyptian forces succeeded in penetrating those fortifications in which the men had been ordered to take shelter on the assumption that what they were experiencing was only an artillery attack. The reaction in each fortification reflected the determination of the commander on the spot, but in many cases the officers were the first casualties.

Each of the stories of the fortifications proved to be a saga in itself. Before authority was received to evacuate the fortifications on the morning of 7 October, most of the tank forces that had fought on the 6th and the night of the 6/7th, in an endeavour to reinforce the fortifications, were decimated. The units in the fortifications were cut off by surrounding Egyptian forces. Some succeeded in breaking through the Egyptian lines in hair-raising escapades. Others lost most of their personnel. The rest were taken prisoner.

A typical story is that of the unit holding the fortification codenamed 'Ketuba' in the northern sector of the Canal. They were being led in prayer by three boys from a religious seminary in Jerusalem when the Egyptian attack took place. The commander was wounded, Corporal Or-Lev took command and succeeded in beating back the Egyptian attack, sinking many of the Egyptian boats crossing the Canal. Again, in the darkness of the early morning of 7 October, Or-Lev — who was left with twelve fighting men, three of them wounded — fought back a renewed attack by two companies of Egyptian troops, who left the area before the fortification strewn with dead soldiers. When his force was down to seven soldiers, exhausted from battle, shell-shocked and with ammunition running out, Or-Lev saw that he was about to be attacked by more than a battalion of infantry backed by six tanks. He prepared for a final stand. Just as he did so, he received permission to evacuate. Under intense fire, with his whole force and the wounded loaded in one half-track, the men of 'Ketuba' fought their way out of the position, crossed a track through the swamps and finally reached the Israeli lines.

The southern end of the Suez Canal was held by the 'Quay' fortification built on the breakwater of Port Tewfik opposite Suez. It was manned by 42 regular army soldiers under the command of Lieutenant Shlomo Ardinest. As the Egyptian artillery bombardment opened up, a force of inflatable boats moved across the Canal and was beaten off by the Israeli garrison, which sank most of the boats. Ardinest, a 'yeshiva'* student, was soon the only unwounded officer in the position. On Sunday night, 7 October, an Egyptian unit managed to break into the fortification from the south with the help of flame-throwers and set the stronghold's fuel stores alight. The defending garrison wiped out the attackers in hand-to-hand fighting. For three days, this position, surrounded by water on three sides and connected to the mainland by a single road on a breakwater six yards wide, endured an intense artillery barrage and attacks by thousands of Egyptian soldiers supported by tanks. The Egyptian tanks were picked off by the guns of four severely damaged Israeli tanks, which had managed to reach the fortification on the first day of fighting; ranging their guns by

* Orthodox seminary.

improvisation, the crews of the Israeli tanks set one after another on fire. The medical officer in the position had by now run out of morphine, and was without infusions or syringes, while bandages were also rapidly running out.

By Tuesday morning, 9 October, the position had only ten men trained for combat capable of bearing arms, in addition to ten support personnel, including the doctor, the medical orderly, the cook, and two yeshiva students who had come to organize the prayers on Yom Kippur. The doctor performed the first tracheotomy of his life without any form of anaesthetic on a soldier who was hit by a bazooka shell, and saved his life. On Thursday 11 October, Headquarters queried Ardinest as to whether he could hold out for another 48 hours. The doctor, who had by now no means with which to treat another wounded man, suggested surrendering through the Red Cross, but Ardinest and his garrison sergeant would not hear of it. On Saturday morning, after holding out for a week against forces of the Egyptian Third Army, when the garrison was left with only twenty hand grenades and a few belts of light-machine-gun ammunition, the fortification was authorized to surrender via the Red Cross at 11.00 hours on the Saturday morning. Ordering his troops to wash themselves in the few drops of water left in the jerry cans and to change their battle-soiled clothes, Lieutenant Ardinest paraded his men and marched into captivity, led by a soldier carrying a Torah scroll from the fortification. The thousands of Egyptians surrounding the position watched the proceedings in awe. After the evacuation, the Egyptian officers searched high and low for non-existent heavy machine-guns in the position, unwilling to believe that the garrison had held out for a week with only four light machine-guns.

At the northern end of the Israeli line, on a sandbank some seven miles east of Port Fouad, was the fortification codenamed 'Budapest'. It was commanded by a reserve officer, Captain Motti Ashkenazi, and manned by eighteen men. 'Budapest' was the only position along the line to be reinforced by a platoon of Israeli tanks in accordance with standing orders. On the Saturday afternoon, the Egyptians mounted a mixed armour and artillery attack from the direction of Port Fouad, with a force that included sixteen tanks, sixteen armoured personnel carriers and jeeps mounting recoilless anti-tank guns, followed by trucks loaded with infantry. In the battle that ensued, eight armoured personnel carriers and seven tanks were set on fire. In the meantime, however, a force of Egyptian commandos established itself on the sandbank one mile east of 'Budapest', thus cutting-off the fortification completely from the Israeli lines. The position was engaged heavily by Egyptian air attack, and the Egyptian commando force that had isolated the fortification ambushed an Israeli relief force supported by armour and destroyed it. Heavy artillery harassment of the position continued without let-up. Meanwhile, Israeli pressure on the commando force was stepped up and, on the night of Tuesday 9 October, the Egyptian force was evacuated by sea. The Israeli Air Force attacked on the Wednesday, in an attempt to relieve the position, but lost seven aircraft shot down in the process. Then, on that same day, Brigadier-General Magen, commander of the northern sector of the Canal, led a force, with ammunition and food, which finally broke through to 'Budapest'. On the Thursday, Ashkenazi's unit was relieved by friendly forces. The Israeli forces, however, had not learned from the lessons of the previous mistakes, and once again 'Budapest' was cut-off by an Egyptian commando unit and the route had to be opened after heavy fighting by an Israeli unit. 'Budapest' held out until the end of the War and achieved the distinction of being the only front-line position in the Bar-Lev Line that did not fall to the Egyptians. (Captain Ashkenazi subsequently became one of the leaders of the protest movements against the Government, placing responsibility for what had occurred at the outbreak of war on the Minister of Defence, Moshe Dayan, and demanding his resignation: it was submitted in due course.)

The performance of the various fortifications in defence varied according to the standard of command in each position. In general, where the command was determined and experienced and had at its disposal a basis of well-trained soldiers, the fortifications held out for days. Most of the positions gave a good account of themselves, having regard to the overwhelming odds in favour of the Egyptians, the comparatively low standard of training that characterized the garrison troops along the Canal, and the incessant pounding by anti-tank missiles and tank guns being fired by the Egyptians point-blank at the Israeli positions from the ramp on the Egyptian side of the Canal. Some of the fortifications fought to the bitter end. Not one position was abandoned without orders. Many of the commanders exercised great ingenuity and skill in leading the remnants of the garrisons and carrying their wounded out through the Egyptian lines. Some came under attack as they endeavoured to cross into the Israeli lines, and in one case a young subaltern convinced an Israeli force, which was sweeping the sand dunes with murderous fire, to desist by having the ingenuity to wave to and fro a 'talith', a prayer shawl, tied to the muzzle of a rifle.

Despite all this heroism, however, the fortifications proved to be a liability. Over the years, they had become a compromise — between strongpoints designed to hold the Canal against Egyptian attack, and warning and observation outposts. As the former they were too weak and dispersed; as the latter they were too strongly manned. There is no doubt that the Egyptians would have succeeded in establishing a foothold even if the original concept of the Bar-Lev Line (including the complete Israeli plan to move forces to the front-line) had been executed on time, and the quality of the troops in the front-line raised (as was envisaged in the event of an emergency). But they would have found their task a much more difficult one, would have incurred very heavy losses, and their attack may conceivably have been beaten back in the final analysis. The Egyptian forces on the east bank of the Canal would in any event have been highly vulnerable to an Israeli counterattack. But perhaps the worst result of the Israeli error in relation to the fortifications was the absence of a clear picture of the situation along the Canal until the morning of Sunday 7 October.

'Shovach Yonim'

At an orders group that General Mandler had convened on the Saturday morning, all operations plans including 'Shovach Yonim' had been recapitulated. Because of the information that had been received that the attack would begin at 18.00 hours, the forces were to deploy in accordance with the 'Shovach Yonim' plan not later than 17.00 hours, but on no account before 16.00 hours, in case the forward movement of Israeli forces should lead to a deterioration and an escalation that could bring the Egyptians to open fire. However, before the Israeli moves could be set in motion, the Egyptian tank attack had begun.

At Mandler's headquarters, the picture of the situation along the Canal was confused. His armoured forces were moving towards the Canal but there was no clear indication of their situation. The general estimate had been that the main brunt of the attack would fall on the northern sector, so the armoured brigade under Colonel Gaby Amir was directed to the north. Colonel Amnon Reshef's brigade moved westwards in the centre while, in the southern sector, Colonel Dan Shomron's brigade was ordered through the Gidi Pass to a position south of the Bitter Lakes.

In the northern sector of the front as Amir's forces moved forward, they were attacked, so he divided and attempted to link up with the Mifreket fortification at the northern end of El-Balah Island. As he advanced, he learned that the forces in the area had been practically wiped out. Another part of his brigade moved east of Kantara to link up with the fortification known as 'Milano'. Three times during the Saturday night, units of his force linked up with the Mifreket stronghold. Early on Sunday morning, General Kalman Magen, who had assumed command of the sector north of Kantara, authorized Amir to withdraw his force with his casualties and to evacuate the Mifreket fortification. The attempt to reach the fortifications had caused losses that left Amir's entire brigade with only some twenty tanks. Amir gradually extricated what was left of his force and moved back to reorganize.

The central sector of the Canal, from El-Balah Island to Ras Sudar in the south, was the responsibility of Colonel Amnon Reshef's brigade. Tall, fair, with an owlish look behind his spectacles, and distinguished by his neatly-kept handlebar moustache, he had commanded his brigade for over a year. As ordered, Reshef's tanks rushed forward to their pre-planned positions — only to find that Egyptian tank-hunting units had occupied them and were launching forth a hail of RPG bazooka shells. At the same time, from the rampart on the Egyptian side overlooking the Israeli approaches, Israeli tanks were engaged by tanks and Sagger anti-tank missiles. The Israeli tank units fought and suffered their first casualties. The Egyptian infantry fought stubbornly. Hundreds were killed by the advancing tanks, but the wave of Egyptian infantry continued to advance. Of the two companies of Reshef's brigade in the area facing Ismailia and Firdan, only two tanks continued to fight. They held the crossroads opposite Firdan all night against 50 Egyptian tanks. All day long on 7 October, the fighting continued as Reshef's brigade was gradually worn down.

To the south of Reshef's brigade was Dan Shomron's brigade. Shomron was a well-built, determined-looking Sabra born on a kibbutz, who had commanded a crack paratroop battalion. (Years later, this able young officer was to attain international renown when he commanded the famous Israeli rescue operation of the hostages held at Entebbe.) He too had been ordered not to move his tanks forward until the afternoon and, as they were preparing to move, Egyptian aircraft swooped in to attack his camp at 14.00 hours. Shomron divided his forces, sending one battalion through the Mitla Pass, one battalion through the Gidi Pass and a third one in between the two, in case either one of them had been blocked by the enemy. His brigade was now responsible for a front some 35 miles wide, stretching from the junction of the two Bitter Lakes south to Ras Masala, some twelve miles south of Suez. Facing his sector was the Egyptian 19th Infantry Division, 7th Infantry Division, 6th Mechanized Division, and behind it the 4th Armoured Division. These forces totalled some 650 tanks, in addition to 130 Marine Brigade, which was due to cross the Bitter Lakes in amphibious vehicles in an attempt to block the Mitla and Gidi Passes. The Egyptians thus outnumbered Shomron by over six to one in tanks.

Shomron's first objective was to link-up with the various Israeli fortifications that were being besieged by the Egyptians. By the evening of 6 October, his units had reached all the fortifications with the exception of the one on the quay at Port Tewfik, whose approaches had been mined and were swarming with Egyptian anti-tank ambushes. As he fought back and blocked the Egyptian attempts to cross in his sector, he pleaded with Mandler either to evacuate the fortifications or to reinforce them; but no authority was granted. The intensity of the battle that Shomron fought can be gauged from the fact that when he had moved through the Mitla and Gidi Passes on Saturday afternoon at 16.00 hours, he did so with a force of approximately 100 tanks; by 08.00 hours on the morning of Sunday the 7th, he was left with 23 tanks. Two-thirds of all the losses incurred in men and vehicles by his brigade during the War were lost on that first night. He was now authorized to break contact with the fortifications and concentrate on holding the Egyptian advance. He had three batteries of artillery and faced 75 batteries of Egyptian artillery.

Realizing that he was outnumbered on all points, Shomron concentrated the remnants of his brigade into one armoured fist and decided to launch a pre-emptive attack on the fast-growing Egyptian concentrations. Carefully husbanding his forces, firing at long range in a classic battle of fire and movement, he did not give the Egyptians a chance to develop any effort against him. On Tuesday 9 October, the Egyptians mounted a first concentrated attack of two mechanized brigades across Artillery Road in the direction of the Mitla Pass. In a battle of manoeuvre, Shomron counterattacked, destroying twenty Egyptian tanks and many armoured personnel vehicles. The Egyptians withdrew in disarray.

The impression at divisional headquarters by Saturday evening was that the armoured forces had reached all the fortifications, apart from those located on the narrow dyke north of Kantara, at Firdan bridge and on the quayside at Port Tewfik. There were five tanks in the latter position, but the position itself was by then cut off.

In the first few hours of the fighting, Brigadier-General Pinko, who had become Mandler's second-in-command two months earlier, had tried to piece together a coherent picture. Unable to do so from the reports, he had taken a helicopter and flown along Artillery Road as far south as the Gidi and Mitla Passes. On numerous occasions, the helicopter had had to avoid Egyptian MiGs and M18 helicopters, but he had succeeded in bringing back what he believed to be the first comparatively clear picture of the situation to his divisional commander. By 01.00 hours on the morning of the 7th, the picture that Gonen received in his headquarters was that the Israeli forces had returned to the water line apart from the area north of Kantara, two fortifications in the central sector and the quayside position at Port Tewfik. Neither Gonen nor Mandler felt any urgency about evacuating the strongpoints along the Canal at this time.

The problem of inaccurate front-line reporting was highlighted by the fact that, on Saturday evening, the situation on the ground as reflected in the picture received at Command Headquarters and GHQ was a satisfactory one. Hence, there was no point in giving orders to evacuate the fortifications because the reports indicated that the Israeli tanks had reached the Canal on Saturday evening and had linked up with them. At 18.00 hours on Saturday evening, General Elazar spoke to Gonen, advising him that if there were fortifications that did not obstruct the main effort of the enemy and only endangered the occupants, he was authorized to evacuate them. He emphasized that he did not want to defend the whole Canal by means of these fortifications, but rather to hold strongpoints that would hinder the development of the enemy's major efforts. At this point Elazar was thinking two days ahead. Realizing that he could influence little of what was happening on the ground at any given moment (except in special circumstances), he understood that the holding battle would be a very difficult one and that the Egyptians would be bound to penetrate in some places. On Sunday, the holding battle would continue, but he was already thinking in terms of a series of counterattacks on Monday. At midnight on Saturday, as soon as he was satisfied that the communications system from the forward headquarters was effective, Gonen moved forward from his headquarters in Beersheba into his advanced headquarters at Um Kusheiba in the forward area of the Sinai. All night he received reports that tanks were patrolling between the Canal fortifications and were linking up with them. In the northern sector near the Mifreket strongpoint, Amir's forces reported that they had knocked out an Egyptian bridge.

All through the night of 6/7 October, the Egyptian bridging units had worked feverishly establishing bridges across the Canal. The next day these bridges came under heavy and persistent attack by the Israeli Air Force and many of them were seriously damaged. However, their sectional construction and the ease with which they could be handled allowed, as General Shazli was later to point out, for a very rapid replacement of damaged sections and also enabled the Egyptians, when any area came under heavy attack, to float the bridge down the Canal to an alternative site or to lash it to one of the banks during daylight hours. Thus, the Israeli claims that nearly all the bridges had been hit on the first day were correct, as indeed were the Egyptian claims that forces were crossing on their bridges without let-up.

On Sunday morning, the Egyptians renewed their attack. Now the very alarming results of the night's fighting were dawning on the Israeli Command: Amir's forces were left with ten tanks, and Mandler reported that, of the 290 tanks with which he had started fighting, he was left with but one-third of that number along the entire length of the Suez Canal. Egyptian pressure was growing as, foiled in their attempt to hose open the Israeli rampart by water jet in the southern sector, they began to bulldoze it. The reserves were far away while the regular holding forces were being worn down. Without air support, Gonen saw no solution until the reserves arrived. Mandler repeatedly requested air support, and Gonen advised him that help would arrive within twenty minutes. 'I don't have twenty minutes', came Mandler's tired reply. At 06.45 hours, the Israeli Air Force made a number of preparatory strikes against the missile system before coming in for close support, and then suddenly General Peled, the commander of the Air Force, notified Gonen that there would be no more air support because of the situation in the north. During the morning, Gonen advised Peled: 'Unless you deploy your force here I have nothing with which to hold the attack.' At 09.30 hours, following the approval of the Chief of Staff, he authorized Mandler to evacuate the fortifications where feasible.

Meanwhile, mobilization in Israel was being accomplished at full speed. As the various headquarters and formations were formed, a new allocation of responsibility along the Suez Canal was made by General Gonen. In addition to Mandler's divisional headquarters, two further divisions were activated, one under command of Major-General Avraham ('Bren') Adan and the other under Major-General Ariel ('Arik') Sharon. Thus, by Sunday afternoon, the northern sector was held by Adan, the central sector by Sharon and the southern sector by Mandler.

Gonen ordered Adan to evacuate the fortifications at approximately 11.00 hours on the 7th. The Minister of Defence, General Dayan, visited the Command Headquarters and recommended Gonen to abandon the fortifications and forward positions now held by the forces of Southern Command, and to withdraw to the high ground passing through the mountains of Jebel Ma'ara and Jebel Yalek. Gonen agreed to the order to withdraw from the fortifications and issued it, but did not accept Dayan's recommendations with regard to the extent of withdrawal. Meanwhile, as the reserves arrived, most of Southern Command by the evening of 7 October was deployed along Artillery Road, with reserves along the main lateral road. The Egyptian advance was being held all along the line. That afternoon, Dayan recommended to the Prime Minister a withdrawal to a more readily defensible line, namely the line of the Mitla and Gidi Passes in the south (and, on the Syrian front, withdrawing from the Golan Heights and consolidating before the escarpment overlooking the Jordan

Valley). General Elazar refused to accept the Defence Minister's recommendation, but at the same time vetoed the recommendation by Sharon to counterattack immediately and to cross the Suez Canal.

By midday on 7 October, the Egyptian 7th Infantry Division had crossed with all its forces south of the Bitter Lakes, as had the 25th Armoured Brigade. Until sundown, Egypt's forces were organized for defence against counterattacks, for a further advance into the Sinai and a deepening of the bridgeheads to a depth of between four and five miles; during this period, all units of the infantry division crossed and, that night, the armoured brigades attached to the infantry divisions crossed too. By the evening of Monday 8 October, the infantry divisions (with an addition of a tank brigade to each division) were in position in full strength on the east bank of the Canal. After fending off the anticipated Israeli counterattacks, the forces attempted to widen each bridgehead, having been ordered to fan out and meet each other, to a depth of six to eight miles. Following this, a mechanized brigade of the 6th Mechanized Division crossed on the southern flank of the 19th Infantry Division (the southernmost division) in readiness to move down Wadi Sudar, when the attack eastwards would be developed.

The next phase, ending by the morning of Thursday 11 October, was to be devoted entirely to the defensive − to causing the Israelis maximum possible losses in their counterattacks. At the same time, the Egyptians planned to push down the coast of the Sinai towards Ras Sudar and Sharm El-Sheikh. Then, from Thursday until Monday 15 October, the 4th and 21st Armoured Divisions were to cross the bridgehead to mount a major attack, the main effort of which was to be directed towards the capture of the nerve centre of Refidim (Bir Gafgafa). The 4th Armoured Division with the 25th Armoured Brigade was to advance from the area of the Gidi Pass through Um Mahza to Refidim; the northern arm of the pincer was to be mounted by the 21st Armoured Division from the area of Ismailia and Deversoir through Tasa to Refidim. Secondary efforts were also to be developed.

The first counterattack

Armed with the authority of the Prime Minister, General Elazar proceeded to Southern Command in the evening of 7 October, and presented the plan for a counterattack against the Egyptian forces on the eastern bank of the Suez Canal on the following day. The Command order was to launch a concentrated divisional attack rolling down from north to south along the east bank of the Canal, but leaving a distance of some two miles between the Canal and the right flank of the attacking forces in order to avoid the danger of infantry anti-tank fire from the Canal-side ramparts. The plan called for an attack by Adan's division against the Egyptian Second Army, striking south from the area of Kantara, with Sharon's division being held in reserve in the area of Tasa. Should Adan's attack succeed, Sharon would then launch an attack against the Egyptian Third

Army, moving from the area of the Great Bitter Lake southward. Should Adan's attack be unsuccessful, however, Sharon's forces would be thrown in to reinforce it. Elazar emphasized that Sharon's forces would be held as a reserve to Adan's northern attack and their activation would be subject

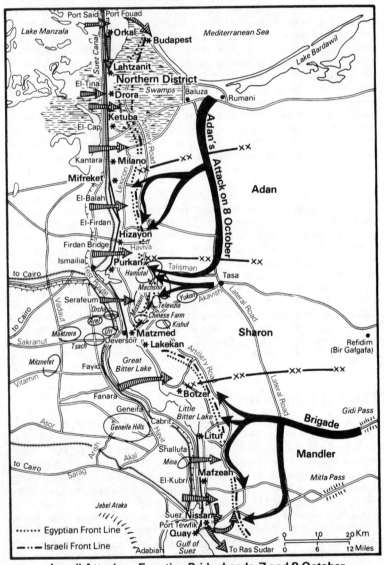

Israeli Attack on Egyptian Bridgeheads, 7 and 8 October

to his, Elazar's, personal approval; furthermore, the attacking forces should not reach the Canal, because of the danger of infantry anti-tank fire from the ramparts. It was assumed that, should the attack be successful, it might be possible to effect a limited crossing to the west bank at the southern extremity of each sector.

Adan's division was deployed along the main lateral road, namely the Baluza-Tasa road. His first brigade (Amir's) was to move southwards between the Canal road and Artillery Road, to destroy the enemy in the area and reach the fortifications opposite Firdan and Ismailia respectively. On the left flank of this brigade, but still west of Artillery Road, Colonel Natke Nir's brigade was to advance southwards towards the Purkan fortifications opposite Ismailia. A third brigade, commanded by Colonel Arieh Keren, was to move southwards east of Artillery Road towards Matzmed, at the northern extremity of the Great Bitter Lake, where a limited crossing of the Canal would be attempted on Egyptian bridges if they were taken intact. After the destruction of the enemy forces by Adan's division, Brigadier-General Magen's forces were to come in from the north and mop-up along the east bank of the Canal.

The forces moved from north to south according to plan, but, as the morning advanced, it became clear that Adan's forces were in fact moving too far to the east along Artillery Road and away from the bulk of the enemy forces. This mistake was not corrected in time; as a result, instead of rolling down the northern flank of the narrow Egyptian bridgehead and hitting the Egyptians where they least expected it, the massed forces of Adan's division were moving across the *front* of the Egyptian bridgehead. And thus, when they turned towards the Canal, their attack developed from east to west — right into the Egyptian positions waiting for them.

The first to join battle was Amir's force at about midday, which was engaged by hundreds of Egyptian infantry firing anti-tank weapons at short range, who appeared out of the sand dunes. The leading battalion withdrew, leaving twelve tanks burning on the battlefield.

Meanwhile, because the main force was moving too far to the east across the front of the concentrated Egyptian forces, and was not encountering any serious resistance, the impression gained at Gonen's headquarters was that all was going well. Thus, at 11.00 hours, he ordered Sharon's division to move southwards to the area of the Gidi Pass in order to hold it in readiness for a push against the Egyptian Third Army.

Meanwhile, in the early afternoon, Adan ordered a two-brigade attack (Nir's and Amir's) towards the Firdan bridge. Eight hundred yards from the Canal, Nir's forces found themselves surrounded by thousands of Egyptian infantry, and eighteen of his tanks were set on fire and destroyed. Nir is an unusual example of perseverence and courage overcoming disability. While serving as battalion commander in the Six Day War, he had been seriously wounded in his legs, and had undergone more than twenty operations. He refused to be retired from combat duty, and by sheer perseverence was awarded a fighting command in a reserve tank brigade, despite his disability. Like the knights of old, he had to be assisted or hoisted in order to mount or dismount from a tank, but his bulldog nature brought him to a combat command. When he withdrew his forces from the inferno in which they found themselves in attacking in the direction of the Canal, only four tanks were capable of withdrawing with him.

No Israeli infantry or armoured infantry had been deployed in this attack, which had no air force support and which had only two batteries of artillery backing it. Facing this attack were the forces of the Egyptian 2nd Infantry Division, commanded by General Hassan Abu Saada, in co-ordination with the forces of the 18th Infantry Division reinforced by the anti-tank reserves of Second Army.

In the meantime, the Egyptians launched an attack on Keren's forces to the south, in the general area of the northern end of the Great Bitter Lake, and occupied a number of Israeli strongpoints. And, in addition, two Egyptian counterattacks each comprising a mechanized brigade and a tank brigade, one from the area of the Firdan bridge and one from the south towards the Ismailia road, were mounted against Adan's forces. Adan authorized Amir and Nir to improve their positions by making tactical withdrawals and, at about 14.00 hours on 8 October, Gonen realized that Adan's attack had been a failure. He therefore ordered Sharon to return from the southern to the central sector — so Sharon's division had spent a critical day travelling southwards and northwards without in any way exercising influence on the battlefield. Meanwhile, Adan's division was fighting back the Egyptian counterattack. As the sun, which was blinding the Israeli forces, set, visibility improved and the Egyptian attackers suffered very heavy casualties among their tanks and armoured personnel vehicles. The Egyptian counterattack was halted.

It was clear now to the Israeli Command that they must conserve forces and allow time for the reserve army to deploy with all its supporting arms. Many errors in Israeli military thinking, particularly that of the armoured forces, were highlighted by the developments on 8 October. The Israeli armour mounted what looked like old-fashioned cavalry charges, without infantry support and with inadequate artillery support. This made no sense whatever in the face of the masses of anti-tank weapons that the Egyptians had concentrated on the battlefield. Again, Adan's armoured force was at no stage concentrated, but frittered away piecemeal. Had Southern Command mounted a two-divisional attack concentrated against the area of the Firdan bridge with the necessary support, it could well have succeeded in punching a hole in the Egyptian lines from which the Israeli forces could then have rolled up the Egyptian bridgehead from its flanks. The Israeli forces on that day suffered heavy casualties and lost a number of important positions, and the day's fighting represented a lost opportunity. On a personal level, the events of 8 October were to bring to expression the very difficult relationship between Sharon and GOC Southern Command, General Gonen, not to mention open mistrust and hostility that developed between him and the General Staff and his other divisional commanders. On Tuesday afternoon, 9 October, Sharon's forces attacked the Egyptians in order to retake a second-line fortification that had fallen to the Egyptians the day before. Despite Gonen's instructions to him to stop the attack, Sharon persisted in developing it, with the result that Gonen requested from the Chief of Staff that Sharon be relieved of his command.

Meanwhile, Amnon Reshef's brigade, under command of Sharon, was now facing the so-called 'Chinese Farm' (an experimental agricultural area in which Japanese instructors had been used before the 1967 War; seeing Japanese inscriptions on the walls, the Israeli troops, not particularly well versed in East Asian scripts, had named the place 'Chinese Farm'). Reshef's units and the divisional reconnaissance unit attached to them, continued their probing, reaching the water's edge along the Great Bitter Lake and then turning northwards towards the Chinese Farm, hugging the edge of the lake. On the morning of 10 October, however, the reconnaissance forces were ordered to withdraw from this area because it was obvious to the Israeli Command that, unbeknown to the Egyptians, these probes had revealed the boundary between the Egyptian Second and Third Armies — and the soft underbelly of Second Army.

The crisis

On Tuesday 9 October, General Dayan briefed the editors of the Israeli press. His talk exuded pessimism, and he hinted at the possibility of a defence line in the southern Sinai to cover only Sharm El-Sheikh. He believed that it would be necessary to decide on new and shorter lines. He also indicated his intention of going on Israeli television that night and of revealing to the public the scope of the losses incurred by the Israeli forces to date, including the loss in three days of fifty aircraft and hundreds of tanks. The atmosphere he created gave rise to much concern, so Golda Meir, the Prime Minister, sent General Aharon Yariv, the former Chief of Intelligence, to appear in his place.

On 9 October, General Chaim Bar-Lev, the former Chief of Staff who was now Minister of Trade and Industry, was asked by General Elazar to go to Southern Command and, in effect, to take command there as personal representative of the Chief of Staff with full command authority over General Gonen. As he surveyed the situation in Southern Command, it became evident to Bar-Lev that it would be very difficult to exercise command over General Sharon and, on 12 October, he proposed to the Chief of Staff that Sharon be relieved. Dayan, however, vetoed that proposal, on the grounds that it would create unnecessary internal political problems. Twice during the War did Bar-Lev recommend relieving Sharon of his post. . . .

As from 9 October, the Israeli forces succeeded in stabilizing the line and holding the Egyptian forces, who thereafter did not succeed in making additional territorial gains during the remainder of the war. The Egyptians daily launched a number of attacks, but gradually the Israeli forces got the measure of the Egyptian Army with its new equipment and, in particular, developed new methods for dealing with the Sagger anti-missile threat. By the use of co-ordinated smokescreens and concentrated artillery fire, the

Israeli forces succeeded in minimizing the effect of the Egyptian anti-tank missile concentrations.

As the Egyptian infantry attacked again and again, incurring heavy losses, Israeli respect for the determination and daring of their opponents grew. On 9 October, the Egyptians mounted a divisional attack on Amir's brigade, penetrating the Israeli lines, but Adan, concentrating his armour, crushed the Egyptians by drawing them on to Amir's brigade and then unleashing his other two brigades, one on their northern flank and one on their southern flank. On Wednesday 10 October, the Egyptians mounted five separate attacks against Adan's division and, on the same day, Sharon's division was attacked by units of the Egyptian 21st Armoured Division. Manoeuvring carefully in the desert, he smashed the Egyptian attack, which cost them some 50 tanks left on the field of battle. Also on the 10th, the Egyptian 1st Mechanized Brigade advanced southwards along the Gulf of Suez, but was held by an armoured force under General Yeshayahu Gavish, who was commanding the southern Sinai. The Egyptian force of some 50 tanks joined battle with the Israelis in the area of Ras Sudar — out of range of the Egyptian missile umbrella covering the Suez Canal. Consequently, the Israeli Air Force was able to attack and destroy the entire brigade. According to General Shazli, the Egyptian Chief of Staff, in his subsequent description of the war, he used this experience to oppose the pressure put on him by the Egyptian Minister of War, General Ahmed Ismail Ali, to advance and attack the Mitla and Gidi Passes. Shazli at all times opposed the emergence of the Egyptian forces from beneath the missile umbrella. This difference of opinion was ultimately to explode into a very serious controversy.

Gradually, the Israeli forces took control of the battlefield, allowing the Egyptian assaults to break up on the Israeli anvil. Confidence was growing. The ratio of losses had changed markedly, with the Israeli losses dropping and those of Egypt increasing. Israeli reserves were arriving, and the ordnance units were repairing tanks. Southern Command was gathering strength.

The Israeli Command was of the opinion that no decision in the field of battle could be made unless the Israeli Army crossed the Canal into Egypt proper and then developed its natural tendency for speed and manoeuvre. It must not get bogged-down in a static war for which it was not suited. The Israelis had all along planned the roads and the concentration areas, including the bridging equipment, for such a contingency. The concept of attack was now developed. It would be a two-divisional attack at the vulnerable boundary between the Egyptian Second and Third Armies at Deversoir, at which point, it will be recalled, a reconnaissance force had noted that the link in the Egyptian line was a weak one. Orders were given to assemble a preconstructed bridge, which would be rolled into position. Gonen presented his plan, which was accepted in principle by Bar-Lev. Deversoir was chosen as the point of crossing because one flank would be protected by the Great Bitter Lake; furthermore, the west bank at this point was far more conducive to a battle of manoeuvre than other areas that had been proposed. Above all, this was the junction point between two Egyptian armies and, by the very nature of things, constituted a weak link.

But the Israelis faced a dilemma. The Egyptian armoured divisions were concentrated on the west bank of the Canal, and this fact made the plan almost impracticable. The Egyptian force concentrated on the west bank — fresh forces that had not yet been deployed in battle — included two armoured divisions, two mechanized divisions and two independent armoured brigades, with a total of some 900 Egyptian tanks. Both Elazar and Bar-Lev felt that it was inadvisable to make the crossing until a serious dent had been made in the Egyptian armoured forces.

On both sides of the line, there was a sharp division of opinion that focused on the Egyptian armoured concentrations still on the west bank. On the Israeli side, pressure was developing to cross the Canal as rapidly as possible and not to wait for the Egyptian armoured forces to cross to the east; against this view, Elazar and Bar-Lev felt that it was essential to wait for the Egyptian armoured concentrations to cross over to the east bank, to lure them into committing themselves in battle, and only then to launch an attack across the Canal against an Egyptian army that had lost most of its armoured strength. On the Egyptian side, the Minister of War, backed by President Sadat, was pressurizing General Shazli to move the armour across to the east bank and to mount an attack against the Mitla and Gidi Passes. Three times in the course of 24 hours, he issued orders to this effect, and three times Shazli resisted the order, explaining the dangerous situation that might thereby be created. Finally, a direct order was issued to mount the armoured attack on 14 October.

In the original crossing of the Canal, the Egyptians had moved over 1,000 out of a total of 1,700 front-line tanks, leaving behind some 350 tanks in the vicinity of the west bank of the Canal, and 250 as a strategic reserve: the 21st Armoured Division was the reserve behind Second Army, and the 4th Armoured Division was the reserve behind Third Army. The decision to move them across the Canal has been characterized by Shazli as the major Egyptian error in the war. This move, in fact, left only one armoured brigade to protect the west bank of the Canal.

Meanwhile, in Israel, on Friday 12 October, Generals Elazar and Bar-Lev presented their plan for the crossing of the Canal to the Minister of Defence. Elazar proposed waiting for the Egyptian attack and dealing with it before the Israelis crossed the Canal. Dayan was sceptical and not very enthusiastic about the operation, but added that he was not prepared to 'wage a jihad against it': the Israeli crossing of the Canal would not decide anything, nor would it bring the Egyptians to ask for a cease-fire. He was sharply at variance with Elazar on the plan. Dayan brought the matter to a meeting chaired by the Prime Minister and attended by members of the ad hoc Cabinet in addition to a number of generals. During the discussion after Bar-Lev had presented the plan, many doubts were expressed by those participating as to the feasibility of the operation. It seemed to many that basing such an operation on one supply road would be in defiance of accepted military doctrine. In the course of the meeting, intelligence was received that the movement of the Egyptian armour across the Canal to the east bank had begun, and Bar-Lev there-upon proposed postponing a decision in order to enable Southern Command to prepare itself to receive the Egyptian attack and to break it. Indeed, indications were growing that, with the crossing of the Egyptian armoured forces, the long-awaited Egyptian attack was imminent. Elazar, the Chief of Staff, decided to postpone the crossing until after the main armoured battle, in which the Israeli forces would attempt to destroy the maximum number of Egyptian tanks and draw into the bridgeheads from the west bank as much Egyptian armour as possible.

General Shazli had been overruled by the Egyptian Minister of War on the specific instructions of President Sadat, but the Minister of War had agreed to postpone the attack from 13 to 14 October. However, on Saturday 13 October, the Egyptians launched probing attacks all along the line. The 4th and 21st Armoured Divisions were concentrated on the east bank of the Canal and prepared, against the advice of the Chief of Staff, to launch an attack towards the passes out of the range of the missile umbrella that covered the Egyptian bridgeheads. Their plan was to make for the Refidim (Bir Gafgafa) nerve centre by means of a wide pincer movement, with an armoured division and an armoured brigade advancing from the Gidi crossroads through Um Mahza to Refidim, and another armoured division advancing to Refidim from the area of Ismailia-Deversoir via Tasa.

Gonen meanwhile deployed the forces of Israel's Southern Command with instructions that the efforts along the Mediterranean coast in the north and the Gulf of Suez in the south were to be blocked by armoured forces, and that thereafter the air force — out of range of the Egyptian surface-to-air missile system — would deal with the attacking forces. As for the central and southern sectors, should the attack be a frontal one, Mandler and Sharon were to hold it; if the effort continued towards Refidim, Adan's division (in addition to part of Sharon's forces) was to be held in reserve for a counterattack from the flank. One of Adan's brigades was moved to the area of Refidim.

In the morning, the Chief of Staff went to Southern Command and flew on to Sharon's advanced headquarters to review the plans for the armoured battle, which seemed imminent, and for the projected crossing of the Canal. Gonen flew to this meeting by helicopter. Seated beside him was Ezer Weizman, (then reserve major-general, former commander of the Israeli Air Force and subsequently chief of the Operations Branch at the General Staff Headquarters). Gonen advised Mandler by radio that he would come to visit him at his headquarters after he had finished with Sharon, and they agreed a meeting place by codewords. Suddenly Mandler went off the air. He had been killed by Egyptian missile fire, which had zeroed-in on the observation point from which he had been speaking to Gonen by radio. Elazar issued immediate orders for Brigadier-General Kalman Magen, who was commanding the northern sector, to replace him.

With Mandler's death, an officer of unusual integrity was lost to the Israel Defence Forces. His sense of loyalty to his superiors and to those under his command was most marked. After the outbreak of war, those near him could sense that he felt a degree of personal responsibility for not having acted according to his instincts, which had told him that war was imminent. He believed that the situation would have been radically different had his forces been in position according to the overall plan. He was, however, one of the most disciplined officers in the army, and not one person had heard a word of reproach from him after the outbreak of war.

On Sunday morning, 14 October, the Egyptian armoured forces launched their attack between 06.00 and 08.00 hours. In the northern sector, the Egyptian 18th Infantry Division, strengthened by a tank brigade equipped with Soviet-built T-62 tanks, attacked from the area of Kantara with the object of reaching Rumani. Commando units were heliported to points in the salt marshlands to the east. In the central sector opposite Sharon, the Egyptian 21st Armoured Division, which had completed crossing into the Sinai that morning, with a tank brigade from the 23rd Mechanized Division, broke out of the bridgehead along the central route leading from Ismailia. In Magen's southern sector, two tank brigades attempted to break out eastwards towards the Gidi and Mitla Passes, one brigade on each axis. Part of this force endeavoured to insinuate itself along the wadis towards the passes. To the south, a special task force (comprising an infantry brigade from the 19th Infantry Division, a tank brigade and 113 Mechanized Brigade from the 6th Mechanized Division) moved towards Ras Sudar in a southerly push along the Gulf of Suez. Three of the six Egyptian thrusts were directed by General Mamoun's Second Army from its headquarters near Ismailia. Three further thrusts were mounted by General Wassel's Third Army, the northernmost of which was directed due eastwards towards the Gidi Pass and the Israeli Southern Command headquarters at Um Kusheiba. Farther south, there was a similar armoured drive towards the Mitla Pass, some nine miles away, while the southern thrust was south-eastwards towards Ras Sudar.

Thus began one of the largest tank battles in history (apart from the battle of Kursk in the Second World War), with some 2,000 tanks locked in battle along the entire front. It was a heavy, sultry morning. The Egyptians opened with a heavy artillery attack. The Israeli forces had carefully prepared themselves for this battle and were waiting. In the north, the Egyptians pressed against the over-extended Israeli lines, and Gonen ordered Adan's division to move in and assume responsibility. By early afternoon, Adan had thrown the Egyptians back to their starting point with a loss of some 50 tanks. In the central sector, the Egyptians fared no better against Sharon's division: Colonel Reshef, who had sited his tanks well on high ground, allowed the Egyptians to advance in headlong attack against his fire base and, as they closed on the Israeli tanks, the Egyptian forces were engaged at ranges frequently down to 100 yards. Simultaneously, he threw the divisional reconnaissance unit, reinforced by a company of tanks, against the southern flank of the attacking forces. When the battle ended, the Egyptian 1st Mechanized Brigade had been destroyed; 93 knocked-out tanks had been counted, while Reshef's brigade had suffered only three tanks hit, all by missiles — not one tank had been hit by Egyptian tank fire. On Reshef's southern flank, an Israeli brigade commanded by Colonel Haim Erez successfully beat back a parallel Egyptian attack. By the end of the day, the Egyptian 21st Division, which had been ranged against Sharon's forces, had lost a total of 110 tanks.

To the south of Sharon, Magen's division held the thrusts towards the Gidi and Mitla Passes, containing the Egyptian attack after initially giving up some ground before counterattacking and taking a toll of some 60 Egyptian tanks. The Egyptian southern effort, which endeavoured to make a deep flanking movement to the south and turn northwards to reach the Mitla Pass from the south, came up against Israeli paratroop forces holding the pass at Ras Sudar. Magen's tanks were deployed in anticipation of such a possible flanking movement, and Shomron's brigade was waiting at the Mitla Pass itself. A fierce battle ensued, in which the Egyptians were engaged by the Israeli paratroop forces and Israeli armour. After two hours of fighting, most of the 3rd Armoured Brigade of the Egyptian 4th Armoured Division had been wiped out. Brought to a halt by the Israeli forces, the concentrated Egyptian armour attempting to move southwards, by now out of range of the anti-aircraft, surface-to-air protective missiles, came under attack by the Israeli Air Force. Within two hours some 60 Egyptian tanks and a large quantity of armoured personnel carriers and artillery were in flames as a result. By the time this column retraced its steps towards evening, it had lost more than half its strength, approximately 90 tanks.

During the day, the Egyptians issued optimistic reports that were broadcast around the world and reflected reports being received from the two field army headquarters. However, towards evening it became quite clear to General Ismail Ali, the Minister of War, that these reports did not reflect the true situation, and that his forces were now exposed without the essential surface-to-air missile protection against the Israeli Air Force. He describes in one of his interviews after the war how, when he realized the true situation, he ordered all formations back to their original positions. Israeli Southern Command waited in vain for the Egyptian attack to develop further, with increased strength, and to penetrate deeper. But the Egyptian forces were poorly led and their tactics were unimaginative. The Israeli forces had a field day. Not a single lasting gain was registered by the enemy. In the northern sector, the Israelis counterattacked and re-established contact with the 'Budapest' fortification, which had been cut off.

This battle was a major turning point in the war in the Sinai: 264 knocked-out Egyptian tanks were counted on the battlefield, and the attackers had suffered more than 1,000 casualties. The Israeli tank losses on that day totalled only some ten tanks. As the results of this, in many ways, major and fateful battle and its significance dawned on General Saad Mamoun, he suffered a heart attack: he was replaced as GOC, Second Army, by General Abd el Munem Halil. The Egyptian Command realized the seriousness of the defeat. General Saad el Din Shazli, Chief of Staff of the Egyptian armed forces, admitted in a document circulated to all the commanders, that the Egyptian attacking forces had been surprised on all axes of advance by Israeli tanks and anti-tank battalions equipped with anti-tank guided missiles of the SS11 type, which had succeeded in blocking their attacks and inflicting very heavy tank losses. Analysing the losses sustained by the Israelis in their initial counterattack to the Canal and against the Egyptian bridgeheads on 6 October, and the heavy losses sustained by the Egyptians by their attack on the 14th, he reached the conclusion that it was impossible to ensure the success of any attack — whether by tanks or by armoured infantry — without destroying or silencing in advance the anti-tank missile defences.

On the morning of 15 October, General Shazli proposed that the remnants of the 21st Armoured Division and the 4th Armoured Division be once again returned to the west bank of the Canal and concentrated there, so as to achieve the required military balance as he saw it. The Minister of War, General Ismail Ali, opposed this move, maintaining that the removal of these forces would affect adversely the morale of the Egyptian Army on the east bank, and that the Israelis would interpret such a move as a sign of weakness, which would invite additional pressure on the Egyptian forces. Shazli maintains to this day that the decision was a political one, because on the next day, 16 October, President Sadat was scheduled to deliver a political speech to the Egyptian parliament, the People's Council, and he wanted to speak from a position of strength.

On the possibility of a major Egyptian offensive Dayan had been sceptical. Sharon had urged that the Israeli forces not wait for the Egyptian offensives but attack the bridgeheads and attempt to nibble away at them. In the final analysis, the position taken jointly by Elazar, Bar-Lev and Gonen was fully vindicated. The Egyptians had decided on the offensive under pressure from the Syrians, who had hoped that such an attack would relieve some of the Israeli pressure on the Syrian front. However, when the offensive was finally mounted, it was spread out along a front over 100 miles long, in six major thrusts. Had the armour that had been brought over to the east of the Canal been concentrated in one, or at most two, strong armoured fists directed towards one or two of the passes, it would certainly have had a better chance of success than the spread-out effort the Egyptians actually mounted. Furthermore, the Egyptians did not learn from their initial success in crossing the Canal, and did not provide adequate forces of infantry to support their attack against the Israelis. In retrospect, it is clear that General Ismail Ali's decision, based on direct instructions from President Sadat, stood a good chance of success only if the attacking forces were concentrated in a major armoured fist. In the manner in which the attack was mounted, it is quite clear that the Egyptians erred, and that they walked into the trap Elazar had prepared for them. His evaluation of the developments that should take place along the Canal before an Israeli crossing was a correct one, and one of the most important decisions he made in the course of the war.

So, on the Israeli side, the conclusion to be drawn from the battle was clear: Elazar issued orders for the Canal crossing to take place on the following night.

The Israeli plan

Sharon's division was given the task of leading the Canal crossing with a brigade of paratroopers reinforced by tanks. His mission was to cross in the area of Deversoir, with his left flank hinging on, and protected by, the Great Bitter Lake, and to establish and hold a bridgehead three miles wide northwards from the lake, thus putting Egyptian mortars and anti-tank missiles out of range of the preconstructed bridge, which in the meantime would be towed to the Canal and laid across it. The tanks would pass through the agricultural strip running parallel to the Canal along the sweet-water (irrigation) canal and begin, in the initial phase, to knock out Egyptian surface-to-air missile sites, thus clearing the air above the bridgehead for the Israeli Air Force. Adan's division would be held in readiness to cross immediately after Sharon, while Magen's division was to be prepared to cross on a given order. It was expected that at least one of the pontoon bridges would be operational early on the 16th.

Later, the plan was issued in a more detailed manner. In addition to effecting the first crossing, Sharon's division was ordered at the same time to widen the corridor to the Canal on the east bank — capturing the Chinese Farm and the stronghold codenamed 'Missouri' — up to a point three miles from the water-line. This move would open the two axes leading to the Canal, 'Akavish' and 'Tirtur' (the latter a ruler-straight road that had been built for the specific purpose of towing the preconstructed bridge to the Canal). The initial crossing would be carried out by a brigade of paratroopers in inflatable boats, supported by ten tanks, which would cross on rafts. Two bridges would be established: a preconstructed bridge and a pontoon. The assault force would secure the bridgehead and, when additional forces crossed, move southwards. Should any difficulty be encountered in widening the corridor on the east bank, Adan's division would cross after the assault units, and only thereafter would the remainder of Sharon's forces cross. Adan was to cross the bridge on the morning after Sharon's crossing, and sweep southwards on the eastern flank of Sharon's southern sweep. His mission was to destroy the surface-to-air missile batteries in the area, and thus enable the Israeli Air Force to establish supremacy in the air over the battlefield. The attack was to develop in order to cut off the Egyptian Third Army and to destroy it. Simultaneous with the crossing, the northern force under Brigadier-General Sasoon (who had replaced Magen) and Magen's division in the south, were to launch attacks along their fronts in order to pin down the enemy forces.

The Israeli forces had, over the years, prepared the infrastructure for a possible crossing of the Canal within the framework of normal military planning. They had built roads, such as the one codenamed 'Tirtur' in the Deversoir area, along which preconstructed bridges could be towed on rollers. The area facing the planned crossing point at Deversoir had been prepared as a concentration area with high sand walls scooped out, creating a large protected 'yard' where the necessary last-minute organizing and arrangements could be made.

It was quite clear to Sharon, however, as he prepared to launch the attack, that he would not be able to carry it out in the framework of the timetable. His plan was for an armoured brigade under the command of Colonel Tuvia Raviv to launch a holding attack against the Egyptian bridgehead of Second Army at its southern flank, while Reshef's brigade would make a wide, southerly, flanking movement through the sand dunes to the Canal. One force of Reshef's brigade would capture the Egyptian-held fortification of Matzmed, where the Suez Canal enters the Great Bitter Lake; a second force would clear Akavish Road; while the third force would move northwards to widen the corridor in the direction of the Chinese Farm and would clear Tirtur Road. A paratroop brigade under Colonel Danny Matt would follow Reshef's brigade along Akavish; while yet another brigade under Colonel Erez would follow Matt's brigade, and the divisional crossing would be completed by Reshef's brigade. The basic assumption of the entire plan was that the preconstructed bridge would be across the water by the next morning. While Raviv was securing the corridor on the east bank, one force of Erez's brigade was to cross with Danny Matt, with another towing the preconstructed bridge along Tirtur to the banks of the Canal. At the same time, Raviv's brigade was to launch an attack in order to draw the main weight of the Egyptian 16th Infantry Division and 21st Armoured Division north, in the direction of the Tasa-Ismailia road, and to focus the Egyptian Command's attention on the northern sector of the front.

Opening the gap

When Reshef started out at 16.00 hours, he had four tank battalions and three infantry battalions on half-tracks. At nightfall, he moved down from the high ground in a south-westerly direction (along the route that the divisional reconnaissance unit had reconnoitred to the Great Bitter Lake on 9 October). His force reached Lexicon on the Great Bitter Lake without encountering any resistance and then turned northwards. The divisional reconnaissance unit that led Reshef's brigade divided into three sub-units; one unit skirted the north-east shore of the Great Bitter Lake and moved towards Matzmed; the second moved to the north of the first to reach the Canal; while the third moved to the north of the second and also reached the Canal. Thus this reconnaissance unit closed in on the Canal in a three-pronged advance, with the southern prong taking Matzmed.

The 7th Battalion continued to the west of Lexicon, passing the Chinese Farm on its right, attacking northwards in an endeavour to reach an Egyptian bridge six miles north of Matzmed; the 18th Battalion followed the 7th on its east flank and attacked east of Lexicon in a north-easterly direction towards 'Missouri', while the 40th Battalion attacked in a north-easterly direction, with one company at Tirtur and one company at Akavish, taking the Egyptian forces deployed along these two routes from the rear. The 42nd Infantry Battalion — with half a company of tanks —

followed the divisional reconnaissance unit to the west of Lexicon to mop-up the Egyptian infantry. An additional infantry force ('Force Shmulik'), composed of two regular paratroop companies and half a company of tanks, followed the 40th Infantry Battalion to clear up the Chinese Farm east of Lexicon; a third reserve infantry battalion under Major Nathan was held in reserve.

The divisional reconnaissance unit reached Matzmed and the points north of it along the Canal according to plan. After Reshef had passed the Lexicon-Tirtur crossroads heading northwards with the two battalions, fire was opened from the same area on the 18th Battalion as it moved forward east of Lexicon towards 'Missouri'. Although tank, missile and bazooka fire hit the battalion, knocking out eleven tanks, the battalion commander continued on his mission with the remaining tanks.

But, unknown to Reshef, his force had moved into the administrative centre of the Egyptian 16th Infantry Division, to which the 21st Armoured Division had also withdrawn after being so badly mauled on 14 October. His force found itself suddenly in the midst of a vast army with concentrations of hundreds of trucks, guns, tanks, missiles, radar units and thousands of troops milling around as far as the eye could see. The Israeli force had come up through the unprotected southern flank of the Egyptian Second Army at the junction of the Egyptian Second and Third Armies — had entered by the 'back door', as it were — and had suddenly found itself plumb in the centre of the administrative areas of two Egyptian divisions and literally at the entrance to the 16th Infantry Division headquarters. Pandemonium broke out in the Egyptian forces. Thousands of weapons of all types opened fire in all direction, and the whole area seemed to go up in flames. The 40th Armoured Battalion reached the Tirtur-Lexicon crossroads and attacked, but the deputy battalion commander, Major Butel, was wounded and the attack was disrupted; a second company, under Major Ehud, moved up Akavish and cleared the route. The situation now was that the divisional reconnaissance unit had reached Matzmed and the Canal to the north of Matzmed, while Reshef was north of the Chinese Farm attacking northwards with two battalions; the Tirtur-Lexicon crossroads was closed and the remainder of the brigade, with a large number of casualties, was to the south of the crossroads. The infantry forces were suffering very heavily.

The 7th Battalion, between Lexicon and the Canal, continued northwards according to plan; but the 18th, half a mile north of the Chinese Farm, came up against an enemy force including dug-in tanks and entered a fire-fight. Reshef described the situation to Sharon and Matt, who was following him, and proposed that Matt's brigade move along the Nahala road hugging the north-eastern shore of the Great Bitter Lake, with the crossroads 800 yards on his right flank closed.

It was by now 21.00 hours. There were indications that the enemy was preparing for a counterattack from the north; pressure on the 7th Battalion and the 18th Battalion increased. The numerous casualties could not be evacuated because the Tirtur-Lexicon crossroads was blocked, so a battalion evacuation centre formed itself with all wounded next to

Reshef's tank. At 22.00 hours, the 7th Battalion commander, who was now six miles north of Matzmed, reported that he was down to one-third of his strength. Realizing that the brigade was spread far too wide, Reshef ordered the 7th Battalion to withdraw some two miles and form a line with the 18th Battalion, half a mile north of the Chinese Farm. As they were moving, the battalion commander, Lieutenant-Colonel Amram, was wounded in the leg, and was evacuated in the tank that was picking up the wounded on the battlefield. (This tank stood all night next to Reshef's with the wounded battalion commander acting as loader/communications man inside.)

The battle for the Tirtur road increased in intensity as units of the Egyptian 14th Armoured Brigade attacked from the north, while the 7th Battalion was pulling back at approximately midnight. The scene in the area was one of utter confusion: along the Lexicon road raced Egyptian ambulances; units of Egyptian infantry were rushing around in all directions, as were Egyptian tanks. The impression was that nobody knew what was happening or what to do. On all sides, lorries, ammunition, tanks, surface-to-air missiles on lorries and radar stations were in flames in one huge conflagration which covered the desert. It was like Hades. Days later, the entire area between the Canal and 'Missouri' was to appear from the west bank as one vast, eerie, unbelievable graveyard. As a background to this scene, the concentrated forces of artillery on both sides fired with everything they had.

Again and again, the reserve paratroop battalion under Reshef attacked the crossroads, the paratroopers not realizing that they were attacking a major, concentrated Egyptian force of at least a division in strength. During the attack, part of the paratroop force was trapped and, despite several attempts to extricate them, was wiped out.

With two battalions to the west of the Chinese Farm and the remainder of his brigade to the south of the crossroads evacuating casualties and reorganizing, Reshef decided that he would attack the crossroads from the rear. This attack, which took place at 04.00 hours in the morning of the 16th, failed.

At dawn on the 16th, Amnon Reshef moved to high ground and surveyed the scene of the night's battles. In all directions, the desert was covered with a vast fleet of burning and smoking tanks, vehicles, guns, transporters. Dead infantry lay everywhere. It seemed as if there was not a single item of military equipment that had escaped destruction: there were command caravans, mobile workshops, huge transporters carrying SAM-2 missiles, mobile kitchens. . . . The remnants of the Israeli forces were there too, and frequently the distances between them and the Egyptians were no more than a few yards.

Shortly thereafter, Reshef made another attempt to take the Lexicon-Tirtur crossroads. This time, Reshef and the company or so of tanks that he took with him did not storm the crossroads. Using daylight observation, and basing himself on alternate fire and movement, he gradually wore down the Egyptian force firing from maximum ranges. Exhausted by the night's fighting and having sustained very heavy casualties, the Egyptians were unable to stand up to this slow battle of attrition — they suddenly broke and fled. Reshef occupied the crossroads. As he attempted to advance north-eastwards up the Tirtur road, however, he was forced to stop as Egyptian tanks, anti-tank guns and missiles opened up from the slopes of the 'Missouri' position; Reshef fell back to the crossroads. His brigade had now been very severely mauled, and he had lost over half of his force; a very high percentage of the officers and tank commanders were casualties. Tirtur was still closed. Although the crossroads was now held by the Israelis, the Egyptians were pressing from the north against the forces holding the line west of the Chinese Farm. Leaving a battalion to hold this northern line, Reshef withdrew his brigade to Lakekan on the shores of the lake to reorganize. During that night of intense fighting, Sharon's division had suffered more than 300 men killed and had lost over a quarter of its 280 tanks. About 150 Egyptian tanks had been knocked out.

Meanwhile, at 21.30 hours on the 15th, Sharon, who had been misled into believing that the Egyptian forces were collapsing, had reported that Akavish Road was open. He had a force north of the Chinese Farm, but there was contact with the enemy armour at the Tirtur-Lexicon crossroads and he had incurred casualties there. The basis of this first, optimistic report had been the fact that Reshef's brigade had advanced and occupied Matzmed after securing Akavish. However, after Reshef's force had passed, the Egyptians had regrouped with their anti-tank weapons and — unknown to the advancing Israelis — had closed Akavish again. Subsequently, reports were received at Sharon's headquarters that heavy anti-tank resistance was being encountered at Tirtur and the Chinese Farm, while the main Israeli move to the Canal was taking place some hundreds of yards to the south. Despite this very dangerous situation, Sharon ordered Danny Matt to follow Reshef's forces.

The crossing

Colonel Danny Matt, a tall, distinguished-looking man with a nicely trimmed beard and well-kept moustache, had received many wounds in battle over the years. In the Six Day War, he had commanded a paratroop brigade under Sharon in the Sinai, and twice landed by helicopter during the fighting in Syria towards the end of that war. During 1968, he had commanded the daring 120-mile raid into Egypt at Najh Hamadi. From 1969, he had held an appointment as commander of the reserve paratroop brigade that, under General Mordechai Gur, captured the Old City of Jerusalem during the fighting in the Six Day War. In later years, he was to rise to the rank of major-general, serving as President of the Military Courts and as Chief Co-ordinator of the territories administered by Israel in the West Bank and Gaza.

Early in the morning of the 15th, Matt received instructions to move his brigade, which was concentrated at the Mitla Pass, with orders to cross the Canal that night. The orders were that his brigade reconnaissance company and the company of engineers under his second-in-command would lead the crossing of the Canal and establish the first foothold on the west bank. The engineer company would cross at four points with demolition equipment. Everything had been prepared for the breakthrough. A special brigade second-in-command had been appointed to take charge of the 'yard'. This was a brick-surfaced, hard stand at the western end of Tirtur Road and was located a few yards north of the point where the Canal joins the Great Bitter Lake, and just south-west of the Matzmed fortification. The area of the 'yard', measuring 700 yards by 150 yards, had been prepared by Sharon during his period as GOC Southern Command: protective sand walls surrounded it, and it marked the exact point for the crossing. There were positions in it for units to act as a fire base to engage enemy forces on the other side of the Canal, and the necessary arrangements for troop movement headquarters.

Following the initial foothold on the Egyptian side of the Canal, a battalion commanded by Lieutenant-Colonel Dan would widen the bridgehead to the south, while a battalion under Lieutenant-Colonel Zvi would widen it northwards. This bridgehead was to be no less in width than three miles northwards, and the crossings of the sweet-water canal one to one-and-a-half miles westwards were to be seized. Matt was informed that he had 60 inflatable boats available and that they would be delivered to the brigade by 10.00 hours; by early afternoon, however, he had received none of the inflatable boats and only half of the 60 half-tracks that had been promised to him. The boats and half-tracks were only discovered by members of his staff in the mid-afternoon. Matt's brigade moved out towards the rendezvous, but Israeli traffic control had apparently broken down completely — the roads were blocked for miles and there was an almost impassable traffic jam on the road leading to Tasa. Matt's troops negotiated only three miles in some two hours. The traffic was limited to the roads because it was impossible to move off them into the sand dunes, in which all the wheeled vehicles remained stuck in the sand. Working its way forward under the most difficult conditions, part of Matt's forces finally reached the embarkation area of the 'yard'. He had only reached the inflatable boats that were supposed to have been delivered to him in the morning at 21.00 hours; because of the large number of soft vehicles in his brigade carrying the troops, Matt was obliged to adapt his programme accordingly, and he had to leave behind the brigade reconnaissance company, which was to have attacked the bridgehead on the west bank, together with the battalion of Lieutenant-Colonel Dan. It was discovered, too, that the hard stand at the 'yard' was incomplete at one of the two planned crossing points, so only the southern one was was to be used.

As Matt's brigade advanced, led by a company of tanks, followed by the second-in-command of the brigade with the assault crossing force, the brigade forward headquarters and Dan's battalion with the rest of the brigade following as best it could, the column came under artillery, missile and heavy machine-gun fire from the Akavish-Tirtur crossroads, some 1,000 yards distant. A force that Matt sent to establish itself on the crossroads to afford protection against any possible intervention from

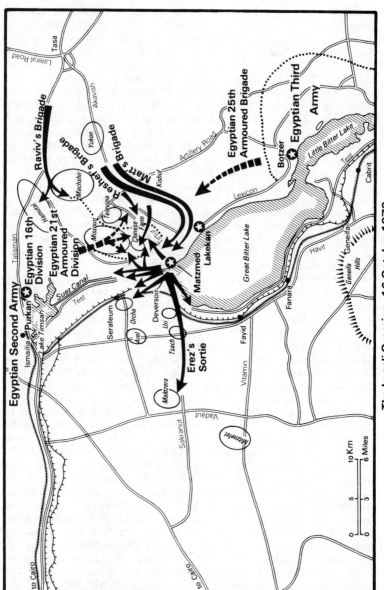

The Israeli Crossing, 16 October 1973

north or east was completely destroyed. Thus, Matt continued this precarious move towards the Canal for the crossing with his very tenuous axis of advance and supply line under intense fire from the enemy. By 00.30 hours in the morning of the 16th, the assault group under the second-in-command of the brigade had entered the 'yard'. Matt now ordered the entire artillery support at his disposal to open up on an area of the west bank some 1,000 yards wide by 220 yards deep.

Meanwhile, the half-tracks which had carried Matt's forces to the 'yard' could not move as planned along the road running northwards and eastwards because the Egyptians had already occupied the road some 700 yards from Matt's headquarters, and so the column of empty half-tracks moved back that night along the road on which the remaining loaded half-tracks were advancing. The situation was precarious in the extreme. However, despite the proximity of the Egyptians to the crossing point and the near pandemonium that reigned in the area, Sharon urged his division on.

At 01.35 hours on 16 October, the first wave of Israeli troops crossed the Canal and set foot on the west bank — ten days after the Egyptian onslaught on the east bank. The leading forces crossed the Canal as planned, with the Israeli artillery plastering the narrow landing strip with tons of shells. Brigade advanced headquarters crossed at 02.40 and, by 05.00 hours, all infantry forces had crossed; at 06.43, the first tank of Erez's brigade crossed on a raft; by 08.00 hours, Matt's forces held a bridgehead that extended three miles northwards from the Great Bitter Lake as had been planned. Resistance had been weak and, as his forces moved along the Egyptian ramp northwards, they came upon thirty Egyptians manning electronic equipment a mile to the north; part of the force was killed and part was taken prisoner. When isolated Egyptian armoured personnel carriers appeared, they were wiped out by the advancing Israeli forces. As they waited in position, the forces facing northwards observed a convoy of seven trucks loaded with 150 troops approaching unsuspectingly. They destroyed it and seized the four main crossings over the sweet-water canal. During the morning, leaving seven tanks to protect Matt's forces, Erez took 21 tanks westward on his mission to seek out the surface-to-air missile sites.

However, the problem of the Chinese Farm hung as a black cloud over the Israeli Command, which was only too aware of the fact that, unless the lines of communication on the east bank were secured, the entire operation would be doomed. Aware of the pressure of the Egyptian 14th Armoured Brigade from 'Missouri' position on Reshef's brigade from the north, Bar-Lev gave advance warning to Adan's division, being held in readiness to cross the first bridge, that it might have to intervene in the battle to open the roads to the Canal.

The situation at Southern Command Headquarters was indeed tense. Seeing what was happening on the east bank, and conscious of the bitter struggle that was going on in the corridor, the Minister of Defence, Moshe Dayan, proposed pulling back the paratroopers from the west bank: 'We tried. It has been no go.' He suggested giving up the idea of the crossing: 'In the morning they will slaughter them on the other side.' Gonen's reaction was: 'Had we known that this would happen in advance, we probably would not have initiated the crossing. But now that we are across we shall carry through to the bitter end. If there is no bridgehead today there will be one tomorrow, and if there is no bridgehead tomorrow there will be one in two days' time.' Bar-Lev overheard the conversation and, in his characteristically quiet voice, drawing out his words in an exaggeratedly slow manner, asked what they were talking about. When Gonen told him, he replied: 'There is nothing at all to discuss.'

Once again, a major debate was developing between Sharon and Southern Command. Sharon was of the opinion that the success in establishing a bridgehead across the Canal must be exploited immediately, irrespective of whether or not a bridge was erected. In his view, Adan's division should be transported on rafts to the other side and then the Israeli forces on the west bank should push on. Bar-Lev turned down this proposal on the 16th, and again on the 17th when Sharon renewed it, pointing out that this was not a raid across the Canal. He considered it would be the height of irresponsibility to launch an attack in corps strength numbering hundreds of tanks across the Canal, with a supply route that had not yet been secured and without a bridge. In his view, the tanks would run to a standstill within 24 hours; above all, he did not wish to rely on vulnerable rafts. He was of the opinion that Adan's division must first complete the clearing of the corridor on the east bank of the Canal before moving over to the west bank.

The preconstructed bridge, which had broken down while being towed, was now being repaired, and the pontoon bridge had been moved forward, but all awaited the clearing of the roads to the Canal in order to move the bridges down. On the afternoon of the 16th, at the conference attended by Dayan, Bar-Lev and Gonen, the latter said that, if neither bridge nor pontoons reached the Canal, they would have to withdraw from the west bank. If there were pontoons but no bridge, the force would remain there, but Adan's division could not be transferred to join it. As soon as a bridge was in position, all the forces could cross as planned.

Adan was already moving his forces forward in order to begin crossing on rafts when he was ordered to open Akavish and Tirtur. Southern Command had sent a paratroop force to deal with the Egyptian forces closing these roads, but they had moved along at night into action without adequate preparation and sustained very heavy casualties. Adan now ordered the paratroopers to leave Tirtur and concentrate on Akavish, but the fire was so heavy that the paratroopers could not disengage. While the paratroopers were fighting desperately between the two roads, Adan decided to make one more attempt. He sent a force of armoured personnel carriers along Akavish to report on the situation; the road was clear. Taking advantage of this situation, the pontoon bridging equipment was gradually moved towards the Canal. Protecting this move of the bridging equipment was a paratroop battalion, whose battalion commander realized that he must now hold the line facing the Egyptians at all costs. He created a line some 75–100 yards from the Egyptian lines with his paratroopers constantly risking their lives by rushing into no man's land to evacuate the wounded. Despite the intense and murderous Egyptian fire, the paratroopers held on grimly in a battle that lasted for fourteen hours, facing a divisional position while, to the rear, movement towards the Canal continued.

Meanwhile, two armoured brigades moved to clear the area of Akavish and Tirtur under Adan's command. Natke Nir's brigade deployed to the south of Akavish, moving northwards across the road and continuing in the direction of Tirtur. Amir's brigade pushed from east to west. Raviv's brigade also joined in, and Adan pressed on the Egyptian forces in the Israeli corridor from east to west with three concentrated armoured brigades.

The battle for the corridor

The Egyptian headquarters had now received news of the existence of Israeli forces on the west side of the Canal. The information was scant and such as not to arouse very considerable concern. Indeed, the initial Egyptian reaction to the crossing was one of incredulity and light-hearted dismissal, with the various levels of command so blinded by self-adulation at their initial success that they tended to brush the operation off as a tiresome nuisance that could be dealt with. The feeling was that this was a move designed by the Israelis to boost morale, and was characterized by President Sadat as a spectacular 'television operation' and no more. On the afternoon of 16 October, the Egyptian General Staff met and decided to strike against the area of the Israeli operation on the morning of 17 October. Here again, sharp divisions of opinion emerged between the Minister of War and the Chief of Staff. General Shazli continued to favour withdrawing part of the forces from the east bank to the west, but, in the light of the new situation, he realized that it would be difficult to pull out the 21st Armoured Division, which was being engaged by the Israeli forces attempting to widen the corridor on the east bank. He therefore proposed withdrawing to the west bank the 4th Armoured Division and also the 25th Armoured Brigade from Third Army, and to strike with two armoured brigades at the Israeli bridgehead on the west of the Canal, attacking from a north-easterly direction. The Minister of War, however, opposed the withdrawal of any forces from the east bank, including the 4th Armoured Division. He also was of the opinion that the counterattack should be mounted on the east bank against the Israeli corridor, and that only a secondary effort be made on the west bank. When President Sadat came to the Headquarters, General Shazli presented his proposal to him: Sadat lost his temper and cut him short, shouting at him that if he mentioned once again the possibility of moving forces back from the east to the west bank he would have him court-martialled.

Early next morning, at 03.00 hours on 17 October, General Wassel, the commander of Third Army, expressed great doubts to Shazli about the idea of moving the 25th Armoured Brigade to counterattack on the east bank. Both he and the commander of the brigade, according to Shazli, were of the opinion that the brigade would be walking into a very dangerous trap. After a long discussion, again according to Shazli, Wassel said resignedly: 'I will carry out the instructions, but I must advise you that this brigade will be destroyed.' Thus, the Egyptian Command, appreciating that a major effort was being made by the Israeli forces to open a corridor north of the Great Bitter Lake, did not realize that while fighting of such intensity was going on in the area of the corridor, the Israeli Command was nevertheless launching a major effort across the Canal without an assured supply route.

So, following instructions, a determined effort was made on 17 October by the Egyptian Second and Third Armies to close the Israeli corridor and cut off all Israeli forces between Lexicon and the Canal. The Egyptian 14th Armoured Brigade had fought for two days against a lone tank battalion commanded by Lieutenant-Colonel Amir Jaffe to the west of the Chinese Farm and, by the evening of the 17th, had been largely destroyed, while the forces of the Egyptian 16th Infantry and 21st Armoured Divisions launched two major attacks against Adan's forces at Tirtur and Akavish.

The Egyptian counterattack was mounted from 'Missouri' and the Chinese Farm towards Akavish. The sand dunes were covered by Egyptian tanks as they moved forward. Colonel Nir and Colonel Amir waited for them and engaged them in a major armoured battle, while Lieutenant-Colonel Amir Jaffe, who was to the west of the Egyptian attack, harassed them from the rear. Twice the Egyptians mounted a major attack; when they finally withdrew, they left a large number of tanks on the field — losses sufficient to seal the fate of the Chinese Farm. At this stage, the Egyptian Third Army launched the 25th Armoured Brigade from the south in order to complete the joint operation. It advanced northwards along the Great Bitter Lake in the direction of the Egyptian 16th Division bridgehead north of the Israeli corridor, with the mission of cutting the corridor and destroying the Israeli forces that had penetrated the bridgehead.

Meanwhile, on the morning of the 17th, a conference was held at Adan's command post on the hills near Kishuf, attended by Adan, Elazar and Bar-Lev. The situation now looked somewhat better, as Akavish Road was open, Tirtur Road was being cleared, the paratroopers had been extricated, the Egyptian counterattacks had been repulsed, and one bridge was already being launched and would be ready for traffic in a few hours. A violent dispute broke out between Sharon and Adan, with Sharon proposing that Adan's division should deal with the corridor and the east bank, and that he would cross over to the west bank with his division. Adan opposed this proposal, maintaining that he had been fighting continuously for 30 hours to perform tasks that in his view Sharon had been supposed to do. He felt that his division deserved to share some of the glory that Sharon had already won by his crossing. Elazar decided in favour of Adan's proposal, ordering Sharon to clean up the corridor and widen it; only then was he to cross. Raviv's brigade would revert to Sharon and would exert pressure against the enemy, enabling Amir's brigade to rejoin and cross with Adan. As the conference continued, Reshef (whose brigade was reorganizing in the area of Lakekan on the shores of the Great Bitter Lake) reported that the dust raised by an approaching Egyptian armoured brigade was coming dangerously near. Aerial reconnaissance confirmed that this was a column of about 100 T-62 tanks. It was the Egyptian 25th Armoured Brigade.

Adan left the conference in order to take command and direct this new battle personally. Before leaving, he received permission from Bar-Lev to release his third brigade under Arieh Keren from reserve. Battle was joined at midday, with Reshef's tanks opening fire at long range and knocking out the first two tanks in the Egyptian column. During the conference, as Reshef's reports came in, Adan had already ordered Natke Nir to leave one battalion in the area of Akavish and Tirtur and to place an armoured ambush with the rest of his forces to the east of Lexicon facing the Great Bitter Lake. At the same time, he ordered Arieh Keren, moving with his brigade along the lateral road, to sweep around and come across country on a secondary road, deploying to the east of Botzer at the southern end of the Great Bitter Lake, thus placing himself to the east and to the rear of the advancing Egyptian brigade. So the Egyptian 25th Armoured Brigade, comprising 96 tanks and large numbers of armoured personnel carriers, artillery, fuel and supply lorries, moved slowly into a trap — to the north, blocking the road at Lakekan was a small unit of Reshef's forces; to the west was the lake; between it and the road, there was an Israeli minefield; to the east, Natke Nir was deployed; and, to the south-east, Arieh Keren's brigade closed off the Egyptian rear.

Nir's brigade opened fire first. Part of the Egyptian force turned to leave the road, moved towards the lake and tried to go back on its tracks. It ran into the Israeli minefield along the lake. The remainder charged towards Nir's forces waiting for them in the sand dunes, and began to be destroyed by his tanks. When the Egyptian forces had been locked in battle with Nir's forces for half an hour, Keren's brigade moved from the Gidi road in a wide, left flanking movement towards Botzer. His force opened fire: the Egyptian brigade was completely boxed in, and the shore of the lake became a line of fire and smoke as, one by one, the tanks and vehicles in the Egyptian force were picked off. Magen's division from the south meanwhile lent artillery support to Keren's attack. Some of the Egyptian tanks turned to flee. Part of Keren's force followed them, but ran into an Israeli minefield near Botzer. By 17.30 hours, the battle, a classic of its kind and the dream of any armoured commander, was over: 86 T-62 tanks out of a total of 96 had been destroyed; four of them, including the tank carrying the Egyptian brigade commander, escaped into the Botzer fortification. All the armoured personnel carriers were destroyed, as were all the supply trains. Israeli losses were four tanks that had run into the minefield near Botzer when pursuing the Egyptians.

At 16.00 hours, while the battle along the Great Bitter Lake was being waged, the pontoon bridge across the Canal had been completed. Adan regrouped his division, refuelled under heavy enemy shelling and prepared to cross the Canal. He had borne the brunt of the fighting on the 16th and 17th. The 17th had been a good day for him: he had cleared most of Tirtur and Akavish, and had destroyed the Egyptian 25th Armoured Brigade. On the night of 17/18 October, his division crossed the Canal.

Meanwhile, Reshef's brigade had reorganized and, on 18 October, under Sharon's orders, it attacked the Chinese Farm from the rear. The Egyptian forces had by now been worn down by the intense fighting and this time the Israeli attack was successful. The Chinese Farm fell. Before the eyes of the Israelis there unfolded a picture of a highly organized infantry, anti-tank, defensive locality with very heavy concentrations of anti-tank weapons, anti-tank guns and Sagger missiles abandoned on all sides. Following the fall of this position, Reshef pressed northwards, widening the corridor for some three miles. In the afternoon, the Minister of Defence arrived on the battlefield with Sharon. As he looked down and saw the scene of destruction and the evidence of the incredibly bitter and cruel battle that had taken place, he was visibly shaken. Reshef said to him: 'Look at this valley of death.' Dayan murmured in astonishment: 'What you people have done here!'

On the west bank

On the morning of 17 October — after the Israelis had been on the west bank of the Canal for one full day and two nights — the bridgehead came under artillery fire. Matt's headquarters received a direct hit and his deputy was wounded. From this moment until the cease-fire, the bridgehead and the area of the bridge were under constant heavy artillery fire as guns, mortars and Katyushas combined to pour tens of thousands of shells into the area of the crossing. Aircraft attempted to bomb every afternoon, but large numbers were shot down both by the Israeli Air Force, which was now patrolling over the bridgehead, and by the ground forces. Egyptian helicopters came in on suicide missions to drop barrels of napalm on the bridge and the bridgehead; large numbers were shot down. FROG surface-to-surface missiles were employed, but the Israeli forces soon learned how to bring them down with anti-aircraft fire.

Matt's paratroopers were now under heavy attack from Egyptian commandos thrown into the battle. An Israeli force was cut off from the main body of the force, and the Egyptians closed in on them in a bitter hand-to-hand struggle. For four hours the battle raged. One Israeli captain, Asa Kadmoni, single-handed held off the attacks, with a rifle, a grenade and a LAW anti-tank weapon. Kadmoni was finally relieved by a fresh Israeli force when he was down to seven bullets.

Haim Erez a regular officer, who as a small boy had fled to the Soviet Union when the Germans invaded Poland and finally arrived in Palestine via Teheran in 1943, had been raised in a harsh world. After his force — numbering twenty tanks and seven armoured personnel carriers — had crossed the Canal on the 15th, it moved westwards, destroying two surface-to-surface missile bases, a large number of Egyptian vehicles and, by midday on the 16th, had reached a distance of some fifteen miles west of the Canal. His force had taken the Egyptians by surprise, and was moving about freely and with impunity, destroying four surface-to-air missile positions, twenty tanks and twelve armoured personnel carriers, for the loss of one man wounded. On the morning of the 17th, however, the first Egyptian counterattack was mounted by the 23rd Armoured Brigade. Erez's brigade suffered casualties, but the counterattack was broken and the Egyptians withdrew, leaving ten tanks in the field.

The last of Erez's forces had crossed on the 16th at 11.30 hours and, for 37 hours thereafter, no more tanks crossed. This fact was to be heavily criticized by Sharon. At this point, the preconstructed bridge, a 190-yard-long construction on rollers, was being inched forward by a dozen tanks under a concentrated artillery barrage, with Egyptian aircraft bombing and strafing the bridge and Israeli aircraft shooting down the attacking Egyptians. With a continuous artillery barrage bracketing the slow convoy, it creaked and strained into the setting sun towards the Canal, which it reached on the evening of the 18th; shortly after midnight it was operational; one day later a third bridge made up of pontoons would also be in position. The bridging organization under Colonel Even had performed heroically. A total of 100 men of Even's task force − 41 in one night alone − were killed and many hundreds wounded in the course of the operation.

Meanwhile, the reports received by the Egyptian High Command persisted in a considerable measure of wishful thinking, repeating the initial story about small number of amphibious tanks, playing down the scope of the operation, emphasizing that it was purely to boost the morale of the Israeli people and army; a general impression was given that the matter was well in hand, and that the Israeli forces would soon be seen off the west bank. General Shazli describes how, in the afternoon of 18 October, President Sadat came to General Headquarters and asked him to go to Second Army in order to try to raise morale. On his return, on 19 October, Shazli had a fairly clear picture of the situation, estimating that to the west of the Canal were four armoured brigades, a mechanized infantry brigade and a paratroop brigade. The most disturbing element of all as far as the Egyptians were concerned, according to Shazli, was the fact that the Israeli forces had succeeded in neutralizing or destroying the concentrations of SAM missiles west of the Canal to a depth of nine miles and that the Israeli superiority in the air was now coming to full expression in close ground-support. Because of what Shazli claims were the unfortunate decisions of President Sadat, the deployment of the Egyptian forces was widely spread out, and lacked the necessary concentration in order to mount a proper counterattack. He maintains that he pressed again for a redeployment of the Egyptian forces, but was unable to convince either the President or the Minister of War. The increase in Israeli armoured forces on the west bank of the Canal augured ill, particularly for the Third Army, and Shazli again pressed for withdrawal of four brigades from the east to the west bank within 24 hours. He insisted that Sadat come to the general headquarters. The Minister of War, Ahmed Ismail Ali, tried to dissuade him from this move, but Shazli insisted. At 01.00 hours on the morning of 20 October, Shazli again presented his case; after he had finished, the President replied that not one soldier would be withdrawn from the east bank.

According to some reports, Shazli* was by now in a state of total collapse, maintaining that a catastrophe was impending and that the Egyptians must withdraw from Sinai. At this point Sadat, in fact, relieved Shazli of his duties (although the formal changeover took place some weeks later) and appointed General Abdel Ghani Gamasy in his place. Sadat, however, did realize the seriousness of the situation and activated the Soviet Premier, Alexei Kosygin, who had been in Cairo from 16 October, to convene the United Nations Security Council in order to obtain a cease-fire.

Bar-Lev now changed the plan on the east bank, ordering Magen's division to push southwards to the west of, and parallel to, Adan's division towards Suez. The Israeli sweep southwards would therefore be in the form of a fan, with Adan to his east and Magen to his west and rear, thus giving depth to his attack and providing a firm base in the event of any mishap to his front. Sharon would remain at the bridgehead and push northwards towards the Egyptian Second Army.

Reshef's force, which had crossed the Canal on the 19th, moved forward on Sharon's instructions to the west of Matt's forces at Serafeum with orders to attack the position known as 'Orcha'. An armoured infantry company attacked an Egyptian platoon here and, when the 'Orcha' position was finally taken, over 300 dead Egyptian troops were found in the trenches of the fortification, testimony to their extremely obstinate and brave stand. Reshef's forces, together with the paratroopers, reached the outskirts of Ismailia, where an infantry brigade and commando units faced Sharon's forces. To the west, on the Ismailia-Cairo road, a mechanized division was positioned to defend Cairo.

Sharon now pressed for a wide, flanking operation in depth towards Damiette-Balatin on the Mediterranean coast which would cut off the entire Second Army from Egypt. Southern Command insisted on the east-bank 'Missouri' position being taken first, because it was still endangering the corridor to the Israeli bridgehead. Sharon dragged his feet on this order. In the fighting launched by Raviv's brigade, one-third of 'Missouri' was taken.

Adan's division, from the morning of 18 October, attacked southwards along two brigade axes. Facing his forces were an Egyptian mechanized division and the 4th Armoured Division. With Nir's brigade attacking due westwards and Amir's brigade to the south, the Israeli forces advanced. Meanwhile both brigades assigned a battalion each to fan out and destroy surface-to-air missile batteries. On the morning of 19 October, Adan attacked with the full support of the air force, which was no longer

---

* Shazli was later appointed Egyptian Ambassador to London. After some critical remarks about Sadat's régime he was moved to the Embassy in Lisbon. He subsequently resigned and set himself up with Libyan support at a headquarters in Tripoli (later in Algiers) as the leader of the Egyptian opposition to Sadat. Following Sadat's assassination on 6 October 1981, Shazli hailed the event and implied his involvement in the plot. The indications are, however, that he was not involved.

hampered by the surface-to-air missiles, and captured the area of the Fayid airfield, which was rapidly established as an air bridgehead for the resupply of the advancing Israeli forces.

In the area between Ismailia and Suez, there were three principal north-south roads and six major east-west roads. Close to the Canal, and running parallel both to the sweet-water canal and the railway was the road codenamed by the Israelis 'Test'. Farther west and running through Fayid and Geneifa was the main road known to the Israelis as 'Havit'. About six miles to the west of this was the road codenamed 'Vadaut'. Due west from Ismailia was a road parallel to the main railway and the Canal, which went to Cairo by way of the Nile Delta. The main Ismailia-Cairo road extended in a south-westerly direction from Ismailia across the desert. Running due west from Deversoir was a road codenamed 'Sakranut' by the Israelis, intersecting the main Ismailia-Cairo road about twenty miles west of Deversoir. Seven miles farther south ran an east-west road from Fayid called 'Vitamin' and, another twelve miles to the south was a road called 'Asor', the northernmost of the two principal routes from Suez to Cairo; 'Asor' intersected 'Havit' about midway between Geneifa and Shallufa. Five or ten miles farther south was the road the Israelis called 'Sarag', the main Suez-Cairo road. The six hills or hill masses of major importance in this general area were codenamed by the Israelis 'Tsach', 'Arel', 'Maktzera', Mitznefet', and the region known as the Geneifa Hills; south of the 'Sarag' road and west of Suez was Jebel Ataka.

Adan was now located on the Geneifa Hills. Amir was deployed to the east of 'Mitznefet', and Nir and Keren were ordered to move along the Geneifa Hills. They knocked out a number of surface-to-air missile sites on these heights and reached the secondary 'Vitamin' road leading to the lake. Nir's brigade continued southwards crossing the main road, 'Asor', and clearing missile sites as they went, while Keren's brigade continued along the eastern Geneifa Hills.

On the 19th, Magen's division moved through Adan's division and headed westwards towards 'Maktzera'. Along the main Cairo-Bitter Lake road it overcame the 'Tsach' crossroads position from the rear and moved on to relieve Amir's forces facing 'Mitznefet', while Amir moved eastwards along 'Vitamin' to open the main Ismailia-Suez road ('Havit'). Heavy Egyptian resistance broke this attack and Amir's forces sustained losses. Adan received under command a battalion of infantry and a battalion of engineers, which moved down in parallel lines along 'Test', the sweet-water canal road and 'Havit'. The vital airfield of Fayid fell, thus affording the Israeli forces a very important air bridgehead, which could now supply the forces on the west bank.

Adan's move in rushing to the Geneifa Hills was an important element in guaranteeing the success of the southward dash of the Israeli forces. Had these heights been ignored and been occupied by Egyptian commando units, any further advance by the Israeli forces would have been extremely difficult and very questionable. Keren was encountering heavy fighting on the eastern Geneifa Hills, while Amir was moving slowly southwards along the three parallel roads by the lakeside. The Egyptian

Third Army moved the 22nd Tank Brigade of the 6th Mechanized Division back to the west bank. Meanwhile, on Adan's left flank a task force comprising an armoured battalion, an armoured infantry battalion, a paratroop battalion and a battalion of engineers was making its way slowly southwards along 'Test' through successive concentrations of army camps, fighting against Egyptian, Palestinian and Kuwaiti forces.

To the west, Magen was pushing down as planned towards the Cairo-Suez road, having placed Shomron's brigade to protect his west flank at Jebel Um Katib to the south of Mitznefet. By noon on the 19th, Shomron was seventeen miles west of the Canal. On the next day, he moved south to Jebel Um Katib and took up positions facing 'Mitznefet', where for three days his brigade conducted a battle with an Egyptian brigade of tanks, inflicting heavy losses on them.

Meanwhile, elements of the Egyptian 4th Armoured Division were fighting back desperately and attacking Nir's brigade south of the 'Asor' road. On the 21st, this brigade was already a mile north of the main Suez-Cairo road ('Sarag') and controlled it by fire. Thus, from midday on the 21st, the Egyptian Third Army − apart from the southerly road leading south along the Gulf of Suez − was in effect cut off from its rear headquarters and its main supply bases.

The cease-fire

As the full significance of the deteriorating military situation dawned on the Soviet leadership, it became clear to them that the time had come to halt the fighting and to take full advantage of the Egyptian achievements to date. Kosygin assured Sadat that the Soviet Union was prepared, if necessary on its own, to guarantee a cease-fire. The Soviets by now realized that the entire gamble was at risk, and that once again they were in danger of facing a total Arab military collapse. It was clear to them that, given a few more days, the Egyptian Third Army would be doomed, and this in turn could have a direct effect on Sadat's chances of survival. Accordingly, Ambassador Dobrynin of the Soviet Union brought a message from Brezhnev to Kissinger, asking him to fly to Moscow for urgent consultations. During the meeting in Moscow, Kissinger agreed on the necessity for an immediate cease-fire, but insisted that it must, as opposed to previous occasions, be linked to peace talks. At 21.00 hours in the evening of 20 October, the telephone next to Sadat's chair in the war room rang to advise him that Soviet Ambassador Vladimir Vinogradoff requested an urgent meeting to deliver a message from Brezhnev, meeting at the moment with Kissinger in Moscow. Within half an hour Vinogradoff presented the message to Sadat in which Brezhnev requested him to agree to an immediate cease-fire and attached the resolution that the two superpowers were planning to submit to the Security Council, which was about to be convened. The note included also a reiteration of the Soviet undertaking to guarantee the cease-fire in the event of Israeli violation. Brezhnev clearly undertook to transfer Soviet troops to Egypt in order to maintain the cease-fire, and hints about this undertaking were made but a few days later both by Sadat and Heikal.*

In Israel, there was great scepticism about a cease-fire. Few believed that one was imminent. Addressing the editors of the press whom he met every second day during the war, Dayan on 20 October saw no prospect of a cease-fire. Visiting Sharon's division on 21 October, Deputy Prime Minister Yigal Allon assured them that they had ample time and that there was no hurry.

Following the agreement on the text of the proposed Security Council resolution to be submitted by the Soviet Union and the United States, Kissinger flew from Moscow to Tel Aviv and obtained Israel's agreement. The Security Council met at dawn on Monday morning, 22 October, and passed Security Council Resolution No. 338, calling for a cease-fire within twelve hours, and not later than 18.52 hours on the evening of the 22nd. Shortly before the cease-fire was to take effect, the weapon whose introduction to the Middle East had led to the final decision to go to war was activated for the first time anywhere in the world. On that day, according to Sadat, a SCUD missile was launched against Israel. It landed in the desert of the Sinai.

The Israeli push forward was now becoming urgent. The paratroopers in Sharon's division ran into very heavy resistance as they moved northward towards Ismailia, sustaining casualties from infantry and artillery forces. The attack was now taking place along the sweet-water canal and along the main Ismailia-Suez road ('Havit') to the west. Egyptian commandos blocked the advance, and Reshef's brigade lost tanks in the battle at a sewage farm on the outskirts of the town. As the bridges on the main road and across the sweet-water canal were being taken, the cease-fire came into force and Sharon's division was ordered to remain in place.

Adan, to the south, launched his forces in a pincer movement in order to clear the shores of the Little Bitter Lake and the routes running alongside it. Amir's brigade moved along the Geneifa Hills down to the routes along the lake, while Arieh Keren advanced along 'Asor' route to the 'Havit' road in the direction of Lituf. A third southerly prong in the form of Nir's brigade pushed along the main Cairo road ('Sarag') in the direction of Suez, turned in a north-easterly direction along the connecting 'Akal' road and headed for Mina, half-way along the Canal between the two lakes and Suez. The Egyptian Third Army was now fighting desperately along the two main routes, 'Asor' and 'Sarag', leading to Suez from Cairo, and mounted counterattacks against Nir's and Keren's forces as they advanced. The Israelis enjoyed complete mastery of the air now that the surface-to-air missile danger had to a great degree been removed by the destruction of the sites, so the Israeli Air Force were able to knock out the tanks blocking the advance. On orders from Bar-Lev, Adan concentrated two brigades in an attack on 'Asor'. In the afternoon, he issued orders to his three brigades to storm the enemy forces and reach the Canal before 18.00 hours. Abandoning caution, the forces charged

* Mohammed Hassanein Heikal, Editor of *Al Ahram* and Sadat's principal adviser.

forward, breaking into the line of camps along the Little Bitter Lake and reaching the Canal. The Egyptian resistance broke, and thousands of their troops withdrew in disorder.

The cease-fire on the evening of the 22nd found the Egyptian Third Army with its main supply lines cut, with thousands of troops fleeing in disorder, with entire formations and units cut off and with the forces in the bridgehead on the east of the Canal in considerable danger. The Army's main headquarters was cut off from its rear headquarters; in many places, panic reigned as units tried to flee; in other parts, the local commanders organized their units to breakout. In the 19th Division area, the commander transferred units to the west bank and particularly into the town of Suez, where large numbers who had been cut off were already fleeing. Urgent requests were directed to the Egyptian forces pressing from the direction of Cairo to support the forces cut off in the pocket.

By midday on 22 October, the commander of the 19th Division informed General Wassel, the Third Army commander, that the cutting of the Cairo-Suez road at 'Kilometre 109' by the Israeli forces meant in effect that the Army was cut off and isolated. For his part, Wassel made it clear immediately thereafter to the Minister of War that it was surrounded, cut off from supplies, and in danger of complete destruction.

Thus, as opposed to the position along the Egyptian Second Army front, where the cease-fire was being observed, numerous Egyptian units in the Third Army area, who had been cut off one from the other, were endeavouring to join together or break out. As dawn broke, those units on the east bank began to engage the Israeli forces who were facing them from the old Egyptian ramparts on the west bank. The orders to the Israeli forces were to respect the cease-fire, but, if the Egyptians were to break it, then they were to deal with the attacks and continue with their mission. As the Egyptian forces attacked in a desperate effort to escape from the Israeli trap, fighting broke out along the entire front. Gonen issued orders to Adan and Magen to deploy their divisions in such a way as to tighten the noose.

Deploying two brigades, those of Amir and Keren, on a seven-and-a-half-mile front westwards from Mina, Adan's forces pushed southwards in a concerted armoured attack towards the town of Suez. They passed through an area teeming with large numbers of tanks, thousands of infantry, administrative units and supply trains moving round in confusion, numerous anti-tank missile positions and a very heavy concentration of surface-to-air missile batteries. The shock of the armoured punch broke the Egyptian resistance, and Adan's force stormed southwards to the town of Suez, cutting it off from Third Army completely. A large number of surface-to-air missile sites were captured, and thousands of prisoners fell into Israeli hands.

Magen moved down towards Suez along Adan's west flank, leaving a small unit of tanks at 'Kilometre 101' on the Cairo-Suez road to protect his west flank in the event of a counterattack from the direction of Cairo. (Kilometre 101 was to be the site of the disengagement talks between the Israeli and Egyptian military leadership, which were ultimately to lead to

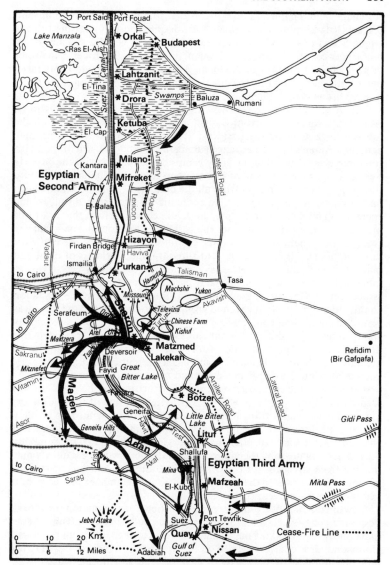

Israeli Advance West of the Canal and Cease-Fire Line

the disengagement of Israeli forces from the Egyptian forces and their
subsequent withdrawal to the east bank.) Magen's division moved through
Adan's forces along the main Suez road and then around the slopes of
Jebel Ataka, which dominates the entire area southwards to the port of

Adabiah, and charged along the route southwards. Dan Shomron's brigade led the push to Adabiah and, despite the fact that his brigade strength was now down to seventeen tanks, he covered a distance of 30 miles between 14.00 hours and midnight. As dawn broke, Shomron's brigade entered the port of Adabiah. Two Egyptian torpedo-boats raced out of the harbour in a desperate attempt to escape. Shomron's tanks opened fire and sank them.

On the morning of the 24th, with the Egyptian forces still fighting, Adan, following advice from Dayan, asked for permission to attack the town of Suez. Gonen's reaction was: 'If it is empty, okay. If it is strongly held, no.' Keren's brigade advanced along the main boulevard of the Cairo road into Suez, capturing the army camps on the outskirts of the city. He was followed by a battalion of paratroopers and, as the tanks moved into the town, they were fired on from all the buildings. This operation, which had been envisaged as a routine mopping-up against a disintegrating enemy, had not been properly prepared. Somehow or other, the tank force managed to extricate itself from the city along the coastal road, but the two groups of paratroopers became cut off in the centre of the city. One unit comprising 70 men managed to slip out under darkness of night and make its way through the dark alleyways and narrow side streets, trying to move without making a sound and carrying the wounded back to the Israeli lines. One of the wounded in this group was the battalion commander himself. In the second group, the commander of the force was wounded and semi-conscious. His place was taken by a company commander who did not want to evacuate because the Egyptians dominated their position. For four hours through the night, in an incredible exchange, Gonen personally coaxed and cajoled the company commander into leaving his position and making a dash for freedom. At first there was the nerve-racking process of getting the besieged unit to identify on air photographs where it was. After a period of trial and error, Gonen finally identified the actual building. He then planned an artillery box in the centre of which the besieged unit would move until it reached freedom. After hours of planning and urging on the radio, the company commander finally took the plunge and led the besieged forces quietly out, moving from street to street under the directions of Gonen as he read an air photograph, back to the Israeli lines. The attack on Suez proved to be a very grave error indeed, costing some 80 killed.

Viewed from the Egyptian point of view, the situation now was desperate. The Israeli forces had completed the isolation of Third Army units on the east bank of the Canal, and had cut them off from the Army Command Headquarters located on the west bank — indeed, Israeli tanks attacked and destroyed the HQ of General Abd al Moneim Wassel, who saved himself in the nick of time. In all, a force of some 45,000 officers and men, and 250 tanks, together with the city of Suez, were completely cut off. Furthermore, all the forces no longer enjoyed the protection of the surface-to-air missile system, and were easy prey for the continued attacks mounted by the Israeli Air Force. The Egyptian Chief of Staff, General Shazli, describes how massive concentrated attacks by the Israeli Air Force on 24 October, mounted against Third Army, destroyed all the crossing equipment left in the army area on the Canal, thus preventing any effective withdrawal of the forces from the east bank to the west.

The elements of Third Army under siege included the 7th Infantry Division commanded by Brigadier-General Ahmed Badawy, holding the northern portion of the east bank bridgehead, and the 19th Infantry Division commanded by Brigadier-General Yussef Afifi, holding the southern half of the bridgehead and also responsible for the city of Suez. Also in the bridgehead were two independent tank brigades and miscellaneous other units. In Suez itself there was a mixture of units, including elements of the 4th Armoured Division and the 6th Mechanized Division. General Badawy, commanding the 7th Division, assumed command of the isolated portion of Third Army on the east bank. He organized the forces under his command for defence and, indeed, repulsed a number of Israeli attacks between 20 and 23 October. He even managed to organize a tenuous supply route across the upper Suez Gulf. However, his supply situation, particularly concerning ammunition, water and food, was very serious indeed. (Badawy was confirmed later as an army commander, and became ultimately the Egyptian Minister of War, replacing General Gamasy, who was to assume the position after the death of General Ismail Ali. In 1981, General Badawy was killed in a tragic helicopter crash while inspecting troops along the Libyan border.)

The Israelis prepared for an all-out assault on the two components of Third Army, particularly on the elements on the east bank. While the Egyptian forces would doubtless have fought a stubborn and effective battle in defence, it is quite clear that, given their desperate situation as far as supplies were concerned, and the total Israeli superiority in the air, the destruction of Third Army could have been achieved by the Israeli forces within a matter of days.

The situation was now assessed by the Russians and the Americans, and both came to a similar conclusion, although not for the same reasons. The Soviets realized that the destruction of the Egyptian Third Army would mean a clear-cut defeat for a country they had supported. Russian prestige would suffer if such a client country, armed with Soviet weapons and equipment, were again to suffer a decisive military defeat. Kissinger, for his part, now appreciated that rescuing the army could be an important bargaining factor in achieving an ultimate arrangement between the sides, with each having a trump card of its own: the Israelis, the besieged Third Army and a presence on the west bank; the Egyptians, a bridgehead on the east bank. Kissinger exerted pressure on Israel through the Israeli Ambassador in Washington and, on the 24th, a second Security Council Resolution was passed, again calling for a cease-fire. Thus, on 24 October, with Sharon's division on the outskirts of Ismailia, threatening its links with Cairo; with Adan's and Magen's divisions completely sealing off the Egyptian Third Army; and with the Israeli forces holding a corridor to the east bank with three bridges across it, and occupying an area of 1,000 square miles inside Egypt down to the port of Adabiah on the Gulf of Suez, a second cease-fire came into effect.

After being caught in circumstances that could well have been fatal, the forces of the Israeli Southern Command had succeeded in turning the tables by carrying out a most daring operation against tremendous odds and in the face of great adversity. They had achieved a major victory by any military standards and had manoeuvred themselves into a position to destroy the Egyptian Third Army, whose saviour was the United Nations Security Council. The Soviet Union had not only made available all the necessary prerequisites for the Egyptian attack, it had also guaranteed against a total débâcle: indeed, as the Egyptian Third Army had turned to Sadat in desperation for supplies, the Soviet Union had moved ominously to the brink and readied its airborne divisions for a move to the Middle East.

2

THE NORTHERN FRONT

The area of the Golan Heights has already been described in the previous chapter on the Six Day War. Five main routes ascended to the Heights from Israel at the 'Green Line', the original 1949 armistice line which runs along the Jordan and the east bank of the Sea of Galilee. They are, from north to south: the road from Kibbutz Dan to Mas'ada and Mount Hermon; the road from Gonen to Wasset; the main road to Damascus crossing the Bnot Ya'akov Bridge to Kuneitra; the Yehudia road ascending from the so-called 'Arik Bridge' across the Jordan where it enters the Sea of Galilee; and the Gamla Rise and El Al route ascending from the Sea of Galilee. Two roads of importance traverse the Golan Heights from north to south. The first is the road running along the so-called 'Purple Line', the 1967 cease-fire line; the second is the maintenance road, known as the 'Tapline Road' which runs alongside the oil Tapline, which originates in Saudi Arabia, crosses the Golan Heights and continues to the Mediterranean Sea via Lebanon.

The Syrian forces manning the Golan Heights were composed, from north to south, of the 7th Infantry Division (which included Moroccan troops), commanded by Brigadier-General Omar Abrash, the 9th Infantry Division, commanded by Colonel Hassan Tourmkmani, and the 5th Infantry Division, commanded by Brigadier-General Ali Aslan. Each was organized on Soviet lines, with an armoured brigade (in addition to other armoured elements in the division) giving a total of some 130-200 tanks per division. Behind these forward infantry divisions were concentrated the 1st and 3rd Armoured Divisions, commanded respectively by Colonel Tewfiq Jehani and Brigadier-General Mustafa Sharba, each with approximately 250 tanks and some independent brigades. The total Syrian force facing Israel numbered approximately 1,500 tanks supported by some 1,000 guns, including heavy mortars and a surface-to-air missile system protecting Damascus. The Syrian tanks were of the Russian T-55 and T-62 models, the latter being the most modern Russian tank in operation at the time, mounting a 115mm smooth-bore gun.

Against these forces were ranged two Israeli armoured brigades, the 7th in the northern sector and 188 Brigade in the southern sector, disposing of a total of approximately 170 tanks and some 60 artillery pieces. The Israeli armoured forces disposed of United States type M60 tanks and British Centurions. The northern sector, in which the 7th Brigade was deployed, was the responsibility of a divisional headquarters commanded by Major-General 'Raful' Eitan, based on Nafekh. Along the 45-mile front-line, there were seventeen Israeli fortifications — well-defended lookout posts, each manned by approximately twenty men and supported by a platoon of three tanks — behind anti-tank ditches.

The Syrian plan was to mount a major breakthrough attempt in the north by the 7th Infantry Division supported by elements of the 3rd Armoured Division; the main thrust, however, was to be farther south in

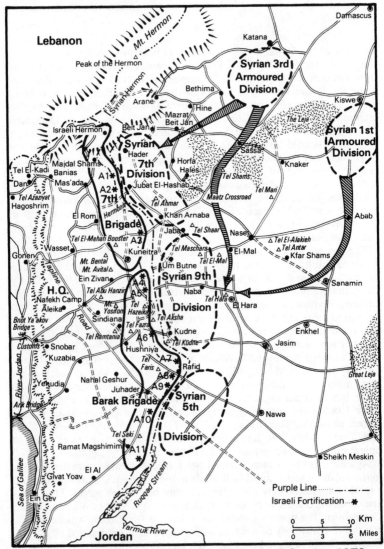

Deployment of Forces, 14.00 hours, Saturday 6 October 1973

the area of the Rafid Opening. This was to be carried out by the 5th Infantry Division, the 9th Infantry Division, the 1st Armoured Division and elements of the 3rd Armoured Division, all concentrated against 188 Brigade which could field but 57 tanks. The Syrian plan called for the occupation of the whole of the Golan Heights by the evening of Sunday 7 October, followed by a reorganization in the area along the River Jordan on Israeli soil in preparation for a further breakthrough into Galilee.

Major-General Yitzhak Hofi, commanding Israel's Northern Command, had been concerned for some time about the growing Syrian concentration of armoured forces. He had expressed his concern to the Minister of Defence, Moshe Dayan, and authorization had been given for units of the 7th Armoured Brigade, which were being held in GHQ Reserve in the southern part of Israel, to move up to the Golan Heights. This move increased the number of Israeli tanks on the Golan Heights from an initial number of some 60 to 170.

The Syrian attack

At 14.00 hours on Saturday 6 October, the Syrian attack opened with a massive artillery and air attack lasting approximately 50 minutes. Under cover of this attack, the massed Syrian armoured forces moved forward, while an independent move was made against the Israeli position on Mount Hermon by helicopter-borne Syrian troops. This position was of vital importance to the Israelis, providing as it did a perfect observation post covering the whole field of battle and the approaches to Damascus. In addition, it was an ideal radar outpost and a site for sensitive electronic equipment. The fortification on the mountain top was well built, but the upper system of fortifications had not yet been completed. There were many signs of negligence in the position: the main gate had been damaged and swung open on its hinges unrepaired; no communication trenches had been dug outside the main fortification; and the total force allotted to defend this very sensitive position was one officer and thirteen men. The fortifications were built to withstand artillery fire and aerial bombing, but the trench system which would enable the infantry to defend the locality effectively had not yet been completed. Four Syrian helicopters loaded with troops of a commando battalion approached the peak of the mountain approximately a mile from the position. One helicopter exploded. The three others landed and discharged their troops. Advancing in two columns, the Syrians broke into the Israeli position, which, because of negligence, was not properly organized for defence. That afternoon the position fell to the Syrians. For the Soviet advisers of the Syrians, who arrived shortly after the fall of the position, the electronic equipment captured there was of singular value.

In the northern sector, the Israeli 7th Armoured Brigade was attacked by the Syrian 7th Infantry Division supported by elements of the 3rd Armoured Division and a Moroccan brigade. Simultaneously, the main effort of the Syrians was developed at the Rafid Opening, through which they developed a major thrust along the Tapline Road. 188 Brigade, with 57 tanks, was facing the main effort developed by the Syrians with approximately 600 tanks participating in the attack. The Syrian 5th and 9th Infantry Divisions were supported in this attack by elements of the 1st Armoured Division. The Israeli forces, outnumbered and outgunned, fought desperately for every inch of territory.

188 Brigade clung on to its position with grim determination: the Syrian Armoured Brigade advancing along Tapline Road was held up for some twenty hours by a handful of tanks commanded by a young Israeli lieutenant, Zwicka Gringold, who rushed back to the battlefield from leave, removed the bodies of those who had been killed from a number of tanks, and created a hastily improvised force known as 'Force Zwicka', which rushed into battle with four tanks along Tapline Road to meet the oncoming onslaught led by the Syrian 90th Armoured Brigade. Utilizing his small force with flexibility, darting in and out of the Syrian columns at night, destroying enemy tanks wherever he could, and creating an impression of a much larger force, Zwicka succeeded in holding up the Syrian advance along the Tapline Road. Engaging the Syrians constantly, changing tanks as they were damaged, and continuing doggedly to harass the Syrians, Zwicka's final effort was to appear in the last surviving tank of his 'force' out of the rolling terrain of the Golan Heights as the first Syrian tank broke through the defences of the Divisional Headquarters at Nafekh on 7 October, and to destroy that tank. He was later to be awarded the Order of Courage, Israel's highest decoration for bravery.

By Sunday morning, 188 Brigade had been almost completely destroyed. When the brigade commander, Colonel Ben-Shoham, with his deputy and operations officer, manning a few remaining tanks, moved from Nafekh along the Tapline Road to meet the Syrian attack in a desperate last move, the entire group was wiped out in battle. By midday Sunday 7 October, 90 per cent of the officers of 188 Brigade had been either killed or wounded, including the brigade commander and his deputy. By late Sunday afternoon, the last remaining senior officer active in the Brigade was the intelligence officer.

However, this incredibly brave battle paid off − it gave time to mobilize the reserves and move them up to the front. On the Sunday night, Major-General Dan Laner, a divisional commander whose divisional headquarters had been given responsibility by General Hofi for the southern half of the Golan Heights, was standing at the Arik Bridge literally directing tanks, platoons and companies as they arrived, up the road rising to the front. That Sunday, 24 hours after the first blow, the advance Syrian forces in the southern sector were within ten minutes tank travelling time of the River Jordan and the Sea of Galilee. In the centre of the southern sector, they had reached General Eitan's Nafekh Headquarters − he managed to slip out from one side of the camp as they moved in on the other side − and the Syrian advance was blocked only in the middle of the camp. Farther south, the Syrians had taken the Israeli village of Ramat Magshimim and were poised to advance. To block this Syrian advance, the Israeli units were rushed piecemeal up to the front-line.

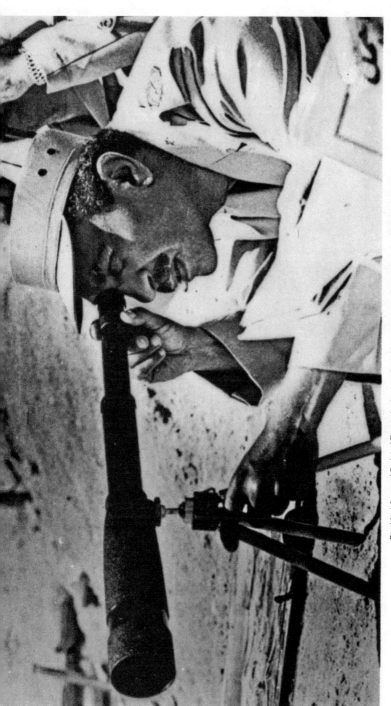

President Anwar el Sadat of Egypt viewing Israeli positions across the Suez Canal, four months before the Egyptian Army carried out its surprise attack of 6 October 1973. Sadat was the architect and chief planner of the war, which was known to the Egyptians as the October War and to Israelis as the Yom Kippur War (so called because the Egyptian attack was launched on the Jewish Day of Atonement). (UPI)

Left: General Saad el Din Shazli, Egyptian Chief of Staff. Shazli was dismissed by Sadat and sent as Ambassador to Great Britain and later Portugal. He subsequently resigned and exiled himself to Tunisia. He disagreed violently with President Sadat over the latter's visit to Jerusalem in 1977, and remained a vociferous opponent of the peace process. (AP)

Below: General Ahmed Ismail Ali, Egyptian Minister of War, arrives in Moscow for consultations. To his right is Alexander Grechko, the Soviet Minister of Defence. (TASS)

Opposite page: Staff conferences at IDF Headquarters at a critical point on the second day of the fighting. **Above:** The Chief of Staff, Lieutenant-General David Elazar, flanked by Major-General Avraham ('Bren') Adan on his left and Major-General Shmuel Gonen ('Gorodish') on his right. Divisional commander Major-General Albert Mandler, who is pointing to the map, was killed the following day. **Below:** On the same day, the Minister of Defence, Moshe Dayan, confers with the commander of the southern front, Major-General Shmuel Gonen. To Dayan's right is Major-General Rehavam ('Ghandi') Zeevi (retd.). (Arad)

Left: A Soviet-made SAM-2 missile on its launching pad on the West Bank of the Suez Canal, after its capture by Israeli troops. (GPO)

Right: The Phantom was the Israeli Air Force's main fighter aircraft in the 1973 War.

Below: The East (Israeli) Bank of the Canal, showing clearly one of the ruptures made in the sand barrier by Egyptian water cannon which enabled Egyptian troops to cross and breach the Bar-Lev Line. This photograph was taken after the Israelis had recaptured the area and constructed a pontoon bridge across to the West Bank.

A chance meeting in the midst of the battle in the Sinai, 1973. Moments after this photograph was taken, the armoured personnel carrier received a direct hit which killed all its occupants, including the son of the lieutenant-colonel (centre). (Arad)

The Israeli counteroffensive on the Golan Heights opened on 8 October 1973, supported by heavy artillery and air-strikes.

Right: An Israeli Skyhawk goes into action. (Gamma, Paris)

Below: A barrage from Israeli artillery at the start of the counterattack. These are Russian-built 130mm guns captured by the Israelis and turned against their former owners. (Michael Freidin)

Far right: Men of the Armoured Corps carry out field repairs on a damaged tank track near the Syrian town of Kuneitra. (Agence France-Presse)

Left: Israeli Centurion tanks advancing against the Syrian lines on the Golan Heights. (Starphot) **Above:** Israeli troops advancing above the snow line near the peak of Mount Hermon. (Shmuel Rachmani)

Below: IDF reinforcements moving into position on the Golan Heights. The self-propelled gun in the foreground is an American-built 175mm. (GPO)

Below: A portable roller bridge being towed laboriously towards the Canal. ('Arad)

Inset: A bridge in place, with supplies beginning to move across.

Left, top: Arrangements for transferring non-military supplies to the encircled and cut-off Egyptian Third Army are made between Egyptian and Israeli officers with the help of UN personnel. (GPO)

Left, below: The operation to relieve the Third Army is underway with Egyptian soldiers loading amphibious armoured vehicles with much-needed supplies for their stranded colleagues. On the far side of the Canal, the break in the rampart is clearly visible.

Right: Major-General Abdel Gamasy of Egypt (right) and Major-General Aharon Yariv of Israel at Kilometre 101 during the cease-fire discussions terminating the 1973 War. (Israel Sun)

Below right: US Secretary of State, Henry Kissinger arriving at Lod Airport and being met by Foreign Minister Eban. Kissinger made herculean efforts to arrive at a cease-fire settlement through his long drawn-out 'shuttle diplomacy'. (Braun)

Above: The Israeli Defence Minister, Moshe Dayan, stares across the Suez Canal. Many Israelis held him mainly responsible for the Israeli Army's unpreparedness on 6 October 1973, although he was exonerated by the Agranat Commission. (However, the full report of the commission's findings has still not been made public.) (Arad)

Right: Israel's Prime Minister, Golda Meir, in a broadcast on US television, March 1973. She, too, was criticized for misjudging the situation, thereby allowing Israel to be caught unawares. (GPO)

Meanwhile, in the northern sector, the Israeli 7th Armoured Brigade under Colonel Avigdor Ben-Gal ('Yanush'), with an initial force of approximately 100 tanks, was holding its ground in the area between Mas'ada and Kuneitra, and was ranged against the attack of the Syrian 7th Infantry Division supported by elements of the 3rd Armoured Division, with a total attacking force of some 500 tanks. For four days and three nights the battle raged relentlessly without let-up, with two to three attacks being mounted by day and at least two attacks by night. The battle had commenced on Saturday at 14.00 hours. By the Tuesday afternoon, Syrian tanks had broken through the Israeli lines and were everywhere. The crew of each Israeli tank was fighting for its life. Ben-Gal's force numbered now only seven tanks and, with his ammunition situation already critical, he prepared to withdraw.

A battalion commander, Lieutenant-Colonel Yossi, was caught on his honeymoon in the Himalayan Mountains when the war broke out. By superhuman efforts he managed to return to Israel, rushed to the battlefield and improvised a force of thirteen damaged tanks that had been towed back to the support echelons for repair. He organized crews (including many wounded who discharged themselves from hospital) and, on the Tuesday afternoon, moved up into the 7th Brigade's sector at the head of his makeshift force. He arrived on the scene of battle just as the remnants of the 7th Brigade were about to withdraw. The seven remaining tanks of the brigade joined Lieutenant-Colonel Yossi's force and moved over to counterattack the Syrians. Taken by surprise, the Syrians, who had been extended, had been fought to a standstill, and who had lost some 500 tanks and armoured vehicles in the killing ground which came to be known as the 'Valley of Tears', before the 7th Brigade's positions, broke. The Israeli outposts in the fortifications, which had all held out in the midst of the Syrian advance (apart from three whose men had withdrawn under orders), reported that the Syrian supply trains were turning east which indicated that the force was about to withdraw. The Syrian attack was broken, and their forces withdrew before the 7th Brigade, which followed them to the cease-fire 'Purple Line'.

In the southern sector, an armoured division under Major-General Moshe Peled, which had been held in reserve by GHQ, moved up on Sunday night along the El Al road on the Israeli right, and launched a counterattack against the Syrians. General Moshe Peled, known by the Arab nickname of 'Mussa', was a heavy-set officer who grew up in the Armoured Corps, moving through various command posts until he became a divisional commander. A gruff, decisive man hailing from a farming village in the valley of Jezreel, he was ultimately to become commander of the Armoured Corps in the Israel Defence Forces. The attack succeeded, and Peled's division advanced against the forces of the Syrian 9th Infantry Division along the El Al route towards Rafid. General Dan Laner's division meanwhile advanced along the Yehudia road, relieved Nafekh and closed in on Hushniya. By noon, the Israeli 20th Brigade on the right flank of the attack mounted by Peled's division had reached the vicinity of Tel Faris after wearing down the Syrian 46th Tank

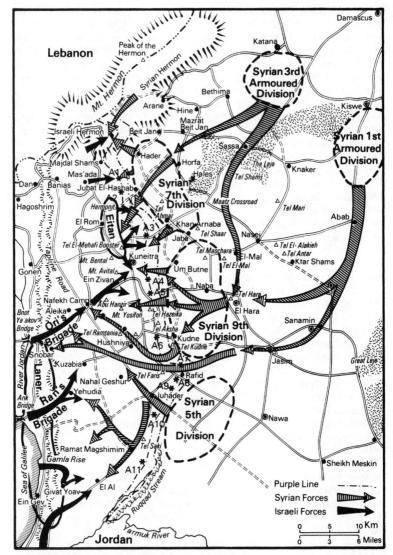

Maximum Syrian Penetration, Midnight Sunday 7 October

Brigade. But Syrian opposition was fierce, and their armoured forces continued to move in from Syria across the 'Purple Line'. Peled's division was in fact straddling two of the Syrian 1st Armoured Division's three axes of advance (Kudne-Ramtaniya-Hushniya, the Tapline Road and the Rafid-Juhader-Ramat Magshimim road), and the 20th Brigade had by now become a wedge penetrating the mass of enemy armour. By noon on Tuesday 9 October, the 20th Brigade's situation was precarious.

Meanwhile on the other side of the fence, Colonel Jehani, commander of the Syrian 1st Armoured Division, was facing a serious dilemma. Repeated attacks by Colonel Uri Orr's 79th Brigade (in Laner's division) had decimated the Syrian 91st Brigade commanded by Colonel Fiyad; the Israeli forces under General 'Raful' Eitan, north of Kuneitra, were holding the line that the northern Syrian attackers had failed to penetrate. He had concentrated his divisional supply system in the area of Hushniya prior to developing his attack towards Israel, but the entire area was now threatened by the pincers of Laner's forces from the west and north and of Peled's forces from the south — if the armoured forces Jehani was throwing desperately against Peled's sweep could not block it, his entire division would be doomed. In addition, the Israeli Air Force was now in battle, having dealt with many of the threatening surface-to-air missile sites, and the area of the Hushniya camps was under effective air bombardment. The situation was beginning to look very serious to Colonel Jehani. He ordered his forces in the Hushniya pocket to exert pressure eastwards against Peled's encircling force in an attempt to break out of the pocket, with the result that part of Peled's division found itself under pressure from two opposing directions.

Peled was not yet aware of Jehani's predicament. He ordered his 14th Brigade to continue its advance eastwards, and to launch an attack in the centre of his divisional front, in an attempt to achieve the greatest possible depth, thus relieving the left flank of his right-hand brigade, and reducing the pressure on that force. Peled's attack gained the high ground of Tel Faris which was invaluable as an artillery observation point. (However, unknown to the Israelis, a small Syrian unit remained camouflaged and hidden on the slopes of the hill and continued to direct Syrian fire until it was discovered two days later on 11 October.) Peled's 19th Brigade now took up the attack with close air support, clashing with the 40th Mechanized Brigade of the Syrian 1st Armoured Division. After an initial success by the Israelis, the Syrian forces moved back under cover of darkness, as the Syrian 15th Mechanized Brigade of the 3rd Armoured Division attempted to break through and relieve the units of the 1st Armoured Division, which had been cut off in the Hushniya pocket.

Early on Wednesday morning, 10 October, Peled ordered all his brigades forward with the purpose of taking Tel Kudne, where the Syrian forward headquarters was located. He suffered heavy losses in the attack, and was ordered by General Hofi, GOC Northern Command, to remain in position while General Laner launched his forces, the 79th Brigade under Colonel Orr and the 17th Brigade under Colonel Ran Sarig, against Hushniya from the north. Thus, the area between the Hushniya crossroads and Tel Fazra became the killing ground for the Israeli forces: gradually, Laner's forces reduced the Hushniya pocket while Peled's forces moved up with tanks on Tel Fazra.

By midday on Wednesday 10 October, almost exactly four days after some 1,400 Syrian tanks had stormed across the 'Purple Line' in a massive attack against Israel, not a single Syrian tank remained in fighting condition west of that line. The Hushniya pocket, in which two Syrian brigades had been destroyed, was one large graveyard of Syrian vehicles and equipment. Hundreds of guns, supply vehicles, armoured personnel

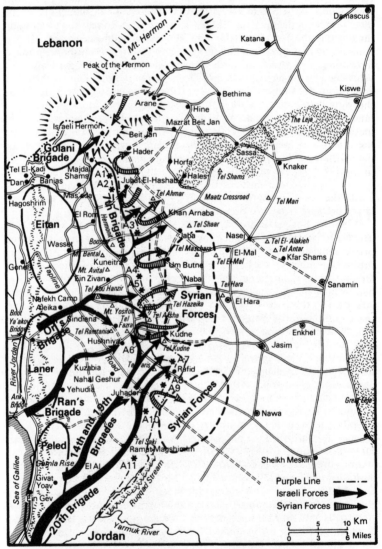

**Israeli Counterattack Reaches Purple Line, Wednesday
Morning 10 October**

carriers, fuel vehicles, BRDM Sagger armoured missile carriers, tanks and tons of ammunition were dotted about the hills and slopes surrounding Hushniya.

The pride of the Syrian Army lay smoking and burnt-out along their earlier axes of advance. Each individual Israeli force had gained a great victory in itself. The Israeli 17th Brigade under Colonel Sarig (in Laner's division), numbering some 40-50 tanks, had destroyed over 200 Syrian tanks along the Yehudia road. The Syrians had left behind in the Israeli-controlled area of the Golan Heights 867 tanks, some of which were of the most modern T-62 type, in addition to thousands of vehicles, anti-tank vehicles, guns and sundry equipment. The most modern arms and equipment that the Soviet Union had supplied to any foreign army dotted the undulating hills of the Golan Heights, testimony to one of the great tank victories in history against the most incredible odds, and to the indomitable spirit of the Israeli forces, which within a period of four days had suffered a crushing disaster, had recovered and, in one of the heroic battles in modern military history, had turned the tables and driven the invading force back to its starting line.

The Israeli break-in

The strategic decision of the Israeli General Staff had been in favour of priority for the Golan Heights. In this area there was no depth, such as in the Sinai, and any local Syrian breakthrough could well endanger the Israeli centres of population in northern Galilee. The Syrians therefore had to be seen off the area as rapidly as possible, after which the Syrian Army had to be broken, thus removing the military threat poised against the country's northern frontier. Only then could the weight of Israel's military force be turned against the Egyptian forces. An additional consideration was the fact that help in the form of reinforcements – above all from Iraq, but also from Saudi Arabia and Kuwait – was on the way. And it was obvious that King Hussein of Jordan, until now sitting awkwardly on the fence of non-intervention, would be influenced in his future decisions by the fate of the Syrian Army. Time was of the essence, as reports of the Iraqi troop movements towards Syria were received. Furthermore, the withdrawing Syrian Army must not be given a chance to recover and absorb the equipment beginning to flow in from the Soviet Union.

At 22.00 hours on Wednesday 10 October, the General Staff held a conference to decide whether to consolidate positions along the 'Purple Line' or to continue the attack into Syria. Minister of Defence Dayan entered during the conference and Elazar outlined the pros and cons of the problem to him. Dayan was hesitant about an advance into Syria, mindful as he was of the danger of the possibility that such an advance could spark off Soviet intervention in order to defend Damascus. The Chief of Staff, General Elazar, however, was of the view that the Israelis had to achieve a penetration some twelve miles in depth: an advance to such a line would bring the Israeli forces to a point where an adequate defence line could be established, and also from where Damascus could be threatened by long-range artillery. Elazar believed that the establishment of the Israeli forces along such a line would neutralize Syria as an element in such a war and bring pressure to bear on Egypt. Dayan took Elazar and a number of officers to see Golda Meir. Following a discussion, the Prime Minister decided in favour of continuing the push into Syria, and General Elazar issued orders to Northern Command accordingly. The counterattack would commence on Thursday 11 October.

Hofi decided to launch the attack in the northernmost sector of the Golan, choosing this area because the left flank of the attacking forces would rest on the slopes of Mount Hermon, which would be impassable to Syrian armoured forces. The axis of advance constituted the shortest route to Damascus, 30 miles away, and the resultant threat to their capital city could influence the Syrian deployment. The terrain was rolling ground, affording good observation on the main Kuneitra-Damascus highway, along which Laner's forces were due to advance. 'Raful' Eitan, with the 7th Brigade in the lead, was to command the break-in. Laner's division, with Orr's 79th Brigade and Sarig's 17th Brigade under command, was to attack two hours after Eitan's division along the heavily-fortified main Damascus road. Should Laner's division be blocked, it would follow Eitan's; if, however, Laner were to succeed along the Damascus road, Eitan would cover him and support him from the high ground to the north as he advanced. H-Hour was 11.00 hours on Thursday (it being difficult for the Israeli forces to attack earlier in the morning because the sun would be in their eyes). Laner would move at 13.00 hours.

Meanwhile the 7th Brigade was feverishly being refitted, tanks were being repaired, replacement equipment was being absorbed, and reinforcements were joining the units. As a result, two days after he was down to his last reserves in battle, Ben-Gal was ready to move into battle with a re-equipped and reinforced brigade.

The 7th Brigade mission was to take Tel Shams and Mazrat Beit Jan. Its southern boundary was to be the main Kuneitra-Damascus route passing through Khan Arnaba, Tel Shams and Sassa. The break-in point was chosen on what proved to be the correct assumption that the area was less-strongly defended in the north. As Ben-Gal saw it, one of his main problems would be to get through the Syrian minefields as rapidly as possible, because success or failure would be dictated by the rapidity with which he managed to deploy all his forces in battle. The break-in area was rocky, hilly and well-wooded. Ben-Gal divided his brigade into two forces. The northern force was composed of Avigdor Kahalani's 7th Battalion and Amos's newly-arrived reserve battalion − its mission was to capture Hader and Mazrat Beit Jan. The southern force, led by the remnants of 188 Brigade commanded by Lieutenant-Colonel Yossi, consisted of two battalions of tanks with additional forces: the 5th Battalion under Lieutenant-Colonel Josh, a battalion under Yossi, and the remnants of the 4th Battalion. Their mission was to capture Jubata, the high ground north of Khan Arnaba, the Syrian Army camps at Hales and Tel Shams.

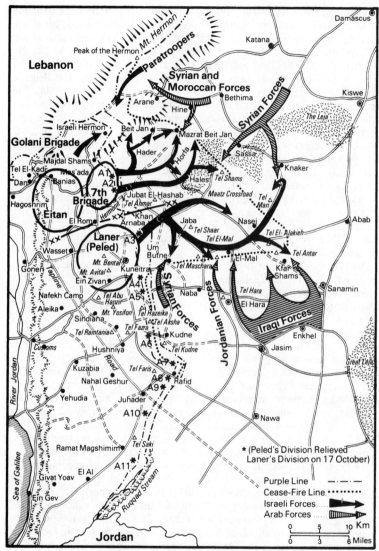

The Breakthrough, 11 October 1973

On Wednesday evening, after the Command orders group, Ben-Gal addressed all his assembled commanders. Looking at them, and recalling what they had been through in the past four days (many with difficulty managing to keep their eyes open), men to whom he knew the country owed so much, a strange emotion moved him. He launched into a touching address. In their logical sequence, the dry recital of the elements of an operation order, instinctive to every officer in every army, became a moving pronouncement. He was inspired as he faced the red-eyed, weary officers who had led their men so valiantly in so fateful a battle. He outlined the plan for the break-in to Syria and the exploitation of success.

At 11.00 hours on 11 October, units of what had been 188 Brigade crossed the 'Purple Line' and led the 7th Brigade forces into Syria. The remnants of a brigade that had been decimated in battle had reorganized and were leading the Israeli attack. 188 was a brigade in which 90 per cent of the commanders had died or had been wounded — only one original company second-in-command and two platoon commanders remained, not one company commander having survived the first battles. And yet here again the Brigade was in action. Facing Ben-Gal's forces was the Moroccan Expeditionary Force in brigade strength, backed by some 40 tanks and covering the approaches to Mazrat Beit Jan. To the south of these forces was a Syrian infantry brigade reinforced with anti-tank weapons and some 35 tanks. The advance forces found the breaches through the Syrian minefields and, backed by artillery and air support, broke through them.

The 7th Brigade's northern effort broke through the wooded area and, in bitter fighting, gradually gained the high ground and captured the Hader crossroads, forcing the Syrian 68th Brigade of the 7th Infantry Division to withdraw. Several days later the commander of this brigade, a Druze, Colonel Rafiq Hilawi, was paraded in a camp on the outskirts of Damascus: his badges of rank were torn off him as, with eyes blindfolded, he faced a firing squad. He had been court-martialled and sentenced to death for withdrawing, his guilt having been compounded by the intense suspicion with which the Syrian régime regarded the Druze people. The northern advance continued against Mazrat Beit Jan. After being held up initially by a counterattack mounted by Syrian armour backed by air support, the Israeli forces broke into the village on Friday 12 October. Heavy fighting took place in the village for some six hours. By 17.00 hours, Mazrat Beit Jan and the hills surrounding it were in Israeli hands. Golani infantry with armoured elements moved in to hold the area.

In the southern sector, General Eitan's advancing division captured Tel Ahmar overlooking Khan Arnaba from the north. Eitan's right flank and Laner's left flank were now parallel one to another. By Thursday afternoon, the Druze village of Horfa had been taken, while on Friday morning the Maatz crossroads was taken. The leading battalion under Yossi was ordered to attack and capture the dominating feature facing the attacking forces along the Damascus road, Tel Shams. Three times his battalion was beaten back by intense anti-tank fire from Sagger anti-tank units positioned among the rocks and boulders in the volcanic plain on both sides of the road — the rocky nature of the terrain made it extremely difficult for tanks to deploy off the road. An attempt by Ben-Gal with two battalions failed to develop a wide sweep across the well-nigh impassable plain, despite the fact that some twenty Syrian tanks were knocked out at extreme ranges of some two miles in the fighting.

With two battalions deployed on the main road as a firm base engaging Tel Shams, Yossi cautiously led two companies totalling twenty tanks through the boulders and rocks along a path that they had discovered. The plan was to circle Tel Shams and attack it from the rear. Of his total tank force, eight arrived in the vicinity of the rear slopes of Tel Shams, took the Syrian force by surprise and destroyed ten of the Syrian tanks at close range. Covered by a heavy artillery bombardment, Yossi led his small force and stormed Tel Shams, with two tanks covering the attack and six attacking. As they neared the top of the hill, a hidden anti-tank battery opened fire, destroying four of the attacking tanks. Yossi himself was thrown out of his tank and lay wounded among the rocks. The covering force on the main Damascus road endeavoured to extricate Yossi but failed. Ultimately under cover of darkness a special paratroop unit, led by a young officer called 'Yoni', made its way through Syrian-occupied territory and, in a dramatic rescue operation, evacuated Yossi from under the noses of the Syrian forces on Tel Shams. (Three years later, the same 'Yoni', now Lieutenant-Colonel Jonathan Netanyahu, was to lead the attacking forces in one of the most remarkable rescue missions ever mounted, and saved over 100 Israeli hostages held at Entebbe airport; in that operation, Yoni, a Harvard graduate and an outstanding officer, was killed.) The ill-fated attack on Tel Shams was considered to have been a mistake, especially as it had not been co-ordinated by Ben-Gal with Eitan. Indeed it constituted a classic misuse of armour. This fact was emphasized when, on the night of Saturday 13 October, Eitan ordered units of the 31st Parachute Brigade to attack Tel Shams. Storming the dominating height at night, these crack units of the Israeli Army, fighting in their element, captured the position with a total loss of four wounded.

Meanwhile, to the south of Eitan's forces, Laner's division broke through the Syrian positions on the main Damascus road. The 17th Brigade was led by Colonel Sarig, who had been wounded in the initial attack across the 'Purple Line' and, heavily bandaged, had discharged himself from hospital to assume his command. Born in a kibbutz, Ran Sarig was the son of Nahum Sarig, who had commanded the 'Negev' Brigade in the War of Independence. When Ran was wounded in battle, his younger brother, who was serving in the Army, was lying seriously injured following a road accident. And, but a week before, a third brother, one of Israel's promising young music composers, an officer in a paratroop brigade, had been killed while stemming the tide of the Syrian onslaught.

As the 17th Brigade moved forward in attack, a murderous concentration of artillery opened up on them, and seventeen of Sarig's reconnaissance tanks were knocked out. Seeing the difficulties Sarig was experiencing, Laner moved forward units of the 79th Brigade to extricate him from the battle. However, as the situation looked its most desperate, Sarig's remaining battalion mounted a second charge, and two tanks of the leading platoon reached the Khan Arnaba crossroads. Laner immediately altered his instructions and ordered the 79th Brigade to exploit Sarig's success and move through Khan Arnaba, followed by the 19th Brigade, which had been transferred to Laner from Peled's division.

As the 79th Brigade moved forward and the 19th Brigade moved southwards to Jaba and took Tel Shaar, the Syrians counterattacked and cut the main road in the area of Khan Arnaba, thus cutting-off and endangering those elements of Laner's division that had moved forward. Moving stealthily under cover of darkness through the rocks and boulders of the lava plain, Syrian infantry with anti-tank bazookas turned the area into a virtual deathtrap for the Israeli tanks. Faced with this situation, Laner sent in a paratroop battalion, which fought all night mopping up the Syrian forces and evacuating the Israeli wounded.

Syria's plight

The Syrian Command was by now showing signs of desperation. A note of hysteria was replacing the tone of confident victory that had characterized the Arab broadcasts for the past five days. The Israeli forces were advancing into Syria against a very depleted Syrian Army. The Israeli Air Force had come into its own. By trial and error, it had discovered the weaknesses in the Syrian surface-to-air missile system and had succeeded in destroying part of it; now its aircraft were ranging far and wide into Syria to bomb strategic targets, such as the country's oil stores and power stations. At one stage, Syrian aircraft returning from missions could not find an undamaged airfield in which to land. (Some landed on motor routes specifically constructed for the purpose.) Israeli aircraft were continually rendering Syrian airfields unusable, thus hindering the massive Soviet airlift that was daily flying in dozens of heavy transports, while Israeli naval attacks on Syrian ports were endangering the sea supply line from the Soviet Union. The bulk of the Syrian Army was being concentrated along the approaches to Damascus, and the allied Arab forces, comprising units from Morocco, Saudi Arabia, Iraq and later Jordan, was assigned the task of delaying the Israeli advance. Announcements were made to the effect that, even if Damascus were to fall, Syria would continue to fight.

The Syrian Government issued desperate pleas for help. But, a few days earlier, when the Syrian forces were within a short distance of the Jordan in the southern part of the Golan Heights, having broken the initial Israeli resistance, President Assad had endeavoured to achieve a cease-fire through the offices of the Soviet Union, in order to head off the Israeli counterattack that was ultimately launched, and to remain in control of the Golan Heights. President Sadat, who had succeeded in crossing the Suez Canal and establishing bridgeheads from which his forces planned to break out, would not agree to such a cease-fire. Now, as the Israelis pressed their advantage and pushed into Syria, President Assad was only too aware of the seriousness of the error in failing to press for a cease-fire at the outset. And now, while Syria was bleeding and fighting on the approaches to its capital city, its ally, the Egyptian Army, was sitting placidly on the east bank of the Suez Canal content to consolidate its gains and hesitant to endanger its success by advancing. Assad pleaded with the

Egyptians to apply pressure on the Israeli forces and thus relieve his front. General Ismail Ali, the Egyptian Minister of War, promised action. (And, indeed, he later explained that the armoured battle of 14 October had been motivated by a desire to relieve the pressure on Syria.) The Syrians also turned to their Soviet allies, who stepped up the airlift and increased supplies to their sorely-pressed forces. Aware of the fact that the Syrian front was in danger of collapsing, Moscow issued veiled threats, such as an announcement in the Soviet media that 'the Soviet Union cannot remain indifferent to the criminal acts of the Israeli Army'. The Soviet ambassador to the United States, Anatoly Dobrynin, presented the Soviet threat to the American Secretary of State, Dr. Henry Kissinger, indicating to him that Soviet airborne forces were now on the alert to move to the defence of Damascus.

As the war in the Middle East developed, additional units of the United States Navy moved to join the US Sixth Fleet in the Mediterranean, while Soviet warships moved to protect the ports of Latakia and Tartus in Syria. The Soviet Union began to urge Arab countries to join their fellow Arabs in battle. The Chairman of the Soviet Communist Party, Leonid Brezhnev, sent a message to Houari Boumedienne, the Algerian ruler, urging him to 'do his Arab duty'; and Soviet tanks were shipped via Yugoslavia to the Algerian units assigned to the Egyptian front.

Independent of these developments, a decision had been taken in Israel not to become involved in the capture of Damascus. The effect of such a move on the Arab world could be a very serious one, and its military value would at best be dubious. Furthermore, involvement in the conquest of a city of a million hostile inhabitants could be a very costly proposition indeed, while the Israeli Command was only too aware of the danger of being drawn with its limited forces into the wide, open spaces of Syria. When to these considerations were added the Soviet interest in the security of Damascus and the Soviet threats, it was obviously not in Israel's interest to advance beyond a point from which Damascus could be threatened by Israeli artillery fire. Consequently, only a few pinpoint air attacks against specific military targets in Damascus were approved by the Israeli Government, including a very successful one against the Syrian General Staff building. Indeed, these attacks were approved only after the Syrians had launched surface-to-surface FROG missiles at civilian targets in Galilee, including the immigrant town of Migdal Haemek near Nazareth and Kibbutz Geva: little damage was caused, but the significance of such indiscriminate attacks against civilian targets was not lost on the Government. Nevertheless, at no stage was advantage taken of Israel's capability to shell Damascus. Merely the threat remained.

Iraqi and Jordanian counterattacks

On the morning of Friday 12 October, Laner's division moved forward. The 19th Brigade captured the village of Nasej and was joined by the 17th Brigade, with the 79th Brigade following-up. Laner established his headquarters on Tel Shaar, a dominating feature giving good visibility over the volcanic plain on the approaches to Damascus. He ordered the 17th and 19th Brigades to advance towards Knaker, which would outflank the Syrian positions at Sassa, and bring both his and Eitan's divisions well forward on the main road to Damascus. A battalion of the 19th Brigade reached Tel El-Mal, thus reinforcing Laner's southern flank as his forces moved in a north-easterly sweep towards Knaker. Despite the heavy losses they had sustained, the 17th and 19th Brigades were already less than three miles south of Knaker, and all the indications were that the Syrian forces were breaking. Laner's forces pressed on with renewed vigour. Standing on the dominating height of Tel Shaar, Laner followed through binoculars the clearly-visible advance of his forces along the Nasej-Knaker road. During a lull in the advance, he began to survey the entire scope of the Syrian plain. As he looked southwards he suddenly froze. Some six miles away a force of approximately 100-150 tanks in two major groups was deploying and moving northwards towards his open flank. For a moment, he thought that this might be Peled's division moving after it had broken into Syria, but Northern Command assured him that this division was stuck at Rafid and that these were not Israeli forces. Realizing that he was about to be attacked on his exposed flank while his forces were pursuing the rapidly-withdrawing Syrians to the north-east, he immediately ordered Orr's 79th Brigade to stop refuelling and to deploy to the south of Nasej as rapidly as possible. Sarig's force and the 19th Brigade were ordered to stop in their tracks on the road to Knaker and pull back to cover his southern flank. The order flabbergasted them. The brigade commanders pleaded with him. Here, after all they had been through, they had the Syrians on the run, and now the fruits of victory were to be snatched from their grasp! But he refused to entertain their pleas and ordered them to turn southwards immediately.

In the meantime, without reference to the developments on Laner's southern flank, Hofi had decided to strengthen his force and had ordered Peled to transfer the 20th Brigade to Laner. Thus, a few minutes after Laner had sighted the enemy force advancing across the plain towards his southern flank, the 20th Brigade commander reported for duty in Laner's advance headquarters. He was ordered to deploy his brigade in the area of Tel Maschara and Tel El-Mal.

In accordance with the undertakings it had given to Egypt's General Ismail Ali, the Iraqi Government had despatched its 3rd Armoured Division to Syria upon the outbreak of war. Two brigades arrived in the first week (ending 11 October): an armoured brigade with 130 tanks and a mechanized brigade with 50 tanks. These were to be joined by another armoured brigade with 130 tanks some days later. Reaching the volcanic plain to the south-west of Damascus known as the Great Leja on Friday 12 October, before dawn the Iraqi tanks were taken off their transporters and advanced across the plain towards the southern flank of the Israeli forces, which were moving towards Knaker and were endangering the Kiswe military camps west of Damascus. The armoured brigade moved in a northerly direction, while the mechanized brigade moved in a north-westerly direction towards Tel Maschara. The first Iraqi tanks came up against Orr's 79th Brigade that day, which engaged them at 300 yards distance; they knocked out seventeen tanks and the Iraqi force stopped in its tracks.

Night came on, and it was clear to Laner that the force he now knew to be Iraqi would launch a major concentrated attack. The commander of the 20th Brigade was disturbed because one of his battalions was late in arriving, so he sent out a brigade headquarters officer in a jeep to look for it. Driving in the darkness the jeep collided with a tank. When the officer stood up to advise the tank crew that they were off course, he discovered to his horror that he had bumped into an Iraqi vehicle. He beat a hasty retreat. (The Israeli battalion, which had gone astray, was finally extricated with artillery support from amidst the newly-arrived Iraqis.)

As darkness fell, Laner prepared for battle. The 19th Brigade was deployed along the road at the foot of Tel Shaar; Orr's 79th Brigade was deployed from the 19th Brigade northwards to the crossroads and then southwards towards Nasej; Sarig's 17th Brigade was spread south along the road from Orr's to Nasej, while the 20th Brigade was sited along the Maschara-Jaba road. Thus, Laner created a 'box' from Maschara to Jaba to Maatz to Nasej, leaving an opening of some four and a half miles between Maschara and Nasej. The situation was one that armour commanders dream about.

It was a bright, moonlit night when Laner's deputy, Brigadier-General Moshe Brill, and his intelligence officer informed him that the Iraqis were advancing into the opening between Nasej and Maschara. Laner could hardly believe them and went to the observation point to ascertain for himself. All divisional guns and tanks were turned inwards to the centre of the box, ready to fire at any moving target. Suddenly, the Iraqis stopped. By 21.00 hours, there was complete quiet. Laner's reports had created an atmosphere of tension and expectancy, and, as the hours passed without developments, snide comments began to be made by the staff officers of Northern Command. Laner was feeling uncomfortable. The Iraqi 3rd Armoured Division had in the meantime been reinforced by its 6th Armoured Brigade and, at 03.00 hours on Saturday 13 October, they launched a divisional attack, moving right into Laner's box. Laner's forces held their fire as the Iraqi division moved into the trap. The first streaks of light were appearing in the east when the Sherman tanks of the 19th Brigade opened fire. Their range was 200 yards. Battle was joined and the Iraqis withdrew in disorder, leaving behind some 80 destroyed tanks. Not one Israeli tank was hit. The Iraqi 8th Mechanized Brigade suffered the brunt of the casualties in the first major armoured battle in which the Iraqi Army had ever engaged. Indeed, almost a complete brigade was lost in a matter of minutes. Laner's forces moved on to capture Tel Maschara and Tel Nasej, while paratroopers mopped-up in the hills.

With the advent of the Iraqi armoured force in the field of battle, the 3rd Armoured Division was later followed by another armoured division. Hofi decided to cover his flanks, while at the same time developing local efforts to improve the Israeli positions. The 7th Brigade, by now very spread out, took the hills north and south of Nasej and fought back counterattacks by day and night at Mazrat Beit Jan, Tel Shams and Tel El-Mal until the cease-fire. The discovery that arms taken in one battle, including French-built AML armoured cars, were Western revealed that Saudi Arabian troops had entered the line and were fighting. All during this period Eitan initiated very successful night raids with paratroopers and units of the 'Golani' Brigade against tanks, positions and supply routes behind the enemy lines. The 'Golani' Brigade alone accounted for the destruction of at least twenty enemy tanks in these raids and, indeed, in this respect Eitan was the one outstanding Israeli commander who maintained the traditions that had been established in the Israeli forces over the years.

Laner's forces were by now utterly exhausted and at the end of their tether. Yet the 19th Brigade captured two heights of great tactical and strategic importance — Tel Antar and Tel El-Alakieh — which were later to prove vital in holding the Israeli line. By this time, a shortage of 155mm artillery ammunition was being felt, and the forces were advised that tank ammunition was in short supply. The order was to hold.

On Tuesday, 16 October, Laner's division was again under attack. His forces reported that Centurion tanks were advancing and, when they saw the red pennants on the antennae, they realized that these were tanks of the Jordanian 40th Armoured Brigade, which had entered Syria on the 13th. It was one of the quirks of history that Jordan's crack 40th Armoured Brigade should rush to save Syria from the threat posed to its army and capital city by the Israeli forces, for, in September 1970 during the civil war in Jordan (when King Hussein was fighting for his existence against the Palestinian terrorist organizations in the streets of his capital city), the Syrians had attempted to 'stab him in the back' by launching an armoured force of divisional strength against Jordan in the area of Irbid-Ramthia. The 40th Armoured Brigade had fought bravely against the invasion and held the superior Syrian forces until the Syrians were urged by their Soviet advisers to withdraw when various moves in the area indicated the possibility of American and Israeli involvement.

War had caught King Hussein by surprise — according to his own admission. He was soon under pressure to enter the war, but he realized that, while he was pinning down Israeli forces along his border, an attack against Israel itself would bring the full force of the Israeli Air Force against his armoured forces. His experience in 1967 in this respect was sufficient. Furthermore, he owed little to his northern Arab neighbour: he could recall only too well how he had borne the brunt of the Israeli counterattack in 1967 while the Syrians looked on and did not intervene to help him. As pressure grew among his officers, Hussein mobilized his reserves and, on 13 October, the 40th Armoured Brigade crossed into Syria at Dera'a, entering the line between Syrian and Iraqi forces on the south of the Israeli enclave pushing into Syria. The Jordanians moved towards Tel Maschara and suddenly broke to the west before Tel El-Mal. Sarig moved his brigade up to the slopes of the Tel and waited until the Jordanian tanks drew near before opening fire. His fire hit 28 tanks, and the Jordanian brigade withdrew. At this point, in an uncoordinated manner, the Iraqis began to move from Kfar Shams in the east towards Tel Antar and Tel El-Alakieh. The 20th and 19th Brigades held the attack while Laner ordered Sarig's 17th Brigade to move in a wide, outflanking movement to the south. Battle was joined and after a number of hours the Iraqis withdrew, leaving some 60 tanks burning on the battlefield.

Inter-Arab co-ordination proved to be very faulty on the battlefield. Every morning between 10.00 and 11.00 hours, a counterattack was mounted against the southern flank of the Israeli enclave by the Iraqis and Jordanians, supported by the Syrian and Iraqi Air Forces. Rarely did they succeed in co-ordinating and establishing a common language: on two occasions the Jordanians attacked while the Iraqis failed to join in; frequently Iraqi artillery support fell on the advancing or withdrawing Jordanians; and, on a number of occasions, Syrian aircraft attacked and shot down Iraqi aircraft. In general, the Iraqi forces moved slowly and cautiously, and were led without any imagination or flair. (This hesitant behaviour in battle was to be reflected once again in its performance when the Iraqi Army invaded Iran in the Iraqi-Iranian War along the Shatt al Arab in September 1980. Its leadership was hesitant, its movement was slow, and its performance, despite its overwhelming preponderance in equipment, was disappointing.)

On 17 October, Peled's division relieved Laner and took over responsibility for the southern sector of the Israeli enclave. Hofi ordered him to capture Um Butne, a village with dominating high ground around it, some four miles due east of Kuneitra and controlling the Kuneitra opening. It was essential to widen the Israeli opening into the enclave now held in Syria, and the capture of Um Butne would give more depth to the southern flank. Furthermore, taking Um Butne would add an additional element of security to the Kuneitra opening and obtain control of a north-south road within the enclave. Units of the 31st Parachute Brigade, which had captured Tel Shams so successfully only a few nights before, attacked at night and captured the village. Northern Command then ordered the paratroopers to be relieved by armoured infantry. In the midst of the handover, eight Syrian tanks equipped with optical night-fighting equipment approached and attacked the relieving battalion headquarters. An Israeli counterattack saved the situation, but not before severe losses had been incurred as a result of the costly error of committing reserves during an attack before the inevitable enemy counterattack.

The 20th Brigade in Peled's division was attacked on Friday morning, in the area of Tel Antar and Tel El-Alakieh, by a battalion of Iraqi commandos. Thereafter, an Iraqi attack in divisional strength was mounted across the plain by a force outnumbering the Israelis by three to one: 130 tanks and over 100 armoured personnel carriers supported by heavy artillery concentrations advanced on units of the 20th Brigade. Peled deployed the 19th Brigade on the western flank of the 20th. All morning, a fierce battle raged as the Iraqis tried desperately to retake these two hills dominating the Great Leja. Three major attacks were mounted as the battle raged for some seven hours. It was a day in which Northern Command could not hope for air support (the Israeli Air Force being entirely preoccupied on the Suez front with the Egyptian Third Army about to be cut off by the Israeli sweep towards the city of Suez on the west bank of the Canal). It succeeded in making up for the lack of air power, however, by very effective use of concentrated artillery support.

During the first Iraqi attack against the 20th Brigade, the 19th Brigade came under heavy fire and was pinned down. By dint of armoured manoeuvre, it managed to extricate itself from this situation and made a broad sweep towards the southern flank of the Iraqi attack. This move broke their first attack in the early morning. At 10.00 hours, as the Iraqis mounted their second attack, the Jordanian 40th Armoured Brigade moved out of the area of Tel Hara towards the western flank of Peled's division at Tel El-Mal and Tel Maschara. The Jordanians advanced — in a formation much wider than the Iraqi formation — against Tel Maschara, which was held by a small Israeli force of a company of tanks with supporting infantry. It was obvious that something had gone wrong on the Arab side: the Jordanian and Iraqi attacks were uncoordinated, while the Israeli forces were only too well prepared to take advantage of this; the Jordanian attack this time was late. Peled's orders were that the force on Tel Maschara, which would not be reinforced, should hold the Jordanian attacking force by allowing it to advance to within short range. The reconnaissance unit on the Um Butne hills to the west would attack the left flank of the Jordanians as soon as they had become involved with the Israeli force at Tel Maschara. The Jordanians advanced slowly, taking over an hour to move towards their objective. This enabled the Israeli artillery to concentrate entirely on the attack of the Iraqi force that had come to grips with the 20th Brigade. (In the meantime, the sun had risen and was no longer blinding the Israeli forces.) By noon the Jordanian forces had reached Tel Maschara and began to climb up the hill. The Israeli force holding the hill engaged them and destroyed the leading elements. At this point, the reconnaissance unit launched its attack on the Jordanian flank. The Jordanians left some twelve tanks burning on the hill and began to withdraw, with the Israeli forces harrying them in their flight until 15.00 hours. The total Jordanian armoured loss that day was some twenty tanks.

Meanwhile, the third and final Iraqi attack was being mounted with determination as wave after wave of armour moved up to attack the 20th Brigade. The Israelis had suffered heavily during the day and the brigade commander felt that it was touch and go. In the middle of the battle, he created a reserve of three tanks and placed it in the rear. The Iraqis advanced up the hill against the heavily-depleted Israeli forces, with tanks sometimes firing at ranges down to five yards. Iraqi tanks became interspersed among the defending Israeli tanks: the situation was critical as the battle swayed to and fro on the two hills. At this point, the 20th Brigade commander ordered his reserve of three tanks to move out across the plain in a wide, flanking movement to the north and attack the Iraqi forces from their northern flank. They moved in a wide sweep and came in from the north — which the Iraqis believed to be protected by Syrian forces — taking the Iraqi forces by surprise. The sudden appearance of a force on their northern flank knocked them off balance and, at the last and most critical moment, they turned and withdrew. Some 60 burning Iraqi tanks dotted the plain and the slopes of Tel Antar and Tel El-Alakieh, with about the same number of armoured personnel carriers; columns of dead Iraqi infantry clearly marked the line of approach in the three major attacks. Although Arab counterattacks continued daily against the Israeli enclave until the cease-fire, this was the last major armoured battle to be fought on the northern front.

The recapture of Mount Hermon

On the night of 20 October, Hofi ordered units of an Israeli parachute brigade and those of the 'Golani' Brigade to recapture the Israeli position on Mount Hermon. The paratroopers, who were to attack from the heights of the Hermon downwards, were ordered to capture the Syrian positions while the 'Golani' units, who were ordered to move up from below, were directed towards the Israeli position that had fallen with the outbreak of war. At 14.00 hours on 21 October, the paratroop forces were lifted by helicopter with fighter aircraft covering them. A battalion under Lieutenant-Colonel Hezi secured the helicopter landing areas, and its mission was to clear the area up to half a mile from the Syrian position, the taking of which would be the responsibility of Lieutenant-Colonel Elisha's battalion. Taking the Syrians by surprise with an unexpected attack early in the afternoon, and supported by the Air Force and by Israeli artillery, the leading force under Hezi had to advance about five miles along the crest of Mount Hermon (8,200 feet high) with Syrian artillery endeavouring to intervene. Three Syrian helicopters approached, but all crashed on the hillside, apparently hit by artillery. The Syrians threw in their Air Force and Hezi's advancing forces looked down on the dogfights taking place below them. As darkness came on, his battalion stormed the Syrian so-called 'Serpentine' position: the officer leading the attack was killed, but the Syrian commandos in the position broke and fled, leaving seven dead. Hezi continued to mop-up until they reached another Syrian position. On their way they reached a rocky formation, which they mopped-up without loss. Later, they were to discover that this position, which was the Syrian command post on the Hermon, had received a direct hit from Israeli artillery. There were twelve Syrian dead inside and this fact could account for the comparatively poor showing of the Syrian commandos in defence of the Hermon. Elisha's battalion now moved through with artillery support and stormed the main Syrian position, which was found to be empty. By 03.30 hours in the morning of 22 October, the Syrian part of Mount Hermon was in the hands of the paratroopers for the loss of one killed. Elisha prepared his forces to move towards the Israeli position on Hermon in case they should be ordered to do so by the Northern Command.

Meanwhile, the 'Golani' forces moved up along three routes, advancing as they had in the fruitless counterattack early in the war. They were led on the main road by five tanks. When they reached the area where their attack had been broken on 7 October, they were engaged by covering Syrian forces, which lay in readiness observing their advance. A comparatively large enemy force of commandos, over a battalion in strength, was scattered over the rocky hillside in holes and behind rocks, each soldier equipped with telescopic sights for day and night firing, and with anti-tank missiles deployed to prevent the advance of the supporting Israeli tanks. The Syrians, difficult to identify in the darkness, picked off the Israeli soldiers one by one. The Israeli brigade commander and a battalion commander, who were with the leading group, were wounded. Two companies of 'Golani' reinforcements were flown up and the paratroopers were ordered to begin to move down, but the 'Golani' forces, fighting desperately without their commanders, and in a situation that had now become critical, achieved their mission without outside help. As things looked their blackest and the situation seemed hopeless, the brigade operations officer took command, gathered his broken forces under heavy fire and personally led the last desperate assault. The Syrians broke as, one by one, they were winkled out of their holes and from behind the boulders. By 10.00 hours on 22 October Mount Hermon was again in Israeli hands. This attack alone cost the 'Golani' Brigade 51 killed and 100 wounded. Some days later a young sergeant of 'Golani', speaking in a heavy oriental accent, told the story of the battle on Israeli television in a matter-of-fact manner: 'We were told that Mount Hermon is the eyes of the State of Israel, and we knew we had to take it, whatever the cost.'

On the evening of 22 October, the Syrians accepted a cease-fire proposed by the United Nations Security Council. They had lost some 1,150 tanks in the battle, in addition to well over 100 Iraqi tanks and some 50 Jordanian tanks. In the Golan Heights alone, 867 Syrian tanks were recovered by the Israelis (of great significance being the fact that many of them were in good running order); 370 Syrian prisoners fell into Israeli hands and it was estimated that they had lost some 3,500 troops killed.

On the Israeli side, every single Israeli tank in battle was hit at one stage or another, but the men of the Ordnance Corps excelled in their heroism and ability to improvise, moving around in battle and repairing the tanks under fire. Some 250 Israeli tanks were knocked out, of which almost 100 were a total loss; the remainder were repaired. Israeli casualties were some 772 killed, 2,453 wounded and 65 prisoners, including pilots. In his characteristically quiet and unassuming manner, General Hofi had led the forces of Northern Command to a brilliant victory in a battle waged initially under the most adverse circumstances. He commanded his team of outstanding divisional commanders in a resolute and effective manner. The absence of controversy and recrimination about the Golan campaign reflects in no small measure the success of his leadership. The Israel Defence Forces had fought a battle which, perhaps more than any other, revealed the true quality of the Israeli troops and of the Israeli people.

3

THE AIR AND
NAVAL WAR

SAMs v. 'Flying artillery'

Unlike other wars in which the Israel Defence Forces participated, the air
and naval battles that took place in the Yom Kippur War were in many
ways a reflection of the new developments in the fields of technology and
tactics that had evolved as a result of the introduction of new types of
aircraft and, above all, of the introduction of missiles into the field of
battle. The Egyptian Air Force, in planning a future air war, was deeply
influenced by the trauma of the three hours on the morning of 5 June 1967
– when the Israeli Air Force had surprised all the Arab air forces poised
to attack Israel, and particularly that of Egypt. A second major factor that
guided the Egyptian strategy was the overall influence of Soviet thinking
on Egyptian military thought and planning ever since the Soviet Union
became the main supplier of arms to Egypt. Large numbers of Egyptian
pilots and officers were sent to train in the Soviet Union. Gradually, over
the years, the Egyptians as well as the Syrians became imbued with Soviet
doctrine. As the Egyptian planners prepared for war, the air problem was
a paramount one, predominant in their thoughts. They realized that they
had to find an effective answer to Israeli air supremacy; otherwise there
would be no point in launching a war. For this purpose, their front-line
must be covered in such a way that Israeli air intervention would have little
or no effect on the initial stages of the attack, and would allow the Arab
preponderance in artillery, troops and armour to be concentrated fully at
the point of attack.

For this purpose, the Soviet Union gradually evolved, during the War of
Attrition and thereafter, a system of surface-to-air missile air defence
batteries along the Suez Canal. This provided a 'mix' of SAM-2, SAM-3
and SAM-6 batteries. There were 150 batteries in Egypt at the outbreak of
war, composed of SAM-2 and SAM-3 batteries (with six launching pads
per battery) and SAM-6 batteries (each with twelve missiles ready for
launching on four tanks). Of the 150 batteries, some 50 were concentrated
along the Suez Canal front. The mobile SAM-6, with an effective range of
24,000 yards, fitted into a comprehensive pattern provided by the
comparatively static SAM-2 (with a range of 55,000 yards) and the more
mobile SAM-3 (33,000 yards). Each of these weapons possessed different
electronic guidance characteristics, which complicated the application of
electronic countermeasures. The main advantage of the SAM-6 lay in its
mobility: mounted on a tank chassis, it could be moved into action
rapidly, requiring only minutes to be folded up before being moved to an

alternative site and then another short period to be ready for action again. To seek out a SAM-6 missile launcher, an aircraft would of necessity enter the range of the SAM-2. If one adds to this formidable interlocked system hundreds of SAM-7s — portable, Strela missile launchers organized in platoons in the ground forces — together with conventional anti-aircraft weapons (in particular the multi-barrelled ZSU 23), there is little wonder that the Egyptians and their Soviet advisers were convinced that, from the point of view of anti-aircraft defence, their forces were well protected.

The second problem exercising the Egyptian Command as it prepared for war was the Israeli ability to attack targets in depth in Egypt and Syria without any adequate response, because it was felt that once outside the range of missile surface-to-air defence systems, the Egyptian and Syrian air forces would be no match for the Israeli fighters. The answer to this was given by the Russians. They supplied FROG (Free Rocket Over Ground) battlefield support missiles (with a range of up to 55 miles) to Syria, and these were near enough to engage urban centres of population in Israel. In March 1973, following the visit of a very high-level Soviet military delegation to Cairo, the Soviet Union began to ship the SCUD battlefield support surface-to-surface missile to the Egyptian Army. Capable of carrying either a high-explosive warhead or a nuclear warhead, this had a range of some 180 miles, enabling it to engage centres of population in Israel from Egypt. President Sadat believed that with this deterrent in his hands he could replace the deterrent that would have been created by a medium-range bomber force, and he is on record as saying that his final decision to go to war was made in April 1973 — when the first SCUD missiles arrived on Egyptian soil.

On 13 September 1973, a routine Israeli patrol off the coast of Syria, in the area of Latakia, tangled with Syrian air units. In the course of the ensuing dogfight, the Israeli force shot down thirteen Syrian aircraft for the loss of one Israeli machine. General Benjamin Peled, the commander of the Israeli Air Force, realized that such a result was bound to bring on a retaliatory Syrian move, such as mass artillery bombardment. If the Syrians reacted in this way, the problem, as he saw it, posed by over 30 Syrian surface-to-air missile batteries of hypersensitive SAM-6s would be a very serious one. When the air force was placed on a very high level of preparedness on 5 October, with its combat effectives fully mobilized, Peled ordered his planners to prepare a pre-emptive strike. This strike, it will be recalled, was not approved by the Government by 6 October.

General Peled was the first Israeli Air Force commander produced entirely in Israel. A fighter pilot, he had been shot down by ground fire at Sharm El-Sheikh in the 1956 Sinai Campaign, and had evaded capture when an Israeli Piper Cub literally snatched him from the hands of his would-be captors. He proved himself in the war to be an outstanding commander of an élite force. His restraint, calm confidence and cool-headedness, inspired all around him with confidence. He at no time underestimated his adversaries, but neither did he underestimate the force he led. After he retired from the air force some years later, he became the head of a highly sophisticated electronics concern. In his public utterances he became noted for an ill-concealed disdain for the type of democracy in Israel, and his views could be characterized as reactionary in the extreme.

Ranged against the Israeli Air Force, which comprised principally among its fighters the A4 Skyhawk, the F4 Phantom and the French Mirage, the Egyptian and Syrian air forces were armed principally with the MiG-21, the MiG-19 and the MiG-17. The ratio was approximately 3:1 in favour of the Arab air forces, with the Egyptian and Syrian air forces alone accounting for approximately 900 fighters against some 350 Israeli fighter aircraft.

The attack of the Egyptian Air Force, which was commanded by General Hosni Mubarak, heralded the major onslaught on 6 October. General Mubarak, a heavily-built, quiet, dour bomber pilot, rose through the ranks of the Air Force, and displayed considerable ability throughout his career. He received air pilot and staff training twice in the Soviet Union. After the 1973 War, President Sadat appointed him to be his Vice-President and, on the assassination of Sadat in 1981, he succeeded him as President of Egypt.

The attacks of the Egyptian Air Force were not directed in particular against Israeli formations, but were concentrated rather on airfields, radar installations, headquarters and camps in Sinai, all comparatively close to the front-line. (The normal depth of their penetration was west of a line passing through Baluza, Refidim, Tasa and the Mitla Pass.) The Syrians, on the other hand, concentrated their attacks on the Israeli combat forces. The very limited depth of penetration by the Arab air forces was adhered to throughout, with some exceptions. The deepest penetration was an attempt late in the war by six Egyptian Mirages (supplied by the French to the Libyans) to attack the area of El-Arish, flying in from the sea; three of them were shot down over the sea. Other attempts included two Egyptian Tupolev Tu-16 bombers that failed in a mission to reach Eilat, with one crashing near Abu Rudeis; and two Syrian Sukhoi Su-20s bound for the Haifa Bay area, one of which crashed over Nahariya while the second fled to Syria. The second Syrian attempt at deep penetration was with four Sukhoi Su-20s, three of which crashed in the area of Mount Miron in upper Galilee. The Egyptians tried to make up for their failure to bomb in depth by launching Kelt air-to-surface stand-off missiles from over Egyptian territory. (In general these missiles were launched from deep inside Egypt.) One such missile aimed at Tel Aviv on the afternoon of 6 October was shot out of the air by an Israeli pilot on patrol; of 25 Kelts fired at Israeli targets, it was reported that twenty were shot down by the Israeli Air Force and only two succeeded in causing damage.

The Israeli air planning had been based all along on the assumption that the initial operations of the air force would constitute an all-out attack against the missile systems in order to free the air force later to support the ground effort. The Egyptian and Syrian initiative, the massive nature of the attack with its effect on the Israeli ground forces, the desperate battle being waged by the Israeli forces along the Canal and on the Golan Heights — all these prevented the Israeli Air Force from attacking as planned, and obliged it to throw caution to the winds and give close support to the harassed ground forces without dealing adequately with the missile threat and achieving complete air superiority. Consequently, losses were comparatively heavy. As the situation of the Israeli forces on the ground became more and more desperate in the first two days of fighting, the Israeli Air Force was thrown into battle against unacceptable odds and incurred very heavy losses. After three days of fighting, General Dayan reported to the editors of the Israeli press that some 50 fighter aircraft had been lost. Despite the very heavy losses, however, the Israeli Air Force persevered in its attacks. As the Israeli ground forces advanced into Syria, the Israeli Air Force succeeded in destroying part of the Syrian missile system and began to range far and wide into Syria, attacking strategic targets (oil installations, power plants and bridges) and causing considerable damage to the Syrian infrastructure. The Syrian fighters fought back and, of 222 Syrian aircraft lost in the war, 162 were destroyed in aerial combat.

On the Egyptian front the Israeli Air Force attacked missile sites and enemy airfields, but above all gave close support whenever an Egyptian force emerged from under the protection of the missile umbrella − as in the case of the Egyptian brigade that advanced on Abu Rudeis on the southern Egyptian flank in the large armoured battle on 14 October, when the Israeli Air Force was a major element in destroying the attacking Egyptian forces. As from 18 October, when the Egyptian Command at last appreciated the significance of the Israeli crossing to the west bank of the Suez Canal, the Egyptian Air Force proved to be more daring and more persistent in attack. Aerial encounters reminiscent of the Second World War were seen again, with 40-50 aircraft in the air at times. The Israelis, however, held the upper hand. Indeed, throughout the war the Egyptians succeeded in downing only five Israeli aircraft in air battles, as against 172 Egyptian aircraft lost in the same manner, making a total of 334 Arab aircraft against 5 Israelis shot down in air-to-air combat.

On the west bank of the Suez Canal, an unusual example of mutual co-ordination emerged between the advancing ground forces and the Israeli Air Force. As the armoured forces on the west bank of the Canal destroyed one surface-to-air missile battery after another, the Israeli Air Force gained a freer hand and became a major factor in supporting the advancing Israeli forces. But the Israeli Air Force had dealt directly with the missile batteries according to plan after the initial onslaught of the Egyptian ground forces, particularly in Port Said which, after 13 October, was without any missile defences until the end of the war. By 14 October, Israeli Air Force air attacks against nine missile batteries in the area of Kantara made this area missile-free too. From 21 October, most of the area of the Egyptian Second Army, the whole area of the Egyptian Third Army on the east bank of the Canal and the area of the Gulf of Suez to Ras Adabiah were missile-free.

The Israeli Air Force was instrumental in protecting the area of Sharm El-Sheikh by interdicting the helicopter-borne commando forces. Furthermore, the skies over Israel remained 'clean' throughout the war:

not one bomb fell in Israel, and the air force infrastructure remained unaffected. The maintenance of air superiority also had major strategic implications. King Hussein explained to his Arab colleagues that a major consideration in Jordan's unwillingness to commit its forces against Israeli territory was Israel's control of the air over the potential battlefield.

During the war, the total losses of the Egyptians and the Syrians were 514 aircraft, some 58 of which were shot down by their own forces; Israeli losses totalled 102, of which, according to Minister of Defence Dayan, 50 were lost in the first three days. The bulk of the Israeli losses were caused by missiles and conventional anti-aircraft fire, with honours roughly even between the two, particularly during close-support missions. The conflict was a major proving ground from which many will have drawn their lessons. Despite the manner in which the Israeli Air Force acquitted itself in the face of the missiles, there was no doubt that many of the accepted concepts about air war would have to be re-evaluated. The role of aircraft in war had changed, and new strategies and uses of air power would have to be evolved. Obviously, the whole new generation of stand-off air-launched weapons and tactical surface-to-surface missiles, enabling anti-missile battery operations to be mounted out of the range of the enemy missiles, would change considerably the conditions in the field of battle, while surface-to-air missilery would be based to an increasing degree on highly mobile platforms, such as the SAM-6. To a degree, air power would not be as influential as it had been, and would affect the immediate battlefield less than hitherto. The proliferation of light, portable missile launchers in the front-lines meant that close support would be the exception to the rule in the future, with the air force being obliged to concentrate on isolating the field of battle, maintaining supremacy in the air, and destroying the forces in and near the field of battle. Considerable emphasis in the use of air power in the future would be placed on the protection of the home front, in addition to attacks against the surface-to-surface missile systems threatening the home front and also the battlefield.

Missiles at sea

The war found the main Egyptian naval forces based in the Mediterranean. They consisted of twelve Osa-type missile boats, ten submarines, six advanced-type torpedo-boats and some twenty regular torpedo-boats, in addition to three destroyers and two frigates, minesweepers, patrol boats and eleven LCT landing craft. The Syrian order of battle included nine missile-boats (three Osa-type and six Komar-type), eleven torpedo-boats and two minesweepers. Against this combined force was ranged a force of fourteen Israeli missile-boats.

On the night of 6/7 October, a force of five Israeli missile-boats set out to patrol the coast of Syria to a distance of some 200 miles from their base. At 22.28 hours, as the Israeli naval forces moved north past the Lebanese coast, parallel to the Syrian coast opposite Cyprus, a Syrian torpedo-boat to the north was identified. The Israelis closed in, and then it turned to withdraw rapidly eastwards towards the Syrian coast. Fire was opened, and in the ensuing battle the Syrian torpedo-boat sank. The Israeli force had by now turned eastwards and was sweeping towards the Syrian coast opposite Latakia in two parallel forces, the southern force including the INS *Reshef* (the first Israeli-designed and constructed naval vessel ever to enter naval combat). As the force closed in on the coast, it sighted a minesweeper, which was engaged by *Reshef* with missile fire and sunk. But, lying in wait due south of the minesweeper, the force now observed a Syrian force of three missile boats — the torpedo-boat had been a warning outpost, the minesweeper a form of decoy, while the Syrian force was deployed to attack the Israeli vessels from the flank as they were engaging it. The Israelis turned south and joined battle with the missile-boats, which fired a volley of missiles at their approach. The Israeli force sailed in parallel columns southwards and manoeuvred so that the Syrian force found itself sandwiched between them. At 23.35 hours, battle was joined. Volleys of missiles were fired by both sides and, within 25 minutes, the three Syrian vessels had been sunk. The battle of Latakia, the first naval missile battle in history, had been won by the Israeli Navy without sustaining any casualties.

The Israeli naval forces persisted in their aggressive action, closing in night after night on the Syrian and Egyptian coasts and obliging both countries to tie down comparatively large forces, both armour and artillery, along the coasts. (An entire armoured brigade was deployed to protect the Syrian coast.)

The second naval battle of significance, that of Damiette-Balatin on the Mediterranean coast of Egypt, took place on the night of 8/9 October. A force of six Israeli missile-boats approached the Egyptian coast to shell the military installations and coastal defences in the area of Damiette. Just on midnight, an Egyptian force of four missile-boats engaged the Israelis with missile fire. Still outranged, the Israeli force moved in at full speed. As they observed the Israelis approaching undeterred by the missile fire, the Egyptians turned and began to withdraw. Three of the Israeli boats launched their missiles and, in a matter of 40 minutes, three Egyptian boats were sunk, while the fourth disappeared out of range.

The Israeli forces continued to harass the Egyptian and Syrian naval forces and coasts with ever-increasing daring and initiative. The ferocity and dash of the Israeli attacks had their effect on the Syrian and Egyptian navies. As Israeli pressure mounted, the Arab navies concentrated around their harbours without emerging into the open seas, firing their missiles from there while relying for protection on very heavy concentrations of coastal artillery strengthened by armoured forces along the coast. The Egyptians had planned a large fleet of small vessels in anchorages and fishing ports along the Gulf of Suez, which was to ferry forces and supplies across the Gulf to the advancing Egyptian forces. On the first night of the war, the Israelis identified a concentration of boats in the Bay of Mersa Talamat, south of Ras Za'afrana. The Israelis attacked and created havoc, and the Egyptian operation was disrupted before it got under way.

Israeli Naval Raids

On a number of occasions the Egyptians attacked along the Israeli-held Sinai coast, but Israeli pressure developed and within a few days the Israeli Navy was in complete command of the Gulf of Suez. On the night of 8/9 October, a battle took place off the Egyptian coast at Ras-a-Sadat, in which an Egyptian patrol-boat was sunk despite the support it received from radar-operated, land-based 130mm guns. Five nights later, a force of five Israeli patrol-boats entered the anchorage at Ras Ghareb, where over fifty Egyptian small craft were concentrated to move across the Gulf of Suez. In the ensuing close-range mêlée, nineteen Egyptian armed fishing boats were sunk.

With the outbreak of war, the Egyptians had declared a naval blockade in the Red Sea, in the area north of the 23rd parallel. Two Skory-type destroyers and some ancillary craft were based on the port of Aden, and two submarines were based on Port Sudan. The Israelis, for their part, blockaded the Gulf of Suez, basing themselves on Sharm El-Sheikh and the Sinai coast in the Gulf of Suez. Thus, both sides were blockaded from a naval point of view as far as their outlets to East Africa and Asia were concerned. (Despite attempts by the Egyptian Navy to impose a blockade on the Mediterranean approaches to Israel, the shipping lanes to and from Israel were kept open during the war.)

The Israeli naval planners had given considerable thought and study to Israel's naval problem, and had managed to concentrate the maximum firepower feasible in a small vessel. The fast, compact Israeli Navy, which had suddenly appeared in the arena, took the Arab navies by surprise. Its degree of effectiveness can be gauged from the fact that, in the course of the war, it suffered a total loss of three killed at sea and 24 wounded — not a single Israeli vessel sank, despite the fact that the Egyptian and Syrian navies fired a total of some 52 missiles at Israeli targets at sea, and sustained a confirmed loss (not counting vessels damaged and later repaired) of nineteen naval vessels, including ten missile-boats.

While the naval battles in the Yom Kippur War did not have a decisive influence on its outcome, this small naval war in the Middle East was such as to enable naval architects and planners to have a closer look at the sea war of the future. The battle of Latakia, the first naval missile battle in history, confirmed the fact that naval warfare had entered a new era.

SUMMARY
A New Era

The war aims of the Arabs were comparatively limited from a military point of view, but had as a prime purpose political gains. President Sadat had reached the conclusion for some time that war was desirable, even essential, to enable an advance in the political process. Sadat's directives, as far as the strategic aim of the war was concerned, were to upset Israel's security doctrine by initiating a military operation that would cause heavy casualties to Israel and directly affect her national morale. The immediate military purpose of the Arabs was to neutralize Israeli air strength by creating a surface-to-air missile system capable of so doing; by cancelling out Israel's advantage from operating along interior lines of communication by mounting a simultaneous attack on both fronts; and by capturing a limited area from the Israelis while causing heavy casualties. As far as the Arabs were concerned, the mere fact of initiating the attack was in itself a major move forward and constituted an important political change.

Despite the massive land and air offensive of Egypt and Syria against Israel in the Yom Kippur War, the strategic aims of both countries were comparatively limited. This was, as emerges from the material that has been published about the war in the Arab world and from Arab sources, a result of the very considerable measure of respect the Arab armies had for the Israel Defence Forces after the Six Day War. The political purpose of Egypt and Syria was to strike two heavy blows against Israel in order to break the log-jam which had occurred in the Israeli-Arab conflict since the cease-fire in August 1970. These strategic blows were designed to force the hands of the superpowers and oblige them to pressurize Israel to return to the 1967 borders, without requiring any Arab country actually to sign a peace treaty with Israel — a development that, in the eyes of the Arabs, would have to be avoided in order to prevent granting any form of legitimacy to Israel in the Middle East. In short, their aim was to move the clock back to the eve of the Six Day War in 1967 as far as Israel-Arab relations were concerned.

An analysis of the Israeli position shows that war was considered to be against Israel's interests, and therefore to be avoided as much as possible. It was realized that the mere fact alone of war breaking out would constitute a political advantage for the Arabs. So every effort must be made to prevent any meaningful military advantage being gained initially by the Arabs. Furthermore, the result of Israel's reaction must be to destroy as much of the Arab forces and their military infrastructure as possible, in order to leave Israel with a marked advantage for a number of years. Thus, Israel's aims were to avoid war if possible by deterrence; to prevent the Arabs from gaining any territorial advantage in the initial attack; to gain and maintain the upper hand in the air by destroying the Arab missile system; to destroy Arab forces; and to capture territory for use as a political bargaining factor.

Ever since the wargames held in Israel in the summer of 1972, the Israeli General Staff had evaluated correctly the type of attack the Egyptians would mount against them in the event of a war. The basic assumption in Israel was that there would be adequate intelligence warning, which would enable Israel to mobilize her reserves rapidly, and that these forces would be deployed to the front under the full protection of the air force. For their part, Egypt and Syria assumed that the simultaneous attack on both fronts would pin the Israeli forces down to the respective fronts, without being able to utilize the Israeli Air Force effectively. It was assumed that the initial Arab onslaught would enable the Egyptians and Syrians rapidly to capture the Golan Heights in the north and a strip along the east bank of the Suez Canal.

The Egyptian ground forces who were to cross the Suez were to be equipped to saturation point in anti-tank weapons and missiles in order to wear down the Israeli armour, which would obviously counterattack as an Egyptian bridgehead was widened and broadened. The Egyptian plan was that, following the attrition of Israeli armour, they would then deploy their armoured reserves together with additional heavy anti-aircraft equipment (particularly surface-to-air missiles) on the east bank with the purpose of mounting an advance into the Sinai in order to capture the Mitla and Gidi Passes some 30 miles east of the Canal, and Ras Sudar on the eastern coast of the Gulf of Suez. With these advances, international action prompted by the superpowers would bring about a cease-fire and would leave the Egyptians with the fruits of victory in their hands. In the north, the Syrians planned a massive armoured attack designed to capture the whole of the Golan Heights in a period of one to three days; to assume defensive positions along the River Jordan and the Sea of Galilee; to advance their anti-aircraft missile system and then meet the inevitable Israeli counter-attack head-on; and thereafter to engage in a war of attrition designed to cause the maximum number of casualties to the Israeli forces. Plans were prepared, in the event of a successful occupation of the Golan Heights, to mount a subsequent attack into Galilee with the primary object of cutting off the area of the 'finger' of eastern Galilee.

The first outstanding Arab military success – and indeed the most important – was the strategic and tactical surprise they achieved. While this success was aided to no small degree by mistakes made by Israeli Intelligence and the political and military leadership in Israel, the bulk of the credit must go to the highly sophisticated deception plan mounted by the Egyptians and Syrians. They succeeded in convincing the Israeli Command that the intensive military activity in Egypt to the west of the Canal during the summer and autumn of 1973 was nothing more than a series of training operations and manoeuvres. This deception must be marked out as one of the outstanding plans of deception mounted in the course of military history. Its success proved that the tactical and operational defence system of the Israel Defence Forces, both along the Suez Canal and in the Golan Heights, was inadequate.

Undoubtedly, had the Israeli static defence system been fully manned as planned, with the necessary artillery, armour and air support, the enemy advance would have been slowed down considerably. The Egyptians would have been prevented from making meaningful gains in a number of sectors, and the attack would have been channelled in the directions desired by the Israelis, thus facilitating the Israeli armoured counter-attack. In the event, a forward, static defence system proved to be very vulnerable and was comparatively easy prey for a surprise attack. It seems that a much more flexible and mobile system of defence would have been more effective in the circumstances.

The massive Egyptian crossing of the Suez Canal, including the transfer of five divisions simultaneously in the course of 24 hours while engaged in battle with a surprised enemy, must be considered a major military achievement. In general, both the planning and the execution of the Egyptian Army, and above all the technical and organizational ability which enabled them in the course of a night to throw across the Canal ten bridges over which they transferred tanks and vehicles, and a further ten bridges for infantry, all point to a very successful organizational military operation.

The Israelis had made no secret of their armoured philosophy, which envisaged the immediate launch of a massive, rapidly deployed, armoured counterattack. Accordingly, the Egyptians assiduously developed an answer to such an attack and also, of course, to the concomitant Israeli air attack. The answer lay in equipping the attacking forces across the Canal with enormous quantities of Sagger anti-tank rockets and Strela SAM-7 light anti-aircraft missiles. The massive use of these missiles and rockets, combined with artillery fire, provided the initial solution for the challenge posed by possible Israeli counterattacks. The Israeli mistake seems to have been in launching previously-planned counterattacks − which had been observed during training periods by the Egyptians, and had been suitably mapped out so that they could prepare the necessary reply. This tactic on the part of the Israelis was a very costly one, and many armoured vehicles were lost as a result. With hindsight, one can see that, had the Israelis adopted a more cautious policy, made better use of battlefield intelligence and air reconnaissance, and thus read more clearly the Egyptian tactics, it would have been possible to have mounted a co-ordinated attack of armour, artillery and armoured infantry, thus avoiding a great number of casualties. Such a tactic could well have avoided the failures of the major Israeli attack on 8 October and the linking-up of the Egyptian bridgeheads to create a long, contiguous bridgehead that later proved impossible to dislodge.

A further important achievement on the part of the Arab armies was the success of the Syrian Army (supported by two armoured divisions from Iraq and an armoured brigade task force from Jordan) in blocking the advance of the Israel Defence Forces towards Damascus. True, the Israelis had no intention of taking Damascus proper, but aimed merely to create a threat to the city; however, despite their defeat at the hands of the Israel Defence Forces in the Golan Heights, the Syrians succeeded in withdrawing in an orderly manner, in conserving some of their reserves (particularly the 3rd Armoured Division) and in establishing a strong defence line some eighteen miles south of Damascus. There is no doubt that the ability of the Iraqis to move from Iraq over a distance of some 300-400 miles two armoured divisions, and to activate the first in the battle against the advancing Israelis on 12 October, is worthy of note from a military point of view. In contrast to the mediocre ability displayed by the Iraqi Army in battle with the Israelis, its ability at very short notice to organize the move of formations to the Golan Heights in such a comparatively short time was something of a logistic feat.

Nevertheless, despite initial successes achieved by the Arab armies both at the strategic and tactical levels, and the general improvement shown by them in combat as compared with their record in previous wars, the Israel Defence Forces emerged the military victor. In the course of the war, the Israelis succeeded in blocking the advance of the respective Arab armies in the two strategic theatres; in causing very heavy casualties to the attacking forces; in pushing the Syrian Army in the Golan Heights back across its starting line; in breaking into its operational depth in the Golan Heights and into the Egyptian strategic depth on the western bank of the Suez Canal; and finally in bringing the Egyptian Army to the brink of disaster, a situation which forced it to ask for a cease-fire.

The two main successes of the Israel Defence Forces were in blocking the Arab advances in the course of a few days and mounting attacks respectively against Syria and Egypt. Having initially suffered losses in their headlong counterattacks (particularly on the Suez front where heavy losses of armour were incurred), the Israelis rapidly adapted themselves to the new situation. The new Israeli deployment gradually took control of the situation and wore down the attacks by both the Syrians and the Egyptians. Basing themselves on armoured 'anvils', which combined with armoured infantry and artillery to slow down and ultimately hold the advances, the Israelis then began to attack from the flanks, leading, for instance, to the almost complete encirclement of the Syrian 1st Armoured Division in the Hushniya area of the Golan Heights on 8 and 9 October. The Israeli forces reached their peak in this phase in the armoured battle of 14 October, in which the Egyptians attempted to increase the depth of their penetration to the line of the passes some 30 miles east of the Canal. The result was a major victory for the Israeli forces, involving the loss of over 250 Egyptian tanks. It was this victory that paved the way for an immediate decision to cross the Canal.

Once the line had been stabilized on both fronts, Israel was faced with the strategic question of whether to transfer the main effort to the Sinai front, for the Israeli forces had returned to the 'Purple Line' on the Golan Heights. The purpose of such an operation would be either to entice the Egyptian armoured forces from across the Suez Canal to the east bank in order to draw them into battle and defeat them in a war of manoeuvre, or to make a number of snap attacks across the Canal, such as an attempt to take Port Said or areas on the west coast of the Gulf of Suez. This latter alternative was supported, amongst others, by the Minister of Defence. The alternative school of thought was in favour of launching a major attack into Syria in order to seize territory that could later be used in political bargaining against the Egyptian enclaves on the east bank of the Suez Canal. The plan was to come as near as possible to the outskirts of Damascus in order to threaten that city − an action that would take the Syrians out of the war and force them to ask for an immediate cease-fire. This plan was supported by the Chief of Staff and the commander of the Air Force, and they succeeded in convincing the Minister of Defence. The decision was taken on 10 October.

The Israeli forces advanced some fifteen miles into Syria, but the attack was stopped some eighteen miles south of Damascus when, on 12 October, the Iraqi 1st Armoured Division established contact with the Israeli forces. From a strategic point of view, the Israeli attack did not succeed in destroying the Syrian and Iraqi forces. Syria was not taken out of the war, and it appeared at this point that the Israeli military effort was coming to an end; indeed, the Chief of Staff pointed out to the Israeli Government on 12 October that the attack in the north had been stopped in its tracks by the joint Syrian and Iraqi forces, and that there was little prospect of mounting a major effective attack on the Egyptian enclaves and bridgeheads on the east bank of the Canal. Hence, he was of the opinion that Israel should now be interested in a cease-fire. However, new human elements entered the considerations affecting the new moves.

In Egypt, there had been a debate as to whether or not the 4th and 21st Armoured Divisions should be moved to the east bank. The Minister of War, General Ahmed Ismail Ali, had turned down this proposal, being unwilling to move these forces to the east bank without an adequate ground-to-air missile system preceding them: this would protect them as they attacked out of the bridgehead towards the passes. However, on 12 October, following the Israeli attacks in the direction of Damascus, the Syrians exerted pressure on the Egyptians to ease their situation by mounting an attack to draw Israeli forces from the Syrian front to the Sinai. It was this that changed the Egyptian attitude to the transfer of armoured forces to the east bank of the Canal; the 4th and 21st Armoured Divisions were transferred on the instructions of the President of Egypt, with orders to attack the Israelis on 13 and 14 October along six parallel axes of advance in order to reach the line of the passes at Mitla and Gidi. This led to the major battle of 14 October and the Israeli victory that led ultimately to their crossing of the Canal.

A further strategic debate that took place in the Israeli High Command was whether or not to mount a major attack across the Suez Canal before the Egyptian armoured reserves had been transferred to the east bank. One school of thought favoured an immediate attack, maintaining that it would be possible to wear down the Egyptian armoured forces on the other side of the Canal. This school of thought felt, too, that even if there were difficulties in bringing forward bridges to the Canal, it would be possible if sufficient forces were introduced across the Canal to take some of the Egyptian bridges from behind, from inside Egypt. The second school of thought favoured waiting for the Egyptians to transfer their armoured forces to the east bank and only then, once they had been committed, to make the crossing. While this debate was going on, the Egyptians resolved it for the Israelis by transferring the armoured divisions to the east bank.

It is possible at this point to compare the moves made by the respective Egyptian and Syrian Commands in respect of armoured reserves. The transfer of the Egyptian 4th and 21st Armoured Divisions to the east bank gave the Israelis the necessary opening to cross the Canal and to be comparatively free to widen and broaden their bridgehead on the west bank of the Canal and to strengthen their forces even before the bridging equipment was put into position. It should be recorded here that the first Israeli bridge was finally put into position 36 hours after the time planned therefor. The Syrians, for their part, persisted in retaining the 3rd Armoured Division in reserve, and this force was the main opposition to the Israeli forces advancing on Damascus on 11 and 12 October. Its retention in reserve by the Syrians paid off handsomely when the Israeli attack was mounted.

It is therefore of great interest to the military historian to note that the event that brought about the strategic change on the Suez front – a change that was to give rise to the military situation finally forcing the Egyptians to ask for a cease-fire – occurred not on this front but far away on the Syrian front. While it was not planned as such, it was the decision to mount an Israeli offensive into *Syria*, in the direction of Damascus, that finally brought about the strategic change on the *Suez* front, which ultimately was to influence events leading to the conclusion of the war. The war came to an end because the Israel Defence Forces managed to pass three divisions across to the west bank of the Suez Canal and the Egyptian Army was unable to block this force. The result was the encirclement of the Egyptian Third Army and a threat to the rear administrative and supply areas of the entire Egyptian Army along the Suez Canal. Furthermore, a threat to Cairo itself was being developed. As this situation was obviously getting out of hand, the Egyptians asked for a cease-fire. In his message to President Assad, President Sadat wrote: 'I cannot . . . accept the responsibility before history for the destruction of our armed forces for a second time. I have therefore informed the Soviet Union that I am prepared to accept a cease-fire on existing positions . . . My heart bleeds to tell you this, but I feel that my office compels me to take this decision.'

Thus, the military victory went to Israel. The Israel Defence Forces achieved almost fully the strategic task it had been set, 'to deny the enemy any military advantage'. In the north, the Syrians had been thrown out of the Golan Heights and the Israeli forces had advanced towards Damascus. On the southern front the Egyptians had left themselves a certain territorial advantage, although a very limited one, in the form of bridgeheads to the east of the Suez Canal. But, against this, the Israel Defence Forces managed to recover, to cross the Canal westwards between the two Egyptian armies, to break into the Egyptian operational depth, to surround the Third Army and cut it off, and to be in a position to threaten the entire military deployment of the Egyptians on both sides of the Canal — so much so that the Egyptians asked for an immediate cease-fire.

But Israel did not reap the political benefits of the war. President Sadat had initially launched the attack in order to break the military and political log-jam. This he had succeeded in doing. He proceeded to develop his political strategy, which ultimately led him first to an interim agreement in the Sinai, and ultimately to a peace treaty with Israel, which gave him back the valuable oilfields and the entire area of the peninsula.

The United States also benefitted considerably, from a political point of view, from the outcome of the war. At the conclusion of the Yom Kippur War, the United States held the key to impose a cease-fire and to extract the political dividends from the situation created. The Russians were obliged to invite the United States Secretary of State, Henry Kissinger, to Moscow on 21 October in order to work out the details of a cease-fire between Israel and Egypt, which was due to come into effect at 18.00 hours on 22 October. All parallel arrangements in the Security Council of the United Nations were also guided by the United States. President Sadat appreciated immediately the vital centrality of the United States position. From 23 October, he established a direct relationship with Washington, assuming that the most effective way in which to pressurize Israel was to operate through Washington. And, in return for American pressure on Israel, he began gradually to enable the United States to improve its position in Egypt at the expense of the Soviet Union. The United States negotiated Israeli military concessions, including the cease-fire on the west bank of the Canal, opening a supply line to the beleaguered Egyptian Third Army, and the disengagement by the Israeli forces from the west bank of the Canal to the east bank, without the Egyptians being obliged to give up any of their territorial gains on the east bank. This was just a prelude to the political developments that were to create a situation over the years, planned and developed by President Sadat, giving Egypt a special position in the overall American strategic plan in the Middle East.

From a military point of view, the imbalance in the composition of Israeli forces became evident as the war developed. Because of a lack of armoured personnel carriers, the Israeli infantry lacked mobility, and thus tanks did not operate as part of a team but rather on their own. There was a failure to take into account available intelligence, such as that on the SAGGER anti-tank missile, and to apply its lessons organizationally and operationally. Furthermore, because the Israeli forces placed so much emphasis on airpower, the artillery arm had been neglected. In general, one can say that the Israeli forces tended initially to fight the previous war until, after a few days, they gradually got the measure of the enemy and were capable of supplying the answer. The Israeli infantry did not come into its own in the Yom Kippur War: on few occasions was it correctly used to full advantage. In this war, the Israeli forces faced an Egyptian

Army better led at the tactical level than they had known before. The Egyptian and the Syrian armies accounted for themselves much better in combat than in any of the previous encounters which the Israeli forces had had with them. At most stages in the fighting, the Syrian forces acted as a well-disciplined army. This came to very vivid expression in the withdrawal which they carried out into Syria after the Israeli attack on 10 October. This withdrawal was carried out in an orderly, controlled manner.

One of the basic errors in the Israeli evaluation of Arab strategy was a failure to appreciate that the Egyptians would decide on a *limited* military solution to their problem based on the missile umbrella, and would accordingly develop a limited strategy. The mistake of the Israeli General Staff was to judge the Arab General Staffs by its own standards of military thinking.

In the course of the war, the two superpowers mounted resupply operations, the Soviet Union to Syria and Egypt, and the United States to Israel. The intensity of the war took the quartermasters' staffs by surprise. The expenditure of ammunition was inordinately high, the losses of aircraft were serious, and the figures of tanks destroyed were alarming. It was clear that the staff tables on the basis of which ammunition was stocked over the years required drastic revision. The American airlift was obviously of vital importance militarily to Israel at a critical juncture, but it was perhaps even more significant politically. Its unequivocal nature was undoubtedly a major factor in bringing about a cease-fire, and in turning the United States into the central figure on the stage of the Middle East in the subsequent months. (This was implied by President Sadat in his letter to President Assad advising him that he was seeking a cease-fire.)

In the events leading up to the war, there were two fatal errors on the part of the Israelis. The first was that in intelligence evaluation, and the failure at the command level and the ministerial level to appreciate the significance of the parallel developments on the Syrian and Egyptian fronts. The second major error was the stubborn assumption of the Israeli defence and military establishment that the unrealistic and unfavourable ratio of forces along the borders was adequate to hold any Egyptian or Syrian attack. This in turn was based on erroneous readings of developments in the field of war, particularly of the air force's ability to deal with the surface-to-air missile systems, and failure to appreciate the significance of various developments, such as the construction of the high rampart on the Egyptian side of the Canal.

The principal immediate results of the Yom Kippur War were disengagement agreements between Egypt and Israel on the one hand, and Syria and Israel on the other hand, followed by an interim agreement in the Sinai signed between Israel and Egypt in September 1975. This interim agreement called for the withdrawal of Israeli forces to the Mitla and Gidi Passes, the establishment of an electronic surveillance system manned by Americans in the Sinai, and the return of the Abu Rudeis oilfields to Egypt. The Suez Canal was opened to shipping bound to and from Israel. These developments ultimately led to the historic visit of President Sadat to Jerusalem and his appearance before the Israeli parliament, the Knesset, which in turn brought about a peace treaty — the first signed between Israel and an Arab state. There is no doubt that the intitial Arab successes in the Yom Kippur War satisfied their feelings of national honour, and facilitated Sadat's* ability to develop a dialogue between the two sides, ultimately reaching a peace treaty. The Yom Kippur War gains in perspective as it recedes into history, and assumes its place as a war of great historic significance. It ushered in a new era of military conflict. This was the first war in which the various types of missiles — surface-to-surface, surface-to-air, air-to-surface and sea-to-sea — were used on a major scale, and during which there took place the first naval missile battles in history. Indeed, the entire science of military strategy and technique has had to be re-evaluated in the light of the lessons of this war.

From a global point of view, the 1973 war saw the first attempt by the Arab oil-producing nations to use oil as a weapon. True, the oil boycott was not very effective, but its effect was essentially psychological and not practical: it was not universally observed even by the Arab states. However, it did have an effect of 'sounding the alarm' for the free world. The volatility and instability of the Arab world, with its prodigious glut of wealth, only highlights the danger of this situation.

* On 6 October 1981, while reviewing a military parade commemorating the Egyptian crossing of the Suez Canal in 1973, President Sadat was assassinated by a small group of Moslem fundamentalists who, posing as soldiers, jumped from a vehicle towing artillery as it passed the reviewing stand. They stormed the crowded stand, pumping automatic weapons fire at Sadat as they advanced.

BOOK VI

THE WAR AGAINST TERRORISM:
Entebbe

THE WAR
AGAINST TERRORISM:
Entebbe

Since the early 1950s, Israel has been subjected at various periods to terrorist attacks from across the borders, and has invariably reacted in reprisal raids. In 1968, the Palestine Liberation Organization launched its first attack against Israel overseas, by hijacking an El Al airliner flying from Rome to Tel Aviv and diverting it to Algeria. Thereafter, civil aircraft bound to and from Israel, Israeli offices abroad and Israeli embassy buildings were subjected to attack by various components of the PLO — frequently aided by other groupings within the international terrorist community. An attack on Puerto Rican pilgrims in Lod Airport was carried out by members of the Japanese Red Army and, on numerous occasions, German and French terrorists bent on PLO missions have been apprehended in Israel.

The policy adopted by Israel from the outset rejected any form of compromise with terrorism, and was designed to stamp it out wherever it might appear. Thus, when terrorists hijacked a Belgian Sabena airliner, which was forced back to Ben-Gurion Airport in Israel in May 1972, Israeli commandos disguised as mechanics and ground attendants recaptured it, killed two Arab gunmen and saved 97 passengers. When children were taken hostage in a school in the northern Galilee town of Maalot in May 1974, the building was stormed by Israeli military units, despite the danger to the children: the terrorists were killed, but 22 children lost their lives. In an attack on the Haifa-Tel Aviv coastal road on 13 March 1978, when terrorists hijacked a bus, a battle ensued in which all but two of the terrorists were killed, as were over 30 passengers. In an attack on an Israeli El Al airliner at Kloten Airport in Zurich, an Israeli security guard stormed the Palestinian terrorists who were firing at the plane, killing one with his pistol.

The same pattern has characterized the instinctive Israeli reaction to terror throughout: compromise with terrorism would lead to an impossible situation. Every terrorist must know, when embarking on an action against an Israeli target, that he will in all probability have to fight his way out.

The Israel Defence Forces set up an élite unit highly trained in counter-terrorist activities. The policy guiding the Israelis on this issue was set out very clearly by Shimon Peres, who was the Minister of Defence in the Government of Israel during the Entebbe hostage rescue operation in 1976. At a conference on international terrorism, he enunciated Israeli policy. He emphasized that there should never be surrender to terrorism, that Israel must have an elaborate intelligence system and an early warning system with properly trained people in order to nullify the terrorist advantage of surprise and indiscriminate attack. He emphasized the importance of fighting terrorism not only in the operational field but also in the psychological field. As he put it, 'The tendency of terrorist groups to bedeck themselves with titles such as the "Red Army" or the "Liberation Organization" should not beguile us or our often-bewitched media . . . Terrorist groups should be described in their true colours — groups which are impatient with democracy, which are undisciplined, corrupt in their attitude to life, and unable to free themselves from the domination of murder and hatred.' He pointed out that terror has become international and must be fought internationally. The terrorists consider most free nations and peoples as their enemies; countermeasures must therefore be internationally co-ordinated.

The most dramatic reaction to international terrorism so far has undoubtedly been the Israeli operation that brought the release of 100 Israeli hostages who had been hijacked to Entebbe in Uganda in an Air France airliner.

On Sunday 27 June 1976, Air France flight 139, flying from Tel Aviv to Paris via Athens, was hijacked by four PLO terrorists after leaving Athens. Two of them, a man and a woman, were Germans, members of the Baader-Meinhof urban guerrilla organization; and two of them were Arabs, members of the terrorist Popular Front for the Liberation of Palestine. In the aircraft were 256 passengers and 12 crew members. Taking advantage of the lax security arrangements at Athens, the terrorists had succeeded in bringing on board guns and hand grenades. After being hijacked, the aircraft landed for refuelling at Benghazi, Libya, and then continued south, landing at Entebbe in Uganda, where the terrorists were joined by additional Palestinian terrorists and by units of the Ugandan Army, who moved the hostages into the old terminal building at the airport.

Uganda Radio made known on 29 June the demands of the hijackers, which included the handing over of 53 convicted terrorists — 40 held in Israel, six in West Germany, five in Kenya, one in Switzerland and one in France. Meanwhile, the Israelis had been separated from the other passengers and, in the course of the week, the non-Israelis were flown back to France. The Israeli Government was faced with the problem of achieving the release of the Israeli hostages, and a negotiating machinery was set up using intermediaries.

On the evening of 28 June, Lieutenant-General Mordechai ('Motta') Gur, the Chief of Staff, issued instructions to prepare immediately a paratroop force which would be ready to parachute into Entebbe, or arrive there across Lake Victoria, and capture the airport terminal, kill the terrorists and defend the hostages until arrangements had been concluded with the Government of Uganda to release them. But the Prime Minister, Yitzhak Rabin, refused to contemplate the operational plans presented to him, maintaining that they did not provide a complete solution to the problem. Indeed, at this stage of the developments, his general attitude as to the feasibility of a military operation was negative.

The Minister of Defence, Shimon Peres, took an entirely different view. In all the discussions, he emphasized the paramount importance of refusing to submit to the terrorists: their success in this operation would constitute a political and moral defeat for Israel of major proportions, and would constitute a most dangerous precedent for the future in the struggle against terror and hijacking. Apart from discussing the matter with the Chief of Staff, he discussed it in detail with the various senior officers directly involved. General Gur, for his part, emphasized the importance of success in such an operation and the catastrophic results of failure: unequivocally, he told the Minister of Defence that he would not recommend an operation unless he personally reached a conclusion that the risk was reasonable and that the proposal was feasible. On the Wednesday, the Israeli Cabinet met again on the subject, and the Prime Minister reiterated that, unless he received a proposal for a military operation backed by the General Staff, he would advise the Cabinet to accept the ultimatum of the terrorists and their conditions in order to bring about the release of the hostages.

Parallel to the planning efforts mounted by the General Staff, however, Major-General Dan Shomron, who was Chief Infantry and Paratroop Officer in the Israel Defence Forces (and who had commanded an armoured brigade in the Sinai during the 1973 War), had decided on Monday 28 June — without any instructions from above — to commence planning the release of the hostages in Entebbe. As soon as the separation of the Israelis from the other passengers had begun, he had recalled the selection process used by the Nazis in the concentration camps, and had given immediate instructions to his staff to begin planning. By Wednesday evening, his staff had already crystallized a plan on an airborne landing on the new airfield at Entebbe, movement in vehicles (adapted to the local background in Uganda) to the old airport, liquidation of the terrorists and release of the hostages. It became evident to the planners that it would be unrealistic to plan in terms of an operation designed to capture the airport entirely, because this could mean the killing of the hostages by the terrorists and Ugandans. The first strike would take place against the terrorists and the operation would develop from this central focal point outwards. The Air Force advised Shomron's staff that their Hercules aircraft could reach Entebbe, but that there would be a problem with refuelling on the way back. The solution to this problem would be to refuel at Entebbe, using the existing fuel supplies and tanks at the international airport there.

On the morning of Thursday 1 July, the Prime Minister, by now under increasing pressure from the public and from the families of the hostages, asked the Cabinet for a quick decision approving the release of the imprisoned terrorists whose freedom had been demanded by the terrorists, in order to bring home the hostages. He made a similar appeal to the Leader of the Opposition, Mr. Menachem Begin, and the Chairman of the Defence and Foreign Affairs Committee in the Knesset, and received their approval. However, that same afternoon, Shomron was invited by the Chief of the Operations Branch, Major-General Yekutiel Adam, to come to the General Staff to present his plan. Present were Shimon Peres, the Minister of Defence; the Chief of Staff, General Gur; the Chief of the Operations Branch, General Adam; the Commander of the Air Force, Major-General Benjamin-Peled; and the Assistant Chief of the Operations Branch, Brigadier-General Avigdor Ben-Gal. This was the first time the plan was presented in full detail. It called for a landing at Entebbe on Saturday 3 July at 23.00 hours, and for a 'dry' rehearsal on the Friday evening using a model. The assumption was that, since the MiG aircraft of the Ugandan Air Force were parked in the old airport, there must be a tarmac taxiing runway leading from there to the new airport.

At the conclusion of Shomron's presentation, Shimon Peres turned to each one of those present, asking him for his views, what were the prospects for success, how many casualties he anticipated and whether or not he recommended carrying out the operation. There were those who opposed the operation; there were those who gave it a 50-50 chance. Shomron's reply was that there was one weak point — landing the first aircraft without arousing suspicion. If this were possible, then there was a 100 per cent chance of success. With luck, there would be no casualties. Should a fire-fight develop, he estimated that there would be ten casualties, and he recommended without hesitation that the operation be mounted. Peres indicated his approval of the plan subject to the final approval of the Cabinet, and ordered them to continue with all the preparations. As they rose to leave the room, Shomron turned to Peres and said, 'I understand that I am to command the operation.' Peres turned and looked at the Chief of Staff, and then said, 'Fine. You are the commander of the operation.' Shomron was given the authority to choose the units that would participate in the operation, and it was agreed that on Friday evening the plan would be tried on a model. On Saturday, they would take off from Sharm El-Sheikh at 15.30 hours for Entebbe.

In order not to give rise to any suspicion that a military operation was being planned, all the diplomatic negotiations in France and Uganda continued meanwhile, indicating that Israel would give in to the demands of the terrorists and make the necessary arrangements to meet these demands by Sunday 4 July. It therefore became imperative to release these hostages before this date. This consideration left Saturday night as the last possibility.

The units participating were assembled immediately, the telephone communications to and from their base were cut, and the men were forbidden to leave there. Two hundred highly trained personnel were assembled, most of them regulars, with battle experience.

Leaving open the involved problem of the landing at Entebbe (for which additional intelligence information was necessary), the General Staff laid down the general outline of the operation from the point of landing and allotted units and tasks. These would be:
1. A force to illuminate and secure the runway
2. A force to occupy the old terminal and release the hostages
3. A force to take control of the new terminal
4. A force to secure the airfield and destroy the Ugandan fighter aircraft.
5. A force to evacuate the hostages from the terminal to the aircraft.

In the course of the planning and preparation for the operation, considerable use was made of the photographs taken by Israeli Air Force personnel some years before, when they were training the Ugandan Air Force. (In one of the home movies that they studied, Idi Amin, the ruler of Uganda, arrived at the airport in a black Mercedes, accompanied by a Land Rover, and it was this that gave birth to the idea to look for a Mercedes car which would be used for deception purposes in the operation.) To this information was added intelligence collected by special interrogators who interviewed the non-Jewish passengers released by the terrorists, after their arrival in Paris. From their reports, a clear picture of the daily routine at the terminal was obtained: where they slept; where the various conveniences were located and how they reached them; what was the guard routine and in which rooms the terrorists lived; the nature and character of the terrorists and their behaviour towards the hostages; the location of the Ugandan soldiers in the building and around, and their guard routine.

On the Friday, Israeli television broadcast a film that had been made by a foreign press correspondent, which showed the new terminal in Entebbe. From this they learned that the new terminal was a two-storey building. There were also photographs of the old terminal where the Israeli hostages were being held. The passengers who had been released described how the terrorists had placed boxes in the terminal; leading from each was a white detonating wire, and it was presumed that the boxes contained explosives. However, since information also indicated that Ugandan soldiers were stationed on the roof, the conclusion was drawn that the boxes were but a ruse to frighten the hostages, and that the building was not really wired for detonation.

As the intelligence material accumulated, General Gur decided that the operation was entirely feasible, and that he could recommend to the Minister of Defence that it be set into motion. At the same time, he issued instructions that he would command the operation from his headquarters at the General Staff, while the head of the Operations Branch, Major-General Yekutiel Adam, and the Commander of the Air Force, Major-General Benjamin Peled, would constitute an advanced General Staff Headquarters in an aircraft flying over the scene of the operation. It was decided, too, that a second aircraft accompanying the advanced headquarters, would include a fully-equipped field hospital; this was scheduled to land at Nairobi without any advance warning in order to set up a field hospital to deal with those hostages or soldiers who might be wounded.

Gur was very concerned about whether or not the aircraft could land safely in darkness until, on Friday, he and Peled flew in a Hercules to ensure that it was capable of a 'blind' landing. The indications were that the weather would be good on the night of the operation, and that the night would be dark without any moonlight.

On the Friday, as exercises were carried out on a model, a debate was continuing in the Cabinet. The Prime Minister expressed serious doubts about the feasibility of the operation. Meanwhile, the Chief of Staff met all the commanders involved in the operation. He asked each one how he estimated the chances. All expressed the opinion that the mission was possible, and that the prospects of success were good. Gur addressed each one of them, asking them if they appreciated what the price of failure would be. However, he advised them that on the morrow, on the Sabbath, he would go to the Cabinet and recommend carrying out the operation.

On the Saturday morning at 08.00 hours, Gur presented his plan to the Minister of Defence, and then they together presented it to the Prime Minister. Gur opened his remarks by saying, 'I present to you a plan for execution this evening. The troops are on their way, and the entire operation is now in motion according to a pre-arranged plan.' The Prime Minister gave his approval, subject to the approval of the Cabinet. Three hours later the final briefing of the troops took place. Take-off was set for 15.30 hours.

The plan was as follows. The first aircraft would land on the runway and disembark a unit of paratroopers, whose task would be emergency lighting of the runway in addition to the existing lighting arrangements. The aircraft would taxi rapidly to the end of the runway, and there the assault unit designated to take control of the two terminals would disembark. The unit under Lieutenant-Colonel Jonathan ('Yoni') Netanyahu, riding in two Land Rovers and the Mercedes, would move directly to the old terminal in order to release the hostages. The paratroopers, under Colonel Matan Vilnai, would move on foot to the new terminal and take control of it, the control tower and the refuelling tarmac. The commander of the operation, Major-General Dan Shomron, would disembark with these two advance units together with his advanced headquarters staff.

The second aircraft would land seven minutes after the first, thus giving time to Netanyahu's force to take the old terminal by surprise and release the hostages. This aircraft would taxi to the end of the runway and disembark the remainder of the forces, including two armoured cars that would secure the immediate surroundings of the terminal and release the hostages. This aircraft would also carry Shomron's headquarters jeep in order to enable him to move rapidly between the units and control them as well as maintaining direct contact with the command aircraft circling above.

The third aircraft would land immediately after the second and would disembark two additional armoured cars for Lieutenant-Colonel Netanyahu's force and a unit of the 'Golani' Infantry Brigade commanded by Colonel Orr, which would take control of the area linking the two runways, would act as a reserve in the event of any untoward development in various parts of the airfield, and would assist the hostages to embark on the rescue aircraft.

The fourth and last aircraft would disembark the remainder of the reserve forces and a Peugeot tender for the rapid evacuation of the wounded. It would carry a medical team and also a refuelling team. This aircraft was ordered to taxi to the old terminal in order to embark the hostages.

It was envisaged that the critical elements in the operation would be the actual landing of the aircraft; the storming of the old terminal; prevention of the arrival of Ugandan reinforcements; and securing the runway in order to guarantee a safe take-off home.

At 15.20 hours, the Cabinet, still discussing the operation, authorized the 15.30 take-off; however, the actual operation was not yet approved. It was understood that, should approval not be given, the aircraft could be returned to their base. By 16.00 hours, all the aircraft were airborne, and it was after this by the time the Cabinet approved the operation unanimously.

After seven hours of flying, the force came within range of the Entebbe control tower. The operation had been planned so that the first aircraft could dovetail behind a scheduled British cargo flight, thus arousing no suspicion. Exactly as planned, they came behind the British aircraft as its captain was asking the terminal for permission to land. They flew in over Lake Victoria in a heavy rainstorm, and the approach for landing was made by instruments. Suddenly, the rain stopped and the skies cleared, and there before their eyes were the landing lights of Entebbe Airport.

The British cargo aircraft landed, and the first Israeli Hercules glided in immediately behind it without arousing any suspicion in the control tower. As they touched down, the pilot slowed according to plan, and the advance party jumped out while the aircraft was still taxiing. They doubled along the side of the airfield, placing goosenecks (mobile landing lights) ready to provide alternative lights for the three aircraft that were following, in the event that the airfield lights would be switched off. The aircraft taxied to a dark corner of the field without lights, the rest of the initial landing force disembarked, and the Mercedes car and the Land Rovers were rolled off. All around there was an atmosphere of quiet and peace. The only noise was that of the British cargo aircraft taxiing towards the terminal, which drowned the noise of the Israeli party. Major-General Shomron looked around and said to his men, 'Boys, this operation is a success despite the fact that not one bullet has yet been fired.'

The men mounted the vehicles, which drove with their headlights on slowly towards where the hostages were being held. The Mercedes led, followed by the two Land Rovers. The area was well lit up and there was no difficulty in finding the way to the objective. Approximately 100 yards from the control tower, two Ugandan soldiers came into full view in the Israelis' headlights. Netanyahu and another officer drew pistols equipped with silencers. One of the Ugandans pointed his rifle at the vehicle and called on it to halt. Netanyahu and the second officer fired at the Ugandan soldier from 10 yards range and hit him. Because of this unplanned encounter, the unit disembarked on the spot, some 50 yards from the terminal, instead of driving right up to it, and raced on foot towards the terminal. One of the entrances to the terminal had been blocked, so the entire force entered by the remaining entrance instead of two entrances as had been planned. The point section broke into the hall where the hostages were lying, most of them fast asleep on the floor. A terrorist on the right of the hall opened fire and was killed. Two more terrorists — one of them a woman — were by the window on the left of the hall, and were shot by the leading soldiers. A fourth terrorist at the end of the hall was identified and shot. The hall was fully lit up and the terrorists were easily identifiable because they were all standing with weapons. They were completely taken by surprise.

From the moment that the Ugandan sentry had been shot outside the terminal until the four terrorists inside the terminal had been killed, only 15 seconds had passed. This speed with which the operation was carried out was undoubtedly the main factor in the initial success. One of the soldiers called out in Hebrew and English to all the hostages to remain lying on the floor — but one of the hostages, who in his excitement failed to obey the order, jumped up and was shot too. Lieutenant-Colonel Netanyahu followed the assault unit. He reached the entrance to the hall and paused in the garden before the entrance. Suddenly, fire was directed towards the attacking unit from the control tower. Netanyahu was hit by a bullet in the neck. Although evacuated safely, he died later.

The second aircraft had been scheduled to land exactly seven minutes after the first plane, thus giving an opportunity to the attacking forces to take the terrorists completely by surprise. As planned, the additional three aircraft landed, discharging their armoured cars. These drove to the terminal, with Shomron in a jeep. Inside the terminal, the assault units continued to mop-up and kill any terrorists or Ugandan troops that engaged them. Two European terrorists endeavoured to slip out of the terminal, pretending that they were hostages. A section commander called on them to halt when he noticed a grenade hanging on one of their belts. But they continued moving and were fired at, being blown up by the grenade, which detonated. Additional units searched and cleared the VIP lounges and the customs hall: 60 Ugandan soldiers on the second floor fled. In all, in the course of this operation, 35 Ugandan troops were killed. Thirteen terrorists were surprised, some of them in their sleep, and were shot dead at short range.

The Ugandan troops on the control tower continued to fire at the Israeli troops, as the hostages were being bundled out of the hall. The armoured personnel carrier with the force was directed to neutralize the control tower. This was done by means of concentrated heavy machine-gun fire and RPG fire. It was now possible, as aircraft number three taxied up to the vicinity of the old terminal, for Colonel Orr and two units with him to evacuate the hostages from the terminal. By the evacuating plane was the medical team which immediately began to treat the wounded. Loading the hostages, the wounded and the dead took some fifteen minutes.

Meanwhile, as the shooting erupted in the old terminal, Colonel Vilnai was ordered by Shomron to move. One unit went directly towards the new terminal while a second unit searched the aircraft parking area opposite the terminal. The unit directed towards the terminal stormed the building, searched the entrance, the two storeys of the building and the roof. According to their instructions, the troops were ordered not to fire at the Ugandan troops in the new terminal unless fired upon by them. All Ugandans were to be allowed to flee, but fifteen Ugandans who surrendered were locked in one of the rooms and warned not to leave. Within fifteen minutes of the commencement of the operation, Vilnai's force had taken control of the new terminal, and the Peugeot tender arrived with the refuelling equipment. At this point, Vilnai and the captain of the leading aircraft (who was the squadron commander), recommended that the refuelling should not be done in Entebbe. Shomron accepted their recommendation and asked for permission to take off without refuelling from GHQ advanced headquarters, which was flying above in a Boeing 707. Permission was given: instructions were issued not to refuel in Entebbe but instead to do so in Nairobi.

The first aircraft had landed at 23.01 hours; at 23.58 hours — 57 minutes after the commencement of the operation — the first aircraft loaded with the hostages took off from Entebbe in the direction of Nairobi. Forty-two minutes later, the last aircraft left after one of the final units to leave the airport had set fire to eight Ugandan Air Force MiGs by machine-gun fire. Shomron with his headquarters remained with the rearguard unit and took off with it in the last plane to leave.

The aircraft landed for refuelling in Nairobi Airport, and thereafter made their way back to Israel, to arrive to a joyous and victorious welcome, having accomplished one of the most electrifying, imaginative and universally applauded rescue operations in history. Back at his control headquarters at the General Staff in Tel Aviv, General Gur, the Prime Minister, the Minister of Defence and members of the General Staff drank a toast to those who were winging their way back from Entebbe.

This had been an operation with a high risk factor. It was not planned in order to capture territory or to cause casualties by use of concentrated fire: it was planned to release hostages under guard, and in such circumstances the use of concentrated firepower would have been futile, and indeed counter-productive. Such an operation had, of necessity, to be highly sophisticated, like using a sharp stiletto instead of a sledgehammer, and was therefore a highly involved operation. Speed was of the essence, because any hesitation would have cost the lives of Israeli hostages. The force was up against between ten and thirteen trigger-happy terrorists stationed amongst the hostages. Around the whole force were hundreds of Ugandans. The main problem had been to release the hostages alive. This guiding fact influenced the entire plan and mode of operation. Furthermore, the operation had no safety margin. In the field of battle, if an attack does not succeed, then one tries again or moves to another sector. If one battalion fails then another one is thrown into the battle. Artillery support and air support can be added at will. But there is always a margin of safety. In an operation such as that at Entebbe, all elements are interdependent. The slightest error, the slightest lack of co-ordination, and the whole structure is liable to collapse like a pack of cards. This lesson emerged in the ill-fated United States attempt to rescue their hostages in Iran in 1980. Such operations leave little or no margin for security.

The planning had been carried out under the most difficult circumstances, because there were a large number of unknowns. All the subsequent stories about agents in Uganda and on Lake Victoria are complete fabrications and without foundation. The operation at Entebbe was the culmination of years of training for such eventualities on the part of the counter-terrorist unit and the other commando units that accompanied it, and testimony to the fact that the Israel Defence Forces leaves nothing to chance. All eventualities are thought out and planned for well in advance, so it was possible to plan and execute such an operation at very short notice. The rescue at Entebbe was a resounding blow to international terrorism, and gave rise to a new resolve, both in the United Nations and elsewhere, to fight this dangerous phenomenon and to emulate the Israeli example.

In the debate at the United Nations Security Council, in which an unsuccessful attempt was made to condemn Israel for carrying out the rescue operation in Entebbe, the author of this book, who represented Israel, said:

'It has fallen to the lot of my small country, embattled as we are, facing the problems which we do, to demonstrate to the world that there is an alternative to surrender to terrorism and blackmail. It has fallen to our lot to prove to the world that this scourge of international terror can be dealt with. It is now for the nations of the world, regardless of political differences which may divide them, to unite against this common enemy which recognizes no authority, knows no borders, respects no sovereignty, ignores all basic human decencies, and places no limits on human bestiality.

'We come with a simple message to the Council: we are proud of what we have done, because we have demonstrated to the world that in a small country, in Israel's circumstances, with which the members of this Council are by now all too familiar, the dignity of man, human life and human freedom constitute the highest values. We are proud not only because we have saved the lives of over 100 innocent people — men, women and children — but because of the significance of our act for the cause of human freedom.

'We call on this body to declare war on international terror, to outlaw it and eradicate it wherever it may be. We call on this body, and above all we call on the Member States and countries of the world, to unite in a common effort to place these criminals outside the pale of human society, and with them to place any country which co-operates in any way in their nefarious activities . . .'

Below: A Palestine Liberation Army soldier in the Gaza Strip.

Inset: The banner of the PLA as flown in Gaza before the Six Day War of 1967. (Y. Aharonot)

Above: One of the dozens of improvised booby-trap methods used by terrorists: a bomb concealed in a watermelon. (Israel Police)

Right, top: Kozo Okamoto, who was one of the three members of the Japanese 'Red Army' group that carried out an attack at Lod Airport in May 1972, killing 24 Puerto Rican pilgrims and other passengers. Okamoto is presently serving a life sentence in an Israeli jail.

Right: The coffins of the Puerto Rican victims of the Lod Airport massacre before being flown back to the United States. (Israel Sun)

Left: The Olympic flag flies at half-mast inside the Munich Olympic Stadium during a memorial service for the eleven Israeli team members killed by Palestinian terrorists during the 1972 Games. 80,000 people filled the stadium to capacity. (AP)

Below: The surviving members of the Israeli Olympic team before embarking at Munich airport for their flight home. (AP)

Long Live Marxism
Leninism! P.F.L.P

Left: The tragic results of two separate terrorist attacks on civilian buses. The bus in the top photograph was ambushed by fedayeen at Scorpion's Pass while on its way to Eilat in 1954. (GPO) In the lower photograph, victims of the 1978 coastal road attack just outside Tel Aviv are evacuated from the gutted vehicle, which had been hijacked by a group of PLO terrorists. (Jerusalem Post)

Top: A police specialist investigates the aftermath of a terrorist grenade attack on a cinema in Tel Aviv, December 1974. (GPO)

Below: A note left by the terrorists on an adjoining seat. (Shalom Bar-Tal)

Above: Evacuating a wounded child in Maalot, northern Galilee, where more than twenty children were killed during a PLO attack in May 1974. (Rubinger)

Right, top: The three PLO terrorists held their 8[...] hostages in the Netiv Meir school building, whic[...] is seen here being attacked by Israeli soldie[...] during their rescue bid. (GPO)

Right: The coffins of the Maalot victims. (GPO[...]

This page: The three PLO terrorists who attacked Maalot, photographed in their training camps shortly before their mission. **1,** Aly Ahmed Hassan ('Lino'); **2,** Ahmed Saleh Nayef ('Harbi'); **3,** Ziyeid Abdul-Rahive ('Kamal Hassan'). (Jerusalem Post)

Opposite: The Fourth of July 1976. A unit of specially trained commandos led by Lieutenant-Colonel Jonathan ('Yoni') Netanyahu (top left) rescued the passengers of a hijacked Air France airbus from Entebbe Airport, Uganda. (GPO) Netanyahu was killed in the action. Brigadier-General Dan Shomron (top right) commanded the operation. (Jerusalem Post)

Right: The Air France captain leads the rescued hostages from an Israeli Air Force Hercules on their arrival at Lod Airport. Deputy Prime Minister Yigal Allon (back to camera) is there to welcome them. (GPO)

Above: Prime Minister Menachem Begin addresses the Knesset on the occasion of President Sadat's visit to Jerusalem in November 1977. To Sadat's left is Yitzak Shamir, the Speaker of the Knesset. (GPO)

Below: President Sadat, United States President Jimmy Carter, and Menachem Begin demonstrate the new spirit of understanding between the two nations after the signing of the peace treaty in March 1979. (GPO)

BOOK VII

OPERATION 'OPERA'
THE DESTRUCTION OF OSIRAK

OPERATION 'OPERA'
THE DESTRUCTION OF OSIRAK

Since the early 1960s, the Middle East has figured very prominently on the list of world regions which may be on the verge of nuclearization. Specialists claimed that this was true not only in terms of a potential for the production of a military nuclear device, but also of the actual existence (albeit not officially acknowledged) of nuclear bombs in the hands of Israel. Indeed, many Arab leaders, strategists and commentators have stated their belief that Israel is in possession of an arsenal of A-bombs. This perception, as well as frustration in many parts of the Arab World with the military results of the October 1973 War, after it had started with an initial Arab operational advantage, and the availability of extremely large sums of petro-dollars, created new incentives for the acquisition of a nuclear capability in the Arab world.

Iraq, an oil-rich Arab country, aware of its technological advantages, chose the slow and more expensive route: the procurement and development of its own nuclear infrastructure.

Iraq's nuclear programme

Iraq commenced its nuclear programme in the mid-1950s. In 1959 Iraq concluded an agreement on nuclear co-operation with the Soviet Union. In 1963, the USSR began construction of the Tuwaitha Nuclear Centre near Baghdad, a complex of nuclear facilities and laboratories, including an IRT2000-type research reactor with a capacity of 2 megawatts thermal [mW(th)], which became operational in July 1968 (in 1978 its power was reported to have been upgraded to 5mW(th) by increasing its fuel enrichment).

By 1974, however, Iraq had changed course and commenced a series of prolonged and complicated high-level negotiations with France for the supply of nuclear facilities and expertise. Iraq and France concluded a nuclear co-operation agreement at the end of 1975. Iraq was reported to have requested that France supply it with a double-purpose gas-graphite type power reactor (with a capacity of 500 megawatts electrical [mW(e)] and 1,500mW(th), designed to produce both plutonium and electricity. The Iraqis chose a very advanced and powerful Osiris-type research reactor, the 'Osirak' (the acronym for Osiris-Iraq).

From the outset, the intensification of Iraq's activities in the field of nuclear research and development was a source of serious concern to a number of close and remote observers. Their reactions were manifested in two main forms: diplomatic pressures exerted by Israel and the US, primarily on France and Italy; and a series of mishaps to Iraq's nuclear programme – some of which were widely believed to be the work of Israeli intelligence agents. These actions did not, however, significantly impede Iraq's progress.

Soon after the flare-up of the Iraq–Iran War in September 1980, the Osirak nuclear reactor was hit twice – apparently from the air by Iranian aircraft – on 30 September and 1 October 1980. In both cases Israel denied any connection with the attacks, which had also caused only superficial damage. Another consequence of the war was the evacuation of most foreign scientists and technicians from Iraq, including those involved in the nuclear programme, except a dozen volunteers who remained in Tuwaitha after the 30 September air raid

On 6 November 1980 it was reported that Iraq had blocked until further notice International Atomic Energy Agency (IAEA) inspection of its nuclear installations. The *Washington Post* reported (on 7 November 1980) that: 'French officials are indicating extreme embarrassment at the uncertainty surrounding the reactors... in a war situation. It places the whole problem of nuclear proliferation in a new light – not foreseen in any international treaties... '

The concern in Israel

In November 1980, Israeli diplomats in the UN announced that Israel now supported Egypt's proposal with regard to establishing a nuclear-free-zone in the Middle East as expressed in a debate during the 29th UN General Assembly session. Israel now proposed that a treaty-writing conference be convened, with the participation of all Middle East nations. This conference should work out a binding treaty with a rigorous safeguard and inspection system. Explaining the timing for this move, an Israeli diplomat stated that it was prompted by: 'the attempt of a number of countries in the Middle East to achieve a nuclear capability, principally Iraq, and, in the adjacent region, Pakistan.' In the same month, Israel's Chief of Staff stated in a public address that: 'the Iraqis openly say so and, indeed, intend to use their nuclear weapons against Israel.' And on 8 December, an Israeli newspaper, reporting on Foreign Minister Shamir's visit to France, said that, 'in spite of the efforts by France to soothe Israel's concerns, Israel would continue its close watch on nuclear developments in Iraq and sound the alarm about the danger inherent in the existence of nuclear installations in the hands of such an irresponsible Government.'

Towards the end of February 1981, the IAEA announced that in a routine inspection of the Osirak research reactor, held the previous month, all the nuclear fuel had been satisfactorily accounted for. The *New York Times*, reporting from Vienna, added: 'Although Iraq has renounced nuclear weapons by signing the [Non-Proliferation] Treaty, western officials have expressed growing concern in recent months that it may be secretly attempting to develop an atomic bomb.'

Towards the end of April 1981, the French Foreign Ministry announced that French scientists and technicians, evacuated when the Iraq–Iran War broke out, had returned to Iraq to resume work in the nuclear research centre.

The political backdrop

On 28 May, Israel and Egypt announced a one-day summit meeting for 4 June in Sinai between President Sadat and Prime Minister Begin. The summit, the first in nearly 18 months, concentrated on three issues: the Lebanese crisis, the bilateral Israeli-Egyptian talks on automony for the Palestinians in the administered territories, and the negotiations for the setting up of a multi-national peacekeeping force to monitor the demilitarization of the Sinai following the completion of Israel's evacuation.

On 4 June, the White House announced that Sadat and Begin had been invited to visit the US on 5–6 August and 9–10 September, respectively. Yet, by the end of the first week of June, the situation was still very tense, and all regional attention was riveted on South Lebanon. It was then that Israel launched yet another surprise, its air raid on Osirak.

Prime Minister Begin calls for a decision

On 14 October 1979, Prime Minister Begin summoned a group of ministers to consider Israel's response to the Iraqi threat. Also attending were the Chief of Staff and the Air Force commander, as well as the heads of the Mossad (Israel's secret intelligence service) and Military Intelligence and others. Begin opened the discussion with a dramatic statement: 'We have the choice of two evils.'

The first 'evil' was an attack on the reactor, with the risk of adverse reactions. Iraq was at war with Iran, Iraq's hopes of a rapid victory had failed to materialize, and its military situation was deteriorating; but an Israeli attack on the reactor could induce Iraq to direct its military might against Israel, an end for which Baghdad might even make its peace with Syria. Consideration also had to be given to the Egyptian position. Egypt was awaiting 26 April 1982, the date of Israel's final withdrawal from Sinai under the peace treaty between the two countries. An Israeli attack on the Iraqi reactor could in no way be interpreted as a violation of that bilateral treaty, and Cairo was aware that, in the event of an Egyptian violation, Israel would respond accordingly; nevertheless, Sadat's reaction to a strike at the reactor was impossible to predict. The operation was therefore, risky.

The second 'evil' was to refrain from action. In other words, to sit by idly and do nothing to prevent Iraq's continued efforts toward manufacture of nuclear weapons.

After thorough consideration, Begin declared, 'I have come to the conclusion that we must choose the first of the two evils. Why? First, because now is an opportune moment. The Gulf War has weakened Iraq and has also put a halt to work at the reactor, which is still "cold". That means it is feasible to destroy it without the risk of radioactive contamination of its vicinity. Who knows if such an opportune moment will recur? It must be clear that if Israel does not prevent it, Iraq will manufacture nuclear weapons.'

In the ensuing vote, the raid was endorsed by five ministers (including Begin). Four voted against it, demanding that a final decision be left to the full Cabinet. On 28 October 1980, Begin duly summoned the Cabinet. After Begin wound up the deliberations, a vote was called. The Prime Minister's proposal won ten votes. Six voted against.

Planning Operation 'Opera'

The generally accepted consensus among Israeli intelligence experts at the end of 1979 was as follows:

- Within a few months – by March 1980 at the latest – France would dispatch the first shipment of 93%-grade uranium, comprising 12–12.5kg out of an overall total of 70kg promised. On delivery of the fuel, the small Tammuz 2 (Isis) reactor would go into immediate operation, its Iraqi staff receiving French guidance in operating the various systems.

- Within three to four months – by July 1980 approximately – the larger Tammuz 1 reactor (Osirak) would be ready for activation.

- Between May and December 1980, the second phase of the Italian project would reach completion, giving Iraq the facilities for extracting plutonium from the spent fuel rods.

Following a directive from Prime Minister Begin of November 1979, the IDF General Staff had begun examining various proposals for the destruction of the reactor. Early in 1980, directives were issued to extend groundwork for the raid. A consultation attended by representatives of the various bodies linked to the operation concluded that technical preparations must be complemented by a wide range of information, to come from the Mossad, Military Intelligence and the Air Force's own intelligence department, whether independently or in co-ordination. At the same time, work went on to muster all available information about the reactor's internal construction, its components and similar details.

Under Air Force Commander Major-General David Ivry's systematic direction, Colonel Aviem Sella, his deputy and head of the Operations Division, continued to polish up the Air Force's plans. By February Ivry was in a position to put on an advanced 'display' for the edification of the Defence Minister and the Chief of Staff.

On 27 April 1981, a final decision designated F-16s as the planes to attack the reactor. Almost all the bombs were to be directed at the main objective, Tammuz 1, on the assumption that adjoining targets would also be damaged. According to preliminary estimates, the number of planes chosen for the mission gave odds of 99.88 per cent that the reactor would be hit, and 100 per cent certainty of some damage to the structure. The directives specified the number of bombs to be carried by each plane, and there were precise instructions about communications. After a number of delays, the date set for the raid was Sunday, 7 June 1981.

The squadrons designated to take part in the operation were placed on top alert. Initially, only two squadrons were alerted, but for reasons of security the alert was extended to additional squadrons unconnected with the reactor raid. Their commanders were told that a strike into Lebanon might be in the offing. The order 'Prepare for execution of mission' was issued on 6 June. The F-16 squadrons summoned all technical crews and armourers from their homes; special flights ferried them to the operational base, which they reached that evening. In the coming hours they would test the armament and bomb loads and prepare to receive the planes as they flew in from their home base.

Operation 'Opera'

In the morning hours of Sunday, 7 June, Lieutenant-Colonel Zeev Raz, the commander of the leading formation and Lieutenant-Colonel Amir Nachumi, commander of the second formation, together with their eight F-16 planes, flew down to the Etzion forward field (in southern Sinai). The Chief of Staff and the Air Force Commander also came.

The crew members were called together for an additional briefing. In the afternoon, as zero hour approached, the pilots started their engines and taxied to the take-off positions, to await the thumbs-up signal from the squadron technical officer. The sign was given at 16:01. After take-off was completed without hitches the F-16s were accompanied by six F-15 fighters ready to support them with air defence. One F-15 served as a flying command post with Colonel Aviem Sella in charge. The planes cruised at a low altitude, maintaining radio silence. They had a long flight ahead of them. Everything had been calculated with split-second accuracy. Navigation was entrusted to the most precise and reliable systems ever manufactured.

If the Saudi-leased AWACS surveillance planes were in flight at the time, they failed to detect the Israeli assault force and the planes entered Iraqi airspace without incident. Once there, though, the head of the leading formation picked out a potential hazard and hastened to warn his fliers: 'Watch out for the antennas and columns! They are very tall'. Near the Tigris, the planes climbed to an altitude of 1,000 feet. Becoming aware of sporadic anti-aircraft fire, Lieutenant-Colonel Raz warned his colleagues to be careful.

Suddenly, the planes got their first glimpse of the objective. They saw the ramps around the reactor, erected after the Iranian raid. Towering as high as the dome, they were part of a fortified defensive system which included anti-aircraft cannon and Soviet-made surface-to-air missiles. There was no sign of activity from the missile batteries.

The planes attacked precisely according to plan. Diving from an attack altitude of several thousand feet, they achieved the correct positions to release their bombs. The reactor attack was completed in a single swoop, with only the briefest of intervals – mere seconds – between one plane and the next.

The pilots scored a total success. Under the impact of the bomb blasts, the reactor dome collapsed into the core housing, which filled up with rubble. The cylindrical structure supporting the dome was hurled sideways, and its lower section totally destroyed. The building's foundations were also damaged. Water – probably from an underground source – inundated the structure as a result of the tremendous blast. All electric circuits and control systems suffered severe damage.

'The homeward route', recalls Lt-Colonel Nachumi, 'was just as it says in the books – an anticlimax. Everything was dwarfed in comparison with the assignment we had accomplished. True, there was a problem: we had no reserve fuel, but that was dwarfed too. In effect, it was all behind us, even though we would still be over enemy territory for some time.'

Prior to the operation, there had been some apprehension over enemy planes or surface anti-aircraft systems attempting to down the Israeli aircraft on course to target or homeward bound. Pilots of the escort planes which provided a protective umbrella were cautioned to keep a sharp look out. It was learned later that enemy planes took off after the attack in an attempt to intercept the departing Israeli assault force, but, failing to make contact, they turned back on their tracks.

At 18:47, as the planes approached base, David Ivry radioed to the pilots to congratulate them on their brilliant performance. The sun was setting when the assault commander's voice resounded over the radio: 'We are touching down. We are home!'

Flying back to their home base in central Israel, the pilots deliberately set off a number of supersonic booms within earshot of a million citizens. With the Shavuot festival already in full swing, the civilians failed to understand what the noise was all about. It was only the following day that they grasped that the pilots had been indulging in a celebration of their triumph.

The international reaction

World reactions immediately after the raid were characterized by a mixture of astonishment, appreciation of the military aspects of the raid and its 'surgical precision', and milder, or stronger, condemnation of the act itself. Unlike the Entebbe Operation of July 1976, which was met with relief and almost universal approval and justification, the Osirak raid brought forth a series of strong political reactions, ranging from outright indignation (from parts of the Arab world and the USSR) to questioning the wisdom of the military act, its justification and its potential repercussions. Naturally, there were also different assessments as to possible, imminent or delayed, Iraqi or even all-Arab retaliation capabilities.

A number of points were recurrent in the international debate that followed the raid. Some were of a general nature and concerned issues such as:

- The legality or illegality of the use of military force as a means to solve international disputes or conflicts, including the justifiability of pre-emptive strikes.

- The quality and adequacy of existing international non-proliferation arrangements and the security which they provided in a variety of circumstances, some unforeseen.

- Whether Israel 'did the world a favour' by destroying the Iraqi reactor or established a very dangerous precedent.

Other, more specific, questions related to:

- Iraq's intentions. Arguments for the raid centred on the specifications of Iraq's nuclear installation and that there was proof that Iraq's nuclear programme was designed to provide it with nuclear weapons. Counter-arguments were that Iraq was a signatory to the Non-Proliferation Treaty and to International Atomic Energy Agency safeguard agreements (while Israel, itself considered a nuclear power, was not); and that the combination of IAEA safeguards and inspections, coupled with special precautions which the French government had taken, would prevent Iraq from being able either to produce a bomb at all, or to produce one clandestinely without any warning.

- The timing of the raid. Much of the argument and counter-argument related to this issue. Questions were raised as to whether Israel had indeed fully exhausted the diplomatic alternative. The Israeli government's statement that the decision to act was influenced by the possibility that once Osirak became operational it would be impossible to destroy it without endangering the inhabitants of Baghdad with radioactive fallout was not universally accepted by specialists.

The UN anti-Israeli resolution

The UN Security Council opened a debate about the raid at Iraq's request. The hard-line Arab states initially pushed for a resolution that would boycott or expel Israel from the UN, eager to force a US veto, and thus to deepen the split between the US and the Arab world. Following complicated bargaining between Jeanne J. Kirkpatrick, the chief American delegate to the UN, and the Iraqi Foreign Minister, they finally agreed on a compromise resolution which was unanimously adopted by the Security Council on 19 June. Resolution 487 (1981) strongly condemned: 'the military attack by Israel in clear violation of the Charter of the UN and the norms of international conduct', and called upon Israel to refrain in the future from any such acts or threats. It also considered the raid: 'a serious threat to the entire IAEA safeguard regime', and called upon Israel: 'urgently to place its nuclear facilities under IAEA safeguards', and considered that Iraq was: 'entitled to appropriate redress for the destruction it has suffered'.

The IAEA addressed itself to the Israeli raid twice – immediately after the attack, and during its 25th regular session convened at the end of September 1981. In two official statements, on 9 and 12 June 1981, Dr. Sigvard Eklund, the Director-General of the IAEA, stated that Iraq had fully and satisfactorily complied with the IAEA safeguard regime.

Ten years later, in preparation for the First Gulf War, for the liberation of Kuwait, all those parties which had condemned the Israeli raid, were now extremely thankful. Were it not for Israel's Operation Opera Iraq would have long since been a nuclear power.

BOOK VIII

THE WAR IN
THE LEBANON

1

OPERATION 'PEACE FOR GALILEE'

In spring 1981 the continuing civil war in Lebanon, which had been ravaging that unhappy country since 1975, took a new turn as the Syrian forces manning the Damascus–Beirut road pushed northwards in order to penetrate the mountainous area north of the road and northeast of Beirut, held by the Christian Phalangist forces commanded by the Christian leader Bashir Jemayel. These forces had since 1976 been receiving military supplies from Israel, and had been urging the Israelis to become militarily involved in Lebanon in order to evict the Syrian forces and the PLO.

This renewed outburst of fighting in Lebanon erupted around the Christian town of Zahle in the Beqa'a Valley and on the main highway linking Beirut with Damascus. The citizens of Zahle had attempted to construct an alternative road to this highway, which was controlled by the Syrians; this would enable them to be in direct contact with the mountainous area further east controlled by the Christian Phalangist forces. The Syrians were opposed to the construction of such a road and began a systematic shelling of the town of Zahle. Fighting erupted between the Syrian Army and reinforced Christian units as the Syrians began to destroy the town indiscriminately. Heavy casualties and loss of matériel resulted from the fight around Zahle, which was placed under siege by the Syrians.

Late in April 1981 the Syrians attacked the Christian position on Mount Sanine known as the 'French Room'. This strategic position affords artillery control of both Zahle and the port of Jounieh, which had become the capital city of the Christian Phalangist enclave to the north of Beirut. Through this port the Christians received all their supplies.

When the Syrians encountered heavy resistance on the 'French Room' and on Mount Lebanon, they launched attacks by assault helicopters on 25–27 April 1981. Their very effective use of helicopter missile fire directed point-blank at the Christian mountain positions placed the Christians in a very serious predicament, and in danger of being overrun by the Syrian Army.

The Phalangists appealed in desperation to Israel for help, maintaining that the Lebanese Christian community without protection from air attack faced slaughter and possible annihilation. Prime Minister Begin ordered the Israeli Air Force to lend support to the Christians, maintaining that the Christian community faced the danger of a holocaust.

As the Israelis saw it, for the first time in four years of Syrian intervention in Lebanon, the threat of annihilation of the Christians meant that the tacit 'red line' with Israel had been crossed.

In pursuance of Mr. Begin's decision, on 28 April the Israeli Air Force shot down two Russian-built MI-8 Syrian helicopters engaged in supplying the attacking Syrian forces. This action too broke one of the unwritten, tacit agreements which characterized the Israeli–Syrian relations in Lebanon. Thereupon the Syrians, in order to protect their forces against the Israeli Air Force, moved their surface-to-air missiles – which covered from Syrian territory the Beqa'a Valley in east Lebanon held by the Syrians – into the Beqa'a Valley, thus violating another unwritten Syrian–Israeli agreement. For the presence of the Syrian surface-to-air batteries in the Beqa'a Valley hampered the regular Israeli reconnaissance flights taking place over Lebanese territory, in which hitherto the Syrians had tacitly acquiesced.

The Israelis requested through Ambassador Philip Habib, the US mediator who had been sent to the area by President Reagan, that the Syrians withdraw their missile sites from inside Lebanese territory. The Syrians refused. According to Mr. Begin at a political rally (Israel was in the throes of a campaign in national elections which were to be held on 30 June), Israeli aircraft had been sent to attack these missile sites in April, but had failed to do so because of heavy clouds in the area. Ambassador Habib continued his efforts, with little success.

Mr. Begin's Likud Party won a slight majority over the Labour Alignment, which made a spectacular come-back, gaining 47 seats in place of the previous 32. Mr. Begin was able, with the aid of the three religious parties in the Knesset, to form a coalition government.

In July 1981 PLO units in southern Lebanon opened heavy and indiscriminate fire from long-range 130mm Soviet-type guns and Katyusha rocket launchers against some 33 Israeli towns and villages in northern Galilee. The battle on the northern border of Israel was waged for some ten days, with the Israeli population driven into shelters.

It became clear that Israel could not afford to live with such a situation, which had brought to a halt normal life in northern Galilee. In Kiryat Shmoneh, industry came to a standstill with a high proportion of the population leaving the town. In the northern resort town of Nahariya the tourist industry came to a halt.

The Israeli reaction, which included the bombing of PLO headquarters and stores in Beirut and PLO bases throughout Lebanon, was wide-ranging, fierce and massive. At this point, Ambassador Philip Habib instituted negotiations in order to achieve a cease-fire, to which both sides – the Israelis for whom life in Upper Galilee was being disrupted, and the PLO who were suffering heavily from Israeli counter-action – were receptive. On 24 July 1981, using Saudi Arabian mediation with the PLO, Ambassador Habib arranged a cease-fire. Life in Galilee began to return to normal.

Soon, however, differences of opinion emerged as to the nature of the cease-fire. The Israelis maintained that they understood the cease-fire to be a complete cease-fire in which no action would be taken against Israeli targets in Israel or Israeli and Jewish targets abroad. The PLO maintained that the agreement covered only operations across the Lebanese–Israeli border. The American interpretation tended in favour of accepting the cease-fire as applying to targets in Israel from whatever direction the attack came, but not to targets abroad. Soon, while the northern border remained peaceful, other PLO-mounted operations took place. There were clashes and encounters with PLO units which crossed the border into Israel from Jordan across the River Jordan; terrorist activities took place within Israel; an Israeli diplomat was assassinated in Paris; Israeli and Jewish targets were attacked in various parts of Europe. Israel made it clear that all these activities were a violation of the cease-fire. Over 240 terrorist actions were mounted by the PLO against Israeli targets during the cease-fire.

On a number of occasions tension rose almost to breaking-point as Israeli forces were mobilised and poised to cross the Lebanese border. The Israeli Defence Minister, Mr. Ariel Sharon, made it clear that Israel's intention was to cross the border in force and wipe out the PLO infrastructure. In his various discussions, including those with representatives of the US Government, he stated his desire to link up with the Christians north of Beirut and by so doing, to influence the creation of a stable government in Lebanon, thereby ridding Lebanon of PLO and Syrian forces, and conceivably achieving normal relations with Israel.

A major consideration at the time was that Israel was due to withdraw finally from Sinai on 26 April in accordance with the Israel–Egypt peace treaty, and it was felt that neither Egypt nor the USA would react adversely to Israel's intention to cross the border lest such opposition would give Israel second thoughts about withdrawing from Sinai. However, powerful US pressure and opposition within the Cabinet led to the postponement of this operation.

The Israeli withdrawal from Sinai was completed against heavy internal opposition, forcing the Israeli armed forces to evict many who refused to vacate Israeli settlements in Sinai and the town of Yamit. Thereafter the process of normalisation between Israel and Egypt proceeded apace.

There were increasing signs of unrest within the PLO camp because a cease-fire with Israel in effect removed much of the *raison d'être* of that organization. Pressures were growing to resume hostile activities.

On Thursday, 3 June, the Israeli Ambassador to the Court of St. James's, Mr. Shlomo Argov, was leaving a dinner party at the Dorchester Hotel in London when a would-be assassin fired at him, causing him critical injuries in the head. The assailant was shot down by a Scotland Yard special security officer, and his accomplices were apprehended a short while thereafter by the London police, who uncovered a terrorist gang with quantities of arms and lists of prominent Israelis and Jews in Britain marked for assassination. The three men apprehended included an Iranian, a Jordanian and an Iraqi. They apparently belonged to an Iraqi terrorist group which had broken away from the PLO when led by one Abu Nidal, and had been adopted by the Syrians. The PLO denied complicity in the assassination attempt.

The Israeli Cabinet met and decided that it could no longer remain passive in face of such provocation, and on Friday, 4 June, heavy Israeli

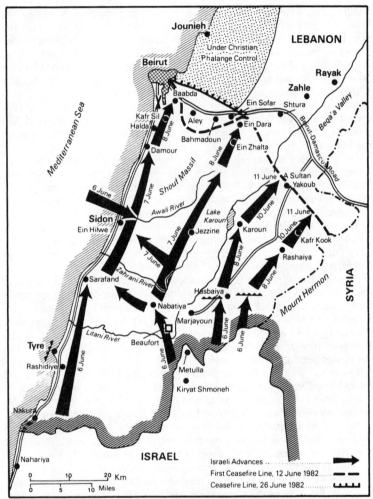

Operation "Peace for Galilee"

air attacks were launched against PLO targets in the area of Beirut and throughout the Lebanon. The PLO reacted immediately with artillery and Katyusha fire on the Israeli settlements in northern Galilee, causing considerable damage and some loss of life.

On 6 June at 11.00 hours, a large Israeli armoured force crossed the Lebanese border in Operation 'Peace for Galilee'. The Government of Israel declared that the purpose of this operation was to ensure that the area north of the Lebanese border would be demilitarised from all hostile elements for a distance which would place the Israeli towns and villages along the border out of range. As the Government spokesman announced, the purpose of the operation was to put '. . . all settlements in Galilee out of range of terrorist artillery . . . positioned in Lebanon'. In other words, this would mean an operation encompassing an area to a distance of some 25 miles north of the Israeli border.

The main features of Lebanon are two alpine mountain ranges (the Lebanon, reaching a height of 7,000 feet, south of Beirut, and the Anti-Lebanon, reaching a height of 9,000 feet at Mount Hermon). These ranges divide the country into four parallel zones running from north to south. These are: the coastal plain; the Lebanon ridge; the Beqa'a Valley; and the Anti-Lebanon ridge, the crests of which mark the border between Lebanon and Syria.

The mountainous area is particularly difficult for armoured fighting vehicles: the mountain roads are narrow, poorly maintained and easily defended. The coastal area varies between a width ranging from a few hundred metres to a few kilometres, with towns and villages such as Tyre, Sidon and Damour constituting effective road-blocks along the route.

The Beqa'a Valley can be easily covered by fire from the surrounding mountain slopes and the extensive agriculture in the area makes it easy for defending forces to conceal themselves. The River Litani crosses a good part of Lebanon from east to west from the area of the Beqa'a Valley to the Mediterranean, and the southern Beqa'a and its approaches from Israel are dominated by the Beaufort Heights rising to a height of 2,400 feet near the bend of the River Litani. Manning this highly defensible area were two military forces – the PLO forces and the Syrian Army. The PLO controlled some 15,000 fighters organized in military formations, under the overall command of its Supreme Military Council. This force was deployed along the western slopes of the Hermon range, known generally as 'Fatahland'; in the Nabatiya area comprising the Arnoun Heights and commanding the bend of the Litani River; and along the main axis between the southern tip of the Beqa'a Valley and the Mediterranean shore south of Sidon. The Nabatiya area also controls the so-called central axis to the north from Israel, the Aichiye-Rihane area, the Tyre region, the area south and east of Tyre based on Jouaiya, the Greater Sidon area and the north coast region between Damour and Beirut. In each of these areas the PLO forces ranged in size between approximately 1,500 fighters and brigade strength, armed with a wide assortment of light and heavy weapons, artillery ranging up to calibres of 130mm and 155mm and Katyusha rocket launchers including some capable of firing forty 122mm rockets. Over 100 obsolescent Russian-type T-34 tanks and a number of UR-416 personnel carriers completed the PLO armoury, which included a very large variety of anti-tank and anti-aircraft weapons.

The PLO had, in fact, taken over a considerable part of the area of southern Lebanon and had created within it a 'state within a state'. Lebanese authority was superseded by the brutal PLO terrorist methods which created a nightmare for the Lebanese inhabitants. Much of their military infrastructure was located in the midst of urban and rural areas; thus the cellars of large apartment houses were converted to storage areas for weapons and high-explosive ammunition, and apartments in many buildings were turned into weapon emplacements. The deployment of PLO forces was planned in such a way as to turn the civilian population into a living shield, and in fact into hostages in the hands of the PLO.

Since 1976 the Syrian Army, which had intervened and had entered Lebanon at the request of the Christian forces to protect them from the attacks of the PLO, had established itself with a force of approximately 30,000 troops in Lebanon. Ostensibly, this was part of an Arab peace-keeping force designed to impose a cease-fire in the Lebanese civil war, but gradually the other Arab contingents withdrew when it became clear that the Syrian 'peace-keeping force' was in effect a Syrian occupation force intent on turning Lebanon into a vassal state.*

The Syrian forces in Lebanon included a division-size force including a tank brigade and two infantry brigades of the so-called Palestinian Liberation Army (PLA). A further tank brigade and support troops were deployed in the area between the Syrian border and Joub Jannine, covering batteries of SAM-2, SAM-3 and SAM-6 surface-to-air missiles positioned in Lebanon. Further south a brigade-size force was deployed in the Beqa'a Valley on both sides of Lake Karoun down to the area of Hasbaiya. The Syrian force in Lebanon included some 200 tanks with an additional 100 tanks on the Lebanese border. In most of the areas controlled by the Syrians, particularly in the south-eastern sector, PLO forces positioned themselves behind the cover of the forward Syrian troops.

The Israelis concentrated a large armoured force in order to move into Lebanon. The figures published indicate a force of eight divisional groups. The Israeli plan was for a three-pronged push: one along the coastal plain which would bring the Israeli forces to the area north of Damour or the southern suburbs of Beirut and the international airport; a central force which would advance through the Shouf Massif, and would cut the Beirut–Damascus road in the area of Ein Dara to the west of Shtura; and an eastern force which would roll up 'Fatahland' to the southern part of the Beqa'a Valley.

The purpose of the three-pronged attack was to destroy the PLO military infrastructure, and clear the area north of Israel for a distance of 25 miles. The strategic purpose of the central advance was to reach the Damascus–Beirut road, turn eastwards along that road, and by feinting in the direction of the Syrian border to cause the Syrian forces in the Beqa'a Valley, who would thus be in danger of being outflanked, to withdraw eastwards towards the Syrian border.

The assumption was that the main strategic key to the operation must be the establishing of a presence on the Beirut–Damascus road. This was Syria's first strategic aim when its forces entered Lebanon in 1976. The isolation of Beirut from Damascus was considered to be essential.

---

*Syria never recognized Lebanon as an independent country, and in fact had no formal diplomatic relations with Lebanon. There was never any Syrian embassy in Beirut. It maintains that Lebanon is part of Greater Syria.

The operation was commanded by Major-General Amir Drori, GOC Northern Command. A product of Israel's Military Academy, he had advanced in rank in combat units. In the 1973 Yom Kippur War he commanded the Golani Infantry Brigade, which took part in the heavily fought battle for the recapture of Mount Hermon. He himself was severely wounded. He rose to command a division, to head the Training Branch at GHQ, and finally to be GOC Northern Command. A quiet, soft-spoken, intellectual man, he was rather typical of the new professional officer that had grown up in the Israel Defence Forces.

The forces operating in the eastern sectors were commanded by Major-General Avigdor Ben-Gal ('Yanush'), who a year earlier had left his post as GOC Northern Command for a year of academic studies in the United States. He returned in the midst of his studies to assume a field command. Once again, he was to find himself in military confrontation with the Syrian armoured forces.

Shortly after the central thrust, two columns to the west crossed the border – one column advancing along the coastal road towards Tyre with a parallel column moving along an internal road towards the foothills overlooking the coast and parallel to the coastal operation.

The coastal column was led by an armoured brigade commanded by Colonel Eli Geva, who had been a company commander in the tank force that fought so desperately against the Syrian invasion of the Golan Heights in 1973.

The policy laid down was for the forces to advance and reach the final objectives as rapidly as possible, thus closing off the escape and reinforcement routes of the PLO, and only thereafter to mount a mopping-up operation and engage the PLO forces.

Thus the forces advancing along the coastal road by-passed a heavy concentration of PLO units and moved forward rapidly in order to join up with the task force which was to be landed by the navy from the sea. By midnight, 6–7 June, the advance units had reached the town of Sarafand. As the coastal column advanced, a landing was effected near the mouth of the River Litani at Qasmiya, and the town of Tyre was closed off.

To the east of this force the Syrian task force moved along the slopes of the Hermon towards Rashaiya El-Foukhar while another force advanced from Metulla on Hasbaiya. Yet another force moved in a north-easterly direction, by-passing the Beaufort positions and moving towards the strongly held area of Nabatiya.

On the second day of the fighting, the advancing forces along the coastal road reinforced by the eastern arm of the coastal attack, which had crossed the Aqiya Bridge across the River Litani and had been advancing in the foothills above the coastal road, linked up with the task force which had been landed from the sea to the north of Sidon.

Meanwhile, Tyre was completely isolated, and its inhabitants were advised to leave the town and to congregate along the seashore in order to enable the Israeli forces to proceed with the task of evicting the PLO terrorists who had taken up positions in the buildings throughout the town. This move undoubtedly saved a large number of civilian lives, because the fighting against the PLO in the town was to prove to be fierce and bitter.

In the central sector, shortly after midnight on 7 June, the well-nigh inaccessible Beaufort Crusader fortress was captured after heavy fighting and serious casualties by the Golani Brigade reconnaissance unit. From this fortress the PLO had dominated northern Galilee and were able to direct their artillery fire against targets in northern Galilee and in the southern part of Lebanon held by forces commanded by Major Sa'ad Haddad, a Lebanese officer who had created an enclave of approximately 100,000 Christians and Shi'ite Moslems which was linked to, and supported by, Israel.

Meanwhile, in the central sector the troops of the central task force stormed the Arnoun Heights and established themselves in the Nabatiya sector. The Hardale Bridge across the River Litani was taken and in the central sector the forces commenced to advance, against strong resistance, along the narrow mountain roads. The Israeli forces came up against the first strong concentration of Syrian forces in the area of the town of Jezzine. The task force to the east advanced slowly along narrow roads and gorges which were easily defended, past Hasbaiya. The Syrians moved the 91st Armoured Brigade to the southern Beqa'a Valley.

The problem facing the Israeli command now in the central and eastern sectors was that the Syrians were blocking any possibility of achieving the 25-mile limit from the border of eastern Galilee. The Government of Israel announced officially that it would not engage the Syrian Army unless its forces were engaged by the Syrian Army. Messages were passed via Washington, suggesting that the Syrians take control of the PLO and prevent them shelling targets in Israel. The problem for Israel was complicated by the fact that the PLO units in the eastern sector had withdrawn behind the covering screen of the Syrian forces, and indeed for the first two days fired sporadically into the eastern panhandle of the Galilee.

When the Israeli proposal evoked no response on the part of the Syrians, whose reaction was to strengthen considerably their forces in the eastern sector, the sporadic firing which had taken place along the Israeli–Syrian front line now developed into full-scale fighting. In the general area to the south of Lake Karoun, the Israeli forces were facing a Syrian commando battalion in addition to an armoured battalion from the 62nd Syrian Brigade, which was deployed along the Damascus–Beirut road. Additional Syrian reinforcements in the form of the 51st Brigade were moved southwards from the Shtura area to the area south of Jezzine.

On the third day of the fighting, the parallel forces which had joined together on the coast road now advanced towards Damour. Operations against the PLO units in Tyre and Sidon were escalated; the Israeli forces faced the problem of endeavouring to avoid civilian casualties while at the same time the PLO held large groups of civilians as hostages in order to prevent Israeli attacks. In many cases the Israelis endangered the lives of their own troops in order to avoid causing heavy casualties to the civilians, but the severe fighting inevitably took its toll of civilians too.

In the central sector, the armoured battle developed in the Jezzine area with an Israeli task force ranged against a Syrian armoured brigade strengthened by an infantry battalion and a commando battalion. The Syrian 1st Armoured Division assumed responsibility south of the area of Lake Karoun. After a day's battle the Syrian forces withdrew from the Jezzine Heights, and the central task force advanced some 12 miles, thus threatening the whole area to the east of Lake Karoun and the roads leading down to the Mediterranean. The outskirts of Beit El-Din and Ein Dara were reached. This advance was beginning to threaten the Syrian hold over Beirut.

Heavy fighting continued in the eastern sector, with the Syrians making full use of their commandos manning anti-tank missile units, which were effective in the narrow passes and tortuously narrow roads in the mountainous area. The roads were mined, the passes were blown up, and the advance, because of the nature of the territory, was very slow. The Israeli Air Force became a central factor in this fighting. Meanwhile the Syrian Air Force began to intervene in the fighting, and in three separate dogfights six of their Soviet-built MiG aircraft were shot down: there were no Israeli losses.

Probably one of the most significant events of the war, within the purely military connotation, occurred on 9 June, the fourth day of the fighting. Once the Israelis had decided to push the Syrian forces in Lebanon back to the 25-mile limit from the Israeli border, it was clear that air support in such an operation was essential if casualties were to be kept to a minimum. The terrain was mountainous, with narrow roads, deep gorges, heavily wooded and easily defended, and was much more suited to defence than to an armoured attack. But the air space over the battlefield was covered by the surface-to-air missile batteries which the Syrians had brought into the Beqa'a Valley a year earlier and had now reinforced. These batteries, of the SAM-2, SAM-3 and SAM-6 types, hampered the operations of the Israeli Air Force over the battlefield. Accordingly, the Israeli Government decided on an attack against these surface-to-air missiles. At 14.00 hours the Israeli Air Force attacked, with the result that 19 batteries were completely annihilated and four were severely damaged, without the loss of a single Israeli plane.

The Syrian Air Force reacted in strength to this Israeli operation, and one of the major dogfights to have taken place in the history of air warfare developed over the Beqa'a Valley. According to the Syrians, some 100 Israeli planes participated in the operation and 100 Syrian planes were ranged against them. In the battle which followed, 29 Syrian planes were shot down, without any Israeli losses. In the ensuing days the Syrians renewed their air attacks as the Israeli Air Force intervened to prevent the entry of additional surface-to-air batteries into Lebanon.

In the course of the first week's fighting in the war, a total of 86 Syrian planes, all first line, of the MiG-21, MiG-23 and Sukhoi-22 types, were shot down without the loss of a single Israeli plane. The only Israeli air losses had been two helicopters and a Skyhawk which had been shot down by PLO missile fire.

The Israeli victory over the missiles gave Israel complete mastery of the air. There had been much conjecture as to whether or not the Syrians would attack the Golan Heights in the event of a Syrian–Israeli clash in Lebanon. The destruction by Israel of the missile system in Lebanon and of some 15 per cent of the first-line aircraft of the Syrian Air Force doubtless affected Syrian considerations in this respect. The air victory was a dramatic one which gave rise to considerable concern in the Warsaw Pact headquarters, and to considerable interest in the Western countries, particularly NATO. This new development now enabled the Israeli forces to take full advantage of Israeli air power and to dominate the battlefield.

Meanwhile, on the western sector the Israeli forces tightened their grip on the PLO in Sidon, and on the Ein Hilwe refugee camp from which area the PLO forces were resisting. Once again an attempt was made to divide the civilian population from the combatants by calling on the civilians to congregate on the seashore and thus avoid unnecessary civilian bloodshed.

The armoured and infantry forces now advanced to the township of Damour, some 11 miles south of Beirut. Damour, which had been a beautiful Christian township, had been destroyed by the PLO in 1976, when they massacred a considerable part of the Christian population and drove the rest out. The town was occupied by PLO camps and headquarters, with ammunition dumps and weapons storage warehouses located everywhere. Heavy fighting took place in this town, which fell after a bitter battle.

Meanwhile, in the central sector, heavy tank battles with the Syrians were taking place around Ein Dara, which commands the Damascus–Beirut highway from a distance of 3km. Here the Syrians, using heavy concentrations of anti-tank weapons manned by special commando units, fought stubbornly in order to prevent Israeli forces from reaching the strategic road.

In the eastern sector, the easterly effort of Ben-Gal's corps finally broke through the Syrian defences and advanced in the area east of Lake Karoun, joined in battle as it was with the 1st Syrian Armoured Division, which fought stubbornly and contested every position. Ben-Gal sent part of his force around the western shores of Lake Karoun. This force was able to attack the right-hand rear flank of the Syrian 1st Armoured Division which was resisting the Israeli advance up the Beqa'a Valley to the east of Lake Karoun.

The manoeuvre was effective, and in the battle that ensued the Syrian armoured division suffered considerable losses. One Syrian armoured brigade was totally destroyed, and in all the Syrians lost in this battle some 150 tanks. At one stage in the fighting, an Israeli armoured battalion discovered that it had moved into a Syrian-defended locality in the Beqa'a Valley and was being engaged on all sides, especially from the high ground on both flanks of the valley. Its situation appeared to be desperate, but it was finally relieved by a heavy concentration of artillery fire backed by air support, after having suffered considerable losses.

The advance in the western sector was held up near Kafr Sil, where the Syrians and the PLO had planned an armoured ambush with commando units and special anti-tank forces. The advancing force pinned down the Syrian and PLO forces facing it from the north, and developed an outflanking thrust to the east aimed at cutting off Beirut and the terrorist forces in its western and southern outskirts from the east and the Damascus road.

Meanwhile, as the battle in the central and eastern sectors had developed, Syrian reinforcements were moved into Lebanon; a Syrian armoured brigade *en route* to the front was completely destroyed by an Israeli Air Force interdiction action, while the Syrian 3rd Armoured Division, which was equipped with the T-72 tank – the most modern in the Soviet arsenal – moved into the Beqa'a Valley. Syrian tank strength in the Lebanon was thus in the region of 700.

The battle on the eastern front sector continued on Friday, 11 June, with the Israeli forces deploying the new Israeli main battle tank, the Merkeva (Chariot), against the T-72. As the 91st and 76th Syrian Tank Brigades of the 1st Armoured Division fought in the area of Lake Karoun, elements of the 3rd Armoured Division engaged Israeli forces in the Beqa'a Valley. In the course of the fighting, nine T-72 tanks were destroyed by Israeli fire.

Israel announced a unilateral cease-fire, to come into effect at midday on Friday, 11 June. Immediately after the Israeli announcement, Syria announced that it would observe the cease-fire too. Israel made it clear that the cease-fire did not apply to the PLO forces. At the outset of the cease-fire, the Israeli forces in the eastern sector were established on the Beqa'a Joub Jannine line with the easternmost elements being some 5km from the Syrian border to the east. Israeli forces in the central sector held the line in the area of Ein Dara, just south, but in range of, the Beirut–Damascus road.

In the western sector, in the area of Kafr Sil held by the Syrian 85th Brigade – by now completely cut off in Beirut – the cease-fire broke down after two hours. The Syrians blocked the road which would enable the Israeli forces to link up with East Beirut via Halde and Baabde. As evening fell, the Israeli forces outflanked the Syrian positions.

Fighting continued in the area of the Ein Hilwe refugee camp near Sidon, with the Israelis calling on the PLO to lay down their arms. They refused, and the fighting continued. Meanwhile hundreds of PLO fighters were giving themselves up or being captured in the Israeli-occupied area.

The fighting continued into 12 June to the south of Beirut, with an Israeli armoured force breaking through after capturing Kafr Sil and moving in the direction of Halde and Baabde, the seat of the President of Lebanon.

A second cease-fire was negotiated by the US Ambassador, Philip Habib, after the Israeli forces had completely surrounded West Beirut and linked up with the Christian Phalangist forces in East Beirut.

Not until Monday, 14 June, was the Ein Hilwe camp, in which the PLO forces fought stubbornly, taken.

The uneasy cease-fire continued, with frequent eruptions as each side tried to improve its position. On Tuesday, 22 June, Israeli forces attacked the Syrian and PLO positions on the Beirut–Damascus road in the area of Aley-Bahmadoun. This move was designed to push eastwards the Syrian forces which endangered the flanks of the Israeli forces laying siege to Beirut. Once again, the Israeli Air Force was brought into action. The Syrians sent in reinforcements along the Beirut–Damascus road, and

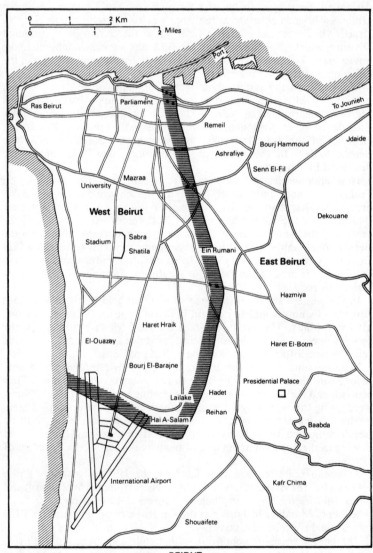

BEIRUT

Syrian commando forces engaged the Israeli forces from the area of Al Mansouriya which they had taken the day before. After 60 hours of heavy fighting against the determined Syrian forces, the Israel Defence Forces succeeded in removing the Syrians from the area of Aley-Bahmadoun on the Damascus road. Both sides suffered heavy losses, with the Israelis admitting to 28 killed and 168 wounded in that sector in three days' fighting. The Syrian forces withdrew eastwards from Bahmadoun.

An uneasy cease-fire took effect, with the Israel Defence Forces tightening their hold around Beirut, from the international airport in the south to the city's port in the north. From mid-July, Ambassador Habib was again negotiating, through the mediation of the Lebanese Government, to bring about the total evacuation of some 8,000 PLO fighters besieged in Beirut, and the remnants of the Syrian 85th Brigade.

On 14 July, the Lebanese Government officially issued a call for the removal of all foreign forces. This was the first time that the Government had come out in favour of the policy supported both by Israel and the United States. The Israelis announced that while they would retain the military option to move into West Beirut, they would accede to the various requests for more time to allow the negotiations to take their course. During these negotiations the cease-fire broke down repeatedly.

In Israel, voices were raised against any move by their forces into West Beirut. Clearly, such an operation could be costly, not only to the Israel Defence Forces, but also in terms of civilian casualties in the city. The Israelis applied pressure to the western sector of the city by periodically cutting off electricity and water supplies, and this was also bitterly debated in Israel. Not unmindful of this, the PLO leader, Yasser Arafat, prolonged the negotiations, but with the Israel Defence Forces intensifying the siege by artillery attacks from land and sea, and bombing raids, it became clear to him that the Israelis would not desist until the PLO forces had left Beirut.

On 4 August 1982, the Israelis mounted a limited attack in the city, capturing two southern districts and completing the occupation of Beirut's international airport. At the same time they exerted pressure westwards along the vital Corniche el-Mazra'a highway from the area of the Museum. The tactical implications of these moves were not lost on the PLO leadership, who became more and more aware of the untenable situation in which they found themselves. Meanwhile, Philip Habib continued his efforts to secure the evacuation of the PLO, his main problem being the unwillingness of the Arab states to accept them.

On 12 August 1982, Israeli aircraft attacked West Beirut for about eleven hours which prompted the President of the United States, Ronald Reagan, to telephone Prime Minister Begin and express his concern. Mr. Begin ordered an immediate cease-fire, and considerable criticism was directed against Ariel Sharon, the Minister of Defence. Accused of exceeding the terms of reference which had been laid down by the Cabinet, he found himself isolated, with only one Minister supporting him. The ensuing Cabinet debate mirrored the widespread public feeling that the Minister of Defence had on a number of occasions acted without sufficient authority from the Government and that more than once he had presented it with a *fait accompli*. Again, Ariel Sharon found himself at the centre of a public storm over military decisions and operations.

Gradually Philip Habib managed to negotiate arrangements for the evacuation of PLO and Syrian forces from Beirut and the transfer of PLO personnel to those Arab countries which agreed to absorb them. In part this was accomplished with the help of Saudi Arabian pressure and promises of economic aid to the host countries. Under the supervision of the Multi-National Force, composed of US Marines and French and Italian troops, some 14,000 Syrians, PLO and Palestinian Liberation Army personnel were evacuated from Beirut. Of these, approximately 8,000 PLO personnel were evacuated by sea to eight Arab countries, while Yasser Arafat with part of his headquarters was moved to Tunis. The Syrian forces, the remnants of the 85th Brigade, were evacuated by land to the Beqa'a Valley in eastern Lebanon. By the first week in September the evacuation had been completed.

At the end of August 1982, elections for a new President took place in the Lebanese parliament and Bashir Jemayel, the leader of the Christian Phalangists, the only candidate presented, was elected. He was due to assume the Presidency from Elias Sarkis on 23 September. On 14 September 1982, however, while Bashir Jemayel was conducting a staff conference in the Phalangist headquarters in Beirut, the building was blown up by a 200kg bomb. Bashir Jemayel's lifeless body was found in the ruins. With his passing, the hopes which had attended his election, that he would succeed in creating a strong independent government in Lebanon which would maintain close relations with Israel, evaporated. Bashir Jemayel had had many enemies, both in Lebanon and elsewhere, but all the indications are that the act was planned by the Syrians and perpetrated by Bashir Jemayel's enemies within the Lebanese Christian camp.

Syria has always been jealous of her special position in Lebanon and, indeed, has never recognized Lebanon's independence. Hence the prospect of a strong government in Beirut under Bashir Jemayel was irreconcilable with the Syrian approach which called, in effect, for the existence of a vassal state in Lebanon, under the indirect control of Syria. Following the murder of Bashir Jemayel, Israel's Minister of Defence, Ariel Sharon, with the approval of the Prime Minister, ordered the Israel Defence Forces to enter West Beirut. The Government of Israel announced that this move had been taken to prevent an outbreak of inter-communal strife and massacre. At a later stage Ariel Sharon announced that the purpose of the operation was to clear out the remnants of the PLO. He maintained that 2,000 such operatives with large quantities of equipment and ammunition had remained in West Beirut. Two days after the entry of the Israel Defence Forces into West Beirut, both Sharon and General Eitan, the Israeli Chief of Staff, announced in interviews to the Press that all the centres of control in West Beirut were in the hands of the Israel Defence Forces, and that the Palestinian refugee camps were surrounded.

For some weeks, the Israel Defence Forces had been urging the Lebanese Army to accept responsibility for the Palestinian refugee camps.

Until Bashir Jemayel's murder, the Lebanese forces had assumed responsibility for a number of camps, but after his assassination they stopped doing so. On 15 September 1982, the Israeli General Officer Commanding in Beirut, acting on the instructions of the Minister of Defence, coordinated the entry of Lebanese Phalangist forces into two Palestinian refugee camps, Shatilla and Sabra. These camps were in fact urban districts; one of them had some 2,000 buildings. The purpose of the entry of the Phalangists was to root out the remainder of the PLO forces who were believed to be in the camps. During the evening of 16 September, the Phalangists entered the camps, having been warned by Israeli officers to ensure that no civilians be harmed in the course of the operation. Israeli Cabinet approval of the operation was given shortly after the Phalangists had gone in. Sounds of shooting in the camps were heard by Israeli and Lebanese forces in the area, but were assumed to be the sounds of battle between PLO forces and Phalangists. Soon, however, a grisly picture emerged; the Phalangist forces had carried out a massacre, killing hundreds of defenceless men, women and children. On the morning of 17 September, General Amir Drori, the GOC Northern Command, summoned the representatives of the Phalangists and demanded that they withdraw from the camps. They did so on the morning of Saturday, 18 September.

News of the massacre shocked Israel, and there was world-wide protest. World Jewish opinion was alienated, and in Israel the opposition parties demanded an emergency meeting of the Knesset, the establishment of a State commission of inquiry and the resignation of the Prime Minister and the Minister of Defence. The opposition parties had warned against the dangers of entering West Beirut, and maintained that the fact that Israel had announced that it was assuming responsibility for law and order in West Beirut, placed on it a degree of indirect responsibility for the tragic events which had taken place in the camps. Furthermore, the permission given to the Phalangist forces to enter the camps was seen as a major error on the part of those who had taken that decision.

Initially, Begin resisted public pressure to establish a commission of inquiry, maintaining that it would suffice to appoint an investigator without the authority granted under the law to a formal Commission of Inquiry. The Minister of Energy in Begin's Government, Yitzhak Berman, and another member of the ruling Coalition Liberal Party voted in the Knesset against the Government and supported the call for a Commission of Inquiry. Berman resigned from the Cabinet.

The National Religious Party and the Tami Party, both members of the ruling coalition, demanded a formal inquiry, thus jeopardizing the majority of the Government in the Knesset should their demand not be met. Public demand for the establishment of a Commission of Inquiry reached its climax in a mass protest which took place in Tel Aviv with the participation of some 400,000 people. About 10 per cent of the total population attended this rally, which was in all probability the largest ever seen in Israel. In the light of the growing demand for a formal inquiry, both at home and abroad, Begin retracted, and a Commission of Inquiry was established under the chairmanship of the President of the Supreme Court, Justice Yitzhak Kahan, with the participation of a member of the Supreme Court, Judge Aharon Barak, and Major-General (res) Yona Efrat.

The Commission deliberated for several months and heard the testimony of a large number of witnesses, including the Prime Minister, the Minister of Defence and other members of the Cabinet. In February 1983, the Commission's report was published. It blamed the Prime Minister for a lack of effective control; the Minister of Defence; the Chief of Staff; the GOC Northern Command, General Drori; the GOC Forces in Beirut, Brigadier-General Amos Yaron; the Director of Military Intelligence, General Yehoshua Saguy; and the Minister of Foreign Affairs, Yitzhak Shamir. In its conclusions, the Commission called for the resignation of the Minister of Defence, the dismissal of the Director of Military Intelligence, and the removal from a command position for three years of Brigadier-General Yaron. The Commission claimed that the Chief-of-Staff, General 'Raful' Eitan, should have foreseen the possibility of Christian vengeance against the camp residents and his failure to avoid such a danger was 'tantamount to a breach of duty'. Nevertheless, Eitan's dismissal was not called for, but only because of the imminence of his retirement. These recommendations were implemented by the government, although Begin decided to retain Sharon in the Cabinet as a Minister without Portfolio. Moshe Arens, Israel's Ambassador to the United States, replaced Sharon as Minister of Defence.

A week after the murder of Bashir Jemayel, his brother Amin was elected President of Lebanon in his place. Unlike his brother, he did not arouse any great enthusiasm in the Christian Lebanese Front and among the Phalangist forces. He was known for his close relations with Syria and for his reservations about the maintenance of close relations with Israel in contrast to the policy of his brother Bashir. It looked as if the Israeli plan had come to nought.

Meanwhile the Multi-National Force of US Marines and French and Italian troops – which had departed with undue haste before the termination of its mandate, after the evacuation of the Syrian and PLO forces from the city – returned. Its numbers were doubled to about 3,000 troops. The Israeli forces withdrew from Beirut, handing over to Lebanese forces and troops of the Multi-National Force. Once again Lebanon was racked by inter-communal fighting, with bloody outbreaks between pro-Syrian and pro-PLO supporters in the northern city of Tripoli, which was under the control of Syrian forces. The internecine strife which had characterized relations between the Christian and Druze communities in the Shouf Mountains, erupted, with entire communities being driven from their villages, and the Israeli forces in the area being hard-pressed to stop the fighting and maintain uneasy cease-fires.

The Israeli and Lebanese Governments began negotiations, with US participation, and meetings were held alternately in Halde near Beirut, and Kiryat Shmoneh in northern Israel or in Natanya. Israel demanded a withdrawal of all foreign forces from Lebanon, Syrian, PLO and Israeli; the establishment of adequate security arrangements in southern Lebanon to ensure that it would never again become a base for PLO attacks on northern Israel; the establishment of normal relations between Lebanon and Israel, including freedom of travel, tourism, trade and other links, and the maintenance of offices in the two countries for reciprocal government representation.

During the negotiations, the Israelis withdrew their initial demand for the maintenance of Israeli-manned warning outposts on Lebanese soil. Arrangements were negotiated for joint Israeli-Lebanese Army patrols to be active in southern Lebanon, and for Israeli reconnaissance flights and sea patrols to take place over Lebanese air space and along the Lebanese coast. Israel's demands included the retention of Major Sa'ad Haddad – the commander of a mixed Christian and Shi'ite Moslem force which had co-operated with the Israel Defence Forces in fighting the PLO – as commander of the southern Lebanon area, namely for a distance of 25 miles from the Israeli border, within the framework of the Lebanese Army. This demand became a major problem in the negotiations, with the Lebanese Government refusing to recognize Major Haddad, whom they regarded as a renegade, and the Israeli Government refusing to abandon a man who had proved a trusted friend in difficult and adverse times.

The negotiations were being conducted against a backcloth of uncertainty as to whether the Syrians intended to withdraw their forces. The Israelis were adamant that they would not withdraw unless adequate arrangements were made for the withdrawal of the Syrian and PLO forces from Lebanon. The Syrians indicated to the US Government that they would withdraw if they could be assured of an Israeli withdrawal. They later changed this position to one which limited itself to undertaking to consider such a withdrawal after examining the Israeli-Lebanese agreement if and when reached.

Meanwhile, tension was growing as Syria tested the vast quantities of brand-new equipment received from the Soviet Union, and reinforced its front line facing the Israeli forces in the Beqa'a Valley.

At this point, the Soviet Union, which had been comparatively passive during the Israeli operation in Lebanon, stepped up its involvement in the crisis. In February 1983 the Russians installed SAM-5 surface-to-air missiles, with a range of some 185 miles, in two major sites in Syria, thus giving them adequate range to cover the skies over Tel Aviv, and the eastern half of Cyprus, including the area over the Levant Sea in which the US Sixth Fleet was then deployed, and southwards to the area of Amman in Jordan. These sites were manned by Soviet troops and protected by them in fenced-off areas which became, in effect, extra-territorial Soviet territory in Syria. This Soviet deployment, which was regarded with considerable concern by the United States, Israel and Jordan, was interpreted as a Soviet reply to the massive destruction of Syrian Soviet-built ground-to-air missiles in the Lebanese war, as a means to bolster Syrian morale, and as a Soviet reaction to the stationing of US Marines in Beirut within the Multi-National Force – a move which Soviet commentators tended to interpret as the creation of a base for the US Rapid Deployment Force in the Middle East. Once again the Soviet Union had taken steps to heighten tension in the Middle East, to threaten Israel and to embarrass the United States in its efforts to achieve a peaceful solution to the Arab-Israeli problem.

The negotiations with Lebanon took place against the background of a move by President Reagan to advance the Israeli–Arab negotiations on the basis of his so-called Reagan Plan, which was designed to encourage Jordan to enter into negotiations with Israel. The plan, while rejecting the idea of an independent Palestinian state on the West Bank and in Gaza, called in effect for Jordan to act for the Palestinian people in negotiations which envisaged territorial compromise between Israel and Jordan in the West Bank and Gaza.

King Hussein had made it clear that he would not endanger himself by entering into negotiations with Israel without receiving a mandate from the PLO to act for the Palestinians. In April 1983, after prolonged negotiations between King Hussein and Yasser Arafat, the PLO, following its National Council Meeting which had been held in Algiers a month earlier, rejected out of hand the Reagan Plan – which had previously been rejected by Mr. Begin – and withheld from King Hussein authority to enter into negotiations with Israel. At this point, angered by Arafat's rejection (despite the urging of the Saudi Arabians and King Hussein) of the Reagan Plan and of Jordanian negotiations with Israel, the United States gave expression to its frustration and disappointment in a statement by the US Secretary of State, George Shultz, which questioned the sole representation of the Palestinians by the PLO.

An additional complicating factor was the strained relationship between Syria and the PLO leadership. Syria, backed by the Russians, played a major role in encouraging opposition to any inclination on the part of Arafat to authorize King Hussein to negotiate with Israel, and indeed threatened military action should the Jordanians enter into such negotiations. Syria – with its ominous threats of military action, its massive acquisition of weapons from the Soviet Union, with surface-to-air missile units stationed on Syrian soil in addition to 4,500 Soviet military advisers – was gradually becoming the main force in the Middle East, opposing all moves in the Arab world to open negotiations with Israel.

Thus the end of April 1983 found the Middle East in a stalemate as far as Jordanian–Israeli negotiations were concerned, because of Arafat's unwillingness to split the PLO's ranks on such an issue. At the same time, with the help of the United States, slow but sure progress was being made in bilateral negotiations between Israel and Lebanon as to the future relations of the two countries; the whole played out against a backcloth of ominously increasing Soviet involvement in the area.

Sharon resigned from his post as minister of defence. His successor, Moshe Arens, though considered a hawk in the Israeli political spectrum, was not himself identified with the war in Lebanon and did not share the quest for far-reaching gains in the subsequent negotiations, in this he represented an increasing body of opinion both in the Israeli establishment and among the public, who saw little potential profit in a continued massive Israeli investment in Lebanon. From this perspective, and because of his belief in the value of close co-operation with the US, there emerged a new willingness to follow a softer line in the negotiations.

This softer line was matched by a fresh American approach to the negotiations which crystallized in April. The most notable manifestation of this new attitude was the arrival in the area, at the end of April, of the Secretary of State, George Shultz, to join in the negotiating process.

By the end of the first week in May, the main elements of an agreement had been arrived at. Shultz made a deliberate decision to postpone the negotiations with Syria over the agreement's implementation (which requested the withdrawal of all foreign forces) until after it had been signed on 17 May. Its main elements can be summed up under five headings:

- Abolition of the state of war between the two countries.

- Re-affirmation of the territorial integrity of the two states, and an Israeli undertaking to withdraw all its forces from Lebanon.

- Agreement on a series of normalization measures. Most importantly, the re-establishment by the two parties, if they so desired, of 'liaison offices' in the territories of the other state, and the assumption that there would be 'movement of goods', products and persons between the two states.

- Agreement on a series of security arrangements. These included Israeli undertakings, but were primarily meant to provide Israel with guarantees against attacks from either regular or irregular forces from Lebanese territory.

- Integration of Major Haddad and his militia into the Lebanese Army and its auxiliary forces.

The agreement left many questions unanswered, and despite the fact that it was a second agreement between Israel and an Arab country, did not arouse any enthusiasm within Israel, because it was assumed that the agreement was being made with a weak Lebanese government whose authority did not extend far beyond the municipal confines of Beirut.

In June 1983, both the Knesset in Israel and the Lebanese parliament ratified the agreement. Linked to it was the issue of the withdrawal of all foreign forces from Lebanon, and it was envisaged that, should the withdrawal not take place, the agreement would be void. The key now lay with Syria, but despite considerable Arab and international pressure, Syria, basing itself on an all-out condemnation of the Israeli–Lebanese agreement – which President Assad maintained was prejudicial to the security of Syria – made it quite clear that it had no intention of withdrawing.

Syria was obviously strengthened in its hard line by the considerable political pressure being exerted in Israel on the government, either in favour of a partial withdrawal of the Israeli forces from the Shouf Mountains and the area of Beirut to the line of the River Awali, or in the case of other political elements, a total withdrawal from Lebanon. The

Syrians, as is the case with most dictatorships, failed to understand the various nuances within the political struggle in Israel. The assumption of President Assad was that the steady bleeding of Israel by the infliction of casualties, the continuing economic burden which Lebanon was creating for Israel, and the increasing number of days which reservists were having to serve, were all factors, coupled with the political pressure within Israel, that would lead to an Israeli withdrawal without a concurrent Syrian withdrawal being required.

The US Government exercised its influence, activating Saudi Arabia and moderate Arab countries, in an effort to obtain Syrian agreement to withdrawal. Secretary of State Shultz made a number of visits to the area and discussed the matter in the course of difficult and tough negotiations with President Assad against a backcloth of growing strife in the Shouf Mountains between the Druze community and the Christians. Bloody outbreaks took place between them, and the only element preventing a major disaster was the Israeli forces. Voices were raised in Israel against its forces being used to police an area between feuding Lebanese factions, with resultant casualties for Israeli troops. The Government of Israel began to consider redeploying its troops along the River Awali, thus excluding the Shouf Mountains and the district of Beirut from the area held by Israelis, with a resultant lightening of the burden. However, as the significance of the Israeli partial withdrawal dawned on the Americans and Lebanese, Israel found itself, paradoxically enough, being pressurized not to withdraw. It was feared that a partial withdrawal would mean a *de facto* partition of Lebanon, with the Syrians holding the Beqa'a Valley in the north of Lebanon and the Israelis holding the area south of the River Awali. Furthermore, there was a suspicion that the Lebanese Army was incapable of taking over from the Israel Defence Forces and maintaining order between the warring Lebanese factions, and that the Multi-National Force, of some 3,000 American, French, Italian and British troops, was not strong enough to cope with the situation that would result from the Israeli withdrawal. Israel found itself under considerable international pressure – American, Lebanese and European – not to withdraw its forces from Lebanon until an arrangement for a total withdrawal of all forces could be reached.

However, the losses caused to the Israeli forces by Lebanese and Palestinian terrorist groups, which had infiltrated back into the area of Beirut and other parts of Lebanon, plus the economic burden, led the Israeli Government to decide in principle on a redeployment of its forces with a view to shortening its lines, thereby reducing the burden and ensuring greater security for its troops. The actual execution of such a plan was the subject of negotiations between the Israeli Government and the US and Lebanese Governments. It became evident that prospects of a Syrian agreement to withdraw seemed to be very dim, but unless such Syrian agreement could be achieved, the prospects of a *de facto* partition of Lebanon into Syrian and Israeli zones of influence, with the central Lebanese Government being propped up for a long period of time by a multi-national force, were very real indeed.

In the meantime, a further development occurred in the area which was bound to affect developments in relation to the Palestinian problem.

For months, under American and moderate Arab pressure, King Hussein had been urged to come to the negotiating table with Israel, but he was unwilling to do this unless given a mandate from the PLO. Many elements within the PLO favoured such a change in policy, and King Hussein and Yasser Arafat negotiated the issue over a long period. But the results of the Palestine National Council meeting in Algiers, and growing pressure from extremists against any form of compromise on the extreme policy set out by the Palestinian Covenant calling for the annihilation of Israel, led to the failure of their talks.

The prolonged negotiations between Arafat and Hussein, however, brought to a head an internal struggle within the ranks of the PLO. The dispersal of the PLO; the distance of its headquarters in Tunis from the planned area of conflict on the Israeli borders; the reducing of Arafat to an itinerant politician with little to offer; the internecine strife between the various Arab and Palestinian elements in northern Lebanon – all combined to create an atmosphere of frustration and disenchantment with Arafat's leadership.

Late June and early July 1983 saw the outbreak of an armed revolution against Arafat's leadership. This revolution sprang from the ranks of Al Fatah, Arafat's own organization and the largest component within the PLO. The ostensible reason was dissatisfaction with military appointments made by Arafat to strengthen his hold on the organization, but the real reason was a demand on the part of the anti-Arafat element for a more extreme policy based on military struggle rather than political effort.

At this point the incipient hostility which had characterized the deterioration of relations between Arafat and President Assad came to a head. The Syrians actively supported the anti-Arafat forces fighting in the Beqa'a Valley and, in the midst of the struggle, Arafat was summarily ordered to leave Syria.

It was clear that so long as the PLO forces remained in Syria and northern Lebanon, they would gradually become a tool of Syrian policy, and Arafat's hold on them would be weakened. Arafat, for his part, to save his skin and his position, would in all probability have to give in and adopt an extreme intransigent policy, favouring the military over the political struggle.

What was occurring in the PLO in July 1983 was typical of the tragedy which had beset the Palestinians from the outset of their struggle against Zionism – internal strife and discord, a move away from any form of compromise and negotiation, and an inherent inability to agree on anything less than the most extreme position. Despite its success in achieving an international image, the growing irrelevance of the PLO within the framework of developments in the Middle East was becoming more and more evident. These developments did emphasize the very fragile nature of the situation in Lebanon. They did reveal the inherent weakness of any Lebanese Government at the time committed to maintaining law and order in a country torn by communal and religious strife.

So, in mid-1983, Israel found itself facing a seemingly insoluble situation: the Christians engaged in mortal combat with the Druze; the various Moslem elements locked in internecine battle in northern Lebanon; the Syrians fighting the Phalange forces in the Christian enclave; the PLO torn by an internal revolt as the Syrians backed the more extreme elements; Libyan and Iranian contingents in the Beqa'a Valley adding to the turmoil.

In the midst of this chaos, the Multi-National Force found itself in the unenviable position of attempting to bolster up the central Lebanese Government, while the UN UNIFIL Forces in southern Lebanon were finding themselves more and more irrelevant within the framework of their terms of reference.

Israel was in the process of redeploying its forces from the Shouf Mountains to the line of the River Awali. Further redeployment would, doubtless, be dependent on satisfactory security arrangements being made to guarantee that no terrorist forces would enter the area threatening Israel. Such arrangements would doubtless depend on Major Haddad's troops being strengthened in order to replace the withdrawing Israeli forces. In the Beqa'a Valley the Israeli forces would continue to face the Syrian Army, until such time as the Syrians agreed to withdraw from Lebanon. This complex situation was developing against a backcloth of ominous moves by the Soviet Union which was stepping-up its involvement in Syria.

SUMMARY

The Lebanese operation mounted by the Israelis was brought on directly by the indiscriminate shelling of Israeli territory by the PLO batteries and Katyusha rockets based in Lebanon, but the issues involved were far more complex than a mere reaction to artillery fire across the border.

Since 1970, when the PLO had failed to destroy the Hashemite Kingdom of Jordan in a bitter war against King Hussein, the PLO had moved its area of operations from Jordan to Lebanon. With its arrival in Lebanon the border between Israel and Lebanon, which had been a peaceful one, became an area of major confrontation. The Lebanese Government came to agreements with the PLO leadership delineating exactly the scope of operation that would be permitted to the PLO against Israel. In an agreement that was signed with the Lebanese Chief of Staff, the PLO agreed not to fire against Israeli territory from Lebanese territory. But none of the agreements reached over the years between the PLO and the Lebanese Government – over 100 in number – have ever been honoured.

Gradually the PLO achieved in Lebanon what King Hussein fought to prevent in Jordan, namely, the establishment of a 'state within a state'. The area of southern Lebanon and the coastal area including Tyre and Sidon came under PLO control. Lebanese authority in great part ceased to exist in the areas taken over by the PLO, and an effective form of PLO sovereignty was imposed on a considerable part of Lebanon. This situation led to eruptions along the border culminating in the 1978 Litani Operation, when the Israeli forces attacked and pushed the PLO forces back to the River Litani. The United Nations force UNIFIL was interposed between Israel and the PLO area. The villages of southern Lebanon – some 60 per cent Shi'ite Moslem and 40 per cent Christian, totalling a population of about 100,000 and led by a Christian Lebanese officer, Major Sa'ad Haddad – joined together to create an enclave linked to Israel, while remaining part of Lebanon. The UN force, numbering some 6,000 troops, was not sufficiently effective because of the weak terms of reference it had received from the Security Council, which did not authorize it to evict PLO elements from the area under its control, although at the same time it was very effective in preventing the mounting of hostile operations by PLO units from the area under its control.

Eventually the PLO acquired modern equipment, primarily Katyusha rocket launchers and medium guns, and was able to engage targets in Israel by firing over the UNIFIL area without entering their territory. This finally led to Operation 'Peace for Galilee'.

Perhaps the most significant point of all was the total isolation in which the PLO found itself once the Israeli forces attacked in southern Lebanon. Apart from the inevitable lip service, the Arab nations did not lift a finger to help the embattled PLO forces. Indeed, the Syrian forces in Lebanon remained silent and motionless as the Israeli forces dealt with the PLO, and at no point attempted to intervene in their support.

For some time it had been evident that relations between the PLO and the Syrians were, to say the least, strained. This was borne out by the behaviour of the Syrians when the PLO forces were fighting the Israelis. There is no doubt but that the PLO in its behaviour, its lack of flexibility, its internal feuding and the uncontrollable terrorist idiom which it introduced, isolated itself among its own Arab people. The unwillingness of the Arab countries to accept the PLO forces besieged in Beirut during the negotiations conducted in July 1982 was eloquent testimony to the true attitude of the Arab countries towards the PLO. Indeed, its eclipse created in many parts of the Arab world a tacit sigh of relief.

Similarly, President Assad had found himself to be completely isolated from the Arab world which, while paying the usual lip service to Arab solidarity where Israel was concerned, was not unduly disturbed by the discomfiture of President Assad's regime and by the losses which his army and, above all, his air force, incurred.

By May 1983, Syrian losses were between 350 and 400 tanks. Israeli tank losses (total loss) were some 50. Israeli casualties were some 480 killed, some 2,600 wounded and 11 prisoners. Syrian casualties were approximately 370 killed, some 1,000 wounded and almost 250 prisoners of war. Syria lost 86 combat aircraft, five helicopters and 19 surface-to-air missile batteries. Israel's losses were one Skyhawk and two helicopters. PLO losses were estimated to be approximately 1,000 killed and 6,000 prisoners.

As Israel gradually took control of the territory of southern Lebanon and mopped up the PLO centres, a vast network of stores of weapons, ammunition dumps and military supplies was revealed throughout the entire area. It was estimated that sufficient small arms were revealed to equip five infantry brigades, and that some 100 trucks a day for a period of more than a month would be required to remove what had been discovered. Huge underground stores tunnelled into the mountains were found, in addition to major dumps located in the cellars beneath large civilian apartment buildings.

It is clear that Operation 'Peace for Galilee' found the PLO at a crossroads in its military development. It seemed that it was in transition from a loosely organized band of terrorists to a formal military framework. The types of weapons discovered, the tanks and artillery, indicated this. There were those who considered that this was a case of pre-positioning of equipment by the Soviets, but the type of equipment which was discovered, the greater part of which was obviously destined for terrorist and guerrilla activities, tends to negate this view. It seems that the solution to this puzzle is more simple and more mundane. The PLO disposed of vast quantities of money supplied by the Arab countries. The international arms merchants found in it a ready market; and doubtless the discreet side benefits accruing to the purchasers of arms were enjoyed by those involved in this activity in the PLO. Furthermore, it must be recalled that Israel was not the only problem facing the PLO. In 1970 the PLO had waged a major, bloody battle against the Jordanian Army. In 1976 it had suffered heavy casualties at the hands of the Syrian Army. Indeed, its losses in one battle against the Syrian Army – in the battle for the Za'ater refugee camp – were six times its losses against the Israel Defence Forces in 1982, with over 6,000 killed and many thousands wounded and rendered homeless.

The vast amount of military equipment, ammunition and infrastructure which was discovered indicates that the PLO had decided to turn its 'state within a state' in southern Lebanon into a stronghold which would guarantee it against attacks from the fraternal Arab forces. This would appear to have been a major consideration with the PLO in building up considerable quantities of equipment and arms – in addition, of course, to its major purpose, that of fighting Israel.

It is impossible to compare the Israeli Army's problems in this war with the problems it faced in previous wars. This time the initiative was entirely in Israel's hands, with the resultant benefits emerging from such a situation. Israel was fighting on one front, and had the luxury of being able to concentrate the bulk of its armed forces along that front. It had been evident to the planners of the operation from the outset that from a geopolitical point of view, Israel was in an advantageous position. Peace reigned along the Egyptian border, and Egyptian involvement could be regarded as highly unlikely. Indeed, the war brought about a political gain for the Egyptians when the PLO, which had derided the Israel–Egypt Peace Treaty and had danced in the streets when President Sadat had been assassinated, turned in desperation to President Mubarak of Egypt and asked for his political intervention. It was clear that King Hussein of Jordan and many of the other Arab rulers had no intention of committing themselves either to the PLO or to Syria, and indeed could barely conceal their satisfaction at the predicament in which both found themselves.

The Americans had opposed the idea of such an operation all along but, again, a reading of the atmosphere in Washington indicated that should such an operation remove a central point of friction along the Lebanese–Israeli border and lead to the removal of the PLO and Syrian forces from Lebanon, American approval, tacit or explicit, would be forthcoming. Furthermore, it was quite clear that the Soviet Union had a commitment to the Syrian Army in Syria, but had no such commitment to the Syrian Army in Lebanon.

Thus Israel went to war for the first time in its history with the odds on its side, and with a preponderant military advantage over the forces it was fighting. What is clear is that the Israeli Army in 1982 was the best force fielded by Israel in battle to that time. It was superbly equipped, highly trained and highly motivated and, as usual, well led. From a logistic point of view, the army was far superior to anything that had been known hitherto. Elements which had been criticised in previous wars, such as the logistic command and control, the artillery corps and the engineers, were outstanding, and proved that Israel had learnt the lessons of the 1973 Yom Kippur War. Lieutenant-General 'Raful' Eitan, the Chief of Staff, had raised the standard of discipline to a degree hitherto unknown in the army, and his leadership added a dimension of calm confidence wherever he moved in the field.

Once again, Western technology was pitted against Eastern technology. The Western technology now also included many of the advances made by Israel and the Israeli improvements to American technology. The results were evident for all to see. In 1973, 50 Israeli aircraft were lost to anti-aircraft missiles in the first three days of the war, and in all over 100 aircraft were shot down by missiles. In 1982, the Israeli Air Force succeeded in destroying the entire surface-to-air missile system of the Syrians in Lebanon without sustaining a single loss. In the armoured battles, despite the fact that the Syrians had the benefit of defending terrain favourable to the defenders, their losses were some ten times the Israeli losses.

These were the first battles in which the new Soviet T-72 tank was tested. It had been considered to be impregnable to the anti-tank shells or missiles then in use, and yet the Israeli forces succeeded in destroying nine such tanks in battle. Indeed, this tank, as opposed to its predecessor the T-62, often exploded immediately on being hit, giving no time for its crew to escape.

Facing it was the new Israeli tank, the Merkava, experiencing its baptism of fire. Designed by Major-General Israel Tal, it embodied revolutionary changes in tank design reflecting the lessons which Israel had learnt in tank warfare. The effectiveness of the safety devices included in this tank to protect the members of the crew resulted in its being nicknamed 'the insurance company' by the Israeli troops. It came through its battle tests with flying colours. Its design saved many lives, and its survivability in battle was beyond what many experts had previously credited.

Once again, as opposed to the 1973 war, the Israeli artillery came into its own, operating effectively and imaginatively. The accuracy and devastating effectiveness of the artillery in this operation enabled the Israeli armoured forces to advance rapidly through areas which were very easily defended. But not only were the various supporting arms that much more effective this time than in the past, the co-ordination and inter-service and inter-arm orchestration achieved was of a very high standard.

On the battlefield, the Israeli forces operated with a real-time intelligence capability. It was obvious in this war that very considerable advances had been made in the Israeli military intelligence organization in this respect. The field commanders benefited from almost instant intelligence which facilitated their task of reaching immediate decisions. The development of effective reconnaissance drones produced over recent years by Israeli industry played an important part in this success of battlefield intelligence.

The greatest advantage that the Israeli forces had in this confrontation was that of complete air superiority. The lessons of the 1973 war had led the Syrians to believe that Israeli air power would be seriously restricted by concentrations of surface-to-air missiles. They planned their deployment accordingly. The destruction of the missiles in the Beqa'a Valley on 9 June with the resultant destruction of this doctrinal theory, knocked the Syrian command off balance, and it was clear, as they threw air units desperately into battle, thus incurring additional heavy air losses, that they were urgently seeking a reply to a situation for which they had not planned.

Israel's air victory appears to have been a major element in the decision of the Syrian Government to seek an immediate cease-fire. Indeed, when on Friday, 11 June 1982, Israel announced unilaterally its decision to observe a cease-fire, the Syrians immediately followed suit. The developments in the air undoubtedly led to the Syrian decision not to widen the scope of the fighting to the Golan Heights, and also to cut their losses in the Beirut area, where in effect they abandoned militarily the remnants of their 85th Brigade.

There was much discussion in the Israeli Air Force command, following the heavy losses sustained in the 1973 war, particularly at the hands of the Syrian surface-to-air missile complex. The Syrians had reached the conclusion that a dense surface-to-air missile system was an answer to Israeli air superiority, and there were those in the Israel Defence Forces who doubted whether there was a valid answer to the problem posed by the missile system. However, Israel's Air Force Commander in the 1973 war, Major-General Benny Peled, was of a different opinion, and he initiated a very heavy investment in resources and in very effective research work with the purpose of finding a solution to this vexing problem. The Israeli Air Force learnt its lessons, drew its conclusions, trained and prepared for the future. Its new Commander, Major-General David Ivry, who had been Peled's deputy in the 1973 war, was convinced in advance, together with his staff, of the complete success of Israel's new methods when used in the planned attack on the missile sites.

However, when evaluating the results of the Beqa'a air battle, sight should not be lost of the fact that the confrontation which took place was not merely one between the aircraft and the missile. It was one between two complex technological systems, including most modern and highly sophisticated air control and electronic communications equipment. These two systems were tested in battle, both in the destruction of the missiles and in one of the major air battles in modern history. The control and direction of such an operation, and the orchestration required for all the elements involved, is highly complex and thus, despite the very sophistication of the equipment, the human element still remains a dominant one.

The Israeli Air Force was successful in interdiction and in preventing reinforcements from reaching the battlefield, as when a brigade of the Syrian 3rd Armoured Division was caught in a narrow defile and badly mauled. However, the opinion held in the Israeli Air Command was that, while the American planes flown by the Israeli Air Force were superior, it was impossible to draw conclusions from these battles about the Russian equipment. The general consensus in Israel was that the Russian planes were good and highly effective. The failure this time was that of the Syrian pilot and his command. The Syrian pilots fought bravely, but they were thrown into battle in an ineffectual manner, with the result that they were unable to bring to expression the technological advantages of their equipment, losing in the process over 80 planes and a high percentage of pilots. The fault, in the Israeli view, lay not with the Russian equipment but with the Syrian command, which handled its forces poorly, and with the training of the pilots.

On the ground, the Syrian Army fought well; at no stage did the command lose control of its forces. The Syrian soldier, once again, proved to be brave and fought determinedly. The Syrians could best be characterized as inflexibly stubborn. Their artillery fought well; they inevitably withdrew in an orderly manner; and they succeeded in achieving very effective co-ordination between their tank and anti-tank commando units. The weakness of the Syrian Army was an inflexibility in manoeuvre at the level of major formations.

The PLO fought determinedly and desperately. Their use of children from the age of 12 upwards, known as the 'RPG kids' because they used to great effectiveness the Soviet RPG (rocket-propelled grenade) from buildings and plantations against Israeli vehicles, created many problems for Israeli troops. Once the PLO realized that they would be taken prisoner, they gave themselves up in large numbers. Despite their organization in brigades and battalions, they operated in the field in small-unit groups.

The Israeli war aim was to create conditions which would prevent southern Lebanon from being used again as a base for attack on Israeli territory. This required the destruction of the PLO infrastructure in that area. While Israel made it clear that she would not have gone to war to evict the Syrian forces from Lebanon or to create a strong Lebanese government, at least one of the aims, namely the withdrawal of the Syrians, remained a possibility; but the prospects of a strong central Lebanese government seemed to be very uncertain.

While there was near national consensus on the aims of the war as enunciated by Prime Minister Begin in the Knesset at the outset, namely the clearing of an area to a depth of 25 miles from Israel's borders in order to ensure peace for Galilee, voices were raised against the prolongation of the conflict around Beirut. There were those who opposed a departure from the original parameters laid down by the government. Mr. Sharon was accused by opposition voices of overstepping the authority he had received from the Cabinet. He resolutely maintained in the public debate that he had received authorization in the Cabinet for each move and that, without removing the PLO presence from Beirut, it would be impossible to create a basis on which a strong Lebanese government could be established.

2

ENDING THE ENTANGLEMENT

The Israeli effort to work out a nationally acceptable, cost-effective – in terms of both life and money – Lebanese policy during the first half of 1984 was made against the back-drop of an increasingly unstable political framework. The coalition, led and inspired by the Likud since 1977, and reconfirmed in power by the elections of 1981, suffered an almost irreparable blow with the resignation of Menachem Begin in September 1983. The resignation was not merely an indication of a personal sense of inadequacy by a hitherto revered leader, but a confession of failure by this leader with regard to actual policies he pursued in Lebanon and policies he allowed his colleagues to pursue in the economy.

In September 1983, the Israel Defence Forces had withdrawn from the southern part of the areas held by them since 1982 (namely the Shouf Mountains and the environs of Beirut) and had redeployed on a new line further south, along the Awali River.

This withdrawal was generally considered a prelude to a further or even a total evacuation from south Lebanon, once new security arrangements had been made there. The major step taken by Israel towards such security arrangements was the formation of the South Lebanon Army (SLA), based on the militias created there by Major Sa'ad Haddad. When Major Haddad died (on 17 January 1984) the choice for replacing him fell on Major-General Antoine Lahad, a retired Lebanese officer, who took command in April 1984.

In Israel, Yitzhak Shamir, almost immediately after his appointment as the new Prime Minister, signaled his lack of confidence in the ability of the existing coalition to carry on, and the message came across clearly: the Likud and the coalition it headed had reached the end of its tether. New general elections were held on 23 July, more than a year ahead of the scheduled date of October 1985.

The general elections failed to produce a clear winner and created a stalemate unprecedented in Israel's annals. The concept of the 'National Unity Government' became central and even dominant in the national political agenda. Eventually, the result was the establishment of such a government.

On the political front proper, not much was expected. The two major partners in the coalition were clearly divided on all major issues, the time-framework of the Government was greatly affected by the agreement that the Prime Minister and the Foreign Minister would rotate in 25 months and, of course, the uncertainty whether the coalition would survive in the first place made thinking about long-range political planning even less likely.

Israel's withdrawal to the Awali River did not put an end to local military operations against IDF forces in Lebanon. The number of such incidents was on the rise. They were aimed at IDF installations as well as against members of the SLA, with an average of some 15–20 incidents with casualties every month. By far the most serious incident was on 4 November, when a Shi'ite suicide-driver succeeded in breaking through the security gate of IDF local headquarters in Tyre. Sixty people were killed (28 were men of the IDF and the Israeli Security Service and 32 were local men held there on suspicion of terrorist activity. In addition, there were 32 Israelis and 12 local Palestinians wounded. Indeed, this very special incident was the first suicide bombing operation against an Israeli target.

The main organization claiming responsibility for terrorist operations at the time was the Lebanese National Resistance Front (LNRF), an organization first noted in 1983. It was made up of various political and religious elements united by the common aim of liberating Lebanon from Israeli occupation by using force. The LNRF itself claimed that it was raising the necessary funds from its own sources, but Israeli sources assessed that it was supported by Syria.

Another source of terrorist operations (as well as of attacks on the Multi-National Force in Beirut) were the Iranian affiliated Shi'ite groups.

Israel's Labour politicians were strongly committed to a speedy general withdrawal. They were under pressure from their constituency and the entire public mood in Israel was one of resignation to cutting the country's losses in an enterprise that had turned into an unsustainable failure. There was no real support from the Israeli public for Israel's continuing massive military presence in Lebanon and the hopes that Israel's proxy in the field, the South Lebanon Army, would become a substantial asset were not taken seriously by most authoritative observers. Israel tried for a while to persist in negotiating with a Lebanese military delegation in the border town of Naqura, but it became evident that this was a farce. The voice was that of Beirut, but the hands were those of Damascus.

The failure of the Naqura talks brought the message home even more forcefully. Labour's leaders were anxious to reach a decision, while the Likud was split. This made the results of the deliberations inside the Israeli Cabinet a foregone conclusion. Almost symbolically, the architect of Israel's Lebanese enterprise, Ariel Sharon, not only served throughout the deliberations in the irrelevant post of Minister of Commerce and Industry, but was physically absent from the country practically throughout the entire process, prosecuting *Time* magazine in a libel suit in New York.

Also symbolically in 1984, the Lebanese–Israeli Agreement of 17 May 1983 was abrogated by the Lebanese, further underscoring the inability of the Lebanese government to deal with Israel independently of Syria. Symbolically as well in 1984 Pierre Jemayel, founder of the clan whose two sons had played such a prominent role in the vortex of Middle East politics in the early 1980s, died. All in all, there was in Lebanon a clash of national wills between Syria and Israel.

Armed operations in Lebanon against Israel Defence Force and South

Lebanon Army targets were particularly intense until the redeployment of Israeli troops in late April 1985 in a security zone that stretched from three to twelve miles north of the international border.

The war for the security zone

On 10 June 1985, the Israeli Government headed by Shimon Peres resolved upon a complete withdrawal from Lebanese territory. The decision was passed by a majority of a single vote, that of David Levy, a Likud minister in the government coalition who joined the Labour ministers in supporting withdrawal. But the pull-out did not bring an end to Israeli involvement in south Lebanon. Out of loyalty to the South Lebanon Army, the IDF transferred responsibility for the security zone to this force. This step implied a continuous commitment to provide the SLA with military advice, guidance, weapons and ammunition, and funding.

Initially, the pull-out appeared to have served its purpose; for some time there were almost no attempted attacks on Israeli territory. But the apparent calm soon proved an illusion.

The various Shi'ite militias in south Lebanon rejected the existence of the SLA and its control of the southern zone of the country. Hostile incidents and conflicts became ever more frequent, and the IDF, which could not remain indifferent, was soon dragged into direct involvement, deploying forces throughout the zone. Within a short time, reality in south Lebanon had changed; the IDF was once again the controlling, operative force in the 'security zone', while the SLA became a relatively marginal auxiliary factor.

Fifteen more years of almost continuous military activity would pass until, in 2000, Prime Minister Ehud Barak decided on a final retreat, in which the security zone was completely vacated, the SLA ceased to exist, and the IDF redeployed south of the international border, with the UN certifying that Israeli forces had, indeed, completely withdrawn from Lebanese soil.

These fifteen years can be divided into four main periods.

The first period was that immediately following the IDF pull-out of 1985. Ostensibly, an umbrella organization called the Lebanese National Resistance Front was to co-ordinate Lebanese activities in the region, but in reality, four organizations contended for primacy and control of the Shi'ite south. These were the Believers' Resistance, organized by Shi'ite Al-Amal; the Islamic Resistance, organized by Hizballah (the Party of God); the Comprehensive Resistance; and the National Resistance, strongly dependent on the Syrian Ba'ath party. Also active was the Palestinian factor, which comprised both pro-Arafat and anti-Arafat factions.

The Hizballah movement soon gained primacy and became the principal, if not the only, Lebanese organization active in the south.

In the midst of these was UNIFIL (United Nations Interim Force in Lebanon), which attempted at first to impose its authority and enforce calm. Its Swedish commander, General Haaglund, went so far as to threaten that, 'if the attacks continue I will be the first to demand the departure of the force.' But the attacks, far from ceasing, actually multiplied, and UNIFIL forces remain in the region to this day, lacking any operational function whatsoever.

Hizballah operations against the SLA became a matter of almost daily routine. Nevertheless, from the Israeli standpoint, the security zone fulfilled its purpose: preventing penetration into Israeli territory.

Palestinian organizations attempted to bypass the land barrier and enter Israel from the sea, departing from Lebanese coastal bases north of the security zone. The Israeli Navy reacted by positioning vessels along the Lebanese coast, detecting such attempts and destroying the intruding units *en route*.

The night of the hang gliders

On the night of 25 November 1985, an attempt to infiltrate into Israel was made by two men flying motorized hang gliders. One was discovered and shot after having landed in the security zone. The other landed near an IDF camp on the outskirts of Kiryat Shmoneh. Upon landing he opened fire on a passing military vehicle, killing an officer and injuring a woman soldier. He then broke into the camp, shooting and hurling hand-grenades. The attack resulted in the death of five more soldiers and the injury of six others. The attacker was then shot dead.

This attack turned out to be the most lethal in years. It was also the first successful operation initiated from Lebanon since the Israeli withdrawal in February 1985. Responsibility for the attack was claimed by the PFLP-GC (the Popular Front for the Liberation of Palestine – General Command, an extreme Palestinian terrorist organization operating from Syria..

Israel, for its part, was shocked and embarrassed. The IDF launched an extensive investigation within its ranks, and those found responsible for negligence were punished. Israeli Prime Minister Yitzhak Shamir pointed to Syria as the principal culprit behind the attack. Obviously, he said, 'the organization which... perpetrated these murders... [could not] carry this out without the auspices and help of the Syrians.'

The Lebanese border during the first *intifada*

The second period of the Israeli presence in south Lebanon began soon afterward, with the outbreak of violence in the administered territories on 7 December 1987 which became known as the 'first *intifada*'. In this period, the objective of organizations in Lebanon was clearly to aid the Palestinian uprising by igniting a 'second front' on the Lebanese border. The bulk of their activities took place inside the security zone, and consisted of Katyusha rocket fire, armed attacks, and explosive charges placed along IDF and SLA movement routes.

These organizations also tried to penetrate south into Israeli territory. In 1988 there were 25 such attempts, as compared to seven in the previous year. All or most of these attempted incursions were carried out by units of the various Palestinian organizations in Lebanon, which competed among themselves to demonstrate support for their fellow Palestinians in Israeli-controlled territories. They were aided by local Lebanese, who guided them through the security zone to the Israeli border.

On 2 May 1988, in response to these increasingly frequent incidents, the IDF launched a major operation both inside the security zone and to its north: the 72-hour Operation 'Law and Order'. This operation constituted a turning point in Israeli security policy in south Lebanon, as it was the first time the IDF initiated a large-scale confrontation with Hizballah.

The background was a recent intensification of cross-border infiltration attempts into Israel. It had culminated in April, when four squads reached the border area. Some of them came very close to reaching Israeli settlements. The interception of these squads took a relatively high toll in IDF casualties.

Operation 'Law and Order' was designed to regain the once-effective Israeli deterrence in south Lebanon and, more specifically, to eliminate the infrastructure of Palestinian armed activity in the area by apprehending those behind the recent upsurge of border-crossing attempts and their local accomplices. The task force, comprising several hundred IDF troops, cut off four small villages north of the zone which were suspected havens for Palestinian squads and Lebanese collaborators. Concurrently, SLA troops conducted house-to-house searches. Arms caches were confiscated and the population was warned not to collaborate with terrorist organizations; however no arrests were reported, seemingly because all members of the Palestinian and left-wing groups had already fled north.

Later in the day, the task force attacked Maydun village. Recently deserted by its inhabitants, Maydun served as a forward position for Hizballah armed action against IDF and SLA targets in the security zone and the border area. Moreover, the Hizballah influence in the Maydun area threatened to drive a wedge between the Christian enclave in Jezzine and the security zone which, if it succeeded, could have ominous consequences for the SLA.

Hitherto, IDF activity against Hizballah had consisted mostly of air raids, though at times IDF patrols clashed with Hizballah men inside the security zone. Never before had Israel initiated such a large-scale confrontation with the organization outside the zone. The fact that Maydun was not inhabited by a civilian population defined it as a purely military target and enabled the IDF to unleash a massive conventional attack.

Heavy artillery shelling on surrounding targets was followed by an assault on the village. Several hundred IDF paratroopers, backed by tanks and helicopter gunships, raided the village. They were met with fierce resistance from Hizballah men, well entrenched and using mortars, rocket-propelled grenades (RPG), and artillery from within the village and the surrounding hills. The village was taken after ten hours. IDF casualties were three dead and 17 wounded, while Hizballah casualties amounted to over 40.

Following Operation 'Law and Order', the SLA was reinforced to number 3,000 troops, and was encouraged to initiate aggressive actions. SLA military successes were the probable cause of two attempts to assassinate the force's commander, General Antoine Lahad. In the second of these attempts, in November 1988, a young female activist of the Lebanese Communist Party succeeded in severely wounding Lahad.

The Al-Naima raid

On 9 December 1988, a combined IDF force comprising naval, land and air units raided Al-Naima, a PFLP-GC base some nine miles south of Beirut. Over 20 PFLP members were killed, including the commander of the organization's south Lebanon forces, Abu Jamil, who had been responsible for planning terrorist incursions into Israel. A senior Israeli officer was also killed in the raid, and three soldiers were wounded.

When the order to withdraw was given at the end of the operation, it was discovered that four soldiers were missing. Nevertheless, due to the late hour, the decision was taken to withdraw as planned. Only later were the missing men retrieved by air. The decision to pull out while soldiers were still behind enemy lines – a very exceptional step in the light of IDF fighting traditions – provoked intense controversy in Israel. Justifying the decision, Chief of Staff Dan Shomron cited the fear of involving Israel in open political-military conflict with Syria, which supported Ahmed Jibril's terrorist organization and had military units stationed near the area of the raid. Defence Minister Yitzhak Rabin stated that he would not have approved the operation had he foreseen the complications.

Car bomb near Metula

Fanatic Hizballah volunteers developed a new method of attacking IDF forces: explosive charges carried by suicide bombers. Beginning in 1985, Hizballah made 16 such attempts, but these were unsuccessful thanks to the precautions of IDF and SLA forces at points of entry into the security zone from the north. On 19 October 1988, however, a Lebanese car charged with explosives was driven up to an IDF convoy on its way back into Israel, only a few hundred metres north of the border crossing at Metula. The driver, a Hizballah suicide bomber, detonated the charge, killing eight soldiers and wounding seven. This suicide operation was intended to show that Hizballah could still cause Israel heavy casualties despite the IDF's extensive strikes against the organization's bases. It was the deadliest such action against IDF forces since March 1985, when a suicide bomber belonging to a pro-Syrian organization killed 12 soldiers.

The IDF launched a detailed inquiry into how the driver had succeeded in coming so close to the Israeli border unimpeded. Investigation revealed that the explosives had been smuggled into the security zone from the north with the help of local collaborators, while the car carrying the charge had been prepared inside the security zone.

In July 1989 an IDF helicopter force raided the village of Jibshit and kidnapped Sheikh Abd al-Karim Ubayd, the commander of Hizballah forces in south Lebanon, and two of his assistants. Israel intended to hold Ubayd hostage in order to exchange him for three IDF soldiers held captive by Hizballah. Israel also hoped it could use Ubayd to help obtain the release of the 19 Western hostages (Americans, British and Germans) being held in Lebanon. All these hopes were disappointed.

The end of the Lebanese civil war

The third period began with the end of the Lebanese civil war, and the warring factions' acceptance of the so-called 'Syrian peace'. The Ta'if accords had been signed as early as October 1989, at the initiative and with the mediation of Saudi Arabia and the United States. Three weeks of discussions among members of the Lebanese Chamber of Deputies in Taif produced a 'Document of National Accord', in line with Syrian conceptions, bringing an end to 15 years of civil war, while tacitly accepting the continued presence of Syrian troops in Lebanon. However, it was not until two years later that the Syrian Ba'ath party was able to assume control of the Lebanese political system, when Damascus capitalized on its support of the international coalition to free Kuwait from Iraqi occupation.

The direct result of Syrian hegemony was the disarming of the Lebanese Christian militias, the Druze Progressive Socialist Party, and the Shi'ite Al-Amal movement. The only movement which was not disarmed was Hizballah, in the south of the country. Syria's proffered justification for its failure to disarm Hizballah was that this force was not involved in the internal Lebanese conflict, but was fighting to liberate national territory from the Israeli occupiers.

The traditional Lebanese leadership desired peace and stability, in order to rebuild the national economy, devastated by 15 years of war. Though Lebanese public opinion was severely critical of the surrender to Syrian dictates, national weariness proved the stronger. These developments took formal shape in the Treaty of Brotherhood, Co-operation and Co-ordination, signed on 22 May 1991, and the Defence and Security Pact of 7 September of that year. These agreements defined the special status of Damascus in the relationship, in conformance with the Ta'if accords.

The new reality in Lebanon had two apparently contradictory consequences. On the one hand, Lebanon's primary interest was to be free of the damage and perils of continued warfare, in order to begin a comprehensive rebuilding of the country. On the other hand, Syria's failure to disarm Hizballah militias, on the pretext that they were fighting to liberate the south of the country, granted these militias greater freedom to operate.

The practical result was a considerable increase in hostilities in the security zone. The IDF tried to take advantage of Lebanon's desire for reconstruction and normalization by attacking Shi'ite villages with artillery fire and aerial bombardment, assuming that the inhabitants would respond by pressuring Hizballah commanders to end their attacks. But the outcome was different: Hizballah launched massive Katyusha attacks against Israeli towns on the Lebanese border, the main target being the town of Kiryat Shmoneh. The increase in hostilities cost the IDF and SLA greater losses than before. The ratio of casualties worsened significantly: whereas in 1990 it was 5.2:1 in Israel's favour, in 1992–3 the ratio dropped to 1.7:1.

Israel was reluctant to launch large-scale land operations in Lebanon, for two reasons: the inevitable Hizballah Katyusha attacks, which could cause loss of lives and heavy damage, and the fear of severe international criticism.

On 25 July 1993, however, the Israeli forces launched Operation 'Accountability', which continued until the 31st of that month. The operation aimed to exploit the rebuilding process of Lebanon's economy and society by bombarding cities and villages in the south with artillery and from the air, in order to cause a massive exodus to the north, towards Beirut. Israel hoped and assumed that this would induce the Lebanese and Syrian governments to rein-in Hizballah.

After six days of fighting a cease-fire was agreed. The international community was severely critical of the massive displacement of population and, instead of Beirut and Damascus, it was Israel which found itself under pressure to end the attack. Moreover, US mediating efforts were aided by Syria, helping boost Syrian president Hafez al-Assad's position in Washington. Under the terms of the cease-fire agreement, Hizballah gave a written pledge not to initiate Katyusha attacks either against Israel or into the security zone. However, the organization remained free to continue operations against IDF forces in the zone.

These operations indeed continued: on 19 August 1993, nine Israelis were killed in the security zone.

Following the Oslo accords of August–September 1993 (discussed from page 415 below) and the parallel attempts at negotiation toward an Israeli–Syrian political agreement, the fourth period of the IDF presence in the security zone began.

Damascus was extremely cautious to preserve absolute calm along the Golan Heights, so as to avoid being drawn into a military confrontation with Israel (well aware that the balance of power was not in Syria's favour). However, the Syrians encouraged the activities of Hizballah, in the hope that the killing of Israeli soldiers would wear out Israel and pressure Jerusalem into greater flexibility, gaining concessions for Syria in the bilateral talks. Peace on the Lebanese border, Damascus implied, would only arrive once Syria and Israel had signed a political agreement, which would embrace the issue of Lebanon. Besides Syria, Iran also played a significant role in funding, arming, organizing and encouraging Hizballah violence. It was always clear, however, that it was Damascus which decided when to escalate attacks and when to reduce them.

Clashes between Hizballah and the IDF and SLA continued, but the local population in south Lebanon sensed it was only a matter of time before a solution was found and the IDF pulled out. Increasing numbers of local residents therefore began to co-operate with Hizballah, so that the IDF found itself compelled to get more directly involved in the fighting, and to depend less and less on the SLA.

There were three main causes for Hizballah's increased success. The first factor was political: Hizballah activity gradually lost its terrorist character, and international public opinion came to accept it as a legitimate armed struggle to liberate Lebanese territory from Israeli occupiers. Secondly, Hizballah's fighting capacity improved, as a result of better organization, weaponry and training, and also thanks to its ability to learn swift, effective lessons from every clash with the IDF. The third cause was the shrewd use of psychological warfare. Hizballah used every type of media to disseminate reports, true or distorted, of all confrontations with the IDF. It took full advantage of the IDF's policy not to report incidents before it possessed full, detailed data, and not to release information on casualties before the families had been notified. Thus, Hizballah reports became a source of information even for many Israelis.

Operation 'Grapes of Wrath'

In November 1995, Israeli Prime Minister Yitzhak Rabin was assassinated, and Shimon Peres was appointed his successor. Although the planned date for general elections was October 1996, Mr. Peres decided to profit by the Israeli public's shock at the assassination and move the elections forward by several months.

In January 1996, Prime Minister Peres authorized the assassination of Yahya Ayyash, the man behind most of the Hamas terrorist attacks, who was in hiding in the Gaza Strip (the emergence of Hamas is discussed in the section on the first *intifada* from page 393). This action greatly undermined the relative calm then prevailing, and gave rise to several deadly suicide attacks in late February and early March, which caused especially high casualties. The inevitable result was a drop in public support for Mr. Peres as elections approached.

In April, Mr. Peres yielded to pressure from IDF officials who recommended an extensive military operation. The goal was to improve the military balance in south Lebanon and significantly curb Hizballah activities. Operation 'Grapes of Wrath' was launched on 11 April 1996.

This was a kind of expanded repeat of Operation 'Accountability' of three years earlier (July 1993). Israel's declared aim was to bring about renewed international intervention which would put a complete end to Katyusha rocket attacks on Israeli towns south of the border. But its real objective was more far-reaching: Israel hoped to obtain a nine-month cease-fire, in return for which it would pledge a complete withdrawal from the security zone at the end of this period.

To increase the pressure, the IDF did not limit itself to bombing southern villages. Massive artillery bombardment caused the evacuation of the entire population of the city of Tyre, and this time even Beirut itself was not exempt, and was attacked from the air for the first time since 1982. In Beirut, the Israeli Air Force targeted Hizballah offices and facilities in the south of the city. Also, in response to a Katyusha attack which brought down the Kiryat Shmoneh power system, a Beirut power station was bombed, blacking out the city.

Despite the Israeli hope that public opinion in Beirut would blame Hizballah and demand the organization be restrained, it was Israel that received the brunt of the blame. Syria, meanwhile, took no action but waited for military complications which would serve its interests, and these were not long in coming.

Israel had assumed that the flight of the entire civilian population of the south would grant the IDF freedom to act against Hizballah. This proved to be a fond hope. The turning point of the operation came on 18 April. Israeli artillery targeted Katyusha rocket launchers belonging to Hizballah but, lamentably, the shells hit a large concentration of civilian refugees who, rather than flee to the north, had sought protection near a UNIFIL base at Qana. Over a hundred Lebanese were killed in this tragic carnage, the highest number of casualties since the Israel–Hizballah conflict began. The Lebanese government and public accused Israel of deliberately planning the killing, while UNIFIL officials claimed Israel had purposely targeted the organization.

The tragedy at Qana had two results. The political advantage Israel had enjoyed during the first eight days of the operation swung abruptly in Syria's favour, and Damascus came to play a central role in seeking a solution to the conflict. The United States, which throughout the operation had supported Israel and its desire for radical change in the situation, was now obliged to find a way of extricating Prime Minister Peres from his failed adventure. President Clinton sent Secretary of State Warren Christopher to the region to forge a reasonable compromise.

The cease-fire agreement of 26 April reaffirmed the understandings of July 1993. These were put in writing, but were not signed. Also, a special monitoring commission was formed, including representatives of Lebanon, Israel, Syria, the United States, and France. The Hizballah leadership presented this agreement as a victory: the organization was free to attack the IDF in the south, Israel had promised not to act against Shi'ite villages in the region, Hizballah's military and logistical infrastructure had survived the operation, and the southern population's hatred of Israel had become extreme.

The Four Mothers movement

Many Israelis supported a unilateral IDF withdrawal from south Lebanon.

The debate over withdrawal involved media figures, politicians, military officials and the general public. At the government level, however, there was a near consensus against a unilateral withdrawal without a comprehensive political treaty with Syria. Government ministers endorsed this position as long as intelligence officials and IDF commanders unequivocally recommended it. (The opinion of the GOC Northern Command, Major-General Amiram Levine, who supported the withdrawal, was not brought to the ministers' knowledge and therefore never discussed.)

It was the 'Four Mothers' movement which achieved the breakthrough in gaining public support for a unilateral pull-out. The founders of this movement were a group of mothers whose sons were serving in the security zone, who embarked on a relentless popular campaign demanding an IDF withdrawal. They were motivated by the increasing danger to IDF soldiers in Lebanon and the ever-rising number of casualties, without a clear, convincing justification for Israel's continued presence in the region.

1997 was an especially difficult year. 39 IDF soldiers were killed in action, and another 73 soldiers were killed in a collision between two helicopters that were flying them to their security zone bases (as the IDF's policy was to avoid moving troops by the dangerous Lebanese roads).

Also, on the night of 4 September 1997, the IDF suffered an especially grave operational mishap. A naval commando force (Flotilla 13) attacked a Hizballah maritime base at Ansariyya, some 12 miles south of Sidon. The unit was ambushed by a Shi'ite force which included Hizballah and Amal members. 11 commando soldiers were killed. The remaining soldiers were retrieved by IDF helicopters, as were the bodies of those killed. But parts of corpses remained at the site, and Hizballah used these in an arduous ten-month negotiation, at the end of which Israel returned the bodies of 40 Lebanese fighters in return for the slain soldiers' body parts.

The helicopter disaster and the miscarriage of the naval commando operation gave the final push to the Four Mothers' public campaign, and support for the movement steadily rose. In early 1999 an opinion poll found that 55 per cent of Israelis backed an immediate IDF pull-out from Lebanon, as compared to 44 per cent one year earlier.

The Yitzhak Mordechai initiative

Defence Minister Yitzhak Mordechai proposed a new political initiative in an interview for the Paris-based Arabic weekly *Al-Watan al-Arabi*. Mordechai declared that Israel was willing to implement UN Security Council resolution 425, of 1977, which called for a complete IDF retreat from Lebanon. But for the withdrawal to take place, the Lebanon government must fulfill its own obligation according to the resolution, and assume effective military control of the areas vacated by Israel. 'Let's place resolution 425 on the negotiation table and discuss new security arrangements,' Mordechai said. 'I am not calling for peace or normalization – only security arrangements.'

Initially, Lebanon's President Elias Hirawi was enthusiastic, describing Mordechai's initiative as 'the first positive sign in 20 years', but, within days, Lebanese Prime Minister Rafik al-Hariri put a damper on hopes for a breakthrough. On 9 January 1997 he declared that there had been no official Israeli proposal, and described Mordechai's remarks as 'strictly for media consumption'. In the interim, between Hirawi's enthusiasm and Hariri's dismissal, the Syrians had warned the Lebanese off. Syrian Vice-President Abd al-Halim Khaddam and Foreign Minister Faruq al-Shar'a also rushed to Paris to warn the French against trying to mediate. They said they saw the Israeli initiative as a thinly-veiled attempt to get a separate peace with Lebanon and evade negotiations with Syria over the Golan Heights.

Despite the clear Lebanese rejection of the Mordechai initiative, Israel continued to go through the motions. On 1 March, Prime Minister Netanyahu confirmed to the cabinet that Israel was prepared to accept 425 and pull its forces out of Lebanon, if the Lebanese Government 'co-operates with us in the establishment of security arrangements in south Lebanon'. The initiative was finally laid to rest by Hariri on a visit to Washington in mid-June. He told President Clinton that a peace deal with both Syria and Lebanon was the only game in town.

Changing military conditions

The military conditions of the conflict were growing steadily worse for Israel. There was the threat of Katyusha rocket attacks on Kiryat Shmoneh and other Israeli towns on one hand, while the SLA and the south Lebanese population realized that the Israeli presence was drawing to a close, be it as part of a deal with Syria or by a unilateral retreat. They therefore saw little reason to continue co-operating with the IDF, and many began to look for ways to rehabilitate themselves in the eyes of the Lebanese authorities.

But the most important factor was Hizballah's operational development. Hizballah fighters had created intelligence systems which kept them closely informed of IDF activities, and thus scored significant military successes. In parallel, they exploited every such incident for psychological purposes, to increase Israeli public support for a withdrawal.

On 28 February 1999, an Israeli vehicle was ambushed by Hizballah. Four soldiers were killed, including Brigadier-General Erez Gerstein, the IDF's regional commander. He was the highest-ranking IDF officer killed in Lebanon since 1982. This dramatic event caused heated public debate in Israel, and strengthened the various movements calling for a withdrawal.

In June 1999, the SLA pulled out of the Christian enclave of Jezzine, north of the security zone. This step, though of no important operational consequence, dealt a severe blow to co-operation between the local population and the IDF.

Ehud Barak's unilateral pledge

The turning point came during Israel's 1999 general elections. Prime Ministerial candidate Ehud Barak, shrewdly reading Israeli public opinion and relying on his own military experience, did not hesitate in stating a view diametrically opposed to the IDF's appraisal and its recommendations to the cabinet. Barak set himself a one-year period for a new attempt at reaching a peace treaty with Syria, which he believed stood a realistic chance of success. Such a treaty would, of course, include a solution to the problem of the Lebanon border.

Barak's commitment involved a self-imposed time constraint: if, within 12 months, an agreement with Damascus proved unattainable, he promised a unilateral IDF withdrawal. Indeed, immediately after his election in May, Barak instructed the IDF Chief of Staff to prepare for such an eventuality.

The political negotiations failed and, as Barak had pledged, IDF forces withdrew from the security zone on 24 May 2000. Some 6,500 Lebanese – SLA fighters and their families – were admitted into Israel. During the year preceding the pull-out, the official border line was determined; Israel began constructing a security fence and a line of military fortifications along the entire border; and the IDF removed most of the large amounts of equipment it had deployed in the region in the 18 years since Israeli forces entered Lebanon. Out of desire to complete the pull-out without clashes or casualties, the last stage was hasty and almost resembled a rout. Though performed cleanly and without casualties, this aspect of the withdrawal produced severe criticism in Israel and cries of victory from Hizballah and the Palestinians.

In pulling out of Lebanon , Barak had taken a huge strategic gamble. For nearly two decades Israel had defended its northern border by holding on to a strip of south Lebanon. The price was being bled by Hizballah, which sought to end the occupation, but who functioned as a Syrian tool prodding Israel to give up the Golan Heights. By withdrawing – against the advice of his generals – Barak robbed Hizballah of its main justification for fighting, and Syria of its main lever for pressure on Israel.

While his gamble on the Lebanese front did pay off, there was still one glaring weakness in his overall strategy of which he and the Israeli defence establishment were all too well aware. The Palestinians could, and did, interpret the withdrawal as capitulation by Israel in the face of determined military pressure, and adopt similar tactics themselves. When a violent Palestinian uprising erupted in September of that year, many analysts and politicians were quick to make the connection.

SUMMARY

Operation 'Peace for Galilee' opened up new political vistas for peace in the Middle East because it seemed to be the beginning of a process of eclipse of an insidious, destructive force in the Middle East, namely the PLO, which wreaked havoc and destruction in Lebanon, and which was abandoned by the Arab world during its struggle. The proceedings of the Palestine National Council meeting in Algiers in March 1983 and the resultant failure of Yasser Arafat to give King Hussein of Jordan the necessary backing to enter into negotiations with Israel, were indicators of the basic weakness of the PLO; Arafat hesitated and finally decided against any positive move by King Hussein because of his fear of a split in the PLO led by the extreme so-called Rejectionist Front elements within the organization. And, indeed, the revolt in late June and early July against Arafat's authority in the ranks of the PLO in the Beqa'a Valley, with the resultant internecine strife, heralded what seemed like an eclipse of Arafat's leadership, since his only way of saving himself seemed to be the taking of an extreme line and the abandoning of any thought of negotiation and compromise.

The events surrounding the entry into West Beirut and those following the massacre in the refugee camps dimmed many of the achievements of the operation, which liberated northern Israel from the threat of attack by PLO forces and which brought about the withdrawal of the PLO and the Syrians from Beirut. The balance sheet was further affected by a mounting series of attacks on Israeli forces in Lebanon by various terrorist groups, which caused many casualties, and also by terrorist actions which included the destruction of the American Embassy in Beirut with a loss of more than 50 lives.

In retrospect it would appear that, had Israel withdrawn from Beirut immediately after the evacuation of the PLO forces, it would have avoided becoming bogged down in the morass of Lebanese political reality, its forces would not have entered West Beirut and would not have been connected in any way, however indirectly, with the slaughter of Palestinians by the Phalangist forces. The continued presence of the Israel Defence Forces in Beirut after the withdrawal of the PLO and the Syrians was an example of biting off more than one can chew. This created a situation which brought about a bitter debate and polarization within Israel, and adversely affected Israel's international image. Even so, it took 18 more years for the Israeli political leadership and public to recognize the futility of the continued presence in Lebanon, and the need for a complete withdrawal.

In August 1982, two months after military activities began, Operation Peace for Galilee seemed to be a success. The PLO's political leadership and most of its military forces had gone into exile, and no longer posed a threat to Israel. At that point, Israel should have withdrawn from Lebanon immediately and completely. But it did not do so. During these two months, it had been fighting a military conflict, one which most Lebanese supported, as the Israeli actions relieved them, too, of the Palestinian threat. But from that point on, the IDF became a foreign occupying power in Lebanon – a situation which would give rise to the Shi'ite resistance movements in the south, chief among which was Hizballah.

What prevented Israel from making a timely decision to withdraw?

The first cause, and in the early stages possibly the main one, was reluctance to admit the strategic error Israel had committed in trusting the Maronite Christian leadership as a loyal partner – a belief that underpinned the entire operation. The Israeli Prime Minister and Defence Minister were not content simply with defeating the PLO, but deluded themselves that an Israeli–Lebanese peace treaty was within reach. The murder of President-elect Bashir Jemayel, and even the public outcry that followed the Phalangist massacre of Palestinian refugees in the Sabra and Shatilla camps, did not change the Israeli Government's position. It was only with the appointment of a new Defence Minister who was not committed to the previous strategic conception – Moshe Arens – that the IDF withdrew from the region of Beirut.

Another factor, which was doubtlessly influential throughout the 1980s, was the continued Lebanese civil war. The lack of internal stability in Lebanon meant there was no ruling power which could be relied on to maintain peace. This consideration became irrelevant when the civil war came to an end and a central government was established, with the primary goal of rebuilding the Lebanese nation, infrastructure and economy.

The South Lebanon Army had been created by Israel in the early stages of the Lebanese internal conflict, in order to maintain quiet along Israel's northern border. But the SLA gradually lost its usefulness to Israeli security and, from being a means to an end, became an end in itself which must be preserved and defended.

Lastly, the peace process of the 1990s created a link between the Israeli presence in south Lebanon and the political negotiations with Damascus. Syrian President Hafez al-Assad used the continued IDF presence as a source of leverage, hoping to soften Israel's position and gain more favourable terms in a possible peace treaty.

Despite this criticism of the protracted, futile Israeli occupation of south Lebanon, we must keep in mind that Operation Peace for Galilee accomplished three major goals:

- Israel achieved its purpose of destroying the PLO's military infrastructure in Lebanon and forcing the organization into exile;

- The PLO was left without a border from which to launch military operations against Israeli targets, and was therefore obliged to change its strategy and seek a political solution to the conflict;

- On a military level the war, and especially the sweeping destruction of Syrian surface-to-air missiles, brought about a Syrian strategic decision to renounce military confrontation with the IDF in the foreseeable future.

Above: Yasser Arafat, head of the PLO, in conversation with some of his officers outside one of the PLO offices in Beirut at the beginning of Operation 'Peace for Galilee'. (UP)

Right: A battery of Soviet SA-6 Gainful SAMs mounted on a PT-76 tank chassis. (Army Spokesman)

Above: An American-built M88 armoured recovery vehicle leads a Merkava MBT.

Right: Major-General Yekutiel Adam shortly before he was killed in the battle for Damur. (Bamahane)

Top right: Major Sa'ad Haddad, commander of the Lebanese forces in South Lebanon, unfurls the flag of Lebanon at Beaufort Castle. (Army Spokesman)

Far right: Prime Minister Menachem Begin (right) and Minister of Defence Ariel Sharon at the newly captured Beaufort Castle.

Right: Lieutenant-General Rafael Eitan. (Shalom Bar Tal)

Below: Major-General Amir Drori (left) takes over Northern Command from Major-General Avigdor Ben Gal a year before Operation 'Peace for Galilee'. During the war General Ben Gal returned to an operational command at the front. (Camera 2)

Far right, top: An IDF checkpoint on the Beirut-Damascus road. (Chanoch Gutman)

Far right, below: Foreign Minister Yitzhak Shamir (right) in conversation with US special envoy Philip Habib. (Zoom 77)

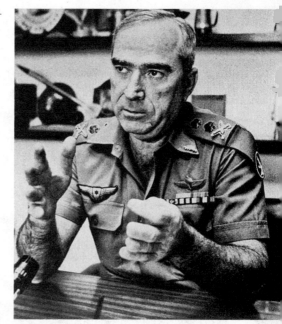

Evacuation: PLO members preparatory to embarkation on ships taking them from Beirut. (Habakkuk Levison)

The Israeli Army evacuate from Lebanon, 1985. (Harnik Nati/GPO)

American Patriot missiles being launched to intercept an Iraqi Scud missile over Tel Aviv, Gulf War, 1991. (Alpert Nathan/GPO)

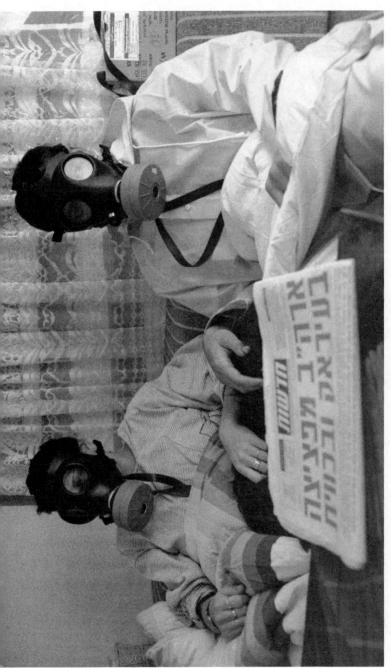

An Israeli family in its sealed room, with gas masks, during an alarm in the Gulf War, 1991. (Alpert Nathan/GPO)

The famous photograph of Yitzhak Rabin and Yasser Arafat shaking hands after signature of the Oslo 2 Accord at the White House. King Hussein applauds and President Clinton watches, 1995. (Sa'Ar Ya'Acov/GPO)

Above: Rescue teams search through the remains of a Jerusalem bus blown up in a Hamas suicide bomb, 1995. (Ohayon Avi/GPO)

Below: Palestinian demonstrators in the Occupied Territories, 2000. (Ohayon Avi/GPO)

Prime Minister Ariel Sharon meeting with UN Secretary General Kofi Annan in Jerusalem, 2001. (Ohayon Avi/GPO)

President Chaim Herzog and an American Patriot battery commander in the Gulf War, 1991. (Alpert Nathan/GPO)

Moshe Dayan, with Shlomo Gazit, in a press conference in June 1969 on the second anniversary of the Six Day War.

BOOK IX

THE FIRST
PALESTINIAN UPRISING

THE FIRST
PALESTINIAN UPRISING

A change of government

In 1977 the Gahal party won the Israeli general election and replaced
Labour, which had been in government since Israel was established in
1948. The new prime minister, Menachem Begin, appointed Ezer Weizman
as his minister of defence, and he became the first person to fill that office
who was not from the Labour Party.

Weizman and his deputy, Mordechai Zippori, were not newcomers to
the defence establishment. With no real differences between the two major
parties on security matters, there was no reason to expect new directives
or a change of style. Indeed, once he settled in to the day-to-day routine,
Weizman became a loyal student of his predecessors. Within two years,
however, following Egyptian President Sadat's visit and the
Israeli–Egyptian peace accords, Israel had adopted a total reversal of its
existing policies in the administered-occupied Palestinian territories.

In the 17 September 1978 Camp David accord, Israel accepted the
linkage of the Israeli–Egyptian arrangements in Sinai with a
comprehensive solution of the conflict, based on negotiations to resolve
the Palestinian problem in all its aspects. Prime Minister Begin set himself
a goal to achieve at the end of the final settlement negotiations with the
Palestinians: permanent Israeli control and sovereignty over all of the
territories, with the Arab and Palestinian residents remaining in their place
and enjoying a limited religious-cultural autonomy. Or, in his words:
'Autonomy for the people, not autonomy for the land.' The way he chose
to achieve this was a takeover by Israel of all of the state and public land
in the territories and a massive Israeli settlement campaign in Judea,
Samaria and the Gaza Strip. That campaign gained extra momentum after
Defence Minister Ezer Weizman resigned from his office, the government
and the party.

A new Knesset, a new government

The 1984 election results caused deep frustration both to Israelis and to
Palestinians. In the three years before the Palestinian uprising broke out
large and clear writing appeared on the wall, yet the Israeli authorities
avoided seeing things for what they were and acting accordingly. In those
three years there was a steep rise in the level of disturbances, terrorist
attacks, modes of response, and violence by Jewish settlers.

According to routine, every week the defence minister held a staff meeting with his aides. At those meetings the latest crisis was reviewed in an attempt to explain the immediate causes of the incident at hand. But those discussions failed to address the general trend of events and the inevitable results of 20 years of military occupation.

In 1985 violence rose sharply. Rarely did the Palestinians use firearms (probably out of fear of a severe Israeli reaction), but there was a rise in stone throwing, homemade firebombs and roadblocks. In response to public pressure, the government decided on severe punitive measures, including selective expulsions and administrative detentions.

A key factor that intensified the violent clashes between Palestinians and Israelis was the rise in the number of settlers. They played an important role in two ways: they had a loud and active lobby in the Knesset and they initiated violent retaliatory attacks after nearly every Palestinian terrorist attack.

In August 1985 the Israeli advisor on Arab affairs in the Gaza Strip addressed the appearance of the fundamentalist Islamic movement in the Strip for the first time. In July 1986 he issued an update to his report. From reading both reports it is clear that the emergence of the radical group Hamas (or in its previous name al-Mujama'a al-Islamiya) came as no surprise to the Israeli authorities. The six Islamic movements that acted in the Strip had one common denominator: the wish to establish an Islamic state where life would be governed by Islamic law (Sharia). Hamas, headed by Sheikh Ahmed Yasin, would soon be the strongest and most dominant of those movements.

The writing on the wall

In the years 1986–7 Israeli authorities picked up many signals that something exceptional and dramatic was about to happen in the territories. Those signals were not adequately heeded. The Israeli security establishment was in the custom of conducting inquiries and thoroughly analyzing every violent incident, but it focused directly on the specific event. There was no attempt to look at the broader context and analyze what the disparate incidents had in common.

Not one of the agencies with responsibilities in the administered territories (the IDF, the General Security Service [GSS, the Israeli civilian security service] and the Military Civil Administration) predicted, not to say warned, that a popular uprising of substantial dimensions was in store. From 1967 to the outburst of the *intifada* on 9 December 1987, responsibility for research on the Palestinians in the territories had never been adequately defined in a way that committed one of the intelligence research organs to make assessments for the future. Since then, such explicit responsibility has been assigned to the GSS.

The defence establishment had been locked in the misconception that Israeli security forces could easily overcome any unrest in the territories. Indeed, in the first days of the *intifada* many thought that this wave, like other waves of unrest in the past, would end quickly. But in the second or third week, when the clashes spread beyond the Jebaliya refugee camp, set the whole Gaza Strip on fire and extended to Judea, Samaria and Jerusalem, the GSS realized that Israel was facing a new reality.

The first serious incident that preceded the *intifada*, or perhaps foretold it, occurred at the Balata refugee camp near Nablus. On 31 May 1987, a few months before the *intifada* broke out, an Israeli infantry battalion was sent into the camp to conduct searches and arrests. Hundreds of men were gathered in the local schoolyard for initial selection and interrogation. The camp's women organized a furious demonstration that began marching towards the school, and the local *muezzin*, using the mosque's loud-speaker, incited the crowd to throw stones at the soldiers.

The battalion commander realized that the only way to continue with his mission was to open fire on the demonstrating women. The commanding officer of Israel's Central Command, Amram Mitzna, rushed to the site and ordered the soldiers to stop the operation, even though he knew it would be interpreted as an IDF defeat. Mitzna realized that the alternative, shooting dozens of women to death, was more damaging to Israel. Had Mitzna insisted on completing the mission the *intifada* might have broken out that very day.

The Palestinian uprising

A big Israeli civilian truck was driving through the crowded and narrow alleyways of the Jebaliya refugee camp in the northern Gaza Strip on 8 December 1987. A careless move by the driver caused him to hit a local Arab's car. Four of the car's passengers were killed on the spot and several others were badly injured. That accident was the fuse that set off countless rumours in the Strip to the effect that: 'It was no accident but a planned Israeli revenge attack.' The victims of the accident were buried that night, and thousands of mourners stormed an IDF outpost in Jebaliya.

The next day was the first day of the *intifada*. Spirits in the Gaza Strip did not calm down. People did not go to work and the violent demonstrations went on. That brought to an end the 20 'good' years of Israeli administration. Upon the outbreak of the *intifada* a new phase began in the relations between the parties. It was a phase of violence and militant confrontations – and at the same time of seeking paths towards political dialogue for a settlement.

The Israeli government refused to come to terms with the fact that 9 December 1987 was the watershed line of Israel's military occupation of the territories. It took the army command and the political leadership in Jerusalem several months to realize beyond doubt that the violent incidents in the Gaza Strip and the West Bank were fundamentally different from all the incidents of the past 20 years. A hopeless war had broken out between Israel's military forces and the local residents. It was an all-out confrontation, in which Palestinian residents of the West Bank and the Gaza Strip attacked any Israeli who crossed their path – whether military, settlers or innocent civilians – with rocks, knives, home-made firebombs and, eventually, gunfire. Palestinian violence also spilled out of the region. Attacks apparently carried out by hard-line Palestinian organizations against Western targets caused Jewish and Israeli casualties.

The Israeli government at the time was a national unity coalition but that did not mean it was immune to domestic criticism. Right wing political figures demanded the IDF use its arms against those involved in the uprising, and treat the rioters as if they were Arab enemy troops attacking Israel. They demanded Israel declare the *intifada* was for all intents a war, and treat its participants the way it would treat enemy combatants in war.

On the other hand both the political and the military establishment argued there was not, and could not be, a military solution to the Palestinian uprising. The only way out was political. Yitzhak Rabin, the defence minister at the time, completely rejected all the extreme proposals for putting down the *intifada*. Such proposals were in blatant violation of international law and violated the IDF's regulations and norms.

The *intifada* was the first occasion in the IDF's history when the military were presented with unrealistic expectations by the political establishment, while at the same time the security people made it clear to the politicians they would not let them use the security apparatus to cover up their political problems. They would not take the political echelon's chestnuts out of the fire for them.

The 'Ship of Return'

One of the many Palestinian attempts to embarrass Israel on the political level was a plan initiated by Abdel Jawad Salah, a former mayor of al-Tira, north of Jerusalem, who had been expelled to Jordan by the Israeli authorities. His plan was to organize a boat (the 'Ship of Return') that would carry hundreds of Palestinian refugees to 'Palestine'. The 'Ship of Return' was intended to imitate the 1947 journey to Palestine of several thousand Jewish refugees on board the *Exodus*. Clearly this was a public relations manoeuvre, designed to embarrass Israel by suggesting a similarity between the Jews of 1947 and the Palestinians of 1988, and thus underscoring the Palestinians' right to a homeland.

The operation was regarded by Israel as a hostile act. On 15 February 1988, underwater sabotage crippled the 'Ship of Return', in fact a PLO-owned ferry berthed at Limassol (Cyprus), which was due to carry the refugees on their voyage to Israel. Less than 24 hours earlier the three PLO military officers who had purchased the vessel for the PLO were killed in Limassol by an explosive charge planted in their vehicle. Both incidents were evidently linked. Following these events the PLO pointed to Israel as the only party interested in stopping the ship and vowed to retaliate.

The assasination of Abu Jihad

Khalil al-Wazir, alias Abu Jihad, was regarded as the number-two man within the PLO and as Yasser Arafat's most likely successor. In 1973 he became the man in charge of the 'Western Sector', the PLO's apparatus for armed activity in Israel proper and in the West Bank and Gaza. With the outbreak of the Palestinian uprising in the West Bank and Gaza, he soon reportedly began funneling money and instructions to local operatives in order to sustain the level of activity. In fact, Abu Jihad was quoted as saying that he was commanding the uprising.

On 16 April 1988, Abu Jihad, was assassinated by a crack commando team at his house in Sidi-bu-Sa'id, a suburb of Tunis. According to eyewitnesses and Tunisian security sources, the squad comprised about 30 men, seven or eight of whom carried out the actual killing. The assailants wore military outfits and masks and carried guns with silencers. They broke into the house and killed Abu Jihad and then escaped in three rented vehicles. There were no clues to the attackers' identity.

From press reports it emerged that the operation was carried out by a combined team from the Mossad and a special hand-picked IDF commando unit known as Sayeret Matkal, assisted by the Israeli Navy and Air Force. The operation was monitored and co-ordinated by some of the IDF's leading officers from a Boeing 707 flying over the Mediterranean outside Tunisian airspace.

Some time before the attack, several Arabic-speaking Mossad agents, carrying false Lebanese passports, had arrived in Tunisia to provide the team with operational intelligence and logistical support. On the night of the mission the Mossad agents awaited the commando unit, which arrived by rubber dinghies launched from an IDF missile boat, and drove the unit to its destination in three rented cars.

The killing of the PLO's most senior military figure was a severe blow to the organization and the Palestinians at large, since Abu Jihad was first and foremost a symbol of the armed struggle.

Attacks on Israelis

On 30 October 1988 an Israeli bus near Jericho was fire-bombed, resulting in the death of five Israeli citizens – among them a mother and three children – and the wounding of four others. It was the highest death toll in a single attack since the beginning of the uprising. According to Israeli experts, the attack, which coincided with Israeli general elections, most likely increased the number of votes for the right-wing parties. The PLO, attempting to counter such a development or perhaps promote a moderate image for itself, denounced the attack, calling on Israelis 'to vote for peace'.

Perhaps more than any other incident of the time, the bus attack symbolized how the *intifada* was spilling into Israel. On 6 July, a civilian bus *en route* from Tel Aviv to Jerusalem, was attacked by one of the passengers, an Arab, about half an hour after its departure from Tel Aviv. As the bus was approaching the Neve-Ilan junction, the assailant jumped at the driver, forcefully turned the steering wheel to the right and diverted the bus off the road into an abyss. The steepness of the abyss into which the bus fell imposed extreme difficulties on efforts to rescue the passengers and provide medical aid to those injured, who were trapped inside the bus or lay beside it. Sixteen passengers were killed and 25 were wounded. The attacker, who was only slightly injured, was arrested, and his interrogation revealed that he was a member of the Gaza-based Islamic Jihad.

This incident caused intense anxiety in Israel. The fact that it had occurred on a main highway was a blow to the Israeli public's sense of security while moving on the roads and in public transport. Consequently, measures were taken to step up security in traffic centres, such as central bus stations and new safety devices were introduced on all buses.

On 17 September 1989, this increased alertness paid off when the security forces arrested a Palestinian who tried to board a bus about to leave the Tel Aviv bus station for Jerusalem. A knife was found on his person and he admitted his intention was to perpetrate an attack similar to the previous one.

Two Israeli soldiers were abducted and murdered by two young Hamas members in two separate incidents in Israel proper. On 16 February 1990, the two murderers, disguised as orthodox Jews, stopped at a military pick-up point where a soldier waiting for a lift got into their car. Shortly after, they apparently shot the soldier dead and buried his body, which was found some time later. On 3 May, the same two attackers picked up another soldier waiting for a ride, likewise killed him and buried the body. The two Hamas members escaped to Egypt, but the head of their cell was arrested. These two incidents shocked the Israeli public severely and deepened the feeling of insecurity on the roads.

The Temple Mount tragedy

The most serious single incident in the administered territories since 1967 took place on 8 October 1990 on the Temple Mount (al-Haram al-Sharif) in Jerusalem, during which 19 Palestinians were killed and over 200 Palestinians and 11 Israelis were injured. This tragedy became a major catalyst that served to escalate the *intifada*, and had a deep emotional impact on both sides.

The incident originated with the announcement by an extreme Jewish group, the Temple Mount Faithful, that it intended to march onto the Temple Mount on the Jewish holiday of Sukkot. The fear of a Jewish takeover of al-Haram al-Sharif, the site of the El-Aqsa mosque, the third holiest shrine in Islam, and its displacement by a Jewish temple injected a powerful element into the Israeli–Palestinian conflict. Over 3,000 Moslem worshippers gathered on the Temple Mount in order to prevent the entry of the Jewish contingent, while over 20,000 Jewish worshippers were gathered at the Western Wall below for the Sukkot holiday prayers.

Palestinians at the Temple Mount started stoning both the Jews praying below as well as the police on the Mount with a barrage of heavy rocks, after they had been misled by the Arab preacher at the nearby village of Silwan that Jews were approaching the Mount. The few policemen stationed on the Mount retreated and the Moslem worshippers took control of the area. Largely because of mistaken information that policemen were trapped inside, the police, upon the arrival of reinforcements, then decided to storm the Mount, using live ammunition, rubber bullets, and tear gas. It was at this stage that most of the Palestinian casualties were inflicted.

In a call issued on the day of the incident, the *intifada* UNC (Unified National Command) sought to channel the fury aroused by the tragedy toward an escalation of the *intifada* declaring, 'every soldier and settler on the land of Palestine is a target that should be eliminated.' For the first time since the beginning of the uprising, leaflets produced by the Fatah organization urged the use of 'weapons' and knives, inasmuch as stones and demonstrations had proven ineffective. Hamas leaflets stated that all Jews were legitimate targets for killing to avenge the martyrs.

Reassessing the *intifada*

The list of the Palestinian uprising's gains is quite impressive.

Its first and probably most important gain was spreading and imprinting the desired message – presenting the Palestinian problem to the whole world, while manipulating the world media. The same headlines and pictures appeared in the Israeli media to great effect. Israeli public opinion's *idée fixe* that the military occupation could go on forever was beginning to melt away. Everyone understood the existing situation could not go on indefinitely and that a new policy that strove to break free of the entanglement was badly needed.

The Palestinian uprising also gave rise to a new generation of local leaders on the Palestinian side. These were purely local brave young people who lived there and were known and chosen by their communities. They were authentic leaders. They all achieved leadership status thanks to their leading uprising operations, and most of them had done time in Israeli jails, for short or long periods. It was the first time since the Six Day War that a young and new Palestinian leadership emerged, posing a challenge, a political alternative and a potential threat both to the traditional leadership (which was established, corrupt and old) and to the PLO's leadership in exile.

But the *intifada*'s most important achievements were on the political level. The Palestinian uprising disrupted the stagnation of the ongoing Israeli occupation and forced all sides to re-examine their fixed positions and offer new approaches.

Despite these benefits, the negative impact of the *intifada* on the

Palestinians must not be ignored. In the long term, their losses may have outweighed their gains.

The most obvious loss of the Palestinian uprising was its failure to prevent the building of new Israeli settlements in the West Bank and Gaza Strip. In 1987, when the uprising broke out, there were 67,000 Jewish settlers in the West Bank. In a dozen or so years that population almost tripled, and in mid-2001 was 200,000. In the same time the Jewish population of the Gaza Strip grew from 2,500 to 9,000. That impressive growth occurred mainly in the first five years of the Likud government, and the *intifada* did nothing to thwart it.

Another negative outcome of the *intifada*, that may have long-reaching implications, is the development of hatred between the two national communities. The atrocious attacks by extreme Palestinians against innocent Israelis on the one hand, and the despicable massacre by settler Baruch Goldstein from Kiryat Arba against Moslem worshippers at Hebron's Cave of the Patriarchs on the other, were bad signs. The *intifada* badly poisoned the souls of Israelis and Palestinians and it is doubtful there is a cure for such fierce hatred in the short run.

The *intifada* caused economic and administrative upheaval in the territories in general and the Gaza Strip in particular. Can the hands of the clock be turned back and the destructive results canceled? Ten years of disruption, because of Palestinian workers' irregular attendance at their jobs, forced their Israeli employers to find replacements, either by introducing machines and automation as a substitute for unskilled manual labour, or by the massive import of foreign workers. These foreign workers show up to work regularly and their employment does not entail a security risk.

The *intifada* and the IDF

While at first there was concern that the *intifada* would have dangerous effects on the Israeli Army – to the point of a mutiny among commanders and soldiers, or a wholesale refusal to serve in the administered territories – these fears did not materialize. However, most young Israelis loathed service in the territories, but once they received orders to report to reserve service they did their duty, regardless of their political positions. The number of refusers of military service among those called up was minimal.

The serious harm to the IDF should be sought elsewhere.

One central problem, which had never occurred before, was that the IDF was placed at the centre of a fierce public debate. For the first time in the IDF's history politicians on the right claimed that Israel's failure to quell the *intifada* stemmed from an absence of ideological motivation among the IDF's senior command, who were allegedly not sufficiently committed to winning this war. And if that were not enough, the military command was attacked from the other side of the political spectrum as well. Leftist circles kept on saying the necessity of confronting Palestinian women and children led to declining respect for moral restraints and even a loss of humanity among the soldiers.

Indeed, the IDF soldiers were effected by the burden of the tormenting and frustrating confrontations with the Palestinian rioters. The result was a fierce desire to fight back, including the wish to use firearms. In the first stage of the uprising, such feelings were prevalent mainly among soldiers who were in direct contact with the rioters. Most commanders tried to curb such sentiments, but things could not go on like that for long, and many officers, too, began developing similar feelings to their men.

The *intifada* also led to a crisis of trust towards the IDF spokesman and his statements. The clashes and confrontations with the *intifada* rioters forced the IDF spokesman's office to compete with reports from the Palestinian side, or directly from the media, whose representatives gave 'live' reports from the site of the confrontation. The military command-chain's reporting system was slow and could not provide full, detailed and credible information fast enough to compete and respond to the stories and arguments raised by the Palestinians. Even when the spokesman presented an accurate version, his story usually arrived late, after the Palestinians had told their different version.

Did the effort invested in dealing with the *intifada* effect the IDF's overall operational and professional fitness? The immediate negative effects were:

- A substantial portion of the budgetary burden the army had to bear because of the *intifada* was not reimbursed by the state treasury.

- Because of the *intifada* the IDF greatly reduced the training and exercise programs of most of its army formations, who were forced to go on policing missions in the territories.

SUMMARY

It is hard to determine an exact date when the *intifada* ended. Seemingly, it ended precisely in September 1993, at the festive ceremony on the White House lawn, where the Oslo Accords were signed. Actually, the *intifada* began gradually to subside towards the end of 1990, and especially following the Iraqi occupation of Kuwait, the Gulf War, the Madrid international conference and the bilateral talks to achieve a permanent Israeli–Palestinian settlement, which opened in Washington at the end of 1991.

It is also hard to determine one single, special factor that led to that subsiding. Gradually the *intifada* leadership lost the support of the Palestinian public. The *intifada*'s achievements in its first three years exhausted themselves and, perhaps most importantly, a clear feeling emerged that Israel had learned to live with the *intifada*, and that, in the mutual balance, the Palestinians had become the main victims, when they ceased to interest the international media, while domestically, on the Palestinian street, frustration and internal corruption grew.

The main results of the Palestinian *intifada* were:

- Israel did not break. Five years of violent, cruel and exhausting fighting did not break its spirit, nor did they lead to a withdrawal back to the Green Line. The IDF and the General Security Service were caught off guard. But quickly they recovered and deployed to protect every settlement, while providing adequate security for the traffic on the many and long roads in the territories. The winner in this struggle was the Israeli intelligence community (with the emphasis on the GSS and the IDF's intelligence branch) which quickly prepared to operate under the new conditions. There was tight co-operation between the intelligence bodies, the operational forces, and the IDF reserve divisions that carried most of the burden of service in the field, with a minute number of soldiers refusing to serve in these frustrating positions.

- The new military deployment was carried out with minimal harm to the IDF's strength on the borders, facing the external threat, and with no harm to Israeli deterrence.

- The big failure of the Palestinian struggle was its inability to stop the Israeli settlement momentum in Judea and Samaria. To the contrary, this reached unprecedented proportions, with the express goal of creating a new reality on the ground that would preclude a territorial compromise.

- Nonetheless, the violent struggle led to an about face in Israeli public opinion. Israelis came to believe it was necessary to separate the Israeli from the Palestinian population, and that there was a need for a political solution based on two states, living alongside each other. In that respect, Israeli public opinion was ahead of the political leadership in Jerusalem.

- The Palestinians' greatest achievement was in placing their cause on the international agenda. If it were not for the *intifada* the international conference in Madrid (October 1991) would not have convened to discuss settlement of the Israeli–Arab conflict, and there would not have been bilateral negotiating teams between Israel and the Palestinians, Jordan, Syria and Lebanon.

- The *intifada* created political momentum, first in the US, and then in the Palestinian National Council, which understood that it had to initiate a political move if it did not want to lose support 'in the field'. Eventually Israel, too, recognized its duty to offer political initiatives to establish dialogue and create a solution to the conflict.

- The *intifada* struggle gave rise to a new generation of young Palestinian leaders. Most were 'graduates' of Israeli jails. They were the ones who carried the burden of the violent struggle, but at the same time were very pragmatic and understood the need for a political compromise.

- And finally, the *intifada* failed to sever the local economy in the administered territories from its nearly complete dependence upon the Israeli market. One dubious result of that Palestinian policy is worth emphasis: the *intifada* closed the Israeli labour market to the Palestinian labourers from the territories. Israeli businesses found alternatives to the Palestinian labourers (about 140,000) they had previously employed. Even when the political-security obstacle was removed, it was impossible to return the number of Palestinian workers employed in Israel to its dimensions from before the *intifada*.

BOOK X

ISRAEL AND
THE FIRST GULF WAR

ISRAEL AND
THE FIRST GULF WAR

Iraq occupies Kuwait

The background to the long-standing conflict around Iraq's refusal to accept Kuwait's separate existence was its claim that Kuwait was part of the former Ottoman province of Basra, and was an integral section of the geographical unit situated to the southwest of the Shatt al-Arab River – Iraq's natural access route to the Persian Gulf. In 1990, however, historical argument was more a pretext to justify action than a concrete motive for it.

Iraq's war with Kuwait began on 2 August 1990. The military campaign was easy, speedy and successful. Within seven hours, Iraq's 100,000 soldiers, most of them belonging to the elite Republican Guard force, overran Kuwait and subdued its much smaller inexperienced army of some 20,000 men. Iraqi policy aimed at achieving a single goal after the conquest: the quick annexation of Kuwait. On 8 August, Iraq formally announced a 'merger' with Kuwait.

The US led the global political alliance to isolate Iraq politically, economically, and militarily in order to force it to withdraw. Last-moment efforts were made to stop the wheels of war from rolling on 6 January 1991 when French President François Mitterand proposed a UN Security Council resolution linking an Iraqi pullout to the Arab–Israeli conflict. This was opposed by the US, and on 9 January James Baker met with Iraq's deputy prime minister, Tariq Aziz, in Geneva, with a personal message from President Bush to the Iraqi president: make an immediate and unconditional withdrawal from Kuwait or face terrible consequences. UN Secretary-General Javier Perez de Cuellar's final appeal to Baghdad 'to turn the course of events away from catastrophe' was simply ignored.

The Gulf War

The air campaign, begun on the night of 16–17 January, was the coalition's principal military vehicle for the first 38 days of the operation. During the final four days, air power operated closely with fast-moving ground forces. Strategic bombing was directed at 12 sets of targets in Iraq and Kuwait, ranging from leadership command facilities to military storage sites. The first few days of the air offensive sufficed to establish the superiority of precision-guided munitions over ordinary iron bombs for surgical strikes. This also helped to reduce the extent of collateral damage and civilian casualties in attacks on strategic targets situated in populated areas.

It was Washington's understanding that its ability to lead the military coalition against Iraq – a coalition in which several Arab countries played a major role – depended in large measure on scrupulously keeping Israel out of the war. Indeed, Baghdad, too, understood this, and for this very reason made a particular effort to drag Israel into active involvement in the war.

A major component of Saddam Hussein's strategy was launching Improved Scud missiles with conventional warheads at Israeli population centres. Iraq presumably never considered the possibility that the Israeli government would refrain from responding. On the other hand, though it possessed missiles with chemical warheads, Iraq did not launch them. It is here that we saw Israeli deterrence at work, and sense the Iraqi fear of unrestricted Israeli retaliation.

Saddam Hussein adopted this strategy with the expectation of achieving three goals. First, of course, was the Iraqi desire to settle its account with Israel for the destruction of the Osirak nuclear reactor near Baghdad and to inflict painful casualties and damage. Second, he hoped that Israeli retaliation would transform the war against Iraq into an Israeli–Arab war, which would force the Arab states to withdraw from the coalition under pressure of Arab public opinion. The war would then be seen as a Western assault on the Arabs as a whole, which would deny the legitimacy of the US to pursue it any further. Iraq justified its missile attacks by alleging that Israeli planes had participated in the bombing of Iraq, and more importantly by charging that the entire war was the result of a Zionist conspiracy against Iraq. Israel's decision not to retaliate, however, foiled Saddam's calculation. Although Iraq had the technical capacity, Saddam refrained from attacking Israel with chemical weapons, presumably fearing a nuclear counterstrike by Israel.

Saddam Hussein's third goal in attacking Israeli cities was to earn the admiration of the Arab world as the first Arab leader to inflict a heavy blow on Israel and expose its weakness, thereby restoring Iraqi morale and that of its supporters in the face of Allied superiority. Judging from popular reactions in various Arab states, this goal was largely achieved. Iraqi propaganda continuously reiterated that the missile attacks had broken a psychological barrier for the Arabs, and that the countdown had begun for the demise of the so-called State of Israel.

Some senior Israeli officers demanded taking military action against Iraq. Many of them felt Israel to be unacceptably exposed to attack by both conventional and non-conventional weapons, and considered that the country ought to respond militarily in order to maintain its deterrent capacity. However, since the army was, as always, controlled entirely by the civilian political echelon, its controversies with the government on this issue were not permitted to be made public.

The al-Hussein (Improved Scud) missiles launched from western Iraq against densely populated targets in Israel were designed to provoke Israel and drag it into the war. As noted already, the provocation failed, though the damage caused by missile attacks was heavy. There were 17 missile attacks between 18 January and 25 February 1991. Altogether, 39 missiles were launched. Most hit populated areas and caused damage; others fell wide and caused no damage.

Baghdad was not the only party to be surprised at Israel's restraint. It was a course of action very different from that implied by the deterrent image Israel had been projecting toward the Arab world in general and Iraq in particular, from the very first Iraqi threat 'to burn half of Israel'. Restraint resulted from a combination of several reasons and considerations, probably the most important among them having to do with bilateral US–Israel relations.

One should begin with luck. Thousands of Israeli houses and apartments were destroyed or damaged but only two persons were killed, though some 300 were wounded. The extremely low number of fatal casualties played an important role in facilitating Jerusalem's restraint and in explaining the lack of Israeli public pressure for a military response. Second, the IDF had plans to attack the missiles and the launchers but it was difficult to guarantee complete destruction of every single missile and launcher. This no doubt increased Israeli hesitation about undertaking military action which might still be followed by further Iraqi missile attacks.

But the most complex considerations stemmed from Israel's manifold relations with the US administration. From the very first days of US–Israeli agreement on strategic co-operation, Washington had made it very clear that Israel had no role to play in any inter-Arab conflict. In this particular case, whereby a US confrontation with Saddam Hussein became the focus of American national effort, when success or defeat were almost totally dependent on the ongoing political support of some pivotal Arab states, the possibility of an independent Israeli military operation against Iraq came to be seen as a threat liable to undermine the American position.

The Gulf War was the first military confrontation since 1949 that involved Israel's civilian population in hostilities directly, with part of the population actually on the front line bearing the brunt of the enemy's attack. One manifestation of changed perception in Israeli society during the war related to the issue of patriotism. During most of Israel's previous wars, the criterion for measuring patriotism was military service or some form of volunteerism in the war effort. During the Gulf War, however, the criterion became co-operation in taking the necessary survival measures, a passive acceptance of whatever fate might bring, and a willingness to stay put in the face of missile attacks.

Once the Gulf War ended, Israeli society returned to normal. State control of the broadcasting stations was reduced, the economy resumed its regular activity, and most of the population resumed its former life-style. It became apparent that the democratic system had not been put to any grave test, and that, at least on the surface, the government had demonstrated reasonable efficiency in dealing with a crisis situation of major proportions.

Military lessons for Israel

The invaluable experience gained by Israel in the course of the Gulf crisis and war pointed to the need to introduce profound changes in at least three different dimensions of the defence of Israel's heartland.

As anticipated by many, much confusion, lack of co-ordination and rivalry among the various authorities operating in the rear, surfaced during the war. A uniform command structure in charge of all government emergency functions in this area became absolutely necessary. Indeed, in June 1991, the Israeli Ministry of Defence decided to establish a new military command – the Rear Command – to oversee all relevant IDF activities as well as co-operate with the various civilian agencies in Israel's rear. The Rear Command is for the time being an integral part of the IDF. There were, and there still are, serious arguments against this organizational solution – the alternative would have been the establishment of a civilian command to co-ordinate all civilian agencies and their work with the IDF. One of the major changes, introduced by the new command, was a qualitative improvement of the various resources in the civil defence organization, in terms of manpower, equipment and infrastructure.

Defence against ballistic missiles was also improved. Although only a few Iraqi missiles hit Israeli population centres, they inflicted casualties, caused extensive psychological and property damage, and virtually paralyzed segments of the Israeli economy for several weeks. The point of departure for any effective response against ballistic missiles is early warning. As was repeatedly demonstrated in the course of the Gulf War, the increment of even a few minutes of early-warning time proved invaluable for purposes of alerting the general public and activating defence units. At the outset of the war, Israel enjoyed on average a warning time of roughly one and a half minutes. This was later increased to about five minutes. All of the warnings were based on detection of missile launches by the US DSP (Defence Support Program) satellites.

The Gulf War demonstrated that the existing air-defence systems (principally the Patriot PAC-2) were ill-equipped to deal effectively with the ballistic missiles already present in the Middle East theatre. The possibility that in any future war Israel might be threatened with ballistic missiles carrying non-conventional warheads, led to the decision to develop the Chetz (Hebrew for 'arrow') anti-ballistic missile. The US promised to share the development costs, and indeed, by the end of some nine years of work, Israel has today the only proven and effective anti-ballistic system.

Twelve years later, during the Second Gulf War, Israel did not face any Iraqi threat. It had, however, been well prepared for such a contingency.

Political developments

The background, nature and outcome of the Gulf War opened a 'window of opportunity' for political negotiations between Israel and its Arab neighbours. Three factors contributed to this situation.

First and foremost was the success of the United States in forming an international coalition and obtaining UN approval for its strategy of liberating Kuwait, and especially its overwhelming military victory in Iraq.

A second factor was the change in attitudes within the Arab states themselves. The war, with its purpose of freeing one Arab country from occupation by another, divided the Arab world and damaged its former cohesion, with consequences reaching beyond the war itself. This created a ripe opportunity for political initiatives.

The third factor, which was unrelated to the Gulf War but was in many ways the most important of the three, was the collapse and break-up of the Soviet Union. Almost overnight, 50 years of cold war and conflict between the West and Soviet blocs came to an end – and with them disappeared the chief obstacle which had for years stood in the way of any new initiative.

American President George Bush, Sr., and especially Secretary of State James Baker, decided not to let this opportunity slip by. After securing the agreement of all the states concerned, on 30 October 1991 they convened an international summit in Madrid to seek a political agreement in the Middle East. This meeting was attended by the heads of the region's governments and was co-sponsored by the USA and the Soviet Union. The Israeli delegation was headed by Prime Minister Yitzhak Shamir.

This summit produced decisions in two fields.

The first aim was to open bilateral negotiations in Washington between Israel and Syria, Lebanon, and a joint Jordanian–Palestinian delegation. The Palestinian delegation was headed by representatives of the local population of Gaza and the West Bank, as Israel's condition was that the Palestinians should not be represented by the Tunis-based PLO. But it soon became clear that the Jordanian and Palestinian representatives had little in common, so that the joint delegation was split up and Israel began bilateral talks with two separate groups, Jordanian and Palestinian. It also became apparent from the start that the Palestinian representatives were co-ordinating their every move with the PLO in Tunis and its chairman Yasser Arafat. Thus, Israel's demand that the PLO be kept out of the talks proved to be all but meaningless.

The second consequence of the Madrid summit was the creation (at another international conference in Moscow, on 29 January 1992) of five multi-lateral working groups, each chaired by a neutral country not involved in the conflict. These working groups were intended to provide a forum where the states of the region could discuss matters of importance to all of them. The five groups were:

- The Working Group on Economic Development,
- The Working Group on Arms Control and Security,
- The Working Group on Water,
- The Working Group on Refugees,
- The Working Group on the Environment,

The chairs of these working groups carried out their roles with energy and initiative, but in the absence of real cooperation on the part of the Middle Eastern states, the groups' activities soon died down.

BOOK XI

THE OSLO PROCESS

THE OSLO PROCESS

Following the first Gulf War in 1991, the US initiated the Madrid International Conference, chaired by the US together with the Soviet Union, in an attempt to solve the Arab-Israeli conflict. Among its resolutions was a decision to open bilateral negotiations between Israel and Syria; Israel and Lebanon; Israel and Jordan and Israel and the Palestinians. These negotiations were held in Washington.

The Palestinian delegation was based exclusively on local Arab dignitaries that were representing the local population in the West Bank and the Gaza Strip. The head of the Palestinian delegation was Dr. Haydar Abdel Shafi from Gaza. Israel opposed the inclusion of the PLO in these negotiations, but it was an open secret that the Palestinian delegates followed the advice and instructions of the PLO leadership in Tunis.

But the breakthrough came through other, secret, talks, which two Israeli academics conducted with authorized PLO representatives in Oslo in 1993. They reported their contacts to Israeli deputy foreign minister Yossi Beilin and received guidance from him. At a later stage, Foreign Minister Shimon Peres and Prime Minister Yitzhak Rabin also became involved, and Foreign Ministry director-general Uri Savir was appointed to head the Israeli delegation to the talks. These contacts culminated in a bilateral agreement known as the Oslo Declaration of Principles (DOP), achieved in August 1993. This declaration was signed three weeks later at a solemn ceremony at the White House, where, for the first time, Israeli Prime Minister Rabin shook hands with PLO Chairman Yasser Arafat.

The Oslo DOP put an end to the farce of the Washington negotiations, and three of the participants – Rabin, Peres and Arafat – received the Nobel Peace Prize. The agreement dramatically changed Israel's status in the Middle East. It enabled Israel to sign a peace treaty with the second of its Arab neighbours, Jordan (on 26 October 1994), and to inaugurate contacts in various fields with countries in North Africa and the Persian Gulf.

The first stage of the new Israeli–Palestinian relationship saw the withdrawal of IDF forces from the Gaza Strip and Jericho (May 1994), the arrival of the PLO leadership in Gaza, and the formation of the Palestinian National Authority. Later, in January 1996, general elections were held for the presidency of the Palestinian Authority and for the 88-member Palestinian Legislative Council. Concurrently, the IDF pulled out of six of the main Palestinian cities in the West Bank: Bethlehem, Ramallah, Nablus, Jenin, Tulkarem, and Qalqiliya. The withdrawal from the seventh city, Hebron, was postponed until bypasses could be constructed and other arrangements made to resolve the complex problem of coexistence between the Jews in the area (the settlers of nearby Kiryat-Arba and the small Jewish population of Hebron itself) and the city's Arab residents.

In the administered territories, the initial response to the Oslo accords was a wave of optimism; the first few days following the Washington ceremony saw Palestinians handing flowers to IDF soldiers. But the euphoria was short-lived. Palestinian breaches of the agreement became more and more numerous: increasing the number of 'police' beyond what had been agreed, smuggling weapons and terrorist equipment, and sheltering wanted terrorists in Palestinian Authority territory. Violent incidents also occurred, but the real turning point came on 25 February 1994.

The Hebron massacre

Baruch Goldstein, a medical doctor and a Jewish settler and a member of the extreme right-wing Kach movement, from Kiryat-Arba (near Hebron), opened fire on Moslem worshippers in the Tomb of the Patriarchs (the Ibrahimi Mosque) in Hebron. Twenty-nine Palestinians were killed by Goldstein and numerous others died in the stampede which followed and the riots which ensued. The number of wounded was not known but was large. Goldstein himself was killed by the Arab worshippers when he ran out of ammunition.

In retrospect, the Hebron massacre served as a major catalyst in the escalation of terrorism perpetrated by Palestinian Islamic organizations. Hamas condemned the massacre as an attack on the religion of Islam itself, declaring that it stemmed from the historical hatred of the Jews toward Islam and Moslems. Hamas carried out its threats six weeks later, in Afula and Hadera on 6 and 13 April respectively, by means of suicide bombers who blew themselves up with their victims, killing 13 civilians and wounding dozens of others.

Israeli authorities responded with mass arrests of some 2,500 activists in an attempt to break up the organizational infrastructure of the Islamic movement, which served as Hamas's legal civilian wing, but failed to put an end to the movement's military activities.

The abduction of Nahshon Wachsman

The abduction on 11 October 1994 of an Israeli soldier, Nahshon Wachsman, by Hamas activists – two days after two Islamic militants from Gaza killed two Israelis and injured 13 others in the centre of Jerusalem – raised the tension between the PLO and Israel to new heights. The kidnappers demanded that Israel release 200 prisoners, including Hamas founder Sheikh Ahmed Yasin, in return for Wachsman's life. Israel, misled by circumstantial data, assumed that the soldier was held hostage in Gaza (under PLO control). Consequently, Prime Minister Rabin suspended all negotiations with the PLO and imposed closure on the Gaza Strip, stating that Wachsman's safe return would serve as the ultimate test of the Palestinian Authority's ability to fulfill the obligations it undertook.

Arafat condemned the kidnapping and ordered his security forces to mount an intensive effort to bring about the captive's safe release. He warned Hamas that he would not tolerate the insubordination and indirectly accused Iran of meddling in Palestinian affairs. The Palestinian police carried out widespread searches and arrested some 250 Hamas activists. However, Palestinian Authority officials also contended that the soldier was being held inside administered territory, on the West Bank, and Nabil Sha'th (the Palestinian leader in charge of press relations), for one, argued that Israel shared responsibility for the kidnapping by having refused to release all Palestinian prisoners.

The PLO's assertions on the victim's whereabouts proved correct when the Israeli security service discovered that he was being held in the town of Beit Nabala near Jerusalem. An Israeli rescue attempt resulted in his death, as well as the death of an Israeli officer, along with the three kidnappers. Embarrassed by its false accusations against the PLO, Israel lifted the closure on the Gaza Strip; Rabin, however, insisted that progress in the peace process hinged on the Palestinian Authority's determined action against terrorism from Gaza.

The bombing of a bus in Tel Aviv on 19 October, by a suicidal Hamas activist, which caused the death of 22 and the injury of 42 Israelis, added to the tension between the Palestinian Authority and Israel, although the terrorist came from the Israeli-controlled West Bank and not from the Gaza Strip.

Beit Lid and its aftermath

On 22 January 1995, two Islamic Jihad terrorists from Gaza detonated themselves within minutes of each other at the Beit Lid junction bus stop, near Israel's coastal town of Natanya. The place was full of soldiers returning to their units and 22 Israelis, including civilians, were killed, and 63 wounded.

The attack stunned Israelis who angrily held the Palestinian Authority responsible. In an exceptional partisan statement by a national symbol meant to be above politics. Israeli President Ezer Weizman called on Rabin to suspend the peace talks. While Rabin publicly stated that suspending the talks would be giving the terrorists exactly what they wanted, in effect the negotiations were put on ice and remained there for months to come.

The general feeling in Israel was that Arafat and the Palestinian Authority were not doing enough to prevent terrorism. In a rare televised address to the nation two days after the attack, Rabin called on the public not to be demoralized by the latest act of terror. He warned the terrorists: 'We will keep fighting you... We will chase you down, no border will stop us. We will liquidate you and emerge victorious.' To his Israeli countrymen, Rabin declared: 'Don't be tempted by moments of weakness... We are a strong nation. We have an awesome army. We have the ability to attain our goals, which we define as peace, security, construction and development.' By remaining strong, Israel would 'fulfill the Jewish dream of returning to Zion.'

The most important element in his speech was, however, Rabin's statement that the goal of the peace process was territorial separation of Israelis and Palestinians, which, he said, would make Israelis safer. He voiced, however, support for the peace process, and in a veiled attack on Weizman said, 'we will stick to the path of peace. There is no other alternative. We will attain peace because, despite terror and even though it is difficult now, it is the long term solution... This will bring an end to one nation controlling another.'

On 9 April, there were two suicide attacks against Israeli targets in the Gaza Strip. Seven soldiers and one civilian were killed, and 45 were wounded. On 24 July, six more persons were killed and 32 wounded in a suicide bus bombing in Ramat Gan, adjacent to Tel Aviv. Finally, on 21 August, yet another suicide bomb went off in a bus in Jerusalem, killing four and wounding 106. With every attack, domestic support for the Rabin government weakened and political negotiations were further delayed.

How far this process had gone was shown most clearly on 4 November 1995 when Prime Minister Yitzhak Rabin was assassinated by a young Israeli right-wing zealot in Tel Aviv. Foreign Minister Shimon Peres was elected to replace Rabin.

A new spell of violence

On 1 February 1996 Peres announced early elections, on 29 May 1996. Two weeks after Peres's announcement, however, a nine-day spell of bloody terror shattered Labour's sense of an easy victory and, in retrospect, proved to be the point at which the tide in Israeli public opinion turned in Benyamin Netanyahu's favour.

Fears of suicide bombings had increased after the early killing of Yahya Ayyash, the Hamas suicide bomb mastermind, nicknamed 'the engineer', who was blown up when he answered a call on his booby-trapped cellular phone in his Gaza hideout. Fearing revenge attacks by Islamic militants, Israel imposed stringent security measures, including a tight closure on the West Bank and Gaza Strip.

There were no immediate large-scale attacks by the Islamic fundamentalists, but several weeks later, early on the morning of 25 February, a six-month hiatus in suicide attacks against civilian targets inside Israel was shattered when a bomber detonated himself on a Jerusalem bus, killing 24 people and wounding more than 70. Almost simultaneously, another Palestinian blew himself up at an army pick-up point in Ashkelon, killing another Israeli and injuring dozens. A week later, another bomber attack, again on a Jerusalem bus, killed 19 and wounded

10. The very next day, another bomber blew himself up in Tel Aviv, outside a busy mall; 14 people died in the blast and over 100 were injured.

These bomb blasts highlighted Israel's growing dependence on Arafat for its security. Having pulled out of all major West Bank towns – barring Hebron – by late December 1995 and handed them over to Palestinian control, Israel's intelligence was badly damaged as the network of collaborators it had assembled over the years disintegrated. Prime Minister Peres told the Israeli people that the peace process would not be defeated by terror. But, if necessary, he warned, Israeli soldiers would penetrate areas under Arafat's control, if the Palestinian leader did not crush Hamas's terrorist infrastructure.

Only after the second Jerusalem bombing and the Tel Aviv attack the following day, did Arafat move against the fundamentalists. He realized that they posed a threat not only to the peace process but ultimately to him as well. Thus he decided to act – he outlawed Hamas's military wing, Izz al-Din al-Qassam, and began a roundup of other Hamas and Islamic Jihad activists.

The prime minister's warning and Arafat's actions seemed to put an end to the terrorist threats. Only they came too late to have the effect their authors wanted. On 29 May 1996 Benyamin Netanyahu won the Israeli election.

The tunnel incident

In a surprise move on the night of 23–24 September, Israeli workers completed the excavation of an archaeological tunnel that ran alongside the foundations of the external walls of the Temple Mount and installed a gate at the opening of the Via Dolorosa in the Old City of Jerusalem. Israeli officials claimed that the purpose of the move was to facilitate tourism, but from the moment the news broke, it became clear that the government had taken this controversial step to demonstrate Israel's sovereignty in Jerusalem. Israel had frequently been accused by Moslem fundamentalist groups of planning to demolish the El-Aqsa Mosque by weakening its foundations as a result of archeological excavations, and opening the tunnel did provide the proof, however false. The act ignited opposition in the administered territories and resulted in violent confrontations between the IDF and the Palestinian security forces with fatalities on both sides.

Prior to this incident, referred to by the Palestinians as the 'El-Aqsa Battle', tension in the territories had been mounting due to frustration and uncertainty over the fate of the peace process. Palestinian expectations for a rapid deployment of their forces in Hebron and the release of prisoners did not materialize, and it was against this background that the Palestinians reacted violently to the opening of the tunnel. Riots and clashes between demonstrators and Israeli security forces broke out in East Jerusalem, Ramallah and Bethlehem, rapidly deteriorating into fully-fledged shooting incidents between Israeli soldiers and Palestinian

Authority security forces. The Palestinians depicted the riots as a spontaneous reaction by the masses to Israeli aggression against the El-Aqsa Mosque and accused Israel of deliberately shooting at civilians.

A general strike was called by the Palestinian Authority on 25 September. The next day, Israel closed the territories and imposed a curfew in several West Bank towns. Clashes nevertheless erupted and spread in the Gaza Strip, where protesters invaded two Jewish settlements and attacked IDF outposts. Bloody incidents occurred in Nablus, where demonstrators attacked a Jewish religious school located in the Tomb of Joseph. Six Israeli soldiers, trapped at the site, were killed. As the riots spread, the IDF was obliged to use helicopters and snipers and, for the first time since 1967, tanks were stationed near the Palestinian cities to deter further escalation.

By 27 September the rioting had begun to subside but the toll during the three days of bloody confrontations was 84 Palestinians and 15 Israeli soldiers killed.

According to the Oslo accords Israel had agreed to withdraw its forces and its military government from all major Palestinian cities in the West Bank. By the end of January 1996, Israel had indeed completed its withdrawal from all cities but one. Because of the need to build a by-pass road from Jerusalem to the Jewish parts of Hebron, the withdrawal had been postponed until April 1996.

Following the very painful Palestinian Terrorist acts in February–March 1996, Prime Minister Peres decided not to withdraw from Hebron and to see first how the Palestinian Authority dealt with this spell of terrorism. Three months later Shimon Peres lost the Israeli general elections to Benyamin Netanyahu. Upon coming to power, the new Prime minister delayed the withdrawal from Hebron further.

Netanyahu and Arafat met on 24 December 1996 and completed a draft implementation agreement on 2 January 1997. The Hebron agreement was signed that month.

For Israelis and Palestinians alike, the Hebron agreement was significant, for it contained dual, though unequal, obligations. Of particular significance was that it marked the first agreement between a Likud government and the Palestinians and even more significantly the Hebron agreement indicated the Likud's willingness to divide or partition the West Bank. The concept of territorial compromise had originated after the 1967 war from within the Israeli Labour Party; but until this point it had been abhorrent to Israel's right wing, previous Likud prime ministers, and the settlement community.

Netanyahu served only three years as prime minister. Young and inexperienced, he did not manage to handle his very unstable political coalition and when he lost Knesset support he had to call for new elections for prime minister (held in May 1999).

His successor, Ehud Barak, did not do any better. From the very first days of his term he alienated his political partners as well as the leadership of his own Labour party. His big political gamble was based on the hope of bringing a settlement of the Israeli-Palestinian conflict to the Israeli public. Barak had hoped that President Clinton would convince Palestinian Chairman Arafat to accept a very positive political compromise during the Camp David summit. Coming back from the summit with Arafat's negative response, Barak lost his last hope for political support, and he was forced to call for new Prime Ministerial elections after less than two years in office. He was defeated by Likud leader Ariel Sharon in February 2001.

In the election campaign preceding his victory in 1999, Barak had set definite political goals. He promised immediate negotiations on both fronts – with Syria and the Palestinians – and undertook to bring the IDF out of South Lebanon within a year, whether by agreement with Syria or unilaterally. Once elected, he acted resolutely to fulfill this promise. The talks with Damascus soon reached a dead end, and Barak was obliged to stand by his word and order a unilateral withdrawal from Lebanon.

The failure of the Syrian talks led Barak to focus on negotiations with the Palestinians. He saw no point in following the framework of the Oslo accords (in which Israel was to carry out two further redeployments from West Bank areas), and preferred to proceed directly to a final agreement. Barak reasoned that if such an agreement could be reached, Israel would withdraw to the determined border anyway while, if a final agreement was impossible, it was senseless to give the Palestinians more land in the meantime. But Yasser Arafat, who like Barak had grave doubts about the likelihood of reaching a final agreement, insisted that those promises Israel had already made should be fulfilled in their entirety.

At a summit meeting held on Barak's initiative in July 2000 at Camp David, the peace process foundered. The gap between the two parties' positions proved too wide to be bridged. A little over two months later, following a visit by Ariel Sharon to the Temple Mount, the second or El-Aqsa *intifada* began.

SUMMARY

The Oslo accords marked a new era in Israeli–Palestinian relations, opening discussions toward a permanent bilateral agreement. This process broke down, but its momentum could not be stopped. When, in July 2000, the two sides found themselves at a crossroads, there was no turning back. Israel and the Palestinians faced the choice of seeking an agreement or enduring a crisis which could not be resolved except by violent confrontation.

In the first years of the talks, Israel had adhered to the clear principle that terrorism would not be allowed to derail the peace process. The Israeli formula was, 'We will fight terrorism as if there were no peace process, and pursue peace as if there were no terrorism'. But this elegant precept could not be upheld in practice. Every painful terrorist attack strengthened those who opposed the talks and dealt another blow to the mutual trust that was so vital to their success.

In the first three years following the Oslo accords, terrorist attacks continued in parallel with political negotiations, while Israel stood by its formula. But the wave of brutal attacks in early March 1996 put an end to this policy. Both Israelis and Palestinians now realized that terrorism and peace talks were incompatible. If the process was to go on, there must be relative calm. But this realization came too late. The attacks cost Shimon Peres the elections, and the government of his successor, Benyamin Netanyahu, was opposed to the Oslo process. Although four more years would pass before the outbreak of the second *intifada*, the fate of the peace process was sealed then, in March 1996. The Camp David summit of July 2000 made it finally clear that Israel and the Palestinians could not reach a compromise. The Palestinian Authority then took a decision: what it had been unable to achieve through political means, it would achieve through violent struggle.

The IDF withdrawal from south Lebanon probably played an important role in encouraging the Palestinians to resume hostilities. They hoped and assumed that Israeli society, which had refused to sustain continued IDF casualties in south Lebanon and obliged its government to withdraw, would do the same for them in their struggle to drive Israel out of the administered territories.

Thus began the bloody struggle which became known as the El-Aqsa *intifada*.

BOOK XI

THE EL-AQSA INTIFADA

THE EL-AQSA INTIFADA

Background

In his successful campaign in the Israeli election in 1999, Ehud Barak had set definite political goals. He promised immediate negotiations on both fronts, with Syria and the Palestinians. Once elected, he acted resolutely to achieve a political agreement with Damascus. But these talks soon reached a dead end, and Barak was obliged to fulfill his campaign promise and order a unilateral withdrawal from Lebanon.

The Camp David summit of July 2000 finally made it clear that Israel and the Palestinians could not reach a compromise. The Palestinian Authority then made a decision: what it had been unable to achieve through political means, it would achieve through violent struggle. They hoped and assumed that Israeli society, which had refused to sustain continued IDF casualties in south Lebanon and obliged its government to withdraw, would do the same for them in their struggle to drive Israel entirely out of the administered territories.

After the abortive Camp David Summit, Palestinians began to debate the merits of resorting to violent confrontation. In July, a Jerusalem-based reporter described Fatah's mood in these words: 'Certain Fatah leaders air the view that a clash is required for the world to intervene in favour of the weaker side and force the Israelis to address rights the Palestinians have been unable to persuade them to address through negotiations.' In a late July 2000 poll, 57 per cent of Palestinians thought that a violent confrontation would win them political gains, and 63 per cent thought that Hizballah's resistance methods should be emulated if an agreement were not reached in the coming months. Hearts and minds were being prepared for an uprising, with the goal of reshuffling the political deck.

On 28 September, Likud leader Ariel Sharon visited the Temple Mount (al-Haram al-Sharif) in Jerusalem. The next day, Palestinians rioted, and Israeli police killed five in an attempt to control them. Over the following days, thousands of young Palestinians, backed up by armed members of Fatah's Tanzim organization and Palestinian police officers, marched to Israeli checkpoints in search of confrontation. The Palestinian Authority worked to transform sporadic riots into a sustained uprising, which the Palestinian media immediately dubbed the El-Aqsa *intifada*.

Characteristics of the El-Aqsa *intifada*

There is a natural tendency to equate the first and second *intifadas*. Their basic quality is, of course, the same: a Palestinian uprising intended to drive Israel out of Gaza and the West Bank by force. The two conflicts took place in the same geographic area and involved the same two sides but the similarities end there. In all other aspects, the second, El-Aqsa *intifada*, has been very different from the first.

The El-Aqsa *intifada* broke out when the Oslo process was at an advanced stage. This had two significant consequences. First, there now existed an elected and recognized Palestinian leadership in the administered territories (the Palestinian Authority), which prepared, initiated and directed the armed conflict; and second, Israel had transferred control of 98 per cent of the Palestinian population to the Palestinian Authority, including the entire Gaza Strip and major parts of the West Bank (In its implementation of the Oslo agreement Israel had withdrawn its forces and its military administration from all major Palestinian cities in the West Bank where the PA took over responsibility for both security and civilian affairs. Israel also withdrew from other parts of the West Bank but retain responsibility for security there.) Hence the goal of the Palestinians' violent struggle was not to free themselves from occupation, but to strengthen their position in the political negotiations with Israel.

Because of the basic fact that the Palestinian population was no longer under Israeli rule, the El-Aqsa *intifada* lacked the usual characteristics of a popular uprising. There were almost no mass demonstrations or stone-throwing. Almost from the first, this *intifada* was a war, using firearms and explosive charges. Two striking aspects were the large quantities of weapons available to the Palestinian militants (of much higher quality than before) and the inexhaustible supply of explosives. In spite of its efforts Israel did not succeed in prevent smuggling from Sinai to the Rafah area of the Gaza Strip even though more than 100 tunnels were uncovered, some of them 300 feet deep.

Although the struggle was broadly directed by Palestinian Authority Chairman Yasser Arafat and his associates, the actual operations were carried out by members of the Palestinian security forces and of the many other organizations that had formed in the territories. Attacks were planned and prepared without co-ordination or centralized control, and the relation of individual terrorists to their nominal groups was often vague to the point of being arbitrary.

In contrast to the first *intifada*, this time the attacks targeted innocent Israeli civilians, and made no distinction between the administered territories and Israel proper. The Palestinians used their ultimate weapon – suicide bombers – to strike against Israeli population centres.

The Gaza Strip enjoyed almost complete independence, as well as free communications with the Egyptian border through the Rafah region in the south. This made possible the establishment of a Palestinian military industry, which specialized in manufacturing mortars and mortar bombs, as well as Qassam rockets of various diameters. Also, large quantities of weaponry, especially standard explosives, were smuggled into Gaza from the Sinai region. As the conflict developed, Gaza terrorists began to use locally made high-trajectory weapons, to compensate for the difficulty of penetrating Israeli settlements or infiltrating into Israel itself. In total, about 1,500 mortar bombs and 150 Qassam rockets were fired prior to the cease-fire of June 2003. It has to be said, however, that their main achievement was psychological (only one Israeli was killed by these mortar bombs and rockets).

A final point was the central role of Iran in supporting terrorism. Iranian involvement in terrorism has included logistical aid, funding, training, and various other activities. The Islamic Jihad has been almost completely Iranian-controlled since 1994. Hamas, though maintaining its independence, has also enjoyed generous support. Another aspect of Iranian involvement has been the recruitment of Israeli Arabs for terrorist activities, both directly and through the Lebanese Hizballah.

Stages of the conflict

In the first year of the *intifada*, Israel was reluctant to carry out military operations in A areas and even in B areas, for reasons of both internal and international politics. When IDF forces did enter these areas on limited missions, Israel immediately declared that it would withdraw as soon as the task was complete. This situation changed after the 11 September 2001 attacks on the United States, and especially after Israeli casualties reached intolerable levels (135 Israelis were killed in March 2002 alone).

In the new context of the international war against terrorism, the Palestinian struggle was seen as a terrorist campaign to be condemned and fought against by every possible means. Thus, Israel was given the go-ahead to carry out military reprisals in Palestinian territories.

The Passover Eve suicide bombing at Natanya's Park Hotel, on 27 March 2002, stunned Israeli public opinion and caused Israel to launch a military operation, Operation 'Defensive Shield', against the Palestinian cities of the northern West Bank. This operation began the following day and continued for 18 days, until the IDF withdrawal of 14 April.

When it became evident that the Palestinians saw the operation as an exceptional one-time measure, and terrorist attacks did not significantly decrease, the IDF launched Operation 'Determined Path', reasserting complete freedom of action in all Palestinian territories, with no political restrictions.

Israel regarded Chairman Arafat as being chiefly to blame for the failure of the peace talks, and considered him the leader and director of the *intifada*. However, Israeli policy-makers were sharply divided as to how to act about Arafat: whether he should be banished from the Palestinian territories or physically eliminated. The compromise adopted was to make him a kind of prisoner in the Muqata, the Palestinian Authority government building in Ramallah. Like any compromise, it was a bad decision: the captive Arafat continued to pull political and military strings, and his extreme political views were further inflamed by a sense of indignation and deep humiliation. Moreover, Palestinian public opinion remained in his favour, resenting Israel's affront to the symbol of their national liberation movement.

In the first stage, when Israel was still reluctant to act freely in Palestinian territories, its response to major terrorist attacks was to strike against Palestinian Authority government and security facilities, mainly from the air. But this policy was soon abandoned. Although the targets selected were vacant ones, to avoid harming innocent Palestinians, the images that appeared in the international media were unfavourable.

The new policy was one of specific preventative missions, both against terrorists themselves and against key figures responsible for planning and organizing attacks. This prevention policy owed its success to the intelligence agencies, which kept close, detailed track of the terrorists' preparations. There was remarkably close co-operation between intelligence and operational forces, which translated into effective, real-time prevention missions: Israeli security forces entered Palestinian areas to carry out pre-planned arrests; intelligence alerts enabled immediate blockage of terrorists' expected entrance routes; terrorists were targeted in precise aerial attacks (mainly by helicopter gunships). These measures were carried out with minimal harm to innocent Palestinian civilians.

Aerial attacks ceased after Operation Defensive Shield. Israel preferred to use ground forces to arrest terrorists, who could then be interrogated and provide invaluable intelligence information.

The debate over the security fence

The diametric contrast in the nature of terrorist operations between the Gaza Strip and the West Bank is noteworthy. When the IDF left Gaza in 1994, it built a security fence surrounding the Gaza Strip, which has proved a complete success. In the three years of the conflict from 2000, terrorists failed to penetrate into Israel from Gaza. Thus, Palestinian attacks in Gaza were aimed almost exclusively at IDF forces and Israeli settlements inside the fence. A defensive need arose to prevent terrorists from approaching Israeli settlements and IDF outposts. For this purpose, lookout zones were created by removing Palestinian buildings and orchards, to allow defensive forces an optimal field of vision. All in all, the Gaza Strip saw more than 50 per cent of the total Palestinian attacks (9,600) during the three years of the *intifada*, with only 10 per cent of the Israeli casualties.

In contrast to Gaza, terrorists from the West Bank succeeded in penetrating Israeli city centres with astonishing ease. As a result, several political and popular movements called for a similar security fence to be built around the West Bank. A vigorous public debate ensued, as various Israeli groups opposed such a fence for different reasons. Right-wing groups, especially among the settlers, saw the proposed fence as a precedent for dividing the West Bank between Israel and the Palestinians, a step they fiercely opposed. Left-wing groups, which had at first supported the building of a fence, objected to its planned path, which would place most of the Israeli West Bank settlements west of the fence. This, they argued, would establish a geopolitical fact which would make a future

Israeli–Palestinian agreement impossible. They also opposed the way the fence would be constructed wholly at the expense of Palestinian land, causing severe problems for those Palestinians who would become enclosed within fenced enclaves.

As for the Palestinians, they opposed the fence for much the same reasons as the Israeli left, as well as from fear that the fence would become a closed border, completely separating the two communities and making all human and economic contact impossible.

As long as no continuous fence surrounds the West Bank, penetration from the West Bank is extremely easy. Israelis are under the continuous threat of suicide bomber attacks. The chief problem in dealing with this danger is the impossibility of deterring youths who are motivated by religious fanaticism. Israel has found itself obliged to create a large corps of tens of thousands of security guards to protect the entrance to practically every public building, including educational institutions, restaurants, cinemas, bus stations, and so on. Security guards cannot stop terrorists from striking, but they can prevent them from entering sites and force them to detonate their charges outside. The guards thus risk their own lives to avert an immeasurably higher death toll.

After 1,000 days: a first balance sheet

Between the outbreak of the *intifada* on 29 September 2000, and the Israeli–Palestinian cease-fire signed on 4 June 2003, 820 Israelis were killed and about 4,780 wounded, the great majority of whom were innocent civilians. The total number of Palestinian attacks was over 18,000. Of these, only 0.6 per cent (115) were suicide bomber attacks, but they caused 47 per cent (381) of the total Israeli deaths and 56 per cent (2,677) of the total number of wounded. Palestinian casualties during that same period were some 2,300 killed and some 14,000 wounded.

Israeli casualties dropped dramatically with the start of Operation 'Defensive Shield' in April 2002. Simultaneously, the security forces made impressive achievements in the conflict with the Palestinians. Some 546 terrorists were killed in this period and 2,981 were arrested, of whom 271 were suicide bombers captured before they could carry out their mission.

The following are a few important milestones of the thousand days of the *intifada*:

- The lynching in Ramallah. On 12 October 2000, just two weeks after the opening of the El-Aqsa *intifada*, two non-combatant Israeli reserve soldiers, returning for duty in a military base north of Jerusalem, were stopped at a Palestinian road block near Ramallah. They were brought to the local police station where they were brutally murdered by a local Palestinian mob. One, aged 38, was a father of three, the other, a 35-year-old, was newly wed.

  According to reporters' evidence on the scene, not only did the local Palestinian police not protect the two men slaughtered while in their custody, but they also tried to prevent foreign journalists in the area around the building from filming the incident. Despite these attempts to distance reporters, an Italian television crew managed to film several scenes.

- Suicide bombing at the Dolphinarium Disco. On 1 June 2001, a Palestinian suicide attack in front of a crowded discotheque in Tel Aviv, killed 18 and injured more than 70. Islamic Jihad claimed responsibility for the attack. The suicide bomber joined a line of young people waiting to get into the discotheque at the Dolphinarium Beach, near Tel Aviv's hotel district. The area was crowded at the beginning of the weekend, as young people stayed out late.

- Palestinian gunmen assassinate Minister Ze'evi. Rehav'am Ze'evi (known as 'Gandhi'), Israel's tourism minister and leader of the right-wing National Alliance Party, was shot in the face at point-blank range outside his hotel room in Jerusalem on 17 October 2001. The Popular Front for the Liberation of Palestine, a Marxist-Leninist group which is the second largest faction within the PLO, claimed responsibility. They said they assassinated Ze'evi in revenge for Israel's killing of the group's leader, Abu Ali Mustafa. He had died in a missile attack by an Israeli helicopter gunship on his office in Ramallah, in August 2001.

- Seizing the *Karine A*. On 3 January 2002, the Israeli Navy seized control over the *Karine A*, a small boat that was sailing in international waters, in the Red Sea, on its way to the Suez Canal. The ship was carrying weapons intended for the Palestinian Authority. The boat's cargo included some 50 tons of advanced weaponry, including Katyusha rockets, sniper rifles, mortar shells, anti-tank mines and a variety of anti-tank missiles. From Gaza, the 122mm Katyushas could have threatened Ashkelon and other coastal cities; while from the West Bank, Ben-Gurion International Airport and several major cities would have been within their range. The shipment also included rubber boats and diving equipment, which would have facilitated seaborne attacks from Gaza against Israeli coastal cities.

  Investigation of the crew members revealed that the commanding officer of the boat was Colonel Omar Akawi. The ship had been purchased by the Palestinian Authority and was manned by Palestinian Authority personnel, with the aim of transferring the weapons it carried from Iran to the Palestinian Naval Police near the Gaza beaches.

- Passover suicide bombing in Natanya. On 27 March 2002, 30 people were killed and 140 injured – 20 seriously – in a suicide bombing at the Park Hotel in the coastal city of Natanya, in the midst of the Passover holiday ceremonial *Seder*, with some 250 guests. Hamas claimed responsibility for the attack. The terrorist walked into the dining room of the hotel, in the centre of the city, and detonated an explosive device. The terrorist was identified as a member of the Hamas Izz al-Din al-Qassam brigade, coming from the West Bank city of Tulkarem, which is just some six miles east of Natanya.

- Operation 'Defensive Shield'. The massacre at the Park Hotel could not be left unanswered. After a series of terrorist attacks within Israeli cities that cost 135 civilian lives in one month, Israel launched Operation 'Defensive Shield'. The goal was to dismantle the terrorist infrastructure developed by the Palestinian Authority, or allowed to operate in territory the Palestinian Authority controlled. The operation consisted of moving Israeli forces into Palestinian areas in Judea and Samaria (the West Bank) and the Gaza Strip for the purpose of arresting terrorists, finding and confiscating weapons and destroying workshops for the local manufacture of explosives.

Israeli Prime Minister Ariel Sharon, speaking to the Knesset on 8 April emphasized: 'The orders are clear: target and paralyze anyone who takes up weapons and tries to oppose our troops, resists them or endangers them – and to avoid harming the [innocent] civilian population.'

Among Israel's targets was the terrorist infrastructure in the Jenin refugee camp, the origin of many terrorist attacks against Israel. After days of fierce fighting, the terrorist cells were subdued but not without significant casualties. Palestinians claimed a massacre took place in Jenin, with some 1,000 Palestinians killed, but independent observers found no evidence of anything other than a fierce battle in which the Palestinian terrorists used the civilian population as their shield. The total number of Palestinians killed in Jenin was 55, of which the majority were armed terrorists. IDF casualties in Jenin were 33 soldiers killed.

Operation 'Defensive Shield' marked a new phase in Israeli military measures against Palestinian terrorism. Seven months after the al-Qaeda attack against US targets on 11 September 2001, there was no outside pressure on Israel to withdraw immediately from Palestinian population centres. Indeed, military results were almost immediate – Israeli casualties (an average of 60 killed in January and February 2002, and 135 in March) dropped to an average of 45 in May and June and 21 in July.

Towards the end of the *intifada*?

The El-Aqsa *intifada* has severely damaged the Palestinian economy. The state of war and the Israeli counter-measures – curfews, closures, reduced mobility on West Bank roads – have brought the local economy to an almost complete standstill. Moreover, the security risk has kept Palestinian workers out of Israel, where many had previously earned much higher wages than in the West Bank (where the chances of finding work are scant at any rate). Simultaneously, Israel's actions have brought about the collapse of local government and administration, especially in the West Bank. Ostensibly, Palestinians have a president, a prime minister, a cabinet, and other political and administrative office-holders. But behind these titles, the 'emperor has no clothes'. The majority of Palestinians have tired of the struggle and want a return to relative peace, normalization, and coexistence with Israel. The majority, therefore, does support an end to the *intifada*.

Those who led and directed the struggle, being aware of Palestinian public opinion, now also support a cease fire – not least because of Israel's policy of targeting leaders, which has caused them to fear for their lives as long as the violence continues. This indeed was the main reason for the 'Hoodna' agreement signed (29 June 2003) between the Palestinian Authority leaders and the two major Palestinian organizations (Hamas and Islamic Jihad).

Israelis, too, are showing signs of fatigue, first and foremost because of the high number of casualties during the thousand-day conflict. Israel is at war, its longest and bloodiest war since the War of Independence. Also, it is the first war since 1948 in which the civilian population has sustained most of the damage, and Israel's massive military superiority is of no significance. In the three years up to 2003, Israel also suffered a severe economic crisis which, though not an exclusive result of the *intifada* was indisputably exacerbated by it. In those three years of the *intifada*, the Israeli standard of living dropped by almost 15 per cent and what was of special worry was the fact that this economic crisis took place in an open world, where the option of living abroad was increasingly tempting, especially for the Israeli elite. There is a growing awareness that this crisis cannot be solved until the political situation changes. Another problem, one which was almost unknown during the first *intifada*, was the relatively high number of reserve soldiers who refuse to serve in the administered territories. This form of protest has won considerable sympathy both in Israel and abroad.

An additional threat, with very dangerous long-term consequences, was the increasing number of Israeli Arabs involved in assisting and carrying out terrorist attacks. The first signs of this new phenomenon were perceivable as early as October 2000, when Israeli Arabs echoed the cries of Palestinians to 'save the El-Aqsa mosque'. Violent demonstrations began in the town of Umm Al-Faham and spread to Arab villages in Galilee, and even to the Tel Aviv–Jaffa area. Israeli police intervened to stop the spread of demonstrations, and were forced to open fire. This catastrophic confrontation ended with 13 Israeli Arabs killed and hundreds wounded.

The active involvement of the United States following its decisive victory in Iraq, combined with both sides' willingness to end the fighting, brought about the acceptance of the Quartet's (the USA, Russia, EU and UN) 'road map' (which the Israeli government approved on 23 May 2003) and the signing of the Aqaba cease fire of 4 June 2003.

The first role of the 'road map' was to stop the dangerous escalation of violence, without which there was no chance to renew a political process. Accordingly, Palestinians did commit themselves to put an end to terrorist activities including the destruction of the terrorist infrastructure in Palestinian territories. Israel, on the other hand, committed itself to stop the establishment of new settlements as well as to remove immediately all its unauthorized outposts. Muhammad Abbas (Abu Mazen) had agreed to head a new Palestinian government and to implement all Palestinian commitments according to the 'map', even if he would not always enjoy the support of Chairman Yassir Arafat.

This agreement did not work out.

Neither side implemented its commitments scrupulously. Muhammad Abbas – without Arafat's support – was forced to resign. The 'road map' remained, for the time being, a dead letter.

It did not take long before Israel again became a target for painful suicide-bombings. Israel's response was a series of targeted attacks against Palestinian terrorists getting ready for suicide missions, as well as against the heads of extreme Islamic terrorist organizations.

At the time of writing both sides, as well as other parties in the region were waiting for a new diplomatic initiative.

SUMMARY

The Israeli–Palestinian conflict, known as the second or El-Aqsa *intifada*, falls into two parts. The first stage lasted 18 months, from 29 September 2000 to 27 March 2002. This period was one of constantly growing success for the Palestinians: the number of Israeli casualties steadily rose, and the Palestinian cause enjoyed international support. These achievements were possible not least because of Israel's reluctance to undertake large-scale, continuous military operations in Palestinian territory.

The second stage of this bloody confrontation lasted 14 months, until the cease-fire of 4 June 2003. The turning point was the Passover Eve suicide bombing in March 2002 at the Park Hotel in Natanya. The rising tide of such attacks, all of them prepared in the West Bank, reached its apex in that month, in which 135 Israelis were killed. Israel was left with no choice but to act forcefully inside Palestinian lands, with no political time limit. Israel had in effect received a green light for this decision from the American leadership six months earlier, after the September 11 attacks on the United States. From that day, Palestinian terrorism came to be seen as an inseparable part of international terrorism, to be suppressed by all possible means.

During the 14 months of this second stage, Israel succeeded in compelling the Palestinians to appoint a moderate Prime Minister, Mahmoud Abbas, who openly criticized the continuance of the *intifada*, as well as an Internal Security Minister committed to ending the uprising, Mohammed Dahlan. Israel's success in achieving this goal, despite the fact that it, too, emerged battered and exhausted from the conflict, is due to four main factors.

The first is the fortitude of Israeli society. The Palestinians, misinterpreting the causes for Israel's withdrawal from south Lebanon, had assumed that violent pressure would bring about an instant shift in Israeli public opinion and compel the government to show greater flexibility towards their demands. The opposite occurred: the Israeli public veered strongly to the right. In the Knesset elections of February 2003 right-wing parties received a large majority of the vote, while the two left-wing parties, Labour and Meretz, nearly collapsed. As for the increased number of soldiers who refuse to serve in the administered territories, this phenomenon has not spread, and most Israelis continue to fulfill their military duties with remarkable fidelity.

If there was one field in which the Palestinians expected immediate success, it was settlement construction in the territories. They assumed that the expansion of settlements would stop and that many (if not most) settlers would depart for Israel. Although there were occasional instances of this, on the whole the settlement project continued, and the total number of settlers – in Gaza and especially the West Bank – actually grew during the *intifada*. The massive military deployment both inside settlements and along transport routes meant that not a single settlement (including the smallest and most isolated ones) was abandoned.

The third factor was the Palestinians' great foreign policy failure. Intoxicated by the wide media coverage they enjoyed during the first year of the *intifada*, they believed the international community would intervene in their favour and pressure Israel into accepting their demands. Their mistake was a triple one. They pinned their hopes on the UN and Europe, ignoring the fact that the only international power which could apply pressure on Israel was the United States. They failed to understand that the media, sympathetic as it may be, cannot keep the Palestinian issue in the headlines for very long. Public interest naturally declines with time, and soon ceases to be a source of political pressure. Moreover, the Palestinians' chief weapon – suicide bombings – presents a very unfavourable media image and does not earn sympathy. Their third blunder was not taking into account the dramatic change in international politics that followed September 11.

The fourth and final reason for Israel's success was its security forces. These proved able to meet the new challenge and find operational solutions that significantly reduced terrorist achievements. The impressive contributions of the IDF military intelligence corps and the General Security Service to this success cannot be overlooked. The Israeli public learned almost daily of as many as 50 terrorism alerts, which intelligence agents thoroughly investigated, identifying those involved in the planned attack and when and where it was to take place. Operational forces were then dispatched to intercept the terrorists, either before they set out or on the way to their objectives.

It is, then, easy to understand the Palestinian shift: the change in leadership, the approval of the 'road map', and the cease-fire.

At this writing it is too early to tell how the new situation will develop. The indisputable key to further progress is scrupulous adherence to the stages of the road map. Here US President George W. Bush and his foreign policy team will play a critical role. Without constant pressure on the two sides to progress according to plan, the political process is unlikely to attain its goal. However, neither side has implemented its commitment according to the 'map'. The expected genuine 'cease-fire' was not even seriously tried and political negotiations never started.

It is of no importance which of the two parties was more responsible for the outcome; one should not blame, however, the two parties alone. The US administration also shares the responsibility – it has shown no active involvement or timely intervention in order to salvage the 'map'. America's growing involvement in Iraq and the coming presidential elections are the explanation for these failings. What next? It is quite possible that the two parties and the region will have to wait for the American elections in November 2004 and for a newly-elected President who will be free and willing to get himself involved in Israeli-Palestinian affairs.

CONCLUSION

Since the end of the Second World War, the Middle East, in which some 21 Arab countries and one Jewish state, Israel, achieved their national independence, the area has been torn by war. The central conflict has been that waged between Israel and its Arab neighbours, who were from the outset unwilling to acquiesce in the establishment of a Jewish state in their midst, and who made every effort to annihilate it. Paradoxically enough, however, the majority of the wars that have torn the Middle East apart over the past five decades have been waged between the Arab states themselves. In them, Arab has been pitched against Arab, and Moslem against Moslem. The weapons used originally in the wars in the Middle East were those that had been acquired by the armies existing at the time in the area, and from the vast amount of equipment left in the Middle East by the Allied forces stationed there during the Second World War. Gradually, however, the armies in the region equipped themselves with more modern, advanced weapons, and the degree of sophistication in these armies became more marked.

In 1955, the Soviet Union made its first move after the Second World War to enter the Middle East arena, and in the so-called 'Czech Deal' became the major supplier of modern weapons to Egypt. This move was to be followed by similar developments in other Middle Eastern countries. Gradually, the world superpower rivalry spilled over into the Middle East and came to military expression on the battlefields of the area. As the Arab-Israeli conflict persisted, and as the Arab world itself was torn and racked by revolutions, upheavals and internecine wars, the small armies in the region grew into major military establishments, dwarfing most others in the world with the exception of those of the superpowers. Indeed, apart from the arsenal of the United States of America, the greatest concentration of military hardware and equipment in the modern world is that which exists in the Middle East. In some cases this has brought about major industrial development, particularly in the case of Israel, where the technological sophistication demanded by the use and maintenance of modern weaponry has brought forth a highly advanced industry capable of maintaining, developing and producing these weapons. The human price to pay for this development has been a very costly one indeed. While a refugee problem persists in the area, vast quantities of material resources have been and continue to be squandered on weapons of war. The economic consequence of this development, apart from in those countries enjoying a glut of wealth from oil resources, has been very serious; but the greatest and most damaging of all has been the human cost, from which none of the countries involved in the conflict has escaped.

The Israeli military experience

Israel was born in battle. Its army was forged in the fires of conflict and the continuous struggle for existence that has characterized the State of Israel since its foundation. When the War of Independence ended, it gradually became evident that the new state would be obliged to live by the sword for many years before peace would finally be achieved, but it was clear that Israel would never be able to maintain a large standing army commensurate with the military problems posed by its neighbours. From an economic point of view, such a burden would be crippling. The logical answer was that Israel would have to establish an army of civilians, and that, in effect, the whole nation would have to be an army. Thus one of the most effective reserve systems (based partially on the system obtaining in Switzerland) was created. In periods of quiet, the nation devoted itself to its main objectives – namely, creating a democratic society, absorbing immigrants, developing education and a system of justice, and achieving economic independence. But, in times of crisis and of war, the nation donned uniform, and does so to this day, thus enabling Israel to field in wartime the largest army in the world in relation to the size of the population. The first campaign in which the reserve system was tested in war was the 1956 Campaign. It proved very effective. Indeed, this system has been one of the principal secrets of Israel's military success over the years.

In all her wars, Israel's troops have excelled in their courage, in particular in such classic struggles as the battle of Ammunition Hill between Israeli paratroopers and the Jordanian Arab Legion in East Jerusalem, and the Israeli armoured and infantry assault on what seemed to be impregnable Syrian positions and fortifications on the Golan Heights, during the Six Day War. The standard set by the best of the Israel Defence Forces has always been of the highest. The standards that the Palmach set in the War of Independence were maintained in the Israeli armed forces in their early years of organization by Moshe Dayan when he became Chief of Staff in 1953. 101 Commando Unit, which Mordechai Makleff set up under the command of Major Ariel Sharon and which mounted with great effectiveness the first major reprisal raids by the IDF against the Arab armies, established the fighting standards, and above all the standards of leadership, to which the Israeli Command aspired. Dayan instilled this fighting spirit ruthlessly into the armed forces, and set the paratroop forces, again under the command of Sharon, as the example to be followed by all Israeli fighting units. The success of this policy came to fruition in 1956.

The circumstances of the War of Independence, in which Israel suffered from weakness in manpower and lack of equipment in modern arms and weapons, evolved a military philosophy based on flexibility, surprise and improvisation. Night-fighting, speed, commando-type operations, the strategy of 'indirect approach' – all these became the hallmark of the philosophy evolved by the Israel Defence Forces. Above all, emphasis was laid on the inculcation of a flexibility of thought in the officers in the field, and in particular in the junior leaders, who were trained to be able to adapt themselves in the heat of battle to the inevitable changes that occur, and to avoid a slavish dictation by the book. There thus emerged from the ranks of the underground fighting in the heights and the plains of Galilee, the hills of Judea and the sands of the Negev Desert, an army led by officers who were always at the head of their men.

However, control of a large modern army was learned by a process of trial and error. The Israeli military leadership acquired its experience in battle. Young men trained to command at company and, at most, at battalion level, suddenly found themselves performing the functions of generals handling armies. Initially, therefore, the military leadership was highly inexperienced, and in many cases was not equal to the very heavy task that fate had decreed for it in the field of battle. Many mistakes were made, some of them most tragic.

In the first two wars, the Israelis had a leader of world stature, whose place in history in the ranks of the outstanding leaders in the world is assured. David Ben-Gurion had the necessary foresight, understanding and wisdom to anticipate developments, and to a degree to prepare for them, and he had the ability to rouse the nation to an impressive degree of self-sacrifice. In 1948–49, Ben-Gurion led the Jewish population of Palestine – besieged, cut off, subjected to a British naval blockade, deprived of basic weapons necessary for self-defence on many occasions, and fighting on all fronts against heavy odds. The brunt of this war was borne by the military leadership at the company and battalion level; here the loss of life was heavy. But, from the junior leadership in the field, from the battalion commanders downwards, emerged the future generals of the Israel Defence Forces and the leaders in the four wars that Israel was to fight before the first peace treaty with an Arab state was signed in 1979.

In subsequent wars, the standards set for personal example in Israeli leadership in battle were maintained, and played a very important part in the success of Israeli arms. The Sinai Campaign was the only campaign commanded by the late General Dayan, who, in the War of Independence, had commanded a commando battalion. The opening moves of this classic campaign were a brilliant application of the strategy of 'indirect approach'. Not only were the Arab countries, particularly Egypt and Jordan, led to believe that the Israeli preparations were directed against Jordan and not against Egypt; the brilliant opening moves created a situation whereby the Egyptians were in the dark for some 48 hours as to whether the Israeli attack was indeed a major military offensive or merely yet another reprisal raid in depth across the border. The aims of the strategy were fully achieved. And, again, in the swift attack by the Israeli forces (and particularly by the 7th Armoured Brigade) the flexibility of thought and adaptation that characterized the Israeli moves came to full expression.

In the Six Day War, the Arabs were once more out-generalled – but on three fronts. The extent of such an astounding victory however, led the Israeli Command to ignore many of the shortcomings within their own forces that had been revealed in the war – some of the Israeli achievements were in fact a function of Arab shortcomings and errors. The Israeli political and military leadership, which in matters of security was very much subject to the overriding authority and influence of Moshe Dayan, the Minister of Defence, was more and more guided by a preconceived notion of what they believed would be the considerations on the Arab side. The result was that President Sadat was able to adapt a brilliant deception plan to the concept as evolved in Israel in such a manner as to vindicate the Israeli evaluations. One of the major errors of the Israeli General Staff here was to judge the Arab General Staffs by its own standards of military thinking; as a result, it did not reach the correct conclusions in respect of the limited war strategy adopted by the Arabs in 1973.

The trauma of the Yom Kippur War, the initial success of the Egyptians and Syrians and the comparatively heavy losses sustained in the war – almost 3,000 killed – led to an agonizing public reappraisal of Israel's defence posture and establishment. Many mistakes were revealed: the intelligence evaluation failure; the erroneous political evaluation; the tendency to fight the previous war; and so on. Israel has, however, passed through that fire.

Beside the heroic efforts of a 'civilian' army and inspired leadership, meanwhile, has been the recognition that air power is a vital element in the winning of wars. 1956 was the first campaign in which Israel, thanks to Mystère fighter aircraft supplied by the French, was able to hold its own in the air against the Arab air forces, and indeed succeeded at the outset in establishing command in the air and maintaining it. The Israeli pre-emptive air strike in 1967 was a brilliantly planned and executed operation, which in three hours of air operations accorded Israel command of the skies. This air superiority is an advantage that Israel is always concerned to maintain and, indeed, to use. This was demonstrated graphically in June 1981. Aircraft of the Israeli Air Force, executing a brilliant precision bombing operation, destroyed a nuclear reactor being built with the aid of French technicians in the outskirts of Baghdad. This was a pre-emptive move against the acquisition by Iraq of nuclear weapons, which were avowedly designed for use against Israel. Once again, Israel was making bold use of a weapon of decisive power, honed in combat, and qualitatively equal, if not superior, to any other air force in the world.

In the last 20 years, since the end of the Lebanon War, Israel has not fought a 'conventional' war. It has, however, been involved in three difficult conflicts, which have given rise to a new and wholly different strategic situation. These were the first *intifada*, the first Gulf War, and the second, or El-Aqsa, *intifada*.

The Coalition's decisive victory in the first Gulf War proved the absolute superiority of US weaponry over that made in the Soviet Union. This superiority was demonstrated to even greater effect in the second Gulf War, a dozen years after the collapse of the Soviet empire, when all of

Iraq was occupied within a few days with hardly any Anglo-American casualties. Israel is the only nation in the Middle East which possesses such weaponry and which has the capacity to maintain and operate it. The neighbouring Arab states are well aware of this fact, which contributes greatly to Israel's ability to deter possible military attacks.

Luck also plays a role in Israel's strategic situation. Its four Arab neighbours – Egypt, Jordan, Syria, and Lebanon – are all among the 'poor' Arab states, which either lack oil reserves entirely or possess a very limited amount of them. All four of these states face severe socio-economic difficulties, and would be unable to make preparations for war while simultaneously dealing with their economic crises.

On the other hand, however, three new threats have appeared, threats which make Israel's military superiority more difficult to exploit.

One such threat, which first declared itself in the Gulf War, is ballistic missile attack. These missiles can be launched from a distance of hundreds of miles, so that the attacking country's lack of a border with Israel is no hindrance, and may in fact even offer considerable advantages. Also, ballistic missiles nullify the otherwise decisive supremacy of the Israeli Air Force, enabling Arab countries to strike at Israeli population centres, which they could not do using bomber planes.

The second new threat is the acquisition of weapons of mass destruction by most of the Arab states. Presently, these states possess only chemical and biological weapons. Iraq's attempts to develop nuclear weapons were foiled by Israel in 1981, and later by the two Gulf Wars. Iran's similar attempts are now the focus of worldwide anxiety, but whether any of those concerned will undertake to thwart them remains to be seen.

Faced with these risks, Israel has taken increased precautions. On the defensive side, pre-emptive intelligence coverage has been greatly improved, and the Rear Command has been established to prepare against possible attacks on population centres. On the active side, Israel has developed the Arrow missile, capable of intercepting ballistic missiles. Finally, of course, there is the deterrence aspect; the Arab states estimate that Israel would not hesitate to use its own weapons of mass destruction in the event of a chemical, biological, or nuclear attack.

The third new threat is terrorism. The Palestinians have discovered the ultimate weapon of suicide bombers, who cannot be deterred and can cause heavy casualties. In facing this risk, Israel's principal countermeasure has been to build a passive defence system. This involves a corps of tens of thousands of security guards, stationed at the entrances to all public buildings and other areas where large numbers of people gather. These security guards, with great danger to their own lives, prevent terrorists from entering their targeted areas, leaving them no choice but to detonate their charges outside. Another step, still in its inception, is the construction of a security fence, which is to prevent virtually all passage into Israel from the West Bank.

Israeli attack operations have been just as important. These are made possible by the impressive achievements of the Intelligence Corps and the General Security Service. Thorough, precise and up-to-date intelligence is an essential condition of such military attacks.

One kind of operation involves entering Palestinian territory, with no imposed time limit, in order to search the area, find and arrest suspected terrorists, and destroy any weapons or military infrastructure. The other type of operation is a pinpoint attack against terrorists who cannot be physically reached and arrested. The assassination of relatively high-ranking terrorist leaders was one factor behind the Palestinian decision to propose a cease-fire in 2003.

The Arab military experience

In general, with but few exceptions, the Arab armies gave a good account of themselves in defence, primarily because the scheme of battle could be planned well in advance, and did not have to be departed from. They did not, however, give a good account of themselves in attack because of the inability of the junior leadership to adapt in the heat of battle to changing and unexpected circumstances. They continued to be plagued by the political mistrust between the Arab states and the internal bickering and lack of trust that characterized inter-Arab relationships. Always, the Israelis were able to take advantage of this lack of cohesion and unity between the Arab armies, and at times to deal with them piecemeal and individually. Thus, the Arabs have never been able to take full advantage of their numerical superiority, while the Israelis, usually operating along internal lines of communication, have always been capable of taking advantage of the rifts within the Arab world.

This was the situation in the 1956 war when, in effect, Israel succeeded in isolating Egypt both politically and militarily, creating a situation whereby its attack did not give rise to Arab intervention at Egypt's side. The basic Arab mistake was to assume that the defeat of the Egyptian forces in 1956 was caused by the intervention of British and French forces against Egypt. This assumption led to over-confidence and an under-evaluation of Israel's forces on the eve of the Six Day War in 1967, with the resultant catastrophic outcome for Egypt, Jordan and Syria in the war. In 1967, the Arab world did indeed mobilize its forces at the side of President Nasser of Egypt as he publicly prepared for war against Israel. But here, too, the inherent problem emerged. The Jordanian forces were misled by false Egyptian reports into attacking Israel, and the Syrian Army, despite King Hussein's pleas for support, dragged its feet and did not come to Jordan's aid in its hour of need.

Nevertheless, in some ways, the Arabs did learn from their defeats. President Nasser, and after him President Sadat, analysed together with the Egyptian General Staff the errors made by their forces. The opening phases of the 1973 war as executed by the Egyptian Army proved that the lessons had been learned. President Sadat's war of 1973 was intended to serve primarily a political rather than a military purpose, namely to set in motion a political process that would oblige Israel to return to the 1967 borders without requiring any Arab country to sign a peace treaty with Israel. The strategic and tactical surprise that the Egyptians and the Syrians achieved against Israel was undoubtedly an outstanding military success in itself, and followed the creation of a highly sophisticated and successful deception plan. The Egyptian crossing of the Suez Canal was a major military achievement, and was to be celebrated over the years as one of the great victories of Egyptian arms. (Ironically, in one of the bitter turns of history, it was at a military parade in Cairo to mark the eighth anniversary of the crossing of the Canal that President Sadat was assassinated.)

The Yom Kippur War undoubtedly led to the historic trip of President Sadat to Jerusalem, which in due course brought about the first peace treaty between Israel and an Arab state. The war had a major military and political impact on the Middle East, and must assume its place as a war of great historical significance. The entire science of military strategy and technique was re-evaluated in the light of its lessons. Furthermore, this was a war in which oil was used by the Arab oil-producing nations as a weapon, which became an international factor of consequence in the years after the war. As this war recedes into history, it gains considerably in perspective, because of its military and political implications and lessons. The disengagement agreements between Israel and Syria and between Israel and Egypt; the interim agreement between Israel and Egypt in Sinai in 1975 involving the withdrawal of Israeli troops from the Suez Canal, the Abu Rudeis oilfields in Sinai and other strategic points; the activation of an electronic surveillance system by the United States in Sinai – all of these led ultimately to the peace treaty between Israel and Egypt coupled with the Israeli withdrawal from Sinai, and to a stabilization of the situation along the Israeli–Syrian border in the Golan Heights. Israel's victory in every one of the wars it has been forced into, and the Arab recognition that Israel's ultra-modern weaponry grants it absolute military supremacy, were the main factor behind the signing of the peace treaties.

The role of the superpowers

Arabs and Jews, however, are but two of the elements at work in the political arena of the Middle East. President Nasser was armed by the Soviet Union and the Soviet Union had a hand in bringing on the Six Day War. The Israeli victory, which completely transformed Israel's strategic position, opened prospects for dialogue with the Arab world; a population of over a million Palestinian Arabs came under Israeli control, and the 'open bridges' policy, which allowed freedom of movement between Jordan and the West Bank, created prospects of an understanding between Israel and the Arab world. However, the Soviet Union dissuaded any tendency by the Arabs to move towards negotiation with Israel. Ten days after the war, the Israeli Cabinet voted unanimously to return the Sinai to Egypt and the Golan Heights to Syria in return for peace and demilitarization. It was the Soviet Union that blocked this move. Her subsequent actions and policy encouraged the Arab Summit Conference held at Khartoum in August–September 1967 to reject the Israeli overtures with 'the "three noes" resolution' – no negotiation with Israel, no recognition of Israel, no peace with Israel. Once again, the stage was set for renewed conflict in the Middle East. In the years that followed, the Soviet Union was afforded the opportunity to test much of the strategy and theory of modern air defence; Soviet strength in Egypt grew to some 20,000 troops, and her air force assumed responsibility for part of the air defence of Egypt. However, when President Sadat came to power in 1970, while deciding that he must go to war in order to break the political log-jam with Israel, he also decided to change Egypt's orientation from a pro-Soviet one to one supporting the Americans. In a move characteristic of the imagination and decisiveness of Sadat, he ordered the Russians out of Egypt in July 1972 – and then prepared for war against Israel with Russian support and possibly connivance.

The United States for its part exerted considerable efforts to bridge the gap between the Israeli and the Arab positions on the basis of United Nations Security Council Resolution 242, which was adopted on 22 November 1967. This resolution called, *inter alia*, for: 'withdrawal of Israeli armed forces from territories occupied in the recent conflict' as well as the right of 'every State in the area... to live in peace within secure and recognised boundaries free from threats or acts of force.' Parallel to a policy of maintaining Israel's defensive capability in the face of the growth of Soviet military supplies to Arab countries, the United States initiated moves designed to break the impasse in the area. US Secretary of State William Rogers produced unsuccessfully the so-called 'Rogers Plan' in 1970, while he successfully negotiated the cease fire along the Suez Canal in August 1970. US efforts were directed principally to containing Soviet-backed moves such as the Syrian invasion of Jordan in 1970, to maintaining Israel's deterrent posture and to seeking a political solution by means of negotiations.

Both superpowers were involved in the Yom Kippur War: major resupply operations were mounted by the Soviet Union in favour of the Egyptian and Syrian Armies and by the United States in favour of the Israeli forces. Sadat's decision to ask for a cease-fire was first and foremost influenced by the military facts on the battleground – the IDF crossing of the Canal, the destruction of Egypt's main military trump-card, its anti-aircraft missile batteries, and of course, the encirclement of Egypt's Third Army. One should also mention the effectiveness of the American resupply operation. It was the US Secretary of State, Henry Kissinger, who negotiated a cease-fire between Israel and Egypt, including Israeli military concessions that involved opening a supply line to the beleaguered Egyptian Third Army. From this point, the United States developed a central position in all the negotiations, as President Sadat moved towards a completely pro-American orientation. The role of the United Nations' peace-keeping forces in implementing agreements reached in the negotiations in respect of Sinai, the Golan Heights and at a later date of Lebanon, became an increasingly important one.

Since the Yom Kippur War, the United States has played a central role in all developments in the Middle East, and specifically in attempts to promote political negotiations. American mediation brought about the Separation of Forces agreement between Israel, Egypt and Syria, and later (in October 1975) the active intercession of Secretary of State Kissinger resulted in the interim agreement in Sinai. This was the first agreement since 1967 in which Israeli forces withdrew, leaving the western Sinai to the supervision of an American force, the Sinai Field Mission (SFM).

This pact was to hold for three years, until October 1978. However, it soon became clear that reaching another interim agreement, involving further Israeli withdrawal, was impossible without a real political *quid pro quo* by Egypt.

On 1 October 1977 the USA and the Soviet Union released a joint declaration intended to renew the Geneva Conference. This peace conference, involving Israel and all its Arab neighbors, had been agreed upon after the Yom Kippur War, but an attempt to convene it had ended in total failure three years before. The declaration was irksome to both Israel and Egypt, as neither saw any possible resolution to the crisis.

Egyptian President Anwar Sadat resolved to bypass the American–Soviet initiative. Facing severe socio-economic problems within Egypt, and encouraged by talks between Israeli Foreign Minister Moshe Dayan and Egyptian Deputy Prime Minister Mohammed Tohami, Sadat decided on his dramatic visit to Jerusalem on 19 November 1977. This unexpected visit was not co-ordinated with either of the superpowers. Peace talks now began between Israel and Egypt, and would continue for almost 18 months.

It soon became apparent, however, that without active American involvement no progress would be made. President Jimmy Carter put much time and effort into furthering the talks and staked his prestige on their success – especially at the Camp David summit of 17 September 1978, and later when he visited the two nations' capitals in person to serve as a go-between.

The Camp David accord became the basis for the structure and principles of future Israeli-Arab agreements, especially that with the Palestinians. As the accord required, Israel and Egypt now began negotiations (with American involvement) to create a Palestinian autonomy in the occupied territories. But the gap between the parties' positions was too wide, and American influence, with the Carter presidency nearing its end, was now much less dominant. These talks made no progress and were soon abandoned.

As the focus of military conflict moved north, to the Lebanese border, international bodies began to play central roles on this front. Once again it was the United States that served as chief mediator. Following 1978's Operation Litani, the UN Security Council created UNIFIL, an international force in south Lebanon, as a buffer between Israel and Lebanon. This force's mandate has since been renewed every few months, but it has served no practical purpose either in preventing violence or mediating between the two sides.

Three years later, when serious conflict broke out between the IDF and the PLO in south Lebanon, US State Department envoy Philip Habib was sent to the region. With his mediation, a cease-fire was agreed and carefully adhered to for a year, until the outbreak of the Lebanon War.

Throughout that war, the US once again played an important role. An International Intervention Force, including American Marines, French, British and Italians, had been formed to supervise the evacuation of PLO and Syrian forces from Beirut This force evacuated the area immediately afterwards.

After the Christian militias' massacre of Palestinian refugees in Sabra and Shatila, American Marines had immediately returned to Beirut and political intervention brought the IDF to withdraw from Beirut. Eighteen months later, following two car-bombs in the US embassy's building and in the Marines' barracks, President Reagan ordered the withdrawal of all American troops from Lebanon (February 1983).

There is also another level to the involvement of the superpowers in the Middle East. With the demise of the Soviet Union, many of the Arab states lost their chief source of modern military supplies. The United States gradually became the most important source of advanced military technology. Israel's extensive operational experience contributed to closer relations between the two countries, and to Israel's participation in the United States' sophisticated weapons' development programme.

Following the Soviet collapse and the 1991 Gulf War, the US became the leading power in international affairs, including the Israeli-Arab conflict and its attempted resolution. A 'window of opportunity' was formed, which Washington decided to use by convening the Madrid summit conference.

In a kind of imitation of Sadat's independent initiative of November 1977, Israel began secret talks with PLO representatives in Oslo. These talks led to the famous Declaration of Principles (DOP) which was signed on the White House lawn in Washington. In the years since then, the US has played a key role both in implementing various steps and in acting as an acceptable mediator to both sides.

In the final stage, the US was joined by the other three members of the 'Quartet': Russia, the European Union, and the UN. This development gave rise to the 'road map', which both Israel and the Palestinians accepted as a blueprint for ending the violence and renewing political negotiations with a series of predetermined goals.

The Palestinians

The Israeli victory in the Six Days War radically changed the strategic aspects of the Israeli–Arab conflict. From the 1948 War of Independence up until June 1967, the conflict was between Israel and its four neighbours, Egypt, Jordan, Syria, and Lebanon. But the expulsion of Egypt from the

Gaza Strip and of Jordan from the West Bank resurrected the Palestinian problem. These territories were home to about half of the Palestinian people, who now found themselves under Israeli military rule. As for Israel, it stubbornly insisted on seeking a solution through the Hashemite Kingdom of Jordan, rejecting out of hand the possibility of a direct bilateral agreement with the Palestinians.

The PLO was founded three years earlier, in 1964. The Arab states committed themselves, at least in theory, to destroying Israel and creating a Palestinian state in its place. This position was reasserted at the Arab summit in Khartoum in 1967. In addition to the familiar 'three noes' (no recognition, negotiation, or peace with Israel), an additional resolution was adopted: no compromise or concession on Palestinian rights.

The PLO soon despaired of establishing itself in the Israeli-occupied territories, and became based in neighbouring countries. From there, it prepared attacks against Israel, both in the form of cross-border fire and incursions, and by organizing terrorist cells inside the territories.

After failing in an attempt to take control of Jordan, it moved its base of operations from Jordan to Lebanon – a move that set the scene for the ultimate decimation of Lebanon and the subsequent Syrian intervention in that country. The civil war that broke out in Lebanon in 1975 created a new situation along Israel's northern border. Various Christian elements, rival Moslem communities, the Syrian Army and the PLO became involved, a chaotic state of affairs developed in wartorn Lebanon, and all the while the PLO continued to use Lebanon's territory as a jumping-off ground for terrorist attacks against the Israeli population. And so the war of terror went on.

Despite the brutality of the terrorist campaign, Israel is winning on this front, too. The Lebanon War of 1982 drove the PLO central command out of Beirut, so that the Palestinians were left without any contiguous area from which to keep up terrorist pressure on Israel. The exiled PLO leadership in Tunis reached a correct conclusion: to seek a political agreement with Israel.

Over the years, especially with the rise of the Likud to power in Israel, nationalist movements began to take shape in the Palestinian territories themselves. But the explosion came only in December 1987, 20 years after the Six Day War. The situation of Palestinians in the West Bank and Gaza had reached a boiling point, sparking the first *intifada*. This sudden eruption of violence was a turning point for Israel, too; most Israelis now realized that the 20-year period of relative calm was over, military rule in the territories could no longer be sustained, and a political solution had to be found.

The first Gulf War created a window of opportunity for a settlement in the Middle East. At the initiative of the United States, the international Madrid Conference of October 1991 took place, bilateral talks commenced in Washington, and secret negotiations began in Oslo, later to give rise to the Declaration of Principles signed in Washington in September 1993.

Both sides had high hopes and expectations of this agreement. But the political process miscarried two years later, when Israeli Prime Minister

Yitzhak Rabin was assassinated by a young Jewish radical. After a further six months the Labour government fell, and thus the peace process was gradually derailed. Four years later, following the failed Israeli–Palestinian summit at Camp David, the countdown began toward the second, El-Aqsa, *intifada*.

In June 2003, the two sides agreed to a cease-fire. This was a major achievement for Israel. The IDF had succeeded in convincing the Palestinians of the futility of the violence they had initiated. At this writing, however, it is too early to tell if or when the parties will in fact resume the path of negotiations towards a peace treaty.

In any case, even if an agreement with the Palestinians is signed, it will still be necessary to obtain a treaty with Damascus, in the absence of which lasting peace along Israel's borders cannot be secured.

Were Israel to reach final peace agreements with all its neighbours, Israel would still be a country that remains dependent for its survival on military ability. Yet it is a country that rejects militarism. This fact, and the open and free discussion that characterizes Israeli democracy, have been important factors in Israel's inherent strength. The Israeli Army is not an army for parades; it is an army that rejects the trappings and formalities normally associated with the military, and adheres to the uniform worn in battle, because the armed forces are seen as a necessary evil with the sole purpose of defending the nation's existence. Israel is defended today by the most experienced army in the world. From a professional point of view, it has had the opportunity to test itself in battle again and again. There are few, if any, armies in the world today that have such an accumulation of experience in its ranks as have the Israel Defence Forces.

The Yom Kippur War and the peace treaty with Egypt placed Israel on a course of conciliation with its neighbors. Following the Oslo agreements, an Israeli–Jordanian peace treaty was signed, and Israel has continued to seek a solution for its conflicts with Syria and Lebanon and with the Palestinians.

Realistically speaking, however, even if such peace treaties are achieved, true change in the Israeli–Arab relationship is not to be expected. It will probably be many years before the Arab world ceases from seeing Israel as a foreign intruder in the Middle East and awaiting the opportunity to destroy it. In such conditions, despite the formal state of peace, Israel's military might will continue to be the primary safeguard of its existence.

In the more than 50 years since its foundation, Israel has seen radical changes take place in the nature of the security risks it faces. Its victory in the Yom Kippur War, and its absolute supremacy in modern military technology, have greatly reduced the dangers of conventional war at the borders.

But two other spheres of risk remain. The first of these is the threat from more distant Arab and Islamic states, beyond Israel's immediate neighbours. The danger these countries pose is not that of conventional warfare, but of an attack with weapons of mass destruction (chemical, biological, or even nuclear). Chief among these countries are Iraq and

Iran. At this point, the 2003 Gulf War has done away with the Iraqi threat (although it is too early to tell what the future holds for Iraq), but the Iranian danger remains. Israel must decide whether it will act to prevent these risks (as in 1981, when it destroyed a nuclear plant near Baghdad), or whether it limits itself to deterring potential attackers by threatening a very severe military response.

The second sphere of risk is that of Palestinian and Islamic terrorism. Israel has dealt with this danger with considerable success. The efficient combination of intelligence and operational forces has accomplished impressive results in preventing terrorist attacks. But this is not a complete solution. Israel's task is more difficult in combating Islamic terrorist groups which are not Palestinian at all: the Lebanese Hizballah and the international al-Qaeda. This new reality makes it all the more important for Israel to reach political agreements that remove the ideological basis for these extremist movements.

Finally, two further dangers should be mentioned. One is the participation of more and more Israeli Arabs in terrorist attacks that originate in Palestinian Authority-controlled areas. The other, very different danger is that of demography: within seven or eight years, the Jewish population is set to become a minority in the region between the Jordan River and the Mediterranean.

SELECT
BIBLIOGRAPHY

Abu-Lughod, I. (ed.) *The Arab-Israeli Confrontation of June 1967: An Arab Perspective.* Arab Information Center, New York, 1968.

Adan, A. ('Bren'). *On the Banks of the Suez.* Arms & Armour Press, London, 1980; Presidio Press, San Francisco, 1980; original title: *On Both Banks of the Suez*, Edanim, Jerusalem, 1979.

Allon, Y. *The Making of Israel's Army.* Vallentine, Mitchell, London, 1970; Universe Books, New York, 1971.

——. *Shield of David. The Story of Israel's Armed Forces.* Vallentine, Mitchell/ Weidenfeld and Nicolson, London, 1970; Random House, New York, 1970; Weidenfeld and Nicolson, Jerusalem, 1970.

Associated Press. *Lightning out of Israel: The Six Day War in the Middle East.* The Press, New York, 1967.

Azcárate, P. de. *Mission in Palestine, 1948–1952.* Middle East Institute, Washington, 1966.

Badri, Hassan el, Taha el Magdoub, and Mohommed Die el-Din Zohdy. *The Ramadan War.* T. N. Dupuy, Dunn Loring, Va., 1977.

Barer, S. *The Weekend War.* Yoseloff, New York, 1960; Karni, Jerusalem, 1959.

Barker, A. *Suez: The Seven Day War.* Faber & Faber, London, 1964; Praeger, New York, 1965.

Beaufre, A. *The Suez Expedition 1956*; translated by Richard Barry. Faber, London 1969; Praeger, New York, 1969; original title: *L'Expedition de Suez.* Grasset, Paris, 1967.

——. 'Une Guerre Classique Moderne: La Guerre Israelo-Arabe.' *Strategie*, July/August, 1967, pp. 7-25.

Ben-Gurion, D. *Israel: Years of Challenge.* Blond, London, 1964; Holt, Rinehart and Winston, New York, 1963; Massadah, Tel Aviv, 1963.

Ben-Porat, Y. *Hamechdal* (Hebrew). Hotzaa Meyuchedet, Tel Aviv, 1973.

Berkman, T. *Cast a Giant Shadow: The Story of Mickey Marcus, Who Died to Save Jerusalem.* Doubleday, New York, 1962.

Blanchard, A. 'The Six-Day War'. *Army*, August, 1967, pp. 24–33.

Browne, H. *Suez and Sinai.* Longman, Harlow, 1971.

Bull, O. *War and Peace in the Middle East: The Experiences and Views of a UN Observer.* Leo Cooper, London, 1976.

Burdett, W. *Encounter with the Middle East: An Intimate Report on What Lies Behind the Arab-Israeli Conflict.* Deutsch, London, 1969; Atheneum, New York, 1969.

Burns, E. *Between Arab and Israeli.* Harrap, London, 1962; Obolensky, New York, 1963.

Byford-Jones, W. *The Lightning War.* Hale, London, 1967; Bobbs-Merrill, Indianapolis, 1968.

Carmel, M. *Campaigns of the North* (Hebrew). 'Maarachot' and Kibbutz Hameuhad, Tel Aviv, 1949.

Cavenagh, S. *Airborne to Suez.* Kimber, London, 1965.

Childers, E. *The Road to Suez.* Macgibbon & Kee, London, 1962.

Churchill, R. and W. *The Six Day War.* Heinemann, London, 1967; Houghton Mifflin, Boston, 1967.

Collins, L. and Lapierre, D. *O Jerusalem!* Weidenfeld and Nicolson, London, 1973; Simon and Schuster, New York, 1972.

Dawson, J. 'The Air War in the Middle East'. *Air Force & Space Digest*, August 1967, pp. 26–29.

Dayan, M. *Breakthrough.* Weidenfeld and Nicolson, London, 1981; Knopf, New York, 1981; Edanim, Jerusalem, 1981.

——. *Diary of the Sinai Campaign.* Weidenfeld and Nicolson, London, 1966; Harper and Row, New York, 1966.

——. *Story of My Life.* Weidenfeld and Nicolson, London, 1976; Morrow, New York, 1976; Edanim, Jerusalem, 1976.

Donovan, R. *Israel's Fight for Survival.* Signet Books, New York, 1967.

Draper, T. 'From 1967 to 1973'. *Commentary* (New York), Vol. 56, No. 6, December 1973.

Dupuy, Col. T. N. *Elusive Victory. The Arab-Israeli Wars, 1947–1974.* Macdonald and Janes, London, 1978; Harper and Row, New York, 1978.

Eban, A. *Abba Eban: An Autobiography.* Weidenfeld and Nicolson, London, 1977; Random House, New York, 1977.

Eden, Sir A. *Full Circle: The Memoirs of Anthony Eden.* Cassell, London, 1960; Houghton Mifflin, Boston, 1960.

Eisenhower, D. D. *Waging Peace, 1956–1961.* (Volume 2 of *The White House Years*), Heinemann, London, 1966; Doubleday, New York, 1965.

Gilbert, M. *The Arab-Israeli Conflict. Its History in Maps.* Weidenfeld and Nicolson, London, 1974.

Glubb, Sir J. B. *The Middle East Crisis. A Personal Interpretation.* Hodder & Stoughton, London, 1967.

——. *Peace in the Holy Land. An Historical Analysis of the Palestine Problem.* Hodder & Stoughton, London, 1971.

——. *A Short History of the Arab Peoples.* Hodder & Stoughton, London, 1969; Stein & Day, New York, 1969.

——. *A Soldier with the Arabs.* Hodder & Stoughton, London, 1957; Verry, Mystic, Conn., 1957.

Hadawi, S. *Bitter Harvest: Palestine Between 1914–1967.* New World Press, New York, 1967.

Handel, M. *Perception, Deception and Surprise. The Case of the Yom Kippur War.* Hebrew University, Leonard Davis Institute for International Relations, Jerusalem, 1976.

Heiman, L. 'Infantry in the Middle East War.' *Infantry*, January-February/ March-April 1968, pp. 16–22 and 4–13.

Heikal, M. *The Cairo Documents.* Doubleday, New York, 1973.

——. *The Road to Ramadan.* Collins, London, 1975; Quadrangle/New York Times Book Company, New York, 1975.

Henriques, R. *A Hundred Hours to Suez. An Account of Israel's Campaign in the Sinai Peninsula.* Collins, London, 1957; Viking Press, New York, 1957.

Herzog, C. *Israel's Finest Hour* (Hebrew). Maariv Book Guild, Tel Aviv, 1967.

——. *Days of Awe.* Weidenfeld and Nicolson, Jerusalem, 1973.

——. *War of Atonement.* Weidenfeld and Nicolson, London 1975; Little, Brown, Boston 1974; Edanim, Jerusalem, 1975.

——. 'Middle East War 1973'. *RUSI* (Journal of the Royal United Services Institute for Defence Studies), London, 1975.

——. *Who Stands Accused?: Israel Answers its Critics.* Weidenfeld and Nicolson,

London, 1978; Random House, New York, 1978.

Hirst, D. and Beeson, I. *Sadat*. Faber & Faber, London, 1981.

Horn, C. C. van. *Soldiering for Peace*. Cassell, London, 1966; McKay, New York, 1967.

Hurewitz, J. C. (ed.) *Diplomacy in the Near and Middle East: A Documentary Record*. 2 vols. Macmillan, London, 1956; Van Nostrand, New York, 1956.

——. *Middle East Politics: The Military Dimension*. Pall Mall Press, London, 1969; Praeger, New York, 1969.

——. *Soviet-American Rivalry in the Middle East*. (Published for the Academy of Political Science, Columbia University.) Praeger, New York, 1969.

Hussein, King of Jordan. *My 'War' With Israel*; as told to and with additional material by Vick Vance and Pierre Lauer; translated by J. P. Wilson and W. B. Michaels. Owen, London, 1969; Morrow, New York, 1969.

Israel, Army Historical Branch. *History of the War of Independence* (Hebrew). Tel Aviv, 1975.

——. *The Sinai Campaign*. Tel Aviv, n.d.

Israel, IDF Spokesman's Office. *The Israel-Arab Wars*. Jerusalem, 1975.

Jonathan Institute. *International Terrorism – Challenge and Response*. Jonathan Institute, Jerusalem, 1980.

Joseph, D. *The Faithful City: The Siege of Jerusalem 1948*. Hogarth Press, London, 1962: Simon & Schuster, New York, 1960.

Journal of Palestine Studies. 'The October War and its Aftermath'. Institute of Palestine Studies, Beirut, and Kuwait University, Vol. III, No. 2, 1974.

Kahlany, A. *Fortress Seventy-Seven* (Hebrew). Schocken, Tel Aviv, 1976.

Kalb, M. and B. *Kissinger*. Hutchinson, London, 1974; Little, Brown, Boston, 1974.

'Keesing's Contemporary Archives'. *Arab-Israeli Conflict: The 1967 Campaign*. Keesing's Publications, Bristol; Scribner, New York, 1968.

Kimche, D. and Bawley, D. *The Sandstorm. The Arab-Israeli War of June 1967: Prelude and Aftermath*. Secker & Warburg, London, 1968; Stein and Day, New York, 1968.

Kimche, J. *Seven Fallen Pillars: The Middle East, 1915–1950*. Secker & Warburg, London, 1950.

Kissinger, H. *White House Years*. Weidenfeld and Nicolson, London, 1979; Little, Brown, Boston, 1979.

Kotsch, W. 'The Six Day War of 1967'. US Naval Institute *Proceedings*, June, 1968, pp. 72–81.

Kurzman, D. *Genesis 1948. The First Arab-Israeli War*. Vallentine, Mitchell, London, 1972; World Publishing Company, New York, 1970.

Laquer, W. *Confrontation 1973: The Middle East War and the Great Powers*. Wildwood House, London, 1974. US title: *Confrontation: The Middle East and World Politics*. Quadrangle, New York, 1974.

——. *The Road to War, 1967: The Origins of the Arab-Israeli Conflict*. Weidenfeld and Nicolson, London, 1968; US title: *The Road to Jerusalem: The Origins of the Arab-Israeli Conflict, 1967*. Macmillan, New York, 1968.

——. *The Israel-Arab Reader*. Weidenfeld and Nicolson, London, 1969: Citadel, New York, 1969.

Levine, E. and Shimoni, Y. (eds.) *Political Dictionary of the Middle East in the Twentieth Century*. Weidenfeld and Nicolson, London, 1972; Quadrangle, New York, 1972; Jerusalem Publishing House, Jerusalem, 1972.

Lewis, B. 'The Arab-Israeli War: The Consequences of Defeat'. *Foreign Affairs*, January 1968, pp. 321–335.

Liddell Hart, B. 'Strategy of a War'. *Military Review*, November 1968, pp. 80–85.

Lorch, N. *The Edge of the Sword: Israel's War of Independence, 1947-1949.* Putnam, London and New York, 1961; Massadah, Tel Aviv, 1970.

Love, K. Suez: *The Twice-Fought War. A History.* Longman, Harlow, 1970; McGraw-Hill, New York, 1969.

Luttwak, E. and Horowitz, D. *The Israeli Army.* Allen Lane, Harmondsworth, 1975; Harper, New York, 1975.

Luttwak, E. and Laquer, W. 'Kissinger and the Yom Kippur War'. *Commentary* (New York), Vol. 58, No. 3, September 1974.

Maarachot (Israel Defence Forces Journal) 'The Yom Kippur War' (Hebrew). Tel Aviv, Nov. 1973, Nov. 1980.

MacLeish, R. *The Sun Stood Still: Perspectives on the Arab-Israeli Conflict.* Macdonald, London, 1968; Atheneum, New York, 1967.

Mansfield, P. *The Arab-World: A Comprehensive History.* Thomas Crowell, New York, 1976.

Marshall, S. *Sinai Victory. Command Decisions in History's Shortest War: Israel's Hundred-Hour Conquest of Egypt.* Morrow, New York, 1958.

——. *Swift Sword. The Historical Record of Israel's Victory, June 1967.* American Heritage, New York, 1967.

Meir, G. *My Life.* Weidenfeld and Nicolson, London, 1975; Putnam, New York, 1975; Maariv Book Guild, Tel Aviv, 1975.

Murphy, R. *Diplomat Among Warriors.* Collins, London, 1964; Doubleday, New York, 1964.

Naor, M. *The War After the War* (The War of Attrition) (Hebrew). Ministry of Defence Publications, Tel Aviv, 1971.

Neguib, M. *Egypt's Destiny.* Gollancz, London, 1955; Doubleday, New York, 1955.

Nutting, A. *No End of a Lesson: The Story of Suez.* Constable, London, 1967; Potter, New York, 1967.

——. *Nasser.* Constable, London, 1972; Dutton, New York, 1972.

O'Ballance, E. *The Arab-Israeli War 1948.* Faber & Faber, London, 1956; Praeger, New York, 1957.

——. *The Sinai Campaign 1956.* Faber & Faber, London, 1959; Praeger, New York, 1960.

The Third Arab-Israeli War. Faber & Faber, London, 1972; Shoe String, Hamden, 1972.

O'Brien, P. 'The Six Day War of 1967'. US Naval Institute *Proceedings*, September, 1968, pp. 113-114.

Patai, R. *The Arab Mind.* Scribner, New York, 1976.

Pearlman, M. *The Army of Israel.* Philosophical Library, New York, 1950.

Peres, S. *David's Sling – The Arming of Israel.* Weidenfeld and Nicolson, London, 1970; Random House, New York, 1971.

Perkins, D. *Organization of the Israeli Army Reserve Forces and Their Mobilization in the Six Day War.* US Army War College, Carlisle Barracks, 1972.

Proceedings; International Symposium: 'Military Aspects of the Israeli-Arab Conflict' (Louis Williams, ed). University Publishing Projects, Tel Aviv, 1975.

Proceedings; International Symposium on the 1973 October War. *Al Ahram*, Cairo, 1976.

Quandt, W. B. *Decade of Decision: American Policy Toward the Arab-Israeli Conflict 1967-76.* University of California Press, Berkley and London, 1978.

Rabin, Y. *Rabin Memoirs.* Weidenfeld and Nicolson, London, 1979; Little, Brown, Boston, 1979; Maariv Book Guild, Tel Aviv, 1979.

Roosevelt, K. *Arabs, Oil, and History: The Story of the Middle East.* Gollancz, London, 1949; Harper, New York, 1949.

Rosenne, S. *Israel's Armistice Agreements with the Arab States. A Juridical Interpretation.* International Law Association, Tel Aviv, 1951.

Rothenberg, G. *The Anatomy of the Israeli Army.* Batsford, London, 1979; Hippocrene, New York, 1979.

Sadat, A. el. *In Search of Identity.* Collins, London, 1978; Harper and Row, New York, 1978.

Safran, N. *From War to War: The Arab-Israeli Confrontation, 1948-1967.* Pegasus, New York, 1969.

——. *Israel: The Embattled Ally.* Harvard University Press, London – Cambridge (Mass.), 1978.

Schiff, Z. *La Guerre Israelo-Arabe, 5-10 Juin, 1967.* Julliard, Paris, 1967.

——. *A History of the Israeli Army (1870-1974).* Straight Arrow Books, San Francisco, 1974.

——. *October Earthquake* (Hebrew). Zmora, Beitan, Modan, Tel Aviv, 1974.

Schmidt, D. A. *Armageddon in the Middle East.* John Day, New York, 1974.

Sharef, Z. *Three Days.* W. H. Allen, London, 1962; Doubleday, New York, 1962.

Sherman, A. *When God Judged and Men Died. A Battle Report of the Yom Kippur War.* Bantam Books, New York, 1973.

Shoemaker, R. 'The Arab-Israeli War'. *Military Review,* August 1968, pp. 56–59.

Stevenson, W. *Strike Zion!* Bantam Books, New York, 1967.

——. *90 Minutes at Entebbe.* Corgi, London, 1976; Bantam, New York, 1976.

Strategic Summary. 'The Middle East War'. International Institute for Strategic Studies, London, 1974.

Strategic Survey 1973. International Institute for Strategic Studies, London, 1974.

'Sunday Times' Insight Team. *Insight on the Middle East.* Deutsch, London, 1974.

——. *The Yom Kippur War.* Deutsch, London, 1975.

Teveth, S. *The Tanks of Tammuz.* Weidenfeld and Nicolson, London, 1968; Viking Press, New York, 1969.

Thomas, H. *The Suez Affair.* Weidenfeld and Nicolson, London, 1967; Harper and Row, New York, 1967.

Trevelyan, H. *The Middle East in Revolution.* Macmillan, London, 1970; Gambit, Boston, 1970.

Van Creveld, M. L. *Military Lessons of the Yom Kippur War: Historical Perspectives.* Sage Publications, Beverly Hills, 1975, London, 1976.

Wallach, J. 'The Israeli Armoured Corps in the Six Day War'. *Armor,* May/June 1968, pp. 34–43.

Watt, D. *Documents on the Suez Crisis, 26 July to 6 November 1956.* Royal Institute for International Affairs, London, 1957.

Weizman, E. *The Battle for Peace.* Bantam, London and New York, 1981; Edanim, Jerusalem, 1981.

——. *On Eagles' Wings.* Weidenfeld and Nicolson, London, 1976; Maariv Book Guild, Tel Aviv, 1975.

Weller, J. 'Lessons from the Six Day War'. *Military Review,* November 1971, pp. 44–50.

Wilson, Sir H. *The Chariot of Israel.* Weidenfeld and Nicolson/Michael Joseph, London, 1981.

Yost, C. 'The Arab-Israeli War: How it Began'. *Foreign Affairs,* January 1968, pp. 304–320.

Young, P. 'The Arab-Israeli War'. *RUSI* (Journal of the Royal United Services Institute for Defence Studies), November 1967, pp. 324–339.

——. *The Israeli Campaign 1967.* William Kimber, London, 1967.

Further Reading, Updated Edition

Adan, Avraham. *On the Banks of the Suez: An Israeli General's Personal Account of the Yom Kippur War*. Presidio Press, Novato, California, 1991.

Brynen, Rex. *Echoes of the Intifada*. Westview Press, Boulder, Colorado, 1991.

Bullock, John. *Final Conflict: The War in Lebanon*. Century Publishing, London, 1983.

Creveld, Martin van. *Moshe Dayan*. Weidenfeld & Nicolson, London, 2004.

Dershowitz, Alan. *The Case for Israel*. John Wiley, London, 2003.

——. *Why Terrorism Works: Understanding the Threat, Responding to the Challenge*. Yale University Press, Massachusetts, 2002.

Dupuy, Trevor N. and Martell, Paul. *Flawed Victory: The Arab-Israeli Conflict and the 1982 War in Lebanon*. Hero Books, Fairfax, Virginia, 1986.

Davis, M. Thomas. *40km Into Lebanon: Israel's 1982 Invasion*. National Defense University Press, Washington DC, 1987.

Feldman, Shai. *The Raid on Osiraq*. Center for Strategic Studies, Tel Aviv, 1981.

Feldman, Shai (ed.). *After the War in Iraq: Defining the New Strategic Balance*, Sussex Academic Press, Brighton, 2003.

Freedman, Robert Owen. *The Intifada: Its Impact on Israel, the Arab World and the Superpowers*. Florida International University Press, Florida, 1991.

Gabriel, Richard A. *Operation Peace for Galilee: The Israeli-PLO War in Lebanon*. Hill and Wang, New York, 1984.

Gazit, Shlomo. *Trapped Fools*. Frank Cass, London, 2003.

Hilterman, Joost R. *Behind the Intifada*. Princeton University Press, Princeton, New Jersey, 1992.

Herzog, Chaim. *Living History: A Memoir*. Pantheon Books, New York; Weidenfeld & Nicolson, London, 1996.

Herzog, Chaim. *War of Atonement. Reprinted with a new Introduction by Michael Herzog.* Greenhill Books, London, 1998.

JCSS Study Group. *War in the Gulf: Implications for Israel*. Tel Aviv University, Tel Aviv, 1991.

Jaber, H. *Hezbollah*. Columbia University Press, New York. 1998.

Kench, Henry E. *The Intifada*. New York, 1992.

Mattar, Philip. *The Mufti of Jerusalem: Al-Hajj Amin Al-Husayni and the Palestinian National Movement*. Columbia University Press, New York, 1992.

Nakdimon, Shlomo, translated by Peretz Kidron. *First Strike: The Exclusive Story of How Israel Foiled Iraq's Attempt to Get the Bomb*. Summit Books, New York, 1987.

Olsen, John. *Strategic Air Power in Desert Storm*. Frank Cass, London, 2003.

Oren, Michael. *Six Days of War: June 1967 and the Making of the Modern Middle East*. Oxford University Press, New York, 2002.

Rabinovich, Abraham. *The Yom Kippur War*. Random House, New York, 2004.

INDEX